Red Dot Design Yearbook 2019/2020

Edited by Peter Zec

reddot award
product design

About this book

"Living" presents award-winning products to demonstrate the state of the art in contemporary homes and lives. All of these products are of outstanding design quality and have been successful in one of the world's largest and most renowned design competitions, the Red Dot Design Award. This book documents the current results in the field of "Living", and presents the most important players – the design team of the year, the designers of the best products and the jury members.

Über dieses Buch

„Living" zeigt anhand ausgezeichneter Produkte den State of the Art zeitgemäßen Wohnens und Lebens. All diese Produkte sind von herausragender gestalterischer Qualität, ausgezeichnet in einem der größten und renommiertesten Designwettbewerbe der Welt, dem Red Dot Design Award. Dieses Buch dokumentiert die aktuellen Ergebnisse im Bereich „Living" und stellt zudem seine wichtigsten Akteure vor – das Designteam des Jahres, die Designer der besten Produkte und die Jurymitglieder.

Contents
Inhalt

6	**Preface of the editor**	
	Vorwort des Herausgebers	
8	**Red Dot: Design Team of the Year 2019**	
9	**Flavio Manzoni and Ferrari Design Team**	
28	**The designers of the Red Dot: Best of the Best and their award-winning products**	
	Die Designer der Red Dot: Best of the Best und ihre ausgezeichneten Produkte	
30	Design Group Italia	
	Basalt Architects	
32	Centor Holdings Pty Ltd	
34	AIGANG GmbH	
	Top Design	
36	Dr. Rolf W.-Seifart	
38	David Spielhofer – Orea AG	
40	Shinsaku Miyamoto – Ritzwell & Co.	
42	Andreas Ostwald – ostwalddesign	
44	Keren Hu, Ding Fan, Fang Jianping, Li Yu, Zhuang Jingyang, Liu Fang – Teawith Kettle Design Team	
46	Bosch Home Appliances Design Team	
48	Angelo Po	
	Studio Volpi	
50	Stefan Ambrozus – Studio Ambrozus	
	Peter Ahlmer – berbel Ablufttechnik GmbH	
52	Seonil Yu, Kyukwan Choi, Daesung Lee, Yong Kim, Hyun Choi – LG Electronics Inc.	
54	Ruy Ohtake	
56	Jean-Marie Massaud – Studio Massaud	
58	Grohe Design Team	
60	Andreas Diefenbach, Matthias Oesterle, Marco Flaig – Phoenix Design GmbH + Co. KG	
62	Daniel Fortin, Scott Santoro – Fluxwerx Illumination Inc.	
64	Thomas Turner, Ben Rigby, Nathanael Hunt – Haberdashery	
66	Carlos Pereira – Arpino	
68	Aleš Kachlík, Prof. Jan Němeček, Prof. Michal Froněk – Olgoj Chorchoj Studio	
	The award-winning products of "Red Dot: Best of the Best", "Red Dot" and "Honourable Mention" distinctions	
	Die Siegerprodukte der Auszeichnungen „Red Dot: Best of the Best", „Red Dot" und „Honourable Mention"	
70	Interior design	
	Interior Design	
164	Living rooms and bedrooms	
	Wohnen und Schlafen	
186	Kitchens	
	Küche	
290	Bathrooms and sanitary equipment	
	Bad und Sanitär	
330	Lighting and lamps	
	Licht und Leuchten	
382	Urban design and public spaces	
	Urban Design und öffentlicher Raum	
398	**The jurors of the Red Dot Award: Product Design**	
	Die Juroren des Red Dot Award: Product Design	
400	David Andersen	
402	Prof. Masayo Ave	
404	Martin Beeh	
406	Gordon Bruce	
408	Gisbert L. Brunner	
410	Rüdiger Bucher	
412	Prof. Jun Cai	
414	Vivian Wai-kwan Cheng	
416	Mårten Claesson	
418	Vincent Créance	
420	Martin Darbyshire	
422	Katrin de Louw	
424	Saskia Diez	
426	Stefan Eckstein	
428	Robin Edman	
430	Prof. Lutz Fügener	
432	Hideshi Hamaguchi	
434	Prof. Renke He	
436	Prof. Carlos Hinrichsen	
438	Simon Husslein	
440	Qiong Er Jiang	
442	Prof. Cheng-Neng Kuan	
444	Steve Leung	
446	Dr. Thomas Lockwood	
448	Wolfgang K. Meyer-Hayoz	
450	Prof. Jure Miklavc	
452	Adriana Monk	
454	Prof. Dr. Ken Nah	
456	Alexander Neumeister	
458	Ken Okuyama	
460	Simon Ong	
462	Dr. Sascha Peters	
464	Dirk Schumann	
466	Prof. Song Kee Hong	
468	Dick Spierenburg	
470	Leon Sun	
472	Kazuo Tanaka	
474	Nils Toft	
476	Prof. Danny Venlet	
478	Dr. Joseph Francis Wong	
	Alphabetical index	
	Alphabetisches Register	
480	Manufacturers and distributors	
	Hersteller und Vertrieb	
483	Designers	
	Designer	
492	Imprint	
	Impressum	

Professor Dr. Peter Zec
Preface of the editor
Vorwort des Herausgebers

Dear reader,

The Red Dot Design Yearbook with its four volumes "Living", "Doing", "Working" and "Enjoying" provides a comprehensive overview of the latest developments in product design. As you leaf through the books, you will notice some trends that run through all of the categories. In the competition year 2019/2020, one such trend is the clearly recognisable move toward more eco-friendly and sustainable products on the one hand and products that are more and more intelligent on the other. Other developments unfold within the narrow framework of a certain product segment or geographical region. Frequently, such developments are no less ground-breaking. On the contrary, they often indicate where future trends might lead. Embark on a journey of discovery, and be inspired by the many excellently designed products.

This year once again saw many well-known brands enter their products in the competition. This may come as an initial surprise, as one could be forgiven for thinking that these manufacturers don't need any more awards in order to sell their products or assure themselves of their own expertise. But the lesson to be learned from these companies that are successful as a brand through design is that this success has to be carefully earned – year after year. That's because the credibility of a brand is established by a company being visible over a longer period and also demonstrating a high level of continuity in its products, their design and quality. Many of the best-known brands internationally in the field of consumer and luxury goods have also been winning distinctions in the Red Dot Design Award for years, including Ferrari, Bosch, Apple, hansgrohe, Fiskars, LG Electronics, Lenovo and Sony. Not only are they some of this year's Red Dot: Best of the Best laureates, they can also look back at a consistent brand development. They have a striking corporate design, and above all else they stand for products with outstanding design and high quality.

In order to underscore and enhance the relevance of a comprehensive brand strategy (and ideally a related design strategy), brands have been accorded a larger platform in this year's Red Dot competition for communication design. Within an industry, companies can now enter the running for the distinction "Red Dot: Brand of the Year" in the Red Dot Award: Brands & Communication Design.

Without further ado, allow me to wish you an entertaining read!

Yours sincerely,
Peter Zec

Liebe Leserin, lieber Leser,

das Red Dot Design Yearbook gewährt Ihnen mit seinen vier Bänden „Living", „Doing", „Working" und „Enjoying" einen umfassenden Überblick über die neuesten Entwicklungen im Produktdesign. Wenn Sie durch die Bücher blättern, werden Sie den einen oder anderen Trend erkennen, der sich durch sämtliche Kategorien zieht – im Wettbewerbsjahr 2019/2020 ist dies etwa eine klar erkennbare Tendenz zu umweltfreundlicheren und nachhaltigeren Produkten einerseits sowie zu immer intelligenteren Produkten andererseits. Andere Entwicklungen spielen sich im engen Rahmen eines bestimmten Produktsegments oder einer geografischen Region ab, sind deswegen aber häufig nicht weniger richtungsweisend, sondern zeigen ganz im Gegenteil oft schon an, wohin der Trend in den nächsten Jahren gehen wird. Gehen Sie auf Entdeckungsreise und lassen Sie sich von den vielen ausgezeichnet gestalteten Produkten inspirieren.

Auch in diesem Jahr haben wieder viele bekannte Marken ihre Produkte zum Wettbewerb eingereicht. Auf den ersten Blick mag dies verwundern, denn man sollte meinen, dass diese Hersteller keine Auszeichnung mehr benötigen, um ihre Produkte zu verkaufen oder sich ihres eigenen Könnens zu versichern. Doch kann man von diesen Firmen, die als Marke mit Design erfolgreich sind, lernen, dass auch dieser Erfolg sorgfältig erarbeitet werden muss – Jahr für Jahr aufs Neue. Denn die Glaubwürdigkeit einer Marke kommt erst dadurch zustande, dass ein Unternehmen über einen längeren Zeitraum hinweg sichtbar ist und auch in seinen Produkten, deren Design und Qualität eine hohe Beständigkeit zeigt. Viele der international bekanntesten Marken im Bereich der Konsum- und Luxusgüter sind auch seit Jahren beim Red Dot Design Award erfolgreich, darunter Ferrari, Bosch, Apple, hansgrohe, Fiskars, LG Electronics, Lenovo oder Sony. Sie gehören nicht nur zu den diesjährigen Red Dot: Best of the Best-Preisträgern, sondern können auch auf eine kontinuierliche Markenentwicklung zurückblicken. Sie haben ein Corporate Design, das prägnant ist; vor allem aber stehen sie für Produkte mit herausragendem Design und hoher Qualität.

Um die Relevanz einer umfassenden Marken- und einer damit im Idealfall einhergehenden Designstrategie zu unterstreichen und zu stärken, erhalten Marken bei Red Dot ab diesem Jahr eine größere Plattform im Wettbewerb für Kommunikationsdesign: Beim Red Dot Award: Brands & Communication Design können sich Unternehmen jetzt innerhalb einer Branche um die Auszeichnung „Red Dot: Brand of the Year" bewerben.

Und nun wünsche ich Ihnen viel Vergnügen bei der Lektüre!

Ihr
Peter Zec

The title "Red Dot: Design Team of the Year" is bestowed on a design team that has garnered attention through its outstanding overall design achievements. This year, the title goes to Flavio Manzoni and the Ferrari Design Team. This award is the only one of its kind in the world and is extremely highly regarded even outside of the design scene.

Mit der Auszeichnung „Red Dot: Design Team of the Year" wird ein Designteam geehrt, das durch seine herausragende gestalterische Gesamtleistung auf sich aufmerksam gemacht hat. In diesem Jahr geht sie an Flavio Manzoni und das Ferrari Design Team. Diese Würdigung ist einzigartig auf der Welt und genießt über die Designszene hinaus höchstes Ansehen.

In recognition of its feat, the Red Dot: Design Team of the Year receives the "Radius" trophy. This sculpture was designed and crafted by the Weinstadt-Schnaidt based designer, Simon Peter Eiber.

Als Anerkennung erhält das Red Dot: Design Team of the Year den Wanderpokal „Radius". Die Skulptur wurde entworfen und angefertigt von dem Designer Simon Peter Eiber aus Weinstadt-Schnaidt.

2019	Flavio Manzoni & Ferrari Design Team
2018	Phoenix Design Team
2017	Canyon Design Team
2016	Blackmagic Industrial Design Team led by Simon Kidd
2015	Robert Sachon & Bosch Home Appliances Design Team
2014	Veryday
2013	Lenovo Design & User Experience Team
2012	Michael Mauer & Style Porsche
2011	The Grohe Design Team led by Paul Flowers
2010	Stephan Niehaus & Hilti Design Team
2009	Susan Perkins & Tupperware World Wide Design Team
2008	Michael Laude & Bose Design Team
2007	Chris Bangle & Design Team BMW Group
2006	LG Corporate Design Center
2005	Adidas Design Team
2004	Pininfarina Design Team
2003	Nokia Design Team
2002	Apple Industrial Design Team
2001	Festo Design Team
2000	Sony Design Team
1999	Audi Design Team
1998	Philips Design Team
1997	Michele De Lucchi Design Team
1996	Bill Moggridge & Ideo Design Team
1995	Herbert Schultes & Siemens Design Team
1994	Bruno Sacco & Mercedes-Benz Design Team
1993	Hartmut Esslinger & Frogdesign
1992	Alexander Neumeister & Neumeister Design
1991	Reiner Moll & Partner & Moll Design
1990	Slany Design Team
1989	Braun Design Team
1988	Leybold AG Design Team

Red Dot: Design Team of the Year 2019
Flavio Manzoni and Ferrari Design Team

This year's "Red Dot: Design Team of the Year" title goes to Flavio Manzoni and the Ferrari Design Team in Maranello. Flavio Manzoni became Senior Vice-President for Design at Ferrari in 2010. Since the Italian car manufacturer was founded in 1947, he is the first head designer to have succeeded in building a successful Ferrari Design Team.

This achievement is reflected not only in the new Centro Stile that opened in Maranello in 2018 but also in the Red Dot Award: Product Design. In the last five years, Manzoni and the Ferrari Design Team have won an accolade at the Red Dot Award 14 times and have five times been awarded the highest distinction the competition has to bestow, the Red Dot: Best of the Best.

Ferrari is the first car manufacturer in the history of the competition to win the top distinction five times in a row. Thanks to this achievement, the brand now also leads the Red Dot Ranking in the Automotive Design category for the first time. This is an outstanding accomplishment that will be recognised this year with the honorary title "Red Dot: Design Team of the Year".

Die Auszeichnung „Red Dot: Design Team of the Year" geht in diesem Jahr an Flavio Manzoni und das Ferrari Design Team in Maranello. 2010 wurde Flavio Manzoni Senior Vice-President for Design bei Ferrari. Seit der Gründung des italienischen Automobilherstellers im Jahr 1947 ist er der erste Chefdesigner, dem es gelungen ist, für Ferrari ein erfolgreiches Designteam aufzubauen.

Diese Leistung spiegelt sich nicht nur im neuen Centro Stile wider, das 2018 in Maranello eröffnet wurde, sondern auch im Red Dot Award: Product Design. Manzoni und das Ferrari Design Team wurden in den letzten fünf Jahren 14 Mal im Red Dot Award ausgezeichnet und erhielten fünf Mal die höchste Auszeichnung im Wettbewerb, den Red Dot: Best of the Best.

Ein Novum in der Geschichte des Wettbewerbs: Ferrari ist es als erstem Automobilhersteller gelungen, die höchste Auszeichnung fünf Mal in Folge zu gewinnen. Mit dieser Leistung führt die Marke erstmals auch das Red Dot Ranking im Automotive Design an. Eine herausragende Leistung, die in diesem Jahr mit der Ehrenauszeichnung „Red Dot: Design Team of the Year" gewürdigt wird.

Flavio Manzoni and the Ferrari Design Team of the Monza SP1 and Monza SP2.
Flavio Manzoni und das Ferrari Design Team des Monza SP1 und Monza SP2.

Flavio Manzoni, Senior Vice-President for Design; Matteo De Petris, Responsible Advanced Design;
Francesco Russo, Senior Exterior Designer; Alain Abramo, Senior Exterior Designer; Federico Acuto, Senior Exterior Designer;
Emanuel Salvatore, Responsible Virtual Modelling; Salvo Della Ventura, Responsible Advanced Virtual Modelling;
Luca Casarini, Responsible Interior Design; Fabio Massari, Senior Interior Designer; Guglielmo Galliano, Responsible Graphic & Visual

Designing Dreams
Flavio Manzoni and Ferrari Design Team

Maranello. The small Italian town in the Emilia-Romagna region is synonymous around the world with the brand and the myth that is Ferrari. This is where the dream cars of tomorrow are made, which feature technical innovations that shape our idea of the future and whose timeless language of form endures for generations. Ferrari's company premises are more than a mere ensemble of production halls, workshops and administrative buildings. Since the mid-1990s, site has transformed into a centre of modern industrial architecture. On Viale Enzo Ferrari, the campus street that bears the name of the company founder, a new dream factory that makes customers' dreams come true has emerged between the architectural gems designed by Jean Nouvel, Massimiliano Fuksas, Renzo Piano and Marco Visconti. Its name: Ferrari Centro Stile.

The dream factory

The architectural project of the new design centre was directed by the Ferrari Design Team under the guidance of architect Flavio Manzoni while the engineering project was developed in collaboration with the Design International studio of London and the Planning studio of Bologna. The building has brought together all design-related tasks and activities under one spectacular roof: a structure made from triangular glass and aluminium modules, the exterior of which is decorated with the cavallino rampante or 'prancing horse'. The geometric modules combine to form powerful and elegant areas reminiscent at their points of intersection of the dynamic lines of a Ferrari and that overlie the four-storey building like a wave.

What was once an old warehouse for prototypes is now a design dream factory. On a space of 5,000 square metres, a modern studio has been created for the designers and employees of the in-house design team in addition to a presentation room with a terrace for presenting new models and a Tailor Made area where the company's customers can configure their own customised dream car.

The Tailor Made area turns each Ferrari into a unique piece for its owner. The designers use virtual previews to show the customer his or her individually made vehicle in real time. For example, the aesthetic of the exterior and interior can be previewed on the display. With all of these possibilities for personalising their own Ferrari, customers are given a level of exclusivity that is unparalleled in the automotive sector.

The first floor of Centro Stile houses the Virtual Modelling department, where digital Ferrari models are created in 3D. Modelling involves using software to transform surface data into three-dimensional objects. Although the designers cannot touch or feel the virtual lines and edges, digital cavities and volumes with their hands, their professional eye takes

Maranello. Die kleine italienische Stadt in der Region Emilia-Romagna ist weltweit ein Synonym für die Marke und den Mythos Ferrari. Hier entstehen die Traumautos von morgen, deren technische Innovationen unsere Vorstellung von der Zukunft prägen und deren zeitlose Formensprache Generationen überdauert. Ferraris Betriebsgelände ist nicht nur ein Ensemble aus Fabrikhallen, Werkstätten und Verwaltungsgebäuden: Es hat sich seit Mitte der 1990er Jahre zu einem Zentrum moderner Industriearchitektur entwickelt. Auf dem Campus ist an der Viale Enzo Ferrari, der Straße, die den Namen des Firmengründers trägt, zwischen den architektonischen Glanzstücken von Jean Nouvel, Massimiliano Fuksas, Renzo Piano und Marco Visconti eine neue Traumfabrik entstanden, die die Wünsche der Kunden Wirklichkeit werden lässt: Ferrari Centro Stile.

Die Traumfabrik

Das architektonische Projekt für das neue Designzentrum wurde von dem Ferrari Design Team unter der Leitung des Architekten Flavio Manzoni gesteuert, während das bautechnische Projekt in Zusammenarbeit mit dem Design International Studio in London und dem Planning Studio in Bologna entwickelt wurde. Das Gebäude vereint alle designrelevanten Aufgaben- und Tätigkeitsbereiche unter einer spektakulären Dachkonstruktion: eine Struktur aus dreieckigen Glas- und Aluminiummodulen, deren Äußeres das Cavallino rampante, das sich aufbäumende Pferdchen ziert. Die geometrischen Module verbinden sich zu kraftvollen und eleganten Flächen, die dort, wo sie aufeinandertreffen, an die dynamischen Linien eines Ferrari erinnern und sich wie eine Welle über das vierstöckige Gebäude legen.

Was früher ein altes Lager für Prototypen war, ist heute eine Traumfabrik des Designs. Auf 5.000 m² Fläche ist ein modernes Studio für die Designer und Mitarbeiter des In-house Design Teams entstanden, ein Präsentationsraum mit Terrasse für die Vorstellung neuer Modelle und ein „Tailor Made"-Bereich, welcher den Kunden des Unternehmens erlaubt, ihr Traumauto individuell ausstatten zu lassen.

Im „Tailor Made"-Bereich wird jeder Ferrari zu einem Unikat für seinen Besitzer. In virtuellen Vorschauen präsentieren die Designer dem Kunden sein individuell gefertigtes Fahrzeug in Echtzeit. So lässt sich die Ästhetik des Exteriors und Interieurs bereits am Monitor beurteilen. Mit all diesen Möglichkeiten zur persönlichen Gestaltung des eigenen Ferraris erhalten die Kunden einen Grad an Exklusivität, der in der Automobilbranche seinesgleichen sucht.

Auf der ersten Etage des Centro Stile befindet sich das Virtual Modelling. Hier entstehen digitale Ferrari-Modelle in 3D. Bei der Modellierung werden Daten der Oberflächen mithilfe von Software in dreidimensionale

in these features and 'touches' the surface with its convex and concave forms. This creative interplay with beauty, proportions, contrasts and colour hues is based on the designers' constantly alternating view of the details and the contours of the vehicle.

But alongside state-of-the-art technology, there is still a need for craftsmanship. That's because, in addition to sketches and computer models, Ferrari models are produced by hand. Flavio Manzoni places special emphasis on modelling, where scale models and original-size models are created by digitally controlled milling machines and are formed by a team of experienced artists before the meticulous manual finish. Flavio Manzoni brought the clay modelling approach from Germany in 2010. Particularly in the initial phase of the newly formed design team, Manzoni and his staff literally created new models with their hands. At that time, the Head of Design and his team worked like artists to connect surfaces with each other, to better assess forms and proportions and to refine the models step by step.

Like in many other design studios and in-house design teams, confidentiality was another top priority alongside creativity. Consequently, the geometric elements of the roof construction serve not only as an eye-catching feature but also as a privacy screen. The second skin of the roof construction works like a protective shield that allows daylight through while keeping out unwanted eyes. On the second floor of Centro Stile, which includes a terrace and a large conference and presentation room with a high-resolution LED wall, newly designed models can thus be presented in natural lighting conditions. Not only does Centro Stile make the professional work of the design team easier and more pleasant, it also makes it more effective and efficient for the company, as the draft and development phases are significantly shorter and it's possible to agree on improvements to the models with the engineers right up to the very last moment.

Start-up and warm-up

More than 100 designers work in the Centro Stile building today, but this was not always the case. When Flavio Manzoni was appointed Senior Vice-President for Design at Ferrari in 2010, there were just five people in a small team that lacked not only a structure but also tools and above all else a vision of the future of the Ferrari brand. When the decision was taken to create a dedicated in-house design team, Flavio Manzoni shared his vision with the small group of staff: "I saw their eyes light up, but nobody really believed in it," Flavio Manzoni remembers. "Everyone thought 'Manzoni is a dreamer'." Previously, the design activities were organised in collaboration with external partners such as Pininfarina.

Objekte verwandelt. Auch wenn die Designer die virtuellen Linien und Kanten, die digitalen Hohlräume und Volumen nicht mit den Händen berühren und ertasten können, fährt ihr professionelles Auge an ihnen entlang und berührt die Oberfläche aus konvexen und konkaven Formen. Das gestalterische Spiel mit der Schönheit, den Proportionen, den Kontrasten und Farbnuancen basiert auf dem ständig wechselnden Blick der Designer zwischen den Details und den Konturen des Autos.

Neben neuester Technologie ist aber nach wie vor handwerkliches Können gefragt. Denn neben Skizzen und Computermodellen werden Ferrari-Modelle von Hand gefertigt. Ein besonderes Augenmerk legt Flavio Manzoni auf den Modellbau, wo maßstabsgetreue Modelle und solche in Originalgröße von digital gesteuerten Fräsmaschinen entstehen und von einem Team aus erfahrenen Künstlern geformt werden, bevor dann das Finish sorgfältig von Hand erfolgt. Flavio Manzoni hat das Clay Modelling 2010 aus Deutschland mitgebracht. Insbesondere in der Anfangsphase des neu gebildeten Designteams formen Manzoni und seine Mitarbeiter neue Modelle buchstäblich mit ihren Händen. Der Designchef und sein Team arbeiten zu dieser Zeit wie Künstler, um Oberflächen miteinander zu verbinden, die Formen und Proportionen besser beurteilen zu können und die Modelle Schritt für Schritt weiterzuentwickeln.

Wie bei vielen anderen Designstudios und In-house Design Teams steht mit der Kreativität auch die Diskretion an oberster Stelle. Die geometrischen Elemente der Dachkonstruktion sind daher nicht nur Blickfang, sondern auch Blickschutz. Die zweite Haut der Dachkonstruktion funktioniert wie ein Schutzschild, der zwar Tageslicht hineinlässt, aber ungewünschte Blicke abhält. So können auf der zweiten Ebene des Centro Stile, wo sich eine Terrasse und ein großer Konferenz- und Präsentationsraum mit einer hochauflösenden LED-Wand befinden, neu konzipierte Modelle bei natürlichem Licht präsentiert werden. Das Centro Stile macht die professionelle Arbeit nicht nur für das Designteam angenehmer und leichter, sondern auch für das Unternehmen effektiver und effizienter, da sich die Entwurfs- und Entwicklungsphasen deutlich verkürzen und man in Abstimmung mit den Ingenieuren noch bis zur letzten Minute Verbesserungen an den Modellen vornehmen kann.

Start-up und Warm-up

In den Räumen des Centro Stile arbeiten heute mehr als 100 Designer. Das war nicht immer so. Als Flavio Manzoni im Jahr 2010 zum Senior Vice-President for Design bei Ferrari ernannt wird, bilden gerade einmal fünf Personen ein kleines Team, dem es nicht nur an Struktur fehlt, sondern auch an Werkzeugen, vor allem aber an einer Vorstellung von der Zukunft der Marke Ferrari. Als die Entscheidung fällt, ein eigenes In-house Design Team aufzubauen, teilt Flavio Manzoni mit der kleinen Gruppe von Mitarbeitern seine Vision: „Ich sah das Leuchten in ihren Augen, aber niemand glaubte wirklich daran", erinnert sich Flavio Manzoni. „Jeder dachte: Manzoni ist ein Träumer." Bisher waren Designaktivitäten in Zusammenarbeit mit externen Partnern wie Pininfarina organisiert worden.

The iconic shape of the Ferrari FXX K inspired by aircraft. The perfect fusion of form and function.
Von Flugzeugen inspirierte ikonische Form des Ferrari FXX K. Die perfekte Verschmelzung von Form und Funktion.

When Manzoni became Senior Vice-President for Design at Ferrari in 2010, an old storehouse that housed Ferrari prototypes initially had to be used as a temporary Design Center. And while Manzoni had to improvise on a daily basis, he worked tirelessly on designs for new models. Behind the scenes, he was interviewing hundreds of designers to find out who would fit in his team and be able to understand, reinterpret and transform the Ferrari brand and values.

In the beginning, it was difficult for Manzoni to judge who really understood the Ferrari brand and also fit in the team in terms of their social skills and attitudes. Manzoni quickly noticed that experience does not always pay off. Anyone who wanted to work as a designer for Ferrari would have to be able to approach the brand creatively without preconceptions and be willing to explore Ferrari's brand values again and again in a team with other designers, engineers and marketing experts. Too much experience could sometimes be a disadvantage in this regard. "It was like working in a start-up." That's how Manzoni describes the unimaginable dynamism of this new departure.

Als Manzoni 2010 Senior Vice-President for Design bei Ferrari wird, muss zunächst ein altes Lagerhaus, das Ferraris Prototypen beherbergt, als provisorisches Design Center genutzt werden. Und während Manzoni tagtäglich improvisieren muss, arbeitet er unermüdlich an Entwürfen für neue Modelle. Im Hintergrund führt er Hunderte von Bewerbungsgesprächen mit Designern, um herauszufinden, wer in sein Team passt und in der Lage sein könnte, die Marke und die Werte von Ferrari zu verstehen, sie neu zu interpretieren und zu transformieren.

Zu Beginn ist es für Manzoni schwierig zu beurteilen, wer die Marke Ferrari wirklich versteht und auch mit Blick auf seine sozialen Fähigkeiten und seine Lebenseinstellung ins Team passt. Manzoni merkt schnell, dass sich Erfahrung nicht immer auszahlt. Wer als Designer für Ferrari arbeiten will, muss in der Lage sein, sich auf die Marke einzulassen, und bereit sein, sich immer wieder aufs Neue kreativ und in einem Team mit anderen Designern, Ingenieuren und Marketingexperten mit den Werten, die Ferrari verkörpert, auseinanderzusetzen. Zu viel Erfahrung kann da bisweilen auch hinderlich sein. „Es herrschten Bedingungen wie in einem Start-up-Unternehmen", beschreibt Manzoni die unvorstellbare Dynamik des Neuanfangs.

Ferrari LaFerrari. The balance between organic form and the beauty of complexity.
Ferrari LaFerrari. Die Balance zwischen organischer Form und komplexer Schönheit.

The essence of the brand

The first model developed, designed and built entirely in-house was the LaFerrari, which was designed by the Ferrari Design Team in close cooperation with the technical and development department. The model won a Red Dot in 2015. It was the result of a sporting competition with Pininfarina, where the Ferrari Design Team ultimately emerged as the winner.

The profile of the new vehicle dipped down prominently at the nose and featured a low hood. The nose was reminiscent of the legendary shapes of the Ferrari sports prototypes from the 1960s, for example the "sharknose" of the Ferrari 156. There was a conceptual link between the two, but no formal connection. Of course Manzoni and his design team felt a loyalty to the brand and to Ferrari's mythical aura, but they didn't simply repeat individual elements nostalgically. For them, retro design was an expression of a lack of courage and creativity. With the Ferrari LaFerrari, the designers succeeded in recalling and reinterpreting milestones in the company and design history. Not only did the concave and convex surfaces provide a dramatic tension, they also ensured outstanding wind resistance and downforce values.

Manzoni and his design team have frequently been inspired by ideas and shapes from art and culture, for example the monumental sculptures and installations of the Indian-born British artist Anish Kapoor, whose Marsyas from 2002 was on display in the Turbine Hall of the Tate Modern in London. Like Anish Kapoor, Flavio Manzoni endeavours in his designs to answer the question of how to translate performance-based engineering

Die Essenz der Marke

Das erste Modell, das ausschließlich in-house entwickelt, gestaltet und gebaut wird, ist der LaFerrari, der in enger Zusammenarbeit des Ferrari Design Teams mit der Technik- und Entwicklungsabteilung entworfen wird. 2015 wird er mit dem Red Dot ausgezeichnet. Er geht aus einem sportlichen Wettbewerb mit Pininfarina hervor, bei dem das Ferrari Design Team am Ende als Sieger dasteht.

Im Profil hat das neue Fahrzeug eine scharf nach unten verlaufende Nase und eine tief sitzende Motorhaube. Die Nase erinnert an die legendären Formen der Ferrari Sport-Prototypen der 1960er Jahre, etwa an die „Haifischnase" des Ferrari 156. Zwischen beiden gibt es eine konzeptionelle, aber keine formale Verbindung. Natürlich fühlen sich Manzoni und sein Designteam der Marke und dem Mythos Ferrari verpflichtet, aber sie wiederholen nicht einfach einzelne Elemente in nostalgischer Weise. Für sie ist Retrodesign ein Ausdruck fehlenden Mutes und mangelnder Kreativität. Mit dem Ferrari LaFerrari gelingt es den Designern, Meilensteine der Unternehmens- und Designgeschichte in Erinnerung zu rufen und sie neu zu interpretieren. Die konkaven und konvexen Oberflächen sorgen nicht nur für eine wechselvolle Spannung, sie sorgen auch für herausragende Luftwiderstands- und Abtriebswerte.

Inspiriert werden Manzoni und sein Designteam nicht selten durch Ideen und Formen der Kunst und Kultur, wie etwa durch die monumentalen Skulpturen und Installationen des indisch-britischen Künstlers Anish Kapoor, dessen Marsyas aus dem Jahr 2002 in der Turbinenhalle der Tate Modern in London zu sehen war. Ähnlich wie Anish Kapoor geht

language into an aesthetic body language. "You can only design a Ferrari if you know what's under the surface." That's how Manzoni describes the interplay between technical complexity and aesthetic design.

Manzoni describes the design process as follows: "Designing a new car requires sensitivity, imagination, abstract thought and the ability to combine elements that do not appear to belong together, at least not intuitively." Ferrari endeavours to constantly redefine the limits of technology and design and to gradually push these boundaries towards the future without losing sight of the brand and its values. "Every Ferrari stands for innovation, beauty and driving thrill," says Manzoni, adding that "every model has to embody the essence of the brand."

Naturally, we always have to bear in mind the difference between a Gran Turismo and a supercar when considering the design of Ferrari models. While the Gran Turismo wins fans through its sporting elegance and luxury, a supercar that conveys the adrenaline of the racetrack calls for a higher degree of complexity. Its form hinges on the technical data and on performance. Yet what both of these models share is the idea "that a Ferrari always stems from a dream," says Flavio Manzoni.

One key difference between Ferrari and other manufacturers in automotive design is that the Italian sports car manufacturer does not feature a rhetorical evolution of form. Neither does Ferrari pursue the strategy adopted by other manufacturers that make the models belong to the brand by means of a similarity with other members of the brand family. Although there are lines that connect back to tradition, these are never for stylistic reasons. The focus is on state-of-the-art sports car technology, formal aestheticism and driving thrill. This is also exemplified by the new "Icona" model segment, the design of which draws inspiration from the open Barchettas from the 1950s that Scuderia Ferrari raced in at the time, in particular the 166 MM, but also the 750 Monza and the 860 Monza. The new limited production Monza SP1 and Monza SP2 models with their minimalistic silhouettes are the vanguard in this new series of design icons.

The Monza SP1, which won the Red Dot: Best of the Best in 2019, is designed as a single seater, while the Monza SP2 seats two. The carbon bodywork reduces the weight of the two vehicles to 1,500 kg each. The V12 6.5-litre engine has 810 hp and in both models accelerates from 0 to 100 in 2.9 seconds, reaching 200 km/h just 5 seconds later. Because neither model has a windscreen for the driver, the panelling includes a type of "bypass" that diverts the airflow away from the driver and creates a kind of "virtual windscreen" for the driver. Ferrari has registered a patent for this innovation. The two Monza models are an excellent example of how technology and design, innovation and aesthetics can all be channelled into a unique driving experience. This allows the driver to experience a feeling of speed that is otherwise known only to Formula 1 race drivers.

Flavio Manzoni bei seinen Entwürfen der Frage nach, wie eine leistungsorientierte Ingenieursprache in eine ästhetische Körpersprache umgeformt werden kann. „Man kann einen Ferrari nur gestalten, wenn man weiß, was unter der Oberfläche stattfindet", beschreibt Manzoni das Zusammenspiel von technischer Komplexität und ästhetischer Formgebung.

„Ein neues Auto zu gestalten, erfordert Einfühlungsvermögen, Vorstellungskraft, abstraktes Denken und die Fähigkeit, Elemente zu verbinden, die scheinbar nicht zusammengehören, zumindest nicht auf den ersten Blick", beschreibt Manzoni den Designprozess. Ferrari versucht, die Grenzen der Technik und Gestaltung immer wieder neu zu bestimmen und Schritt für Schritt in Richtung Zukunft zu verschieben, ohne die Marke und ihre Werte aus dem Auge zu verlieren. „Jeder Ferrari steht für Innovation, Schönheit und Fahrleidenschaft", sagt Manzoni und ergänzt, dass „jedes Modell die Essenz der Marke verkörpern muss."

Natürlich muss man bei der Gestaltung von Ferrari-Modellen immer auch den Unterschied zwischen einem Gran Turismo und einem Supersportwagen im Blick behalten. Während der Gran Turismo durch sportliche Eleganz und luxuriösen Komfort begeistert, erfordert ein Supersportwagen, der das Adrenalin der Rennstrecke versprüht, eine höhere Komplexität. Seine Form wird entscheidend von den technischen Daten und der Leistungsfähigkeit geprägt. Aber beide vereint, „dass ein Ferrari immer aus einem Traum entsteht", sagt Flavio Manzoni.

Ein wesentlicher Unterschied zwischen Ferrari und anderen Herstellern im Automobildesign besteht darin, dass es beim italienischen Sportwagenhersteller keine rhetorische Evolution der Form gibt. Ferrari folgt auch nicht der Strategie anderer Hersteller, die Markenzugehörigkeit der Modelle nach dem Vorbild von Familienähnlichkeit zu pflegen. Obgleich es Verbindungslinien zur Tradition gibt, werden diese niemals aus stilistischen Gründen gezogen. Modernste Sportwagentechnik, die Ästhetik der Form und die Fahrleidenschaft stehen im Vordergrund. So auch im neuen Modellsegment „Icona", dessen Design von den offenen Barchettas der 1950er Jahre inspiriert wurde, mit denen die Scuderia Ferrari damals an den Start ging, insbesondere von dem 166 MM, aber auch dem 750 Monza und dem 860 Monza. Die neuen Sondermodelle Monza SP1 und Monza SP2 mit ihren minimalistischen Silhouetten bilden den Auftakt zu dieser neuen Serie von Designikonen.

Der Monza SP1, im Jahr 2019 mit dem Red Dot: Best of the Best ausgezeichnet, ist als Einsitzer konzipiert, im Monza SP2 finden zwei Personen Platz. Die Karosserie aus Carbon drückt das Gewicht der beiden Fahrzeuge auf jeweils 1.500 kg. Der V12-Motor mit 6,5 Litern Hubraum leistet 810 PS und beschleunigt die beiden Fahrzeuge in 2,9 Sekunden aus dem Stand auf Tempo 100, nur 5 Sekunden später ist Tempo 200 erreicht. Da beiden Modellen eine Windschutzscheibe für den Fahrer fehlt, ist in der Verkleidung eine Art „Bypass" eingearbeitet, der den anströmenden Fahrtwind umlenkt und eine „virtuelle Windschutzscheibe" für den Fahrer erzeugt. Ferrari hat auf diese Innovation ein Patent angemeldet. Die beiden Monza-Modelle sind ein gelungenes Beispiel dafür, wie Technik und Design, Innovation und Ästhetik auf ein einzigartiges Fahrerlebnis ausgerichtet sind. So kommt der Fahrer in den Genuss eines Geschwindigkeitsgefühls, wie es sonst nur Formel-1-Fahrer erleben.

Designing values

The dream figures recorded by the sports cars from Maranello aren't limited to the race track – the company is also doing very well in terms of its profitability and share price and market value. The Italian car maker is the most profitable company in the automotive industry and the clear leader amongst premium and luxury car manufacturers. Ferrari understands better than any other company how to make luxury sports cars objects of desire by consistently focusing on the core of the brand and pursuing the strategy of always building one car less than the market requires. If ever any proof were needed that "Good design is good business," as former IBM President Thomas Watson Jr. once said, then Ferrari has delivered that proof impressively in recent years.

The models designed by Flavio Manzoni and the Ferrari Design Team won 14 awards in the Red Dot Design Award in the years 2015 to 2019 alone. Ferrari is the first car manufacturer in the history of the competition to win the top distinction five times in a row – for the Ferrari models FXX-K, 488 GTB, J50, Portofino and Monza SP1. Thanks to this achievement, the brand now also leads the Red Dot Ranking in the Automotive Design category for the first time.

By establishing a Ferrari in-house design team as well as Centro Stile in Maranello and the Ferrari models created under his leadership, Flavio Manzoni has succeeded in his pioneering work. He has created an open and trusting culture of communication, which is the basis for shared success. The further the team progresses together, the better the cars become.

Manzoni likes to compare his team to a jazz ensemble: everyone has his or her own personal strengths and individual skill set, but each person is willing to contribute his or her creativity and social skills to a shared objective and the future of the brand. As a result, the long journey from a blank sheet of paper to a finished car is a magical experience for Manzoni every single time. When a new idea is born and the first strokes and lines put an ideal scenario to paper, he dreams that this ideal and the creative fire that fanned the ideal can permeate the entire project – right through to the finished vehicle. And every new car, every new Ferrari should intuitively express the innovation and the emotion, the values and the philosophy of Ferrari. It has to be a moving sculpture that combines art and science, technology and design into something new and propels Ferrari's mythical aura into the future.

As we know, myths are stories with a significance based on uniquely lived lives that still fascinate us today. Outstanding products follow a similar pattern. They are visionary, stand out from the rest and tell us their story. Places can also carry this myth within them. Maranello is such a place.

Werte gestalten

Traumhafte Werte erzielen die Sportwagen aus Maranello nicht nur auf der Rennstrecke, traumhafte Werte erzielt das Unternehmen auch mit Blick auf die Profitabilität und seine Börsen- und Markenwerte. Der italienische Automobilhersteller ist das profitabelste Unternehmen der Autobranche und mit Abstand der Spitzenreiter unter den Premium- und Luxusherstellern. Kein anderes Unternehmen versteht es besser, luxuriöse Sportwagen zu Objekten der Begierde zu machen, indem man sich konsequent am Markenkern orientiert und der Strategie folgt, immer ein Auto weniger zu bauen, als der Markt verlangt. Wenn die Aussage „Good design is good business" des früheren IBM-Präsidenten, Thomas Watson Jr., noch irgendeines Beweises bedurft hätte, dann hat Ferrari ihn in den zurückliegenden Jahren auf eindrucksvolle Art und Weise geliefert.

Allein in den Jahren 2015–2019 werden die von Flavio Manzoni und dem Ferrari Design Team entworfenen Modelle vierzehn Mal im Red Dot Design Award ausgezeichnet. Ein Novum in der Geschichte des Wettbewerbs: Ferrari ist es als erstem Automobilhersteller gelungen, die höchste Auszeichnung fünf Mal in Folge zu gewinnen – für die Ferrari-Modelle FXX-K, 488 GTB, J50, Portofino und Monza SP1. Mit dieser Leistung führt die Marke erstmals auch das Red Dot Ranking im Automotive Design an.

Mit dem Aufbau eines Ferrari In-house Design Teams, dem Centro Stile in Maranello und den Ferrari-Modellen, die unter seiner Federführung entstanden sind, ist Flavio Manzoni eine Pionierleistung gelungen. Er hat eine offene und vertrauensvolle Kommunikationskultur geschaffen, die die Basis für den gemeinsamen Erfolg ist. Und je weiter das Team gemeinsam voranschreitet, desto besser werden die Autos.

Manzoni vergleicht sein Team gerne mit einem Jazzensemble: Jeder hat seine persönlichen Stärken und sein individuelles Qualifikationsprofil, aber jeder von ihnen ist bereit, seine Kreativität und seine sozialen Fähigkeiten für ein gemeinsames Ziel und die Zukunft der Marke einzubringen. Daher ist der lange Weg vom leeren Blatt Papier zum fertigen Auto für Manzoni jedes Mal und immer wieder ein magisches Ereignis. Wenn eine neue Idee geboren wird und die ersten Striche und Linien eine Idealvorstellung aufs Papier bringen, dann träumt er davon, dass dieses Ideal und das kreative Feuer, das dieses Ideal entfacht hat, das gesamte Projekt durchdringen kann – bis zum fertigen Auto. Und jedes neue Auto, jeder neue Ferrari sollte die Innovation und die Emotion, die Werte und die Philosophie von Ferrari wie selbstverständlich zum Ausdruck bringen. Es muss sich um eine Skulptur in Bewegung handeln, die Wissenschaft und Kunst, Technik und Design zu etwas Neuem verbindet und den Mythos Ferrari in die Zukunft trägt.

Mythen sind bekanntlich Erzählungen, deren Bedeutung auf einzigartigen Lebensgeschichten basiert, die uns heute noch faszinieren. Herausragende Produkte folgen einem ähnlichen Muster. Sie sind visionär, ragen aus der Masse heraus und erzählen uns ihre Geschichte. Auch Orte können diesen Mythos in sich tragen. Maranello ist so ein Ort.

Ferrari's premises are not just an ensemble of factory buildings, workshops and administrative buildings. It is also a center of modern industrial architecture.
Ferraris Betriebsgelände ist nicht nur ein Ensemble aus Fabrikhallen, Werkstätten und Verwaltungsgebäuden: Es ist auch ein Zentrum moderner Industriearchitektur.

Exceeding expectations
Interview with Flavio Manzoni
Senior Vice-President for Design at Ferrari

Flavio Manzoni was born in Sardinia in 1965 and studied architecture with a specialisation in industrial design at the University of Florence, where he graduated in 1993 under Professor Roberto Segoni. His first teacher, however, was his father, who taught him to draw and awakened in him a passion for art, architecture and design. He has been impressed by the approach of the Italian design masters: Bruno Munari, Joe Colombo, Achille Castiglioni, Marco Zanuso, Enzo Mari. In particular, he was fascinated by their attitude to exploring new materials and shapes, by their way of conceiving everyday objects and tools, and by the iconic power of their products. Manzoni's interdisciplinary creativity has accompanied him throughout his career in automotive design.

After graduating, he began his professional career at Lancia in Turin. In 1999, he moved to Seat in Barcelona as the Head of Interior Design before returning to Lancia as Design Director in 2001. In 2004, he took up the role of Design Director for Fiat, Lancia and LCV. From 2007 to 2010, he was Director of Creative Design in the Volkswagen Group, where he designed many of the most recent Škoda, Bentley, Bugatti and Volkswagen models and redefined the aesthetic of those brands.

Manzoni has been Senior Vice-President for Design at Ferrari since 2010. Prof. Dr. Peter Zec and Burkhard Jacob spoke with him in Maranello about design and Ferrari's brand values.

Mr. Manzoni, before joining Ferrari in 2010, you had already worked as a designer for many different automotive brands. Regardless of where and for whom you have already worked, what do you think should be important for a designer?

That's an important question, because there is one aspect that many designers fail to consider in their work, and that's respect for the brand. I think that every designer should first try to understand and interpret the brand rather than expressing himself or herself.

That's pretty surprising to hear, because it sounds very German!

Maybe it's what I learned during my time in Germany. I think it's important for a designer to experience the brand, to feel it and breathe it in, to absorb it and gauge and understand it better without being influenced by the typical design features that may have become embedded in the memory of a designer who has been in the profession for a long time. Together with my team, I try to understand, interpret and transform the Ferrari brand.

And how would you describe the Ferrari brand, its DNA?

There's a short and simple answer to that question. The Ferrari brand is based on three elements: innovation, driving thrill and beauty. These elements are key to understanding the brand. If one of the three is missing, then it's not a Ferrari.

So how do you marry these three aspects of innovation, driving enthusiasm and beauty?

If we think about very complex products like aircraft or cars, their form is heavily informed by the technical and aerodynamic conditions. The Concorde and the Ferrari FXX-K are good examples of this. They are shaped by hundreds of technical requirements, and yet there has always been and will always be a way to make these objects more beautiful without compromising on performance.

Sie sehen uns einigermaßen überrascht, denn das klingt sehr deutsch!

Vielleicht habe ich es während meiner Zeit in Deutschland gelernt. Ich denke, es ist wichtig für einen Designer, die Marke zu erleben, sie zu spüren, einzuatmen und zu absorbieren, um sie besser beurteilen und verstehen zu können, ohne dabei von den typischen Designmerkmalen beeinflusst zu werden, die sich nach einer langen Karriere vielleicht ins Gedächtnis eingebrannt haben. Zusammen mit meinem Team versuche ich, die Marke Ferrari zu verstehen, zu interpretieren und zu transformieren.

Wie würden Sie denn die Marke Ferrari, ihre DNA beschreiben?

Nun, darauf gibt es eine ebenso einfache wie kurze Antwort. Die Marke Ferrari basiert auf drei Elementen: Innovation, Fahrleidenschaft und Schönheit. Sie sind wesentlich für das Verständnis. Fehlt einer dieser drei Faktoren, ist es kein Ferrari.

Wie bringen Sie denn den Dreiklang aus Innovation, Fahrbegeisterung und Schönheit in Einklang?

Wenn wir über sehr komplexe Produkte wie Flugzeuge oder Autos nachdenken, dann wird deren Form stark von den technischen und aerodynamischen Bedingungen bestimmt. Die Concorde und der Ferrari FXX-K sind gute Beispiele dafür. Sie werden von Hunderten technischer Anforderungen bestimmt, und doch hat es und wird es immer einen Weg geben, diese Objekte schöner zu machen, ohne dass sie an Leistung verlieren.

"Every sketch already sets out a certain idea on paper."

Flavio Manzoni – Senior Vice-President for Design

This would mean that form does not necessarily follow function?

The solution has to lie in combining creativity with technology and art with science. In principle, then, form does follow function, but there will always be scope for creativity and aesthetics.

How do you manage to bridge the gap between the past and the future, between tradition and innovation?

Each new Ferrari opens up a whole new chapter and needs its own, independent form. But that doesn't mean our design team suddenly goes crazy and makes nonsensical design suggestions or interprets the product in an absurd way. There are certainly language codes that belong to the Ferrari brand and create a link between the past and the future. However, this is an unspoken, conceptual link rather than a repetition of stylistic features.

If the design of a new Ferrari means the start of a whole new design project, is it even possible to speak of a design language at Ferrari?

Absolutely. A design language does exist, but we do not pursue the strategy adopted by other car manufacturers that make their models belong to the brand by means of a similarity with other members of the brand family. We avoid this déjà vu effect. A new Ferrari always embodies our brand values, but it does not repeat any stylistic elements. That doesn't make any sense for Ferrari.

To what extent then do you even monitor the competition in your industry or compare Ferrari with other brands?

We don't compare ourselves with other brands. That's something we don't do. If we simply wanted to be different from the others, we would only have to add various distinctive elements to the interior or exterior of the car. But that's not Ferrari's approach. Otherwise I would contradict our principles and our understanding of the brand.

Can you describe to us how you and your team arrive at creative and aesthetic solutions?

The solution can either stem from the intuition of one individual or from a brainstorming session with the team. It's especially important to talk to the engineers. When we design a new Ferrari, we don't start with a blank sheet of paper, a stylistic idea or an existing form. Instead, we start with technical questions and content.

How do you start off a new project? Do you give your team a briefing, or do you use draft drawings to provide a certain direction?

Normally, I do not produce any draft drawings before my staff at the start of a new project, as I don't want to restrict the team's creativity. Because every sketch

Inwiefern beobachten Sie denn überhaupt die Konkurrenz in Ihrer Branche oder vergleichen Ferrari mit anderen Marken?

Wir vergleichen uns nicht mit anderen Marken. Das machen wir nicht. Wollten wir einfach nur anders sein als die anderen, müssten wir nur verschiedene, sich unterscheidende Elemente im oder am Auto hinzufügen. Dies ist aber nicht der Ansatz von Ferrari. Ansonsten würde ich unseren Grundsätzen und unserem Markenverständnis widersprechen.

Können Sie uns denn beschreiben, wie Sie und Ihr Team zu kreativen und ästhetischen Lösungen gelangen?

Die Lösung kann entweder in der Intuition eines Einzelnen liegen oder aus einem Brainstorming des Teams hervorgehen. Insbesondere das Gespräch mit Ingenieuren ist wichtig. Wenn wir einen neuen Ferrari gestalten, dann beginnen wir also nicht mit einem leeren Blatt Papier, einer stilistischen Idee oder einer bereits existierenden Form, sondern mit technischen Fragen und Inhalten.

Wie starten Sie in ein neues Projekt? Geben Sie Ihrem Team ein Briefing oder geben Sie durch Entwurfszeichnungen eine bestimmte Richtung vor?

Normalerweise mache ich zu Beginn eines neuen Projektes keine Entwurfszeichnungen vor meinen Mitarbeitern, weil ich die Kreativität des Teams nicht

"Every designer should first try to understand and interpret the brand."

„Jeder Designer sollte zuerst versuchen, die Marke zu verstehen und zu interpretieren."

Flavio Manzoni – Senior Vice-President for Design

already sets out a certain idea on paper. But certainly I sketch a lot, in my office, or during the development process, when it is necessary to converge and finalise ideas.

Is there internal competition in the team when designing a new model?

That's possible. But if there is internal competition, it is always fair and in good spirit. It's important to understand that the personal background and qualifications of each individual are different. That's why the composition of a team changes depending on the project.

What criteria do you use when deciding how to put a team together?

It depends on the project, the technical requirements and the timing. For example, we developed an Advanced Design Department that mainly comprises young designers and artists. Their task is to imagine the future of Ferrari and to sketch it up, far removed from technical specifications or economic restraints. They have to develop visionary ideas without any mental pressure, because the way in which they imagine the future is based on the conditions that we create here and the experiences they have here.

einschränken möchte. Denn mit jeder Skizze hält man bereits eine bestimmte Idee auf Papier fest. Aber ich fertige viele Skizzen in meinem Büro oder während des Entwicklungsprozesses an, wenn es darum geht, Ideen zusammenzuführen und zu finalisieren.

Gibt es denn innerhalb des Teams einen internen Wettbewerb, wenn es um die Gestaltung eines neuen Modells geht?

Das ist möglich. Aber wenn es einen internen Wettbewerb gibt, dann ist er immer fair und sportlich. Es ist wichtig zu verstehen, dass der persönliche Hintergrund und die Qualifikation jedes Einzelnen unterschiedlich sind. Deshalb ändert sich je nach Projekt die Zusammensetzung eines Teams.

Nach welchen Kriterien entscheiden Sie über die Zusammensetzung eines Teams?

Es hängt vom Projekt ab, den technischen Anforderungen und dem Zeitpunkt. Wir haben beispielsweise ein Advanced Design Department ins Leben gerufen, das im Wesentlichen aus jungen Designern und Künstlern besteht. Ihre Aufgabe ist es, sich die Zukunft von Ferrari vorzustellen und sie zu skizzieren, weit entfernt von technischen Vorgaben oder ökonomischen Bedingungen. Sie sollen visionäre Ideen entwickeln ohne mentalen Druck, denn die Art und Weise, wie sie sich die Zukunft vorstellen, basiert auf den Bedingungen, die wir hier schaffen, und den Erfahrungen, die sie hier machen.

You seem to have a very broad understanding of design and see it as more than just the task of finding an aesthetic form for a technical function.

In my view, design is a communicative and cultural process that culminates not just in a car but in a cultural object. I have developed this deeper understanding of design during my time at Ferrari.

If, as you say, design is a cultural process, is a Ferrari more than just a car?

A Ferrari is not just a car, it's an object of desire. We say that it's a dream, a dynamic sculpture. Something that goes far beyond a car. Maybe I'm not a typical car designer in this respect. I have always pursued a multidisciplinary approach, and I try to develop a much broader view of design, particularly automotive design.

Yet there are undeniable technical requirements that the design has to meet.

Of course. But we view the technical specifications or technical limitations as an opportunity for design, because there are limitations in all aspects of life. Limitations should inspire us to find new and unique solutions. We shift the boundaries of what is possible by transcending those boundaries time after time.

Sie scheinen ein sehr weites Verständnis von Design zu haben und sehen darin nicht nur die Aufgabe, eine ästhetische Form für eine technische Funktion zu finden.

Aus meiner Sicht ist Design ein kommunikativer und kultureller Prozess, an dessen Ende nicht einfach nur ein Auto, sondern ein Kulturobjekt steht. Während meiner Zeit bei Ferrari habe ich dieses tiefere Verständnis für Design entwickelt.

Wenn Design ein kultureller Prozess ist, wie Sie sagen: Ist dann ein Ferrari mehr als nur ein Auto?

Ein Ferrari ist nicht nur ein Auto, sondern ein Objekt der Begierde. Es ist ein Traum, wie wir zu sagen pflegen, eine dynamische Skulptur. Das geht weit über ein Auto hinaus. Vielleicht bin ich in dieser Hinsicht auch kein typischer Autodesigner. Ich habe schon immer einen multidisziplinären Ansatz verfolgt und versuche, eine viel breitere Sichtweise auf das Design, insbesondere auf das Automobildesign zu entwickeln.

Und doch gibt es unweigerlich technische Anforderungen, die das Design erfüllen muss.

Natürlich. Wir betrachten die technischen Bedingungen oder technischen Einschränkungen aber als Chance für das Design, denn Einschränkungen sind überall vorhanden. Einschränkungen sollten unsere Fantasie anregen, um neue und einzigartige Lösungen zu finden. Wir verschieben die Grenzen des Möglichen, indem wir sie immer wieder überschreiten.

"The Ferrari brand is based on three elements: innovation, driving thrill and beauty."
„Die Marke Ferrari basiert auf drei Elementen: Innovation, Fahrleidenschaft und Schönheit."

Flavio Manzoni – Senior Vice-President for Design

One of our jury members, Ken Okuyama, always used to say: "I design the cars that I can't afford myself." You and your team design luxury objects. But many of your designers are very young. How is it possible to design luxury that one can potentially not enjoy oneself?

There are different types of enjoyment. The enjoyment of owning a Ferrari, but also the enjoyment of creating a Ferrari.

Is that just a clever dodge?

Not at all. Designing a Ferrari means being allowed to dream and follow an idea that becomes a design object for our customers. Achilles Castiglioni once summarised this feeling very nicely when he said that design is like a delayed conversation with a customer. So there is also always a conversation about the design objects and symbols that we as designers create.

Is there a typical Ferrari customer or a typical Ferrari driver?

We always say: "Different Ferrari for different Ferraristi."

Einer unserer Juroren, Ken Okuyama, pflegte immer zu sagen: „Ich gestalte die Autos, die ich mir selbst nicht leisten kann." Sie und Ihr Team gestalten Luxusobjekte. Aber viele Ihrer Designer sind sehr jung. Wie kann man Luxus gestalten, den man selbst vielleicht nicht ausleben kann?

Nun, es gibt durchaus unterschiedliche Freuden. Die Freude, einen Ferrari zu besitzen, aber auch die Freude, einen Ferrari zu gestalten.

Ist das ein geschicktes Ausweichmanöver?

Keinesfalls. Die Gestaltung eines Ferrari bedeutet, träumen zu dürfen und einer Idee folgen zu können, die für unsere Kunden zu einem Designobjekt wird. Achilles Castiglioni hat dieses Gefühl einmal sehr schön zusammengefasst, indem er sagte, dass Design so etwas wie eine zeitversetzte Konversation mit einem Kunden sei. Es gibt also immer auch eine Konversation über die Designobjekte und Symbole, die wir als Designer schaffen.

Gibt es denn den typischen Ferrari-Kunden oder den typischen Fahrer eines Ferrari?

Wir pflegen immer zu sagen: „Different Ferrari for different Ferraristi."

"Design is a communicative and cultural process."
„Design ist ein kommunikativer und kultureller Prozess."

Flavio Manzoni – Senior Vice-President for Design

That's a clever answer!

It's the truth. The Ferraristi of a GT are not the same as the Ferraristi who drive an XX. They are entirely different people. They also have a completely different idea of what innovation, driving thrill and beauty mean. But ultimately every Ferrari will meet or exceed the different expectations.

How can these different perceptions of the Ferraristi be summed up in a design philosophy?

There's a wonderful quote that is said to have come from Plato: "Beauty is the splendour of truth." That basically explains and describes Ferrari. I think it fits perfectly.

Thank you for talking to us, Mr. Manzoni, and congratulations on winning the title "Red Dot: Design Team of the Year".

Das ist natürlich eine clevere Antwort!

Es ist die Wahrheit. Die Ferraristi eines GT sind nicht identisch mit den Ferraristi, die einen XX fahren. Es sind völlig verschiedene Menschen. Sie haben auch eine völlig unterschiedliche Vorstellung von Innovation, Fahrleidenschaft und Schönheit. Aber am Ende wird jeder Ferrari die unterschiedlichen Erwartungen erfüllen oder übertreffen.

Wie lassen sich denn diese unterschiedlichen Wahrnehmungen der Ferraristi in einer Designphilosophie zusammenfassen?

Es gibt dieses wunderbare Zitat, das angeblich auf Platon zurückgeht: „Schönheit ist der Glanz der Wahrheit." Im Grunde erklärt und beschreibt es Ferrari. Ich denke, es passt perfekt.

Vielen Dank für das Gespräch, Herr Manzoni, und herzlichen Glückwunsch zur Auszeichnung „Red Dot: Design Team of the Year".

Red Dot: Best of the Best
The best designers of their category
Die besten Designer ihrer Kategorie

The designers of the Red Dot: Best of the Best
Only a few products in the Red Dot Design Award receive the "Red Dot: Best of the Best" accolade. In each category, the jury can assign this award to products of outstanding design quality and innovative achievement. Exploring new paths, these products are all exemplary in their design and oriented towards the future.

The following chapter introduces the people who have received one of these prestigious awards. It features the best designers and design teams of the year 2019 together with their products, revealing in interviews and statements what drives these designers and what design means to them.

Die Designer der Red Dot: Best of the Best
Nur sehr wenige Produkte im Red Dot Design Award erhalten die Auszeichnung „Red Dot: Best of the Best". Die Jury kann mit dieser Auszeichnung in jeder Kategorie Design von außerordentlicher Qualität und Innovationsleistung besonders hervorheben. In jeder Hinsicht vorbildlich gestaltet, beschreiten diese Produkte neue Wege und sind zukunftsweisend.

Das folgende Kapitel stellt die Menschen vor, die diese besondere Auszeichnung erhalten haben. Es zeigt die besten Designer und Designteams des Jahres 2019 zusammen mit ihren Produkten. In Interviews und Statements wird deutlich, was diese Designer bewegt und was ihnen Design bedeutet.

Design Group Italia
Basalt Architects

"Design is about people."

„Im Design geht es um Menschen."

What was your goal when you designed your award-winning project?
The Retreat was envisioned as a home away from home on an island on the edge of the Arctic Circle, a place where guests can disengage from their saturated everyday lives and feel connected to nature. Its architecture and design harmonise with the otherworldly volcanic surroundings, erasing the boundary between man and nature. The result is a destination where the seamless interplay of lava, moss and water is woven into every facet of the guest's journey.

Do you have a specific design approach for your work as a designer?
We want to create great work for our clients, one project at a time. Often, this means decades-long partnerships.

Welches Ziel verfolgten Sie bei der Gestaltung Ihres ausgezeichneten Projektes?
The Retreat wurde als ein zweites Zuhause auf einer Insel am Rand des Polarkreises konzipiert – ein Ort, an dem Gäste von ihrem überladenen Alltag abschalten und sich der Natur verbunden fühlen können. Die Architektur und die Gestaltung harmonieren mit der jenseitig wirkenden vulkanischen Umgebung und verwischen die Grenze zwischen Mensch und Natur. Ergebnis ist ein Zielort, an dem das nahtlose Zusammenspiel von Lava, Moos und Wasser für die Gäste mit jeder Facette ihrer Reise verwoben ist.

Liegt Ihrer Arbeit als Designer ein bestimmter Gestaltungsansatz zugrunde?
Wir wollen für unsere Kunden erstklassige Projekte verwirklichen, eines nach dem anderen. Oft bedeutet das jahrzehntelange Partnerschaften.

reddot award 2019
best of the best

Client
The Retreat at Blue Lagoon Iceland,
Grindavík, Iceland

The Retreat at Blue Lagoon Iceland
Luxury Hotel, Restaurant and Spa
Luxushotel, Restaurant und Spa

See page 72
Siehe Seite 72

Centor Holdings Pty Ltd

"There must be joy every single time your design is used. Always and forever."
„Jedes Mal, wenn dein Design verwendet wird, sollte es Freude bereiten. Immer und immer wieder."

What was your goal when you designed your award-winning product?
This is our sixth-generation screen, and we have had a lot of requests for additional features. The real goal was to discern what was truly desirable, and to make it available in a responsible way. The added challenge was designing both for the homeowner and the installer. Their needs are very different and they both must be addressed.

When are you at your most creative?
You cannot turn on a switch to creativity. The trick is to not be scared of failure as the best designs often come from failed learnings.

What is your personal vision for the future?
Our vision is to see a return to products that will last many generations and still give the same joy as on the day they were made.

Welches Ziel verfolgten Sie bei der Gestaltung Ihres ausgezeichneten Produktes?
Dies ist bereits die sechste Generation unseres Insektenschutzsystems. Wir hatten viele Anfragen nach neuen Funktionen erhalten. Das eigentliche Ziel war es, herauszufinden, was wirklich erwünscht war und alles auf eine verantwortliche Weise bereitzustellen. Eine zusätzliche Herausforderung war, sowohl für den Hauseigentümer als auch für den Installateur zu entwickeln, die ganz unterschiedliche Bedürfnisse haben.

Wann sind Sie besonders kreativ?
Man kann keinen Schalter auf Kreativität umlegen. Der Trick besteht darin, keine Angst vor Fehlschlägen zu haben, da die besten Lösungen oft aus misslungenen Versuchen entstehen.

Wie sieht Ihre persönliche Zukunftsvision aus?
Unsere Vision ist eine Rückkehr zu Produkten, die viele Generationen lang halten und immer noch die gleiche Freude bereiten, wie an dem Tag ihrer Entstehung.

reddot award 2019
best of the best

Manufacturer
Centor Holdings Pty Ltd,
Brisbane, Australia

Centor S4
Insect Screen and Shade System
Insekten- und Sonnenschutzsystem

See page 84
Siehe Seite 84

AIGANG GmbH
Top Design

"Good design comes from the heart."
„Gutes Design kommt von Herzen."

When are you at your most creative?
Brainstorming with the team is the most productive time after logical sorting. But when it comes to turning ideas into creative designs, you need a closed, quiet place to be alone.

How do you keep abreast of new developments?
Watching and thinking is the best way. To make products that are truly valuable to people and society, it is important to explore human nature and the laws of nature, and to have access to the latest technology and information so as not to be kidnapped by popular trends.

What does winning the Red Dot: Best of the Best mean to you?
Winning a Red Dot: Best of the Best means that our design team has the ability to produce high-quality design work, which will bring us new challenges and higher goals.

Wann sind Sie besonders kreativ?
Brainstorming im Team ist nach einer logischen Sichtung am produktivsten. Wenn man aus Ideen aber kreative Gestaltungen machen soll, braucht man einen ruhigen, abgetrennten Ort, an dem man allein sein kann.

Wie bleiben Sie über aktuelle Entwicklungen auf dem Laufenden?
Beobachten und Nachdenken sind immer gut. Man sollte das menschliche Wesen und die Gesetze der Natur erforschen und Zugang zu den neuesten Technologien und Informationen haben, um nicht durch gängige Trends vereinnahmt zu werden. So kann man Produkte schaffen, die für Menschen und für die Gesellschaft wirklich wertvoll sind.

Was bedeutet die Auszeichnung mit dem Red Dot: Best of the Best für Sie?
Einen Red Dot: Best of the Best zu gewinnen, bedeutet, dass unser Designteam hochwertige Gestaltungsarbeit zu leisten vermag, die uns neue Herausforderungen und höhere Ziele bringen wird.

reddot award 2019
best of the best

Manufacturer
AIGANG GmbH, Munich, Germany

Multifunctional Smart Lock
Intelligentes Multifunktionsschloss

See page 108
Siehe Seite 108

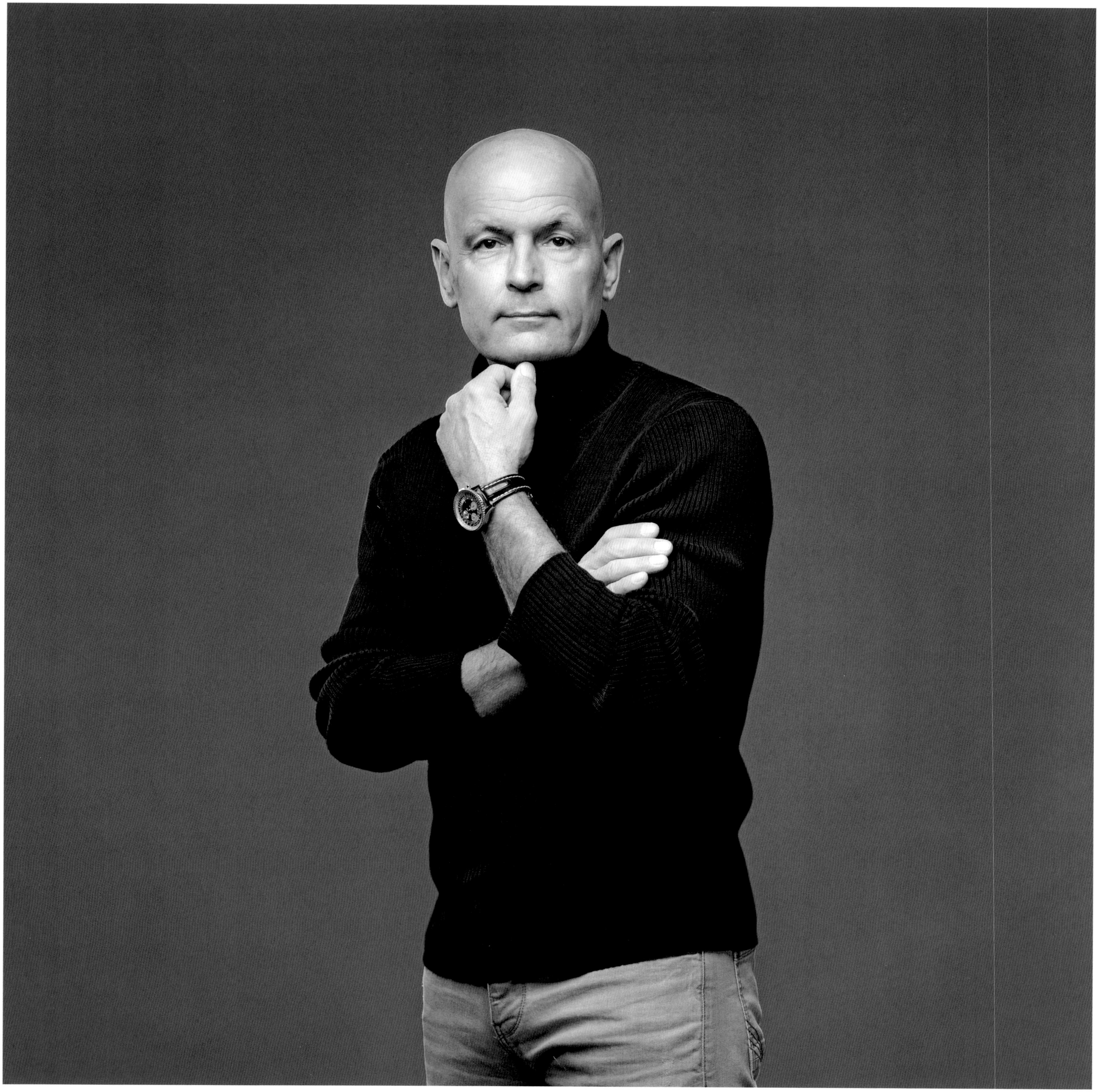

Dr. Rolf W.-Seifart

"Good ideas are always touching."
„Gute Ideen sind immer berührend."

Who or what inspires you?
I like to look for inspiration in history. When visiting the museum, I saw that the armour of the soldiers in the ancient era of cold weapons was inspired by shells from animals. So I designed and created this smart remote control.

When are you at your most creative?
Going all over the world, the symbiosis I notice between modernity and history gives me unlimited creativity, also to design smart home products.

Where will your industry be in ten years?
In the next ten years, more families will live in smart homes. We will continue to present more intelligent products with perfect integration of technology and design that make the life of global users more comfortable and convenient.

Wer oder was inspiriert Sie?
Ich suche Inspiration in der Geschichte. Als ich ins Museum ging, bemerkte ich, dass die Rüstung der Soldaten in der Antike, in der Zeit der kalten Waffen, von Panzern der Tierwelt inspiriert war. So gestaltete und schuf ich diese intelligente Fernbedienung.

Wann sind Sie besonders kreativ?
Da ich durch die ganze Welt reise, sehe ich die Symbiose zwischen der Moderne und der Geschichte. Das gibt mir unbegrenzte Kreativität, die es mir auch erlaubt, Produkte für intelligente Haustechnik zu gestalten.

Wo wird Ihre Branche in zehn Jahren stehen?
In den nächsten zehn Jahren werden mehr Familien in intelligenten Häusern leben. Wir werden mehr intelligente Produkte einführen, die Technik und Gestaltung perfekt integrieren und das Leben der Benutzer weltweit bequemer und komfortabler machen.

reddot award 2019
best of the best

Manufacturer
Moorgen, Shanghai, China

Moorgen Smart Remote Control
Smart Home Automation
Intelligente Hausautomation

See page 124
Siehe Seite 124

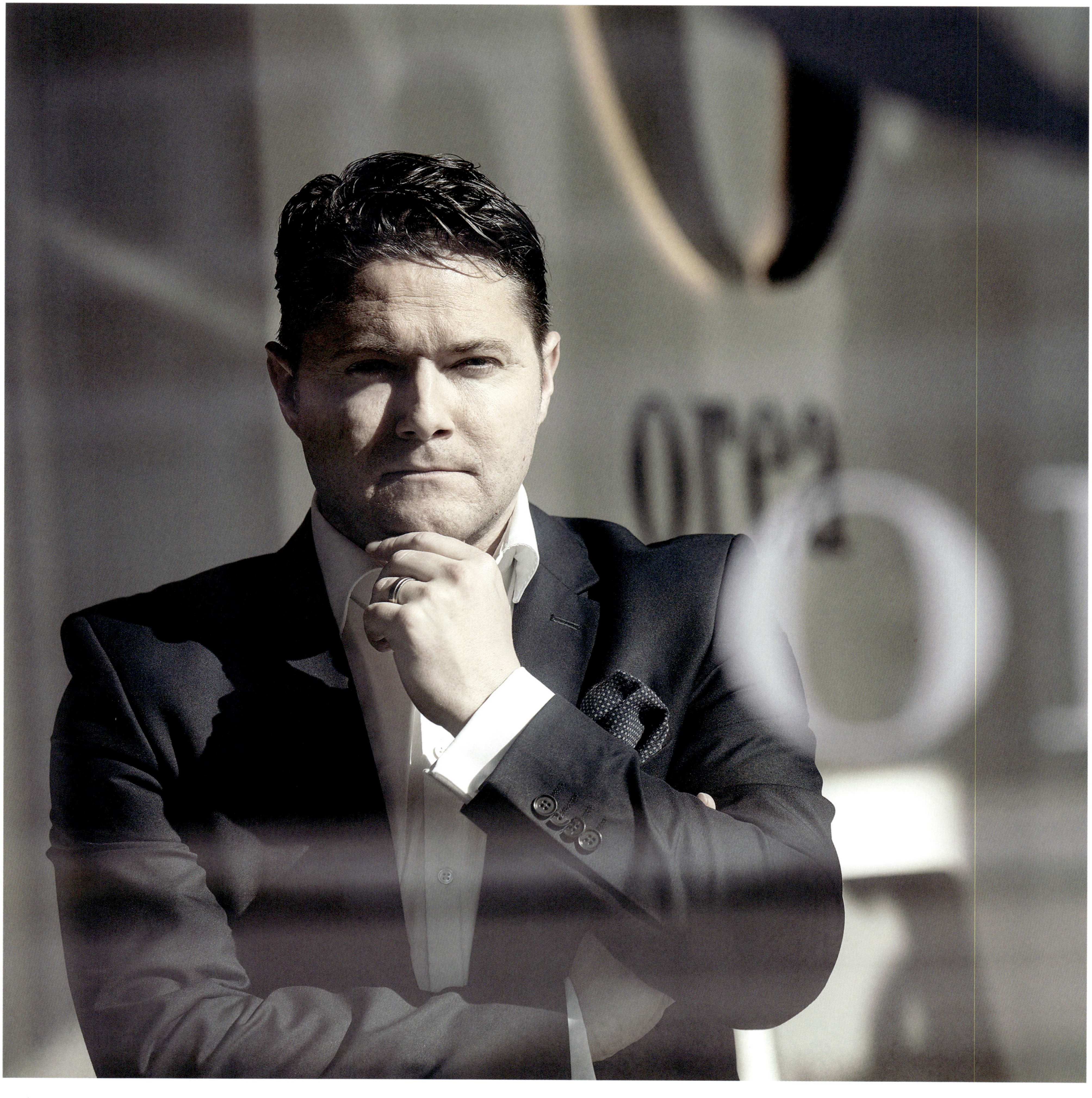

David Spielhofer
Orea AG

"The multifunctional wall combines modern technology with practical application."

„Die Multifunktionswand verbindet moderne Technologie mit praktischer Anwendung."

What was your goal when you designed your award-winning product?
To satisfy the desire for consistent room concepts and the desire for an increasing importance of the living room.

How do you keep abreast of new developments?
My motto is to go through life with your eyes open. Especially also to consider shapes and functions which are not the ones you would have chosen at first sight. It means always being open for a surprise.

Where will your industry be in ten years?
I anticipate three main trends in the years to come: mobility, sociability and health. Focusing on these trends, we will develop our values and products.

Welches Ziel verfolgten Sie bei der Gestaltung Ihres ausgezeichneten Produktes?
Den Wunsch nach konsequenten Raumkonzepten und nach einer größeren Bedeutung des Wohnraums zu befriedigen.

Wie bleiben Sie über aktuelle Entwicklungen auf dem Laufenden?
Mein Motto ist, mit offenen Augen durchs Leben zu gehen. Man sollte vor allem die Formen und Funktionen bedenken, die man auf den ersten Blick nicht gewählt hätte. Das bedeutet, dass man immer für eine Überraschung offen sein muss.

Wo wird Ihre Branche in zehn Jahren stehen?
Ich sehe für die kommenden Jahre drei Haupttrends: Mobilität, Geselligkeit und Gesundheit. Wir werden unsere Werte und Produkte mit einem Fokus auf diese Trends hin entwickeln.

reddot award 2019
best of the best

Manufacturer
Orea AG, Zürich, Switzerland

The Wall
Multifunctional Wall
Multifunktionswand

See page 150
Siehe Seite 150

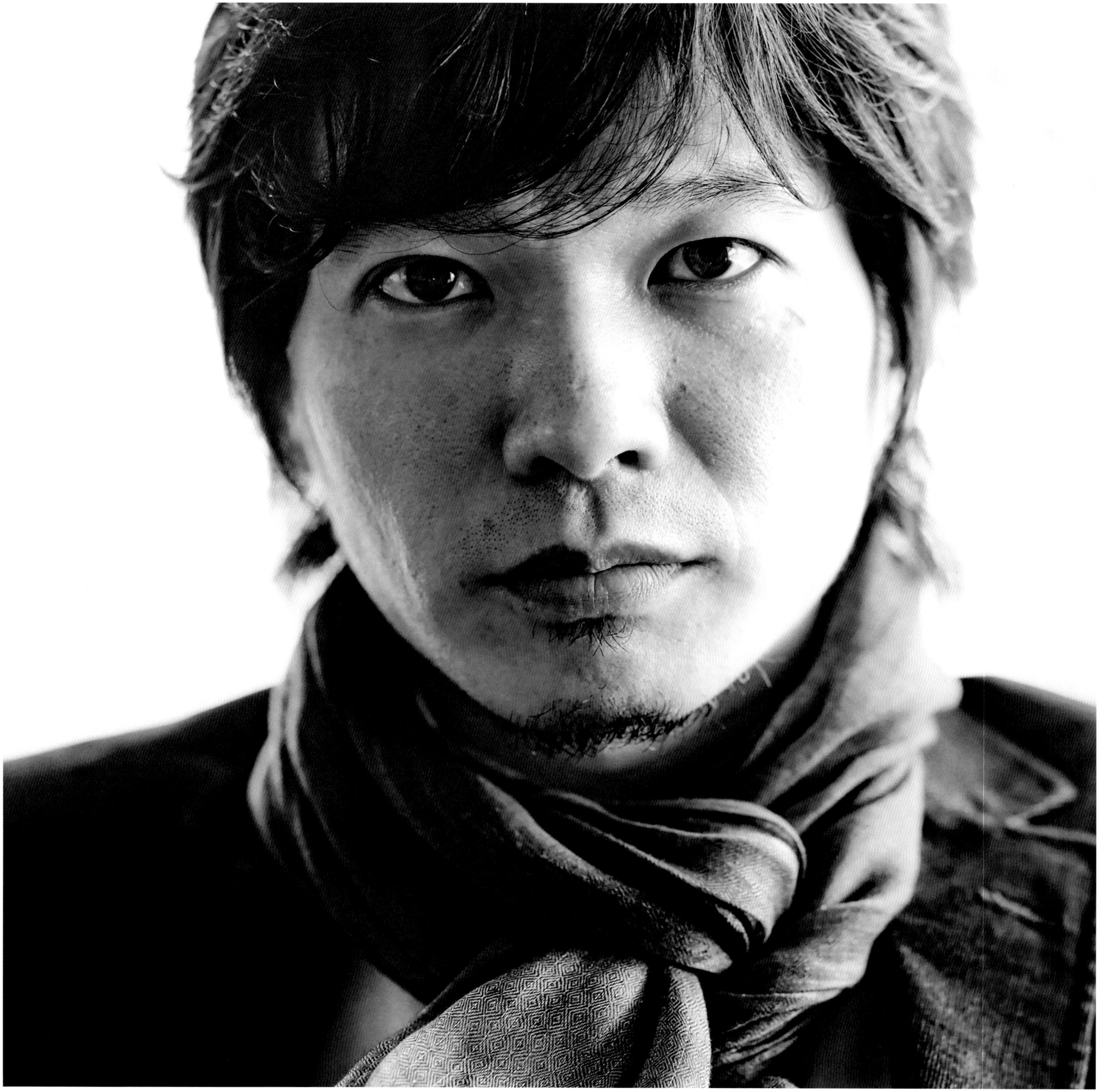

Shinsaku Miyamoto
Ritzwell & Co.

"A product that resonates in the heart is born from thoughtful work."
„Ein Produkt, das im Herzen nachhallt, ist das Ergebnis wohlüberlegter Arbeit."

What was your goal when you designed your award-winning product?
While the world has a tendency to pursue new technologies, productivity, efficiency and trends, I wanted to express the "true value" which appears in the warmth of things made by human hands – a comforting feeling for the five senses.

Do you have a specific design approach for your work as a designer?
I try to be as "analogue" as possible with my specific methods. I face my inner self and search for the fundamental nature of things. I draw by hand and create by hand. I am in constant, thorough dialogue with myself throughout the process.

Welches Ziel verfolgten Sie bei der Gestaltung Ihres ausgezeichneten Produktes?
Während in der Welt die Tendenz herrscht, neuen Technologien, der Produktivität, Leistungskraft und Trends hinterherzulaufen, möchte ich den „wahren Wert", der in den von Menschenhand gemachten Dingen liegt, zum Ausdruck bringen – eine Wohltat für alle fünf Sinne.

Liegt Ihrer Arbeit als Designer ein bestimmter Gestaltungsansatz zugrunde?
Ich versuche, mit meinen Methoden so analog wie möglich zu sein. Ich befrage mein inneres Ich und suche nach der grundlegenden Natur der Dinge. Ich zeichne von Hand und gestalte von Hand. Während des gesamten Prozesses bin ich in ständigem Dialog mit mir selbst.

reddot award 2019
best of the best

Manufacturer
Ritzwell & Co., Fukuoka, Japan

Jabara AV Board
Sideboard

See page 166
Siehe Seite 166

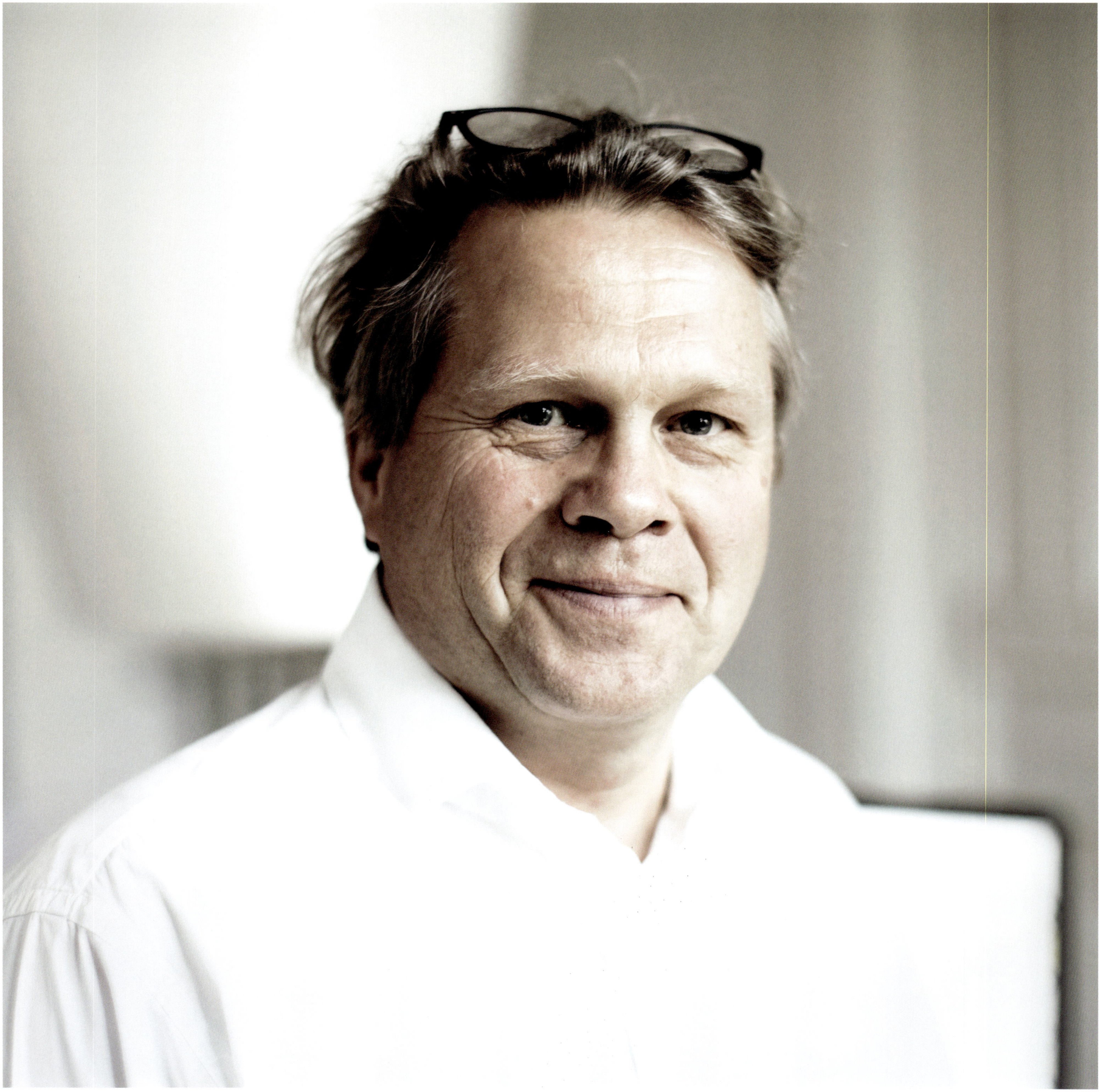

Andreas Ostwald
ostwalddesign

"Coherent and immanent creativity is the basis for successful design."
„Kohärentes und inhärentes Entwerfen sind die Basis für gelungene Gestaltung."

What was your goal when you designed your award-winning product?
The development of numo was not only about the design, but also about the development of a mechanism that was convenient to use. Using the aeris guideline, we have produced a chair that follows the classic genre but that also has a seat shell which moves. This is based on a very dynamic geometry. Here movement also means comfort.

Do you have a specific design approach for your work as a designer?
Design is an attitude. I try to extract the essence of things for every project I take on. That leads to a recognisable signature.

When are you at your most creative?
In development processes, in other words all the time.

Welches Ziel verfolgten Sie bei der Gestaltung Ihres ausgezeichneten Produktes?
Es ging bei der Entwicklung des numo nicht nur um die Gestaltung, sondern auch um die Entwicklung einer sehr komfortablen Mechanik. Der Leitlinie von aeris folgend, haben wir mit der numo-Serie einen klassischen Stuhltypen entwickelt, der auch eine Schwingung der Sitzschale ermöglicht. Diese beruht auf einer sehr dynamischen Geometrie. Bewegung bedeutet hierbei gleichzeitig auch Komfort.

Liegt Ihrer Arbeit als Designer ein bestimmter Gestaltungsansatz zugrunde?
Gestaltung ist Haltung: Ich versuche bei jedem Entwurf, das Wesen der Dinge herauszuarbeiten. Das ergibt dann eine wiedererkennbare Handschrift.

Wann sind Sie besonders kreativ?
In Entwicklungsprozessen, also immer.

reddot award 2019
best of the best

Manufacturer
aeris GmbH, Haar, Germany

numo
Chair
Stuhl

See page 172
Siehe Seite 172

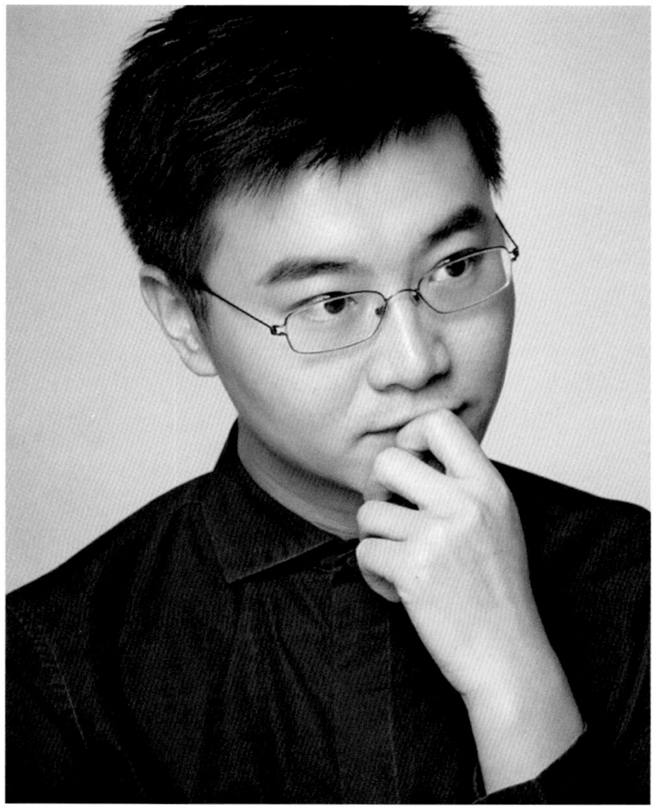
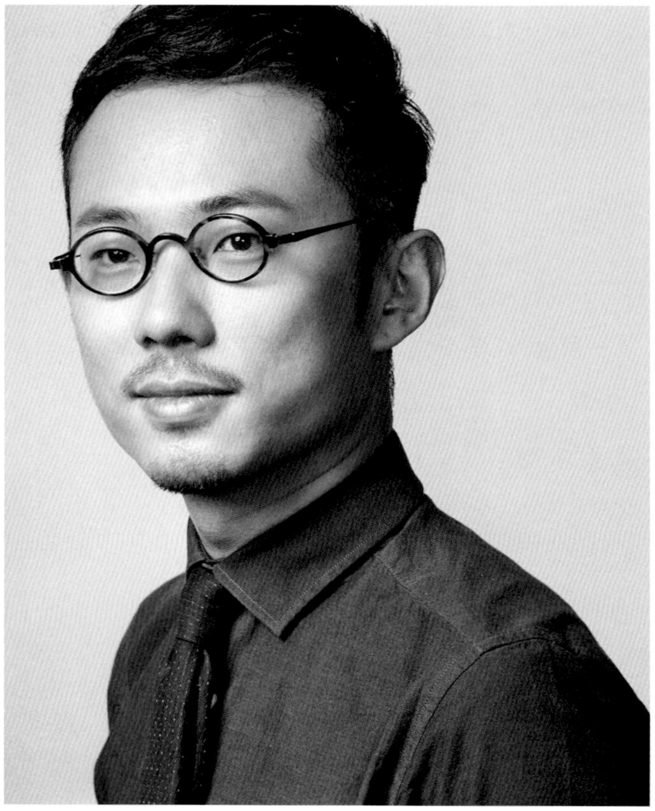
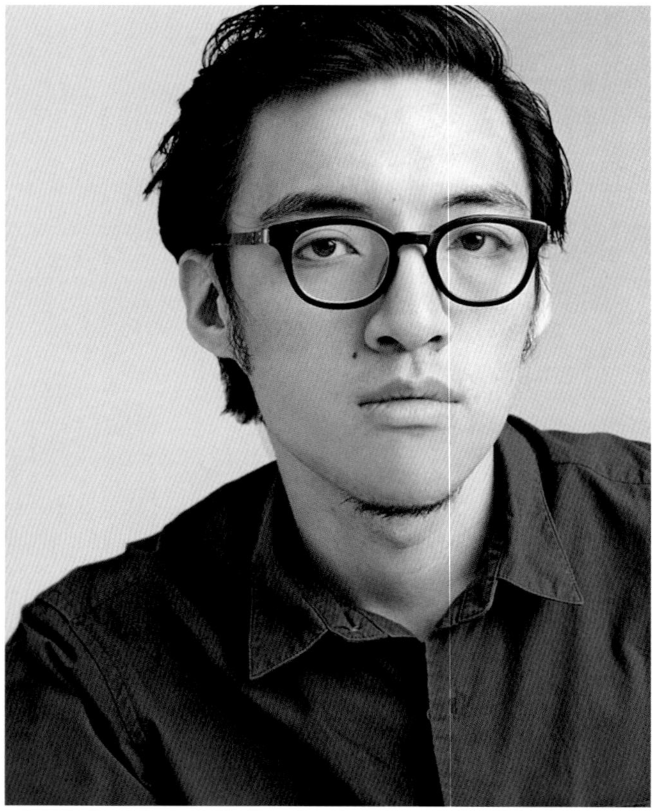
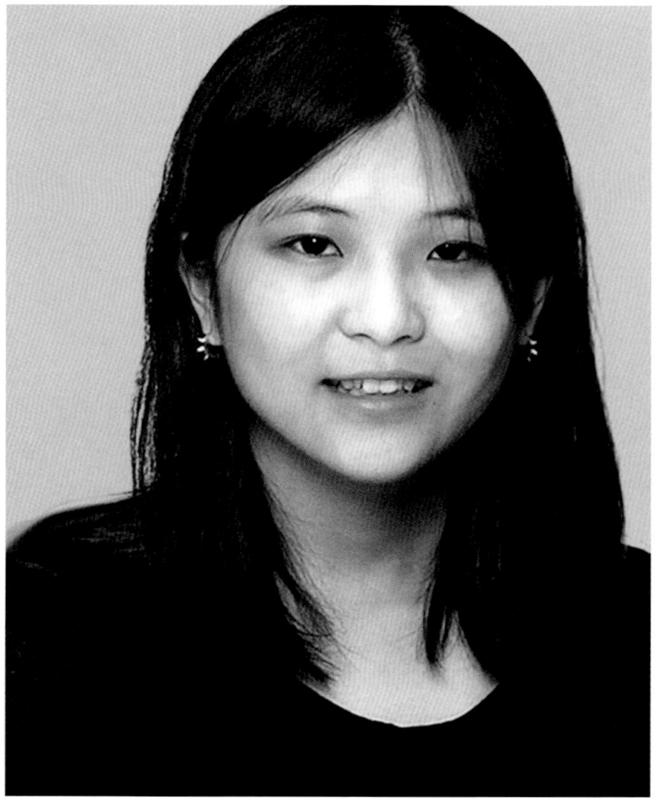
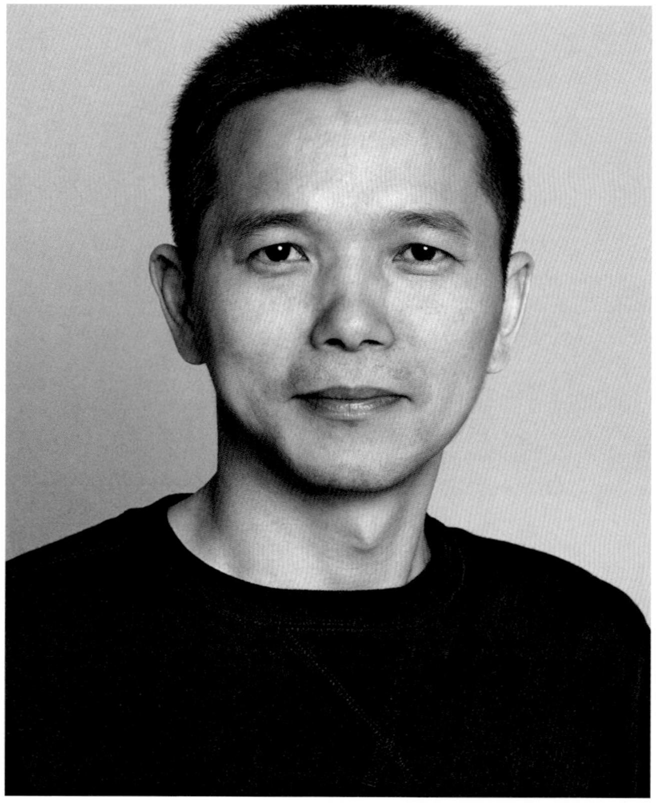
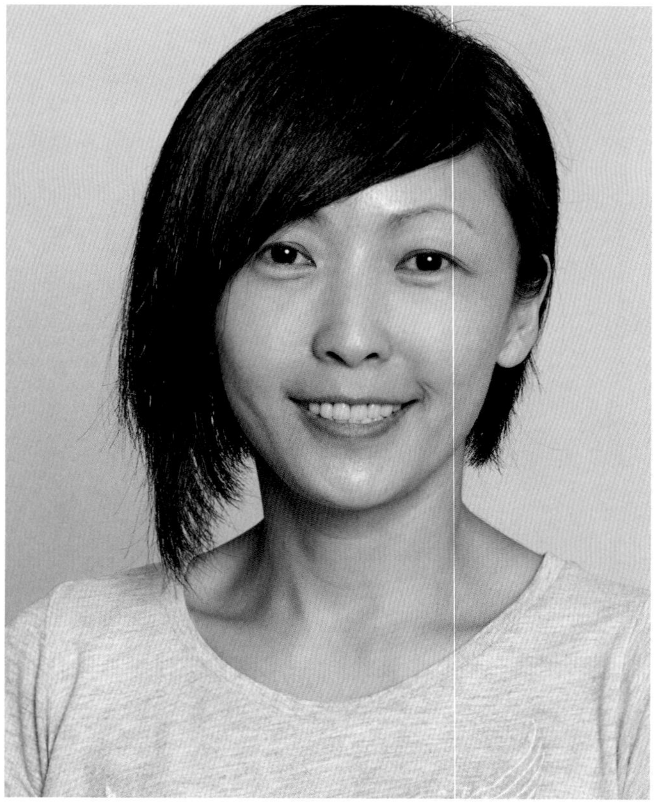

Keren Hu, Ding Fan, Fang Jianping, Li Yu, Zhuang Jingyang, Liu Fang
Teawith Kettle Design Team

"The beauty of the ordinary."
„Die Schönheit des Alltäglichen."

Do you have a specific design approach for your work as a designer?
We try to perceive the small inconveniences of daily life and think about the very nature of things. Our design team is a mix of product designers and graphic designers to enable us to think both from rational and perceptual perspectives.

How do you keep abreast of new developments?
We pay close attention to current technological trends and developments in key sectors of industry, but are not affected by their popularity in design. We feel close to scenic original nature and believe that only the work which moves us is capable of moving anybody else.

Liegt Ihrer Arbeit als Designer ein bestimmter Gestaltungsansatz zugrunde?
Wir versuchen, die kleinen Unannehmlichkeiten des täglichen Lebens wahrzunehmen und über die eigentliche Natur der Dinge nachzudenken. Unser Designteam besteht aus einer Mischung von Produktdesignern und Grafikdesignern, damit wir sowohl rational als auch wahrnehmungsbasiert denken können.

Wie bleiben Sie über aktuelle Entwicklungen auf dem Laufenden?
Wir achten sehr auf aktuelle technische Trends und Entwicklungen in Schlüsselbereichen der Industrie, lassen uns aber von ihrer Popularität im Design nicht beeinflussen. Wir fühlen uns der idyllischen Ursprünglichkeit der Natur verbunden und glauben, dass nur Arbeiten, die uns selbst berühren, auch andere bewegen können.

reddot award 2019
best of the best

Manufacturer
Teawith Essentials Association,
Beijing, China

Teawith Kettle
Tea Kettle
Teekessel

See page 188
Siehe Seite 188

46

Bosch Home Appliances Design Team

"We want to make it possible to experience perfection with all the senses."
„Wir wollen Perfektion mit allen Sinnen erfahrbar machen."

Robert Sachon, Vice President/Head of Global Design Bosch

What was your goal when you designed your award-winning product?
The increasing fusion of kitchen and living environment is accompanied by a call for a high degree of reduction in the design. In the accent | line carbon black range of appliances, the aim was to redefine the balance between kitchen and kitchen appliances. The result was a very discreet, completely black design line whose silhouette is only defined by light and shade.

What is your personal vision for the future?
Our vision is a connected Bosch home in which all Bosch products and services, right through from the domestic appliances and the building management system to the automatic lawn mower, are all seamlessly connected. It is just around the corner and gets nearer to reality every day.

Welches Ziel verfolgten Sie bei der Gestaltung Ihres ausgezeichneten Produktes?
Mit der Verschmelzung von Küche und Wohnraum geht der Wunsch nach einem hohen Maß an gestalterischer Reduktion einher. Bei der Geräteserie accent | line carbon black ging es uns darum, die Balance zwischen Küche und Küchengerät neu zu definieren. Resultat ist eine sehr zurückgenommene, komplett schwarze Designlinie bei der die Silhouette nur durch das Zusammenspiel von Licht und Schatten definiert wird.

Wie sieht Ihre persönliche Zukunftsvision aus?
Unsere Vision vom vernetzten Bosch-Zuhause, in dem vom Hausgerät über das Gebäudemanagement bis hin zum automatisierten Rasenmäher alle Bosch-Produkte und -Services nahtlos miteinander verbunden sind, ist bereits zum Greifen nahe und wird jeden Tag weiterentwickelt.

reddot award 2019
best of the best

Manufacturer
Robert Bosch Hausgeräte GmbH,
Munich, Germany

BOSCH accent | line carbon black
Built-in Appliance Range
Einbaugerätereihe

See page 212
Siehe Seite 212

48

Angelo Po
Studio Volpi

"Enable memorable food experiences."
„Es gilt, unvergessliche kulinarische Erlebnisse zu ermöglichen."

Do you have a specific design approach for your work as a designer?
Style and design are key ingredients of Angelo Po's product development strategy. The brand's equipment combines technologies, performance and long experience in culinary matters with a unique design that constantly evokes "Made in Italy". It is designed to help its customers bring style and elegance to their operations. The design philosophy of the equipment manufacturer for professional restaurant and catering industry is not limited to aesthetics, but also offers functional benefits and improves the quality of work of chefs and operators.
The project was developed in collaboration with Studio Volpi, a leading global partner for companies seeking to implement a winning innovation and design strategy during their industrial process. Aiming to help its customers to create true, meaningful innovation, Studio Volpi prides itself on its unique mix of pioneering spirit, expertise and flawless execution.

Liegt Ihrer Arbeit als Designer ein bestimmter Gestaltungsansatz zugrunde?
In der Produktentwicklungsstrategie von Angelo Po sind Stil und Gestaltung die wichtigsten Bestandteile. Die Geräte verbinden Technologie, Leistung und langjährige Erfahrung in kulinarischen Fragen mit einer einzigartigen Gestaltung, die stets an „Made in Italy" erinnert und Kunden hilft, ihre Arbeit mit Stil und Eleganz auszuüben. Die Gestaltungsphilosophie des Geräteherstellers für die professionelle Gastronomie umfasst neben Ästhetik auch funktionale Vorteile und optimiert die Qualität der Arbeit von Köchen und Bedienpersonal.
Das Projekt wurde in Zusammenarbeit mit Studio Volpi entwickelt, einem führenden, globalen Partner für Unternehmen, die für ihre industriellen Prozesse eine erfolgreiche Innovations- und Gestaltungsstrategie einsetzen wollen. Mit seinem interdisziplinären Ansatz hilft ihnen Studio Volpi, echte, sinnvolle Innovationen hervorzubringen, und ist stolz auf seine einzigartige Mischung aus Pioniergeist, Fachwissen und einwandfreier Umsetzung.

reddot award 2019
best of the best

Manufacturer
Angelo Po, Carpi (Modena), Italy

ACT.O
Combi Oven
Kombiofen

See page 220
Siehe Seite 220

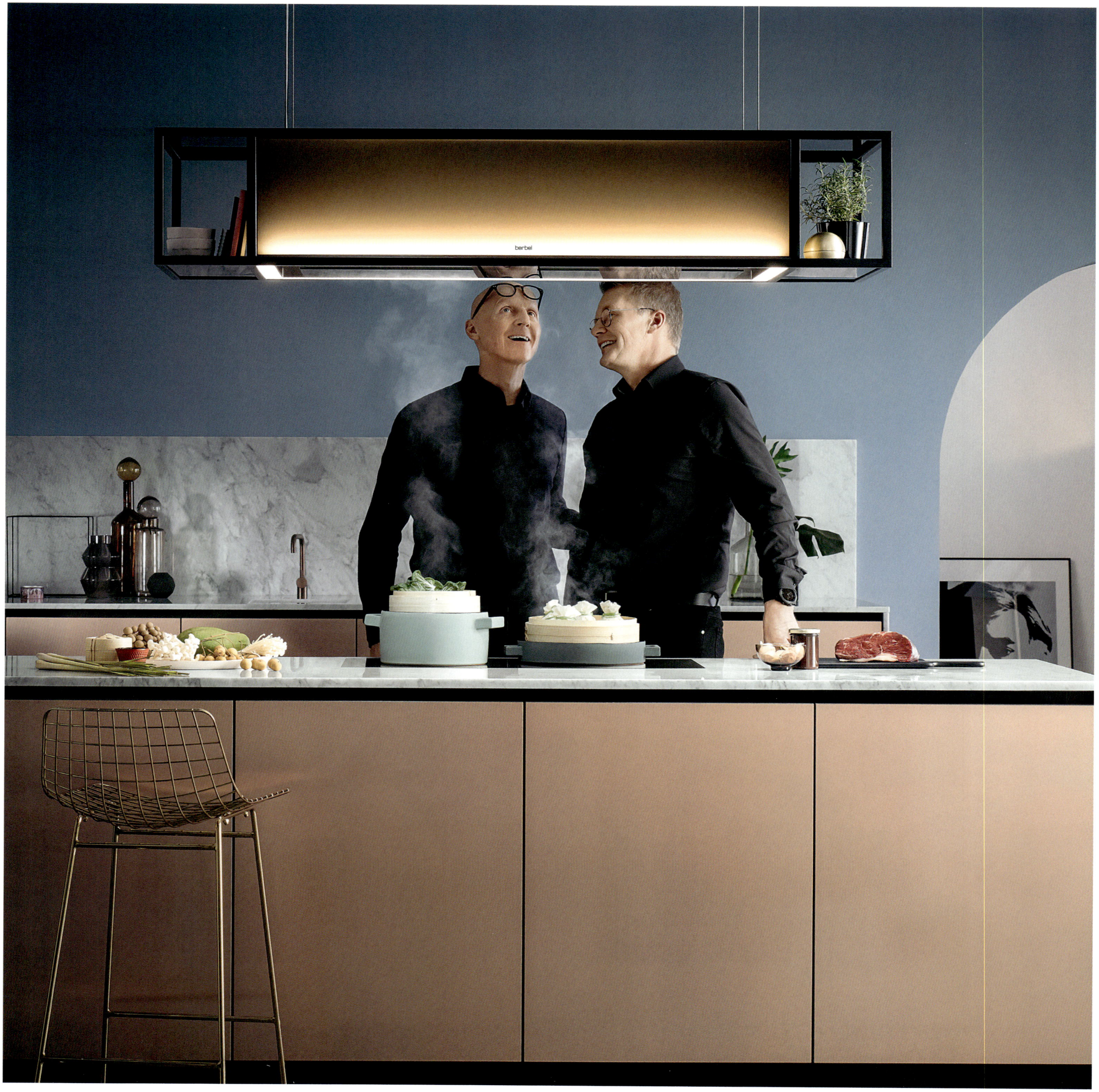
berbel

Stefan Ambrozus – Studio Ambrozus
Peter Ahlmer – berbel Ablufttechnik GmbH

"The berbel principle: the best extractor hoods, patented technology, convincing performance."

„Das berbel Prinzip: beste Dunstabzüge, patentierte Technik, überzeugende Leistung."

What was your goal when you designed your award-winning product?
The Skyline Frame ceiling lift hood was guided by the fusion of kitchen and living room. Its dominant special feature is its emotional treatment of light. The fact that the hood can be raised upwards gives the impression that it is floating in space.

How do you keep abreast of new developments?
We keep our eyes wide open as we go through the world. Colour and use of materials have become bolder in the kitchen sector. The challenge lies in achieving the correct mix of zeitgeist and sustainability.

Where will your industry be in ten years?
From the technical point of view, connectivity of appliances will increase; for example, an extractor hood will notice when something is being cooked and adjust automatically.

Welches Ziel verfolgten Sie bei der Gestaltung Ihres ausgezeichneten Produktes?
Die Deckenlifthaube Skyline Frame orientiert sich an der Verschmelzung von Wohnraum und Küche. Ihre herausragende Besonderheit ist der emotionale Umgang mit Licht. Durch die Möglichkeit, die Haube in der Höhe zu verfahren, scheint sie im Raum zu schweben.

Wie bleiben Sie über aktuelle Entwicklungen auf dem Laufenden?
Wir laufen mit weit geöffneten Augen durch die Welt. In der Küchenbranche ist die Farben- und Materialwelt mutiger geworden. Die Herausforderung liegt in der richtigen Mischung aus Zeitgeist und Nachhaltigkeit.

Wo wird Ihre Branche in zehn Jahren stehen?
Technisch wird die Vernetzung der Geräte Einzug halten, beispielsweise wird die Dunstabzugshaube erkennen, wann gekocht wird, und sich selbständig regeln.

reddot award 2019
best of the best

Manufacturer
berbel Ablufttechnik GmbH,
Rheine, Germany

Skyline Frame
Ceiling Lift Hood
Deckenlifthaube

See page 222
Siehe Seite 222

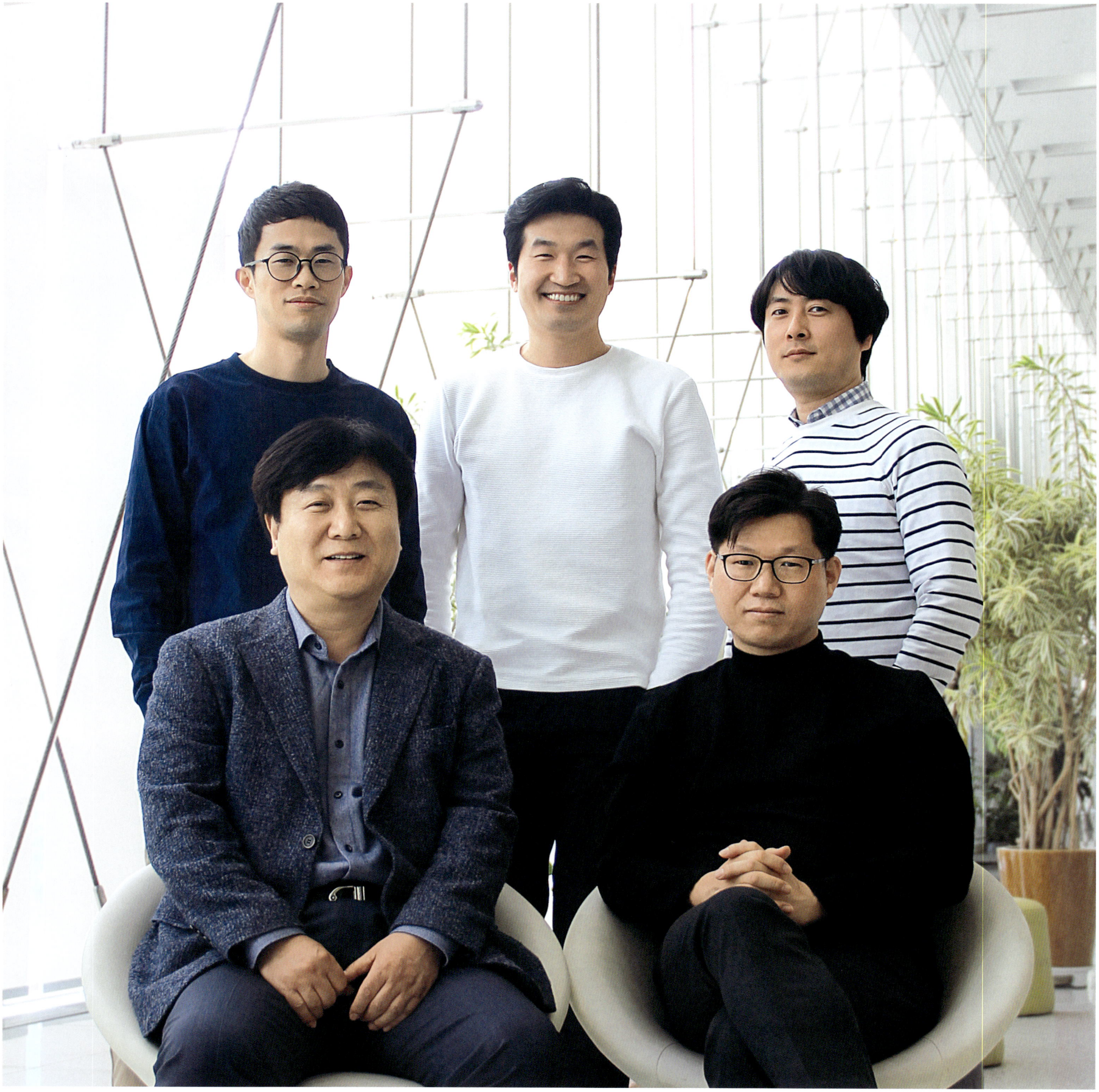

Seonil Yu, Kyukwan Choi, Daesung Lee, Yong Kim, Hyun Choi
LG Electronics Inc.

"Pursue a design that reflects the innovation and customer value, meeting customers' secret needs."

„Design sollte die Innovation und den Kundennutzen widerspiegeln und dabei die geheimen Bedürfnisse der Kunden erfüllen."

What was your goal when you designed your award-winning product?
The LG SIGNATURE Bottom Freezer aims to produce an emotional design value that can "wow" customers. In order to be faithful to the essence of the product and achieve refined perfection, we actively searched out eco-friendly materials for the CMF design (colour, materials and finish). The Auto Smart Door, which opens without touching, and the Auto Smart Lift-up Drawer, which allows users to easily retrieve food stored in the freezer compartment, enable them to experience a usability that has never been available before.

Who or what inspires you?
You can find new design directions and inspiration from customers. We observe and experience the usage environment and usage behaviour of our customers in order to discover their true hidden desires which then inspire the new design.

Welches Ziel verfolgten Sie bei der Gestaltung Ihres ausgezeichneten Produktes?
Der LG SIGNATURE Bottom Freezer sollte einen emotionalen Gestaltungswert bieten, der Kunden begeistert. Um der Essenz des Produkts Rechnung zu tragen und eine perfekte Veredelung zu erreichen, haben wir für das CMF-Design (Farbe, Materialien und Finish) bewusst umweltfreundliche Materialien ausgewählt. Die automatische, intelligente Tür, die sich ohne Berührung öffnet, und die automatische, intelligente Lift-up-Schublade, die das Herausholen von Lebensmitteln aus dem Gefrierfach vereinfacht, ermöglichen es, eine nie zuvor dagewesene Benutzerfreundlichkeit zu erleben.

Wer oder was inspiriert Sie?
Wir finden neue gestalterische Wege und Inspiration bei unseren Kunden. Wir beobachten und erleben ihr Nutzungsumfeld und -verhalten, damit wir ihre versteckten Wünsche erkennen können. Das regt dann den neuen Gestaltungsansatz an.

reddot award 2019
best of the best

Manufacturer
LG Electronics Inc., Seoul, South Korea

LG SIGNATURE Bottom Freezer
Refrigerator
Kühlschrank

See page 274
Siehe Seite 274

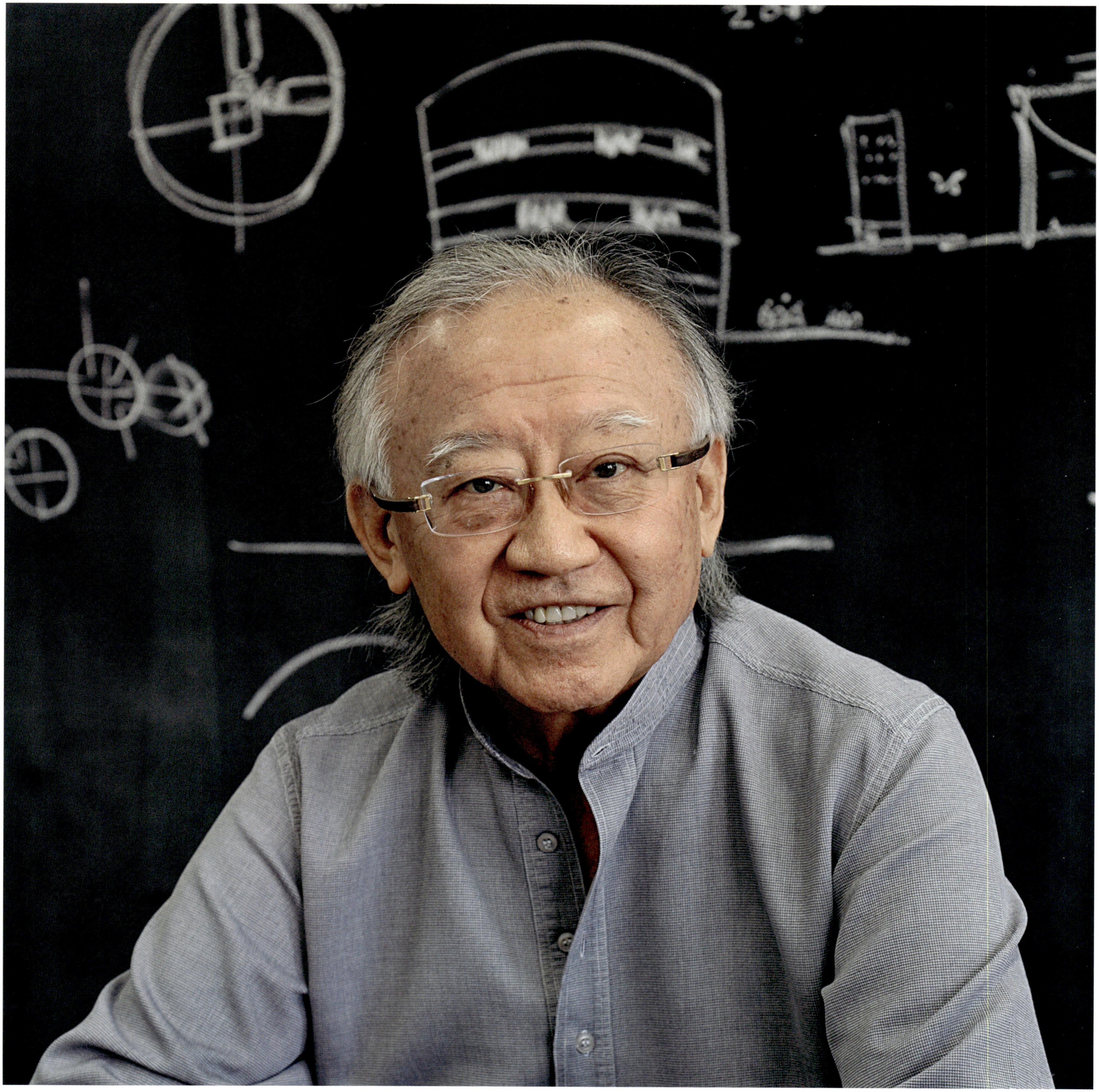

Ruy Ohtake

What was your goal when you designed your award-winning product?
My goal was to develop a product inspired by nature, by the curves of waves, the ever-changing line of the horizon and by the purest shape in design, the egg.

Do you have a specific design approach for your work as a designer?
My work is always unpretentiously simple, but at the same time very bold and unusual. I always try to merge technological innovations with a totally original plasticity. Humanised projects and the sensuality of curves are the biggest trademarks of my work.

Who or what inspires you?
Big names have always inspired me such as Vilanova Artigas and Oscar Niemeyer, but above all, my mother, the plastic artist, Tomie Ohtake.

Welches Ziel verfolgten Sie bei der Gestaltung Ihres ausgezeichneten Produktes?
Mein Ziel war es, ein Produkt zu entwickeln, das von der Natur inspiriert ist, von der Kurvenform der Wellen, der sich immer verändernden Linie des Horizonts und der reinsten Designform, dem Ei.

Liegt Ihrer Arbeit als Designer ein bestimmter Gestaltungsansatz zugrunde?
Meine Arbeit ist immer unprätentiös und schlicht, doch gleichzeitig mutig und ungewöhnlich. Ich bemühe mich immer, technische Innovationen mit einer vollkommen originellen Plastizität zu verbinden. Am Menschen orientierte Projekte und die Sinnlichkeit von Rundungen sind die markantesten Kennzeichen meiner Arbeit.

Wer oder was inspiriert Sie?
Große Namen wie Vilanova Artigas und Oscar Niemeyer haben mich schon immer inspiriert, doch die wichtigste Inspiration ist meine Mutter, die plastische Künstlerin Tomie Ohtake.

reddot award 2019
best of the best

Manufacturer
Roca Brasil, Jundiaí, Brazil

Ruy Ohtake by Roca
Washbasin
Waschtisch

See page 292
Siehe Seite 292

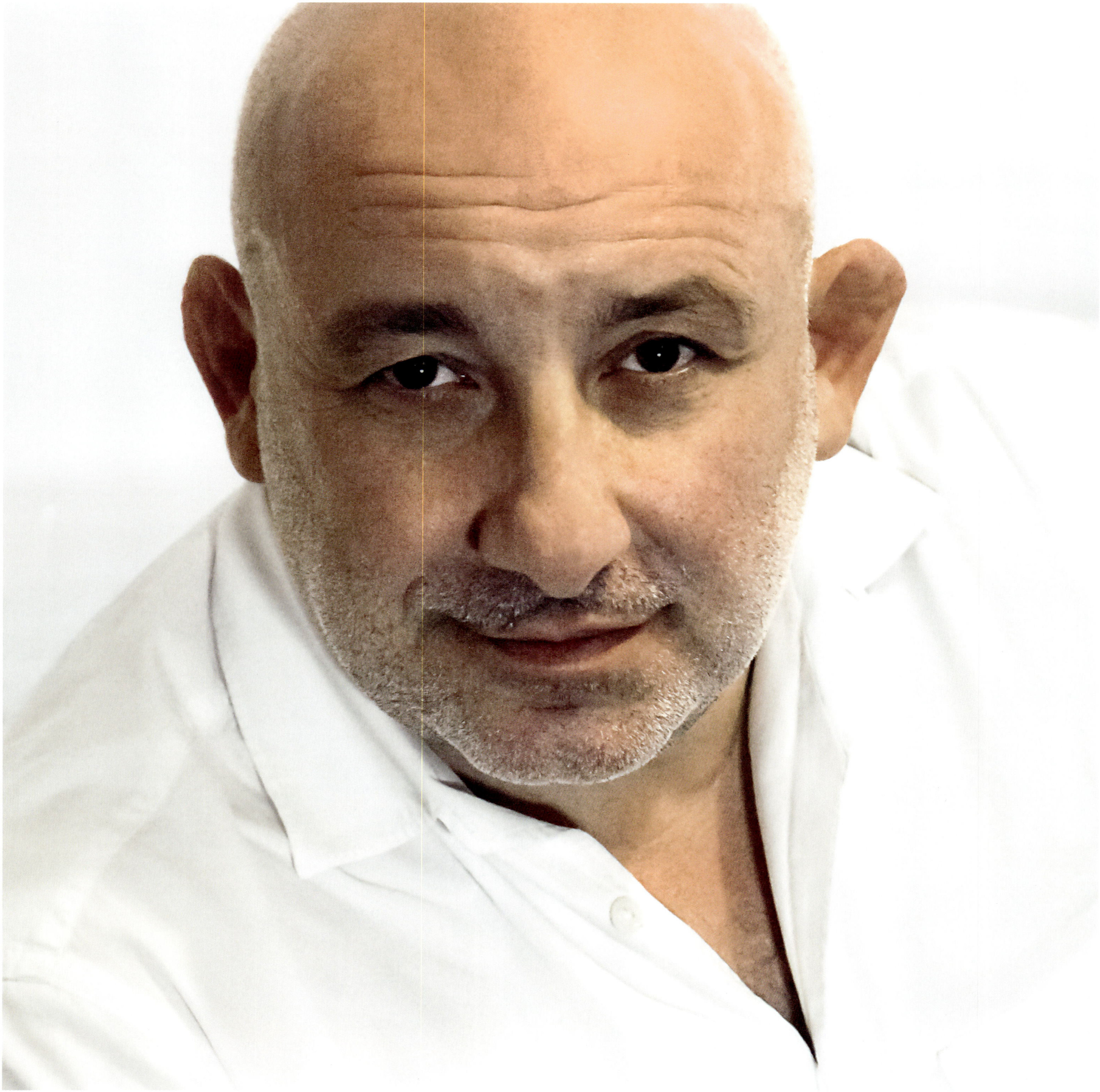

Jean-Marie Massaud
Studio Massaud

"Let's make our life an adventure."
„Wir sollten aus unserem Leben ein Abenteuer machen."

Do you have a specific design approach for your work as a designer?
I have always had a holistic approach, with a symbolic and timeless language. The products that I design tend to be long-lasting, which may be what my partners are searching for when they decide to work with me. In my approach to the AXOR Edge collection specifically, I questioned the concept of the artefact, of cultural legacy and of archetypes.

Why did you become a designer?
I have always been a dreamer. Do you know any other activity in which this is a good quality, not a lack of professionalism?

How do you define design quality?
It's about the quintessence of experience, where competence is a due, quality is a must, and emotion comes first.

Liegt Ihrer Arbeit als Designer ein bestimmter Gestaltungsansatz zugrunde?
Ich habe immer schon einen ganzheitlichen Ansatz mit einer symbolischen und zeitlosen Sprache verfolgt. Die Produkte, die ich gestalte, halten in der Regel sehr lange, was wohl genau das ist, was meine Partner suchen, wenn sie entscheiden, mit mir zusammenzuarbeiten. Speziell bei meinem Ansatz für die AXOR Edge-Kollektion habe ich das Konzept des Artefakts, des kulturellen Erbes und der Archetypen hinterfragt.

Warum sind Sie Designer geworden?
Ich bin schon immer ein Träumer gewesen. Kennen Sie eine andere Tätigkeit, in der das eine gute Eigenschaft und nicht ein Mangel an Professionalität ist?

Wie definieren Sie Designqualität?
Es geht um die Quintessenz der Erfahrung, wo Kompetenz ein Anrecht ist, Qualität ein Muss und Emotion an erster Stelle steht.

reddot award 2019
best of the best

Manufacturer
Hansgrohe SE, Schiltach, Germany

AXOR Edge
Washbasin Tap
Waschtischarmatur

See page 304
Siehe Seite 304

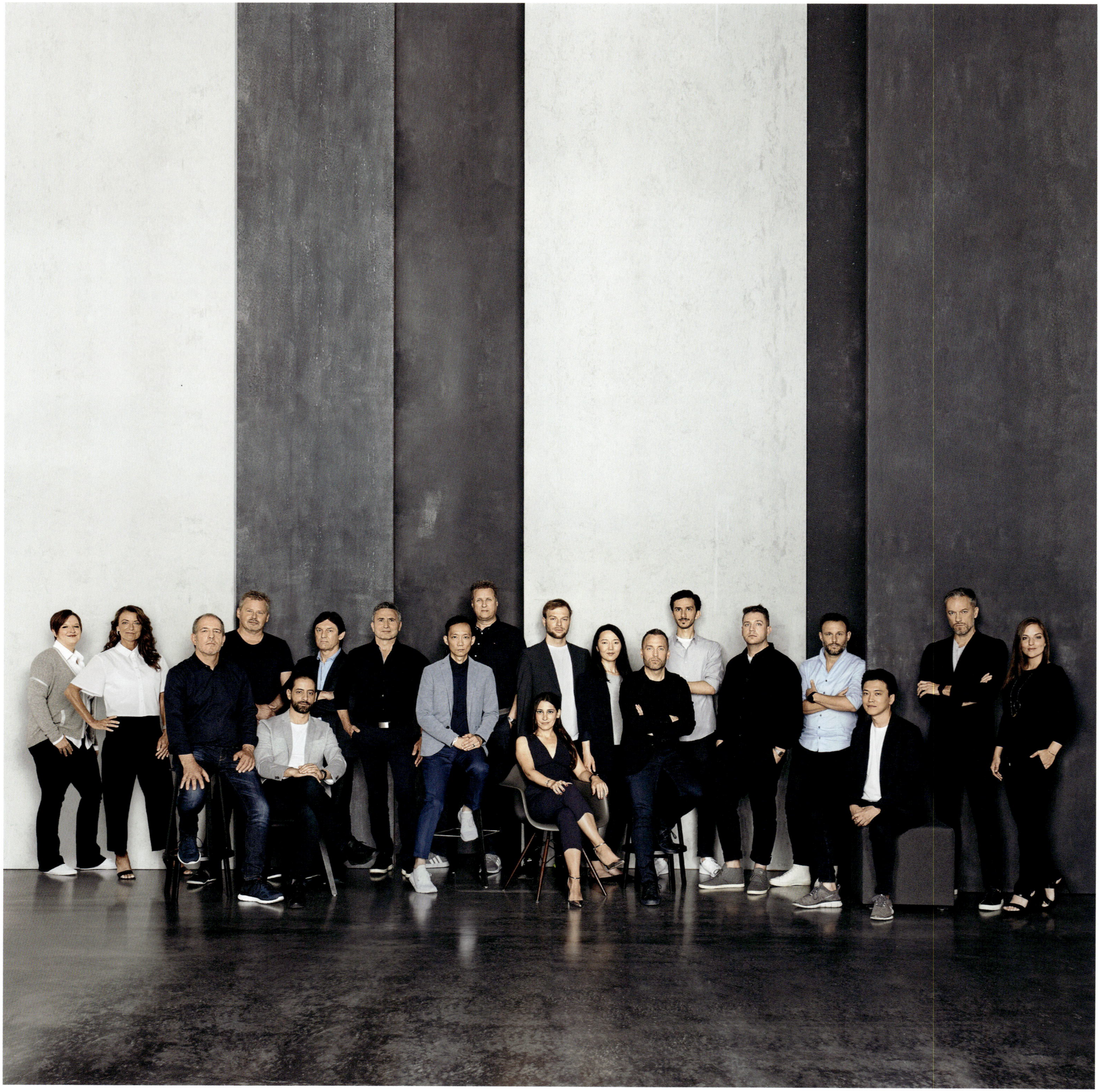

Grohe Design Team

"We believe great design goes beyond form and function."
„Wir glauben, dass großartiges Design über Form und Funktion hinausgeht."

Do you have a specific design approach for your work as a designer?
Simplicity. Every Grohe design is derived from our signature elements, our unique design DNA. It is a minimalist mindset and philosophy, a signature visual interpretation of what we believe consumers desire in their homes.

Who or what inspires you?
Most important is, from our point of view, that the inspiration should come from people. Although we can be inspired by a lot of things, such as by the past, by nature or by a good story, for us, the real inspiration comes from different cultures.

Where will your industry be in ten years?
We will go well beyond standard sanitary products to design more individual and personalised homes. It's clear, the way we live in our homes is rapidly evolving.

Liegt Ihrer Arbeit als Designer ein bestimmter Gestaltungsansatz zugrunde?
Schlichtheit. Jedes Grohe-Design beruht auf unseren unverkennbaren Elementen, unserer einzigartigen Design-DNA. Wir haben eine minimalistische Denkweise und Philosophie, eine unverkennbare visuelle Interpretation dessen, was Konsumenten in ihrem Zuhause haben wollen.

Wer oder was inspiriert Sie?
Unserer Meinung nach ist das Wichtigste, dass wir in Menschen unsere Inspiration finden. Auch wenn uns viele andere Dinge, zum Beispiel die Vergangenheit, die Natur oder eine gute Geschichte, inspirieren können, kommt für uns die wahre Inspiration von den unterschiedlichen Kulturen.

Wo wird Ihre Branche in zehn Jahren stehen?
Wir werden weit über Standardsanitärprodukte hinausgehen und ein Zuhause gestalten, das individualisierter und personalisierter ist. Es ist eindeutig, dass die Art, wie wir in unseren Wohnräumen leben, einem rapiden Wandel unterliegt.

reddot award 2019
best of the best

Manufacturer
Grohe AG, Düsseldorf, Germany

Black Line
Bathroom Tap Collection
Badarmaturen-Kollektion

See page 318
Siehe Seite 318

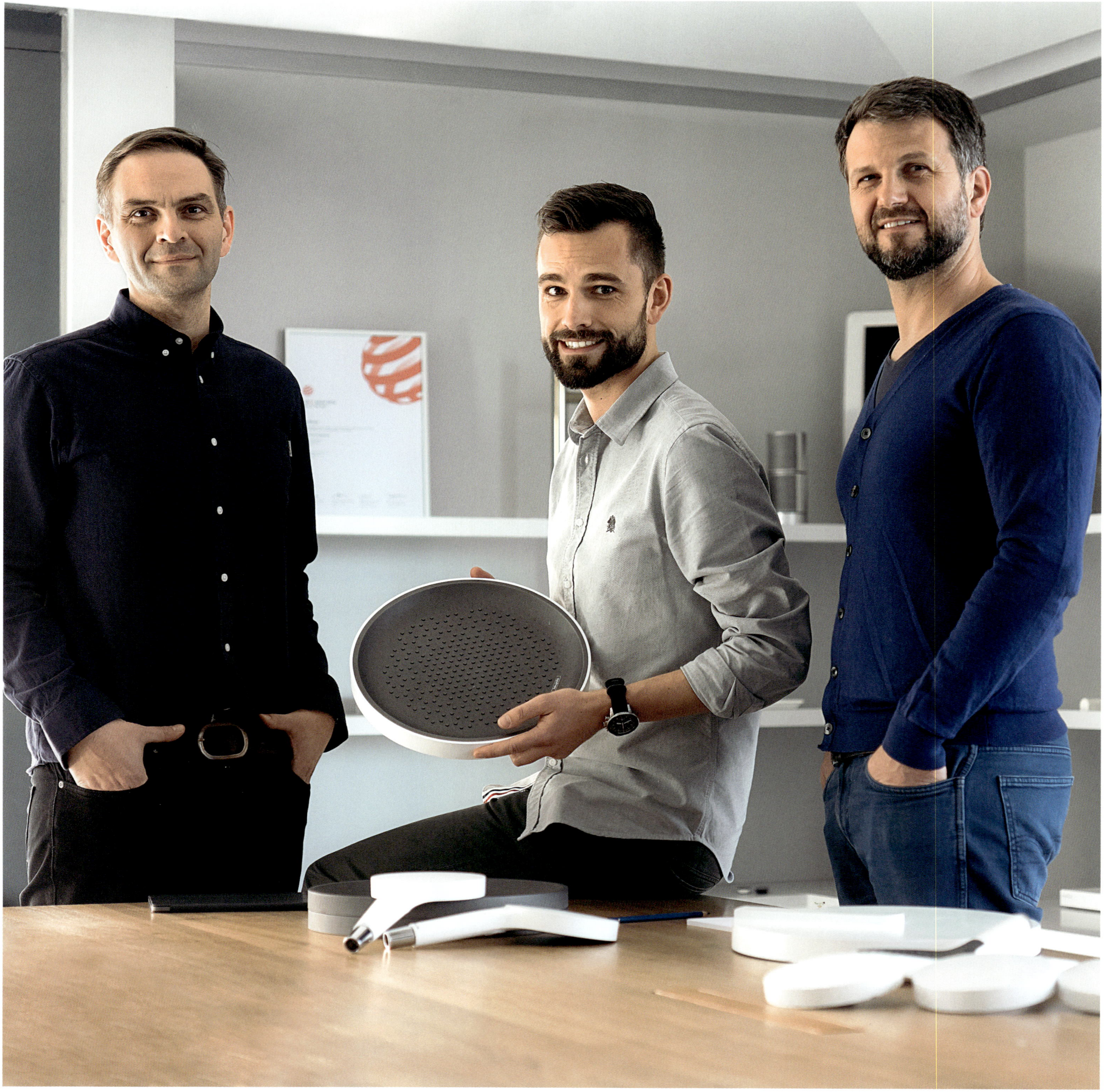

Andreas Diefenbach, Matthias Oesterle, Marco Flaig
Phoenix Design GmbH + Co. KG

"Design with logic, morals and magic."
„Design mit Logik, Moral, Magie."

What was your goal when you designed your award-winning product?
We wanted to create a more immersive water experience and give water a new shape. The Rainfinity shower collection by Hansgrohe is a new archetype that seems progressive yet familiar – it is a design language that fits in perfectly with modern interior design.

Who or what inspires you?
The future inspires us! We constantly question the status quo. Each project has the potential to break new ground. Our aim is to find and explore new paths together with our customers.

How do you define design quality?
Good design must be persuasive in a holistic way. It must take into account social responsibility and have a substantial user value for the people for whom it is created. At the same time, it should also appeal to and move them.

Welches Ziel verfolgten Sie bei der Gestaltung Ihres ausgezeichneten Produktes?
Wasser immersiver und in einer neuartigen Form erlebbar zu machen. Mit der Brausenkollektion Rainfinity für Hansgrohe ist ein neuer Archetyp entstanden, der progressiv und doch vertraut anmutet – eine Designsprache, integriert in das moderne Interior Design.

Wer oder was inspiriert Sie?
Die Zukunft inspiriert uns! Wir hinterfragen permanent den Status quo und suchen immer nach neuen Wegen. Unser Anspruch ist es, in jedem Projekt, gemeinsam mit dem Kunden, Potenzial für Neues zu entdecken.

Wie definieren Sie Designqualität?
Gutes Design muss ganzheitlich überzeugen, es muss der gesellschaftlichen Verantwortung Rechnung tragen und den Menschen, für die es gemacht wird, einen substanziellen Nutzwert geben, sie ansprechen und berühren.

reddot award 2019
best of the best

Manufacturer
Hansgrohe SE, Schiltach, Germany

Rainfinity
Showerpipes, Overhead and Hand Showers
Showerpipes, Kopf- und Handbrausen

See page 320
Siehe Seite 320

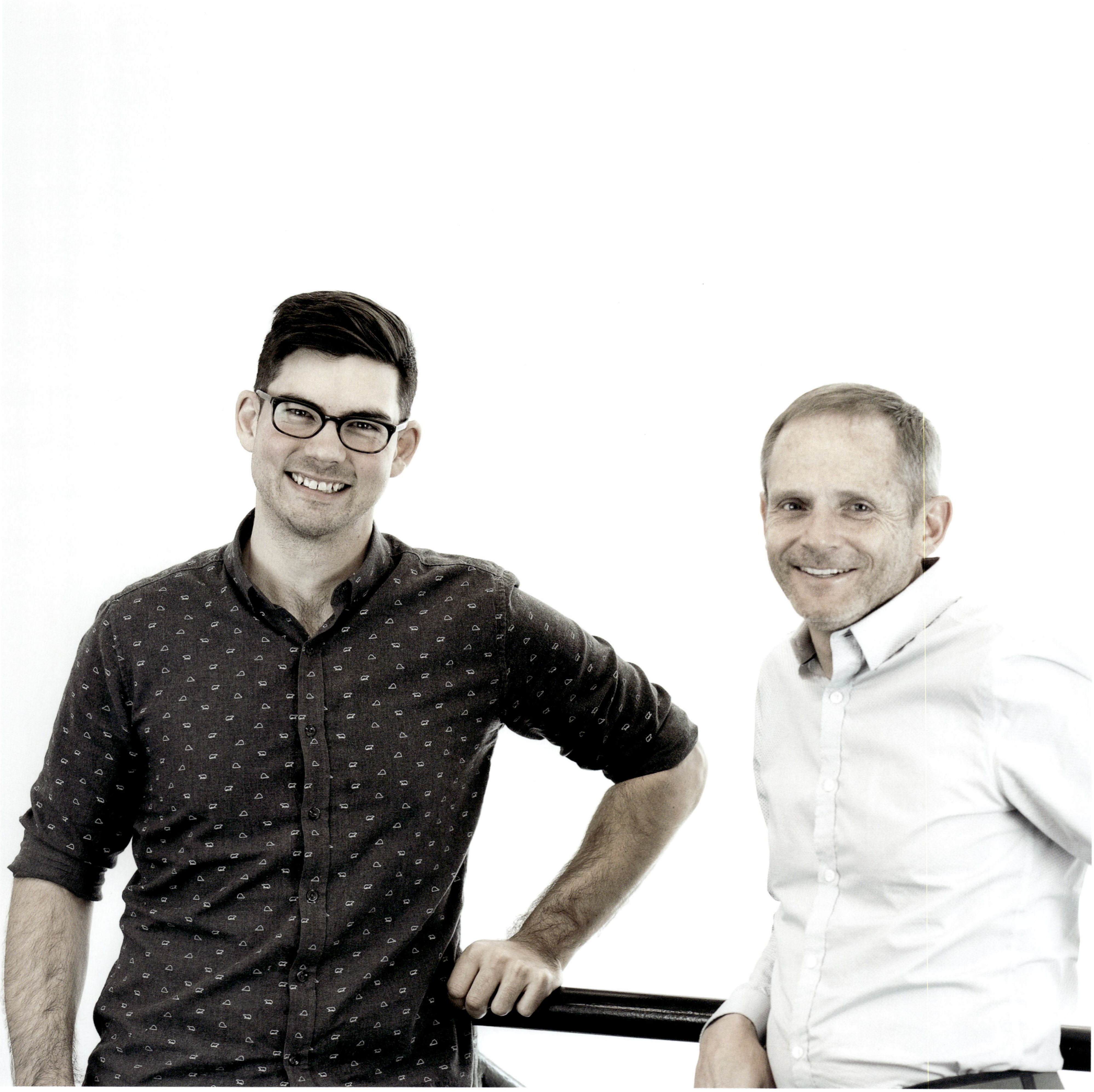

Daniel Fortin, Scott Santoro
Fluxwerx Illumination Inc.

"Light connects architecture and humanity."
„Licht verbindet Architektur mit den Menschen."

What was your goal when you designed your award-winning product?
With Aperture, our intention was to evolve our anidolic optical technology and defy expectations in the general commercial lighting category. Further, we sought to create a luminaire with a simultaneous functional and aesthetic form that sparks the imagination while delivering the precise optical control and performance Fluxwerx is known for.

Who or what inspires you?
Our passion lies at the intersection of the human experience and the architectural condition. We admire the universality and democratisation brought to industrial design by many design greats that preceded us, however our path is more akin to that of great explorers. We only get the sense we are heading along the right path when we are confronted by what seems to be an impossibility.

Welches Ziel verfolgten Sie bei der Gestaltung Ihres ausgezeichneten Produktes?
Mit Aperture wollten wir unsere anidolische optische Technologie weiterentwickeln und uns über die Erwartungen des allgemeinen gewerblichen Leuchtensektors hinwegsetzen. Wir wollten ferner eine Leuchte mit einer sowohl funktionalen als auch ästhetischen Formgebung schaffen, die die Phantasie anregt und gleichzeitig die präzise optische Kontrolle und Leistung bietet, für die Fluxwerx bekannt ist.

Wer oder was inspiriert Sie?
Wir sind leidenschaftlich an der Schnittstelle von Mensch und Architektur interessiert. Wir bewundern die Allgemeingültigkeit und die Demokratisierung des Industriedesigns durch vorausgegangene Designgrößen, doch ähnelt unser Weg eher dem großer Entdecker. Wir haben nur dann den Eindruck, auf dem richtigen Weg zu sein, wenn die Herausforderung, die vor uns liegt, eine Unmöglichkeit zu sein scheint.

reddot award 2019
best of the best

Manufacturer
Fluxwerx Illumination Inc.,
Surrey, British Columbia, Canada

Aperture Circle
Pendant Luminaire
Pendelleuchte

See page 332
Siehe Seite 332

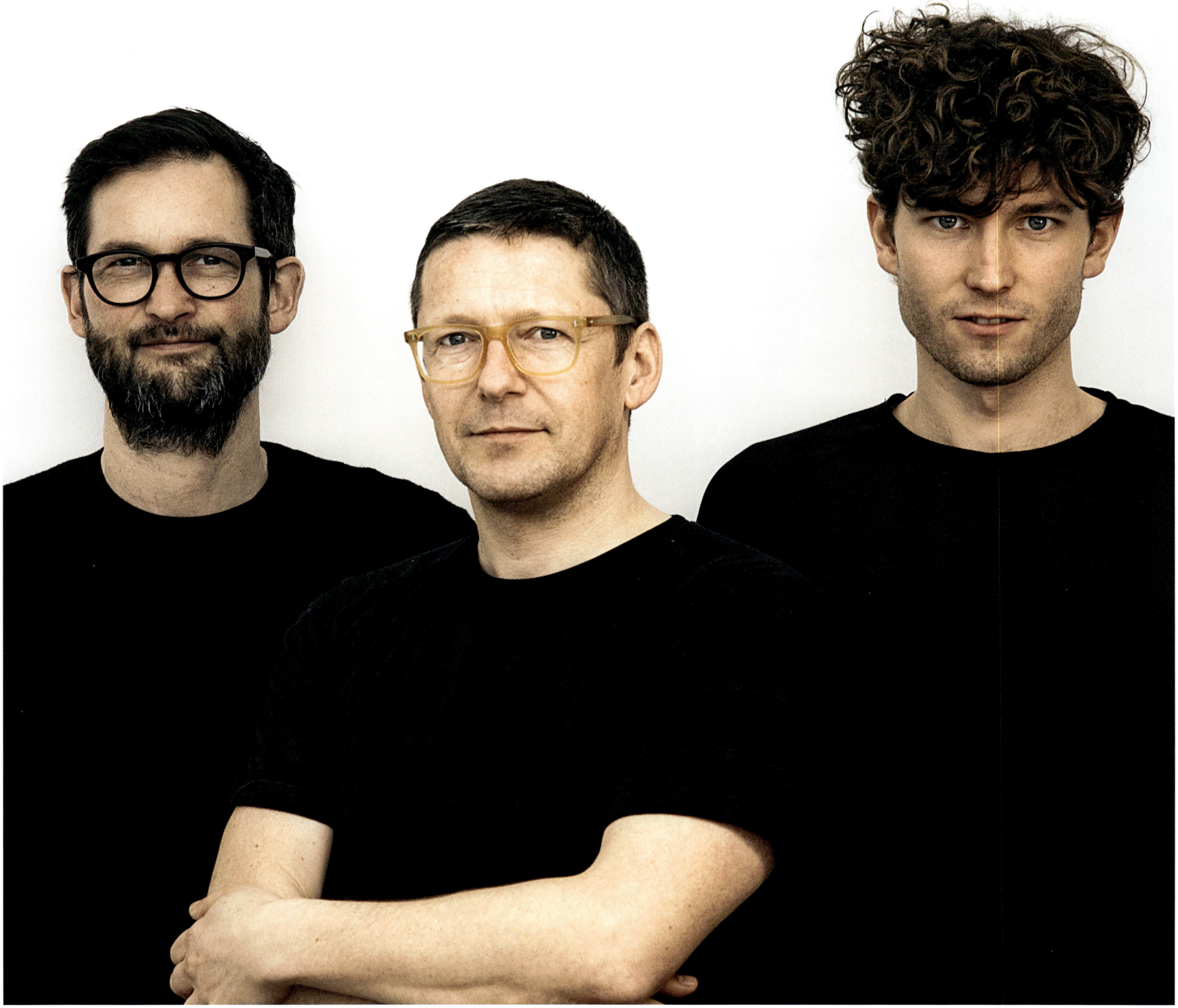

Thomas Turner, Ben Rigby, Nathanael Hunt
Haberdashery

"Haberdashery is a design studio fascinated by the perpetual appeal of light."

„Haberdashery ist ein Designstudio, das von der immerwährenden Anziehungskraft des Lichts fasziniert ist."

Who or what inspires you?
We are inspired by the light in the world around us and how it informs our lives; inspiration is explored on a visceral level, with anything that inspires awe or amazement becoming a source of inspiration.

What is your personal vision for the future?
Haberdashery creates narrative-driven lighting products that connect with our audience on a very human level; we explore continuously, pushing for new ways to connect with the most imaginative parts of the design market through the medium of light.

What does winning the Red Dot: Best of the Best mean to you?
It is hugely important as we are new to the product world; it is verification that the passion and attention to detail we apply to our sculptural projects can be transferred to our product collection.

Wer oder was inspiriert Sie?
Uns inspiriert das Licht in unserer Umgebung und wie es unser Leben prägt. Inspiration spürt man tief im Inneren. Alles, was Ehrfurcht und Staunen hervorruft, wird zu einer Quelle der Inspiration.

Wie sieht Ihre persönliche Zukunftsvision aus?
Haberdashery kreiert Beleuchtungsprodukte, die eine Geschichte erzählen und auf einer sehr menschlichen Ebene eine Verbindung zu unserer Zielgruppe herstellen. Wir sind ständig auf der Suche nach neuen Wegen und erkunden Möglichkeiten, mit denen wir durch das Medium Licht an die erfinderischsten Bereiche des Designmarkts anknüpfen können.

Was bedeutet die Auszeichnung mit dem Red Dot: Best of the Best für Sie?
Sie ist für uns enorm wichtig, da wir Neulinge in der Produktwelt sind. Sie ist eine Bestätigung, dass sich die Leidenschaft und Genauigkeit, die wir in unsere skulpturalen Projekte investieren, auch auf unsere Produktkollektion übertragen lassen.

reddot award 2019
best of the best

Manufacturer
Haberdashery, London, United Kingdom

Dawn to Dusk
Table and Floor Lamp
Tisch- und Stehleuchte

See page 370
Siehe Seite 370

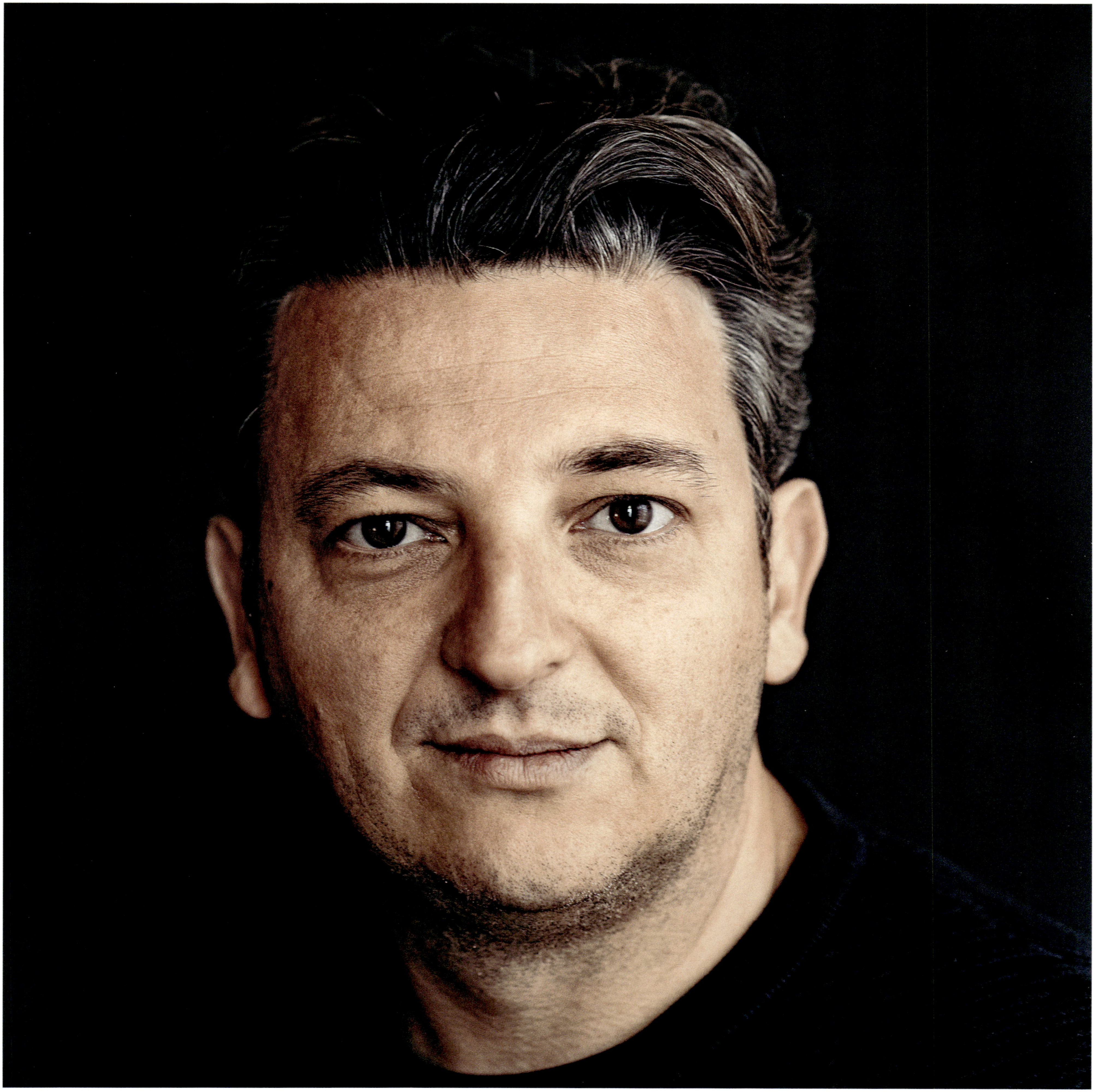

Carlos Pereira
Arpino

"I firmly believe that a product should have its own identity and character."
„Ich bin fest davon überzeugt, dass ein Produkt immer seine eigene Identität und seinen eigenen Charakter haben sollte."

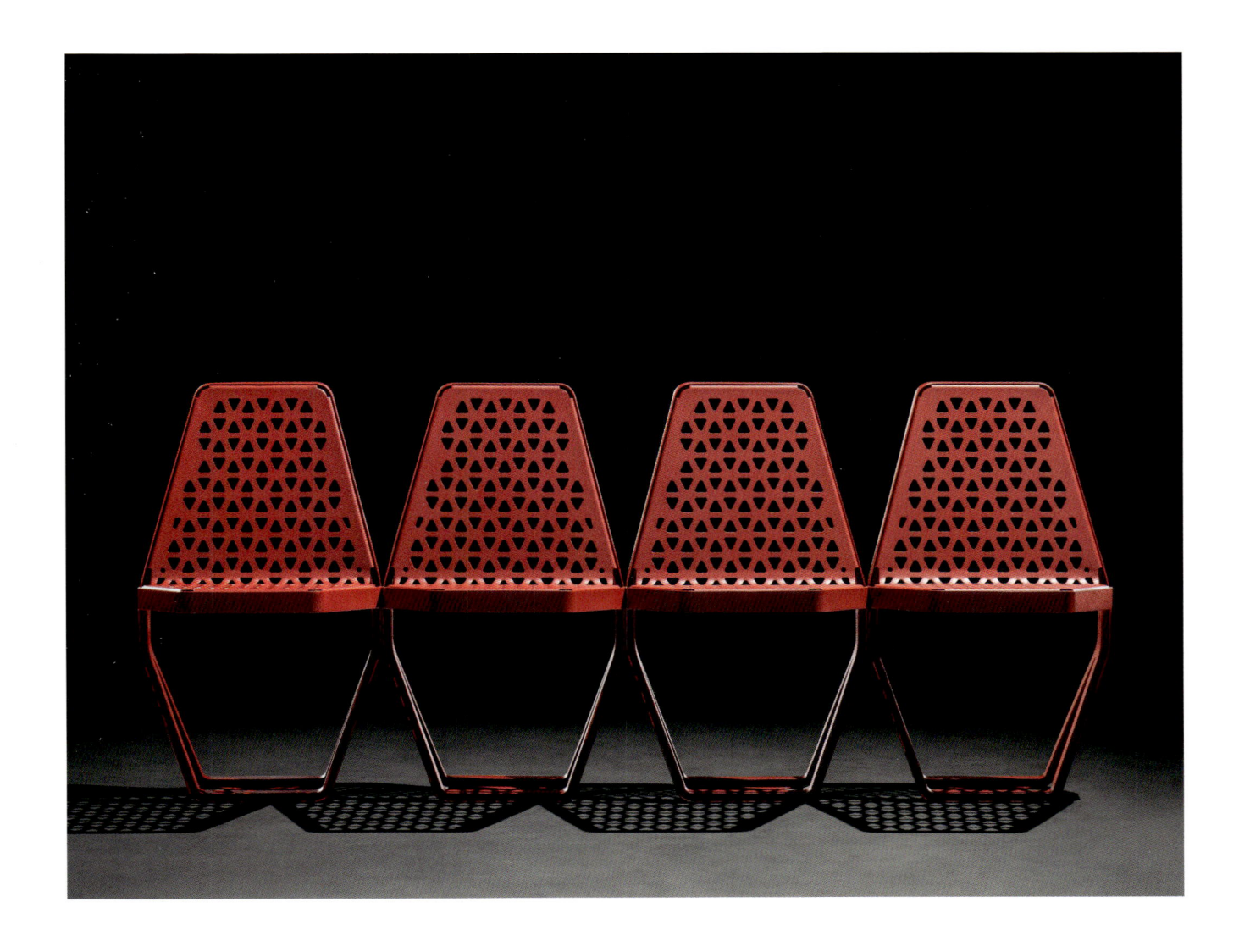

Who or what inspires you?
I am inspired mainly by art and technology, but at the end, just by people, their needs and aspirations.

Why did you become a designer?
I decided to become an industrial designer when I realised the social impact that this profession could have. I was interested in art and architecture at the early age of 16 or 17 and started to read some authors such as Bruno Munari or Gui Bonsiepe, who demonstrated to me the positive social change that design has.

Where will your industry be in ten years?
Wireless and mobile information technology is introducing important changes both in public and urban spaces, and that has immediate consequences for the implementation of the required infrastructure and also for the way people interact with each other and with the space itself.

Wer oder was inspiriert Sie?
Vor allem die Kunst und die Technik, doch letztlich sind es wirklich Menschen, ihre Bedürfnisse und ihre Sehnsüchte, die mich inspirieren.

Warum sind Sie Designer geworden?
Ich bin Industriedesigner geworden, als mir die soziale Wirkung, die dieser Beruf haben kann, bewusst wurde. Bereits im Alter von 16 oder 17 interessierte ich mich für Kunst und Architektur und begann, Autoren wie Bruno Munari und Gui Bonsiepe zu lesen, die mir den positiven sozialen Beitrag von Design klarmachten.

Wo wird Ihre Branche in zehn Jahren stehen?
Drahtlose und mobile Informationstechnologie verändert den öffentlichen und städtischen Raum. Und das hat direkte Auswirkungen auf die Umsetzung der notwendigen Infrastruktur und auch auf die Art, in der Menschen miteinander sowie mit dem Raum selbst umgehen.

reddot award 2019
best of the best

Manufacturer
Arpino,
Luanda, Angola;
Porto, Portugal

Arpino OXS Design Line
Urban Furniture
Stadtmobiliar

See page 384
Siehe Seite 384

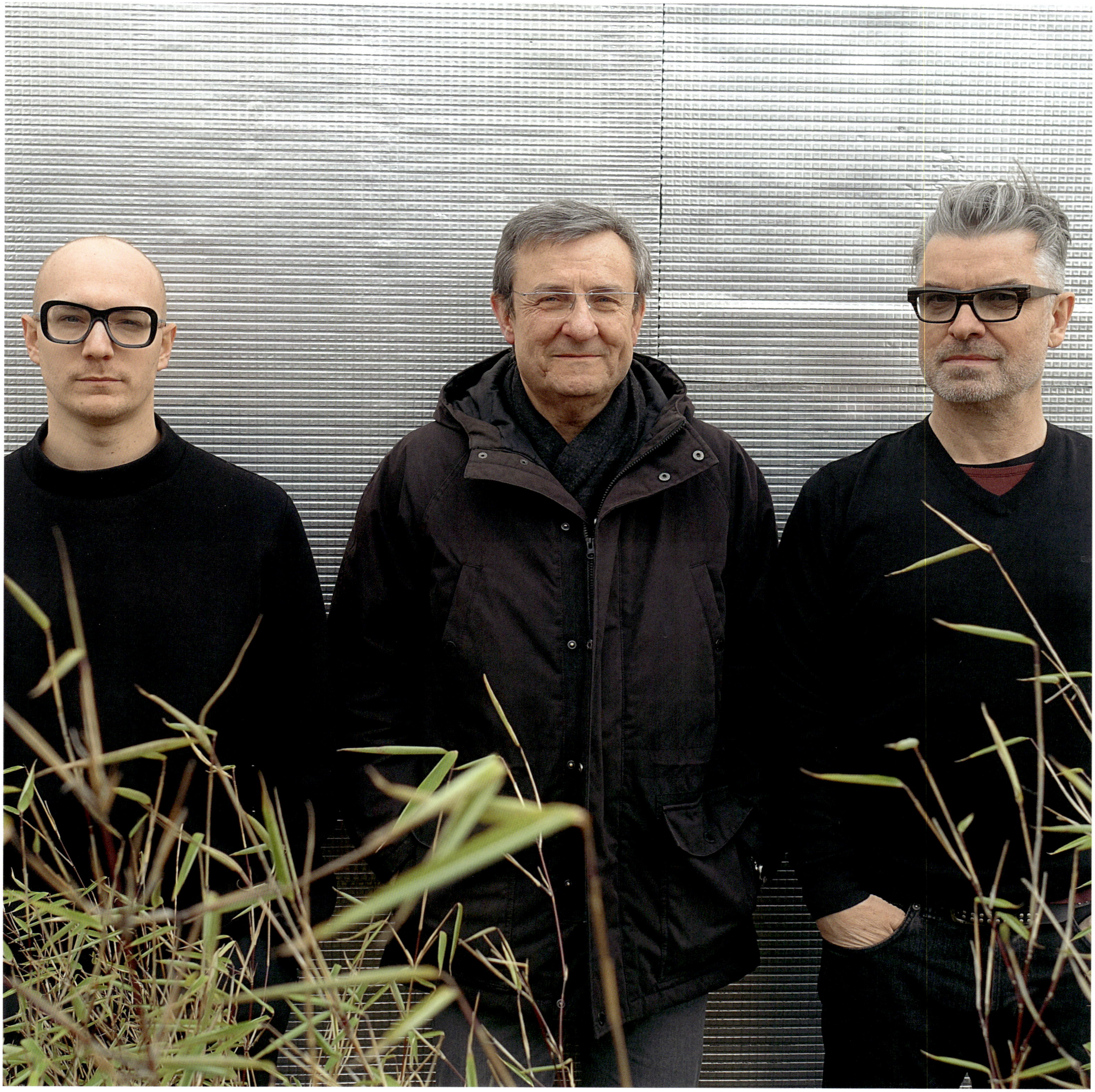

Aleš Kachlík, Prof. Jan Němeček, Prof. Michal Froněk
Olgoj Chorchoj Studio

"Formal design principles with a strong focus on functionality."
„Formale Gestaltungsprinzipien mit einem starken Fokus auf Funktionalität."

What was your goal when you designed your award-winning product?
The goal was to make the public space enjoyable for everyone and make it blend with the city. The design follows traditional post-war Czech urban furniture design, specific to the city of Prague. Its innovation was achieved through the simplified sophisticated design, innovative materials and, most importantly, better ergonomic shapes, which blend into the streets of Prague and bring the public space together.

Who or what inspires you?
Frankly, the whole world inspires us. Objects of everyday life inspire us, meeting unknown people, travelling, seeing new and unknown things, and the city of Prague.

Welches Ziel verfolgten Sie bei der Gestaltung Ihres ausgezeichneten Produktes?
Das Ziel war, den öffentlichen Raum für alle angenehm zu machen und sicherzustellen, dass sich die Abfalleimer in das Stadtbild einfügen. Die Gestaltung folgt dem traditionellen Design des tschechischen Nachkriegs-Stadtmobiliars, das für Prag so typisch ist. Die Innovation beruht auf einer vereinfachten, anspruchsvollen Gestaltung, innovativen Materialien und vor allem besseren ergonomischen Formen, die sich in die Straßen Prags einfügen und den öffentlichen Raum zusammenbringen.

Wer oder was inspiriert Sie?
Ehrlich gesagt, inspiriert uns die ganze Welt. Uns inspirieren Alltagsobjekte, Begegnungen mit unbekannten Menschen, Reisen, Neues und Unbekanntes zu sehen, und natürlich die Stadt Prag.

reddot award 2019
best of the best

Client
City of Prague, Czech Republic

Prague Street Furniture
Bins
Abfalleimer

See page 388
Siehe Seite 388

CD
RADIO
STREAM
TV
VIDEO
VOLUME
TRACK
PLAY / PAUSE
VOLUME
TRACK
PLAY / PAUSE
LIGHT

Interior design
Interior Design

Access control systems
Clubs
Coverings
Display solutions
Doors and door systems
Fire detectors
Handles and handle systems
Hotels
Museums
Office buildings
Postboxes
Real estate
Restaurants
Room acoustics
Room textiles
Screens
Shops
Smart home systems and automation
Smoke alarms
Sockets
Switches and switching systems
Wallpapers and wall panelling
Wellness areas
Window blinds and accessories
Windows

Beschläge
Brandmelder
Briefkästen
Bürobauten
Clubs
Display-Lösungen
Fenster
Fensterverdunkelungen und Zubehör
Griffe und Griffsysteme
Hotels
Immobilien
Museen
Rauchmelder
Raumakustiken
Raumtextilien
Restaurants
Schalter und Schaltsysteme
Shops
Sichtschutz
Smart Home-Systeme und Automation
Steckdosen
Tapeten und Wandverkleidungen
Türen und Türsysteme
Wellnessbereiche
Zutrittskontrollen

The Retreat at Blue Lagoon Iceland
Luxury Hotel, Restaurant and Spa
Luxushotel, Restaurant und Spa

Client
The Retreat at
Blue Lagoon Iceland,
Grindavík, Iceland

Design
Basalt Architects,
Reykjavík, Iceland
Design Group Italia, Milan, Italy

Web
www.bluelagoon.com
www.basalt.is
www.designgroupitalia.com

reddot award 2019
best of the best

Fascinating interplay
To integrate landscape convincingly into architecture is a true challenge and plays a pivotal role in regions with breathtaking nature scenes as can be found in Iceland. Located at the Blue Lagoon in Iceland, The Retreat has been built directly into an 800-year-old lava flow. The overall concept encompasses a subterranean spa, a geothermal lagoon, a restaurant that reimagines Iceland's culinary traditions, as well as a luxury hotel with 62 suites. Encircled by the Blue Lagoon's mineral-rich waters, the architecture and design of the hotel harmonise with the otherworldly volcanic surroundings, erasing the boundary between man and nature. The result is a one-of-a-kind destination where the interplay of lava, moss and water is woven into every facet of the guests' journey. Inspired by the landscape, the interiors feature refined tone-to-tone colour schemes and simple shapes. With all elements converging into unity, the design conveys an atmosphere of restrained luxury. The chromatically defined colour palette has been meticulously chosen to highlight and echo the volcanic vista, conjuring harmony with the water, land, weather and light. The resulting style is truly timeless and a sophisticated incarnation of a self-reliant notion of luxury that is both distinctively Icelandic in that it is rooted in the tradition of Scandinavian design, but at the same time is also infused with Italian craftsmanship and attention to detail.

Faszinierendes Zusammenspiel
Die Einbeziehung der Landschaft in die Architektur ist eine Herausforderung und spielt gerade in Regionen wie der imposanten Natur Islands eine zentrale Rolle. Das The Retreat an der dortigen Blauen Lagune wurde direkt in einen 800 Jahre alten Lavastrom integriert. Als Gesamtkonzept umfasst es ein unterirdisches Spa, eine geothermische Lagune, ein die kulinarische Tradition Islands neu interpretierendes Restaurant sowie ein Luxushotel mit 62 Suiten. Umgeben von den mineralreichen Gewässern der Blauen Lagune harmonieren Architektur und Gestaltung der Räumlichkeiten mit der umliegenden archaischen Vulkanlandschaft und lassen die Grenze zwischen Mensch und Natur verschwimmen. Das Ergebnis ist ein besonderer Aufenthaltsort, an dem das Zusammenspiel von Lava, Moos und Wasser in jeder Facette spürbar wird. Inspiriert von der Landschaft, begeistert das Interieur mit einer feinsinnigen Ton-in-Ton-Farbgebung und einfachen Formen. Mit seiner alle Elemente vereinenden Gestaltung vermittelt es eine Atmosphäre von edlem Understatement. Die chromatisch abgestimmte Farbpalette wurde sorgfältig ausgewählt, um den Blick auf die vulkanische Landschaft zu lenken und dabei eine Harmonie zwischen Wasser, Land, Wetter und Licht zu erzeugen. Der daraus resultierende Stil ist zeitlos und Ausdruck eines differenzierten, spezifisch isländischen Verständnisses von Luxus, das in der Tradition skandinavischen Designs wurzelt und zugleich durchdrungen ist von italienischer Handwerkskunst sowie der Liebe zum Detail.

Statement by the jury
Transforming the spectacular natural lava flow scenery, The Retreat at Blue Lagoon in Iceland has emerged as a wonderful place for relaxation. Its charm resides in its natural simplicity. Establishing a sensual balance, the interior architectural forms have been designed to interact with the elements of the surrounding landscape – creating an atmosphere of noble refinement that is further enhanced by a skilfully implemented colour composition and a clever lighting concept.

Begründung der Jury
Die spektakuläre Umgebung aus Lava transformierend, entstand mit dem The Retreat at Blue Lagoon in Island ein wunderbarer Ort der Entspannung. Sein Reiz liegt in der natürlichen Einfachheit. Eine sensible Balance schaffend, stehen die innenarchitektonischen Formen in Wechselwirkung mit den Elementen der Landschaft – und kreieren eine sehr edle Atmosphäre, die durch die sorgfältige Farbkomposition und das geschickte Lichtkonzept zusätzlich unterstrichen wird.

Designer portrait
See page 30
Siehe Seite 30

73

Stream
Residential Interior Design
Wohnraumgestaltung

Client
Beijing Jinmao, Beijing, China
Design
Design Apartment (Chung-Han Tang), Taipei City, Taiwan
Web
www.da-interior.com

This interior decoration of a show flat manages to create an oasis of calm and naturalness right in the centre of the bustling city centre of Beijing. The main materials used are wood, stone and marble – together with a colour concept based on shades of grey and brown. They exude a feeling of harmony. An important design element is the use of plants, but not only for the outdoor area. They also give a green accent to the interior furnishing, thereby reflecting the contemporary, natural living concept.

Statement by the jury
The interior decoration of this show flat creates a calm and harmonic atmosphere which is a clever antithesis to the bustling urban environment around it.

Dieser Inneneinrichtung einer Musterwohnung gelingt es, inmitten des lebhaften Stadtzentrums von Peking eine Oase der Ruhe und Natürlichkeit zu erschaffen. Vorherrschende Materialien sind Holz, Stein und Marmor – zusammen mit einem Farbkonzept in ruhigen Grau- und Brauntönen strahlen sie Harmonie aus. Ein wichtiges Gestaltungselement sind Pflanzen, die nicht nur auf den Außenbereich beschränkt sind, sondern auch bei der Innengestaltung grüne Akzente setzen und so ein zeitgemäßes, natürliches Wohnkonzept widerspiegeln.

Begründung der Jury
Die Inneneinrichtung dieser Wohnung erzeugt eine ruhige und harmonische Atmosphäre, die gekonnt einen Gegenpol zu ihrem urbanen und betriebsamen Umfeld bildet.

Oriental Palace Club

Client
Seazen Holdings Co., Ltd., Shanghai, China
Design
G-ART Design International, Shanghai, China
Web
www.seazen.com.cn
www.g-artdesign.com

The interior design of the Oriental Palace Club hints at the spirit of ancient, Far Eastern culture. Cultural heritage was the starting point for the design, while perspective is its focal point. The design combines naturalness with an artistic atmosphere. The generous room is defined by natural materials such as stone and wood which can, for example, be found in the shelves, as well as on the walls and ceilings. In combination with rattan and discreetly used plants, the interior with its harmonious colour scheme radiates calm and elegance.

Statement by the jury
The design of this interior architecture, which pays homage to Far Eastern culture, is impressive for its equally harmonious and artistic appearance.

Mit seiner Innengestaltung spiegelt der Oriental Palace Club den Geist einer alten, fernöstlichen Kultur wider. Das kulturelle Erbe steht als Ausgangspunkt und Perspektive im Mittelpunkt, das Design verbindet Natürlichkeit mit einer künstlerischen Atmosphäre. Der großzügige Raum wird von natürlichen Materialien wie Stein und Holz, das sich z. B. in den Regalen sowie in den Decken- und Wandkonstruktionen wiederfindet, bestimmt. Zusammen mit Rattan und dezent eingesetzten Pflanzen verströmt die in harmonischen Farbnuancen gestaltete Einrichtung Ruhe und Eleganz.

Begründung der Jury
Die Gestaltung dieser Inneneinrichtung, die der fernöstlichen Kultur Tribut zollt, beeindruckt mit einer gleichermaßen harmonischen wie künstlerischen Anmutung.

Waldhotel – Health & Medical Excellence

Client
Bürgenstock Hotels AG, Obbürgen, Switzerland
Design
Matteo Thun & Partners (Matteo Thun), Milan, Italy
Web
www.buergenstock.ch/sleep/waldhotel
www.matteothun.com

The modern, sustainable architecture of the Waldhotel is based on the "Healthy by Nature" concept. In addition to 160 rooms and suites, it includes a generously sized restaurant and bar area, meeting rooms, as well as a 4,200 sqm health & medical centre with medical spa. Inspired by Walser architecture and traditional alpine style, local materials were used in the construction of the gabion building. Due to its terrace-like structure and green flat roofs, it easily blends into the landscape.

Statement by the jury
The design of the Waldhotel, which seamlessly blends into its surroundings, achieves an impressive symbiosis of sustainability and exclusivity.

Die moderne, nachhaltige Architektur des Waldhotels setzt das Konzept „Healthy by Nature" um. Neben 160 Zimmern und Suiten umfasst es einen großzügigen Restaurant- und Barbereich, Konferenzräume sowie ein 4.200 qm großes Health & Medical Center mit medizinischem Spa. Inspiriert von der Walser Baukunst und der alpinen Tradition wurden für das Gabionen-Gebäude regionale Materialien verwendet. Dank seines terrassenförmigen Aufbaus und den begrünten Flachdächern fügt es sich problemlos in das Landschaftsbild ein.

Begründung der Jury
Die Gestaltung des nahtlos in sein Umfeld integrierten Waldhotels erreicht auf beeindruckende Weise eine Symbiose aus Nachhaltigkeit und Exklusivität.

Chuan's Kitchen II
Restaurant

Client
Guangzhou ABO Sunny Walk
Restaurant Co., Ltd., Guangzhou, China
Design
Guangdong Infinity Mind Architecture
Design Co., Ltd. (Xiaowen Wang),
Guangzhou, China
Web
www.infinitynide.com

The interior design of Chuan's Kitchen II restaurant is defined by the wall and floor materials used. The most important building material is a waste product resulting from the firing of regional black earthenware. These arched elements are fitted together in such a way that they create the impression of a chain mesh. The tiles, whose gloss radiates energy at dusk, are by contrast made of dismantled soil material of an underground railway construction. They cover the inner walls, the bar area and the floor of the whole restaurant.

Statement by the jury
A fascinating choice of materials characterises the design of Chuan's Kitchen II restaurant which also gains merit for its expressive overall appearance.

Die Inneneinrichtung des Restaurants Chuan's Kitchen II wird von dem verwendeten Wand- und Bodenmaterial bestimmt. Das wichtigste Baumaterial ist ein Abfallprodukt, das in der Region beim Brennen von schwarzem Steingut anfällt. Diese bogenförmigen Elemente werden so zusammengefügt, dass der Eindruck eines Kettennetzes entsteht. Die Fliesen, deren Glanz im Dämmerlicht Lebendigkeit versprüht, bestehen dagegen aus abgebautem Bodenmaterial einer U-Bahn-Anlage. Sie verkleiden die Innenwand, den Barbereich und den Boden des gesamten Restaurants.

Begründung der Jury
Eine faszinierende Materialwahl charakterisiert die Gestaltung des Restaurants Chuan's Kitchen II, die zudem mit einem ausdrucksstarken Gesamteindruck punktet.

Song Chinese Cuisine
Restaurant

Client
Song's Chinese Cusine, Guangzhou, China
Design
Republican Metropolis Architecture
(Yong Cai Huang), Guangzhou, China
Web
www.i-rma.hk

The modern design of the Song Chinese Cuisine restaurant reinterprets an ancient Chinese legend with materials such as stainless steel bricks and glass. The dining area is dominated by a large art installation titled "Crane Wing", which is made of numerous finely wrought feathers. In conjunction with the lighting of the restaurant it turns into a marvellously shimmering object. The walls are curved and, together with the slender copper columns, create a unique room experience which is reinforced by a number of mirrored elements.

Statement by the jury
Artistic and sensual are two words that sum up the design of the Song Chinese Cuisine restaurant. It plays with a range of different materials and shapes.

Die moderne Gestaltung des Restaurants Song Chinese Cuisine interpretiert eine alte chinesische Legende mit Materialien wie z. B. Edelstahlziegeln und Glas. Im Essbereich dominiert eine große Kunstinstallation, die den Titel „Kranichflügel" trägt und aus zahlreichen kunstvoll gearbeiteten Federn besteht. Im Zusammenspiel mit der Beleuchtung wird sie zu einem prachtvoll schimmernden Objekt. Die Wände zeigen eine geschwungene Form und erzeugen zusammen mit schmalen Kupfersäulen ein einzigartiges Raumerlebnis, das durch Verspiegelungen noch verstärkt wird.

Begründung der Jury
Kunstvoll und sinnlich ist die Gestaltung des Restaurants Song Chinese Cuisine, die mit unterschiedlichen Materialien und Formen spielt.

BMW Startup Garage
Office
Büro

Client
BMW Group, Forschungs- und Technologiehaus, Garching, Germany

Design
gravity GmbH (Christopher Black, Sebastian Ritzler), Munich, Germany

Web
www.bmwstartupgarage.com
www.bmwgroup.com
www.gravity-europe.net

Agile collaboration with startups requires innovative and inspirational working environments. Careful consideration was given to this aspect from the outset in the design of the BMW Startup Garage. It features a stratified room-in-room concept with a spacious atrium, plus additional co-working spaces for brainstorming and a large meeting area. The workspaces are located at different levels within the rooms, enabling employees and visitors to enjoy visual and acoustic privacy in an open-plan space.

Für die agile Zusammenarbeit mit Start-ups braucht es eine innovative und inspirierende Arbeitsatmosphäre. Bei der Gestaltung der Räumlichkeiten der BMW Startup Garage wurde dies von Anfang an berücksichtigt. Sie bietet ein geschichtetes Raum-in-Raum-Konzept mit einem großzügigen Atrium, zusätzlichen Co-Working-Spaces für Brainstorming und einem großen Konferenzbereich. Alle Arbeitsbereiche befinden sich auf unterschiedlichen Raumhöhen. Dies ermöglicht eine visuelle und akustische Privatsphäre in einem offenen Raum.

Statement by the jury
The cleverly conceived open space concept for the BMW Startup Garage offers both privacy and an environment which stimulates creative interaction.

Begründung der Jury
Das klug durchdachte Open-Space-Konzept der BMW Startup Garage bietet gleichzeitig Raum für Privatsphäre sowie ein Umfeld, das zum kreativen Austausch einlädt.

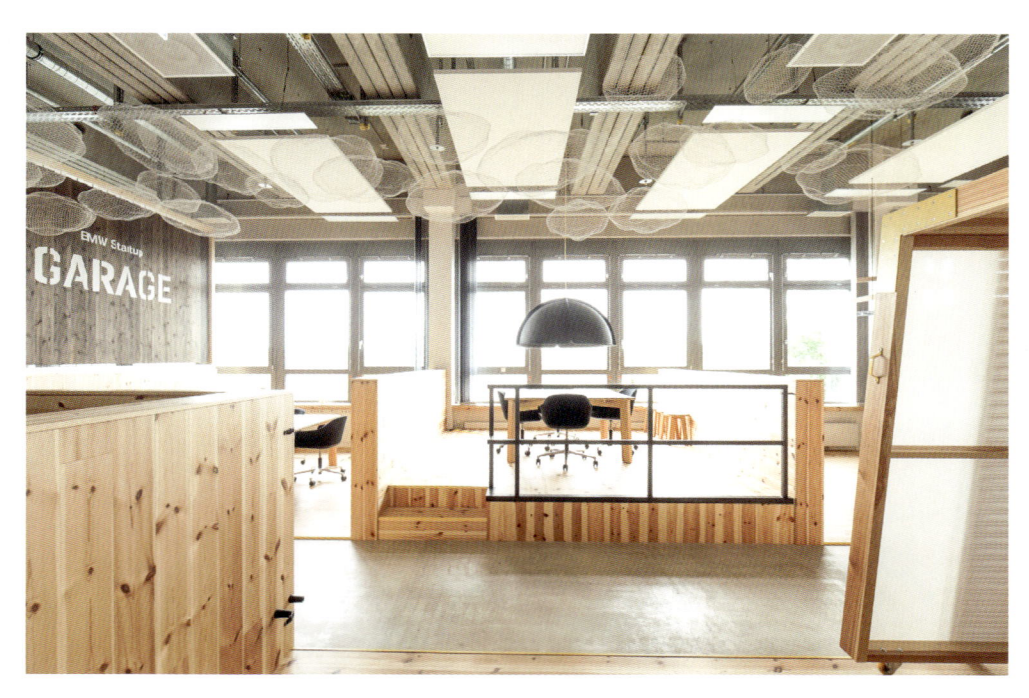

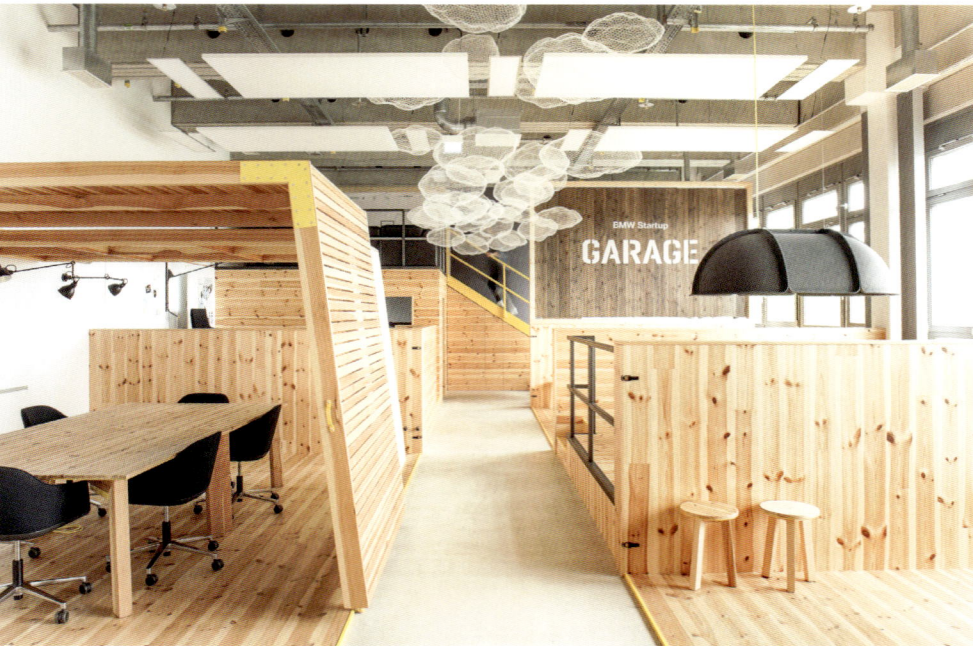

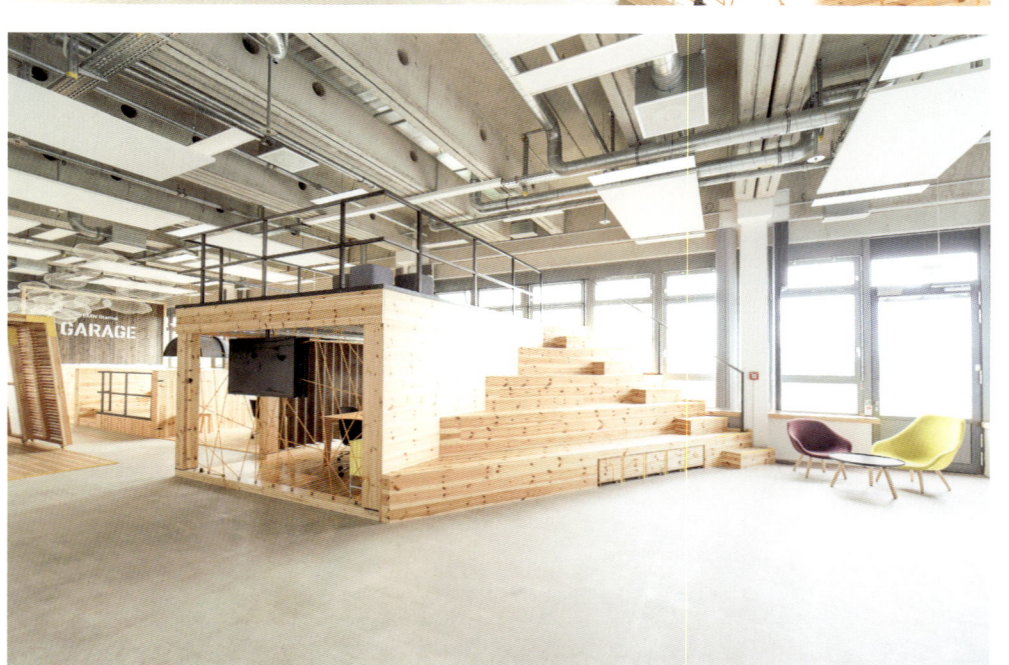

Aekyung Tower
Headquarters
Firmenzentrale

Client
Aekyung, Seoul, South Korea
Design
INNOCEAN Worldwide, Seoul, South Korea
CA PLAN, Seoul, South Korea
Web
www.aekyung.co.kr
www.innocean.com
www.ca-plan.com

The new Aekyung Tower headquarters is a building complex which not only includes offices, but also commercial space and a hotel. The holistic design concept endeavours to convey the company's core value – Share the Life. Its focus is on "togetherness" with the intention of promoting collaboration by everyone in order to reach a common goal. The design of the building complex not only provides employees with an integrated image of the company and a sense of belonging, but also with a platform for communication.

Die neue Firmenzentrale Aekyung Tower ist ein Gebäudekomplex, in dem sich neben Büroflächen auch gewerblich genutzte Räume sowie ein Hotel befinden. Das ganzheitliche Designkonzept zielt darauf ab, den Kernwert des Unternehmens – Share the Life – zu kommunizieren. Es richtet seinen Fokus auf ein „Miteinander", was die Zusammenarbeit aller zum Erreichen gemeinsamer Ziele fördern soll. Die Gestaltung des Gebäudes vermittelt den Mitarbeitern nicht nur ein einheitliches Unternehmensbild und ein Gefühl der Zugehörigkeit, sondern bietet auch eine Plattform für Kommunikation.

Statement by the jury
The Aekyung Tower attracts attention with its consistent and holistic design concept that skilfully reflects the company's values.

Begründung der Jury
Der Aekyung Tower macht mit einem konsequent ganzheitlichen Gestaltungskonzept, das gekonnt die Unternehmenswerte widerspiegelt, auf sich aufmerksam.

Material & Design as an Expression of Transformation
Material & Design als Ausdruck der Transformation
Office
Büro

Client
International Sustainable Chemistry Collaborative Centre (ISC3), Bonn, Germany
Design
Stefanie Jörgens – Gesunde Lebensräume, Meerbusch, Germany
Web
www.isc3.org
www.stefanie-joergens.de
Honourable Mention

This trendsetting interior design meets very high building biology, economic, aesthetic and representative requirements. This resulted in offices that unite a healthy as well as stylish furnishing concept and stand for a fully recyclable material culture. The beauty of the simple is paired with the importance of the invisible. This concept shows that a change in material and work culture is possible even under tight economic conditions.

Statement by the jury
This design concept, which focuses on delivering a healthy work environment, manages to combine ecology and sustainability with classic aesthetics.

Dieses richtungsweisende Interior Design erfüllt sehr hohe baubiologische, ökonomische, ästhetische und repräsentative Anforderungen. Entstanden sind Geschäftsräume, die ein gesundes sowie stilvolles Einrichtungskonzept vereinen und für eine vollständig kreislauffähige Materialkultur stehen. Die Schönheit des Einfachen ist gepaart mit der Wichtigkeit des Unsichtbaren. Dieses Konzept zeigt, dass ein Wandel der Material- und Arbeitskultur auch unter engen ökonomischen Vorgaben möglich ist.

Begründung der Jury
Diesem auf ein gesundes Arbeitsumfeld ausgerichteten Gestaltungskonzept gelingt es, Ökologie und Nachhaltigkeit mit einer klassischen Ästhetik zu vereinen.

Penetrating Perception, Concealing Power
Office
Büro

Client
AD Architecture, Shantou, China
Design
AD Architecture (Peihe Xie), Shantou, China

The design of this office retains the character of the old building in which it is located. In order to accentuate the special quality of the space, due in part to the five metres high walls, it does without unnecessary partitions or embellishments. Instead, the chosen materials create a link to the original space: black paintwork, cement floors and dark grey steel panels echo the original surroundings. New construction elements are made of steel and iron, which corrode naturally with time and take on a strong and beautiful appearance.

Statement by the jury
This office is a winning solution to presenting a powerful interior design that skilfully adapts a historic building to a contemporary use.

Die Gestaltung dieses Büros bewahrt den Charakter des alten Gebäudes, in dem es beheimatet ist. Um das besondere, durch fünf Meter hohe Wände hervorgerufene Raumgefühl zu unterstreichen, wird auf übermäßige Trennwände und Verzierungen verzichtet. Stattdessen stellt die Materialwahl eine Verbindung zum Originalraum her: Schwarze Lackierungen, Zementböden und dunkelgraue Stahlplatten geben die ursprüngliche Atmosphäre wieder. Neue Bauelemente bestehen aus Stahl und Eisen, sie korrodieren auf natürliche Weise und strahlen Stärke und Schönheit aus.

Begründung der Jury
Dieses Büro überzeugt mit einer kraftvoll anmutenden Innenarchitektur, die gekonnt ein historisches Gebäude einer modernen Nutzung zuführt.

Light Waterfall
Real Estate Sales Centre
Immobilien-Verkaufszentrum

Client
Dowell Real Estate, Wuhan, China
Design
KLID – Kris Lin Interior Design (Kris Lin), Shanghai, China
Web
www.chinadydc.com/product/xmyl
www.krislin.com.cn

The alluring design of this estate agency retail space takes water as its theme and showcases it – just like an art exhibition would. The design brings interior, architecture and landscape together to create a whole. Water is always centre stage, albeit in different forms. Right next to the meeting space in the sales centre, there is, for instance, a pond enclosed by a glass wall. A lake has been created just outside the building which reflects a light installation on the facade that creates the impression of flowing water.

Statement by the jury
The design concept skilfully integrates this real estate sales centre into its surroundings and, in doing so, takes a highly sophisticated artistic approach.

Wie eine Kunstausstellung inszeniert die ansprechende Gestaltung das Thema Wasser in diesem Immobilien-Verkaufszentrum. Sie vereint Inneneinrichtung, Architektur und Landschaft zu einem Ganzen, das Element Wasser steht dabei auf unterschiedliche Weise im Mittelpunkt. So befindet sich beispielsweise direkt neben dem Tagungsbereich des Verkaufszentrums ein von einer Glaswand umgebener Teich. Vor dem Gebäude ist ein Gewässer angelegt. Eine Lichtinstallation an der Außenfassade, die den Eindruck fließenden Wassers erweckt, spiegelt sich darin wider.

Begründung der Jury
Das Gestaltungskonzept integriert dieses Immobilien-Verkaufszentrum gekonnt in sein Umfeld und setzt dabei auf hohem Niveau einen künstlerischen Ansatz um.

Envelop 3D
Facade Platform
Fassadenplattform

Manufacturer
Rabel Systems, Nicosia, Cyprus
In-house design
Yiannis Constantinides
Web
www.rabel.com.cy

This system allows the construction of facades using the seamless integration of various modules. A single track without intermediate posts can hold construction elements such as sliding, folding, pivot, pivot-slide doors, casement or fixed windows, curtain walls, glass railings, drywall partitions as well as spider-glass constructions, shading louvres or insect screens. All the modules can lock into each other in a row, or above or below each other to produce a continuous facade. Furthermore, the modules nest into one another without the need for extra frames to create a high level of sound and heat insulation.

Mithilfe dieses Systems lässt sich eine Fassade aus nahtlos integrierbaren Modulen konstruieren. Eine einzelne Schiene, ohne dazwischenliegenden Pfosten, kann Bauteile wie Schiebe-, Falt-, Pivot- und Pivot-Schiebetüren, Flügel- oder fest installierte Fenster, Vorhangfassaden, Glasgeländer, Trockenbauwände sowie Spider-Glas-Konstruktionen, Beschattungslamellen oder Insektenschutzgitter aufnehmen. Sämtliche Module können neben-, unter- und übereinander zu einer durchgehenden Fassade zusammengefügt werden. Auch lassen sich mehrere Module ohne zusätzliche Rahmen ineinander verschachteln und erzielen so eine hohe Schall- und Wärmedämmung.

Statement by the jury
The Envelop 3D facade platform demonstrates a successful architectural construction solution that is characterised by numerous application possibilities.

Begründung der Jury
Die Fassadenplattform Envelop 3D stellt eine gelungene architektonische Baulösung dar, die sich durch vielfältige Einsatzmöglichkeiten auszeichnet.

All-in-one Wall Display System
All-in-one-Wanddisplay-System

Manufacturer
A-John Enterprise Co., Ltd.,
New Taipei City, Taiwan
In-house design
Yun Hui Lin, Fei Wang,
Yu Juung Chang, Chao Sheng Hsu
Design
China University of Technology
(Prof. Ming Chuan Wang, Ruei-Hsing Lin),
Taipei City, Taiwan
Web
www.ajohn.biz

This all-in-one wall display system is made of customisable, aluminium extrusion tracks and modular connectors. Special corner connectors allow for flexible construction at almost any angle. The tracks can be clad with a cover and can also be used for the hanging of display panels as well as cabinet elements. The system, which is eminently suitable for the decor of commercial spaces, can be erected simply and neatly. As no work involving wood or concrete is needed, costs are kept to a minimum.

Statement by the jury
With its flexible construction options, this all-in-one wall display system presents an accomplished and versatile product solution.

Dieses All-in-one-Wanddisplay-System ist aus personalisierbaren, stranggepressten Aluminiumschienen und modularen Steckverbindungen konstruiert. Spezielle Eckverbindungselemente erlauben flexible Aufbauten in beinahe jedem Winkel. Die Schienen können mit einer Bespannung verkleidet werden, es lassen sich zudem Anzeigetafeln und Schrankelemente einhängen. Das System, das sich auch gut zur Dekoration von Geschäftsräumen eignet, lässt sich einfach und sauber aufbauen. Da Holz- und Betonarbeiten entfallen, verringern sich dabei anfallende Kosten.

Begründung der Jury
Mit seinen flexiblen Aufbaumöglichkeiten stellt dieses All-in-one-Wanddisplay-System eine gelungene, vielseitig einsetzbare Produktlösung dar.

Flextile
Textile Display System
Stoff-Display-System

Manufacturer
KG Spennare AB, Nacka, Sweden
In-house design
Johan Spennare, Joel Högberg
Design
Catino (Jonatan Lundén, Petter Polson, Daniel Amosy), Stockholm, Sweden
Web
www.spennare.com
www.catino.se

Flextile is a foldable textile display system that can be erected easily and quickly by any user. It consists of large, square frames of different sizes that can be folded and combined in a number of different ways. Thanks to the innovative design, the fabric print always remains on the frame, even when it is folded, making it fast to assemble and dismantle. If required, it is possible to mount fabrics on both sides of the frame. The appearance of the frame is deliberately unobtrusive in order to focus attention on the fabric print.

Statement by the jury
The innovative design of the Flextile textile display system enthrals with a straightforward assembly and an unostentatious look.

Flextile ist ein faltbares Stoff-Display-System, das einfach und schnell auch von Laien montiert werden kann. Es besteht aus verschieden großen, quadratischen Rahmen, die auf unterschiedliche Weise gefaltet und kombiniert werden können. Dank des innovativen Designs bleibt der Stoffdruck auch im gefalteten Zustand immer auf dem Rahmen, sodass dieser schnell zusammengebaut und zerlegt werden kann. Bei Bedarf lassen sich auch beide Seiten mit Stoff verkleiden. Das Aussehen des Rahmens ist bewusst zurückhaltend, um den Stoffdruck in den Fokus zu stellen.

Begründung der Jury
Die innovative Gestaltung des Stoff-Display-Systems Flextile besticht mit einer unkomplizierten Montage sowie mit einem dezenten Erscheinungsbild.

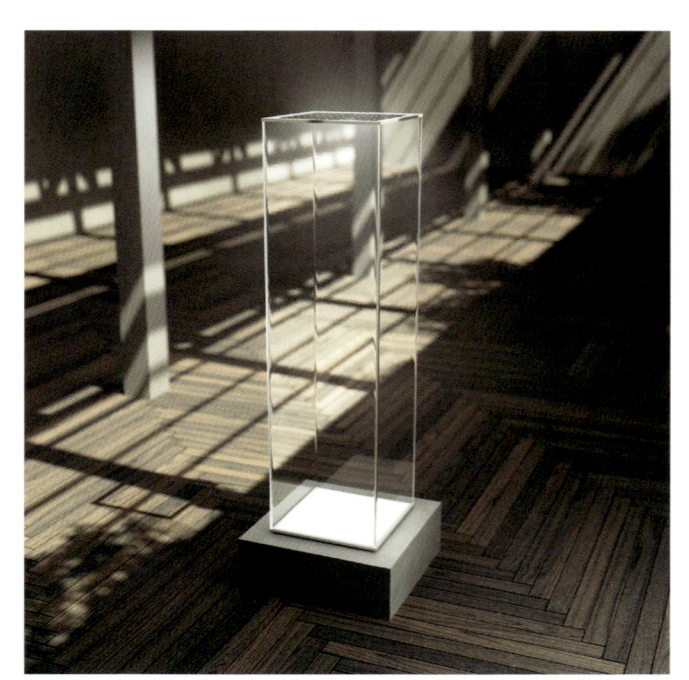

QuickModul Fazila
Glass Display Case
Glasvitrine

Manufacturer
Schreiber Innenausbau GmbH,
Geyer, Germany
In-house design
Web
www.schreiber-innenausbau.de

The QuickModul Fazila is a glass display with a modular design that makes it possible to easily install the display cases in rooms with low ceilings or niches with limited vertical space and is easily extensible. The cases have an aluminium profile of only 10 mm in which the glass plates are glued flush. The profiles are only screwed together in the horizontal plane; in the vertical plane, the mitred edges of the glass form a profile-free joint. The frameless, unassuming design focuses the attention of the viewer on the exhibit.

Statement by the jury
The functionally sophisticated, yet deliberately low-key design of the QuickModul Fazila glass display case meets high standards of exhibition equipment.

QuickModul Fazila ist eine Glasvitrine, deren modularer Aufbau eine einfache Installation auch in niedrigen Räumen oder Nischen mit geringer Einbauhöhe ermöglicht und problemlos erweiterbar ist. Basis ist ein auf 10 mm reduziertes Aluminiumprofil, in das Glasscheiben flächenbündig verklebt werden. Die Profile werden nur in der Waagerechten miteinander verschraubt, in der Senkrechten stoßen die Scheiben profillos in Gehrung aufeinander. Das rahmenlose, zurückhaltende Design rückt das Exponat in den Fokus des Betrachters.

Begründung der Jury
Die funktional ausgereifte, bewusst reduzierte Gestaltung der Glasvitrine QuickModul Fazila wird den hohen Ansprüchen an Ausstellungsmobiliar gerecht.

Museum of the Constitutions

Client
UNAM – National Autonomous University of Mexico, Mexico City, Mexico
Design
Tuux, Mexico City, Mexico
Web
www.unam.mx
www.tuux.mx
www.museodelasconstituciones.unam.mx

The new interior of the Museum of the Constitutions sets out to appeal to the general public and especially to young visitors. The design is dominated by free-standing, up to nine metres high, dynamically shaped constructions that divide the space into different thematic and service areas. The structural frame was built with birch plywood and the flexible plywood cover with native pines and teak veneers from sustainable forestry. The design and production relied on CAD modeling and CNC production methods in combination with highly skilled manual labour.

Mit einem neuen Interieur möchte das Museum of the Constitutions die breite Öffentlichkeit und besonders junge Besucher ansprechen. Das Design wird von freistehenden, bis zu neun Meter hohen, dynamisch geformten Konstruktionen dominiert, die den Raum in verschiedene Themen- und Servicebereiche unterteilen. Das Tragwerk besteht aus Birkensperrholz und die flexible Sperrholzverkleidung aus einheimischer Kiefer und Teakfurnieren aus nachhaltiger Forstwirtschaft. Die Konstruktion und Produktion erfolgte mithilfe von CAD- und CNC-Anwendungen in Kombination mit Handwerkskunst.

Statement by the jury
The inviting redesign of this museum impresses because of its dynamic design vocabulary in conjunction with the use of natural materials.

Begründung der Jury
Die einladende Neugestaltung dieses Museums überzeugt mit einer dynamischen Formensprache und der Verwendung natürlicher Materialien.

G2G Shop – A Mini Mill within The Mills
Retail Shop
Ladengeschäft

Client
The Hong Kong Research Institute of Textiles and Apparel, Hong Kong
Design
Design Department (Ray Zee), Nan Fung Group, Hong Kong
Web
www.hkrita.com
www.nanfungdesign.com

This retail interior combines a sales room with a production site. The G2G shop allows customers to see how new clothes are made from old ones in a glassed-in area framed by container elements. The double-glazing shields the retail space from noise and simultaneously ensures good visibility of the production process. The design pays tribute to both old and new building elements, for example by using traditional metal gates to flank the shopfront. Pillars inside have been left untouched to reflect the design philosophy "old is old, new is new".

Diese Geschäftseinrichtung verbindet einen Verkaufsraum mit einer Produktionsstätte. In diesem G2G-Shop wird die Herstellung neuer Kleidung aus alter in einem verglasten Bereich, der von Containerelementen eingerahmt wird, gezeigt. Die doppelte Verglasung schützt den Verkaufsraum vor Lärm und schafft gleichzeitig visuelle Transparenz. Die Gestaltung zollt alten und neuen Bauelementen Respekt: So flankieren z. B. traditionelle Metalltore die Ladenfront. Pfeiler im Innenraum bleiben unberührt und spiegeln so die Designphilosophie „alt ist alt, neu ist neu" wider.

Statement by the jury
The design of the G2G shop is impressive for the successful transformation of an old building into a modern commercial and production space.

Begründung der Jury
Die Gestaltung des G2G-Shops beeindruckt durch die gelungene Transformation eines alten Gebäudes zu einem modernen Verkaufs- und Produktionsraum.

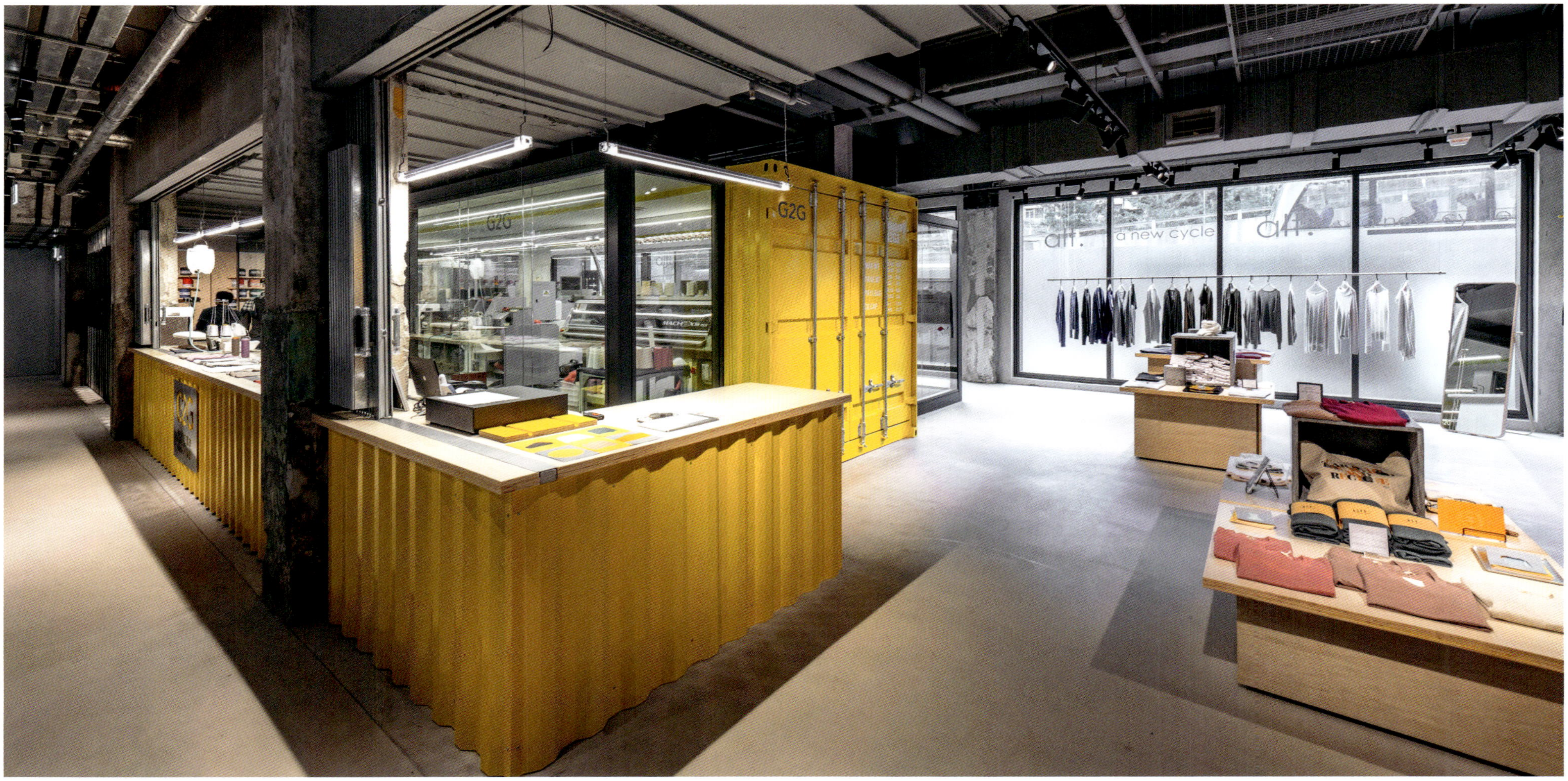
G2G
a new cycle

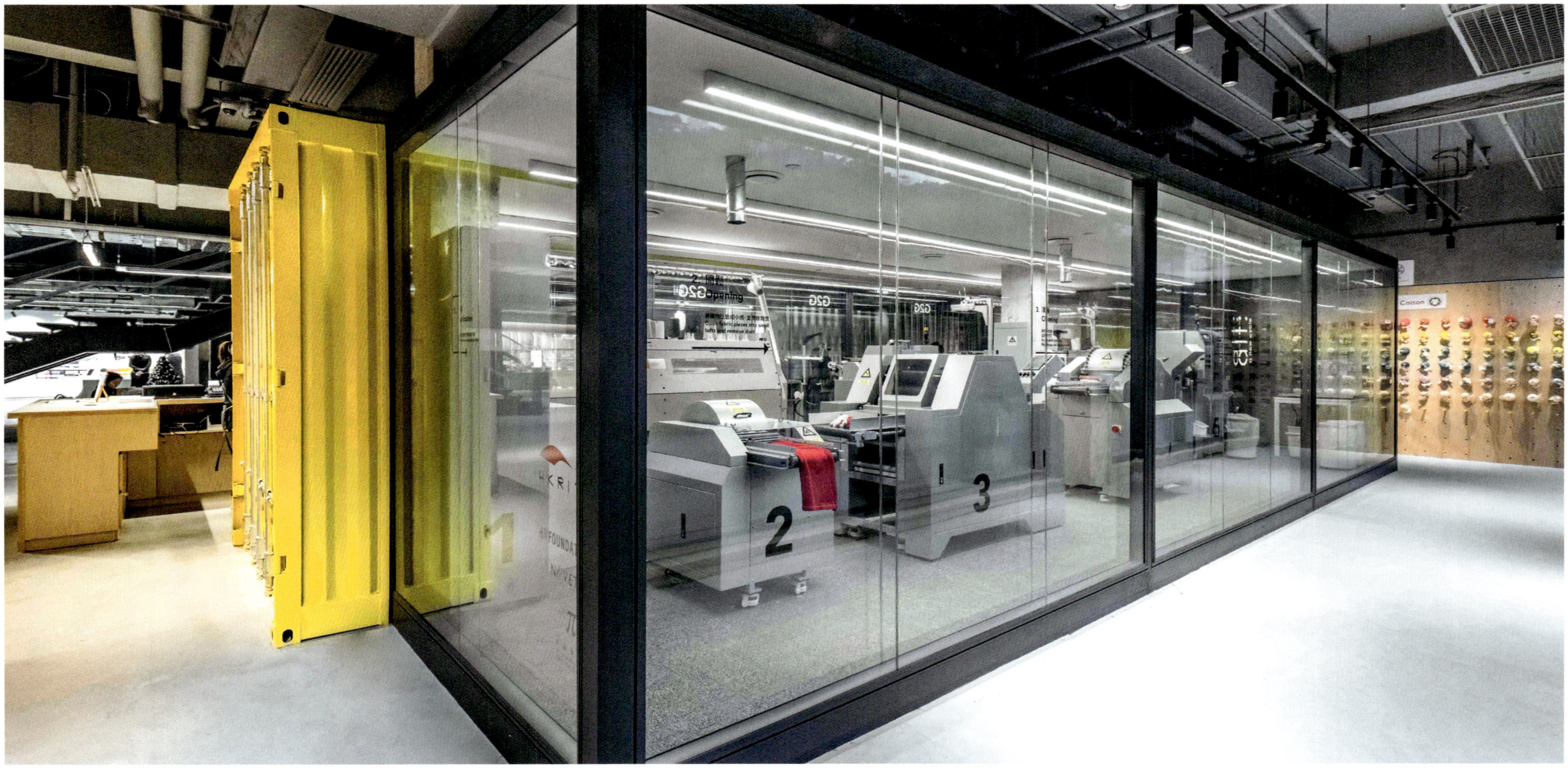
2
3

Centor S4
Insect Screen and Shade System
Insekten- und Sonnenschutzsystem

Manufacturer
Centor Holdings Pty Ltd,
Brisbane, Australia

In-house design
Centor Design Team

Web
www.centor.com

reddot award 2019
best of the best

Without compromise
Connecting to the beautiful world outside as often as possible increases the quality of everyday life. By bringing light, air and views inside, one can experience nature more closely. However, this can also result in harsh sunlight and a higher presence of insects. Against this backdrop, the Centor S4 insect screen and shade system enables owners of houses with larger door openings to enjoy the luxury of inside-outside living without having to face the traditional compromises. The system effectively keeps annoying insects out, protects against sunlight and provides more privacy. Using sophisticated load balancing technology, the screen glides smoothly across the whole door opening at the touch of a fingertip to effortlessly and conveniently stop at any desired position. Another advantage is that it retracts discreetly into the frame when not in use, removing visual distractions to the view outside. When in use, the state-of-the-art screen improves both airflow and visibility by 30 per cent, thanks to an ultra-fine mesh. Screens and shades are held in place by tabs secured in tracks to prevent insect screen blowout and support the hanging of heavier interior shade fabrics, including blackouts. Available in four configurations, including a 90-degree cornerless option, Centor S4 easily adapts to any new or existing door type, while its innovative adjustment technology simplifies the installation process.

Ohne Kompromisse
Häufiger Kontakt mit der Natur steigert die Qualität des Alltagslebens. Licht und Luft in Innenräumen sowie ein schöner Ausblick bringen die Natur näher, was aber auch direkte Sonneneinstrahlung oder das vermehrte Auftreten von Insekten bedeuten kann. Das Insekten- und Sonnenschutzsystem Centor S4 bietet vor diesem Hintergrund Eigentümern von Häusern mit großen Türöffnungen die Möglichkeit, auf luxuriöse Weise das Innen und Außen zu verbinden, ohne die üblichen Kompromisse eingehen zu müssen. Das System schirmt effektiv lästige Insekten und zu viel Sonnenlicht ab, wobei es gleichzeitig die Privatsphäre schützt. Dank einer ausgefeilten Lastausgleichstechnologie gleitet das System, mit nur einem Finger bedient, widerstandslos über die komplette Türöffnungsbreite, um bequem an jeder gewünschten Position anzuhalten. Ein weiterer Vorteil ist zudem, dass es sich bei Nichtgebrauch diskret im Türrahmen verstecken lässt. Dadurch wird auch der Blick nach draußen nicht gestört. Im ausgezogenen Zustand verbessert das hochmoderne System mithilfe eines speziellen Gewebes die Luftdurchlässigkeit sowie die Transparenz um 30 Prozent. Der Sonnen- und Insektenschutz wird durch Laschen am Gewebe fest in der Rahmenschiene gehalten, was auch den Einsatz schwererer Sonnenschutzstoffe bis hin zur Vollverdunkelung ermöglicht. Centor S4 ist in vier Konfigurationen einschließlich einer eckenlosen 90-Grad-Konstruktion erhältlich, während eine innovative Justierungstechnologie den Installationsprozess vereinfacht.

Statement by the jury
The Centor S4 insect screen and shade system fascinates with its sophisticated form and functionality. Its innovative load balancing technology allows for highly convenient operation. The system can be effortlessly stopped in any position or hidden in the door frame when it is not needed. At first glance, it impresses users with its high-quality workmanship. Moreover, it is durable and robust.

Begründung der Jury
Das Insekten- und Sonnenschutzsystem Centor S4 fasziniert mit seiner durchdachten Form und Funktionalität. Seine innovative Lastausgleichstechnologie erlaubt eine ausgesprochen komfortable Bedienung. Das System lässt sich mühelos stoppen oder im Türrahmen verbergen, wenn es nicht mehr gebraucht wird. Auf den ersten Blick begeistert es den Nutzer mit seiner hochwertigen Verarbeitungsqualität. Es ist zudem langlebig und robust.

Designer portrait
See page 32
Siehe Seite 32

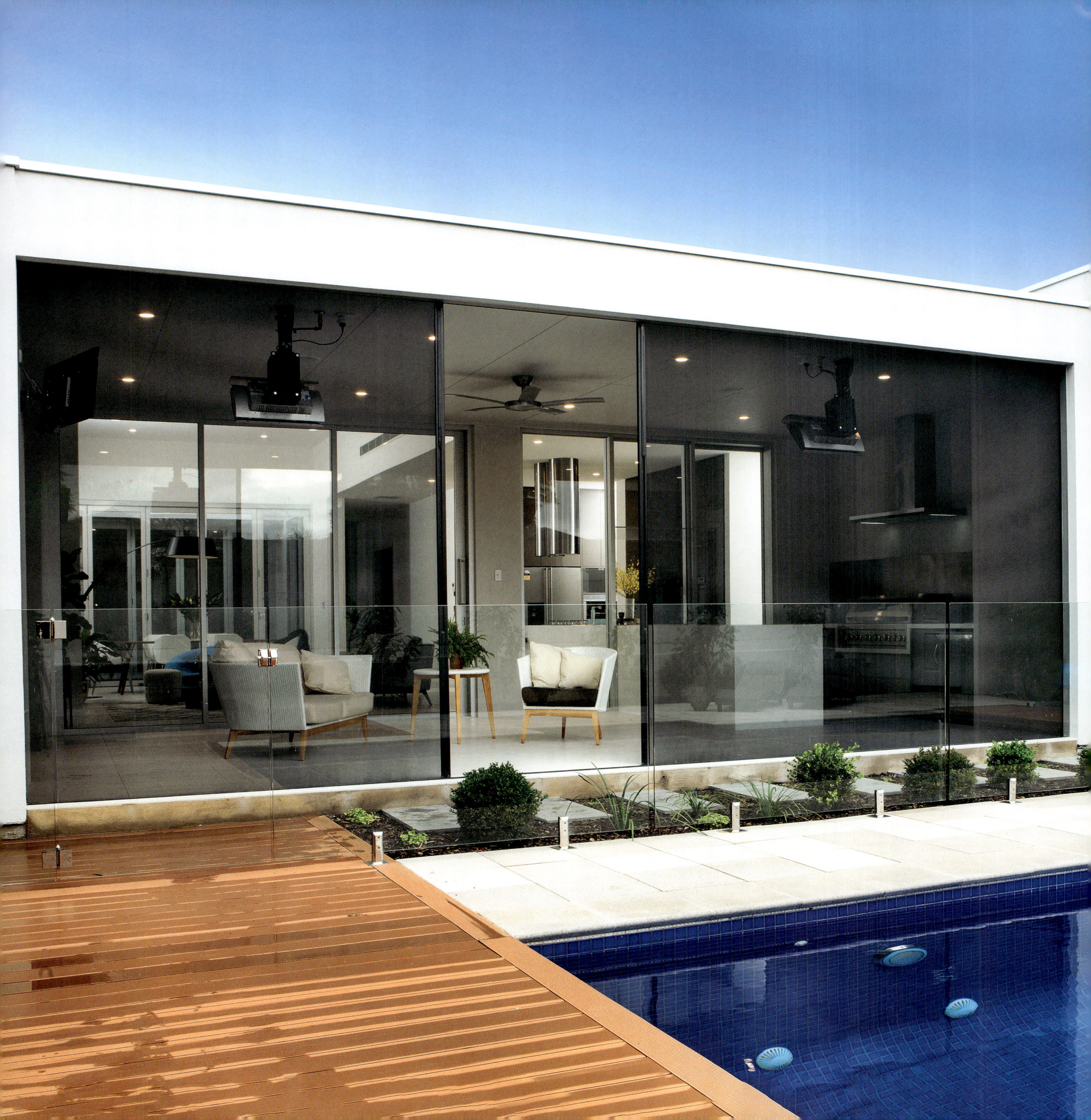

Schüco CSB
Sun Shading System
Sonnenschutzsystem

Manufacturer
Schüco International KG, Bielefeld, Germany
In-house design
Web
www.schueco.de

The Schüco CSB sun shading system is an external aluminium rolling-louvre blade construction. It meets the stringent requirements for wind load despite its low weight of 4.6 kg/sqm. It provides complete protection from direct sunshine when the sun is at an angle greater than 21 degrees. The system, whose surface is weather resistant, can be easily installed in the designated location. The advantage is that the blind is already made to measure and rolled up on the drive shaft before delivery.

Statement by the jury
The Schüco CSB sun shading system is characterised by the use of high-quality materials and an impressive functionality.

Schüco CSB ist ein außen liegendes Aluminium-Rolllamellensystem zum Schutz vor Sonneneinstrahlung. Es erfüllt hohe Anforderungen an Windbelastung, hat dabei aber ein geringes Gewicht von nur 4,6 kg/qm. Es bietet eine vollständige Abschattung direkter Sonneneinstrahlung ab einem Sonnenstandswinkel von 21 Grad. Das mit einer witterungsbeständigen Oberflächenveredelung versehene System lässt sich einfach in dem dafür vorgesehenen Raum montieren. Dabei ist von Vorteil, dass es bereits vorkonfektioniert und auf der Antriebswelle aufgewickelt angeliefert wird.

Begründung der Jury
Ein hochwertiger Materialeinsatz und eine beeindruckende Funktionalität kennzeichnen die Gestaltung des Schüco Sonnenschutzsystems CSB.

Schüco ASE 67 PD
Sliding System
Schiebesystem

Manufacturer
Schüco International KG, Bielefeld, Germany
In-house design
Web
www.schueco.de

The design of the Schüco ASE 67 PD Panorama Design sliding system is both purist and comfortable. A level threshold ensures barrier-free access and the outer frame can be integrated into the walls of the building. The slim profiles give a high degree of transparency. The system envisages sliding elements with a size of up to 3,200 mm × 3,000 mm and a weight of up to 400 kg. A novel mechanism in the interlocking section allows the elements to be locked even when open.

Statement by the jury
Here the focus is on transparency and purism in the technically well-engineered design of the Schüco ASE 67 PD Panorama Design sliding system.

Das Schüco Panorama-Design-Schiebesystem ASE 67 PD ist gleichermaßen puristisch wie auch komfortabel gestaltet. Eine bodengleiche Schwelle sorgt für Barrierefreiheit, und der Blendrahmen ist in die Wände des Gebäudes integrierbar. Dadurch wird mit den schmalen Profilen eine sehr große Transparenz erzielt. Mit dem System lassen sich Schiebeelemente mit Flügelgrößen von bis zu 3.200 mm × 3.000 mm und einem Gewicht von bis zu 400 kg realisieren. Ein neuartiger Schließmechanismus im Verhakungsbereich ermöglicht eine Verriegelung auch bei geöffneten Flügeln.

Begründung der Jury
Transparenz und Purismus stehen im Fokus der technisch ausgereiften Gestaltung des Schüco Panorama-Design-Schiebesystems ASE 67 PD.

Schüco ASE 60/80 TipTronic
Sliding System
Schiebesystem

Manufacturer
Schüco International KG, Bielefeld, Germany
In-house design
Web
www.schueco.de

The new, mechanically controlled Schüco ASE 60/80 TipTronic sliding system is operated with drive elements integrated in the profile. They offer twelve different ways of opening the window, something that greatly expands the design possibilities. Integrated components ensure safe operation of window elements up to a weight of 600 kg. An operating unit with a visual status display is mounted directly on the sliding element. A modular and scalable profile system with hidden fitting components creates rooms that have an unfettered view of the outside area.

Statement by the jury
Due to its carefully considered construction, the Schüco ASE 60/80 TipTronic sliding system can be used in a wide variety of ways.

Das neue mechatronische Schiebesystem Schüco ASE 60/80 TipTronic, das mit profilintegrierten Antriebselementen ausgestattet ist, bietet zwölf Öffnungsvarianten und damit eine große Gestaltungsfreiheit. Integrierte Komponenten sorgen für einen sicheren Betrieb bei jeder Flügelgröße mit einem Gewicht von bis zu 600 kg. Ein Bedienelement mit optischer Zustandsanzeige ist direkt am Flügel angebracht. Das modulare und skalierbare Profilsystem mit verdeckt liegenden Beschlagkomponenten realisiert Räume mit einer sehr hohen Transparenz zum Außenbereich.

Begründung der Jury
Dank einer wohldurchdachten Konstruktion bietet das Schüco Schiebesystem ASE 60/80 TipTronic ein hohes Maß an gestalterischer Freiheit.

LAMILUX Glass Skylight FE
LAMILUX Flachdach Fenster FE
Daylight System
Tageslichtsystem

Manufacturer
LAMILUX Heinrich Strunz GmbH,
Rehau, Germany
In-house design
Joachim Hessemer
Web
www.lamilux.de

The Lamilux Glass Skylight FE allows natural daylight to enter rooms in an aesthetically pleasing way. With the geometric shape and metal surface of the distinctive frame, it deliberately sets out to create a focal point. Together with the upstand, this results in a harmonious unit as all component parts such as motors are integrated into the frame and all connectors such as screws and welding seams are concealed. The frame can be coated in the colour of the user's choice and customised special shapes can also be produced.

Statement by the jury
The well-engineered design of the Lamilux Glass Skylight FE skilfully combines a technically sophisticated construction with the use of high-quality materials.

Tageslichteinfall in einer ästhetischen Art und Weise ermöglicht das Lamilux Flachdach Fenster FE. Der prägnante Einfassrahmen setzt mit seiner geometrischen Form und seinen Metalloberflächen bewusst Akzente. Zusammen mit dem Aufsatzkranz erzeugt er eine harmonische Einheit. Dies wird durch die Integration sämtlicher Komponenten, wie z. B. Antriebe, im Rahmen und durch die Vermeidung sichtbarer Verbindungsmittel wie Schrauben oder Schweißnähte erzielt. Die Farbbeschichtung kann wunschgemäß erfolgen, zudem lassen sich passgenaue Sonderformen realisieren.

Begründung der Jury
Die ausgereifte Gestaltung des Lamilux Flachdach Fensters FE vereint gekonnt eine technisch anspruchsvolle Bauart und einen hochwertigen Materialeinsatz.

Schüco FWS 35 PD
Facade System
Fassadensystem

Manufacturer
Schüco International KG, Bielefeld, Germany
In-house design
Web
www.schueco.de

The Schüco FWS 35 PD facade system enables buildings to have all-glass corners with a slim appearance. This is made possible by doing away with vertical mullion profiles on the corners. This solution creates a harmonious appearance without any distracting elements and lets as much light as possible into the interior. Furthermore, the reliable equipment for opening the window is integrated into the system and concealed from view. If required, a sun-protection system may be installed to reduce the need for cooling and therefore reduce energy consumption.

Statement by the jury
Transparent architecture is made a reality with the innovative construction method of the Schüco FWS 35 PD facade system.

Mithilfe des Schüco Fassadensystems FWS 35 PD lassen sich in Gebäuden schlank anmutende Ganzglasecken realisieren. Ermöglicht wird dies durch den Verzicht auf senkrechte Pfostenprofile in den Eckbereichen. Diese Produktlösung erzeugt ein stimmiges Erscheinungsbild ohne störende Elemente sowie eine maximale Transparenz. Auch die zuverlässigen Öffnungseinheiten sind unsichtbar integriert. Auf Wunsch lässt sich ein Sonnenschutzsystem installieren, wodurch eine mögliche abzuführende Wärmemenge und somit auch der Energieverbrauch reduziert wird.

Begründung der Jury
Dank einer innovativen Konstruktionsweise ist mit dem Schüco Fassadensystem FWS 35 PD die Realisierung einer transparenten Architektur möglich.

ONE by Josko
Window and Sliding Door System
Fenster- und Schiebetürsystem

Manufacturer
Josko Fenster & Türen GmbH,
Kopfing, Austria
In-house design
Johann Scheuringer
Web
www.josko.at

ONE by Josko is a window and sliding door system whose very slim frames have a width of only 5 cm. This filigree construction is a feature of all the products in the series. The interior face of the window may be constructed according to the individual wishes of customers. Thus, they can choose between various sorts of wood, aluminium, glass, concrete and steel. A range of accessories such as a handle, window sill, sun and insect protection and a flat, barrier-free threshold have been developed for this system which also achieves modern insulation values.

Statement by the jury
A strict symmetry and filigree appearance characterise the clever design of the ONE by Josko window and sliding door system.

ONE by Josko ist ein Fenster- und Schiebetürsystem, dessen vier Rahmenseiten eine Ansichtsbreite von nur 5 cm haben. Diese filigrane Konstruktion findet sich bei allen Produkten dieser Serie wieder. Die Innenseite der Fenster lässt sich nach individuellen Wünschen herstellen. Der Nutzer kann dabei zwischen verschiedenen Holzarten, Aluminium, Glas, Beton und Stahl wählen. Für das System, das moderne Dämmwerte erreicht, wurde eigens Zubehör wie ein Griff, eine Fensterbank, ein Sonnen- und Insektenschutz sowie eine barrierefreie Nullschwelle entwickelt.

Begründung der Jury
Eine strikte Symmetrie und ein filigran anmutendes Erscheinungsbild kennzeichnen das ausgeklügelte Design des Fenster- und Schiebetürsystems ONE by Josko.

Dry
Window Collection
Fensterkollektion

Manufacturer
ERCO S.r.l.,
Casnate con Bernate (Como), Italy
Design
Bavuso Design S.r.l. (Giuseppe Bavuso),
Seregno (Monza and Brianza), Italy
Web
www.ercofinestre.it
www.bavuso-design.com

The design of the Dry collection is clean and elegant – minimalist, devoid of superfluous ornaments and of a particularly slim construction. The windows and French windows of this range are made of high-quality materials. Their synthetic resin core for instance provides excellent thermal and sound insulation. The core is enveloped in aluminium profiles for exterior use. For interiors, the range is available in an aluminium or solid wood finish. The locking devices ensure a high level of security, while the hinges are discreetly integrated and concealed.

Statement by the jury
The design of the Dry window collection stands out for its consistent, clear stylistic idiom which ensures usability in numerous different applications.

Klar und elegant ist die Gestaltung der Kollektion Dry – minimal, ohne überflüssige Ornamente und besonders schlank gebaut. Die Fenster und Fenstertüren dieser Serie sind aus hochwertigen Materialien hergestellt: Ihr Kern aus Kunstharz bietet beispielsweise eine sehr gute Wärme- und Schalldämmung. Er ist im Außenbereich von Aluminiumprofilen ummantelt, für den Innenbereich kann eine Ausführung aus Aluminium oder Echtholz gewählt werden. Die Schließelemente bieten ein hohes Maß an Sicherheit, die Scharniere sind dabei verborgen integriert.

Begründung der Jury
Das Design der Fensterkollektion Dry hebt sich durch eine konsequent klare Formensprache hervor, die vielseitige Einsatzmöglichkeiten bietet.

HST-Sky
Lift and Slide Door
Hebe-Schiebetür

Manufacturer
Farko Sp. z o.o., Nowy Sacz, Poland
In-house design
Web
www.fakro.pl

The HST-Sky lift and slide door has the special feature that the glass pane of the fixed part of the window is directly attached to the cladding and threshold. Thus, the field of view is maximised and more daylight enters the room. The cladding is made from a combination of wood and aluminium, thus affording stability and weather resistance. The door can be made with a size of up to 12 × 2.8 metres and comes with a triple or quadruple glazing unit. Despite its size, it is easy to use, but if desired, the unit can be fitted with an electrical window opener.

Statement by the jury
The contemporary design of the HST-Sky lift and slide door stands out due to reliable material properties combined with an ease of use.

Bei der Hebe-Schiebetür HST-Sky wird die Scheibe des fest installierten Flügels direkt in den Rahmen und die flache Bodenschwelle eingebaut. Dadurch vergrößert sich das Sichtfeld und mehr Tageslicht fällt in den Raum. Der Rahmen besteht aus einer Holz-Aluminium-Kombination, was ihm Stabilität sowie Witterungsbeständigkeit verleiht. Die Tür ist bis zu einer Größe von 12 × 2,8 Metern und mit einer Dreifach- oder Vierfachverglasung erhältlich. Trotz ihrer Größe ist sie einfach zu bedienen, optional kann sie mit einem elektrischen Fensteröffner ausgestattet werden.

Begründung der Jury
Die zeitgemäße Gestaltung der Hebe-Schiebetür HST-Sky punktet mit beständigen Materialeigenschaften und einer komfortabel einfachen Handhabung.

Schüco AWS 75 PD.SI
Window System
Fenstersystem

Manufacturer
Schüco International KG, Bielefeld, Germany
In-house design
Web
www.schueco.de

The opening unit, which has narrow profile face widths that perfectly meet all the architectural requirements, is a design characteristic of the Schüco AWS 75 PD.SI window system. What is more, the interior face of the profiles is flush to the window with the sealing being hardly visible, thus giving a unified appearance to the frame. The system offers a range of attachments to the building structure, such as, for example, the option to realise a concealed drainage system. The windows are equipped with built-in anti-burglar properties.

Statement by the jury
A design characteristic of the Schüco AWS 75 PD.SI window system is the minimalist appearance which distracts as little as possible from the view of the outside.

Ein Öffnungselement mit minimierten inneren und äußeren Ansichtsbreiten, das architektonische Anforderungen ganzheitlich erfüllt, ist ein Gestaltungsmerkmal des Schüco Fenstersystems AWS 75 PD.SI. Weiterhin zeichnet es sich durch eine flächenbündige innere Flügelprofiloptik und minimierte Dichtungsansichten aus und sorgt so für ein einheitliches Rahmenbild. Es bietet ein breites Spektrum an Baukörperanschlüssen, so lässt sich z. B. eine verdeckt liegende Entwässerung realisieren. Zudem ist das Fenster mit einbruchhemmenden Eigenschaften ausgestattet.

Begründung der Jury
Ein minimalistisches Erscheinungsbild, das den Blick nicht vom Wesentlichen ablenkt, charakterisiert das Design des Schüco Fenstersystems AWS 75 PD.SI.

Tostem LW
Window
Fenster

Manufacturer
LIXIL Corporation, Tokyo, Japan
In-house design
Web
www.lixil.com

The Tostem LW window contributes to a pleasant domestic environment that is full of light. What is more, it offers very good heat insulation. The aesthetic aspects of it are restrained, for example, the locking system is concealed within the frame. Thanks to the way the window has been made, the view through it is in no way compromised. In a clever manner, it links the interior with the exterior, thus giving a feeling of oneness. The window can be equipped with accessories that protect the interior from the sun or prevent people from outside looking in.

Das Fenster Tostem LW trägt zu einer angenehmen und lichtdurchfluteten häuslichen Umgebung bei. Darüber hinaus bietet es eine hohe Wärmedämmung. Das Fenster hat eine dezente Ästhetik, die Verriegelung lässt sich beispielsweise unsichtbar im Seitenrahmen unterbringen. Dank seiner Konstruktionsweise lenkt nichts Störendes den Blick ab. Auf gekonnte Weise verbindet es so visuell den Innen- und Außenbereich und erzeugt dabei ein Gefühl des Einsseins. Es kann optional mit Zubehör ausgestattet werden, das vor Einblicken oder Sonneneinstrahlung schützt.

Statement by the jury
The design of the Tostem LW window is characterised by a clear and stylish appearance that complements very well a variety of decors.

Begründung der Jury
Ein sowohl klares als auch stilvolles Erscheinungsbild, das sehr gut verschiedene Einrichtungsstile ergänzt, kennzeichnet die Gestaltung des Fensters Tostem LW.

Elegante
Window System
Fenstersystem

Manufacturer
Deceuninck NV, Hooglede-Gits, Belgium
In-house design
Web
www.deceuninck.com

PVC windows demonstrate many positive properties such as good insulation, recyclability and durability. The Elegante window system offers on top of that a particularly slim design. The redesigned profile rebate of only 9 mm guarantees the necessary stability and positions the glass in line with the window surface for an exceptionally minimalist look. The window comes in flush or rebate versions. In combination with the newly developed square glazing beads, the flush version offers a particularly restrained appearance.

Fenster aus PVC zeichnen sich durch zahlreiche positive Eigenschaften wie beispielsweise eine gute Isolierung, Wiederverwertbarkeit und Haltbarkeit aus. Das Fenstersystem Elegante bietet zusätzlich ein besonders schlankes Design. Die neu gestaltete Profilfalz von nur 9 mm gewährleistet die erforderliche Stabilität und platziert das Glas nahezu bündig mit der Rahmenfläche, um ein außergewöhnlich minimalistisches Aussehen zu erzielen. Das Fenster ist in einer flächenbündigen und einer flächenversetzten Ausführung erhältlich. Zusammen mit neu gestalteten rechteckigen Glasleisten bietet die erstere Variante ein besonders zurückhaltendes Aussehen.

Statement by the jury
The minimalist, particularly slim appearance of the Elegante window system allows it easily to integrate into many different house facades.

Begründung der Jury
Dank einer minimalistischen, besonders schlanken Gestaltung integriert sich das Fenstersystem Elegante problemlos in verschiedene Hausfassaden.

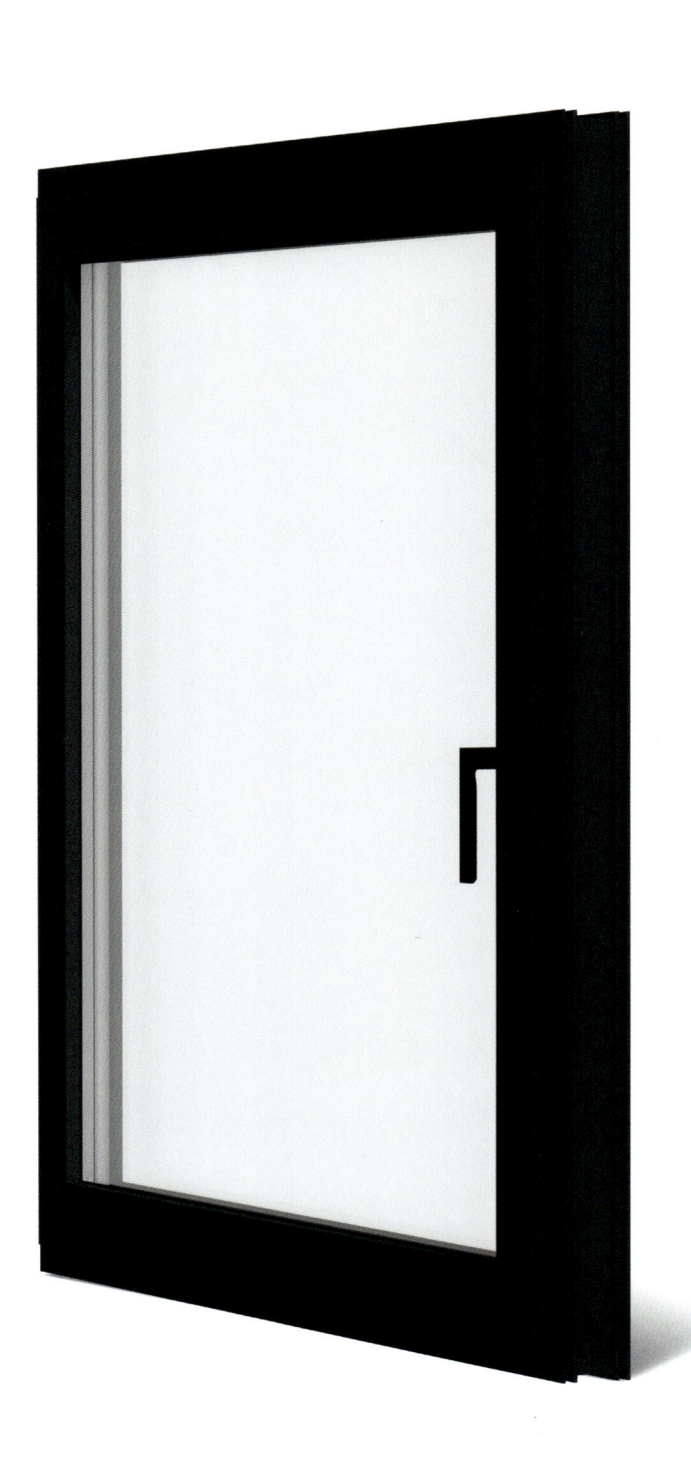

Plial CWS
Stackable Roll Shutter
Faltrollladen

Manufacturer
Regazzi SA, Gordola, Switzerland
In-house design
Ulrich Kollmann
Web
www.plial.de

Plial is a robust roller blind with a self-supporting system that may be surface-, flush- or front-mounted. The compactly made system allows for the stacking of two slats on top of each other in the roller shutter box. Plial CWS was designed specifically for the darkening of corner windows. To achieve this, two separate blinds are installed at an angle of 90 degrees and guarantee complete darkening when closed and a maximum view through the windows when open. In addition, the system offers good thermal and sound insulation as well as burglar protection.

Statement by the jury
Thanks to its functionality and compact construction, the design of the Plial CWS stackable roll shutter system embodies a convincing product solution for corner windows.

Plial ist ein robuster Faltrollladen mit selbsttragender Bauweise, der eine Aufputz-, Einbau- oder Frontmontage ermöglicht. Das kompakt konstruierte System stapelt im Rollladenkasten jeweils zwei Lamellen aufeinander. Plial CWS ist eine spezielle Lösung für die Verdunkelung von Eckfenstern. Dafür werden zwei einzelne Modelle in einem 90-Grad-Winkel montiert – zusammen garantieren sie vollständige Dunkelheit im geschlossenen und maximale Sicht im geöffneten Zustand. Darüber hinaus bietet das System eine gute Wärmedämmung, Schall- sowie Einbruchschutz.

Begründung der Jury
Mit einer hohen Funktionalität und kompakten Konstruktion stellt die Gestaltung des Faltrollladens Plial CWS eine überzeugende Produktlösung für Eckfenster dar.

NM – Motorization Module
NM – Motorisierungsmodul

Manufacturer
Nien Made Enterprise,
Norman – Window Fashions, Taichung, Taiwan
In-house design
Michael Nien, Raymond Jao
Design
LITE-ON Technology Corp., Taipei City, Taiwan
Web
www.nienmade.com.tw
www.liteon.com
Honourable Mention

With the aid of this remote control system shutters can be adjusted either individually or as a group. The device is operated using a remote control or smart device such as phone or tablet and is integrated via the app which is part of the smart home system. The motorization module is powered by rechargeable lithium batteries that last for up to one year. A built-in solar cell boosts the life span of the battery even further, providing both energy efficiency and long-term sustainability.

Statement by the jury
The advantage of this motorization module lies in the well-thought-out use of technology. On top of this, its environmentally friendly way of operation is pleasing.

Mithilfe dieses Motorisierungsmoduls können Jalousien sowohl einzeln als auch als Gruppe gesteuert werden. Es wird mithilfe einer Fernbedienung oder eines intelligenten Geräts wie z. B. einem Smartphone oder Tablet bedient und ist, verbunden über eine App, Teil des Smart Home-Systems. Das Motorisierungsmodul ist mit wiederaufladbaren Lithium-Ionen-Batterien ausgestattet, die bis zu ein Jahr lang halten. Eine integrierte Solarzelle steigert die Lebensdauer der Batterie weiter und bietet sowohl Energieeffizienz als auch langfristig Nachhaltigkeit.

Begründung der Jury
Dieses Motorisierungsmodul punktet mit einem gut durchdachten Technikeinsatz. Darüber hinaus gefällt seine umweltfreundliche Betriebsweise.

NM – Dial Remote Control
NM – Dreh-Fernbedienung

Manufacturer
Nien Made Enterprise,
Norman – Window Fashions, Taichung, Taiwan
In-house design
Michael Nien, Raymond Jao
Design
LITE-ON Technology Corp., Taipei City, Taiwan
Web
www.nienmade.com.tw
www.liteon.com

You can also find this product on page 185.
Dieses Produkt finden Sie auch auf Seite 185.

This remote control uses a dial to operate the shutters easily and precisely. All users need to do, is to turn the outer ring of the dial, and the slats of the shutter will simultaneously tilt to the angle specified. This practical motorization system, which is a useful add-on for any smart home toolkit, can be used to operate not only a single shutter, but also an entire predefined group of shutters or even hundreds of window coverings in a big building. The device comes with a metal casing that delivers both reliability and elegance.

Statement by the jury
The design of this dial remote control for blinds in private homes and building complexes focuses on delivering ease of use.

Diese Fernbedienung verwendet einen Drehring, um Jalousien bequem und präzise zu steuern. Dazu wird einfach nur der äußere Ring gedreht und die Lamellen der Jalousie neigen sich synchron um den gewünschten Winkel. Mit dem praktischen Motorisierungssystem, das eine Smart Home-Ausstattung sinnvoll ergänzt, lässt sich sowohl eine einzelne Jalousie als auch eine definierte Gruppe oder es lassen sich sogar Hunderte von Fensterverkleidungen eines Gebäudes bedienen. Das Gerät besitzt ein Metallgehäuse, das gleichermaßen Verlässlichkeit und Eleganz kommuniziert.

Begründung der Jury
Die Gestaltung dieser Dreh-Fernbedienung für Jalousien in Privathäusern sowie in Gebäudekomplexen ist auf eine einfache Bedienbarkeit ausgerichtet.

DOOYA DC1650
Window Blind Control System
Fensterjalousien-Steuerung

Manufacturer
DOOYA, Ningbo, China
In-house design
Ningbo DOOYA Mechanic & Electronic Technology Co., Ltd.
Web
www.dooya.com

DC1650 is a wireless remote control mounted on the wall. In conjunction with the proprietary curtain motor, it can be used to control blinds. The square-shaped control panel has large buttons that make quick and precise adjustment possible. The panel may be mounted on the wall wherever needed and blends in well with a range of domestic environments. It may also be removed from its bracket to increase the flexibility of use. Thus, blinds can be controlled from anywhere in the house.

DC1650 ist eine an der Wand installierte, kabellose Fernbedienung, die zusammen mit dem herstellereigenen Vorhangmotor zur Steuerung einer Jalousie verwendet werden kann. Das quadratische Bedienelement verfügt über große Tasten, die eine schnelle und präzise Nutzung ermöglichen. Es kann nach individuellem Wunsch an der Wand platziert werden und fügt sich elegant in verschiedene Wohnumgebungen ein. Zur noch flexibleren Bedienung lässt es sich auch aus der Halterung entnehmen. Auf diese Weise können Jalousien von jedem Ort im Haus gesteuert werden.

Statement by the jury
User friendliness and flexibility are the focus of the well-thought-out design concept of the DC1650 window blind control system.

Begründung der Jury
Nutzerfreundlichkeit und Flexibilität stehen im Mittelpunkt des wohldurchdachten Gestaltungskonzeptes der Fensterjalousien-Steuerung DC1650.

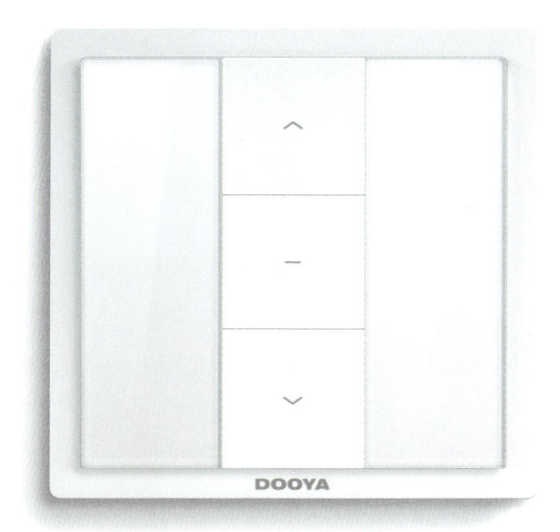

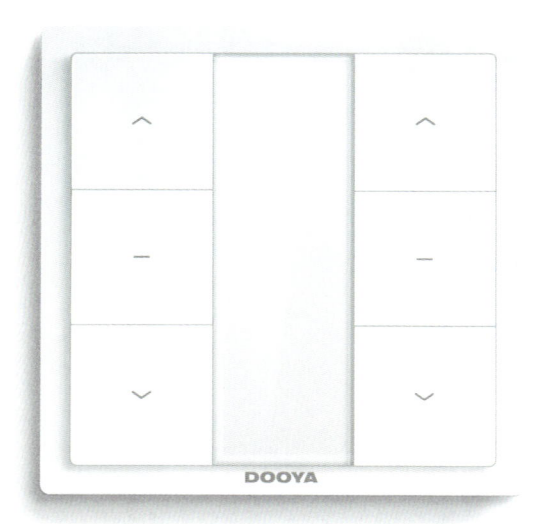

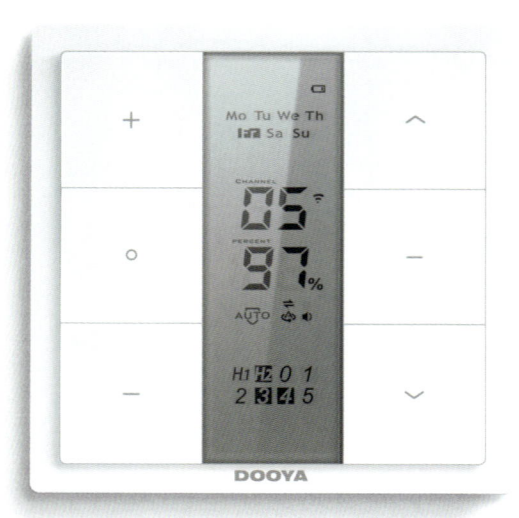

DOOYA DC2700
Window Blind Control System
Fensterjalousien-Steuerung

Manufacturer
DOOYA, Ningbo, China
In-house design
Ningbo DOOYA Mechanic & Electronic Technology Co., Ltd.
Web
www.dooya.com

Depending on the situation, the user of the DC2700 window blind control system can choose between single, double or 15-channel dual control variants. The powerful, but still low-energy transmission technology guarantees that blinds may be controlled from anywhere in the house. The concisely engineered device takes advantage of the elasticity of the material used to create a unity between the surface of the body and the buttons. The distribution of the buttons is logical and such that they are easily reached, which makes for quick and efficient use.

Je nach Anforderung kann der Nutzer der kabellosen Fensterjalousien-Steuerung DC2700 zwischen einer Einkanal-, Zweikanal- sowie 15-Kanal-Dual-Steuerung wählen. Die leistungsstarke, dabei energiesparsame Übertragungstechnologie gewährleistet, dass Jalousien von jedem Ort im Haus gesteuert werden können. Das prägnant gestaltete Gerät nutzt die Elastizität des verwendeten Materials, um eine Einheit von Gehäuseoberfläche und Tastatur zu erzielen. Jede Taste ist sinnvoll und gut erreichbar angeordnet, wodurch eine schnelle und effiziente Bedienung ermöglicht wird.

Statement by the jury
State-of-the-art use of technology and easy handling are the characteristics of the refined design of the DC2700 window blind control system.

Begründung der Jury
Ein zeitgemäßer Technikeinsatz sowie eine einfache Handhabung zeichnen die ausgereifte Gestaltung der Fensterjalousien-Steuerung DC2700 aus.

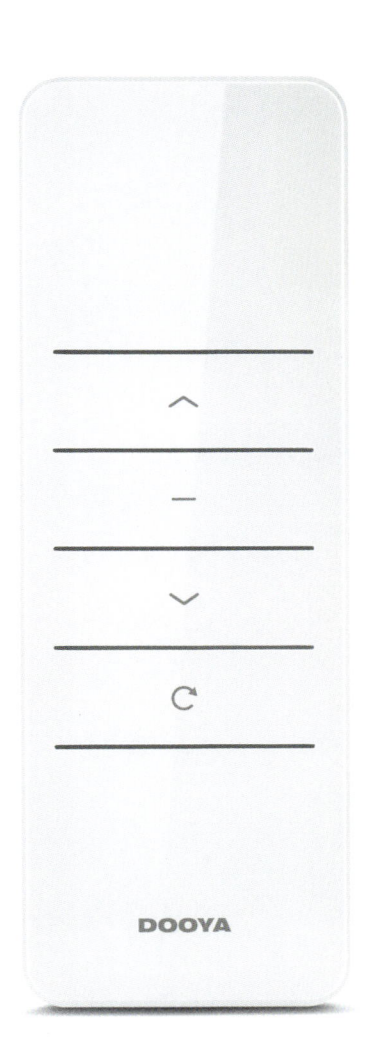

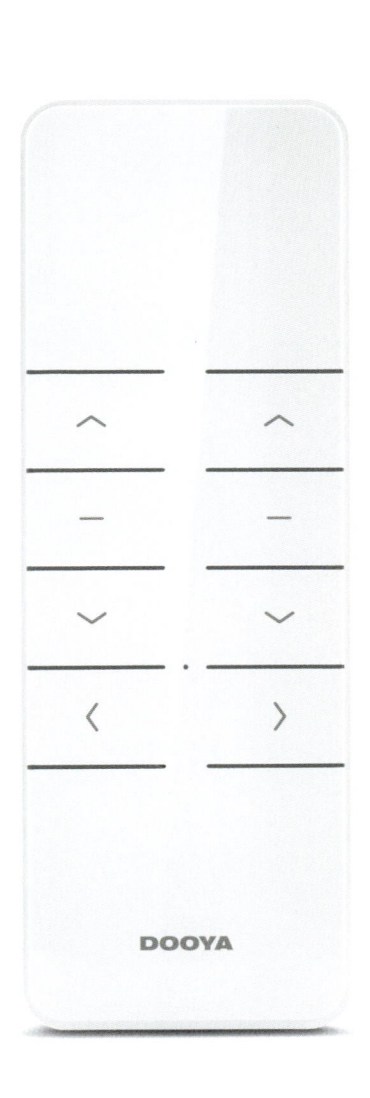

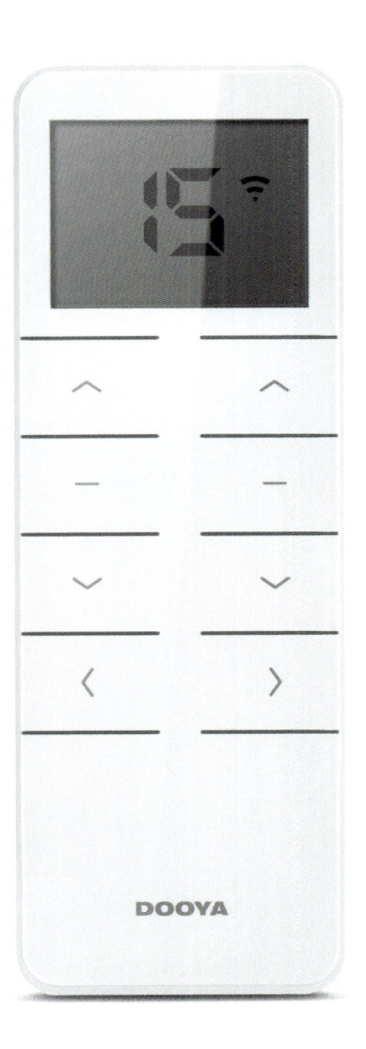

DOOYA DC3700
Window Blind Control System
Fensterjalousien-Steuerung

Manufacturer
DOOYA, Ningbo, China
In-house design
Ningbo DOOYA Mechanic & Electronic Technology Co., Ltd.
Web
www.dooya.com

The clear lines and prominently arranged buttons, together with the screen of the DC3700 remote control give it a seemingly sculptured appearance. The raised buttons simplify the use of the device with which curtains, roller blinds, awnings and automatic window openers may be controlled, indoors as well as outdoors. The wireless remote control possesses powerful features and can, when needed, adjust up to 30 curtains using 15 channels.

Die klare Linienführung und die akzentuiert platzierten Tasten erzeugen zusammen mit dem Bildschirm bei der Fernbedienung DC3700 ein skulptural anmutendes Erscheinungsbild. Die erhabenen Tasten vereinfachen zudem die Handhabung des Geräts, mit dem sich sowohl im Innen- wie auch im Außenbereich elektrisch betriebene Vorhänge, Rollläden, Markisen sowie automatische Fensteröffner einfach kontrollieren lassen. Die Fernbedienung verfügt über leistungsstarke Eigenschaften und kann kabellos mit 15 Kanälen wunschgemäß bis zu 30 Vorhänge steuern.

Statement by the jury
The cleverly conceived design of the DC3700 window blind control system skilfully attracts attention through its expressively aesthetic appearance.

Begründung der Jury
Die klug durchdachte Gestaltung der Fensterjalousien-Steuerung DC3700 zieht mit ihrer ausdrucksstarken Ästhetik gekonnt die Aufmerksamkeit auf sich.

DOOYA

DOOYA DC2150
Window Blind Control System
Fensterjalousien-Steuerung

Manufacturer
DOOYA, Ningbo, China
In-house design
Ningbo DOOYA Mechanic & Electronic Technology Co., Ltd.
Web
www.dooya.com

This remote control panel is mounted on the wall, but can also simply be removed from the bracket if required. This flexibility and convenience means that electrically controlled curtains and roller blinds can be adjusted from any room in the house. What is more, the device may be used outdoors to open and shut awnings. The panel comes with a large screen to simplify configuration. The stepped design of the buttons, which are situated on the sides, makes for easy use.

Dieses Funkfernbedienfeld wird an der Wand montiert, kann aber auch einfach aus der Halterung herausgenommen werden. Auf diese Weise lassen sich flexibel und komfortabel von jedem Raum des Hauses aus elektrisch betriebene Vorhänge und Rollläden steuern. Sogar im Freien kann das Gerät zum Öffnen und Schließen von Markisen genutzt werden. Ausgestattet ist das Bedienpaneel mit einem großen Bildschirm, der die Konfiguration erleichtert. Das stufenförmige Design der seitlich angeordneten Bedientasten garantiert eine einfache Handhabung.

Statement by the jury
The design of the DC2150 window blind control system that blends in well with many interiors conveys a high degree of functionality.

Begründung der Jury
Die Gestaltung der Fensterjalousien-Steuerung DC2150, die sich gut in verschiedene Interieurs einfügt, kommuniziert hohe Funktionalität.

DOOYA DC2100
Window Blind Control System
Fensterjalousien-Steuerung

Manufacturer
DOOYA, Ningbo, China
In-house design
Ningbo DOOYA Mechanic & Electronic Technology Co., Ltd.
Web
www.dooya.com

The DC2100 wireless remote control allows not only for the opening and closing of electrically driven curtains and blinds, but also may be used for outdoor sun protection equipment such as, for example, awnings. The device can control up to 30 pairs of curtains in one home. Thanks to the curved shape of the back of the remote control, it is comfortable to use. The stepped design of the buttons and the large screen make the required configuration and reading of data very easy.

Die kabellose Fernbedienung DC2100 ermöglicht nicht nur das Öffnen und Schließen von elektrisch betriebenen Vorhängen und Rollläden, sondern sie kann auch für Sonnenschutzanlagen im Freien, wie beispielsweise Markisen, verwendet werden. Mit dem Gerät lassen sich bis zu 30 Vorhangpaare in einem Haus steuern. Dabei liegt es dank der bogenförmigen Gestaltung seiner Rückseite komfortabel in der Hand. Die stufenförmig angeordneten Tasten ermöglichen eine schnelle Bedienung, und der große Monitor sorgt für eine einfache Konfiguration und Ablesbarkeit.

Statement by the jury
Good ergonomic properties and a wide range of application possibilities are the design characteristics of the DC2100 window blind control system.

Begründung der Jury
Gute ergonomische Eigenschaften und vielseitige Einsatzmöglichkeiten charakterisieren die Gestaltung der Fensterjalousien-Steuerung DC2100.

DOOYA DC7000
Window Blind Control System
Fensterjalousien-Steuerung

Manufacturer
DOOYA, Ningbo, China
In-house design
Ningbo DOOYA Mechanic & Electronic Technology Co., Ltd.
Web
www.dooya.com

The striking design details of the DC7000 wireless remote control are the large, circular screen and the wave-like contours of the button arrangement which makes for easy use. The powerful device has 15 channels which can control up to 30 electrically powered curtains and roller blinds. It comes with a magnetic bracket which may be installed anywhere in the house. What is more, the unit may be separated from it so that the control of daylight may be carried out throughout the building in a smart way.

Markante Gestaltungsdetails der kabellosen Fernbedienung DC7000 sind der große, kreisförmige Bildschirm sowie die wellenförmig anmutende Anordnung der Tasten, die eine bequeme Bedienung ermöglicht. Das leistungsstarke Gerät verfügt über 15 Kanäle, mit denen sich bis zu 30 elektrisch betriebene Vorhang- und Rollladenpaare steuern lassen. Es ist mit einer Magnethalterung ausgestattet, die überall im Haus angebracht werden kann. Zudem lässt sich das Bedienteil auch abnehmen. Somit kann eine intelligente Tageslichtsteuerung von überall erfolgen.

Statement by the jury
An eye-catching appearance and flexible range of application possibilities are the noticeable features of the DC7000 window blind control system.

Begründung der Jury
Ein auffälliges Erscheinungsbild sowie anpassungsfähige Nutzungsmöglichkeiten kennzeichnen die Fensterjalousien-Steuerung DC7000.

DOOYA DC816
Remote Control
Fernbedienung

Manufacturer
DOOYA, Ningbo, China
In-house design
Ningbo DOOYA Mechanic & Electronic Technology Co., Ltd.
Web
www.dooya.com

The opening, closing, stopping and locking of electrically controlled garage doors becomes easy with the wireless DC816 remote control. Thanks to its low-energy performance that also works over long distances, it is very convenient to use. Its succinct key chain design means it is comfortable to carry. The sliding cover prevents faulty operation and protects the buttons. The contrast between the silver metal and black plastic gives the device a multi-layered, structural appearance.

Das Öffnen, Schließen, Stoppen und Verriegeln eines elektrischen Garagentors lässt sich einfach mit der kabellosen Fernbedienung DC816 steuern. Dank ihrer energiesparsamen Leistung auch über lange Distanzen bietet sie ein hohes Maß an Komfort. Das Gerät ist prägnant als Schlüsselanhänger gestaltet und kann so bequem mitgeführt werden. Die Schiebeabdeckung verhindert dabei Fehlbedienungen und schützt zudem die Tasten. Der Materialübergang vom silbernen Metall zum schwarzen Kunststoff verleiht dem Utensil ein mehrschichtig strukturiertes Design.

Statement by the jury
The refined shape and exciting mix of materials are fascinating and make the DC816 remote control an appealing product solution.

Begründung der Jury
Die raffinierte Formgebung und der spannungsreiche Materialmix begeistern und machen die kabellose Fernbedienung DC816 zu einer ansprechenden Produktlösung.

Tostem Grandel 2 Type 152
Door
Tür

Manufacturer
LIXIL Corporation, Tokyo, Japan
In-house design
Web
www.lixil.com

Tostem Grandel 2 Type 152 is an entrance door made entirely of metal. Although it is an industrially manufactured product, its filigree appearance makes it look as if it had been made from wood by craftsmen using traditional methods. The door panel with its lattice-like structure looks sophisticated but has been designed to be discreet so that it can adapt with subtlety to contemporary architecture. The door comes with a very high level of heat insulation and thus helps to save energy, particularly valuable in regions with large variations in temperature.

Tostem Grandel 2 Type 152 ist eine ausschließlich aus Metall hergestellte Eingangstür. Obwohl es sich hierbei um ein Industrieprodukt handelt, wirkt sie mit ihrem filigranen Aussehen, als wäre sie traditionell handwerklich aus Holz gefertigt worden. Das Türblatt mit Gitterstruktur ist fein, aber auch gleichzeitig bewusst zurückhaltend gestaltet, damit es sich unaufdringlich zeitgenössischer Architektur anpassen kann. Die Tür bietet eine sehr hohe Wärmedämmung und trägt so zur Energieeinsparung, gerade auch in Regionen mit starken Temperaturschwankungen, bei.

Statement by the jury
The classical and discreet design of the Tostem Grandel 2 Type 152 entrance door combines great practical benefits with energy-saving features.

Begründung der Jury
Die klassisch-dezente Gestaltung der Eingangstür Tostem Grandel 2 Type 152 vereint einen hohen praktischen Nutzwert mit energiesparenden Eigenschaften.

Pirnar Theatrica Entrance Wall
Door
Tür

Manufacturer
Pirnar d.o.o., Ljubljana, Slovenia
In-house design
Web
www.pirnar.co.uk
Honourable Mention

The patented entrance door Pirnar Theatrica opens automatically without needing to be touched. It is sufficient just to look at it. A built-in facial recognition system will identify the owner and then gently open the massive door which subsequently closes of its own accord. In addition to the single-door, there is also a double-door version, which creates the impression of a wall that is opening. The door, which does not require a handle, can be produced in wood, stone, glass or aluminium. Installation is straightforward and easy.

Die patentierte Eingangstür Pirnar Theatrica öffnet sich automatisch ohne Berührung. Es reicht aus, sie nur anzusehen. Das integrierte Gesichtserkennungssystem erkennt den Besitzer, öffnet anschließend sanft die massive Tür und schließt sie hinterher von selbst. Neben der einfachen Variante ist auch eine zweiflügelige Ausführung erhältlich, die den Eindruck einer sich öffnenden Wand erweckt. Die Tür, die keinen Griff benötigt, kann beliebig aus Holz, Stein, Glas oder Aluminium gefertigt werden. Ihr Einbau ist unkompliziert und einfach.

Statement by the jury
The use of contemporary, smart technology to enable contactless operation of the Pirnar Theatrica entrance door is fascinating.

Begründung der Jury
Faszinierend ist der Einsatz zeitgemäßer, intelligenter Technik, der die berührungsfreie Handhabung der Eingangstür Pirnar Theatrica ermöglicht.

Muteo
Door System
Türsystem

Manufacturer
Sapeli, a.s., Jihlava, Czech Republic
Design
NOVAGUE, Prague, Czech Republic
Web
www.sapeli.cz
www.novague.com

The innovative design of the Muteo system allows for easy and natural opening of doors – without the need for a handle. Users simply have to pull or push. Everything else happens automatically, thanks to the clever construction of the mechanical catch which forms part of a functional unit with the Z-shaped door. This patented solution changes the way in which viewers perceive rooms and opens up new opportunities for architects to create a unified look for doors and surrounding walls.

Die innovative Gestaltung des Systems Muteo erzielt ein komfortables und natürliches Öffnen einer Tür. Dazu verzichtet sie vollständig auf einen Griff. Der Nutzer muss lediglich drücken oder ziehen – alles Weitere geschieht automatisch durch die raffinierte Konstruktion des mechanischen Schlosses, das zusammen mit der z-förmigen Tür eine funktionale Einheit bildet. Diese patentierte Lösung verändert die Raumwahrnehmung des Betrachters und bietet Architekten neue Möglichkeiten, ein einheitliches Gesamtbild von Türen und umgebenden Wänden zu kreieren.

Statement by the jury
Muteo melds door and handle to a single unit. In doing so, the door system achieves a uniform appearance and offers new interior design possibilities.

Begründung der Jury
Muteo verschmilzt Tür und Griff zu einer Einheit und erzeugt so ein homogenes Erscheinungsbild. Zudem bietet das Türsystem neue Möglichkeiten der Raumgestaltung.

planoglas ultra
Door
Tür

Manufacturer
neuform-Türenwerk Hans Glock GmbH & Co. KG,
Erdmannhausen, Germany
In-house design
Web
www.neuform-tuer.com

The seamlessly glazed door panel of the planoglas ultra inner door consists entirely of safety glass on both sides. This not only allows for maximum transparency, but also creates an elegant impression and a flat, easy-to-clean surface. The technical features can be specified individually or combined to meet current guidelines for sound insulation, fire and smoke protection, as well as anti-burglary requirements. This functional, but also elegant looking model meets all current demands for high-quality interior doors.

Die Innentür planoglas ultra bietet mit der fugenlosen, vollflächigen Verglasung des Türblatts und der Ausstattung mit Sicherheitsglas zu beiden Seiten eine maximale Transparenz, eine edle Anmutung sowie eine plane und damit pflegeleichte Oberfläche. Ihre technischen Merkmale erfüllen aktuelle Vorgaben hinsichtlich Schallschutz, Brand- und Rauchschutz sowie Einbruchschutz – einzeln oder in Kombination. Mit diesem sowohl funktionellen als auch edel anmutenden Modell können alle gängigen Anforderungen an hochwertige Objektinnentüren umgesetzt werden.

Statement by the jury
The sophisticated design of the planoglas ultra interior door fulfils the standards of functionality and is at the same time pleasing for its elegant appearance.

Begründung der Jury
Die anspruchsvolle Gestaltung der Innentür planoglas ultra wird hohen Ansprüchen an Funktionalität gerecht. Darüber hinaus gefällt ihr elegantes Aussehen.

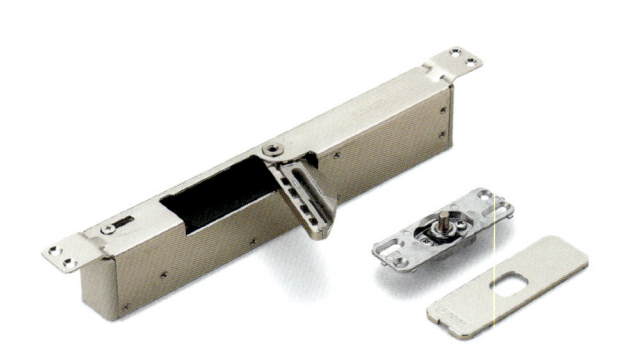

LDD-V100
Door Damper
Türdämpfer

Manufacturer
Sugatsune Kogyo Co., Ltd., Tokyo, Japan
In-house design
Web
www.sugatsune.co.jp

The LDD-V100 door damper makes it possible to gently and silently close room and access doors with a weight of up to 100 kg and a width of up to 90 cm. The mechanism engages during the last 15 degrees and softly pulls the door shut. When opening the door, on the other hand, there is hardly any resistance. The damper works without a visible lever and can be integrated into the door in its entirety. This means it is invisible when the door is closed. The system also has no visually distracting bolt and works without one. A simple door knob is all that is required.

Statement by the jury
With its cleverly conceived design the LDD-V100 damper, which can be recessed invisibly, makes it possible to close even heavy and large doors quietly.

Der Türdämpfer LDD-V100 ermöglicht ein sanftes und lautloses Schließen von Zimmer- und Durchgangstüren mit einem Gewicht von bis zu 100 kg und einer Breite von bis zu 90 cm. Sein Mechanismus greift dabei auf den letzten 15 Grad und zieht die Tür sachte zu. In Öffnungsrichtung besteht dagegen fast kein Widerstand. Der Dämpfer benötigt keinen sichtbaren Arm und kann komplett in die Tür eingelassen werden. Im geschlossenen Zustand ist er daher unsichtbar. Das System funktioniert auch ohne optisch störende Schließriegel, ein schlichter Türknopf reicht aus.

Begründung der Jury
Mit seiner klug durchdachten Gestaltung ermöglicht der unsichtbar integrierbare Dämpfer LDD-V100 das geräuschlose Schließen auch schwerer und großer Türen.

FritsJurgens System M
Hinge System for Pivot Doors
Scharniersystem für Pivot-Türen

Manufacturer
FritsJurgens, Kolham, Netherlands
In-house design
Arjan van der Wal
Web
www.fritsjurgens.com

These hinges for pivot doors are fully integrated into the door leaf both at the top and bottom. They have a load-bearing capacity of up to 500 kg and are suitable for use with wooden, steel or glass doors that are at least 40 mm thick. System M is used for revolving doors and gives users full control of operation. One of its salient features is its smooth operation. The door opens and closes in an elegant, fluent movement. The system is easy and fast to install in new build sites but can also be fitted in older houses.

Statement by the jury
The well-conceived use of technology and cleverly devised construction of System M ensure the elegant opening and closing of pivot doors.

Diese Scharniere für Pivot-Türen sind sowohl oben als auch unten vollständig in die Tür eingelassen. Sie haben eine Tragfähigkeit von bis zu 500 kg und eignen sich für Modelle aus Holz, Stahl oder Glas, die eine Mindeststärke von 40 mm aufweisen. Das System M kommt in Drehtüren zum Einsatz und bietet Nutzern vollständige Kontrolle. Es zeichnet sich durch Laufruhe aus, die Tür öffnet und schließt in einer eleganten, fließenden Bewegung. Das System lässt sich einfach und schnell in Neubauten montieren, aber auch in älteren Häusern einbauen.

Begründung der Jury
Durch einen wohldurchdachten Technikeinsatz und eine ausgeklügelte Konstruktion ermöglicht das System M das elegante Öffnen und Schließen von Pivot-Türen.

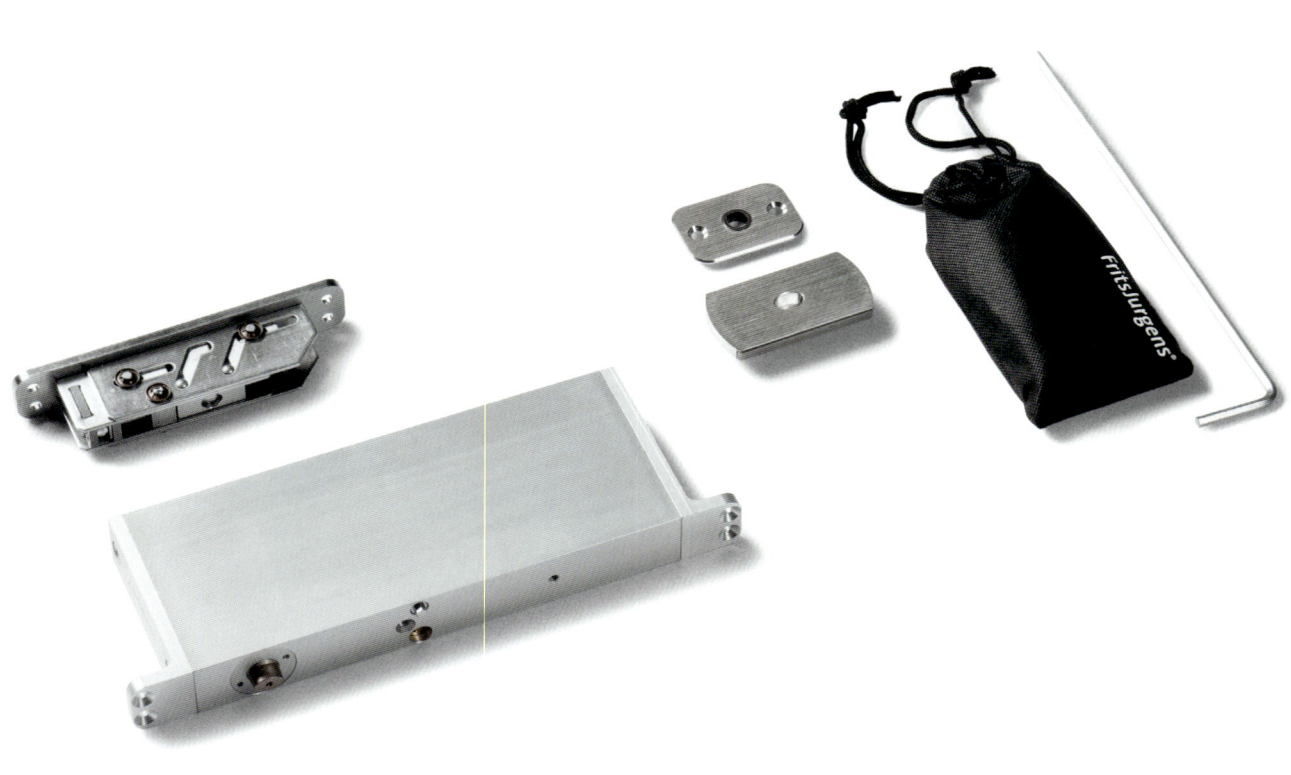

Smart Gateway
Intelligentes Gateway

Manufacturer
Gree Electric Appliances, Inc. of Zhuhai, Zhuhai, China
In-house design
Jianming Tan, Sha Li, Nanfei Chen, Huanlong Wu, Jiahua Liu, Yaxi Dong, Guangyu Chen, Jiachi Liu, Kaining Bao, Zhihong Yang, Fuzhong Tian, Jianbo Dong, Mengquan Wang, Jian Hu
Web
www.gree.com.cn

Gateways, which are used in commercial building complexes such as shopping centres or offices, are generally installed in service rooms. This smart gateway can easily be adapted to suit the de facto situation of the installation site. Its clean design and compact shape convey professionalism. The concealed interfaces work with a sliding cover to ensure high stability and secure operation. The casing is quick to produce and assemble which contributes greatly to manufacturing efficiencies.

Gateways, die in kommerziell genutzten Gebäudekomplexen wie Einkaufszentren oder Büros zum Einsatz kommen, werden oft in Betriebsräumen installiert. Dieses intelligente Gateway lässt sich gut an die tatsächlichen Bedingungen des Aufstellortes anpassen. Sein klares Design mit der kompakten Formgebung kommuniziert Professionalität. Die verborgenen Schnittstellen bedienen sich des Schiebedesigns, was für hohe Stabilität und sicheren Betrieb sorgt. Das Gehäuse lässt sich schnell produzieren und zusammenbauen, was die Fertigungseffizienz steigert.

Statement by the jury
Robustness characterises the design of this smart gateway. With its outstanding adaptability, it can be installed in a wide range of locations.

Begründung der Jury
Robustheit kennzeichnet die Gestaltung dieses intelligenten Gateways. Mit seiner hohen Anpassungsfähigkeit ist es an vielen Orten einsetzbar.

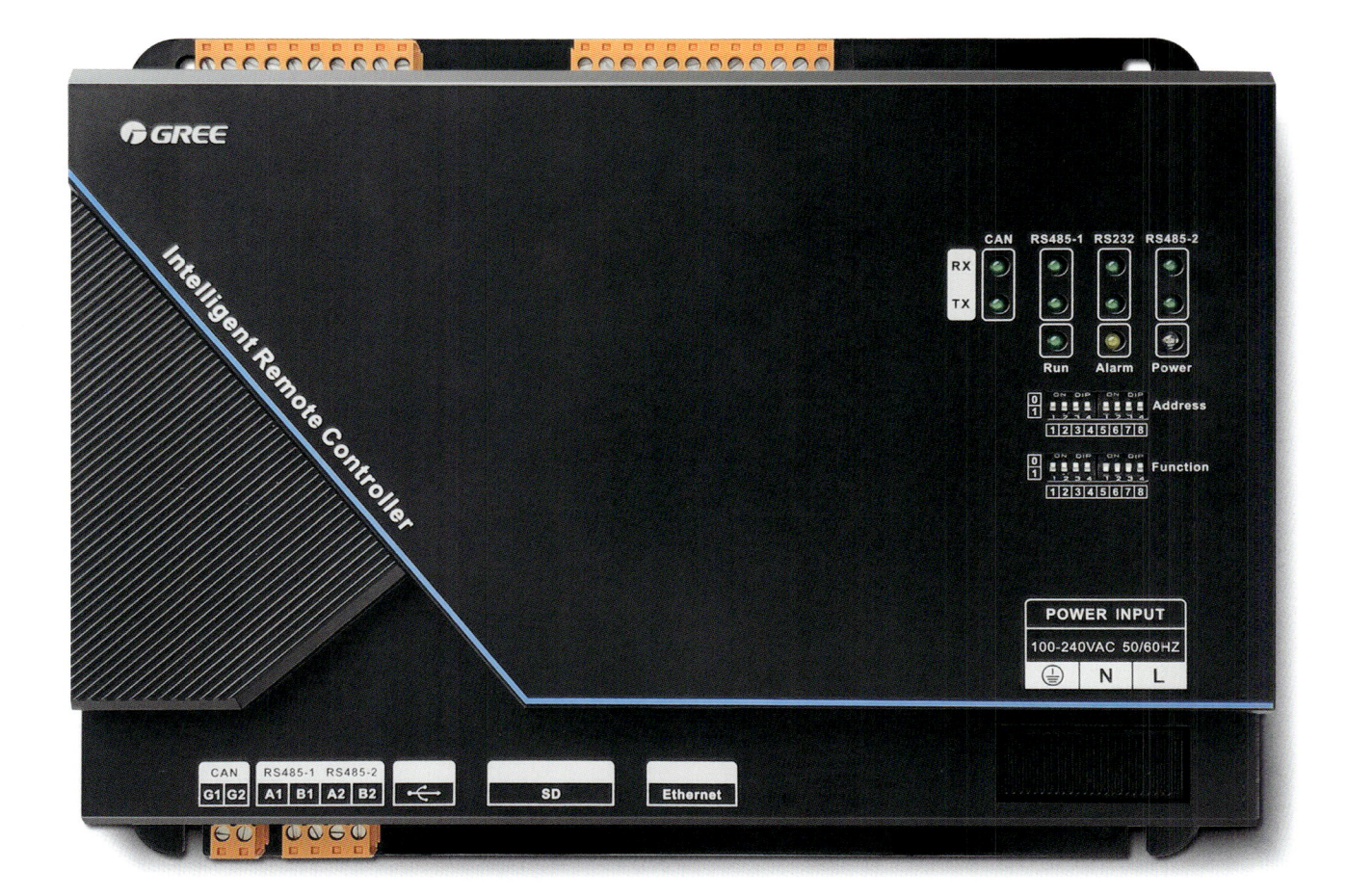

Multifunctional Smart Lock
Intelligentes Multifunktionsschloss

Manufacturer
AIGANG GmbH, Munich, Germany

In-house design
Lijuan Wang

Design
Top Industrial Design Co., Ltd.
(Kaipeng He, Wanqi Li),
Hangzhou, China
Top Design Co., Ltd.
(Jiqing Zhang, Lin Zhou),
Shenzhen, China

Web
www.designt.cn

reddot award 2019
best of the best

Safely integrated

In the same way architecture is ever evolving, the requirements for security concepts are also changing. This multifunctional smart lock is a contemporary solution for older houses, as it can be easily installed even in entrance doors of older buildings. Based on a sophisticated system, it requires only the replacement of the lock itself without the need for any electronic wiring. It is thus highly suitable for listed buildings where only little is allowed to be changed. Furthermore, it is also suitable for small hotels and offices to easily implement access control, without entailing additional high costs. The clear design of the lock has an elegant appearance that enhances the aesthetics of almost every door. Featuring a clear layout, it offers the four easy and intuitive to use functions of finger scan, NFC card, app (Bluetooth) and PIN code. This flexibility helps increase the sense of security among users, even in the event of one of the functions suddenly failing. The option of access via PIN code can be added without the need to install an additional input panel, as it is included already on the body of the lock itself. Thus, there is also no need to drill holes into the wall to install an input panel or do any wiring work. The entire installation is self-explanatory and can be done without professional help.

Sicher integriert

Mit der Entwicklung der Architektur verändern sich auch die Anforderungen an Sicherheitskonzepte. Das intelligente Multifunktionsschloss ist eine zeitgemäße Lösung für ältere Häuser, da es unkompliziert auch in vorhandene Eingangstüren eingebaut werden kann. Auf der Basis eines durchdachten Systems erfordert es lediglich den Austausch des Schlosses selbst und keine weitere elektrische Verkabelung. Es eignet sich daher auch gut für denkmalgeschützte Gebäude, in denen wenig verändert werden darf. Einsatz findet es zudem in kleinen Hotels und Büros, um dort das Problem der Zugangskontrolle ohne zusätzlich entstehende hohe Kosten zu lösen. Dieses Schloss wirkt durch seine klare Gestaltung elegant und wertet die Ästhetik jeder Tür auf. Es ist sehr logisch aufgebaut und bietet eine intuitive und einfache Nutzerführung mit den vier Funktionen Fingerscan, NFC-Karte, App (Bluetooth) und PIN-Code. Diese Flexibilität erhöht das Gefühl der Sicherheit bei den Nutzern auch in dem Fall, dass eine der Funktionen plötzlich einmal ausfallen sollte. Die Option der PIN-Code-Lösung kann ohne die Anbringung einer zusätzlichen Eingabekonsole erfolgen, da sie auf dem Schlossgehäuse selbst angebracht ist. Es müssen somit keine Löcher in die Wand gebohrt werden, um eine solche Konsole zu installieren oder aufwendig zu verkabeln. Die gesamte Installation ist selbsterklärend und kann ohne professionelle Hilfe ausgeführt werden.

Statement by the jury

Featuring a purist design and comprehensive multifunctionality, this smart lock offers new possibilities for installation in older buildings. Specifically designed for retrofitting, the lock has been perfectly adapted to fulfil its function. Allowing effective access control, it provides high security and implies an elegant way of interaction. The high-quality design of the lock consistently extends down to the last detail.

Begründung der Jury

Dieses puristisch gestaltete intelligente Sicherheitsschloss bietet durch seine clevere Multifunktionalität neue Möglichkeiten für ältere Gebäude. Speziell konzipiert für den nachträglichen Einbau, wurde es seinem Einsatzbereich perfekt angepasst. Als effektive Zutrittskontrolle ist es sehr sicher und impliziert eine elegante Art der Interaktion. Die qualitativ hochwertige Gestaltung wurde bis in die Details stringent fortgeführt.

Designer portrait
See page 34
Siehe Seite 34

109

Alarm System
Product Range
Alarmsystem-Produktserie

Manufacturer
Sector Alarm AS, Oslo, Norway
Design
EGGS Design, Oslo, Norway
Sector Alarm AS, Oslo, Norway
Resideo, Mougins, France
Web
www.sectoralarm.com
www.eggsdesign.com
www.resideo.com

The design of these home alarm devices mirrors the company's values and identity. Soft, slightly domed surfaces with precise detailing give an approachable and trustworthy expression. To ensure a pleasant user experience, system status and controls are indicated using both light behaviour and sound signals. A consistent use of visual cues and shapes reinforces simple handling and operational safety. The wall-mounted key pad, motion and door/window sensors are flexible in installation and easy to maintain.

Statement by the jury
Security was the focus of the design for this alarm system whose classical appearance also suits modern interiors.

Die Gestaltung dieses Alarmsystems spiegelt die Markenidentität des Herstellers wider. Weiche, leicht gewölbte Oberflächen mit präzisen Details verleihen ihm eine ansprechende und zuverlässige Ausstrahlung. Licht und Ton, die den Systemstatus und die Bedienelemente anzeigen, sorgen für ein gutes Nutzererlebnis. Die konsequente Verwendung von visuellen Signalen und Formen unterstützt eine einfache Bedienung und Funktionssicherheit. Die an der Wand befestigte Tastatur sowie die Bewegungs-, Tür- und Fenstersensoren lassen sich flexibel installieren und einfach warten.

Begründung der Jury
Sicherheit steht im Fokus der Gestaltung dieses Alarmsystems, das sich zudem mit seinem klassischen Aussehen gut in moderne Interieurs integriert.

TCL T-home
Smart Home Automation
Intelligente Hausautomation

Manufacturer
TCL Corporation, Shenzhen, China
In-house design
Shenzhen TCL Digital Technology Co., Ltd., Shenzhen, China
Web
www.tcl.com

The TCL T-home collection includes six sensors, two Wi-Fi sockets and a visual doorbell. Via Wi-Fi and Zigbee, this allows for gateway control of smart home appliances. The entire suite is simple to use without any complex cabling. All the desired functionalities are quick to set up using an app. The design of T-home and its warm colouring, round shape and smooth surface is deliberately friendly and calm. The rose gold-plated ring subtly echoes the brand's product philosophy.

Statement by the jury
Due to its uncomplicated nature, the harmonious TCL T-home collection makes it possible to retrofit buildings with a smart home system.

Die TCL T-home-Kollektion umfasst sechs Sensoren, zwei Wi-Fi-Steckdosen und eine optische Türklingel. Über ein Gateway können damit per Wi-Fi und Zigbee intelligente Hausgeräte gesteuert werden. Das Set kann einfach, ohne aufwändige Verkabelung, genutzt werden. Über eine App lassen sich schnell alle gewünschten Funktionen einrichten. Die Gestaltung von T-home ist mit dem warmen Farbton, der runden Form und der glatten Oberfläche bewusst freundlich und ruhig. Der aus Roségold plattierte Ring spiegelt dabei subtil die Produktphilosophie der Marke wider.

Begründung der Jury
Dank ihrer Unkompliziertheit lassen sich mit der harmonisch gestalteten Kollektion TCL T-home Gebäude auch nachträglich zu einem Smart Home ausbauen.

Schüco DCS SmartTouch
Building Automation System
Gebäudeautomation

Manufacturer
Schüco International KG, Bielefeld, Germany
In-house design
Web
www.schueco.de

The Schüco DCS SmartTouch combines door communication and access control in a single unit which can be integrated into the wall profile, flush- or surface-mounted. Thanks to an inbuilt HD camera, the entrance area is always visible from anywhere – even when the residents are not at home. Full HD video door communication furthermore also allows for videotelephony with people who are in the entrance area. The device is permanently in receive mode as transmission automatically adapts to local network conditions. Operation and configuration are easy with the help of the Schüco app.

Statement by the jury
The synergy of new technology and high reliability turn the convenient Schüco DCS SmartTouch unit into a highly effective building automation system.

Das Schüco DCS SmartTouch vereint Türkommunikation und Zutrittskontrolle in einem Modul, das sich profilintegriert sowie als Unterputz- oder Aufputzvariante einbauen lässt. Dank der integrierten HD-Kamera ist der Eingangsbereich auch von unterwegs immer einsehbar. Full-HD-Videotürkommunikation ermöglicht zudem Videotelefonie mit Personen, die sich im Eingangsbereich aufhalten. Das Gerät bietet einen ständigen Empfang, da sich die Übertragung automatisch den regionalen Netzgegebenheiten anpasst. Die Bedienung und Konfiguration ist einfach per Schüco-App möglich.

Begründung der Jury
Dank des Zusammenspiels von neuer Technologie und hoher Zuverlässigkeit bietet das komfortable Schüco DCS SmartTouch Gebäudeautomation auf hohem Niveau.

IP Outdoor Station
IP-Außenstation

Manufacturer
Niko NV, Sint-Niklaas, Belgium
In-house design
Arne Desmet
Web
www.niko.eu

This IP Outdoor Station is part of an autonomous entry system. In conjunction with an indoor touchscreen and an app, users can answer calls, even when they are not at home. Accepted, refused and missed calls are stored and recordings are made of visitors. The minimalist style of the device means it easily fits into different facades. Essential information such as nameplate and bell button are included on the front. As the device only needs two wires, it is easy to retrofit.

Statement by the jury
The design of this IP Outdoor Station appeals with a contemporary use of technology and an appearance that is pared down to the essentials.

Diese IP-Außenstation ist Teil eines autonomen Zugangssystems. In Verbindung mit einem Indoor-Touchscreen und einer App können Nutzer ein Gespräch entgegennehmen, auch wenn sie nicht zu Hause sind. Angenommene, abgelehnte und verpasste Anrufe werden gespeichert und Aufzeichnungen von Besuchern erstellt. Das Gerät ist minimalistisch gestaltet und passt sich so gut verschiedenen Fassaden an. Auf der Vorderseite zeigt es mit dem Namensschild und dem Klingelknopf das Wesentliche. Da das Gerät nur zwei Drähte benötigt, kann es einfach nachgerüstet werden.

Begründung der Jury
Die Gestaltung dieser IP-Außenstation begeistert mit einem zeitgemäßen Technikeinsatz und einem auf das Wesentliche reduzierten Erscheinungsbild.

Surface-Mounted Home Station Video 7
Wohnungsstation Video AP 7

Manufacturer
Gira Giersiepen GmbH & Co. KG,
Radevormwald, Germany
In-house design
Design
Schmitz Visuelle Kommunikation,
Wuppertal, Germany
Web
www.gira.de
www.hgschmitz.de

Safety and convenience are the hallmark of the puristic surface-mounted home station video 7. A high-resolution 7" TFT touch display shows who is at the door. The high picture quality of the glass display can be viewed from the sides. All practical functions and settings can easily be controlled via an intuitive operating concept based on icons. The unit can either be mounted on the wall or be placed on an item of furniture with the help of a stand, turning it into a visual eye-catcher.

Statement by the jury
The surface-mounted home station video 7 gains merit for its intuitive handling and the way in which it integrates well with different interiors.

Sicherheit und Komfort kennzeichnen die puristisch gestaltete Wohnungsstation Video AP 7. Ein hochauflösendes, 7" großes TFT-Touchdisplay zeigt an, wer vor der Tür steht. Das Glasdisplay bietet dabei auch beim Betrachten von der Seite eine gute Bildqualität. Über ein intuitives Bedienkonzept, das auf der Verwendung von Icons basiert, lassen sich alle praktischen Funktionen und Einstellungen bequem steuern. Das Gerät kann entweder an der Wand montiert oder mit einem Standfuß versehen als Blickfang auf einem Möbelstück platziert werden.

Begründung der Jury
Die Wohnungsstation Video AP 7 punktet mit einer intuitiven Handhabung. Zudem passt sich das Gerät gut verschiedenen Interieurs an.

Dling
Smart Video Doorbell
Intelligente Video-Türklingel

Manufacturer
Beijing MADV Technology Co., Ltd.,
Beijing, China
In-house design
Yang Jin, Xu Xuexiang
Web
www.dlingsmart.com

Dling is a smart video doorbell. Together with an associated app it allows for easy communication with visitors even when the user is not at home. The unit has a body recognition function and records any disturbances at the front door. In this case, it will immediately notify the user. Paired with a bell receiver, this ensures that Dling provides timely notice of visitors. The discreetly designed unit with rounded edges and low energy consumption will run for six months on only four AA batteries.

Statement by the jury
The harmonious design of the Dling smart video doorbell ensures safety at the front door and allows for interaction with visitors.

Dling ist eine intelligente Video-Türklingel. Sie ermöglicht mithilfe einer begleitenden App die Kommunikation mit Besuchern, auch wenn die Nutzer nicht zuhause sind. Das Gerät hat eine Körpererkennungsfunktion und registriert Unruhe vor der Haustür. In diesen Fällen sendet es direkt eine Information. Durch die Verbindung mit einem Klingelempfänger kann Dling zudem rechtzeitig über Besucher informieren. Das dezent mit abgerundeten Kanten gestaltete Gerät hat einen niedrigen Stromverbrauch und arbeitet mit nur vier AA-Batterien sechs Monate lang.

Begründung der Jury
Die harmonisch gestaltete, intelligente Video-Türklingel Dling sorgt für Sicherheit vor der eigenen Haustür und ermöglicht die Interaktion mit Besuchern.

Q5
Smart Door Lock
Intelligentes Türschloss

Manufacturer
Dessmann (China) Machinery &
Electronic Co., Ltd., Hangzhou, China
Design
LKK Design Shenzhen Co., Ltd.
(Weizhi Shi, Yanhui Zheng), Shenzhen, China
Web
www.dessmann.com.cn
www.lkkdesign.com

The design of the Q5 door lock is modelled on the futuristic aspects of concept cars. The lock is part of a smart home equipment kit and is activated by fingerprint. Door opening is simplified by an automatic process triggered by a slight push. Fingerprint recognition thereby takes less than half a second. The individual parts of the lock are made of a high-quality aluminium alloy and stainless steel. Their surfaces stand out for their smooth texture.

Statement by the jury
The automatic Q5 door lock combines sophisticated technology with an appealing shape to create a high-quality smart home product.

Futuristisch anmutende Elemente von Konzeptfahrzeugen standen Pate bei der Gestaltung des Türschlosses Q5, das Teil einer Smart Home-Ausstattung ist. Die Sperre wird per Fingerabdruck aktiviert und erleichtert das Öffnen einer Tür, indem dieser Prozess durch ein leichtes Drücken automatisch ausgelöst wird. Die Erkennung des Fingerabdrucks dauert dabei nicht einmal 0,5 Sekunden. Die einzelnen Komponenten des Schlosses sind aus einer hochwertigen Aluminiumlegierung und Edelstahl gebaut, ihre Oberfläche zeichnet sich durch eine schmeichelnde Haptik aus.

Begründung der Jury
Das automatische Türschloss Q5 vereint eine ausgereifte Technik mit einer ansprechenden Formgebung zu einem hochwertigen Smart Home-Produkt.

TCL K2
Smart Door Lock
Intelligentes Türschloss

Manufacturer
TCL Corporation, Shenzhen, China
In-house design
Shenzhen TCL Digital Technology Co., Ltd.,
Shenzhen, China
Web
www.tcl.com

The compact design of the TCL K2 smart door lock cuts down on the number of movable components it contains. Equipped with a conveniently large handle which houses the biometric fingerprint unlocking mechanism, this ergonomically well-thought-out design makes the opening and closing of doors quick and easy. The die-cast lock is made of high-quality aluminium as used in the aerospace industry. The operating panel employs IML technology which mimics the texture of metal.

Statement by the jury
Great value in use coupled with a highly individual sense of aesthetics characterise the carefully considered design of the TCL K2 smart door lock.

Die kompakte Gestaltung des intelligenten Türschlosses TCL K2 reduziert den Anteil beweglicher Komponenten. Es ist mit einem komfortabel großen Griff ausgestattet, der das biometrische Fingerabdruck-Entriegelungsmodul beherbergt. Dank der ergonomisch gut durchdachten Platzierung gestaltet sich das Öffnen einer Tür einfach und schnell. Das Schloss wird im Druckgussverfahren aus hochwertigem Aluminium, wie es auch in der Luftfahrt verwendet wird, hergestellt. Für das Bedienfeld wird die IML-Technologie eingesetzt, die die Textur von Metall nachahmt.

Begründung der Jury
Ein hoher Gebrauchswert in Verbindung mit einer eigenständigen Ästhetik charakterisiert die wohldurchdachte Gestaltung des intelligenten Türschlosses TCL K2.

S1
Smart Door Lock
Intelligentes Türschloss

Manufacturer
Shenzhen ORVIBO Technology Co., Ltd., Shenzhen, China
In-house design
Wu Shaobin, Xu Qinglian, Zheng Rongchun
Web
www.orvibo.com

The smart door lock S1 is simple and smooth in design, easy to use, with low power consumption and a battery life of over 500 days. There is a circular fingerprint sensor on the handle to unlock the door with fingerprint recognition. Besides, it can also be unlocked by password, card or app. Users can monitor the security system remotely via the associated HomeMate app to be able to react immediately in case of any abnormal incidents.

Das intelligente Türschloss S1 ist einfach und schlüssig gestaltet und leicht zu bedienen. Darüber hinaus hat es einen geringen Stromverbrauch sowie eine Batterielaufzeit von über 500 Tagen. Auf dem Griff befindet sich ein kreisrunder Fingerabdrucksensor, um die Tür per Fingerabdruckerkennung zu entriegeln. Außerdem kann sie mithilfe eines Passworts, einer Karte oder einer App entsperrt werden. Nutzer können das Sicherheitssystem über die zugehörige HomeMate-App aus der Ferne überwachen, um sofort auf ungewöhnliche Vorkommnisse reagieren zu können.

Statement by the jury
At the core of the design for the S1 smart door lock is the combination of both a user-friendly and energy-saving operation.

Begründung der Jury
Im Mittelpunkt der Gestaltung des intelligenten Türschlosses S1 steht die Vereinigung einer nutzerfreundlichen Handhabung mit einem energiesparsamen Betrieb.

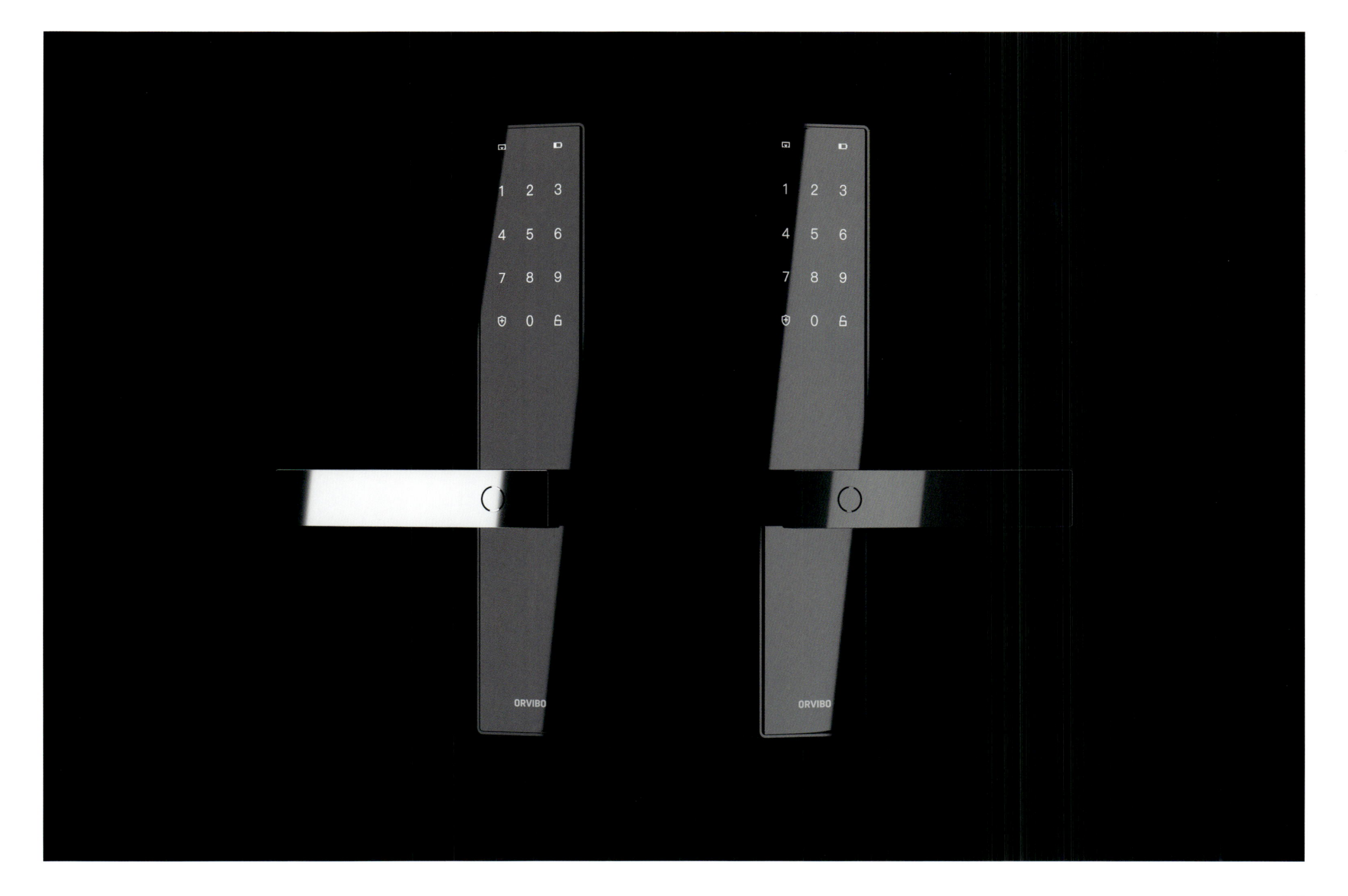

Mi
Smart Door Lock
Intelligentes Türschloss

Manufacturer
Xiaomi Inc., Beijing, China
In-house design
Web
www.mi.com

With its large fingerprint sensor and anti-spoofing facial recognition algorithm, this smart door lock combines security with convenience. Additional unlocking options include codes, NFC, Bluetooth recognition and a physical backup key. The built-in C-class cylinder has seven security sensors to enable real-time monitoring and operation of a remote alarm. The lock is made of a durable zinc alloy. This finely brushed metal results in a modern, minimalist look underscored by the associated IML control panel.

Statement by the jury
Numerous extras that guarantee safety are paired with an appealing minimalist appearance in this smart door lock.

Mit seinem großen Fingerabdrucksensor und dem Gesichts-Anti-Spoofing-Algorithmus vereint dieses intelligente Türschloss Sicherheit und Komfort. Weitere Entsperrungsmöglichkeiten sind bequem via Code, NFC, Bluetooth-Erkennung und physischem Backup-Schlüssel möglich. Der eingebaute Zylinder der C-Klasse hat sieben Sicherheitssensoren, die Echtzeitüberwachung und Fernalarm ermöglichen. Das Schloss ist aus einer robusten Zinklegierung hergestellt. Fein gebürstetes Metall erzeugt zusammen mit dem IML-Bedienfeld ein modernes, minimalistisches Aussehen.

Begründung der Jury
Zahlreiche Extras, die Sicherheit garantieren, verbinden sich bei diesem intelligenten Türschloss mit einer ansprechend minimalistischen Anmutung.

E-lock
Smart Door Lock
Intelligentes Türschloss

Manufacturer
Honeywell China, Shanghai, China
In-house design
HUE Design Studio (Dezhi Yang, Peilin Li)
Web
www.honeywell.com

E-lock is intended primarily for large Chinese families that are looking for a combination of convenient door opening and smart home security. The design of the input field and user interface is focused on their needs and everyday behaviour patterns. The clean, linear use of forms makes entering a code or finger scanning easy. The lock, which complements the manufacturer's proprietary smart home system, is made of extruded aluminium and is both pleasant to the touch and presenting a genteel look.

Statement by the jury
The user-oriented design of the E-lock stands out for its family friendliness. It is also a useful extension of the manufacturer's smart home system.

E-lock richtet sich speziell an chinesische Familien mit mehreren Mitgliedern, die eine Kombination aus komfortabler Türöffnung und intelligenter Haussicherheit suchen. Die Gestaltung des Eingabefeldes und der Benutzeroberfläche fokussiert sich auf deren Bedürfnisse und alltägliches Verhalten. Die klare, geradlinige Formensprache ist hilfreich bei der Eingabe eines Codes oder beim Fingerscan. Das Schloss, welches das herstellereigene Smart Home-System ergänzt, besteht aus extrudiertem Aluminium und bietet eine angenehme Haptik und ein feines Erscheinungsbild.

Begründung der Jury
Die nutzerorientierte Gestaltung des E-lock fällt durch seine Familienfreundlichkeit auf. Außerdem ergänzt es sinnvoll das Smart Home-System des Herstellers.

SHP-DP738
Smart Door Lock
Intelligentes Türschloss

Manufacturer
Samsung SDS, Seoul, South Korea
In-house design
Jeonghoon Ha, Seungryun Lee
Web
www.samsungsds.com

In conjunction with an app, the SHP-DP738 door lock provides smart home security services. Door lock access can thus be controlled in real time via smartphone. In addition, it provides information on unusual events and, in such cases, blocks entry for a few minutes to prevent burglaries. It also detects high temperatures, e.g. in case of a fire, and can trigger an emergency call. The striking lock which comes with a distinctive push/pull switch furthermore complies with the European RoHS directive.

Statement by the jury
The SHP-DP738 door lock attracts attention because of the numerous smart home functions it offers and due to its striking appearance.

Das SHP-DP738 ist ein Türschloss, das zusammen mit einer App Smart Home-Sicherheitsdienste leistet. So lässt sich der Zugriff auf die Türsperre in Echtzeit per Smartphone kontrollieren. Darüber hinaus informiert es über ungewöhnliche Vorkommnisse und blockiert in solchen Situationen den Zugang um einige Minuten, um Einbrüche zu verhindern. Es registriert hohe Temperaturen wie z. B. bei einem Feuer und löst einen Notruf aus. Das ausdrucksstark mit einem markanten Push/Pull-Schalter gestaltete Schloss berücksichtigt zudem die europäische RoHS-Richtlinie.

Begründung der Jury
Das Türschloss SHP-DP738 zieht durch seine zahlreichen Smart Home-Funktionen und sein expressives Aussehen Aufmerksamkeit auf sich.

SHP-DH538, 540
Smart Door Lock
Intelligentes Türschloss

Manufacturer
Samsung SDS, Seoul, South Korea
In-house design
Euncheuk Woo, Jeonghoon Ha
Web
www.samsungsds.com

This timeless door lock with a modern design offers users tailor-made smart home services. With the application of Zigbee wireless network technology, it supports the platform service in conjunction with a smart wall panel and a door camera in order to remotely control real-time access data and the security system, immediately notifying users of illegal entries or burglaries. The lock also offers a wide range of access authentication options such as fingerprint identification, a password, RF ID card, Zigbee and an e-KEY.

Statement by the jury
The functionally mature design and numerous secure, keyless access options account for the appeal of this smart door lock.

Dieses zeitlos modern gestaltete Türschloss bietet maßgeschneiderte Smart Home-Dienste. Dank der Ausstattung mit der Funktechnik Zigbee unterstützt es in Verbindung mit einem intelligenten Wandpaneel und einer Türkamera den Plattformdienst und steuert aus der Entfernung die Echtzeit-Zugriffshistorie sowie das Sicherheitsmanagement. Es informiert zügig bei illegalen Zugriffen oder Einbrüchen. Der Nutzer kann bei diesem Modell zwischen vielfältigen Methoden der Zugriffsauthentifizierung wählen, z. B. Fingerabdruck, Kennwort, RF-ID-Karte, Zigbee oder e-KEY.

Begründung der Jury
Dieses intelligente Türschloss begeistert mit einer funktional ausgereiften Gestaltung und vielen sicheren, schlüssellosen Zugangsmöglichkeiten.

WU-Lock Crown Plus
Smart Door Lock
Intelligentes Türschloss

Manufacturer
Nanjing IoT Sensor Technology Co., Ltd.,
Nanjing, China
In-house design
Zhang Tijun, Liu Jing, Zhu Jian
Web
www.wuliangroup.com

Crown Plus is a smart door lock equipped with a camera which can record videos and unusual incidents at the front door. The lock offers a range of access options to cater for different lifestyles including fingerprint recognition, NFC, password or card. Together with the Wulian Smart Home app it also allows for bidirectional communication with visitors. Moreover, it can also be linked to an existing smart home system – a simple touch on the screen is enough to activate the "home scene".

Statement by the jury
The Crown Plus smart door lock is impressive for the multifunctional choices it offers and for the way in which it thus easily adapts to different lifestyles.

Crown Plus ist eine intelligente, mit einer Kamera ausgestattete Türverriegelung. Es können Videos aufgenommen und ungewöhnliche Vorfälle vor der Haustür festgehalten werden. Sie bietet eine Vielzahl von Zugriffsmethoden, die sich unterschiedlichen Lebensstilen anpassen: Fingerabdruck, NFC, Passwort sowie Karte. Über die Wulian Smart Home-App ist eine bidirektionale Kommunikation mit Besuchern möglich. Darüber hinaus kann sie auch mit einem Smart Home-System verbunden werden – mit nur einem Tastendruck lässt sich bequem eine „Home Scene" aktivieren.

Begründung der Jury
Überzeugend ist die beeindruckende Multifunktionalität, durch die sich der intelligente Türöffner Crown Plus problemlos verschiedenen Lebensstilen anpasst.

Ujia
Smart Door Lock
Intelligentes Türschloss

Manufacturer
Hangzhou You Jia Technology Co., Ltd.,
Hangzhou, China
Design
Propeller Design AB (Jaan Selg),
Stockholm, Sweden
Web
www.aiyoujia.com
www.propeller.se

Equipped with a fingerprint reader, Ujia is a smart door lock that can be operated via an easy to navigate app or NFC tag. Its construction makes the DIY installation simple and it will fit a wide range of doors. The lock is made of zinc alloy with an inbuilt RGB LED indicator. The design deliberately focuses on giving the lock a harmonious appearance to make it look less like an electronic device and more like a complementary addition to the interior decor.

Statement by the jury
The cleverly conceived design of the Ujia smart door lock combines the use of contemporary technology with an appearance that suits the home environment.

Ujia ist ein intelligentes, mit Fingerabdruckleser ausgestattetes Türschloss, das über eine einfach zu navigierenden App oder NFC-Tag gesteuert wird. Seine Bauweise ermöglicht eine leichte, selbstständig ausführbare Installation, zudem passt es sich einer breiten Palette von Türen an. Das mit einem eingebauten RGB-LED-Indikator ausgestattete Schloss ist aus einer Zinklegierung hergestellt. Sein Erscheinungsbild ist bewusst harmonisch gestaltet. Es ähnelt weniger einer elektronischen Vorrichtung, sondern ergänzt die Einrichtung eines Wohnraums.

Begründung der Jury
Die klug durchdachte Gestaltung des intelligenten Türschlosses Ujia vereint einen zeitgemäßen Technikeinsatz mit einem wohnlich anmutenden Aussehen.

Di T91
Smart Door Lock
Intelligentes Türschloss

Manufacturer
Dessmann (China) Machinery &
Electronic Co., Ltd., Hangzhou, China
Design
Hangzhou Hotdesign Co., Ltd.
(Xiaoqiang Yang), Hangzhou, China
Web
www.dessmann.com.cn
www.hz-hotid.com

The Di T91 smart door lock is fitted with fingerprint recognition technology. With the help of an inbuilt AI system, which can predict changes to the fingerprint, it continues to work quickly and reliably even after opening and closing more than 100,000 times. The semi-automatic locking mechanism is integrated into a sliding cover which closes automatically when touched lightly, thereby making it easy to operate. Additional extras include smart cat's eyes, which enable remote monitoring.

Statement by the jury
The clever design of the Di T91 smart fingerprint door lock is focused to a high degree on security and durability aspects.

Das intelligente Türschloss Di T91 ist mit einer Technologie zur Fingerabdruckerkennung ausgerüstet. Dank eines integrierten KI-Systems, das Veränderungen des Fingerabdrucks voraussagen kann, arbeitet es auch nach mehr als 100.000 Öffnungs- und Schließvorgängen noch schnell und zuverlässig. Die halbautomatische Schließvorrichtung ist in einen Schiebedeckel eingesetzt, welcher bei leichter Berührung automatisch schließt und so für eine komfortable Handhabung sorgt. Weitere Extras sind z. B. intelligente Katzenaugen, die eine Fernüberwachung ermöglichen.

Begründung der Jury
Die clevere Gestaltung des intelligenten Fingerabdruck-Türschlosses Di T91 ist auf ein hohes Maß an Sicherheit sowie Langlebigkeit ausgerichtet.

IDL-300
Smart Door Lock
Intelligentes Türschloss

Manufacturer
HDC icontrols, Seongnam, South Korea
In-house design
Hee Sub Jung
Web
www.hdc-icontrols.com

With its slender, lever-shaped design, the handle of the IDL-300 smart door lock is convenient, easy to use and designed for speedy access. Users simply identify themselves per fingerprint by touching the sensor that is built into the handle. Authentication is also possible using a PIN number, an RF card or smartphone NFC. The lock is equipped with Wi-Fi so that verification of identification information can be carried out in real time even if the user is in the open air.

Statement by the jury
The deliberately simple construction and intuitive handling of the IDL-300 smart door lock are hallmarks of clever design.

Mit seinem schlanken, balkenförmigen Design ist der Griff des intelligenten Türschlosses IDL-300 handlich und einfach zu bedienen. Es ermöglicht einen schnellen Durchgang, der Nutzer muss sich lediglich per Fingerabdruck identifizieren. Dazu reicht ein Berühren des im Griff integrierten Sensors. Eine Authentifizierung ist zudem mit einer PIN-Nummer, einer RF-Karte und einem Smartphone über NFC möglich. Das Schloss ist mit Wi-Fi ausgestattet, was eine Überprüfung der Identifikationsdaten in Echtzeit, auch wenn sich der Nutzer im Freien aufhält, ermöglicht.

Begründung der Jury
Eine bewusst einfache Konstruktion und eine intuitive Handhabung charakterisieren die clevere Gestaltung des intelligenten Türschlosses IDL-300.

EN-P8
Smart Door Lock
Intelligentes Türschloss

Manufacturer
Guangdong Mingmen Locks Industry Co., Ltd., Zhongshan, China
Design
Foshan 3&1 Industrial Design Co., Ltd. (Jinfeng Yu, Bing Bai), Foshan, China
Web
www.ming-men.com
www.design3.cn.com

The EN-P8 smart lock for sliding doors is of a very slim construction. Its body consists of an aluminium alloy in combination with a slightly curved sheet of 2.5D glass. The integrated handle exactly follows the contours of this paired-material construction. The body of the lock is made of a durable magnesium alloy and can be opened by fingerprint or with a password. The fingerprint unlocking mode includes a display that mimics the movement of waves, which gives the EN-P8 a particularly lively feel.

Statement by the jury
The resourceful design of the EN-P8 smart sliding door lock gains merit for its mix of high-quality materials and effortless operation.

Das intelligente Schiebetürschloss EN-P8 ist sehr schlank gebaut. Es vereint einen Körper aus einer Aluminiumlegierung mit einer leicht gebogenen Scheibe aus 2.5D-Glas. Der integrierte Griff passt sich dabei exakt den Konturen dieser Kombination an. Das Schlossgehäuse besteht aus einer langlebigen Magnesiumlegierung und lässt sich per Fingerabdruck oder mit einem Passwort öffnen. Der Fingerabdruck-Entsperrmodus ist dabei mit einer Anzeige versehen, die das Spiel von Wellen nachahmt – das verleiht dem EN-P8 eine besonders lebendige Ausstrahlung.

Begründung der Jury
Die raffinierte Gestaltung des intelligenten Schiebetürschlosses EN-P8 punktet mit einem hochwertigen Materialmix und einer mühelosen Bedienung.

Emoji Intelligent-DL1
Smart Door Lock
Intelligentes Türschloss

Manufacturer
Midea Smart Technology Co., Ltd., Shunde, China
In-house design
Ran Peng, Xiao Tao, Ri Hua Ye
Web
www.midea.com

The use of various different emojis gives this smart door lock a human touch. The emojis are associated with a voice recording in order to provide users with an interactive experience, almost as if they were communicating with a friend. They can chat, receive, for example, urgent messages, alerts or recommendations. The design of the smart door look exudes a high-quality impression but is devoid of unnecessary details, which significantly cuts down on production costs.

Statement by the jury
The surprising emoji and sound design of this smart door lock with high-quality look and feel invites users to interact at their front door.

Dieses intelligente Türschloss bekommt durch die Verwendung verschiedener Emojis einen menschlichen Touch. Die Emojis sind mit einer Stimme unterlegt und bescheren so Nutzern ein interaktives Erlebnis, beinahe so, als würde mit einem Freund kommuniziert werden. Man kann chatten und erhält beispielsweise Expressnachrichten, Warnmeldungen oder Empfehlungen. Die Gestaltung des Türschlosses vermittelt einen qualitativ hochwertigen Eindruck. Sie verzichtet jedoch auf überflüssige Details, dadurch reduzieren sich die Produktionskosten erheblich.

Begründung der Jury
Dank der verblüffenden Gestaltung mit Emojis und Sound lädt dieses hochwertig anmutende, intelligente Türschloss zur Interaktion an der Haustür ein.

INC
Door Handle
Türgriff

Manufacturer
FORMANI Holland B.V., Maastricht-Airport, Netherlands
Design
Studio Piet Boon, Oostzaan, Netherlands
Web
www.formani.com
www.pietboon.com

This door handle is part of a range of high-end fittings for doors, windows and wardrobes. Its design combines gentle curves with a good grip. Beginning with a cylinder, the circular shape flattens and then tapers towards the tip. This gives the handle a slight incline from which it also derives its name – INC is here used as the abbreviation of incline. All products from this range are available in stainless steel with a satin finish or PVD gunmetal-coated and so fit equally well into different interiors.

Dieser Türgriff ist Teil einer Serie hochwertiger Beschläge für Türen, Fenster und Schränke. Seine Gestaltung vereint sanfte Kurven mit einer guten Griffigkeit. Ausgehend von einem Zylinder flacht dessen kreisrunde Form zunächst ab und verjüngt sich zum Ende. Dies verleiht dem Griff eine sachte Neigung, durch die er auch seinen Namen erhalten hat – INC ist die Abkürzung von incline (Neigung). Alle Teile dieser Serie sind aus satiniertem Edelstahl oder mit einer PVD-Beschichtung in einem dunklen Anthrazitgrau erhältlich und passen sich so gut verschiedenen Interieurs an.

Statement by the jury
The ingenious design of the INC door handle blends a flowing yet powerful design vocabulary with pleasant haptic properties.

Begründung der Jury
Die ausgeklügelte Gestaltung des Türgriffs INC bringt eine fließende und gleichzeitig starke Formensprache mit angenehmen haptischen Eigenschaften in Einklang.

Cobra Infinity
Door Handle
Türgriff

Manufacturer
COBRA, spol. s r.o., Prague, Czech Republic
Design
NOVAGUE, Prague, Czech Republic
Web
www.cobra-cz.cz
www.novague.com

The design of the Cobra Infinity door handle was inspired by the anatomy of the human hand. With an unfussy shape and pleasant to the touch, it fits the curve of the palm snuggly. The minimalist handle, produced from a single piece of the metal alloy Zamak, has an elegant appearance which is underscored by the matt black or discreet silver finish. The handle is universal in use, as it is compatible with a wide range of doors and interiors.

Statement by the jury
Due to its mature design, the Cobra Infinity door handle satisfies high expectations of good ergonomics, elegance and appearance.

Die Inspirationsquelle für die Gestaltung des Türgriffs Cobra Infinity liegt in der Anatomie einer menschlichen Hand. Mit seiner schnörkellosen Form und angenehmen Haptik schmiegt er sich schmeichelnd der Handfläche an. Der minimalistische Griff, der aus einem einzigen Stück der Metalllegierung Zamak gearbeitet ist, hat eine elegante Ausstrahlung, die durch die Farbgebung in einem matten Schwarz oder dezenten Silber unterstrichen wird. Der Griff ist vielseitig einsetzbar, da er sich problemlos verschiedenen Türen und Einrichtungsstilen anpasst.

Begründung der Jury
Der Türgriff Cobra Infinity wird aufgrund seiner ausgefeilten Gestaltung hohen Erwartungen an eine gute Ergonomie und ein edles Erscheinungsbild gerecht.

Cobra Spectra
Door Handle
Türgriff

Manufacturer
COBRA, spol. s r.o., Prague, Czech Republic
Design
NOVAGUE, Prague, Czech Republic
Web
www.cobra-cz.cz
www.novague.com

The Cobra Spectra door handle is made of the metal alloy Zamak. Due to the use of this high-quality material and well-thought-out ergonomics and construction, it is pleasant to the touch and provides a good grip. The simple, modern design unites a balanced stylistic idiom with precisely drawn lines. The handle is available in black and silver so that it can be used with a wide range of doors and will discreetly fit into the relevant interior.

Statement by the jury
The contemporary design of the Cobra Spectra door handle stands out for the high quality of the material used and for its expressive design vocabulary.

Der Türgriff Cobra Spectra besteht aus der Metalllegierung Zamak. Dank dieses hochwertigen Materialeinsatzes sowie einer ausgeklügelten Ergonomie und Bauart bietet er angenehme haptische Eigenschaften und eine gute Griffigkeit. Die schlichte, moderne Gestaltung vereint eine ausgewogene Formensprache mit klar gezeichneter Linienführung. Der Griff ist in den Farben Schwarz und Silber erhältlich. Dadurch passt er sich sehr gut einer breiten Palette von Türen an und integriert sich dezent in jeweilige Interieurs.

Begründung der Jury
Die zeitgemäße Gestaltung des Türgriffs Cobra Spectra zeichnet sich durch einen hochwertigen Materialeinsatz sowie eine ausdrucksstarke Formensprache aus.

Cobra Ultima
Door Handle
Türgriff

Manufacturer
COBRA, spol. s r.o., Prague, Czech Republic
Design
NOVAGUE, Prague, Czech Republic
Web
www.cobra-cz.cz
www.novague.com

Its bevelled surface and harmonious lines ensure the Cobra Ultima door handle looks both geometrical and sleek. Its shape architecture was carefully thought through in order to offer good ergonomics to support the grip. The handle is available in black and silver which makes it easy to combine with different doors and interiors. It is produced from a single piece of Zamak, a high-quality metal alloy composed of zinc, aluminium, magnesium and copper.

Statement by the jury
The sleek appearance and sophisticated functionality achieved by the design of the Cobra Ultima door handle are bound to attract attention.

Die abgeschrägte, mit harmonischer Linienführung gestaltete Oberfläche verleiht dem Türgriff Cobra Ultima ein gleichermaßen geometrisches wie geschmeidiges Aussehen. Seine Form ist mit Bedacht konstruiert. Sie bietet eine gute Ergonomie und unterstützt so wirkungsvoll die Handhabung des Griffes. Dieser ist in Schwarz und Silber erhältlich – dadurch lässt er sich gut mit unterschiedlichen Türen und Einrichtungen kombinieren. Gefertigt ist er aus einem einzigen Stück Zamak, einer hochwertigen Metalllegierung aus Zink, Aluminium, Magnesium und Kupfer.

Begründung der Jury
Mit einem geschmeidigen Aussehen und einer ausgereiften Funktionalität zieht die Gestaltung des Türgriffs Cobra Ultima die Aufmerksamkeit auf sich.

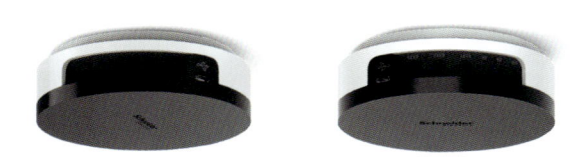

Wiser 360 Degree ZB/IR Convertor
Smart Home Automation
Intelligente Hausautomation

Manufacturer
Schneider Electric (China) Co., Ltd.,
Shenzhen, China
Design
Schneider Electric (Yingzhi Guan,
Leihong Zheng), Shanghai, China
Web
www.schneider-electric.com

As part of a smart home system, this device uses infrared technology and an app to control equipment such as the television, the air conditioning and the stereo system. Assembly is easy. All users need to do is to twist the cover. This applies both for changing a battery or for installing the device on the ceiling. No additional battery cover is required which makes the device more environmentally friendly. Although the USB is not in line with the other interfaces, their layout looks harmonious. With its balanced appearance, this device easily adapts to its surroundings.

Statement by the jury
This smart home device is convincing because of its well-devised, harmonious design. Its environmentally friendly, limited use of materials is also pleasing.

Als Teil einer Smart Home-Ausstattung steuert dieses Gerät über eine App mithilfe der Infrarottechnologie u. a. den Fernseher, die Klimaanlage und das Musiksystem. Der Zusammenbau ist durch Drehen der Abdeckung einfach, selbst wenn der Akku eingebaut oder an der Decke befestigt ist. Umweltfreundlich ist, dass keine weitere Batterieabdeckung nötig ist. Obwohl die USB- und andere Schnittstellen nicht in einer geraden Linie angeordnet sind, passen sie harmonisch zusammen. Mit einem ausgewogenen Erscheinungsbild integriert sich das Gerät gut in seine Umgebung.

Begründung der Jury
Dieses Smart Home-Gerät überzeugt mit seiner wohldurchdachten, harmonischen Gestaltung. Zudem gefällt der umweltfreundlich reduzierte Materialeinsatz.

Anyware Smart Adapter™
Smart Home Automation
Intelligente Hausautomation

Manufacturer
Anyware Solutions ApS,
Copenhagen, Denmark
Design
Ian Mahaffy Industrial Design,
Copenhagen, Denmark
Web
www.anyware.solutions
www.ianmahaffy.com

The Anyware Smart Adapter, which is fitted between the bulb holder and the bulb, comes with a range of different functions. It is easy to install with the help of a physical connection button that is located on the device and an app. Built-in sensors can, amongst others, operate the lighting, but also measure the temperature, humidity and noise levels. The compact adapter also offers Wi-Fi and Bluetooth connectivity, can be used to monitor home security, but at the same time meets stringent safety standards.

Statement by the jury
Thanks to its clever construction, the compact Anyware Smart Adapter manages to offer a great number of smart home functions in a very limited space.

Der Anyware Smart Adapter, der zwischen einer Lampenfassung und einer Glühlampe montiert wird, bietet vielfältige Funktionen. Er wird einfach über eine physische Verbindungstaste, die sich am Gerät befindet, und eine App installiert. Dank integrierter Sensoren steuert er u. a. die Beleuchtung, misst aber auch die Temperatur, die Luftfeuchtigkeit sowie den Geräuschpegel, verfügt über WLAN- und Bluetooth-Verbindungen und dient der Hausüberwachung und somit der Sicherheit. Der kompakt gebaute Adapter entspricht dabei strengen Sicherheitsstandards.

Begründung der Jury
Dank einer cleveren Konstruktion bietet der kompakt gestaltete Anyware Smart Adapter auf begrenztem Raum zahlreiche Smart Home-Funktionen.

TuyaGo
Smart Gateway
Intelligentes Gateway

Manufacturer
Tuya Inc., Hangzhou, China
In-house design
Wenkai Li, Yugen Zhong
Web
www.tuya.com

The TuyaGo Zigbee gateway serves as a control centre for smart home equipment. It can communicate with a cloud or an app via a router. This makes it possible to check and operate smart devices from a smartphone. The minimalist design concept of the gateway comes to the fore in its square shape and smooth, rounded edges. The deliberately unobtrusive appearance means it discreetly fits into different interiors. The housing is made of high-strength and flame-retardant plastic which guarantees the stability of the product.

Statement by the jury
Aesthetic versatility and a sturdy construction were the focus of the sophisticated design of the TuyaGo Zigbee gateway.

Das Zigbee-Gateway TuyaGo dient als Kontrollzentrum für die Smart Home-Ausstattung. Über einen Router kann es mit einer Cloud oder App kommunizieren – so lassen sich intelligente Geräte per Mobiltelefon überprüfen und steuern. Der minimalistische Designansatz des Gateways spiegelt sich u. a. in der quadratischen Formgebung sowie den abgerundeten, glatten Kanten wider. Durch das bewusst unauffällige Aussehen passt es sich dezent verschiedenen Interieurs an. Das Gehäuse ist aus hochfestem, schwer entflammbarem Kunststoff gebaut und garantiert Stabilität.

Begründung der Jury
Eine ästhetische Anpassungsfähigkeit sowie eine solide Konstruktion stehen im Fokus der anspruchsvollen Gestaltung des Zigbee-Gateways TuyaGo.

Aqara Smart Camera G2/Gateway Edition
Smart Home Automation
Intelligente Hausautomation

Manufacturer
Lumi United Technology Co., Ltd.,
Shenzhen, China
In-house design
Lumi United Industrial Design Team
(Meng Meng, Chen Jia, Jiang Minzhen)
Web
www.lumiunited.com

This smart wide-angle camera is notable for its elegantly proportioned outward appearance. It has a viewing angle of 140 degrees and comes with a great many functions like two-way communication, video messaging, user recognition, motion detection as well as time-lapse photography. It also functions as a control centre for Zigbee devices. With the right products, it can be used for home automation, making it possible, if desired, to preset scenarios such as turning off the lights when leaving the home.

Statement by the jury
The clever design of the Aqara Smart Camera G2/Gateway Edition skilfully combines a number of different functions with an engaging look.

Diese intelligente Weitwinkelkamera fällt durch ihr formschönes Erscheinungsbild auf. Sie hat einen Bildwinkel von 140 Grad und bietet zahlreiche Funktionen wie z. B. bidirektionale Kommunikation, Videonachrichten, Personenerkennung, Bewegungsüberwachung sowie Zeitraffer-Fotografie. Gleichzeitig dient sie als Kontrollzentrum für Zigbee-Geräte – zusammen mit entsprechenden Produkten lässt sich so die Automation des eigenen Zuhauses umsetzen. Szenarien wie das Ausschalten von Licht beim Verlassen des Hauses lassen sich auf Wunsch einstellen.

Begründung der Jury
Die clevere Gestaltung der Aqara Smart Camera G2/Gateway Edition vereint gekonnt zahlreiche verschiedene Funktionen mit einem ansprechenden Erscheinungsbild.

Gira System 3000
Control Kit for Light and Blinds
Steuerungsbaukasten für Licht und Jalousien

Manufacturer
Gira Giersiepen GmbH & Co. KG,
Radevormwald, Germany
In-house design
Design
Schmitz Visuelle Kommunikation,
Wuppertal, Germany
Web
www.gira.de
www.hgschmitz.de

Gira System 3000 is a compact control kit for the smart configuration of lights and blinds. The elements of the kit are functional and user-friendly and very easy to install. The unified system of products for the configuration of home devices allows for both a manual and automatic activation of the various functions. The programming and operation of these Bluetooth devices is carried out in a simple manner using a smartphone or tablet and the Gira app.

Statement by the jury
The innovative design of the Gira System 3000 control kit for lights and blinds is impressive due to the high level of functionality and ease of use.

Gira System 3000 ist ein kompakter Baukasten für die intelligente Steuerung von Licht und Jalousien. Das Sortiment ist funktional und nutzerfreundlich und lässt sich einfach und schnell installieren. Einheitliche Systemaufsätze ermöglichen sowohl eine manuelle als auch eine automatische Aktivierung der verschiedenen Funktionen. Die Programmierung und Bedienung der Bluetooth-Geräte erfolgt dabei auf einfache Weise mithilfe eines Smartphones oder Tablets und der Gira App.

Begründung der Jury
Die innovative Gestaltung des Baukastens Gira System 3000 zur Licht- und Jalousiesteuerung beeindruckt mit hoher Funktionalität und einfacher Handhabung.

Physical
Smart Control Panel
Intelligentes Bedienpaneel

Manufacturer
Luxurite (Shenzhen) Smart Home Ltd.,
Shenzhen, China
In-house design
Web
www.insprid.com

The combination of glass, metal and natural wood gives Physical an invitingly informal appearance which turns it into an eye-catcher in the home. The smart control panel is simply mounted on the wall. The device, which combines a home network with a multifunctional switch, can be used to carry out a wide range of tasks. It can, for example, adjust the slats of blinds, the lighting or room temperature and can also be used to open doors or act as an intercom.

Statement by the jury
The design of the Physical smart control panel stands out particularly for its inviting appearance and multifunctionality.

Durch die Kombination von Glas, Metall und dem natürlichen Material Holz erhält Physical eine wohnliche Anmutung, durch die es zu einem Blickfang im Haus wird. Das intelligente Bedienpaneel wird einfach an der Wand montiert. Mithilfe des Geräts, das ein Heimnetzwerk und einen multifunktionalen Schalter kombiniert, lässt sich eine Vielzahl von Aufgaben ausführen. Es können z. B. die Lamellen einer Jalousie, die Beleuchtung oder die Raumtemperatur wunschgemäß eingestellt werden. Darüber hinaus dient das Gerät auch als Türöffner und Gegensprechanlage.

Begründung der Jury
Die Gestaltung des intelligenten Bedienpaneels Physical sticht besonders durch sein wohnliches Erscheinungsbild hervor. Weiterhin gefällt seine Multifunktionalität.

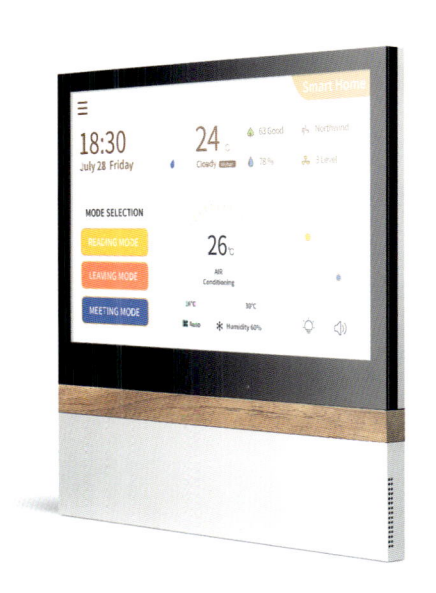

Controlmini
KNX Smart Home Panel
KNX-Panel zur intelligenten
Haussteuerung

Manufacturer
PEAKnx, DOGAWIST Company,
Darmstadt, Germany
In-house design
Gerald Palmsteiner, Greta Pötter
Web
www.peaknx.com

The Controlmini is an A4-sized KNX panel for smart home systems. It is characterised by the high-quality workmanship of its components and the flush-mounted hardened glass front as well as the tailor-made stainless steel casing. The glass cover adheres magnetically and can be replaced and customised. This makes the panel, which is easy to operate thanks to the YOUVI visualisation software, both distinctive and elegant. In addition to the flush-mounted version, it is also available in a 25 mm flat surface-mounted version.

Statement by the jury
The combination of high-quality materials and easy operability of the Controlmini turn it into a very user-friendly smart home KNX panel.

Das Controlmini ist ein DIN-A4-großes KNX-Panel für die intelligente Haussteuerung. Es zeichnet sich durch hochwertig verarbeitete Komponenten wie das bündig aufliegende, gehärtete Frontglas oder das maßgeschneiderte Edelstahlgehäuse aus. Das magnetisch haftende Glas ist austauschbar und kann personalisiert werden. So präsentiert sich das dank der Visualisierungssoftware YOUVI einfach zu bedienende Panel gleichzeitig elegant und individuell. Neben einer Unterputz- ist es auch in einer 25 mm flachen Aufputzvariante erhältlich.

Begründung der Jury
Ein hochwertiger Materialeinsatz und eine leichte Bedienbarkeit vereinen sich bei dem Controlmini zu einem nutzerfreundlichen Smart Home-KNX-Panel.

ABB-tacteo® KNX Sensor
Busch-tacteo® KNX-Sensor

Manufacturer
Busch-Jaeger Elektro GmbH, Mitglied der
ABB-Gruppe, Lüdenscheid, Germany
In-house design
Dörte Thinius
Web
www.busch-jaeger.de

The ABB-tacteo KNX sensor made of glass is an intuitive to use operating unit that is employed for smart building management in hotels, public buildings and apartment blocks. Blinds, lighting, heating and media as well as access controls are easy to operate with the help of the device, which marries modern design with high quality. The control elements are available in different sizes to match a wide range of installation standards. The number of functions is variable and can be configured according to individual needs or desires.

Statement by the jury
The contemporary design of the ABB-tacteo KNX sensor made of glass meets high standards of functionality, convenience and aesthetics.

Der Busch-tacteo KNX-Sensor aus Glas ist ein intuitiv handhabbares Bedienelement, das der intelligenten Gebäudesteuerung von Hotels, öffentlichen Einrichtungen und Wohnblöcken dient. Mit dem Gerät, das ein modernes Design mit hoher Qualität vereint, lassen sich Jalousien, Beleuchtung, Heizung und Medien sowie Zugangskontrollen sehr einfach steuern. Die Bedienelemente sind in verschiedenen Größen für unterschiedliche Installationsstandards erhältlich. Die Anzahl der Funktionen ist variabel und kann nach individuellen Wünschen konfiguriert werden.

Begründung der Jury
Die zeitgemäße Gestaltung des Busch-tacteo KNX-Sensors aus Glas wird hohen Ansprüchen an Funktionalität, Komfort und Ästhetik gerecht.

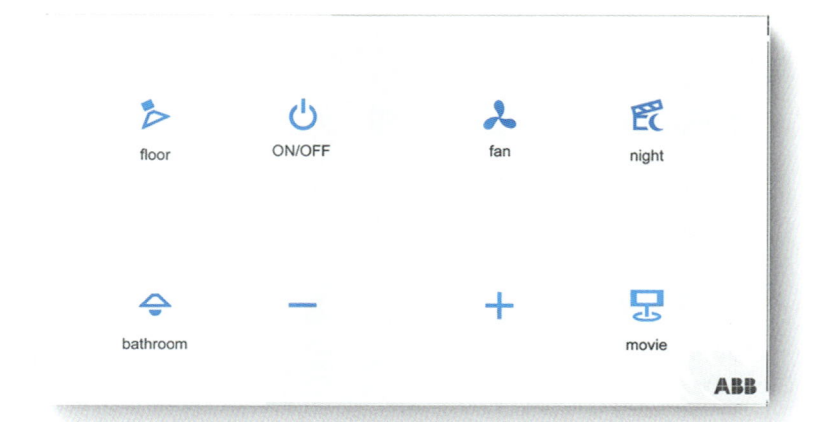

Bright
Smart Switch Panel
Intelligentes Schalterpaneel

Manufacturer
Luxurite (Shenzhen) Smart Home Ltd.,
Shenzhen, China
In-house design
Web
www.insprid.com

The Bright switch panel supports a range of different building automation systems such as KNX, Zigbee and Modbus in order to provide smart controls of home appliances. Its geometric design has a clear structure. The contrasting, coloured light bands on the surface are eye-catching features. The slim device has an easily legible display. Switches may be labelled as requested. A further benefit of the panel is its low energy consumption.

Statement by the jury
The great versatility of the Bright smart switch panel is worthy of note while its expressive design is bound to attract attention.

Das Schalterpaneel Bright unterstützt verschiedene Systeme zur Gebäudeautomation wie beispielsweise KNX, Zigbee oder Modbus, um in jeder Umgebung die intelligente Steuerung von Haustechnik zu gewährleisten. Seine geometrische Gestaltung weist eine klare Struktur auf, einen aufmerksamkeitsstarken Akzent setzen die im Kontrast zur Oberfläche stehenden, farbigen Lichtbandelemente. Das schlank konstruierte Gerät hat ein gut lesbares Anzeigefeld, die Tasten lassen sich wunschgemäß beschriften. Darüber hinaus arbeitet es mit niedrigem Energieverbrauch.

Begründung der Jury
Die vielseitigen Einsatzmöglichkeiten des intelligenten Schalterpaneels Bright begeistern. Zudem zieht es mit seiner ausdrucksstarken Gestaltung die Blicke auf sich.

Horizon™
Keypad Series
Schalter-Serie

Manufacturer
Crestron Electronics, Inc.,
Rockleigh, New Jersey, USA
Design
Noto GmbH (Stefan Hohn),
Hürth, Germany
Web
www.crestron.com
www.noto.design

The Horizon keypad series for the control of lighting, shades and media offers great flexibility. With their elegant appearance, the easy-to-operate keypads are suitable even for more sophisticated interiors. The standard option is available with matching coloured frames in a glossy or satin finish, but they can also be fashioned in other materials as requested by customers. The precisely constructed keypad buttons are illuminated by an LED light which can be produced in any colour desired.

Statement by the jury
The design of the Horizon keypad series focuses on delivering flexibility and customisation and gains merit for its high degree of aesthetic adaptability.

Die Schalter-Serie Horizon, mit der u. a. Beleuchtung, Jalousien sowie Medien gesteuert werden können, bietet große Flexibilität. Mit ihrem edlen Aussehen empfehlen sich die einfach zu bedienenden Schalter auch für anspruchsvoll gestaltete Innenräume. Standardmäßig sind sie mit farblich passenden Blenden in glänzendem oder seidenmattem Finish erhältlich, sie können aber auch in von Kunden gewünschten Materialien hergestellt werden. Die präzise konstruierten Tasten werden von einem LED-Licht, welches in jeder Farbe realisiert werden kann, beleuchtet.

Begründung der Jury
Die auf Flexibilität und Personalisierbarkeit ausgerichtete Gestaltung der Schalter-Serie Horizon punktet mit einem hohen Maß an ästhetischer Anpassungsfähigkeit.

Moorgen Smart Remote Control
Smart Home Automation
Intelligente Hausautomation

Manufacturer
Moorgen, Shanghai, China

In-house design
Moorgen Deutschland GmbH,
Aichtal, Germany

Web
www.moorgen.com

reddot award 2019
best of the best

Stages of comfort

Intelligent houses not only adapt to the general conditions in the form of light, heat and fresh air supply. They also serve and function as part of a far-reaching notion of adaptability to the needs, moods and habits of their inhabitants. The smart remote control by Moorgen delivers a new form and functionality that goes hand in hand with a sophisticated operating concept. Showcasing a design with softly curved lines that lend it a sculptural appearance, it is ergonomically shaped and rests well-balanced in the hands of users. It is made of high-quality materials and possesses a smooth surface texture that is highly pleasing to the touch. The remote control offers a differentiated way of directly controlling processes in the house, such as lighting, curtains, air conditioning and the TV. Moreover, in an intuitive manner, it also allows users to set and individually customise different scene modes. As a result, users can realise unified control of various processes simultaneously with only one click. For example, activating the audiovisual mode can be programmed to not only turn on the audiovisual equipment, but at the same time also gradually dim the light and slowly close the curtains. The content and size of the text on the remote control can be customised to user needs and even engraved on the factory side according to specific user habits.

Szenarien des Komforts

Das intelligente Haus passt sich nicht nur den Rahmenbedingungen in Form von Licht, Wärme oder Frischluftzufuhr an. Es steht auch im Dienste eines weitreichenden Verständnisses der Adaptierung an die Bedürfnisse und aktuellen Empfindungen seiner Bewohner. Die intelligente Fernbedienung von Moorgen bietet hier eine neue Form und Funktionalität, die mit einem hochentwickelten Bedienkonzept einhergeht. Sie ist gestaltet mit weich geschwungenen Linien, die ihr eine skulpturale Anmutung verleihen. Ergonomisch geformt, liegt sie gut austariert in der Hand des Nutzers. Sie besteht aus hochwertigen Materialien und mit der geschmeidigen Textur der Oberflächen ist sie auch haptisch sehr angenehm. Die Fernbedienung bietet eine differenzierte Art der Steuerung der Vorgänge im Haus, wie etwa der Beleuchtung, der Vorhänge, Klimaanlage oder des Fernsehgeräts. Auf intuitive Weise kann der Nutzer zudem auf ihn nahtlos zugeschnittene, unterschiedliche Szenen-Modi einstellen. Dadurch erreicht er eine einheitliche Steuerung mit nur einem Klick auf der Fernbedienung. Ist beispielsweise der audiovisuelle Modus aktiviert, wird das Licht schrittweise reduziert, die Vorhänge werden langsam geschlossen und die audiovisuelle Unterhaltung beginnt. Textinhalt und -größe auf der Fernbedienung können dem individuellen Nutzerverhalten angepasst und vom Hersteller auch entsprechend eingraviert werden.

Statement by the jury

Its simple and detailed design lends the smart remote control by Moorgen a modern and distinctive personality. The user-friendly concept goes hand in hand with a high degree of convenience, as the freely programmable preset modes provide intuitive, unified control of everything in the house. This remote control rests perfectly balanced in the hand and captivates users with the soft and sensuous appeal of the control elements.

Begründung der Jury

Ihre schlichte und detaillierte Gestaltung verleiht der intelligenten Fernbedienung von Moorgen eine moderne und eigenständige Persönlichkeit. Das nutzerfreundliche Konzept geht mit einem hochentwickelten Komfort einher, da voreingestellte Szenen-Modi eine intuitive, einheitliche Steuerung aller Vorgänge im Haus ermöglichen. Diese Fernbedienung liegt perfekt ausbalanciert in der Hand und begeistert mit ihren sensibel und weich ansprechenden Bedienelementen.

Designer portrait
See page 36
Siehe Seite 36

SLEEP
WAKE
GUEST
GAME
MOVIE
MUSIC
REPAST
PARTY
MOTION
READ
RESTING
WORK
MORNING
NIGHT
OVERCAST
SUNNY
moorgen
SLEEP
GUEST
MOVIE
REPAST
MOTION
RESTING
MORNING
OVERCAST

Moorgen Smart Control Knob
Smart Home Automation
Intelligente Hausautomation

Manufacturer
Moorgen, Shanghai, China
In-house design
Moorgen Deutschland GmbH, Aichtal, Germany
Web
www.moorgen.com

This multifunctional control knob is very useful for the operation of smart home devices. A simple push or turn is sufficient to manage lighting, curtains, the HiFi or air conditioning. It is easy and intuitive to use. The artistic design emulates the appearance of a large pebble. The casing is made of black plexiglass and metal which creates a striking contrast. As it comes in a variety of different colours, the knob can be combined with a wide range of interiors.

Dieser multifunktionale Drehknopf unterstützt die intelligente Haussteuerung. Mit seiner Hilfe lassen sich durch leichtes Drehen und Drücken Beleuchtung, Vorhänge, Stereoanlage und Klimaanlage bedienen. Die Handhabung ist dabei einfach und intuitiv. Seine kunstvolle Gestaltung ahmt das Aussehen eines großen Kieselsteins nach. Der Gehäusekörper besteht aus Metall und schwarzem Plexiglas, was einen reizvollen Kontrast erzeugt. Dank verschiedener Farbausführungen kann er gut zu vielen Zimmereinrichtungen kombiniert werden.

Statement by the jury
The playful use of contrasts has been cleverly used to highlight the design of this multifunctional smart control knob.

Begründung der Jury
Durch das Spiel mit Kontrasten setzt die Gestaltung diesen multifunktionalen, intelligenten Drehknopf wirkungsvoll in Szene.

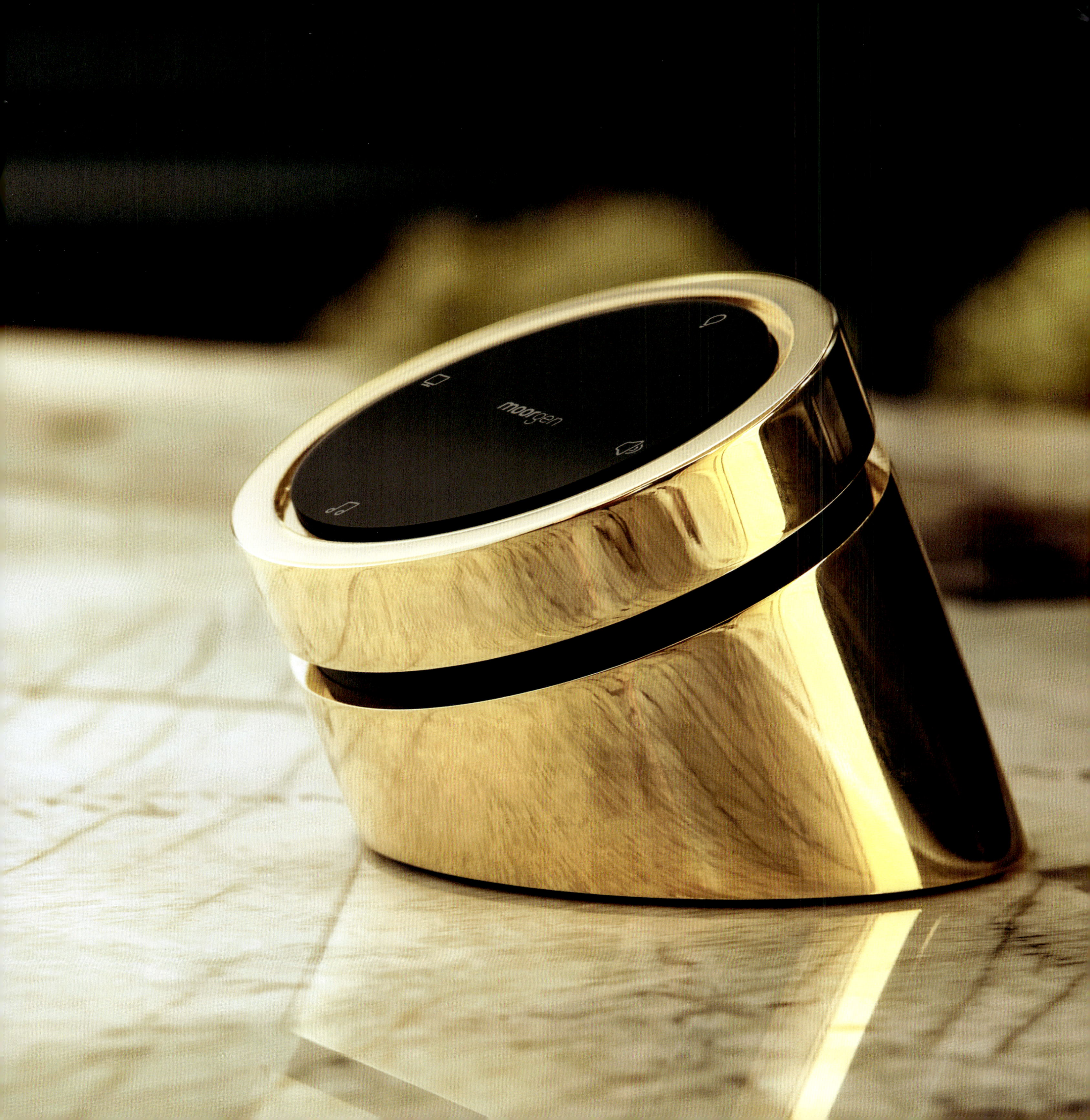

Moorgen Smart Switch Panel
Smart Home Automation
Intelligente Hausautomation

Manufacturer
Moorgen, Shanghai, China
In-house design
Moorgen Deutschland GmbH, Aichtal, Germany
Web
www.moorgen.com

This switch panel can be used to operate smart home systems. If you select the sleep mode, for example, lights are gradually dimmed, curtains gently drawn and the air conditioning is set to a pleasant temperature. The built-in light sensor allows for easy operation, even if light levels are low. The modular design of the panel not only has integrated switches, but also temperature controls, as well as a socket. The enclosing frame is available in a number of different materials and colours.

Mithilfe dieses Schalterpaneels kann eine Smart Home-Ausstattung gesteuert werden. Wird beispielsweise der Schlafmodus aktiviert, wird allmählich das Licht gedimmt, die Vorhänge schließen sich sanft und die Klimaanlage sorgt für eine angenehme Temperatur. Der eingebaute Lichtsensor ermöglicht eine einfache Bedienung auch bei wenig Licht. Das modulare Design des Paneels umfasst neben integrierten Schaltern auch eine Temperatursteuerung sowie eine Steckdose. Der Gehäuserahmen ist in einer Vielzahl von Materialien und Farben erhältlich.

Statement by the jury
The stylish design of this smart switch panel appeals with a wide range of functions and a flexible appearance.

Begründung der Jury
Die stilvolle Gestaltung dieses intelligenten Schalterpaneels gefällt mit einer großen Bandbreite an Funktionen und einem variablen Erscheinungsbild.

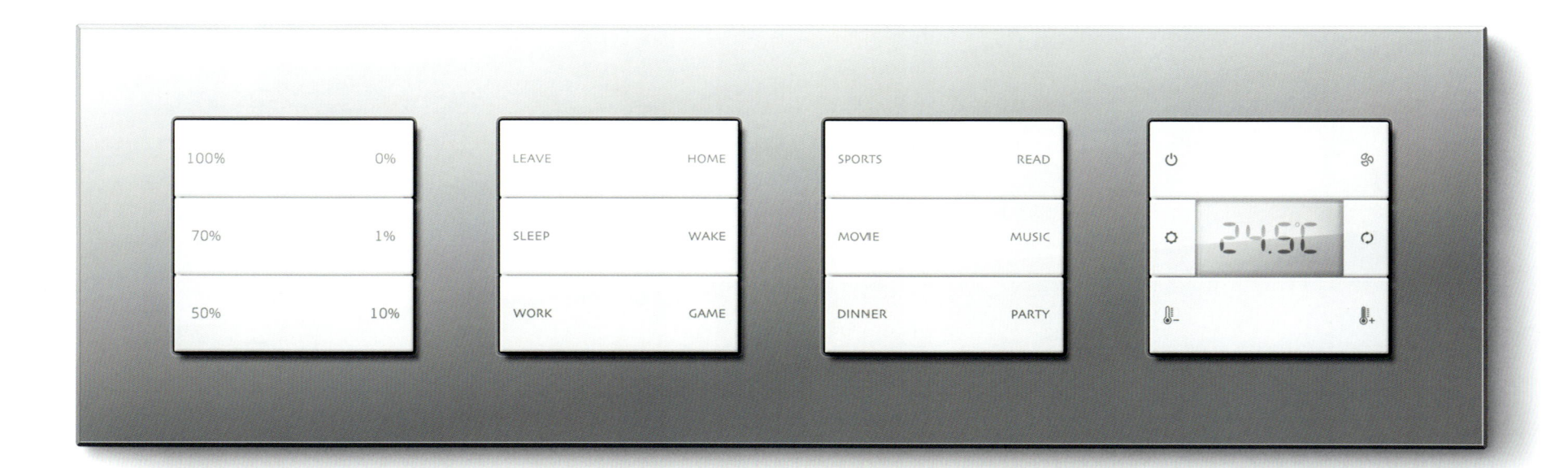

129

Moorgen Smart Control Knob
Smart Home Automation
Intelligente Hausautomation

Manufacturer
Moorgen, Shanghai, China
In-house design
Moorgen Deutschland GmbH, Aichtal, Germany
Web
www.moorgen.com

This compact smart control knob is fixed directly to the wall. The interplay of black or silver metal casing with black plexiglass cover makes the circular device look very appealing. A deliberately subtle design allows it to suit different interiors. The knob, which complements smart home systems, is straightforward to use. By simply turning or pushing it, lighting, music, curtains and much more are easy to operate.

Dieser kompakte, intelligente Drehknopf wird an der Wand montiert. Das Zusammenspiel des Gerätekörpers aus schwarzem oder silberfarbenem Metall und der Abdeckung aus schwarzem Plexiglas verleiht dem runden Utensil eine griffige Anmutung. Mit seiner bewusst dezenten Gestaltung passt es sich verschiedenen Interieurs an. Die Bedienung des Drehknopfs, der eine Smart Home-Ausstattung ergänzt, ist sehr einfach. Durch Drehen und Drücken lassen sich u. a. Licht, Musik und Vorhänge bequem steuern.

Statement by the jury
The design of this smart control knob manages to pair ease of use with a versatile appearance that fits in everywhere.

Begründung der Jury
Die Verbindung einer einfachen Handhabung mit einem vielseitig integrierbaren Aussehen ist bei der Gestaltung dieses intelligenten Drehknopfs gelungen.

moorgen

Moorgen Smart Thermostat
Smart Home Automation
Intelligente Hausautomation

Manufacturer
Moorgen, Shanghai, China
In-house design
Moorgen Deutschland GmbH, Aichtal, Germany
Web
www.moorgen.com

This smart thermostat is suitable for use in the home as well as in public buildings such as hotels or shopping centres. Depending on requirements, it can be connected to an air conditioning unit, underfloor heating or fresh air supply and thus monitor room temperature, humidity as well as levels of particulate matter and carbon dioxide. The device responds quickly to changes in the environment in order to guarantee healthy surroundings in an energy-efficient way. Its modern design combines a black monitor with metal keys.

Dieses intelligente Thermostat eignet sich sowohl für den Hausgebrauch als auch für die Nutzung in öffentlichen Gebäuden wie Hotels oder Einkaufszentren. Je nach Anforderung kann es mit einer Klimaanlage, Fußbodenheizung oder Frischluftzufuhr verbunden werden und so die Innentemperatur, die Feuchtigkeit, den Feinstaub- und den Kohlendioxidgehalt überwachen. Das Gerät reagiert schnell auf Umweltveränderungen, um energiesparend ein gesundes Umfeld zu ermöglichen. Seine moderne Gestaltung verbindet einen schwarzen Monitor mit einer Tastatur aus Metall.

Statement by the jury
The use of modern technology allows this smart thermostat to provide better air quality for interiors and energy-efficient heating.

Begründung der Jury
Dank zeitgemäßer Technik sorgt dieses intelligente Thermostat für bessere Luft in Innenräumen und für einen sparsamen Energieverbrauch bei der Beheizung.

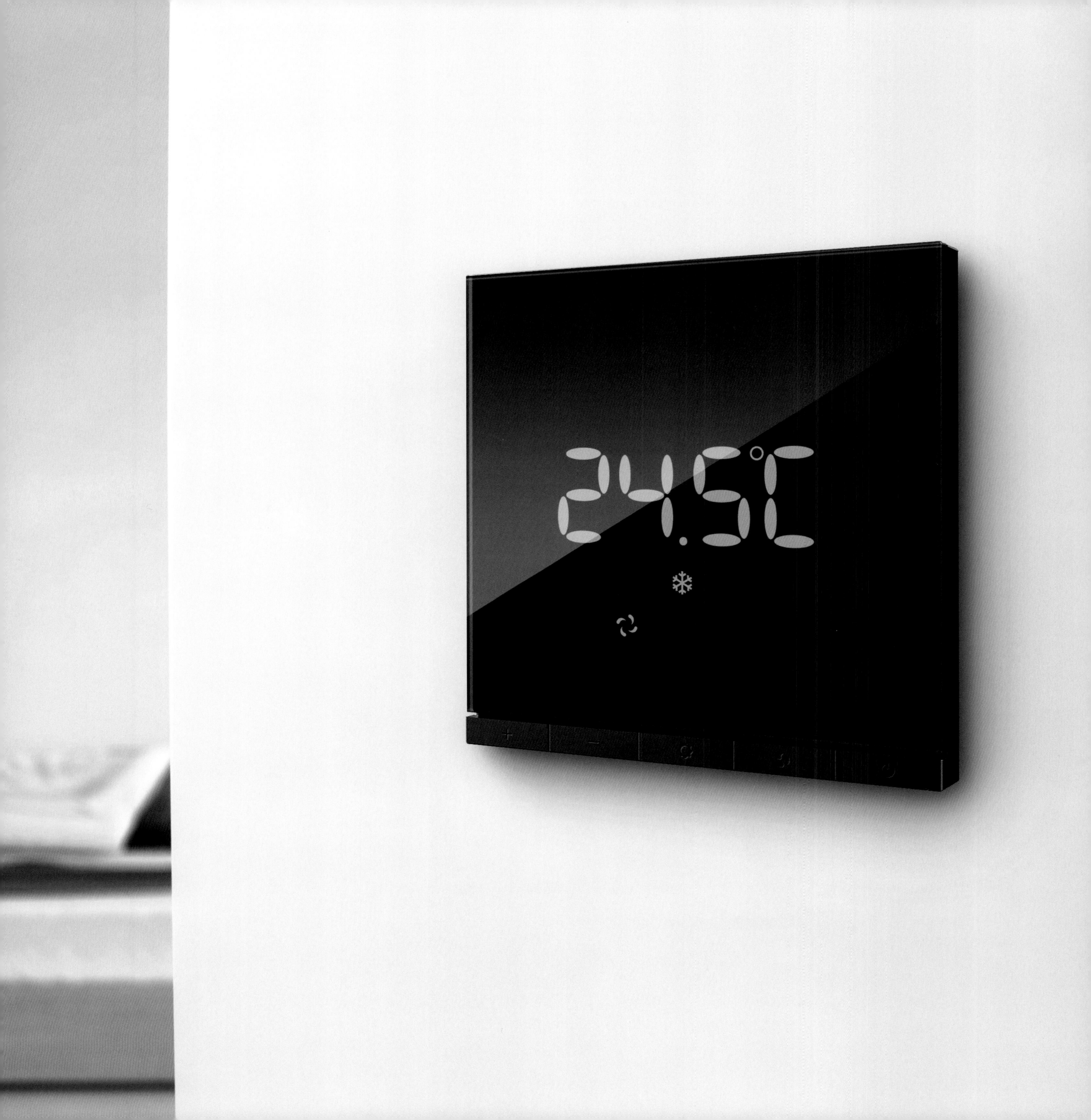
24.5°C

Eikon Tactil
Touch Panel

Manufacturer
Vimar S.p.A., Marostica (Vicenza), Italy
In-house design
Web
www.vimar.com

Eikon Tactil is a touch panel for easy energy management and control of smart home functions such as the operation of lights and blinds. The device can be installed separately or as part of a KNX bus system. The square shape of the panel is designed to be eye-catching. The cover is available in a range of different finishes. In addition to a model in elegantly glossy glass, there are also stone, leather and wooden options. The symbols shown on the surface can be customised.

Eikon Tactil ist ein Touch Panel, mit dem bequem das Energiemanagement betrieben und Smart Home-Funktionen wie z. B. die Steuerung von Licht und Jalousien aktiviert werden können. Das Gerät lässt sich einzeln installieren oder in ein KNX-Bussystem integrieren. Das Panel ist mit seiner quadratischen Form aufmerksamkeitsstark gestaltet. Die Abdeckung ist in verschiedenen Ausführungen erhältlich. So gibt es neben einer Version aus edel glänzendem Glas auch Modelle aus Stein, Leder und Holz. Die auf der Oberfläche gezeigten Symbole sind personalisierbar.

Statement by the jury
With its wide selection of material finishes, the stylish design of the Eikon Tactil touch panel easily fits into any setting and is bound to attract attention.

Begründung der Jury
Mit einer vielfältigen Materialauswahl passt sich das stilvoll gestaltete Touch Panel Eikon Tactil an die Umgebung an und zieht die Aufmerksamkeit auf sich.

Wiser FreeLocate Switch
Smart Home Automation
Intelligente Hausautomation

Manufacturer
Schneider Electric (China) Co., Ltd.,
Shenzhen, China
Design
Schneider Electric (Yingzhi Guan,
Leihong Zheng), Shanghai, China
Web
www.schneider-electric.com

The Wiser FreeLocate Switch is not only an on-off switch, but also a remote control for groups of devices that can be configured by app or E-mode. It is equipped with an elegant, high-gloss faceplate while the LED indicator can be customised to match the surrounding decor. The switch comes with a magnet so that it can easily be attached to the wall, a wall box or iron objects. A range of symbols, which can be replaced as desired make for clear identification of each socket to avoid mix-ups.

Statement by the jury
The Wiser FreeLocate Switch cleverly combines a switch with a remote control to create a practical and elegant smart home device.

Der Wiser FreeLocate Switch ist nicht nur ein Ein/Aus-Schalter, sondern auch eine Fernbedienung für Gerätegruppen, die per App oder E-Mode konfiguriert werden kann. Das Modell ist mit einer eleganten, glänzenden Frontplatte ausgestattet, die LED-Anzeige lässt sich an die jeweilige Einrichtung individuell anpassen. Es ist mit einem Magneten versehen und kann so bequem an der Wand, einer Wanddose oder an Eisengegenständen befestigt werden. Verschiedene Symbole, die leicht ausgewechselt werden können, verhindern ein Verwechseln der einzelnen Schalter und ihrer Funktionen.

Begründung der Jury
Geschickt vereint die Gestaltung des Wiser FreeLocate Switch einen Schalter und eine Fernbedienung zu einem praktischen und eleganten Smart Home-Produkt.

S1
Smart Switch
Intelligenter Schalter

Manufacturer
Midea Smart Technology Co., Ltd.,
Shunde, China
In-house design
Xiao Tao, Ri Hua Ye, Ran Peng
Web
www.midea.com

The design of the S1 smart switch helps users easily to tell which buttons have which function. They are defined according to individual requirements and then combined in one unit. Users can have them marked with different icons and choose from a range of different colour and surface structures. This approach has the advantage of limiting production to standard models and small modules which cuts down on waste by limiting material consumption and therefore also costs.

Statement by the jury
A responsible use of production materials and a personalised look make the design of the S1 smart switch a highly convincing solution.

Die Gestaltung der intelligenten Schalter S1 hilft Nutzern, einfach zu erkennen, welche Tasten welche Funktion haben. Individuellen Bedürfnissen entsprechend werden sie definiert und zu einer Einheit kombiniert. Der Nutzer kann sie mit verschiedenen Symbolen versehen und aus einer Palette unterschiedlicher Farben und Oberflächenstrukturen wählen. Dieses Verfahren bietet den Vorteil, dass nur Basismodelle und kleine Module hergestellt werden müssen, was die Verschwendung von für die Produktion notwendigen Materialien und somit Kosten reduziert.

Begründung der Jury
Mit einem verantwortungsvollen Umgang mit Produktionsmaterialien und einem individuellen Aussehen überzeugt die Gestaltung der intelligenten Schalter S1.

T1
Smart Switch
Intelligenter Schalter

Manufacturer
Midea Smart Technology Co., Ltd.,
Shunde, China
In-house design
Ri Hua Ye, Ran Peng, Xiao Tao
Web
www.midea.com

Household appliances, lights and curtains can all be operated with the help of the T1 smart switch. Users can preprogramme settings and in this way activate a group of appliances by voice command, mobile phone or by pressing physical buttons. The switch can be marked with icons that match certain devices to make identification of the operated appliance quick and easy. The system also allows for customised icons and can so be adapted precisely to different requirements in a resource-efficient way.

Statement by the jury
The design of the T1 smart switch focused on achieving carefully considered functionality. The high level of possible customisation is also very interesting.

Mithilfe der intelligenten Schalter T1 lassen sich u. a. Haushaltsgeräte, Leuchten und Vorhänge steuern. Der Nutzer kann Szenen programmieren und auf diese Weise eine Gruppe von Geräten via Sprache, Mobiltelefon oder physischer Tasten aktivieren. Die Schalter können mit Symbolen versehen werden, die bestimmten Geräten zugeordnet sind – auf diese Weise lässt sich ein gesteuerter Gegenstand schnell identifizieren. Das System ermöglicht personalisierbare Schalter und wird so passgenau auf ressourcenschonende Weise verschiedenen Anforderungen gerecht.

Begründung der Jury
Die Gestaltung der intelligenten Schalter T1 ist auf wohldurchdachte Funktionalität ausgerichtet. Außerdem gefällt das hohe Maß an Personalisierbarkeit.

ABB i-bus® KNX PEONIA Sensor
Smart Home Automation
Intelligente Hausautomation

Manufacturer
ABB (China) Limited, Beijing, China
In-house design
Design
FromD Innovation, Beijing, China
Web
www.new.abb.com
www.fromd.net

The ABB i-bus KNX PEONIA smart home automation sensor offers intuitive operation of all KNX applications found in residential, public and commercial buildings. With its slim, frameless appearance, it looks like a timeless classic. Operation is easy thanks to a rocker switch. The design of the room temperature controls used to switch from heating to cooling and the dynamic display screen contribute to creating a special user experience.

Der ABB i-bus KNX PEONIA Sensor dient der intelligenten Hausautomation. Es lassen sich damit intuitiv alle KNX-Anwendungen in privaten, öffentlichen sowie gewerblichen Gebäuden steuern. Mit seinem rahmenlosen und schlanken Design hat das Gerät ein klassisches, zeitloses Aussehen, die Handhabung erfolgt bequem über Wippschalter. Eine besondere Nutzererfahrung bietet beispielsweise die Gestaltung der Raumtemperaturregelung, die durch ein einfaches Umschalten zwischen Heizen oder Kühlen erfolgt, und des dynamisch anmutenden Anzeigebildschirms.

Statement by the jury
With its both practical and elegantly proportioned design the ABB i-bus KNX PEONIA sensor is suitable for a wide range of different applications.

Begründung der Jury
Mit seiner gleichermaßen praktischen wie formschönen Gestaltung eignet sich der ABB i-bus KNX PEONIA Sensor für vielfältige Einsatzmöglichkeiten.

137

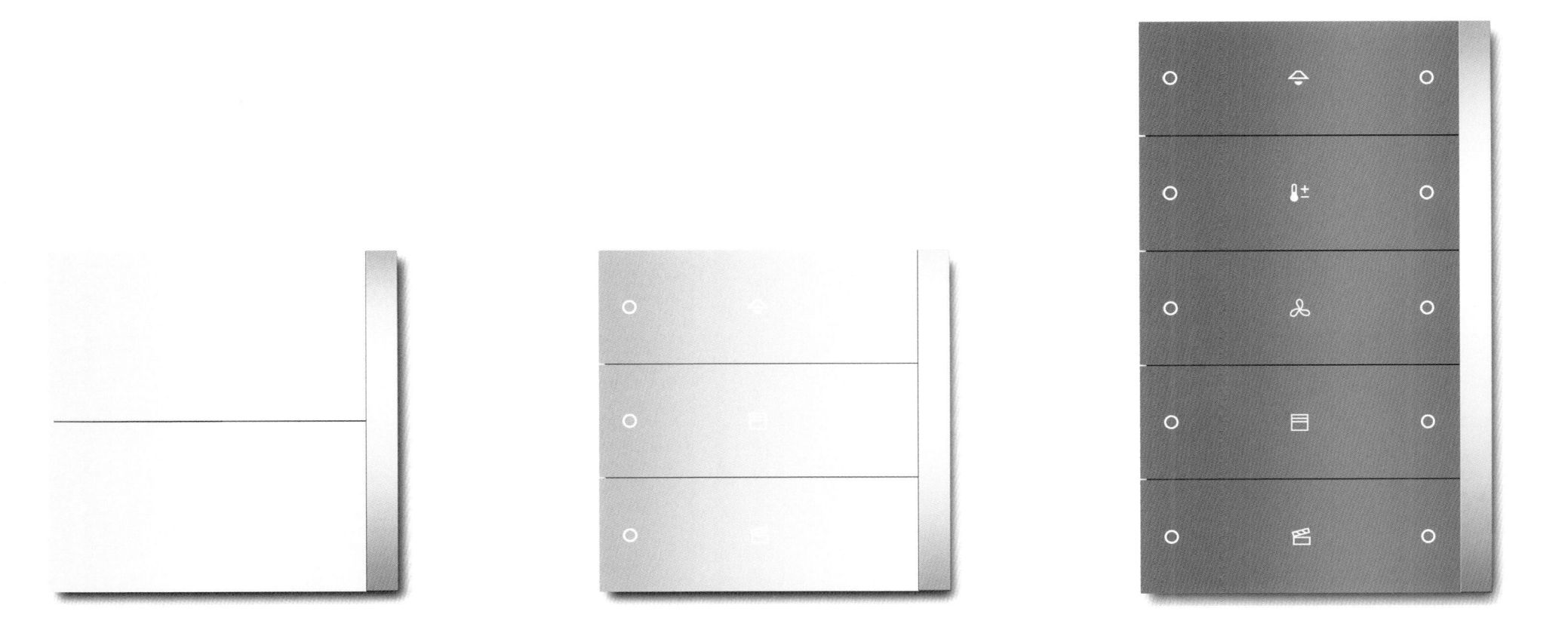

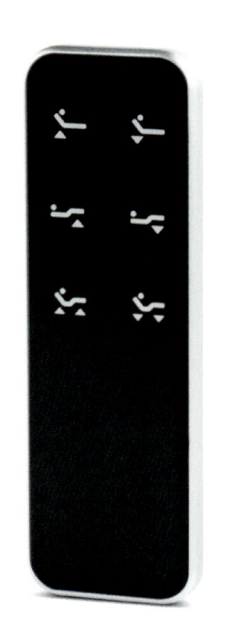

HC338
Radio Hand Control
Funk-Handschalter

Manufacturer
limoss GmbH & Co. KG, Wetter, Germany
In-house design
Sebastian Stoller
Web
www.limoss.de

Beds and chairs can be easily adjusted with the HC338 radio hand control. The slender appearance and high-quality glass surface are attractive and correspond to today's high expectations. This is underlined by the simple design with an aluminium casing and an integrated magnetic bracket. When using the touch panel, that comes with arrow, chair or bed symbols as options, the HC338 has a force feedback function which confirms the action.

Statement by the jury
The design of the HC338 radio hand control combines the use of high-quality materials with an elegant appearance to create a contemporary solution.

Mit dem Funk-Handschalter HC338 können Betten und Sessel bequem gesteuert werden. Das Gerät besticht durch sein schlankes Erscheinungsbild und entspricht mit seiner hochwertigen Glasoberfläche hohen Ansprüchen. Unterstrichen wird dies zudem durch das schlichte Design mit Aluminiumgehäuse und einem integrierten Magneten als Halterung. Um ein Feedback beim Betätigen des Touch-Bedienfelds, das optional mit einer Pfeil-, Sessel- oder Bettsymbolik erhältlich ist, zu bekommen, verfügt der Handschalter über eine Tastendruck-Rückmeldungsfunktion.

Begründung der Jury
Die Gestaltung des Funk-Handschalters HC338 vereint einen hochwertigen Materialeinsatz und eine elegante Anmutung zu einer zeitgemäßen Produktlösung.

F1
Smart Remote Control
Intelligente Fernbedienung

Manufacturer
Shenzhen ORVIBO Technology Co., Ltd., Shenzhen, China
In-house design
Wu Shaobin, Xu Qinglian, Zheng Rongchun
Web
www.orvibo.com

ORVIBO Smart Remote Control F1 has a simple, circular design, adhering to natural, geometric aesthetics. It is entirely made of special infrared transmission material – the surface has a roughened texture, and the device features a refined indicator design as well as a soft light guide treatment. It can replace traditional remote controllers for home appliances and with the help of a timer switch establishes the linkage between various attached devices. By means of the HomeMate app thus the air conditioner, TV, electric fan or set-top box can be remotely controlled.

Statement by the jury
The F1 smart remote control is impressive for its many different application options. Moreover, its geometric shape is very attractive.

Die intelligente Fernbedienung ORVIBO F1 weist mit ihrem einfachen, kreisrunden Design eine geometrische Ästhetik auf. Sie besteht vollständig aus einem Material, das eine Infrarotübertragung ermöglicht – die Oberfläche hat eine raue Beschaffenheit, zudem eine klare Anzeige sowie eine dezente Lichtführung. Sie ersetzt herkömmliche Haushaltsgeräte-Fernbedienungen und stellt mit einem Zeitschalter die Verbindung zu anderen Geräten her. Über die HomeMate-App lassen sich so z. B. die Klimaanlage, das Fernsehgerät, der elektrische Lüfter oder die Set-Top-Box steuern.

Begründung der Jury
Beeindruckend sind die vielfältigen Einsatzmöglichkeiten der intelligenten Fernbedienung F1. Außerdem ist ihre geometrische Formgebung ansprechend.

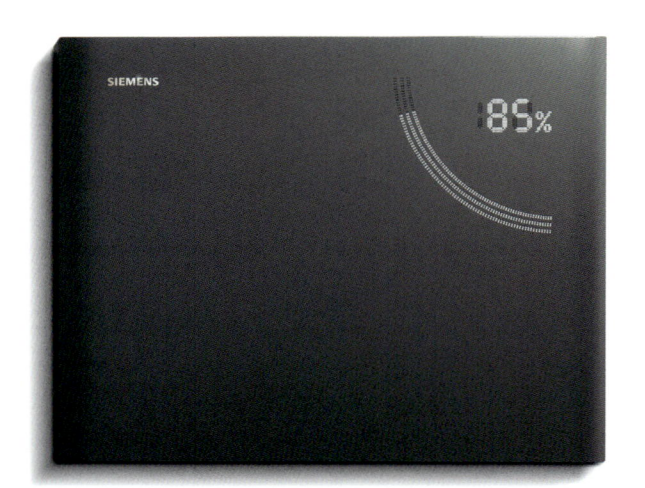

Junelight
Smart Battery
Intelligente Batterie

Manufacturer
Siemens AG, Nuremberg, Germany
In-house design
Vincent Weckert
Design
designaffairs GmbH (Stefan Hillenmayer), Munich, Germany
Web
www.siemens.com
www.designaffairs.com

Junelight is a smart battery for the storage of solar energy, which meets the requirements of modern residential properties. It combines cutting-edge components with a special ventilation concept and thus manages to produce a very flat profile of only 18 cm as well as minimal noise levels. The battery is easy to install in garages, corridors or behind doors. An animated LED display on the front panel indicates whether energy has been stored or consumed. A numerical display provides information on current charge levels.

Statement by the jury
The innovative use of technology as well as space-saving construction define the contemporary design of the Junelight smart battery.

Junelight ist eine intelligente Batterie zur Speicherung von Sonnenenergie, die den Anforderungen moderner Eigenheime gerecht wird. Sie kombiniert zeitgemäße Komponenten mit einem besonderen Lüftungskonzept und erzielt so eine sehr flache Bauweise von nur 18 cm bei minimaler Geräuschentwicklung. Das Gerät lässt sich einfach in Garagen, Fluren und hinter Türen installieren. Auf seiner Front befindet sich eine animierte LED-Anzeige, die wiedergibt, ob Energie gespeichert oder verbraucht wird. Eine numerische Anzeige informiert über den aktuellen Ladestatus.

Begründung der Jury
Ein innovativer Technikeinsatz sowie eine platzsparende Konstruktion charakterisieren die zeitgemäße Gestaltung der intelligenten Batterie Junelight.

DingTalk M1C
Fingerprint
Recognition Device
Fingerabdruckerkennungsgerät

Manufacturer
DingTalk (China) Technology
Information Co., Ltd., Hangzhou, China
In-house design
Web
www.dingtalk.com

DingTalk M1C is a fingerprint recognition device. Its casing is designed to prevent dust from settling, so that it is easy to clean. The module that records the fingerprint is visually demarcated from the body of the device. By using optical technology that is also found in smartphones, it delivers a reliable performance. The surface of the top is chamfered at an angle of 15 degrees which relaxes the wrist when it is being used. To help manage cables, the case is constructed in a partly open manner.

Statement by the jury
The design of the DingTalk M1C fingerprint recognition device is characterised by its ergonomic properties and user-friendly functionality.

DingTalk M1C ist ein Fingerabdruckerkennungsgerät. Sein Gehäuse ist so gestaltet, dass Staubablagerungen reduziert werden und eine leichte Reinigung gewährleistet ist. Das Modul, das den Fingerabdruck erfasst, ist visuell abgegrenzt. Durch die Verwendung optischer Technologie, die sich auch in Smartphones wiederfindet, bietet es eine gute Leistung. Das Gerät hat eine um 15 Grad abgeschrägte Oberfläche, dadurch entspannt sich das Handgelenk bei der Benutzung. Um ein ordentliches Kabelmanagement zu ermöglichen, ist das Gehäuse teilweise offen gestaltet.

Begründung der Jury
Gute ergonomische Eigenschaften und eine nutzerfreundliche Funktionalität zeichnen die Gestaltung des Fingerabdruckerkennungsgeräts DingTalk M1C aus.

DingTalk M1X
Facial Recognition Device
Gesichtserkennungsgerät

Manufacturer
DingTalk (China) Technology
Information Co., Ltd., Hangzhou, China
In-house design
Web
www.dingtalk.com

The small size of the DingTalk M1X facial recognition device makes it stand out. It is equipped with an LED lamp that improves identification in the dark. Even if several faces need to be verified, it offers fast feedback. The circular device can be placed on a table or mounted on a wall. The casing successfully hides cables from view. The screen is designed to be concealed which gives the equipment a harmonious appearance. The user interface matches the round display.

Statement by the jury
The key to the DingTalk M1X facial recognition system is its compact dimensions which do not compromise its fast operation.

Das Gesichtserkennungsgerät DingTalk M1X fällt durch seine geringe Größe auf. Es ist mit einer LED-Leuchte ausgestattet, die die Identifizierung in dunkler Umgebung erleichtert. Auch wenn mehrere Gesichter überprüft werden, erfolgt ein schnelles Feedback. Das kreisrunde Gerät kann sowohl auf einen Tisch gestellt als auch an einer Wand montiert werden. In seinem Gehäuse lassen sich Kabel unsichtbar verstauen. Der Bildschirm ist verborgen gestaltet, was einen stimmigen Gesamteindruck erzeugt. Die Benutzeroberfläche passt sich dabei dem runden Display an.

Begründung der Jury
Eine kompakte Konstruktion mit geringen Ausmaßen bei gleichzeitig schneller Funktionsweise charakterisiert die Gestaltung des Gesichtserkennungsgeräts DingTalk M1X.

Unica
Switch and Socket Collection
Schalter- und Steckdosen-Kollektion

Manufacturer
Schneider-Electric, Eybens, France
In-house design
Guillaume Reiner
Design
Faltazi Design Studio, Nantes, France
EliumStudio, Paris, France
Normal Studio, Paris, France
Web
www.schneider-electric.com
www.faltazi.com
www.eliumstudio.com
www.normalstudio.com

Unica is a modular range that includes switches and sockets and provides 200 functions, often by combining different modules. The design focuses on delivering high quality as well as good ergonomic properties, durability and interoperability. In order to cater for different preferences, the range is available in three different design options: the timeless Unica Studio Line comes in a selection of colours and finishes. Unica Pro offers an innovative approach, while Unica Pure is skilfully designed to blend into high-end interiors.

Unica ist ein modulares Sortiment, das Schalter und Steckdosen umfasst. Es bietet 200 Funktionen, viele Module sind dabei miteinander verbunden. Im Fokus der Gestaltung stehen neben einem hohen Anspruch an Qualität gute ergonomische Eigenschaften, Robustheit sowie Interoperabilität. Um unterschiedlichen Vorlieben gerecht zu werden, ist das Sortiment in drei Designlinien erhältlich. Die zeitlose Unica Studio-Linie gibt es in vielen Farben und Ausführungen. Unica Pro ist ein innovatives Design und Unica Pure fügt sich gekonnt in hochwertige Interieurs ein.

Statement by the jury
The design of the Unica switch and socket collection appeals with its versatility that ensures it meets different design requirements.

Begründung der Jury
Die Gestaltung der Schalter- und Steckdosen-Kollektion Unica begeistert mit einer Vielfältigkeit, die verschiedensten Ansprüchen an Design gerecht wird.

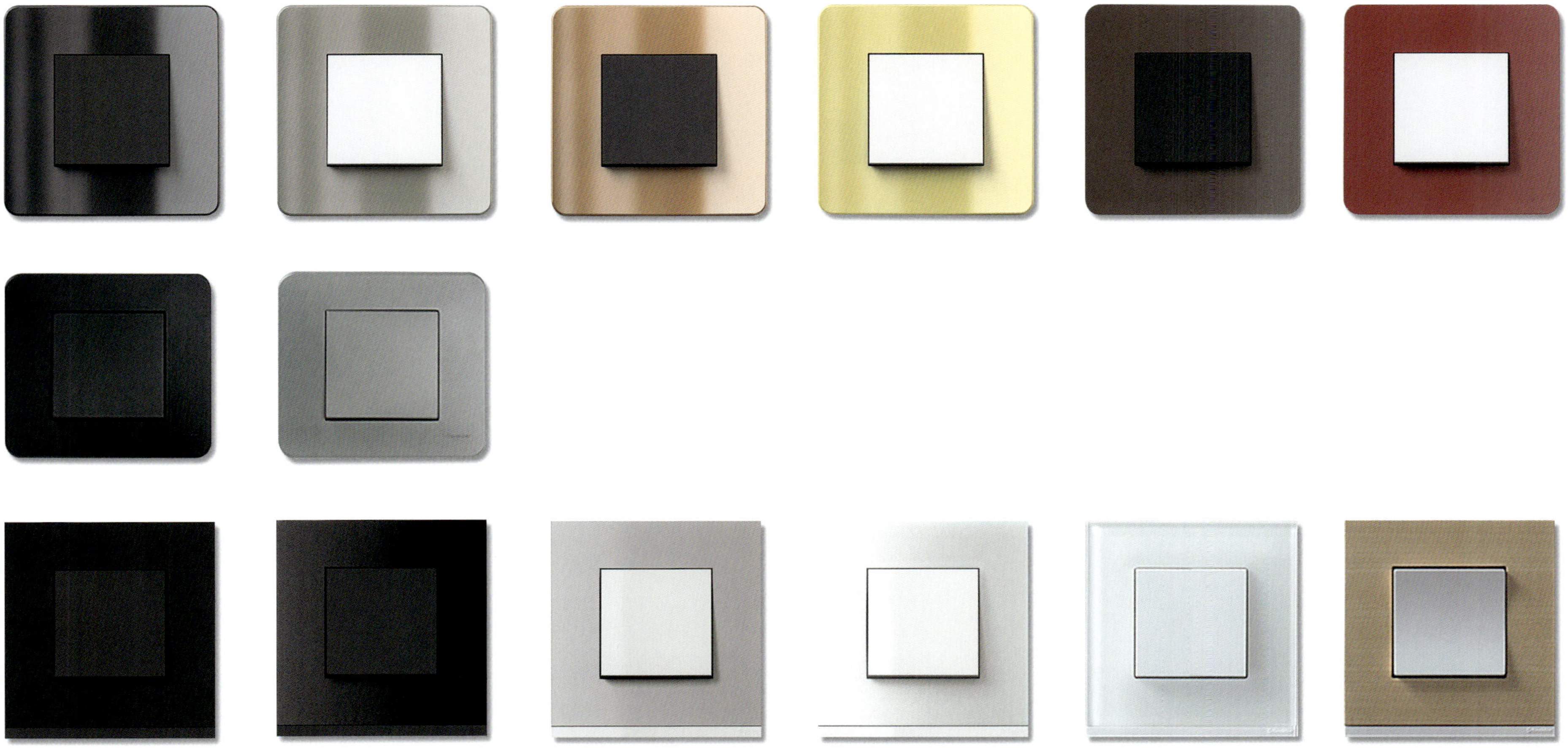

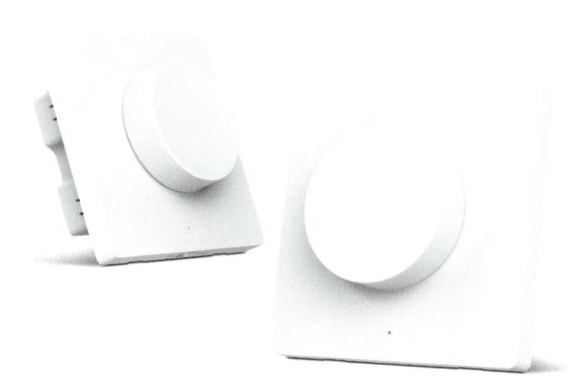

Yeelight
Smart Dimmer
Intelligenter Dimmer

Manufacturer
Qingdao Yeelink Information
Technology Co., Ltd., Qingdao, China
In-house design
Web
www.yeelight.com

Yeelight is a smart dimmer that is equipped with integrated Bluetooth mesh networking technology. It can be used to turn lights on and off and regulate brightness as required. Operation is easy. It can be managed via a remote control or a mobile device. It is furthermore possible to control the switch in real time from anywhere via voice commands or an app. The dimmer with its discreet white design has a concave knob set into the centre of a square frame. The on/off switch is located on the side.

Statement by the jury
With its deliberately understated appearance, the Yeelight dimmer will easily fit into different interiors and support smart lighting management.

Yeelight ist ein mit integrierter Bluetooth Mesh-Technologie ausgestatteter, intelligenter Dimmer, mit dem eine Leuchte ein- und ausgeschaltet und die Helligkeit wunschgemäß reguliert werden kann. Seine Handhabung ist einfach, die Steuerung erfolgt über eine Fernbedienung oder ein Mobilgerät. Darüber hinaus ist von überall eine Echtzeitkontrolle mittels Sprachsteuerung und App möglich. Der in einem dezenten Weiß gestaltete Dimmer hat in der Mitte des quadratischen Gehäuses einen konkav geformten Drehknopf. Der Ein/Aus-Schalter ist an der Seite platziert.

Begründung der Jury
Mit seinem bewusst dezenten Aussehen integriert sich der Dimmer Yeelight, der die intelligente Lichtsteuerung unterstützt, gut in verschiedene Interieurs.

Simon 50E Electronic
Detection and Control Devices
Erkennungs- und Steuergeräte

Manufacturer
Simon Electric (China) Co., Ltd.,
Shanghai, China
In-house design
Simon Electric Group – China Design Team
Web
www.simon.com.cn

The Simon 50E Electronic range includes the detection and operating controls necessary for a smart home system. The range consists of a time-delay switch, a sound/light sensor switch, a high sensitivity PIR sensor, a ground level light with PIR sensor, a dimmer and an all-in-one thermostat. All the devices are round and are set in a square frame. This gives them a cohesive look. As they are manufactured using some identical construction elements, production costs are kept low.

Statement by the jury
Thanks to their well-balanced design, the different smart home devices of the Simon 50E Electronic range form a visual entity.

Die Simon 50E Electronic-Serie umfasst Erkennungs- und Steuergeräte, die für ein Smart Home-System erforderlich sind. Sie besteht aus einem Zeitschalter, einem Ton/Licht-Sensorschalter, einem hochempfindlichen PIR-Sensor, einem Fußlicht mit PIR-Sensor, einem Dimmer sowie einem All-in-One-Thermostat. Alle Geräte haben eine gerundet gestaltete Funktionseinheit, die in ein quadratisches Gehäuse eingelassen ist. Dies sorgt für ein ruhiges Aussehen. Zudem weist ihre Konstruktion mehrere identische Bauteile auf, was die Produktionskosten senkt.

Begründung der Jury
Dank ihrer ausgewogenen Gestaltung bilden die verschiedenen Smart Home-Geräte der Simon 50E Electronic-Serie eine visuelle Einheit.

DELTA zita
Switch and Socket Collection
Schalter- und
Steckdosen-Kollektion

Manufacturer
Siemens Ltd., China, Shanghai, China
In-house design
Web
www.siemens.com.cn

The DELTA zita switch and socket collection stands out for its simple and yet trendy appearance. The fluid operation of the large rocker switch, which is pleasant to the touch, recalls the movement of a wave. The LED indicator is as small as a pinhole and diffuses soft light that is not intrusive even in bedrooms. The entire collection is characterised by a high degree of durability, impact resistance, safety and stability, as well as easy installation. The range is available in different colours including white, gold and silver.

Statement by the jury
The design of the DELTA zita switch and socket collection successfully combines robust material properties with a modern appearance.

Die Schalter- und Steckdosen-Kollektion DELTA zita zeichnet sich durch eine schlichte und dennoch trendbewusste Anmutung aus. Die fließende Bewegung des großen, haptisch angenehmen Wippschalters erinnert an eine Meereswelle. Die LED-Anzeige ist klein wie ein Nadelloch und spendet ein sanftes Licht, das auch im Schlafbereich nicht störend wirkt. Die ganze Kollektion weist ein hohes Maß an Haltbarkeit, Schlagfestigkeit, Sicherheit und Stabilität sowie eine einfache Installation auf. Sie ist in verschiedenen Farben, u. a. in Weiß, Gold und Silber, erhältlich.

Begründung der Jury
Die Gestaltung der Schalter- und Steckdosen-Kollektion DELTA zita vereint überzeugend robuste Materialeigenschaften mit einem modernen Erscheinungsbild.

G28
Socket
Steckdose

Manufacturer
Bull Group Incorporated Company, Cixi, China
In-house design
Web
www.gongniuchazuo.com.cn

G28 is a modular socket that adapts to the user's needs in different situations. Thus, the demands of different environments such as the living room or kitchen can be met in accordance with needs. Although the socket is based on a multi-modular concept, it requires installation of just one cable, which makes it safe and convenient to use. Furthermore, it meets the 86-type models prevalent in China. The socket has an even, smooth surface and is pleasant to the touch and easy to clean.

Statement by the jury
The well-engineered design of the modular G28 socket is convincing because it uses technology in a way that is suitable for the demands of a modern household.

G28 ist eine modulare Steckdose, die den Bedürfnissen des Nutzers mithilfe verschiedener Szenarien entgegenkommt. So lassen sich Ansprüche in verschiedenen Umgebungen, wie z. B. im Wohnzimmer oder in der Küche, wunschgemäß erfüllen. Obwohl die Steckdose das Mehrmodul-Konzept umsetzt, muss nur eine Leitung gelegt werden, was komfortabel und sicher ist. Weiterhin entspricht sie den in China vorhandenen Typ 86-Modellen. Die Steckdose hat eine ebenmäßige, glatte Oberfläche, die eine angenehme Haptik bietet und zudem leicht zu reinigen ist.

Begründung der Jury
Die ausgereifte Gestaltung der modularen Steckdose G28 überzeugt mit einem Technikeinsatz, der den Anforderungen eines modernen Haushalts gerecht wird.

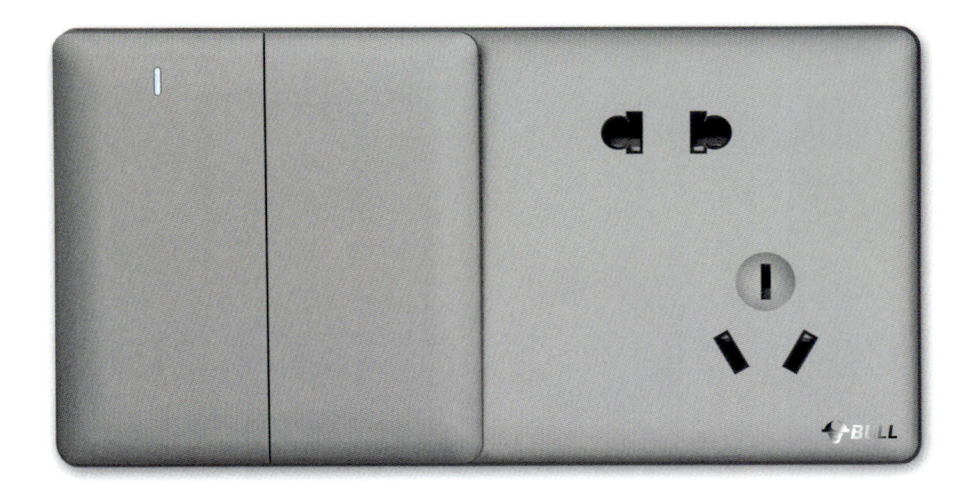

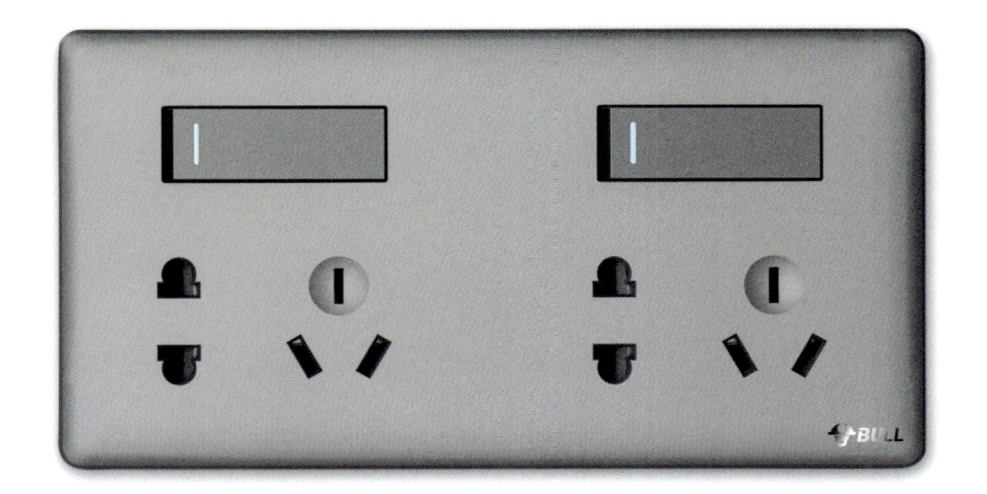

EVOline One
Socket
Steckdose

Manufacturer
Schulte Elektrotechnik GmbH & Co. KG, Lüdenscheid, Germany
In-house design
Siegfried Schulte
Web
www.evoline.com

EVOline One provides power and data access in a compact form both for residential properties and work spaces. The space-saving design of the socket makes it possible to integrate it into all types of sheet material and upholstered furniture both on the horizontal and vertical plane. The round shape allows for quick installation, as a circular hole of 54 mm in diameter is all that is required. Clamps ensure a secure hold on panels that are more than 9 mm thick. By using different modules, the socket can be adapted to suit a very wide range of requirements.

EVOline One bietet sowohl im Privatbereich als auch am Arbeitsplatz einen kompakten Strom- und Datenzugang. Die platzsparend gestaltete Steckdose kann horizontal oder vertikal in alle Plattenmaterialien und in mit Polstern bekleidete Möbel eingebaut werden. Ihr rundes Design ermöglicht eine schnelle Montage, für die lediglich ein Lochausschnitt von 54 mm Durchmesser nötig ist. Klemmstücke sorgen dabei für den sicheren Halt ab einer Plattenstärke von 9 mm. Dank vieler Moduleinsätze lässt sich die Steckdose unterschiedlichen Anforderungen anpassen.

Statement by the jury
The cleverly thought-out concept of the EVOline One socket marries high functionality with an aesthetically pleasing appearance.

Begründung der Jury
Das klug durchdachte Gestaltungskonzept der Steckdose EVOline One bringt hohe Funktionalität mit einem formschönen Erscheinungsbild in Einklang.

Square 1
Socket
Steckdose

Manufacturer
Avolt AB, Stockholm, Sweden
In-house design
Johan Runströmer, Viktor Lundberg
Web
www.avolt.com

Often, apart from built-in sockets, an additional power source is needed. Square 1 solves this problem in a manner that seems timeless. It was inspired by Bruno Munari's trilogy "Square Circle Triangle" and is a homage to the simplicity of shapes. The socket adheres to the principles of minimalism and takes the form of a simple cube, thereby achieving a very individual look without detracting from the interior. Manufacture is environmentally friendly as 20 per cent of the raw materials used are recycled plastics while the packaging is produced entirely from recycled paper.

Oftmals wird neben den fest eingebauten Steckdosen eine weitere Stromquelle benötigt. Dieses Problem löst Square 1 auf zeitlos anmutende Weise. Inspiriert von Bruno Munaris Trilogie „Square Circle Triangle" ist ihre Gestaltung eine Hommage an die einfache Form. Im Sinne des Minimalismus präsentiert sich die Steckdose als schlichter Würfel. Damit erhält sie ein eigenständiges Aussehen, ohne jedoch die Innenarchitektur zu beeinträchtigen. Hergestellt wird sie umweltfreundlich zu 20 Prozent aus recycelten Plastikmaterialien, die Verpackung besteht vollständig aus Recyclingpapier.

Statement by the jury
The uncompromisingly minimalist use of forms and sustainability-focused production make the design of the Square 1 socket stand out.

Begründung der Jury
Die Gestaltung der Steckdose Square 1 begeistert mit einer kompromisslos minimalistischen Formensprache und einer auf Nachhaltigkeit bedachten Herstellung.

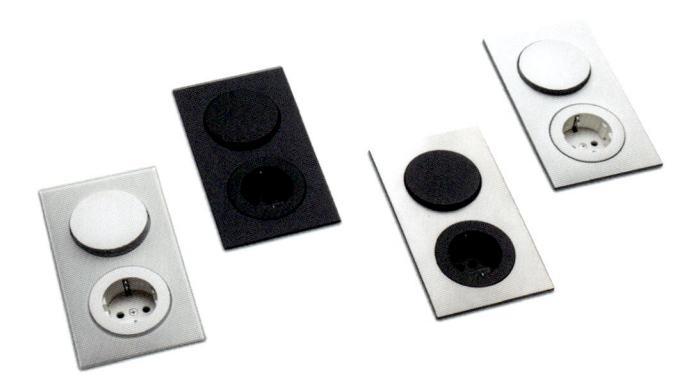

Berker R.8
Switch Collection
Schalter-Kollektion

Manufacturer
Berker GmbH & Co. KG,
Schalksmühle, Germany
Design
Hager Electro SAS, Corporate Design
Hager Group (Erwin van Handenhoven),
Obernai, France
Web
www.berker.com
www.hager.com

The minimalist design of the Berker R.8 range of switches conveys the idea "less is more". The frames of this filigree collection only have a width of 3 mm – thus the socket is almost flush with the wall. They are made of high-quality materials such a glass, aluminium or stainless steel. The rounded central inserts are combined with angular frames. The collection comprises flush-mounted inserts and KNX sensors and offers a platform that can be individually equipped with various inserts.

Statement by the jury
The minimalist and elegant appearance of the Berker R.8 switch collection attracts attention with its very flat construction.

Das minimalistische Design der Schalter-Kollektion Berker R.8 transportiert die Idee „Weniger ist mehr". Das filigrane Sortiment zeichnet sich durch eine Rahmenhöhe von nur 3 mm aus – damit liegen die Schalter beinahe plan auf der Wand. Sie bestehen aus hochwertigen Materialien wie Glas, Aluminium oder Edelstahl. Die runden Zentraleinsätze werden dabei mit kantigen Rahmen kombiniert. Die Kollektion umfasst Unterputz-Einsätze einschließlich KNX-Sensoren. Sie bietet eine Plattform, die mit verschiedenen Einsätzen individuell bestückt werden kann.

Begründung der Jury
Die sowohl minimalistische wie edle Gestaltung der Schalter-Kollektion Berker R.8 zieht die Aufmerksamkeit durch ihre sehr flache Konstruktion auf sich.

Mini Timer
Timer Socket
Timer-Steckdose

Manufacturer
Bull Group Incorporated Company,
Cixi, China
In-house design
Web
www.gongniuchazuo.com.cn

Mini Timer is an easy to manage socket with a timer function suitable for the power supply of mobile phones, batteries and much other equipment. The design concept is noticeable for its break with the typical industrial appearance of existing timer sockets and instead seeks to align with the appeal of digital products. The device is made from a PC/ABS composite which gives it a high level of stability, low flammability, impact resistance and anti-cracking properties. It has a long service life, is non-toxic and recyclable.

Statement by the jury
The contemporary design of this timer socket impresses with a style-conscious appearance and cleverly conceived, environmentally friendly use of materials.

Mini Timer ist eine einfach handhabbare Steckdose mit Timing-Funktion, die sich für die Stromversorgung von Mobiltelefonen, Akkus und vielen anderen Geräten eignet. Sie fällt durch ein Designkonzept auf, das das übliche industrielle Erscheinungsbild durchbricht und sich stattdessen an der Anmutung digitaler Produkte orientiert. Das Gerät ist aus einem PC/ABS-Verbundstoff hergestellt, was für eine hohe Stabilität, Schwerentflammbarkeit, Schlagfestigkeit und Anti-Rissbildung sorgt. Es hat eine lange Lebensdauer, ist ungiftig und recycelbar.

Begründung der Jury
Die zeitgemäße Gestaltung dieser Timer-Steckdose überzeugt mit einer stilbewussten Anmutung und einem klug durchdachten, umweltfreundlichen Materialeinsatz.

Eve Energy Strip
Smart Multiple Socket
Intelligente Mehrfachsteckdose

Manufacturer
Eve Systems, Munich, Germany
Design
Reneltdesign (Oliver Renelt),
Hamburg, Germany
Web
www.evehome.com
www.reneltdesign.de

The matt black body of this smart multiple socket, its aluminium frame and robust cabling all communicate sturdiness. The sockets that also come with power surge protection are arranged to offer sufficient space for large power supply adapters. LED icons indicate the operating status of each of the sockets, which can be operated via Apple mobile devices. It is possible to programme timings so that any connected equipment is switched on and off automatically. Child proofing as well as consumption cost calculations round off the features.

Statement by the jury
The well-engineered design of this smart multiple socket manages to give a technical smart home product a stylish appearance.

Der mattschwarze Korpus dieser intelligenten Mehrfachsteckdose, der Aluminiumrahmen sowie das robuste Kabel vermitteln Solidität. Die mit Überspannungsschutz ausgestatteten Steckdosen sind so angeordnet, dass sie auch großen Netzteilen Platz bieten. LED-Icons zeigen den Betriebszustand der einzelnen Steckdosen, die mit Apple-Mobilgeräten gesteuert werden, an. Es lassen sich Zeitpläne programmieren, sodass sich angeschlossene Geräte selbsttätig an- und ausschalten. Eine Kindersicherung sowie eine Verbrauchskostenberechnung ergänzen die Ausstattung.

Begründung der Jury
Der ausgereiften Gestaltung dieser intelligenten Mehrfachsteckdose gelingt es, einem technischen Smart Home-Produkt eine elegante Anmutung zu verleihen.

Cable Reel
Kabeltrommel

Manufacturer
Bull Group Incorporated Company,
Cixi, China
In-house design
Web
www.gongniuchazuo.com.cn

This small cable reel with a socket is ideal for use in the home. With it, the length of cable can be chosen according to individual needs and it thus helps to get around the problems that arise in situations when it is difficult to manage the cable, for example when charging an electric car or cooking with an electric saucepan. The cable reel is convenient and safe to handle and keeps things tidy after use. If desired, the uniform and compact reel may be hung up to store it.

Statement by the jury
Practical value and a high degree of suitability for daily use characterise the refined design of this compact cable reel.

Diese kleine Kabeltrommel mit Steckdose eignet sich für den Gebrauch im eigenen Zuhause. Mit ihr kann der Nutzer die Länge eines Stromkabels genau seinen Bedürfnissen anpassen. Auf diese Weise lösen sich die Probleme in Situationen, in denen die Handhabung eines Kabels schwierig sein kann, z. B. beim Aufladen eines Elektroautos oder beim Kochen mit einem Elektrotopf. Die Kabelrolle ist einfach und sicher zu handhaben und sorgt zudem für Ordnung nach dem Gebrauch. Zur Aufbewahrung kann die homogen und kompakt gestaltete Kabeltrommel auch aufgehängt werden.

Begründung der Jury
Ein praktischer Nutzwert und ein hohes Maß an Alltagstauglichkeit charakterisieren die raffinierte Gestaltung dieser kompakten Kabeltrommel.

VERVE AIR
Ventilation Outlet
Lüftungsauslass

Manufacturer
Georg Bechter Licht, Langenegg, Austria
In-house design
Web
www.georgbechterlicht.at

Indispensable technical components are often perceived as disruptive elements that are out of place in a room. The design of Verve Air addresses this issue and combines a ventilation outlet with an appealing exterior and built-in lighting while keeping the device's actual function invisible. The ventilation outlet is flush-mounted into ceilings and walls. The shape of the opening ensures that the air evenly disperses before it flows into the room. Depending on position and installation direction, it is therefore possible to achieve different airflow directions.

Statement by the jury
The fascinating design concept of the Verve Air ventilation outlet manages to give a technical building component an elegantly discreet appearance.

Notwendige technische Komponenten werden in einem Raum oft als Fremdkörper wahrgenommen. Die Gestaltung von Verve Air nimmt sich dieser Problematik an und kombiniert einen Lüftungsauslass mit ansprechendem Aussehen und integrierter Beleuchtung, ohne dass dabei die eigentliche Funktion sichtbar ist. Der Lüftungsauslass wird flächenbündig in die Decke oder die Wand eingearbeitet. Durch die Form der Öffnung verteilt sich die Luft, bevor sie in den Raum strömt. Je nach Position und Einbaurichtung können so unterschiedliche Luftströme realisiert werden.

Begründung der Jury
Das faszinierende Gestaltungskonzept des Lüftungsauslasses Verve Air schafft es, einem technischen Bauteil ein edel zurückhaltendes Aussehen zu verleihen.

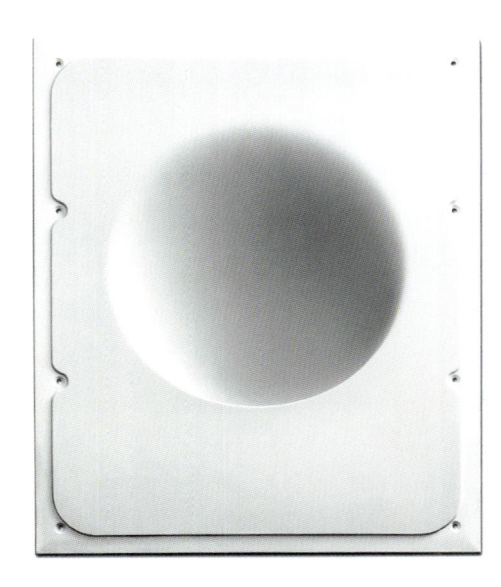

IoT Air Quality Monitor
IoT-Luftqualitätsüberwachungsgerät

Manufacturer
LG Uplus, Seoul, South Korea
In-house design
Seoyeon Lee
Web
www.uplus.co.kr

This device can measure PM 2.5 and 10 fine dust particles, as well as temperature and humidity levels in real time. If readings indicate poor air quality levels, an indicator light and a message delivered via an app alert users and then automatically set the air purifier in motion. The small, compact monitoring device can be powered with batteries and comes equipped with shoulder straps. This makes it easy for users to carry with them and take air-quality readings wherever they may be. The generous LCD display allows for good legibility even from a distance.

Statement by the jury
The clever design of this portable, smart fine dust and air-quality monitoring device captivates attention by its numerous user-friendly details.

Dieses Gerät kann in Echtzeit Feinstaub der Standards PM 2,5 und 10, Temperatur sowie Luftfeuchtigkeit messen. Bei schlechten Werten warnt es den Nutzer durch eine Leuchtanzeige und eine Benachrichtigung per App und steuert automatisch einen Luftreiniger. Das kleine, kompakt gestaltete Überwachungsgerät kann mit Batterien betrieben werden und ist mit einem Trageriemen ausgestattet. Daher eignet es sich gut zur Mitnahme und es lassen sich überall Messungen der Luft durchführen. Die großzügige LCD-Anzeige ermöglicht dabei eine gute Sicht auch von Weitem.

Begründung der Jury
Die clevere Gestaltung dieses tragbaren, intelligenten Feinstaub- und Luftüberwachungsgeräts besticht durch zahlreiche nutzerfreundliche Details.

Cavius Build In System
Safety Devices
Sicherheitsgeräte

Manufacturer
Cavius Aps, Silkeborg, Denmark
In-house design
Web
www.cavius.com

This range of built-in safety devices includes a smoke, a heat and a CO_2 alarm. They are impressively small, have a very shallow profile and are suitable for use as stand-alone models or as part of the Cavius Wireless Alarm family. A special feature of the smoke alarm is its certification status. Due to the use of cutting-edge software, it comes with a fire detection algorithm that offers functions otherwise only found in expensive analogue detection systems.

Statement by the jury
The clever design of this built-in range of safety equipment brings together an impressively small size with technically highly sophisticated features.

Diese Einbau-Serie von Sicherheitsgeräten umfasst einen Rauch-, einen Wärme- sowie einen CO_2-Melder. Sie sind beeindruckend klein konstruiert und weisen ein sehr flaches Profil auf. Sie eignen sich für die Montage als Einzelgerät, ergänzen aber auch die Produkte der Cavius Wireless Alarm Family. Eine Besonderheit ist die Zertifizierung des Rauchmelders. Aufgrund des Einsatzes einer modernen Software enthält er einen Branderkennungsalgorithmus mit ähnlichen Funktionen wie sie sonst in hochpreisigen analogen Erkennungssystemen vorhanden sind.

Begründung der Jury
Die kluge Gestaltung dieser Einbau-Sicherheitsgeräte bringt eine beeindruckend kleine Bauweise mit hohen technischen Ansprüchen in Einklang.

Motion and Presence Detector
Bewegungs- und Präsenzmelder

Manufacturer
Niko NV, Sint-Niklaas, Belgium
In-house design
Arne Desmet, Pieter de Vos
Web
www.niko.eu

This slim motion and presence detector has an innovative mounting bracket system which makes it easier to attach to the ceiling. It consists of two rings that are screwed onto each other. This allows for installation on any type of ceiling material without causing damage. Once installed, the detector can be programmed remotely using Bluetooth and the associated app. It is possible to save and reuse configurations, as well as programme several devices at once.

Statement by the jury
The design of this motion and presence detector is innovative and user-friendly. Its slim structure makes it pleasing to the eye.

Dieser schlanke Bewegungs- und Präsenzmelder verfügt über ein innovatives Befestigungssystem, das die Montage an der Zimmerdecke vereinfacht. Es besteht aus zwei Ringen, die miteinander verschraubt werden. Auf diese Weise kann die Halterung in jedem Deckenmaterial montiert werden, ohne dabei Schaden zu verursachen. Anschließend lässt sich der Detektor sicher aus der Ferne über Bluetooth mithilfe einer App programmieren. Konfigurationen können dabei gespeichert und wiederverwendet werden, auch lassen sich mehrere Geräte gleichzeitig programmieren.

Begründung der Jury
Innovativ und nutzerfreundlich ist die Gestaltung dieses Bewegungs- und Präsenzmelders. Darüber hinaus gefällt seine schlanke Konstruktionsweise.

SieAir
Air Quality Detector
Luftqualitätsmessgerät

Manufacturer
Siemens Ltd., China, Shanghai, China
In-house design
Qi Yu
Web
www.siemens.com.cn

The both simple and stylish looking air quality detector SieAir consists of two components that may be used separately: a cube and a docking station. The easy to transport, two-tone cube can be used anywhere to measure air quality. It is equipped with sensors that accurately measure fine dust and formaldehyde levels as well as temperature and humidity. The readings are displayed on the screen of the docking station, but can also be called up on mobile devices from at a distance.

Statement by the jury
The elegantly proportioned air quality detector SieAir is particularly easy to transport and is therefore very versatile in use.

Das gleichermaßen schlicht wie stilvoll gestaltete Luftqualitätsmessgerät SieAir besteht aus zwei separat verwendbaren Komponenten, einem Kubus und einer Dockingstation. Der einfach zu transportierende, zweifarbige Kubus lässt sich dabei überall zur Messung der Luftqualität einsetzen. Er ist mit Sensoren ausgestattet, die präzise den Feinstaub- sowie den Formaldehydgehalt, die Temperatur und die Luftfeuchtigkeit erfassen. Die Daten werden am Bildschirm der Dockingstation angezeigt, können aber auch über Mobilgeräte aus der Ferne abgerufen werden.

Begründung der Jury
Das formschön gestaltete Luftqualitätsmessgerät SieAir lässt sich besonders leicht transportieren und bietet so vielfältige Einsatzmöglichkeiten.

Siterwell GS546
Smoke Detector
Rauchmelder

Manufacturer
Siterwell Electronics Co., Limited,
Ningbo, China
In-house design
Cheng Chen, Honghe Xiao
Web
www.china-siter.com

With a thickness of only 23.5 mm, this smoke detector is particularly flat and blends discreetly into any setting. The device shows a minimalist design and features a large, flush integrated button which allows intuitive operation. The implied representation of a home conveys a sense of security. The smoke detector is equipped with a reliable self-test function, preventing both failures in the event of fire and false alarms, which could be triggered by the ingress of water vapour.

Statement by the jury
This elegant smoke detector surprises with its slim shape and convinces with a high level of reliability.

Mit einer Korpushöhe von 23,5 mm ist dieser Rauchmelder besonders flach konstruiert und fügt sich so dezent in sein Umfeld ein. Das minimalistisch gestaltete Gerät verfügt über eine große, flächenbündig integrierte Taste, die eine intuitive Bedienung ermöglicht. Die darauf angedeutete Darstellung eines Zuhauses vermittelt Sicherheit. Der Rauchmelder ist mit einer zuverlässigen Selbsttestfunktion ausgestattet, die sowohl Ausfälle im Brandfall als auch Fehlalarme, wie sie durch das Eindringen von Wasserdampf ausgelöst werden können, verhindert.

Begründung der Jury
Dieser elegant anmutende Rauchmelder überrascht durch seinen flachen Korpus, zudem überzeugt er mit Zuverlässigkeit.

Siterwell GS524N
Smart Smoke Detector
Intelligenter Rauchmelder

Manufacturer
Siterwell Electronics Co., Limited,
Ningbo, China
In-house design
Cheng Chen, Honghe Xiao
Web
www.china-siter.com

This smart smoke detector is equipped with NB-IoT technology to guarantee the timely warning of a fire even if the power supply or the Internet connection is down. It can interact with other smart devices, even if remotely located, and it may, for example, automatically trigger a sprinkler system and open smoke ventilation windows. In addition, the device is able to alert the fire department about an emergency independently. In this way, it provides protection even if no one is at home.

Statement by the jury
As a technically sophisticated product solution, this smart smoke detector offers a high degree of safety, especially in combination with other devices.

Um die rechtzeitige Warnung vor einem Brand selbst bei einem Strom- oder Netzwerkausfall zu gewährleisten, ist dieser intelligente Rauchmelder mit NB-IoT-Technologie ausgestattet. Er kann mit anderen Geräten, auch wenn diese entfernt untergebracht sind, interagieren und so beispielsweise die automatische Aktivierung einer Sprinkleranlage auslösen und Rauchabzugsfenster öffnen. Darüber hinaus kann das Gerät selbstständig die Feuerwehr über einen Notfall alarmieren. Auf diese Weise bietet es Schutz, auch wenn niemand zu Hause ist.

Begründung der Jury
Als technisch ausgereifte Produktlösung bietet dieser intelligente Rauchmelder insbesondere im Verbund mit weiteren Geräten ein hohes Maß an Sicherheit.

Dali
Motion and Presence Detector
Bewegungs- und Präsenzmelder

Manufacturer
Niko NV, Sint-Niklaas, Belgium
In-house design
Arne Desmet, Pieter de Vos
Web
www.niko.eu

The Dali motion and presence detector is used to operate lighting. The device, that does not look like a piece of technology, but whose flat shape rather makes it appear like part of the home decor, is programmed via an app. All users require is a Bluetooth connection. They do not need to touch any keys on the device. The imaginative mounting bracket system is easy to use. Instead of the traditional springs, it works with two rings that are screwed onto each other. This allows for installation on any type of ceiling material without causing damage.

Statement by the jury
The Dali motion and presence detector stands out for the successful way in which it combines high functionality with a look that suits the home decor.

Der flach konstruierte Bewegungs- und Präsenzmelder Dali dient der Beleuchtungssteuerung. Programmiert wird das Gerät, das weniger technisch, sondern mehr wie ein Wohnaccessoire anmutet, mittels einer App. Es ist lediglich eine Bluetooth-Verbindung nötig, der Nutzer muss keine Tasten am Gerät bedienen. Einfallsreich ist das einfach zu handhabende Befestigungssystem. Hierbei werden keine Federn verwendet, sondern einfach zwei Ringe miteinander verschraubt. Dies erlaubt die Montage in jedem Deckenmaterial, ohne dass dabei etwas beschädigt wird.

Begründung der Jury
Der Bewegungs- und Präsenzmelder Dali zeichnet sich durch die gelungene Kombination von hoher Funktionalität und einem wohnlich anmutenden Aussehen aus.

The Wall
Multifunctional Wall
Multifunktionswand

Manufacturer
Orea AG, Zürich, Switzerland

In-house design
Orea Design

Web
www.orea-kuechen.ch

reddot award 2019
best of the best

Imagination and design
By creating expressive forms for possible scenarios of future living, design has a significant influence on the planning and realisation of new ideas. Design thus also shapes the zeitgeist. The Wall is a novel modular rear panel system available in different surfaces that are easy to use and configure in a variety of ways thanks to being a sophisticated multifunctional assembly system. Their design combines modern technology with practical interior applications developed for current living environments. The innovative, light sandwich construction integrates mounting rails to form a modular, flexible construction wall. Connected in four phases, the rails allow a diverse range of assemblies, while the 6 mm thin shelves feature integrated LEDs ensuring that, when desired, they effectively catch the eye. USB docks can be added at the planning stage for creating individual arrangements with electricity and light exactly where wanted. Moreover, kitchen scales, contactless charging units, spotlights and other applications can also be added. All the accessories for this multifunctional, luminous rear panel system are freely positionable on the tracks, allowing for fully customisable configurations. The panel can be assembled quickly and easily. The sophisticated structural system features a minimalist and modern design vocabulary for staging and highlighting objects as needed.

Design und Imagination
Indem es möglichen Szenarien künftigen Wohnens formal Ausdruck verleiht, kann Design die Planung und Realisierung neuer Ideen maßgeblich beeinflussen. Es prägt so auch den Zeitgeist. The Wall ist ein neuartiges modulares Rückwandsystem, das in unterschiedlichen Oberflächen erhältlich ist und auf der Grundlage einer durchdachten Multifunktionalität vielfältig konfiguriert werden kann. Seine Gestaltung vereint moderne Technik mit nah an aktuellen Lebenswelten entwickelten Möglichkeiten des Einsatzes im Interieur. Die innovative, leichte Sandwichkonstruktion integriert Aufnahmeschienen als modulare, flexible Bauward. Dabei erlauben vierphasige Stromschienen diverse Nutzungsmöglichkeiten, und die 6 mm dünnen Tablare sorgen durch integrierte LED-Leuchten für einen wirkungsvollen Blickfang im gewünschten Kontext. Individuell den Bedürfnissen angepasst, können in die jeweilige Planung ebenfalls USB-Docks mit einbezogen werden. Sie dienen der Bereitstellung von Licht und Strom dort, wo man es wünscht. Zudem können Küchenwaagen, kontaktlose Aufladegeräte, Spotleuchten und weitere Elemente ergänzt werden. Das gesamte Zubehör der multifunktionalen und leuchtenden Rückwand ist in den Schienen frei positionierbar und ermöglicht eine individuelle Nutzung. Die Wand kann rasch und unkompliziert montiert werden. Das filigrane Tragsystem unterstützt eine minimalistische und moderne Formensprache und setzt gewünschte Objekte als Highlights in Szene.

Statement by the jury
This multifunctional wall fascinates with the idea of creatively expanding an otherwise traditional construction with various elements. It allows to easily plan and precisely add electricity for light, as well as other user-defined elements, wherever needed for customisation. The result are fascinating additions to interiors – additions that are highly technical in nature, but exude a very natural look. The panel thus realises a concept through a captivating simple logic.

Begründung der Jury
Bei dieser Multifunktionswand begeistert die Idee, eine im Grunde klassische Konstruktion auf vielfältige und kreative Weise zu erweitern. Sie ermöglicht ein einfaches Hinzufügen und punktgenaues Bereitstellen von Licht und Strom sowie anderen benutzerdefinierten Elementen. Auf eine hochtechnisch und zugleich natürlich anmutende Weise lassen sich im Interieur so faszinierende Ergebnisse erzielen. Es wird dabei ein in seiner einfachen Logik bestechendes Konzept realisiert.

Designer portrait
See page 38
Siehe Seite 38

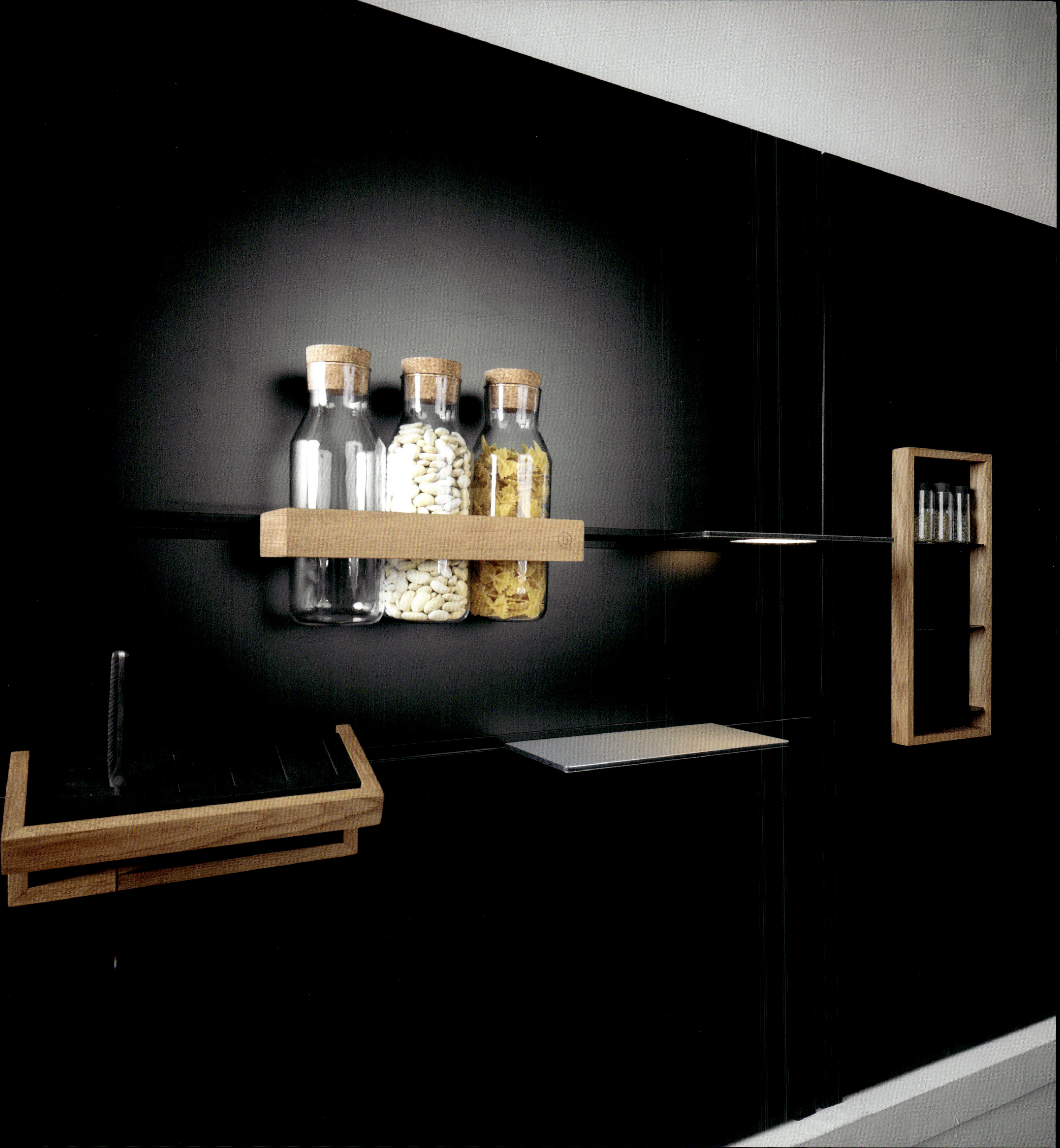

Groveneer
Self-Adhesive Oak Veneer
Selbstklebendes Eichenfurnier

Manufacturer
Groveneer OÜ, Tallinn, Estonia
Design
Mihkel Masso Studio, MMIDS OÜ (Karl Saluveer, Mihkel Masso), Tallinn, Estonia
Web
www.groveneer.com
www.mihkelmasso.com

Groveneer is a self-adhesive natural-oak veneer that can easily be applied to most surfaces. Users simply remove the protective film and it can then be pasted, no tools nor special skills are needed, making it easy to handle for both professionals and DIY enthusiasts. The natural product is finished with a high-quality hard-wax oil to resist the changes of indoor climate. The various designs and colours combine well to form unique patterns. Suitable for both walls and furniture, the veneer can be used to decorate home and office environments.

Groveneer ist ein selbstklebendes Natur-Eichenfurnier, das sich einfach auf den meisten Oberflächen anbringen lässt. Es muss nur die Schutzfolie entfernt und dann aufgeklebt werden. Dafür sind weder Werkzeuge noch spezielle Fähigkeiten nötig, sodass es sich von Profis wie auch von Heimwerkern gut handhaben lässt. Das Naturprodukt ist mit einem hochwertigen Hartwachsöl bearbeitet, um Veränderungen des Raumklimas standzuhalten. Verschiedene Dessins und Farben lassen sich zu unverwechselbaren Mustern kombinieren. Das Furnier ist für Wände und Möbel geeignet und passt sich Wohn- sowie Büroumgebungen an.

Statement by the jury
The concept of this self-adhesive oak veneer is focused on easy application and handling, which encourages creative room and furniture design.

Begründung der Jury
Das Konzept dieses selbstklebenden Eichenfurniers ist auf eine einfache Handhabung ausgerichtet, die zur kreativen Raum- und Möbelgestaltung animiert.

JungleWall
Sound-Absorbing Wall Covering
Schallabsorbierende Wandverkleidung

Manufacturer
Glimakra of Sweden, Glimakra, Sweden
Design
Superlab (Niklas Madsen), Helsingborg, Sweden
Web
www.glimakra.com
www.superlab.se

Nature was the source of inspiration for the design of this wall covering, a product that offers both visual and acoustic relaxation. JungleWall consists of sound-absorbing leaves in different shapes. They are made of felt and come in a range of green tones. They are mounted on the wall so that there is a space between leaf and wall. This gives a very natural appearance and creates the impression as if the leaves were moving. In addition, the choice of material in combination with the distance from the wall creates good sound absorption.

Inspirationsquelle für die Gestaltung dieser Wandverkleidung ist die Natur, die visuell wie auch akustisch Erholung bietet. JungleWall besteht aus schallabsorbierenden Blättern in verschiedenen Mustern. Sie sind aus Filz in unterschiedlichen Grüntönen gefertigt und können so befestigt werden, dass ein Abstand zur Wand entsteht. Dies erzeugt eine natürliche Anmutung, es entsteht der Eindruck, als würden sich die Blätter bewegen. Darüber hinaus unterstützt das verwendete Material zusammen mit dem Abstand zur Wand die gute Schallabsorption.

Statement by the jury
JungleWall captivates with a natural, expressive appearance and creates a calm atmosphere which is pleasant for the senses.

Begründung der Jury
JungleWall besticht mit einer natürlichen und zugleich ausdrucksstarken Anmutung sowie ruhefördernden Eigenschaften und bietet so Erholung für die Sinne.

Wing
Curtain Traversing System
Wellenvorhang-System

Manufacturer
interstil Diedrichsen GmbH & Co. KG,
Steinhagen, Germany
Design
Design AG – Frank Greiser &
Brigitte Adrian GbR,
Rheda-Wiedenbrück, Germany
Web
www.interstil.de
www.design-ag.de

Wing is an internal curtain traversing system of a minimalist design whose wave formations make it appear to float. Conventional tracks of this type generally require two brackets at their ends. This model, by contrast, requires just a single bracket, positioned in the centre. It can support a track with a span of up to 300 cm without the profile ends drooping. This is achieved with the help of the proprietary integral technology which allows poles and profiles to be aligned completely straight.

Statement by the jury
The Wing curtain traversing system attracts attention with a compelling construction method and an elegantly appealing appearance.

Wing ist ein minimalistisch gestaltetes Wellenvorhang-Innenlaufsystem, das einen schwebenden Eindruck vermittelt. Normalerweise benötigen Schienen dieser Art an den äußeren Enden zwei Träger. Dieses Modell kommt hingegen mit nur einem einzigen, mittig positionierten Träger aus. Dieser hält eine Schiene mit einer Spannweite von bis zu 300 cm, ohne dass sich dabei die Profilenden absenken. Dies wird durch die herstellereigene integral-Technik, mit der sich Stangen und Profile einhundertprozentig gerade ausrichten lassen, erreicht.

Begründung der Jury
Das Wellenvorhang-System Wing zieht die Aufmerksamkeit mit einer überzeugenden Konstruktionsweise und einem edel anmutenden Erscheinungsbild auf sich.

W4
Curtain Traversing System
Wellenvorhang-System

Manufacturer
interstil Diedrichsen GmbH & Co. KG,
Steinhagen, Germany
Design
Design AG – Frank Greiser &
Brigitte Adrian GbR,
Rheda-Wiedenbrück, Germany
Web
www.interstil.de
www.design-ag.de

The slightly convex W4 traversing profile is both simple and elegant. What is notable about this curtain traversing system is that the special, organic-looking construction of the wall brackets creates a fluid transition to the profile. The interplay of the high-gloss wall connector with a track of matt silver creates an expressive appearance which allows the system to blend seamlessly into contemporary interiors.

Statement by the jury
The design with matt and high-gloss elements gives the W4 curtain traversing system a both expressive and elegant look.

Schlicht und elegant zugleich präsentiert sich das leicht konvex geformte Innenlauf-Profil W4. Besonders auffällig ist bei diesem Wellenvorhang-System der Wandträger, dessen besondere, organisch anmutende Bauform einen fließenden Übergang zum Profil schafft. Dabei erzielt vor allem das Zusammenspiel des hochglanzpolierten Wandanschlusses mit der Schiene aus einem matten Silber ein ausdrucksstarkes Aussehen, mit dem sich das System nahtlos in zeitgemäße Interieurs integriert.

Begründung der Jury
Die Gestaltung mit matten und hochglänzenden Elementen verleiht dem Wellenvorhang-System W4 ein gleichermaßen expressives wie edles Aussehen.

W5
Curtain Traversing System
Wellenvorhang-System

Manufacturer
interstil Diedrichsen GmbH & Co. KG,
Steinhagen, Germany
Design
Design AG – Frank Greiser &
Brigitte Adrian GbR,
Rheda-Wiedenbrück, Germany
Web
www.interstil.de
www.design-ag.de

W5 is a curtain traversing system whose minimal depth allows for an elegant, but snug fit to the ceiling. Despite the low height, it includes a concealed track channel which even has sufficient space to reliably hide the cords of the complex glide mechanism. The small groove on the visible side of the track accentuates the convex profile shape which tapers off towards the wall. The finials continue the design of the profile and form a harmonious unit with the ceiling.

Statement by the jury
With its harmonious lines, the carefully considered design of the W5 curtain traversing system achieves elegant aesthetics.

W5 ist ein Wellenvorhang-System, das sich dank seiner minimalen Stärke elegant an die Decke schmiegt. Trotz der geringen Bauhöhe verbirgt es einen verdeckten Laufkanal, der darüber hinaus sogar noch über genügend Raum verfügt, um die Schnüre der komplexen Gleitertechnik zuverlässig zu verbergen. Die kleine Nut auf der sichtbaren Seite der Schiene akzentuiert die flach zur Wand abfallende konvexe Profilform. Die Endstücke nehmen die Form des Profils auf und bilden mit der Decke eine harmonische Einheit.

Begründung der Jury
Mit ihrer harmonisch anmutenden Linienführung erzielt die wohldurchdachte Gestaltung des Wellenvorhang-Systems W5 eine elegante Ästhetik.

W6
Curtain Traversing System
Wellenvorhang-System

Manufacturer
interstil Diedrichsen GmbH & Co. KG,
Steinhagen, Germany
Design
Design AG – Frank Greiser &
Brigitte Adrian GbR,
Rheda-Wiedenbrück, Germany
Web
www.interstil.de
www.design-ag.de

The completely symmetrical shape of its inner profile characterises the W6 curtain traversing system. Its adequate width enables the ultra-flat profile to conceal the cords of the glide mechanism with ease despite a very low height of just 13 mm. Gently rounded finials accentuated by a visible groove harmoniously round off the simple, but nonetheless expressive profile which suits a wide variety of interior styles.

Statement by the jury
With its clear use of shapes and minimal height, the W6 curtain traversing system meets the high standards expected of elegant design.

Die absolut symmetrische Form des Innenlauf-Profils zeichnet das Wellenvorhang-System W6 aus. Das ultraflache Profil versteckt die Schnüre der Gleiter trotz der minimalen Höhe von nur 13 mm problemlos. Ermöglicht wird dies dank seiner komfortablen Breite. Sanft abgerundete Endstücke, die durch eine sichtbare Nut betont werden, schließen das schlichte, aber dennoch ausdrucksstarke Profil, das sich gut verschiedenen Einrichtungsstilen anpasst, harmonisch ab.

Begründung der Jury
Mit einer klaren Formensprache und einer geringen Bauhöhe wird das Wellenvorhang-System W6 auch hohen Ansprüchen an stilvolles Design gerecht.

H1910 – Textile
Furniture Handle
Möbelgriff

Manufacturer
Häfele GmbH & Co. KG, Nagold, Germany
Design
byform productdesign (Kristina Meyer, Thorsten Rosenstengel), Bielefeld, Germany
Web
www.hafele.com
www.byform.de

In private homes, rooms are increasingly becoming multifunctional. As a result, functional areas and equipment are taking on a more and more cosy look and feel. The design of the H1910 – Textile furniture handle picks up on this trend. It has a textile-like surface which skilfully manages to give what is generally a technical or functional object a warm, pleasing character. The unmistakable design is furthermore instantly recognisable.

In Privathäusern entwickeln sich Zimmer immer stärker zu Mehrfunktionsräumen. Dies hat zur Folge, dass die Umgebung von Funktionsbereichen einen immer wohnlicheren Charakter annimmt. Die Gestaltung des Möbelgriffs H1910 – Textile greift diesen Trend auf. Er hat eine textil anmutende Oberfläche und verleiht so auf gekonnte Weise auch einem technischen oder funktionalen Gegenstand eine warme, angenehme Ausstrahlung. Das unverwechselbare Design hat dabei eine hohe Wiedererkennbarkeit.

Statement by the jury
The modern design gives the H1910 – Textile furniture handle a markedly winsome appearance which manages to lend even work areas a touch of home-like comfort.

Begründung der Jury
Die zeitgemäße Gestaltung verleiht dem Möbelgriff H1910 – Textile eine betont gefällige Anmutung und setzt so auch in einem Arbeitsumfeld wohnliche Akzente.

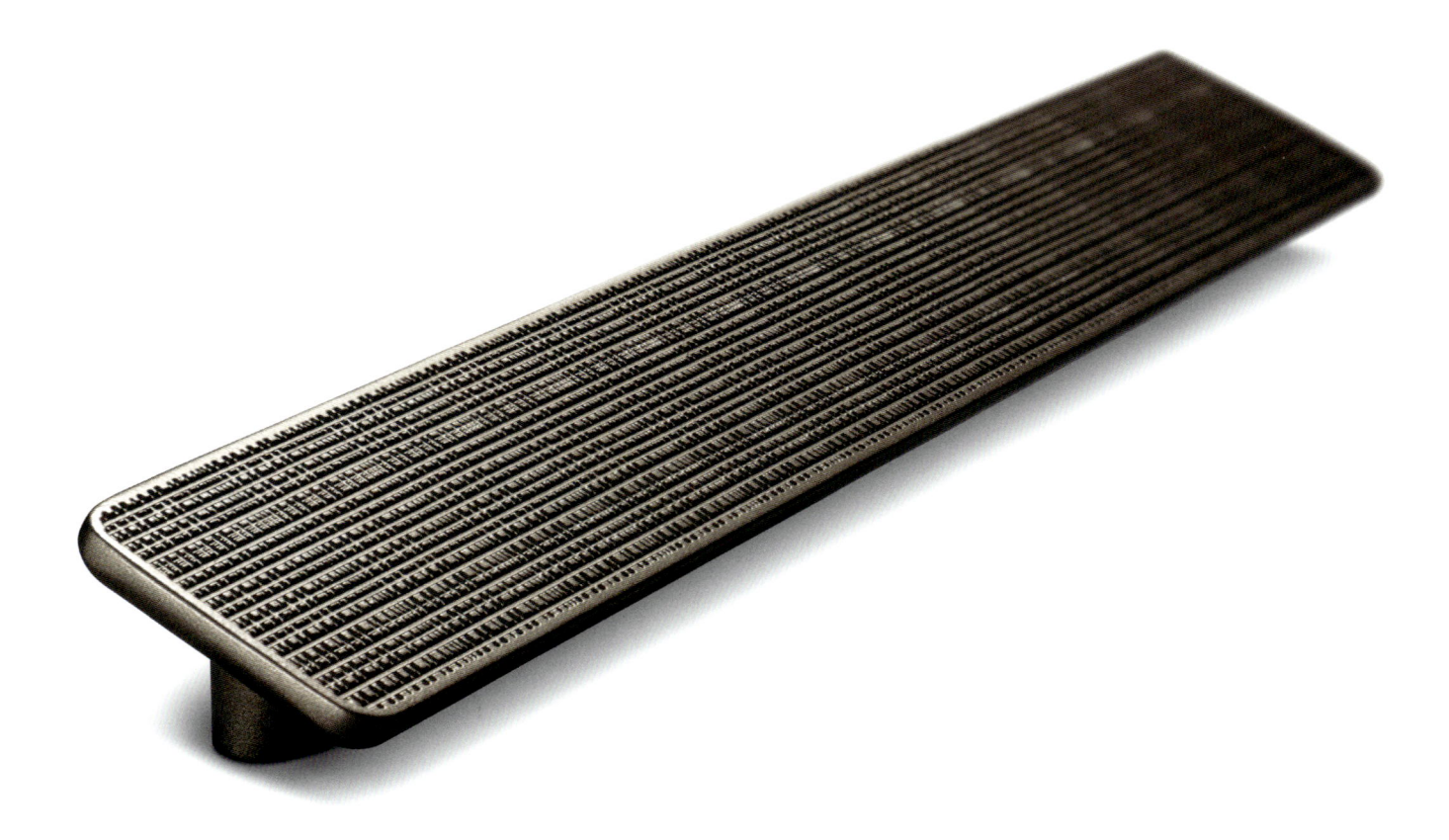

Aquabocci Blade R-47
Drainage System

Manufacturer
Aquabocci Ltd, London, United Kingdom
In-house design
Anthony Milling
Web
www.aquabocci.com

Aquabocci Blade R-47 is a level threshold drainage system for the space between the living area and balcony. The open side entry point features an EPDM silicone sleeve that sits below the door track to carry the water into the drainage channel. At the same time surface water is drained through the top entry point providing complete drainage in the most minimal way possible. The system is available in four anodised colours and therefore easily matches the respective bifold or sliding door.

Aquabocci Blade R-47 ist ein flächenbündiges Drainagesystem für den Bereich zwischen Wohnraum und Balkon. Am offenen seitlichen Eintrittspunkt befindet sich eine EPDM-Silikonbahn, die unterhalb der Türlaufschiene platziert ist, um Wasser in den Abflusskanal zu lenken. Gleichzeitig wird Wasser, das sich an der Oberfläche ansammelt, durch den oberen Eintrittspunkt abgeleitet, was auf einfache Weise eine vollständige Entwässerung ermöglicht. Das System ist in vier eloxierten Farben erhältlich und passt sich daher gut an die jeweilige Doppelfalt- oder Schiebetür an.

Statement by the jury
A carefully thought-out use of technology and a flush-fitting construction characterise the contemporary design of the Aquabocci Blade R-47 drainage system.

Begründung der Jury
Ein wohldurchdachter Technikeinsatz und eine flächenbündige Bauweise zeichnen die zeitgemäße Gestaltung des Drainagesystems Aquabocci Blade R-47 aus.

FREEspace / Free space
Flap Fitting
Klappenbeschlag

Manufacturer
Kesseböhmer GmbH, Bad Essen, Germany
Häfele GmbH & Co. KG, Nagold, Germany
In-house design
Kesseböhmer GmbH
Häfele GmbH & Co. KG
Design
A1 Productdesign, Reindl + Partner GmbH, Cologne, Germany
Web
www.kesseboehmer.de
www.hafele.com
www.a1-productdesign.com

FREEspace / Free space is a hingeless, upward-opening flap fitting of a compact construction that only requires a very shallow installation depth of 63 mm. This makes it suitable for use even with very shallow cupboards. Despite its small size, it can securely support heavy flap weights. A fitting with a 400 mm flap height can for instance support front loads of 1 to 11 kg. Due to its strength and capacity, this model can therefore be used for a wide range of different application areas, thereby saving resources in transport and logistics, and enabling greater standardisation in production.

FREEspace / Free space ist ein kompakt gebauter, scharnierloser Hochklappbeschlag, der eine sehr geringe Einbautiefe von lediglich 63 mm besitzt und sich so auch für den Einbau in sehr flachen Schränken eignet. Trotzdem hält er hohe Klappengewichte sicher und verlässlich. Beispielsweise trägt der Beschlag bei 400 mm Klappenhöhe Frontgewichte von 1 bis 11 kg. Damit kann dieses Modell für viele verschiedene Anwendungsbereiche eingesetzt werden, was Ressourcen bei Transport und Logistik spart und einen höheren Standardisierungsgrad in der Produktion ermöglicht.

Statement by the jury
The innovative design of the FREEspace / Free space flap fitting stands out for its high level of performance and versatility in use.

Begründung der Jury
Die innovative Gestaltung des Klappenbeschlags FREEspace / Free space begeistert mit großer Leistungsstärke und vielfältigen Einsatzmöglichkeiten.

Storage Box with Sockets
Aufbewahrungsbox mit Steckdosen

Manufacturer
Bull Group Incorporated Company,
Cixi, China
In-house design
Web
www.gongniuchazuo.com.cn

This functional design combines an electrical socket with a storage box and ensures tidiness and safety at work or at home. It can be mounted on the wall. Inside, there are several carefully positioned sockets for a range of different plugs and it can even be used for the large power adaptors of laptops. The box, which is both compact and harmonious in appearance, is also able to safely store the cables of the plugs that are connected to it while the sockets are in use.

Statement by the jury
Tidiness and safety are at the centre of the clever design of this storage box with sockets. Its modern appearance is another plus.

Diese funktionelle Gestaltung kombiniert Steckdosen mit einer Aufbewahrungsbox und sorgt so für Ordnung und Sicherheit, beispielsweise am Arbeitsplatz oder im Wohnbereich. Das Utensil wird an der Wand montiert. Es bietet im Inneren mehrere sorgfältig platzierte Steckdosen für unterschiedliche Steckertypen und eignet sich sogar für die großen Netzteile von Laptops. In der Box, die gleichermaßen kompakt wie harmonisch anmutend gestaltet ist, können Gerätekabel während der Nutzung sicher aufbewahrt werden.

Begründung der Jury
Ordnung und Sicherheit stehen im Fokus der raffinierten Gestaltung dieser Aufbewahrungsbox mit Steckdosen. Zudem gefällt ihr modernes Aussehen.

ViZard by ambigence
Flap Fitting
Klappenbeschlag

Manufacturer
Hettich Marketing- und
Vertriebs GmbH & Co. KG, Vlotho, Germany
Design
ambigence GmbH & Co. KG,
Herford, Germany
Web
www.hettich.com
www.ambigence.com

ViZard by ambigence is a new type of flap fitting that can be built into the sidewalls of a piece of furniture so that it is completely invisible. This allows the interior to be purist in design – the space can be used fully without having to allow for mechanisms that get in the way. This opens up a whole array of new functional and design possibilities for furniture manufacturers. The fitting comes with an inbuilt damper so that furniture flaps open and close gently and silently.

Statement by the jury
Advanced technology allows the ViZard by ambigence flap fitting to meet high expectations of aesthetics and of purist design solutions.

Der neuartige Klappenbeschlag ViZard by ambigence lässt sich unsichtbar in den Seitenwänden eines Möbelstücks integrieren. Auf diese Weise wird auch im Inneren ein puristisches Design ermöglicht – der Raum kann vollständig genutzt werden, ohne Rücksicht auf eine störende Mechanik nehmen zu müssen. Dies eröffnet Möbelbauern zahlreiche neue funktionale und gestalterische Möglichkeiten. Der Beschlag ist mit einer integrierten Dämpfung versehen, wodurch sich Möbelklappen sanft und leise öffnen und schließen.

Begründung der Jury
Dank eines fortschrittlichen Technikeinsatzes wird der Klappenbeschlag ViZard by ambigence hohen Ansprüchen an Ästhetik und puristische Designlösungen gerecht.

Smart Package Post Box
Intelligenter Paketbriefkasten

Manufacturer
LIXIL Corporation, Tokyo, Japan
In-house design
Web
www.lixil.com

This smart package post box makes sending and collecting parcels easy. IoT technology connects users and delivery service providers. This saves time for example by eliminating the need for redelivery when recipients are not at home. Collection is not limited to a single box, but is possible from several locations. In this way, this unit, whose elegant design also suits many types of residences, can also replace traditional post boxes.

Dieser intelligente Paketbriefkasten ermöglicht das bequeme Versenden und Abholen von Paketen. Mithilfe der IoT-Technologie werden Nutzer und Zustelldienstanbieter miteinander verbunden. Das bietet einer Zeitgewinn, da z. B. eine erneute Lieferung, wenn der Empfänger nicht zu Hause angetroffen wurde, entfällt. Die Abholung ist dabei nicht auf eine Box beschränkt, sondern an mehreren Standorten möglich. So lassen sich mit diesem Modell, das sich dank seiner edlen Gestaltung problemlos im Wohnumfeld integrieren, auch herkömmliche Briefkästen ersetzen.

Statement by the jury
This smart package post box is markedly user-friendly and its elegantly proportioned design turns it into an eye-catcher in public spaces.

Begründung der Jury
Ausgesprochen nutzerfreundlich präsentiert sich dieser intelligente Paketbriefkasten, der mit seiner formschönen Gestaltung ein Hingucker im öffentlichen Raum ist.

Happig
Storage Container
Sammelbehälter

Manufacturer
Co-Green Design Consultants, Nanjing, China
In-house design
Pan Lefan, Li Rui
Web
www.cogreendesign.com

Happig is a storage container with the shape of a pig. The name intentionally picks up on the word "happiness" in the hope of bringing the user some luck. On its back is an easy-to-open hinged lid whose flowing lines are designed to recall associations with spotted pigs. To give the product a lifelike appearance, paint has been applied in several layers. With its full rounded shape, Happig not only provides a practical storage solution, but also functions as an ornament.

Happig ist ein Sammelbehälter in Form eines Schweins. Der Name lehnt sich an das Wort „happiness" an – damit ist die Hoffnung verbunden, dass dieses Objekt seinen Nutzern Glück bringt. Auf seinem Rücken befindet sich ein leicht zu öffnender Klappdeckel, dessen geschwungene Linienführung eine Assoziation zu gefleckten Schweinen hervorruft. Um eine lebendige Anmutung zu erzielen, wurden verschiedene Farbschichten aufgetragen. Mit seiner rundlichen Form bietet Happig nicht nur eine praktische Aufbewahrungsmöglichkeit, sondern ist auch ein dekorativer Gegenstand.

Statement by the jury
The design of the Happig storage container skilfully combines high practical value with a decorative appearance.

Begründung der Jury
Auf raffinierte Weise kombiniert die Gestaltung des Sammelbehälters Happig einen hohen praktischen Nutzen mit einem dekorativen Erscheinungsbild.

Kopenhagen
Christmas Tree Stand
Christbaumständer

Manufacturer
Krinner GmbH, Straßkirchen, Germany
In-house design
Karsten Eibach
Web
www.krinner.com

Inspired by Nordic design and Scandinavian purism, the design of the Kopenhagen Christmas tree stand deliberately chooses to refrain from using a traditional, contoured shape. With its clean lines, it looks more like an artistic design object and less like a utensil. This impression is reinforced by the combination of black or white steel with pale oak. The stand is equipped with single cable technology which firmly holds the Christmas tree.

Statement by the jury
The design of the Kopenhagen Christmas tree stand combines functionality and aesthetics on a high level and thus skilfully appeals to a style-conscious target group.

Inspiriert von nordischem Design und skandinavischem Purismus verzichtet die Gestaltung des Christbaumständers Kopenhagen bewusst auf eine traditionelle, geschwungene Formgebung. Mit seiner klaren Linienführung mutet er eher wie ein kunstvolles Designobjekt und weniger wie ein Gebrauchsgegenstand an. Dieser Eindruck wird zusätzlich durch die Kombination von schwarzem oder weißem Stahl und hellem Eichenholz verstärkt. Ausgestattet ist das Modell mit einer Rundum-Einseiltechnik, die dem Weihnachtsbaum den nötigen Halt gibt.

Begründung der Jury
Auf hohem Niveau kombiniert die Gestaltung des Christbaumständers Kopenhagen Funktionalität und Ästhetik und spricht so gekonnt eine stilbewusste Zielgruppe an.

Juice Dispenser
Saft-Ausschank

Manufacturer
Nektar Natura, d.o.o., Kamnik, Slovenia
Design
Wilsonic Design, d.o.o. (Metod Burgar, Nina Mihovec), Trzin, Slovenia
Web
www.nektarnatura.com
www.wilsonicdesign.com

This juice dispenser can be used to serve five different freshly prepared fruit and vegetable juices. In order to draw attention to the healthy drinks, it has been designed with the eye-catching appeal of a fruit stand at a farmer's market. It will suit a range of different interior styles. The dispensing system is environmentally friendly and does not waste energy as it cools drinks only to a suitable drinking temperature. The use of appealing glass carafes eliminates the need for disposable packagings.

Statement by the jury
The design of this juice dispenser, which easily fits into different settings and interior styles, is inviting and environmentally friendly.

An diesem Ausschank können fünf verschiedene frische Obst- und Gemüsesäfte angeboten werden. Um die Aufmerksamkeit auf die gesunden Getränke zu richten, ist er aufmerksamkeitsstark wie ein Obststand auf dem Markt gestaltet. Er passt zu vielen Inneneinrichtungen. Das Spendersystem ist umweltfreundlich und kommt ohne unnötigen Energieverbrauch aus, da es die Getränke nur auf eine geeignete Trinktemperatur abkühlt. Dank ansprechender Glasbehälter kann auch auf Einwegverpackungen verzichtet werden.

Begründung der Jury
Einladend und umweltfreundlich ist die Gestaltung dieses Saft-Ausschanks, der sich sehr gut in unterschiedliche Umgebungen und Stile einfügt.

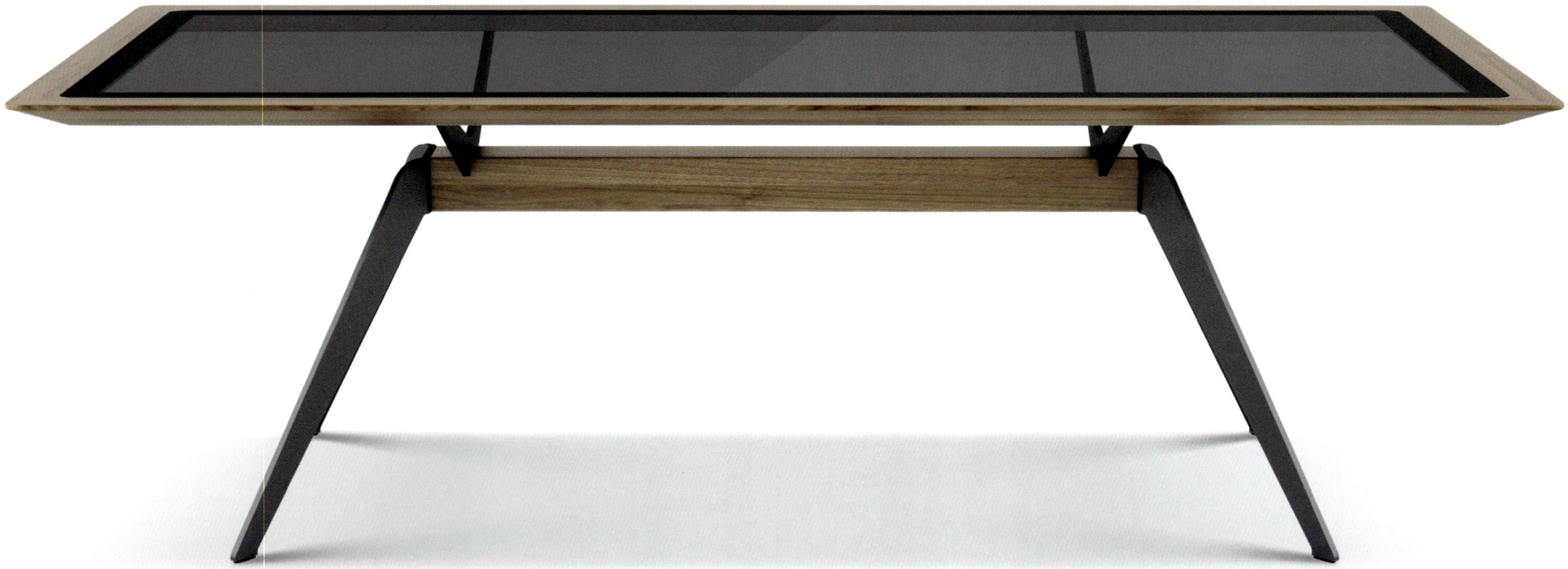

Living rooms and bedrooms
Wohnen und Schlafen

Chairs
Coffee and side tables
Cupboards
Mattresses
Seating
Shelves
Sideboards
Slatted bed bases
Tables
Wardrobes

Anrichten
Couch- und Beistelltische
Kleiderschränke
Küchenschränke
Lattenroste
Matratzen
Regale
Sitzmöbel
Stühle
Tische

Jabara AV Board
Sideboard

Manufacturer
Ritzwell & Co., Fukuoka, Japan

In-house design
Shinsaku Miyamoto

Web
www.ritzwell.com

reddot award 2019
best of the best

Enchanting interpretation
Sideboards have long secured a firm standing in interiors for being both practical and space-saving. The Jabara AV Board lends this type of furniture an extremely appealing aesthetic by skilfully combining tradition with contemporary design. The overall appearance is characterised by harmonious proportions and a striking folding doors design. Crafted in a classic, timeless accordion style, they are reminiscent of the reed-screen doors found in traditional Japanese townhouses. The appeal of this sideboard also rests in the use of carefully selected solid wood, which has been finely cut into thin pieces with chamfered edges to create beautiful contrasting colour shades. The resulting interplay of light and shade evokes the impression that the accordion doors could fold back even further. Opening and closing the sideboard holds a hidden and enchanting charm of its own. It is a slow natural process, accompanied by the feel of a slight stiffness and the soothing sound of the pieces of wood rubbing together. With its functionally well-thought-out arrangement, the Jabara AV Board also showcases an elegant smoked-glass door that hides away any audiovisual equipment. In combination with the accordion-style doors, this sideboard displays a stylish appearance that creates a warm atmosphere in the room.

Reizvoll interpretiert
Das Sideboard hat schon seit langer Zeit einen festen Platz im Interieur, da es praktisch und platzsparend ist. Das Jabara AV Board verleiht dieser Möbelgattung eine überaus reizvolle Ästhetik, wobei sich Tradition gekonnt mit zeitgenössischem Design verbindet. Prägend für seine Anmutung sind ausgewogene Proportionen sowie auffällig gestaltete Rolltüren. Diese sind in einem klassisch-zeitlosen Akkordeon-Stil gefertigt, der an die in Japan vorzufindenden Schilfrohrtüren erinnert. Die Wirkung dieses Sideboards beruht auch auf dem Einsatz sorgfältig ausgewählten Massivholzes, welches bei der Fertigung in dünne Streifen mit abgeschrägten Kanten geschnitten wird, was schöne, kontrastierende Farbtönungen erzeugt. Es entsteht dabei ein Spiel von Licht und Schatten, das dem Betrachter den Eindruck vermittelt, die Harmonikatüren könnten noch weiter zurückklappen. Besonderen Charme hat bei diesem Sideboard auch das Öffnen und Schließen. Es ist ein natürlich wirkender, langsamer Vorgang, der mit einer gewissen Gediegenheit einhergeht und von dem beruhigenden Geräusch aneinander reibenden Holzes begleitet wird. In seiner Aufteilung funktional gut durchdacht, ist das Jabara AV Board zudem mit einer eleganten Rauchglastür gestaltet, hinter der sich das audiovisuelle Equipment verbergen lässt. In Kombination mit der Tür im Akkordeon-Stil stellt dieses Sideboard so eine stilvolle Erscheinung dar, die im Raum eine warme Atmosphäre verbreitet.

Statement by the jury
In an attractive way, this sideboard offers the possibility to both hide and present things. With its purist form and clear proportions, it perfectly embodies the maxims of contemporary design, projecting a delightful composition of selected materials and a filigree-looking construction. Thanks to its well-harmonised colour concept, the Jabara AV Board can also seamlessly integrate into the interiors of young target groups.

Begründung der Jury
Auf attraktive Weise offeriert dieses Sideboard die Möglichkeit, Dinge zu verbergen oder sie zu präsentieren. Mit seiner puristischen Form und klaren Proportionen verkörpert es perfekt Maximen zeitgenössischen Designs. Seine Gestaltung stellt eine reizvolle Komposition aus einer filigran anmutenden Konstruktion und ausgesuchten Materialien dar. Durch sein gut harmonierendes Farbkonzept kann sich das Jabara AV Board auch nahtlos in die Interieurs junger Zielgruppen integrieren.

Designer portrait
See page 40
Siehe Seite 40

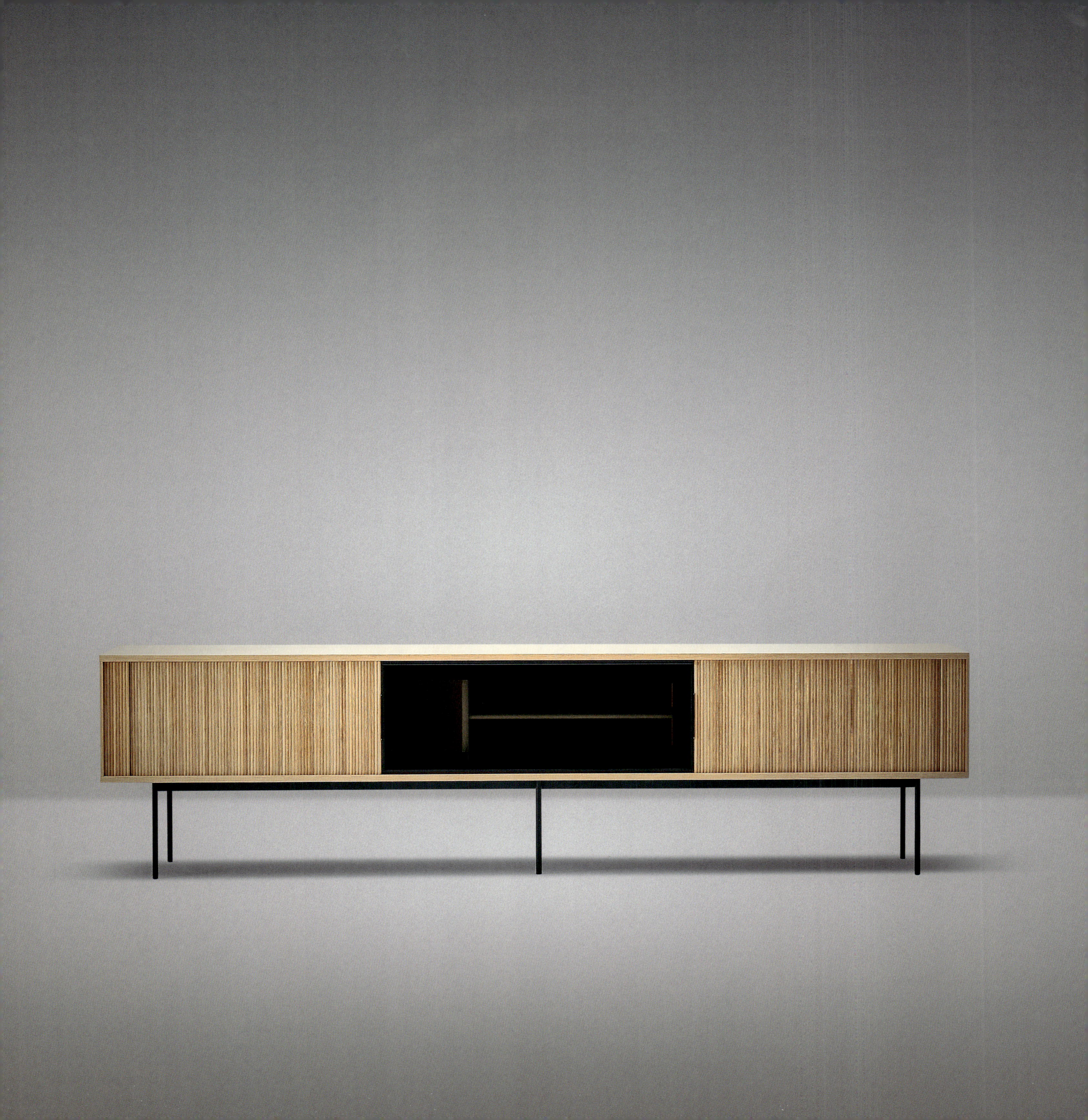

The Farns
Sideboard

Manufacturer
Walter Knoll AG & Co. KG,
Herrenberg, Germany
Design
EOOS Design GmbH, Vienna, Austria
Web
www.walterknoll.de
www.eoos.com

The clean and linear design of the sideboard The Farns pays tribute to Bauhaus. At the heart of the design concept is the interplay of light and shadow, shape and geometry, as well as wood and glass. This distinctive piece of furniture is open on all sides, transparent and accessible, regardless of whether it is freestanding or has been placed up against a wall. Its mirrored walls make the interior look spacious and expansive. The doors can be opened 180 degrees, creating a range of looks suitable for different room situations and lighting effects.

Statement by the jury
With its clear and expressive design, this sideboard will be the centre of attention – as stand-alone piece of furniture or as a complement to the interior.

Die klare und geradlinige Gestaltung des Sideboards The Farns ist eine Hommage an das Bauhaus. Im Mittelpunkt steht das Spiel mit Licht und Schatten, Form und Geometrie sowie Holz und Glas. Das markante Möbelstück wirkt von allen Seiten offen, transparent und zugänglich, unabhängig davon, ob es frei im Raum steht oder an einer Wand platziert ist. Aufgrund seiner verspiegelten Wandscheiben wirkt der Innenraum weitläufig und großzügig. Die Türen lassen sich um 180 Grad öffnen und passen sich so gut unterschiedlichen Raumsituationen und Lichtstimmungen an.

Begründung der Jury
Mit seiner klaren und zugleich expressiven Gestaltung zieht dieses Sideboard – als Solitär oder das Interieur ergänzend – die Aufmerksamkeit auf sich.

Waves
Bar Cabinet
Barschrank

Manufacturer
Mundus Viridis d.o.o., Gradec, Croatia
Design
Thinkobjects, Zagreb, Croatia
Web
www.millamilli.com
www.thinkobjects.eu

The Waves bar cabinet is noteworthy not only for its design vocabulary, which elegantly combines a rectangle with an oval, but also for the structured surface of the door. This creates a fascinating and ever-changing play of light and shadow which inevitably catches the eye. The design of this piece of furniture is dominated by the use of different dark colour tones: dark walnut wood and black metal are paired with tinted reflective glass inside the cabinet, which, in combination with the available lighting, creates a very sophisticated effect.

Statement by the jury
An appealing design idiom, a skilled use of materials and a harmonious colour concept give the Waves bar cabinet a very stylish appearance.

Auffällig ist der Barschrank Waves nicht nur aufgrund seiner Formensprache, die ein Rechteck mit einem Oval kombiniert. Auch die Reliefstruktur der Türoberfläche, die für ein spannungsvolles und faszinierendes Licht- und Schattenspiel sorgt, zieht die Blicke auf sich. Das Design dieses Möbelstücks wird von dunklen Farbnuancen dominiert: Dunkles Walnussholz trifft auf schwarzes Metall. Ergänzt wird dies durch getöntes Spiegelglas im Innenraum des Schranks, das zusammen mit der hier vorhandenen Beleuchtung einen edlen Eindruck erzeugt.

Begründung der Jury
Eine ansprechende Formensprache, ein gekonnter Materialmix sowie ein harmonisches Farbkonzept verleihen dem Barschrank Waves sein edles Erscheinungsbild.

Sliding Door with TV
Gleittür mit TV

Manufacturer
raumplus Besitz- und
Entwicklungs-GmbH & Co. KG,
Bremen, Germany
In-house design
Web
www.raumplus.com

This product brings a sliding door and a media centre together, thus elegantly combining interior design with entertainment. This is made possible by integrating a 55" flat screen with a maximum weight of 25 kg into the door panel. The TV is then easy to operate using a Bluetooth remote control. Users can select door panels from a wide range of different colours and materials and so ensure they harmoniously match the interior. The same applies to the door system's profiles which are also available in a wide selection of models.

Statement by the jury
The inventive design of this furniture item allows for the integration of a flat screen TV into a sliding door and thus meets the demands of a media-related target group.

Dieses Produkt vereint eine Gleittür und ein Medienzentrum und verbindet auf diese Weise Raumgestaltung elegant mit Entertainment. Ermöglicht wird dies durch einen in die Türfüllung integrierten Flachbildschirm, der bis 55" groß und bis 25 kg schwer sein darf. Bedienen lässt er sich bequem über eine Bluetooth-Fernbedienung. Die Türfüllung kann aus einer umfangreichen Farb- und Werkstoffpalette ausgewählt und so harmonisch auf das Interieur abgestimmt werden. Das gilt auch für die Profile des Systems, die in verschiedenen Ausführungen zur Wahl stehen.

Begründung der Jury
Die ideenreiche Gestaltung ermöglicht die Integration eines Flachbildschirms in eine Gleittür und wird so den Ansprüchen einer medienaffinen Zielgruppe gerecht.

Tojo-mehrfach
Shelf
Regal

Manufacturer
Tojo Möbel GmbH, Schorndorf, Germany
Design
Bastian Prieler, Detmold, Germany
Web
www.tojo.de

Tojo-mehrfach is a modular shelving system which shines the spotlight on its real purpose. It can be constructed without needing any additional joins or tools. Also the use of glue, fittings or screws has been deliberately omitted. The shelving system is made of white coated MDF, the natural edges form an elegant contrast. It is available in three different heights and thus fits effortlessly into any room scenario – whether used as a stand-alone piece of furniture, as a sideboard, a room divider or as a continuous shelving unit.

Statement by the jury
The design focus of the Tojo-mehrfach shelf is on providing a range of versatile and flexible uses. Its straightforward assembly is an added bonus.

Tojo-mehrfach ist ein modulares, auf seine eigentliche Funktion konzentriertes Regalsystem, das ohne zusätzliche Verbindungsmittel in verschiedenen Varianten aufgebaut werden kann. Werkzeug ist dazu nicht nötig, auch auf Klebstoff, Beschläge oder Schrauben wird bewusst verzichtet. Das System besteht aus weiß beschichtetem MDF, die naturbelassenen Kanten bilden dazu einen edlen Kontrast. Es ist in drei Höhen erhältlich und passt sich so mühelos der jeweiligen Raumsituation an – ob als Solist, Sideboard, Raumteiler oder endlos zusammenhängendes Regal.

Begründung der Jury
Im Fokus der Gestaltung des Regals Tojo-mehrfach stehen vielseitige und flexible Verwendungsmöglichkeiten. Außerdem gefällt seine unkomplizierte Montage.

Cabas Life
Multifunctional Furniture Item
Multifunktionales Möbelstück

Manufacturer
GID International Design, Shanghai, China
In-house design
Web
www.gid-x.com

The concept behind Cabas Life was to create a space-saving, multifunctional piece of furniture that would combine convenience, versatility and aesthetics. The Asian-influenced design is based on the shape of ancient grocery baskets, but combines this with functions more suited to modern day living. An LED light is integrated into the handle and a USB port has been positioned in its structure. A drawer provides storage space for a variety of equipment while the tray attached to the main structure can be used for a tea ceremony.

Statement by the jury
The modern design of the Cabas Life furniture item, which integrates a range of different functions in a limited amount of space, stands out for its ingenuity.

Hinter Cabas Life verbirgt sich ein platzsparendes, multifunktionales Möbelstück, das Nützlichkeit, Vielseitigkeit und Ästhetik vereint. Die Gestaltung im fernöstlichen Stil orientiert sich an der Form eines altertümlichen Lebensmittelkorbs, bereichert das Möbel aber mit zeitgemäßen Funktionen: Im Henkel befindet sich eine LED-Leuchte und am Korpus eine USB-Schnittstelle. Eine Schublade bietet Stauraum für verschiedene Utensilien, während das Tablett, welches sich auf dem Korpus befindet, zur Durchführung einer Teezeremonie genutzt werden kann.

Begründung der Jury
Die zeitgemäße Gestaltung des Möbelstücks Cabas Life, das auf begrenztem Raum vielfältige Funktionen vereint, besticht mit hohem Einfallsreichtum.

Exclamation
Modular Furniture Item
Modulares Möbelstück

Manufacturer
Zhejiang Horizon Industrial Design Co., Ltd., Hangzhou, China
In-house design
Guojun Wu, Jiao Wu
Web
www.lagomaerbaest.com

The design of Exclamation centres on the interaction between man and furniture. With the help of ten different components, users can create a piece of furniture to match their individual needs; for example, a wardrobe, a side table or a shelving unit. Assembly is easy and no tools are needed. Thanks to the balanced interplay of delicate aluminium and high-quality black walnut, the resulting furniture item always looks harmonious. It can be dismantled and reassembled in a new shape again and again.

Statement by the jury
Exclamation is convincing due to many combination options and a high level of individuality which results from involving the user in the design process.

Im Fokus der Gestaltung von Exclamation steht die Interaktion zwischen Mensch und Möbelstück. Der Nutzer kann aus zehn verschiedenen Komponenten einen Einrichtungsgegenstand nach eigenen Wünschen zusammenfügen und z. B. eine Garderobe, einen Beistelltisch oder ein Regal kreieren. Die einfache Montage erfolgt dabei ohne Einsatz von Werkzeug. Das dank eines ausgewogenen Zusammenspiels von filigran anmutendem Aluminium und hochwertigem schwarzen Walnussholz harmonisch anmutende Möbel lässt sich immer wieder zerlegen und neu zusammensetzen.

Begründung der Jury
Exclamation überzeugt mit vielen Kombinationsmöglichkeiten und, dank der Einbindung des Nutzers in den Gestaltungsprozess, einem hohen Maß an Individualität.

Sendai Pro
Stove
Kaminofen

Manufacturer
Hase Kaminofenbau GmbH, Trier, Germany
In-house design
Fernando Najera
Web
www.hase.de

The Sendai Pro stove is notable for its precise design concept. The large corner firebox positioned high up on the stove – optionally on the right- or left-hand side – provides a generous view of the flames. The shelf on the side, meanwhile, offers plenty of space for wood storage. Thanks to a concealed built-in heat-retaining block, the stove provides long lasting warmth and makes the living room feel cosy. Sendai Pro also comes with a range of different flue connection options: at the top, at the back or on the side through the shelf.

Der Kaminofen Sendai Pro fällt durch sein präzises Gestaltungskonzept auf. Der große, hochliegende Über-Eck-Feuerraum, der in linker und rechter Ausführung erhältlch ist, gestattet einen großzügigen Blick auf das Flammenspiel. Das seitliche Regal bietet ausreichend Platz für den Holzvorrat. Dank des integrierten Wärmespeichers gibt der Ofen langanhaltend Wärme ab und sorgt so für Behaglichkeit im Wohnraum. Sendai Pro bietet variable Rauchrohr-Anschlussmöglichkeiten: nach oben, nach hinten oder seitlich durch das Regal.

Statement by the jury
With a distinctive appearance that also radiates cosiness, the design of the Sendai Pro stove skilfully draws attention to its outstanding feature.

Begründung der Jury
Mit einem markanten, dabei gleichzeitig Behaglichkeit verströmenden Erscheinungsbild setzt die Gestaltung den Kaminofen Sendai Pro gekonnt in Szene.

numo
Chair
Stuhl

Manufacturer
aeris GmbH, Haar, Germany

In-house design
Dietlind Walger-Hutter

Design
ostwalddesign
(Andreas Ostwald),
Hamburg, Germany

Web
www.aeris.de
www.ostwalddesign.net

reddot award 2019
best of the best

Moving shape
Designer and architect George Nelson once defined design as "an expression of the capability of the human mind to step beyond." The aim in designing the numo chair was to lend the familiar cantilever chair a new form, enhanced by an additional dimension. Classic forms were to be combined with innovative technology. At its core is an aeris kinematic system consisting of four flex points, which has been consistently integrated between the frame and the plastic seat shell. This allows the seated person to swing not only backwards, but also forwards. Thus, numo offers excellent ergonomic features and great comfort even when sitting for a long time. Thanks to its timeless and functional design, this chair opens up a wide range of possibilities for use, such as meeting rooms in the office, waiting rooms, restaurants, lounges, but also the home office and dining table. In addition, the version with skid frame is also suitable for outdoor use. Offering five different colours and four frame models, the chair concept provides for numerous customisable design arrangements. This is complemented by the option of freely combinable non-slip seat cushions in matching or contrasting colours. The surprisingly versatile numo chair is fun and offers "moving" features also in a figurative sense.

Form in Bewegung
Der Designer und Architekt George Nelson definierte Design einst als „Ausdruck der Fähigkeit des menschlichen Geistes, seine Grenzen zu überschreiten". Ziel der Gestaltung des Stuhls numo war es, eine neue Form des bekannten Freischwingers hervorzubringen, erweitert um eine zusätzliche Dimension. Klassische Formen sollten mit innovativer Technik vereint werden. Zentral ist dabei eine hochentwickelte aeris Kinematik mit vier Flexpunkten, die schlüssig zwischen der Kunststoff-Sitzschale und dem Gestell integriert wurde. Sie ermöglicht es, dass der Sitzende nicht nur nach hinten, sondern auch nach vorne schwingen kann. numo bietet damit hervorragende ergonomische Eigenschaften und viel Komfort, selbst bei langem Sitzen. Durch seine zeitlose und funktionale Gestaltung eröffnet dieser Stuhl vielfältige Möglichkeiten des Einsatzes, wie für den Besprechungsraum im Office, Warteräume, Restaurants, Lounges, aber auch das Home-Office und den häuslichen Esstisch. In der Variante mit Kufengestell ist er zudem gut für den Außeneinsatz geeignet. Da das Konzept fünf Farb- und vier Gestellvarianten zur Auswahl stellt, ergeben sich zahlreiche individuelle Gestaltungsmöglichkeiten. Diese werden durch die Option farblich passender, aber auch kontrastierend kombinierbarer, rutschfester Sitzpolster komplettiert. Der überraschend vielseitige Stuhl numo macht Spaß und bietet auch im übertragenen Sinne „bewegende" Eigenschaften.

Statement by the jury
The universal numo chair impresses with an elegant balance and the way in which the frame has been connected in a creative manner to the extremely thin seat shell. Based on innovative kinematics, it offers freedom of movement both backwards and forwards, which is perceived by users as natural and supportive. numo embodies the perfect integration of material, technology and aesthetics, which makes for a chair that is outstandingly comfortable and versatile in use.

Begründung der Jury
Der Universalstuhl numo begeistert durch seine elegante Ausgewogenheit und die Art und Weise, wie das Gestell gestalterisch mit der extrem dünnen Sitzschale verbunden wurde. Auf der Basis einer innovativen Kinematik bietet er Bewegungsfreiheit nach hinten und nach vorne, was vom Sitzenden als natürlich und unterstützend empfunden wird. numo verkörpert so die perfekte Integration von Material, Technologie und Ästhetik. Dieser Stuhl ist dabei überaus komfortabel und vielseitig einsetzbar.

Designer portrait
See page 42
Siehe Seite 42

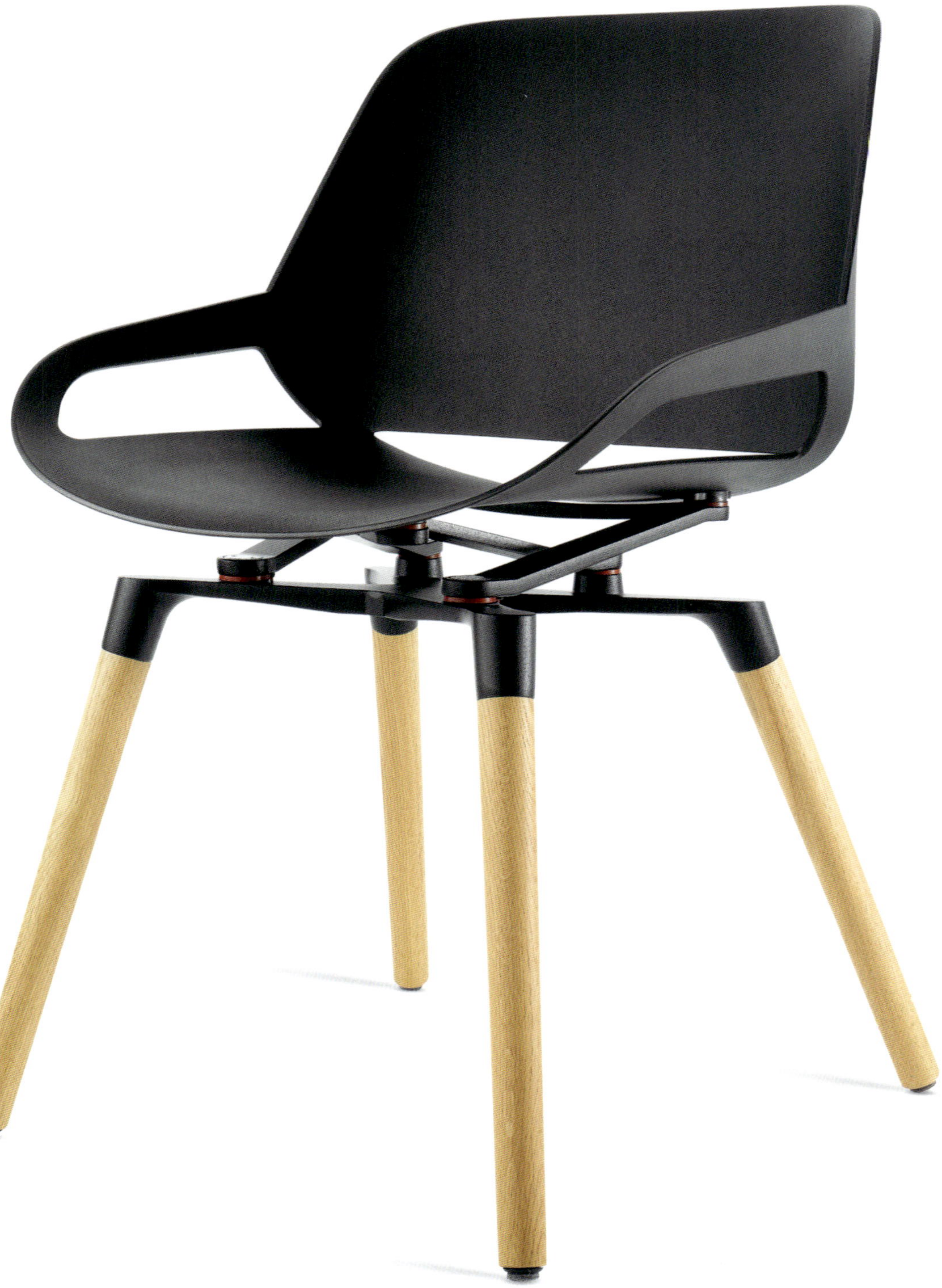

Nix
Chair
Stuhl

Manufacturer
Capdell, Valencia, Spain
Design
Studio Norguet Design (Patrick Norguet), Paris, France
Web
www.capdell.com
www.patricknorguet.com/en

Nix is a chair with a complex construction that is inspired by Nordic design. An outstanding feature of this iconic piece of furniture is the balance it manages to achieve between the use of solid wood and shaped plywood made possible by innovative technology. The pleasing curve of backrest and seat ensure comfort while the careful assembly of the individual components makes the chair both stable and robust. This elegant yet functional chair is suitable for residential spaces as well as public buildings such as hotels, restaurants or museums.

Statement by the jury
The Nix chair, which will fit seamlessly into different spatial settings, stands out for its sophisticated construction and elegant appearance.

Nix ist ein komplex konstruierter, vom nordischen Design inspirierter Stuhl. Ein Merkmal dieses ikonischen Sitzmöbels ist die Ausgewogenheit von Massivholz und mit innovativem Technikeinsatz gebogenem Schichtholz. Die gefällige Krümmung von Rückenlehne und Sitz sorgt für Komfort, während der sorgfältige Zusammenbau der einzelnen Komponenten Stabilität und Langlebigkeit gewährt. Der ebenso elegante wie funktionale Stuhl eignet sich für den Einsatz im privaten Wohnraum sowie in öffentlichen Gebäuden, z. B. in Hotels, Restaurants oder Museen.

Begründung der Jury
Der Stuhl Nix, der sich nahtlos in verschiedene Raumsituationen integriert, zeichnet sich durch eine anspruchsvolle Bauweise sowie eine edle Anmutung aus.

Venice
Chair
Stuhl

Manufacturer
Kartell S.p.A., Noviglio (Milan), Italy
Design
Philippe Starck, Paris, France
Web
www.kartell.com
www.starck.com

The design of the Venice chair pays homage to the eponymous city. Its classic design vocabulary captures the atmosphere of alluring Venetian locations. This distinctive style is complemented by a highly comfortable seat. Made of weather durable polycarbonate, the chair is manufactured using an elaborate injection moulding process. Due to this choice of material, the sturdy chair can be used both in- and outdoors. It is available in a choice of six colours from white to dove grey, grey, sage green, russet and black.

Statement by the jury
Defined by its elegant aesthetics, the Venice chair is an eye-catching item of furniture which is also pleasing for its versatility in use.

Die Gestaltung des Stuhls Venice ist eine Hommage an die gleichnamige Lagunenstadt. Mithilfe einer klassischen Formensprache fängt sie die Stimmung reizvoller venezianischer Schauplätze ein. Der eigenständige Stil wird durch hohen Sitzkomfort ergänzt. Der aus wetterfestem Polycarbonat bestehende Stuhl wird aufwändig in Spritzgusstechnik hergestellt. Durch die Materialwahl kann das stabile Sitzmöbel sowohl im Innen- als auch im Außenbereich verwendet werden. Es ist in den sechs Farben Weiß, Taubengrau, Grau, Salbeigrün, Rostbraun und Schwarz erhältlich.

Begründung der Jury
Durch eine von Eleganz geprägte Ästhetik erzielt der Stuhl Venice hohe Aufmerksamkeit. Darüber hinaus gefallen seine vielfältigen Einsatzmöglichkeiten.

Elipse
Chair
Stuhl

Manufacturer
Zanotta S.p.A., Nova Milanese
(Monza and Brianza), Italy
Design
Patrick Jouin,
Paris, France
Web
www.zanotta.it
www.patrickjouin.com

The Elipse chair stands out for its use of contrasting shapes. The square tubular aluminium alloy structure contrasts with the gentle curves of the seat and the backrest made from a technopolymer based on polypropylene. A characteristic design element of the chair is a circular opening in the backrest which also makes this piece of furniture easy to lift. The chair comes in the colours black, white, anthracite and amaranth.

Statement by the jury
The Elipse chair is memorable for its expressive form which makes it a head-turner in many different interior design settings.

Die Besonderheit des Stuhls Elipse besteht in der Kombination kontrastreicher Formen. Das aus quadratisch geformten Röhren gearbeitete Gestell ist aus einer Aluminiumlegierung gefertigt. Im Gegensatz dazu bestehen Sitz und Rückenlehne aus Technopolymer auf Polypropylenbasis und zeigen eine geschwungene Linienführung. Ein aufmerksamkeitsstarkes Gestaltungselement ist die kreisrunde Aussparung an der Rückenlehne. Diese ermöglicht u. a. ein leichtes Heben des Sitzmöbels, das in den Farben Schwarz, Weiß, Anthrazit und Amarant hergestellt wird.

Begründung der Jury
Der Stuhl Elipse sticht mit seiner expressiven Gestaltung heraus, die ihn in vielen verschiedenen Einrichtungsstilen zu einem Hingucker macht.

Aunglo
Stool
Hocker

Manufacturer
Union Galvanizer Co., Ltd.,
Chachoengsao, Thailand
Design
Dots Studio (Krit Phutpim),
Bangkok, Thailand
Web
www.galvanii.com
www.dots-designstudio.com

Inspired by the "eat and go" style of Asian street food culture, the Aunglo stool is available in two different heights. The design focused on simplifying the structure which consists of individual struts, thus resulting in a light and airy look. Manufactured using durable, hot-dip galvanised steel, the stool can not only be used indoors, but also in demanding outdoor environments. It comes complete with a cushion made of the plastic EVA, which sits loosely on top of the seat.

Statement by the jury
The Aunglo stool gains merit for its functional and shapely design. Thanks to its durable materials, it is also suitable for outdoor use.

Die Inspirationsquelle für den in zwei Höhen erhältlichen Hocker Aunglo liegt in der asiatischen Street-Food-Kultur und drückt „essen und gehen" aus. Dank einer auf Vereinfachung ausgerichteten Gestaltung mutet das aus einzelnen Streben konstruierte Sitzmöbel leicht und luftig an. Es besteht aus langlebigem, feuerverzinktem Stahl und kann nicht nur im Innenraum genutzt werden, sondern wird auch den anspruchsvollen Bedingungen im Outdoorbereich gerecht. Ergänzt wird der Hocker durch ein Kissen aus dem Kunststoff EVA, das lose auf der Sitzfläche aufliegt.

Begründung der Jury
Der Hocker Aunglo punktet mit einer funktionalen und formschönen Gestaltung. Dank seiner Robustheit ist er auch gut für den Outdoorbereich geeignet.

Beatrix
Lounge Chair
Lounge-Sessel

Manufacturer
Ritzwell & Co., Fukuoka, Japan
In-house design
Shinsaku Miyamoto
Web
www.ritzwell.com

With its high backrest, distinctively curved frame and severe bodylines that contrast pleasingly with the softness of the upholstery and the balanced interplay of wood, leather and fabric, the Beatrix lounge chair has an unmistakable aura. Thick, vegetable-tanned leather is proof of the high-quality materials used. Particular attention has been paid to developing a construction that is based on sound ergonomic principles and ensures comfort while at the same time soothing fatigue.

Mit der hohen Rückenlehne, der markant geschwungenen Form des Rahmens, dem Kontrast zwischen der strengen Linienführung des Gestells und der Weichheit der Kissen sowie dem ausgewogenen Zusammenspiel von Holz, Leder und Stoff strahlt der Lounge-Sessel Beatrix eine starke Präsenz aus. Die Verarbeitung von dickem, pflanzlich gegerbtem Leder zeugt von hochwertigem Materialeinsatz. Besonderes Augenmerk liegt auf einer ergonomisch gut durchdachten Konstruktionsweise, die einen hohen Sitzkomfort ermöglicht und Müdigkeitserscheinungen entgegenwirkt.

Statement by the jury
The design of the Beatrix lounge chair is an outstanding example for the combination of a bold look with well-thought-out ergonomic properties.

Begründung der Jury
Die Gestaltung des Lounge-Sessels Beatrix vereint auf hohem Niveau ein kraftvolles Aussehen mit wohldurchdachten ergonomischen Eigenschaften.

Chips
Lounge Chair
Lounge-Sessel

Manufacturer
TON a.s., Bystrice pod Hostynem, Czech Republic
Design
Lucie Koldová Studio, Prague, Czech Republic
Web
www.ton.eu
www.luciekoldova.com

The dominant feature of the Chips lounge chair is its ultra-large backrest made of a perforated fabric set in a manually shaped wooden frame. The backrest, which is reminiscent of a potato crisp, extends to the floor and therefore also acts as the chair's leg. The generous, pocket-sprung seat looks invitingly restful and creates a marked contrast to this airy construction. An ergonomically shaped back cushion, which users can place where it best suits them, adds an extra dimension of comfort.

Dominantes Merkmal des Lounge-Sessels Chips ist seine übergroße Rückenlehne. Sie besteht aus perforiertem Stoff, der von einem handgebogenen Holzrahmen eingefasst wird. Die Lehne, die die Form eines Kartoffelchips nachahmt, reicht bis auf den Boden und dient so auch als Fuß. Einen starken Kontrast zu dieser luftigen Konstruktion bildet der geräumige Sitz, der dank seiner Taschenfederkernpolsterung Bequemlichkeit verspricht. Ein ergonomisch geformtes Rückenkissen, das nach Wunsch des Nutzers positioniert werden kann, erhöht zudem den Sitzkomfort.

Statement by the jury
The fascinating juxtaposition of contrasting elements gives the expertly crafted Chips lounge chair exciting visual appeal.

Begründung der Jury
Das faszinierende Spiel mit Kontrasten verleiht dem mit hoher Handwerkskunst gefertigten Lounge-Sessel Chips eine aufmerksamkeitsstarke Ausstrahlung.

Lido
Chair, Lounge Chair, Table
Stuhl, Lounge-Sessel, Tisch

Manufacturer
Paola Lenti S.r.l., Meda (Monza and Brianza), Italy
Design
Francesco Rota, Milan, Italy
Web
www.paolalenti.it
www.francescorota.com

Designed for outdoor use, the Lido collection comprises a stackable chair, a lounge chair and a table. The robust furniture is made of painted stainless steel. Seat and backrest consist of polypropylene. The innovative feature of this range is a surface made of Diade, a new, single colour material that achieves a surprising textile appearance when used in conjunction with the melange nuances of the Twiggy yarn. This combination of materials is water-repellent and easy to maintain.

Die für den Outdoor-Bereich gestaltete Kollektion Lido umfasst einen stapelbaren Stuhl, einen Lounge-Sessel und einen Tisch. Die robusten Möbel sind aus lackiertem, korrosionsfreiem Stahl hergestellt, Sitz und Rückenlehne bestehen aus Polypropylen. Ihr innovativer Charakter liegt in der aus Diade hergestellten Oberfläche. Dabei handelt es sich um ein neues, unifarbenes Material, das in Kombination mit den Melange-Nuancen des Garns Twiggy eine überraschende Textiloptik bietet. Die Materialkombination ist wasserabstoßend und leicht zu pflegen.

Statement by the jury
The Lido collection captivates with a mix of materials that suits demanding outdoor conditions but at the same time is fascinating to look at.

Begründung der Jury
Die Kollektion Lido überzeugt mit einem Materialmix, der anspruchsvollen Außenbedingungen gerecht wird und zudem ein faszinierendes Aussehen hat.

Any-Way
Table, Stool
Tisch, Hocker

Manufacturer
Beijing Xiao Mo Guai Technology Co., Ltd.,
Beijing, China
Design
Office for Product Design
(Nicol Boyd, Tomas Rosén),
Hong Kong
Web
www.pupupula.com
www.officeforproductdesign.com

The table and stool of the Any-Way range were specially designed for modern families. Made of moulded plywood, they come with lino tabletops and seats. The table can be supplied with an optional felt drawer which offers ample storage space. Designed with children in mind, the tabletop has rounded corners and a raised edge to prevent objects from rolling off it. The easy to assemble furniture items come in three colourways and will add a touch of warmth to a wide variety of interiors.

Statement by the jury
The Any-Way range of furniture is very family-orientated thanks to a design focused on practicality and versality that at the same time radiates positivity.

Tisch und Hocker der Serie Any-Way wurden speziell für die moderne Familie konzipiert. Sie sind aus Formsperrholz gebaut, die Platte und der Sitz bestehen aus Linoleum. Der Tisch ist optional mit einer Filzschublade erhältlich, die einen großzügigen Stauraum bietet. Die Tischplatte hat kinderfreundlich abgerundete Ecken und ist mit einer erhöhten Umrandung versehen, die ein Herunterrollen von Gegenständen verhindert. Die einfach zu montierenden Möbel sind in drei Farben erhältlich und ergänzen mit ihrer warmen Ausstrahlung gut verschiedene Einrichtungen.

Begründung der Jury
Mit ihrer positiven Ausstrahlung und einer auf Praktikabilität und Vielseitigkeit ausgerichteten Gestaltung sind die Any-Way-Möbel sehr familienfreundlich.

Foster 620 Table
Occasional Table
Beistelltisch

Manufacturer
Walter Knoll AG & Co. KG,
Herrenberg, Germany
Design
Norman Foster, London, United Kingdom
Web
www.walterknoll.de
www.fosterandpartners.com

The Foster 620 Table was inspired by nature. The occasional table looks like it has grown out of the floor but is still a natural part of the room. The harmonious shape, elegant tabletop and unique grain of the wood give it a sculptural appearance. The silky-soft surface of the slender tabletop, which comes in three different colours, radiates warmth and well-being. The support is made of solid oak or walnut and has an evenly velvety look as well.

Statement by the jury
The expressive design of the Foster 620 Table combines a natural look with power and elegance to create a piece of furniture with an almost sculptural quality.

Die Inspiration zu dem Foster 620 Table erfolgte aus der Auseinandersetzung mit der Natur. Der Beistelltisch wirkt wie aus dem Boden erwachsen, aber selbstverständlich zum Raum gehörend. Die Harmonie der Form, die elegante Platte und die ausdrucksvolle Maserung verleihen ihm eine skulpturale Anmutung. Die seidigweiche Oberfläche der schlanken, in drei verschiedenen Farben erhältlichen Tischplatte strahlt Wärme und Geborgenheit aus. Der Fuß besteht aus massivem Eichen- oder Nussbaumholz und hat ebenfalls ein gleichmäßig samtenes Aussehen.

Begründung der Jury
Die ausdrucksstarke Gestaltung des Foster 620 Table vereint Natürlichkeit, Kraft und Eleganz zu einem Möbelstück mit skulpturaler Anmutung.

Casattava
Desk
Schreibtisch

Manufacturer
Studio Arredi S.r.l., Narzole (Cuneo), Italy
Design
Prode (Matteo Zaghi), Turin, Italy
Pistejaviiva (Heikki Herranen), Oulu, Finland
Web
www.studioarredi.it
www.designprode.eu
www.pistejaviiva.com

Casattava is a 100 per cent birch plywood desk that adapts to the everyday activities and growth of its users at different ages. The flatpack desk, with its interlocking system of joints, is quickly assembled without any tools, and the height can be adjusted for the user. Casattava has two blackboard covers which can be used to take notes and hide the storage compartments. An engraving serves to hold pens and the tubular bar offers space for a clamp lamp or even a roll of paper.

Statement by the jury
The well-thought-out and straightforward design of the height adjustable Casattava desk is to a high degree focused on delivering functionality.

Casattava ist ein zu 100 Prozent aus Birkensperrholz gefertigter Schreibtisch, der sich den täglichen Aktivitäten sowie dem Wachstum seiner Nutzer in verschiedenen Altersstufen anpasst. Der Flatpack-Schreibtisch und auch dessen Höhe lassen sich dank des ineinandergreifenden Verbindungssystems schnell werkzeugfrei zusammenbauen. Casattava hat zwei Tafelabdeckungen, auf denen Notizen gemacht werden können und die die Aufbewahrungsfächer abdecken. Eine Vertiefung dient als Ablage für Stifte und die Rundstange bietet Platz für eine Klemmleuchte oder sogar eine Papierrolle.

Begründung der Jury
Die wohldurchdachte und unkomplizierte Gestaltung des mitwachsenden Schreibtischs Casattava ist auf ein hohes Maß an Funktionalität ausgerichtet.

Solid
Table
Tisch

Manufacturer
hülsta-werke, Hüls GmbH & Co. KG,
Stadtlohn, Germany
Design
Design Ballendat GmbH (Martin Ballendat),
Simbach am Inn, Germany
Web
www.huelsta.com
www.ballendat.com

The anthracite-tinted glass top of the Solid table is embedded in a protective, hand-made solid wood frame. This allows users to see the clever substructure: slim metal brackets set on an elegant steel cross base support the tabletop and give it the appearance of floating. This steel construction ensures the table is extremely sturdy even when bearing heavy loads. Thanks to the pairing with natural hardwood, the table looks warm and welcoming. All woods have been treated with water-based oils, so that slight scratches can easily be repaired even by the user.

Die anthrazit getönte Glasplatte des Tisches Solid ist in einem schützenden, handwerklich gearbeiteten Massivholzrahmen eingebettet. Sie ermöglicht die Sicht auf die raffinierte Unterkonstruktion: Filigrane Metallbügel auf einem eleganten Kreuzfuß aus Stahl tragen sie fast schwebend. Durch die Stahlkonstruktion wird Stabilität auch bei hoher Belastbarkeit erreicht. Dank der Kombination mit natürlichem Massivholz mutet der Tisch warm und wohnlich an. Alle Hölzer sind auf Wasserbasis geölt – so lassen sich leichte Kratzer sogar selbst reparieren.

Statement by the jury
Solid impresses with a design that combines an inspired construction concept and different materials to create a modern table.

Begründung der Jury
Solid überzeugt mit einer Gestaltung, die eine ausgeklügelte Konstruktionsweise und verschiedene Materialien zu einem modernen Tisch vereint.

tema
Table
Tisch

Manufacturer
Team 7 Natürlich Wohnen GmbH,
Ried im Innkreis, Austria
Design
Produktdesign Tesseraux+Partner,
Potsdam, Germany
Web
www.team7.at
www.tesserauxundpartner.de

tema is a wooden dining table that can be extended by 100 cm. Insertion panels located under the surface and the innovative, very slim 2soft extension mechanism make this simple and intuitive. In a single motion, both halves of the tabletop slide apart simultaneously and the insertion panels automatically swing up in a gently cushioned movement. The advantage of this system is that the bench seats can remain in place when the dining table is extended or contracted, as the frame itself does not move in this process.

Statement by the jury
The carefully thought-out design acquires merit for its innovative use of technology which makes the extendable dining table tema simple and intuitive to handle.

Der Holz-Esstisch tema lässt sich einfach und intuitiv um 100 cm vergrößern. Dafür sorgen unter der Oberfläche integrierte Einlegeplatten sowie die innovative, sehr schlank konstruierte 2soft-Ausschwenktechnik. Mit nur einem Handgriff öffnet sich die synchron ausziehbare Tischplatte in der Mitte und lässt die Einlegeplatten automatisch ausschwenken. Deren Bewegung wird in beide Richtungen gedämpft. Das Gestell bleibt dabei an seinem Platz. So muss eine am Esstisch stehende Sitzbank nicht verschoben werden, wenn dieser vergrößert oder verkleinert wird.

Begründung der Jury
Die wohldurchdachte Gestaltung punktet mit einem innovativen Technikeinsatz, durch den der Auszieh-Esstisch tema einfach und intuitiv handhabbar ist.

Margo Square
Table
Tisch

Manufacturer
vitamin design, DONA Handelsges. mbH,
Hamburg, Germany
In-house design
gg designart, Hamburg, Germany
Web
www.vitamin-design.de

The appearance of the Margo Square table is dominated by its graphic quality. The individual components have clean lines, an impression that is reinforced by the use of a plain, minimalist tabletop, which is made of linoleum or wood. The edge profiling can be customised and either bevelled or finished with a straight edge. The square table is available in a variety of natural woods such as beech, beech heartwood, ash, oak, knotty oak, maple, cherry, walnut or knotty walnut.

Statement by the jury
With its graphic design vocabulary and expressive appearance, the Margo Square table assimilates well with a range of different interior design styles.

Das Erscheinungsbild des Tisches Margo Square wird von seiner grafischen Qualität bestimmt. Die einzelnen Konstruktionselemente weisen eine klare Linienführung auf. Dieser Eindruck wird durch die Verwendung einer schlichten, minimalistisch gestalteten Tischplatte verfestigt, welche aus Linoleum oder Holz hergestellt wird. Deren Kantenprofil erfolgt nach individuellem Wunsch – es kann eine gerade oder abgeschrägte Ausführung gewählt werden. Der quadratische Tisch ist in den naturbehandelten Holzarten Ahorn, Buche, Kernbuche, Esche, Eiche, Asteiche, Kirschbaum, Nussbaum sowie Astnussbaum erhältlich.

Begründung der Jury
Mit seiner grafischen Formensprache und seinem ausdrucksstarken Aussehen integriert sich der Tisch Margo Square gut in unterschiedliche Einrichtungsstile.

Power X
Mattress
Matratze

Manufacturer
Foshan Duo Pu Le Furniture Co., Ltd.,
Foshan, China
In-house design
Prof. Feng Wang
Web
www.dorlux.hk

The appearance of the Power X mattress is defined by its combination of traditional spring and modern design elements. The mattress is manufactured using an innovative 3D CNC cutting technology and includes hundreds of independent support points. Each of these support points consists of four layers of different sponge materials designed optimally to support every part of the human body. The spaces between the support points and the spring-shaped cut serve to aid breathability and elasticity of the mattress.

Das Aussehen der Matratze Power X wird von der Kombination traditioneller Feder- und moderner Designelemente bestimmt. Sie wird mittels der innovativen 3D-CNC-Schneidtechnologie hergestellt und verfügt über Hunderte voneinander unabhängiger Stützpunkte. Jeder dieser Stützpunkte besteht aus vier Schichten unterschiedlicher Schwammmaterialien und bietet eine sehr gute Unterstützung für jeden Teil des menschlichen Körpers. Die Lücken zwischen den Stützpunkten sowie der federförmige Schnitt fördern die Atmungsaktivität und Elastizität der Matratze.

Statement by the jury
The resourceful, functionality-focused design concept of Power X results in a comfortable mattress that also ensures the body is well supported.

Begründung der Jury
Das findige, auf Funktionalität bedachte Gestaltungskonzept verleiht der Matratze Power X angenehme, den Körper unterstützende Liegeeigenschaften.

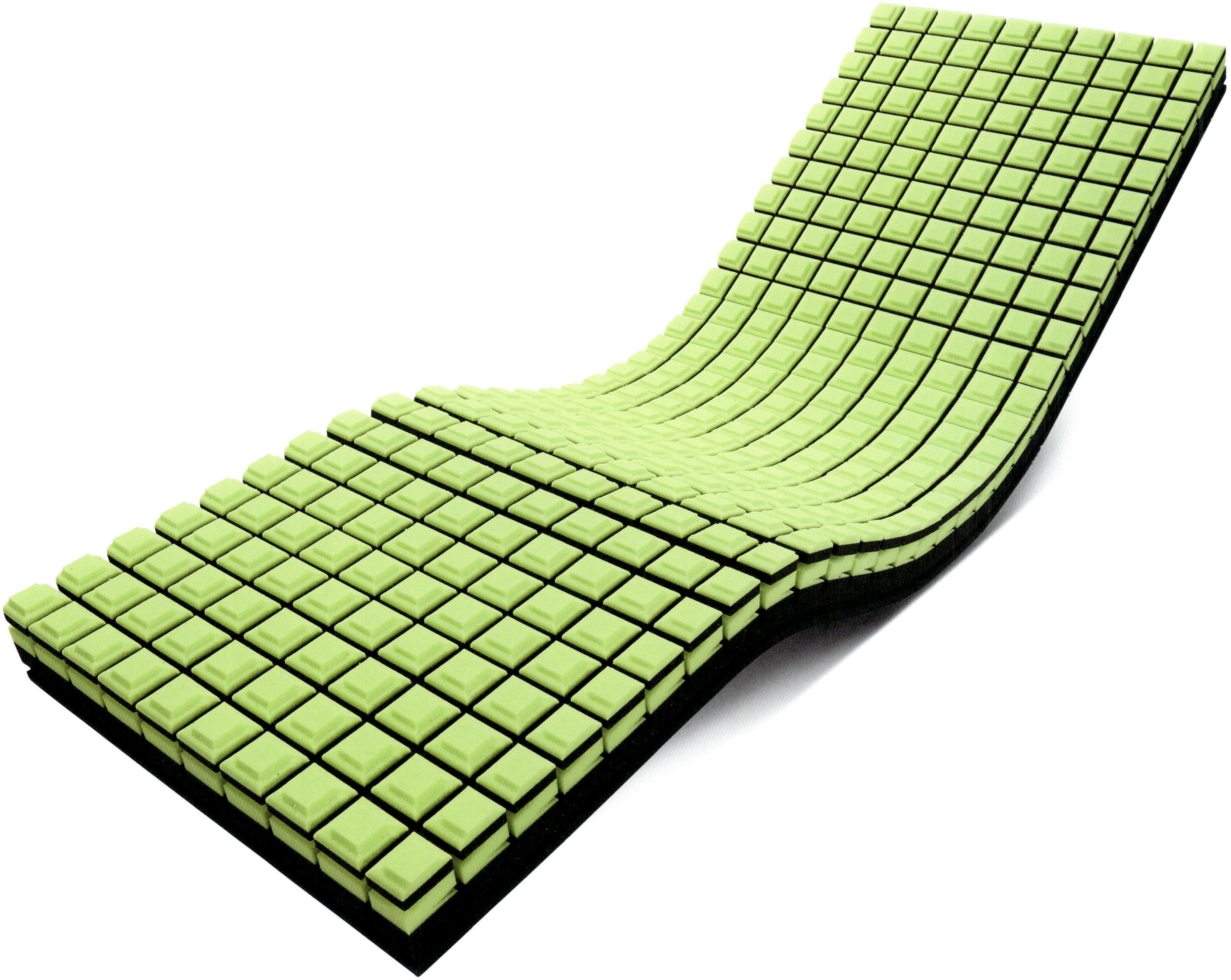

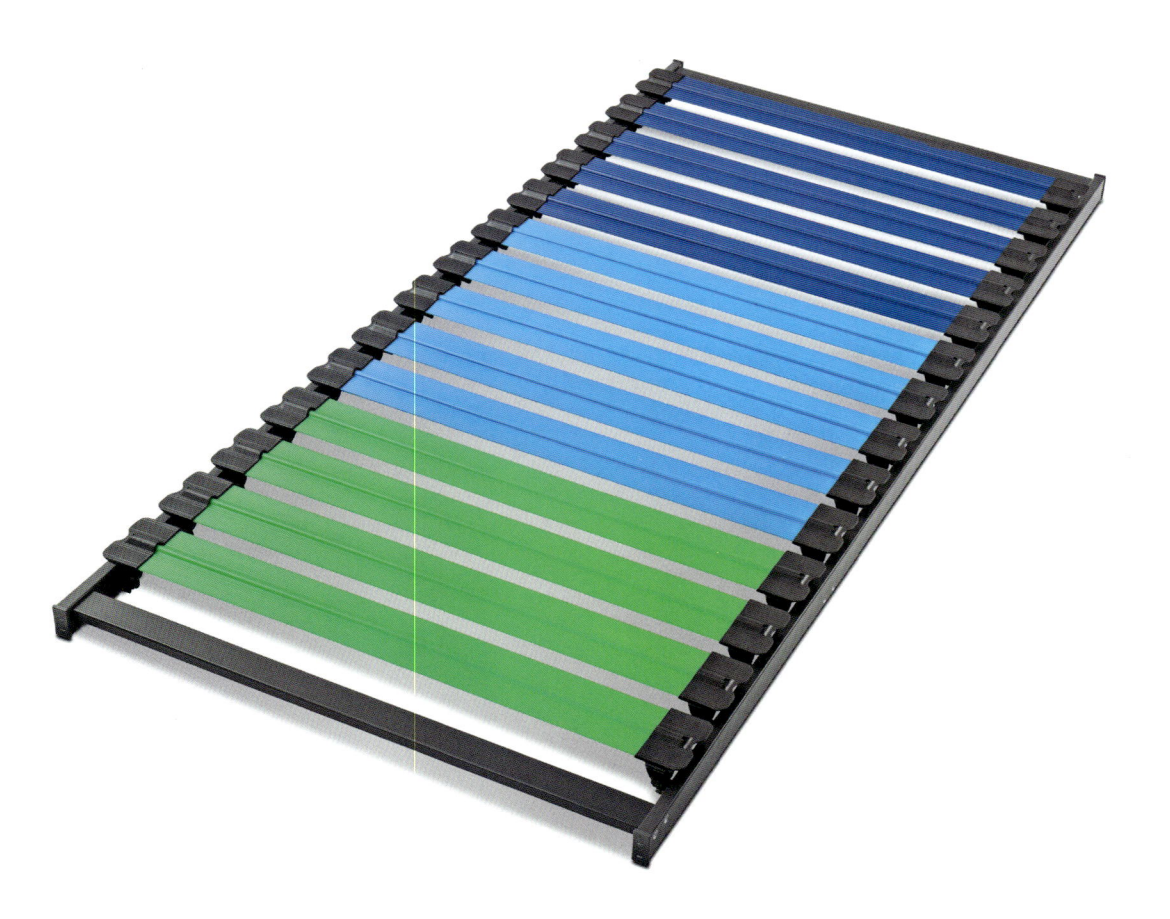

GOODSIDE® 3in1
Slatted Frame
Unterfederung

Manufacturer
OKE Group GmbH, Hörstel, Germany
In-house design
Web
www.oke-group.com

Goodside 3in1 is the name for a bed base made of glass-fibre reinforced plastic slats that perfectly cushion the body all over and prevent it from sinking too far into the mattress. Irrespective of body shape, the back is well supported in any position. The materials used ensure durability and consistent elasticity. The slats are available in various hardness ratings which are characterised by different colours. Depending on the arrangement, the user can choose between a strong, medium or soft hardness rating.

Statement by the jury
With its innovative use of materials and technology, and good ergonomic properties, the Goodside 3in1 slatted frame ensures a comfortable night's sleep.

Hinter Goodside 3in1 verbirgt sich eine Unterfederung aus glasfaserverstärkten Kunststoffleisten. Diese federn den Körper an jeder Stelle einwandfrei ab, ohne dass er zu tief einsinkt. Unabhängig von den Körperproportionen wird der Rücken in jeder Position sehr gut unterstützt. Die verwendeten Materialien garantieren Langlebigkeit und gleichbleibende Elastizität. Die Leisten sind in verschiedenen Härtegraden erhältlich, welche durch unterschiedliche Farben gekennzeichnet sind. Je nach Anordnung kann der Nutzer zwischen den Härtegraden hart, mittel oder weich wählen.

Begründung der Jury
Dank eines innovativen Material- und Technikeinsatzes und guter ergonomischer Eigenschaften bietet die Unterfederung Goodside 3in1 hohen Schlafkomfort.

AiR Conditioning Comforter
Duvet
Bettdecke

Manufacturer
Nishikawa Sangyo Co., Ltd.,
Tokyo, Japan
In-house design
Design
Naoki Takizawa Design Inc.,
Tokyo, Japan
Web
www.nishikawasangyo.co.jp
www.naokitakizawa.com

This duvet comfortably hugs the body thanks to its quilting. Ultra-light fabric was used for the ticking and synthetic fibres for the wadding, so the duvet would be able to retain heat for a long time and be light in weight. Moreover, this filling also has a high bulking power. The cover is encased in a Body Line AiR Quilt which is pleasant to the touch and therefore also aids restorative sleep. In addition, the duvet is very hygienic as it is easy to wash at home.

Statement by the jury
The ambitious design of this duvet succeeds in achieving high thermal insulation at the same time as making it lightweight and pleasant to touch.

Diese Bettdecke schmiegt sich dank ihrer Steppereien angenehm an den Körper an. Ihre hohe Wärmespeicherung sowie ihr geringes Gewicht verdankt sie einem Inlett aus ultraleichtem Stoff sowie einer Einlage aus Kunststofffasern. Diese Füllung besitzt zudem ein hohes Maß an Bauschkraft. Umhüllt wird die Decke von Body-Line-AiR-Quilt, was ein gutes Gefühl auf der Haut gewährleistet und auf diese Weise auch einen erholsamen Schlaf unterstützt. Darüber hinaus ist die Decke sehr hygienisch, da sie bequem zu Hause gewaschen werden kann.

Begründung der Jury
Diese anspruchsvoll gestaltete Bettdecke überzeugt mit einer hohen Wärmeisolierung bei gleichzeitiger Leichtigkeit und behaglicher Haptik.

NM – Dial Remote Control
NM – Dreh-Fernbedienung

Manufacturer
Nien Made Enterprise, Norman – Window Fashions,
Taichung, Taiwan
In-house design
Michael Nien, Raymond Jao
Design
LITE-ON Technology Corp., Taipei City, Taiwan
Web
www.nienmade.com.tw
www.liteon.com

You can also find this product
on page 93.
Dieses Produkt finden Sie auch
auf Seite 93.

As part of the smart home toolkit, the NM dial remote control for shutters transforms any home into a modern, tech-responsive living space. Operation is easy and intuitive, and can be done by iPhone/iPad. Simply by turning the outer ring dial, the louvres adjust instantly to the precise angle desired. Multiple shutters can be controlled at the same time or different sets independently from each other. In this processs, the colour-coordinated ring settings ensure easy identification.

Als Teil des Smart Home-Toolkits verwandelt die NM-Fernbedienung für Rollläden ein Zuhause in einen modernen, technischen Ansprüchen gerecht werdenden Lebensraum. Die Bedienung erfolgt über ein iPhone/iPad und ist mühelos und intuitiv. Durch einfaches Drehen des äußeren Einstellrads passen sich die Lamellen direkt an den gewünschten Winkel an. Es lassen sich mehrere Rollläden gleichzeitig oder verschiedene Gruppen von Rollläden unabhängig voneinander steuern, wobei die farblich abgestimmten Ringeinstellungen die Identifizierung erleichtern.

Statement by the jury
This high-quality dial remote control for blinds presents itself as a functional and at the same time stylish smart home device.

Begründung der Jury
Diese hochwertige Dreh-Fernbedienung für Jalousien präsentiert sich als ein gleichermaßen funktionales wie auch formschönes Smart Home-Utensil.

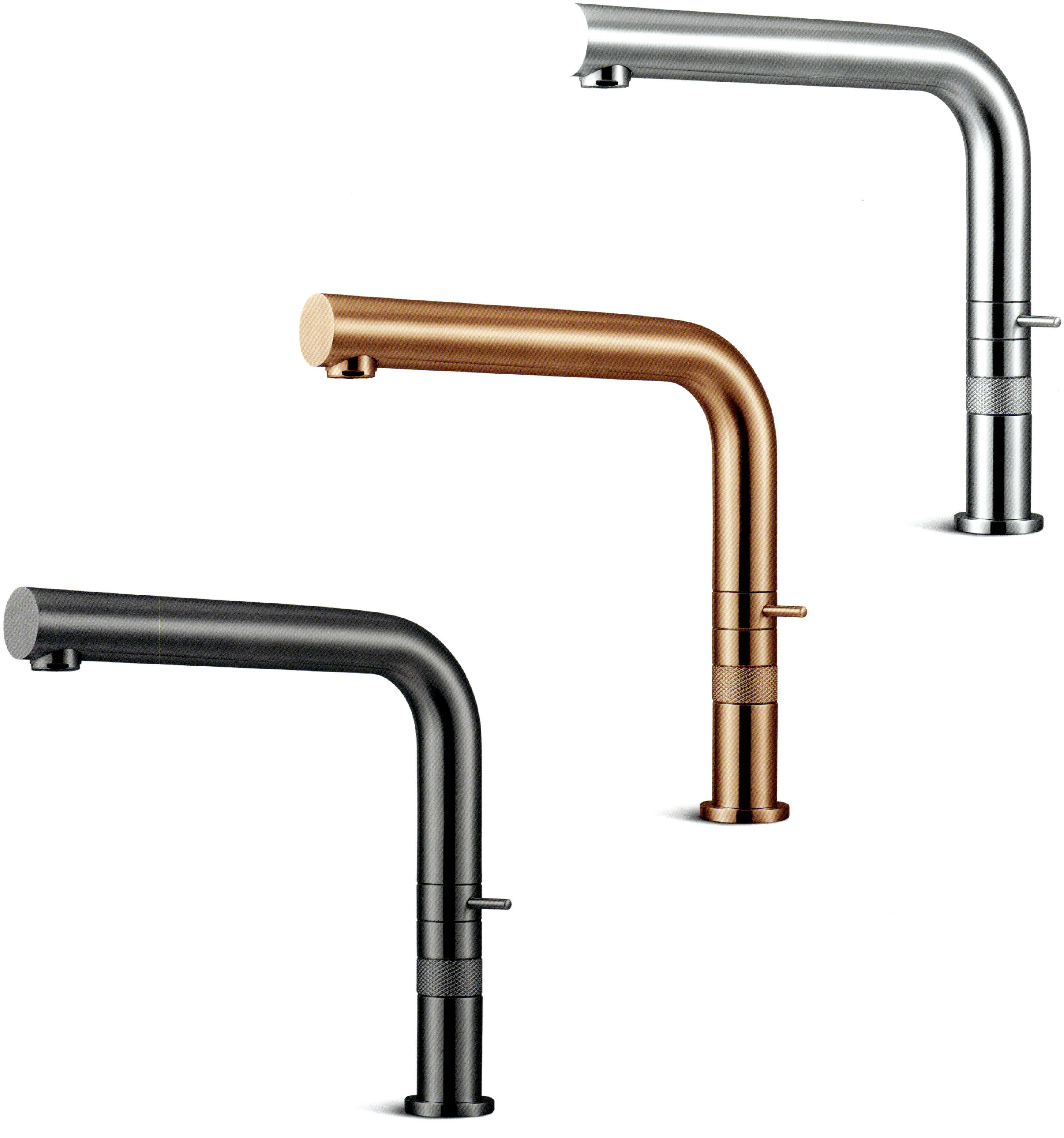

Kitchens
Küche

Coffee machines	Dampfgarer
Dishwashers	Dunstabzugshauben
Eat-in kitchens	Einhebelmischer
Electric kettles	Entsafter
Extractor hoods	Fritteusen
Filter taps	Kaffeemaschinen
Fryers	Kochfelder
Grinders	Küchenarmaturenserien
Hobs	Küchenausstattung
Juicers	Küchenelemente
Kitchen elements	Küchenmaschinen
Kitchen equipment	Kühl- und Gefriergeräte
Kitchen machines	Mikrowellen
Kitchen tap series	Mixer
Microwaves	Mobile Küchen
Mixers	Mühlen
Mobile kitchens	Multifunktionsgeräte
Multifunction devices	Öfen
Ovens	Reiskocher
Refrigerators and freezers	Smoothie-Maker
Rice cookers	Sodaarmaturen
Single lever mixers	Spülbecken
Sinks	Spülmaschinen
Smoothie makers	Teekocher
Steam cookers	Toaster
Tea makers	Unterbaubecken
Toasters	Wasserfiltersysteme
Undermount bowls	Wasserkocher
Water filtration systems	Wohnküchen

Teawith Kettle
Tea Kettle
Teekessel

Manufacturer
Teawith Essentials Association,
Beijing, China

In-house design
Zhuang Jingyang, Liu Fang

Design
United Design Lab (Keren Hu,
Ding Fan, Fang Jianping, Li Yu),
Beijing, China

Web
www.teawith.com
www.u-d-l.com

reddot award 2019
best of the best

It's teatime
Today, kettles continue to be used in households as a utensil to boil water for making tea or coffee. Against the backdrop of changing lifestyles, the Teawith Kettle has been conceived as an electric kettle introducing a new design vocabulary and functionality. The goal was to respond to scenarios in which people are longing for the beauty of taking life slowly while living in big, fast-paced cities. The design has been created to elegantly bridge this gap. This electric kettle fits the modern lifestyle, embodying the cultural essence of both tea making and traditional Far Eastern aesthetics, paired with Western-style design queues. This is expressed in an overall balanced and harmonious-looking design, a round body with a classical shape, as well as a distinctive, arched upright handle and a square base. Made of high-quality materials such as stainless steel for the body, aluminium for the handle and a zinc alloy for the base, the Teawith Kettle is both sturdy and durable. The ergonomic curve of the handle is specially designed for a more comfortable and effortless grip. The narrow spout has also been well thought-out. It offers high control of water flow, promoting an emotionalising experience when preparing tea. Interacting with the kettle is impressively simple, as it is activated by means of a switch integrated in the handle. The handle just needs to be held and pressed – a single flowing, unconscious movement.

It's Teatime
Der Wasserkessel ist ein im Haushalt nach wie vor viel genutztes Gerät für die Zubereitung von Tee oder Kaffee. Vor dem Hintergrund sich verändernder Lebensweisen sollte mit dem Teawith Kettle ein elektrischer Wasserkessel mit neuer Formensprache und Funktionalität kreiert werden. Ziel war es, Szenarien gerecht zu werden, die die Schönheit einer Verlangsamung des Lebens zelebrieren, nach dem sich die Menschen in hektischen Stadtumgebungen sehnen. Die Gestaltung zeigt hier einen eleganten Brückenschlag. Dieser Teekessel passt zum modernen Lifestyle und verkörpert zugleich die Essenz der Kultur der Teezubereitung sowie traditioneller fernöstlicher Ästhetik mit Anleihen westlichen Designs. Zum Ausdruck kommt dies in einer ausgewogen und harmonisch anmutenden Gestaltung, einem runden Korpus mit klassisch geformtem, markantem Griff in aufrechter Position und einem viereckigen Untersatz. Bestehend aus hochwertigen Materialien wie Edelstahl für den Korpus, Aluminium für den Griff und einer Zinklegierung für den Untersatz, ist der Teawith Kettle langlebig und robust. Die ergonomische Kurvatur des Griffs erlaubt dem Teeliebhaber ein komfortables und müheloses Greifen. Funktional durchdacht ist zudem der eng geformte Ausguss. Er bietet ein kontrolliertes Ausgießen des Wassers und emotionalisiert die tägliche Teezubereitung. Beeindruckend einfach ist die Interaktion mit dem Wasserkessel, da er mittels eines in den Griff integrierten Schalters aktiviert wird. Der Griff muss nur gehalten und gedrückt werden – eine einzige fließende, unbewusste Bewegung.

Statement by the jury
The clear design of the Teawith Kettle conveys a strong sense of peace and relaxation. This well-proportioned kettle actively encourages users to prepare a cup of tea and enjoy it while reading a book. Its matte black surface is pleasing to the touch and perfectly suited for long-term use. The shapely, pleasantly high-grip handle with integrated switch is functional and ergonomically sophisticated.

Begründung der Jury
Der Teawith Kettle vermittelt durch seine klare Gestaltung das Gefühl von Ruhe und Entspanntheit. Dieser wohlproportionierte Wasserkessel animiert dazu, sich sofort eine Tasse Tee zuzubereiten und ein Buch zu nehmen. Das matte Schwarz der Oberfläche ist haptisch ansprechend und für den langen Gebrauch perfekt geeignet. Funktional und ergonomisch durchdacht ist der formschöne, komfortable Griff mit integriertem Schalter.

Designer portrait
See page 44
Siehe Seite 44

189

Electric Travelling Kettle
Wasserkocher

Manufacturer
Guangdong Xinbao Electrical Appliances Holdings Co., Ltd.,
Foshan, China
In-house design
Prof. Chen Long Hui, Prof. Yang Bin
Web
www.donlim.com

The Electric Travelling Kettle is perfect for out and about, e.g. when on holiday or in the office. Its shape is reminiscent of a vase and comes without a handle in order to take up as little space as possible. Thanks to a double-walled stainless-steel body, it is well insulated and stays cool on the outside while the water keeps hot for longer. With its slender shape the kettle lies pleasantly in the hand. Power supply cable and plug can be stowed in the base. It is operated by a single button.

Der Electric Travelling Kettle ist ein Wasserkocher für unterwegs, der einen in den Urlaub oder ins Büro begleiten kann. Seine Form erinnert an eine Vase. Auf einen Griff wurde bei der Gestaltung bewusst verzichtet, damit er weniger Platz einnimmt. Dank eines doppelwandigen Edelstahlkörpers ist er gut isoliert und bleibt außen kühl, während das Wasser lange heiß bleibt. Der Wasserkocher liegt mit seiner schlanken Form zudem angenehm in der Hand. Netzkabel und -stecker lassen sich im Boden verstauen. Die Bedienung erfolgt mit einer einzigen Taste.

Statement by the jury
The Electric Travelling Kettle looks more like a living accessory than a kitchen device. It is a compact kettle and especially useful for travelling.

Begründung der Jury
Mehr an ein Wohnaccessoire als an ein Küchengerät erinnernd, ist der Electric Travelling Kettle tatsächlich ein kompakter Wasserkocher, den man gerne mit auf Reisen nimmt.

Jacqueline
Electric Kettle
Wasserkocher

Manufacturer
Ilcar di Bugatti S.r.l., Lumezzane (Brescia), Italy
Design
Habits S.r.l. (Prof. Innocenzo Rifino), Milan, Italy
Studio Narai (Prof. Lorenzo Ruggieri), Milan, Italy
Web
www.casabugatti.com
www.habits.it
www.narai.it

The Jacqueline kettle was designed with regard to an elegant preparation of tea. Its shape recalls an iconic bag and it is inspired by traditional ceramic teapots. It is made of 18/10 stainless steel with a PCT Tritan handle. All stages of the heating process and the infusion can be controlled and regulated: from the temperature, that can be set at a precise degree from 40 to 100 degrees Celsius, to the "keep warm" function. When in use, its base becomes bright. Simple and intuitive, the B Chef app (based on IoT) allows to programme and customise the preparation.

Der Wasserkocher Jacqueline wurde für eine elegante Art der Teezubereitung entworfen. Sein Äußeres erinnert an eine ikonische Handtasche und ist von traditionellen Keramikteekannen inspiriert. Der Wasserkocher besteht aus 18/10 Edelstahl und hat einen Griff aus PCT-Tritan. Alle Stufen des Heizvorgangs können überprüft und gesteuert werden: von der Temperatur, die exakt zwischen 40 und 100 Grad eingestellt werden kann, bis hin zur Warmhaltefunktion. Der Sockel leuchtet, wenn der Wasserkocher in Betrieb ist. Über die IoT-basierte B-Chef-App lässt sich die Teezubereitung einfach und intuitiv programmieren und personalisieren.

Statement by the jury
With its spectacular design, this kettle becomes an eye-catcher on the worktop. It convincingly connects traditional forms with high-tech features.

Begründung der Jury
Mit seiner aufsehenerregenden Gestaltung wird dieser Wasserkocher zum Blickfang auf der Arbeitsplatte. Gelungen ist auch die Verbindung zwischen traditionellen gestalterischen Anleihen und moderner Technologie.

Glass Kettle
Wasserkocher

Manufacturer
GD Midea Consumer Electric MFG, Co., Ltd., Foshan, China
In-house design
Qingxia Wu, Yang Chao
Web
www.midea.com

The can and lid of this water kettle are made of glass. This special design feature enables the user to watch the boiling process from every angle. Even the bottom of the kettle is made of glass, so that, other than with similar devices having metal and plastic elements, it is very easy and convenient to clean, simply with water.

Das besondere Gestaltungsmerkmal dieses Wasserkochers ist, dass bei ihm Kanne und Deckel aus Glas bestehen. Dadurch ist der gesamte Kochvorgang aus jedem Blickwinkel gut sichtbar. Auch die Unterseite des Wasserkochers ist aus Glas gefertigt, sodass er – anders als vergleichbare Geräte mit Metall- und Kunststoffelementen – sehr einfach und komfortabel allein mit Wasser gereinigt werden kann.

Statement by the jury
This kettle with glass body allows users to observe the heating process and thus appeals to the senses. Furthermore, due to the use of glass, it is particularly easy to clean.

Begründung der Jury
Dieser Wasserkocher mit Glaskörper gewährt Nutzern Einblick in den Erhitzungsprozess und spricht damit ihre Sinne an. Zudem ist er durch die Verwendung von Glas besonders leicht zu reinigen.

Tea Maker Compact
Teekocher

Manufacturer
Breville, Sydney, Australia
In-house design
Web
www.breville.com

The Tea Maker Compact makes it possible to prepare various kinds of tea at the touch of a button, paying special attention to the recommended brewing time and temperature for each variety. As soon as the water has reached the ideal temperature, the basket descends and gently agitates the leaves. Once the brewing time has expired, it lifts out automatically. Thanks to a timer function, the tea maker can also be programmed and keeps the prepared tea warm for up to 60 minutes.

Der Tea Maker Compact ermöglicht es, verschiedene Teesorten zu ihren jeweils optimalen Bedingungen hinsichtlich Temperatur und Ziehzeit auf Knopfdruck zuzubereiten. Sobald das Wasser die ideale Temperatur für eine Teesorte erreicht hat, senkt sich das Teesieb in das Wasser hinab, bewegt die Blätter und hebt sich nach der Brühzeit automatisch wieder heraus. Dank einer Timerfunktion kann der Teekocher auch programmiert werden und hält den fertigen Tee danach bis zu 60 Minuten lang warm.

Statement by the jury
Tea preparation with the Tea Maker Compact is remarkably simple, thanks to its automatic functions. The transparent jug also allows the user to observe the tea-making process.

Begründung der Jury
Die Teezubereitung ist mit dem Tea Maker Compact dank seiner Automatikfunktionen denkbar einfach. Das transparente Gefäß ermöglicht es zudem, den Prozess zu beobachten.

BUYDEEM Teamaker K108
Teekocher

Manufacturer
Shenzhen Crastal Technology Co., Ltd., Shenzhen, China
In-house design
Roy Lu, Hao Xin, Wenjin Zhong
Web
www.buydeem.com

The design of this tea maker is based on the concept of the right amount of simplicity in order to achieve a pleasant user experience. The transparent kettle allows a free view of the brewing process and blends in with every kitchen environment. A light band on the base visualises the different steps of the heating process. An NTC thermistor is located in the bottom part of the appliance, ensuring smoothness and easy cleaning. Furthermore, the tea maker is very quiet.

Der Gestaltung dieses Teekochers basiert auf dem Konzept des richtigen Maßes an Einfachheit, um ein besonders angenehmes Nutzererlebnis zu erzielen. Der transparente Kocher gibt den Blick auf den Brühvorgang im Inneren frei und passt in jede Küchenumgebung. Ein Lichtband an der Basis zeigt die Stufen des Heizvorgangs an. Im Boden befindet sich ein Heißleiter (NTC), wodurch der Boden glatt und leicht zu reinigen ist. Darüber hinaus ist der Teekocher sehr leise.

Statement by the jury
By using transparent material, this tea maker is visually reserved and blends harmoniously in the kitchen or office. It is also particularly user friendly.

Begründung der Jury
Durch den Einsatz transparenter Materialien nimmt sich der Teekocher visuell dezent zurück und fügt sich harmonisch in Küche oder Büro ein. Bestechend ist auch seine hohe Benutzerfreundlichkeit.

BUYDEEM Teamaker K165
Multifunctional Tea Maker
Multifunktionaler Teekocher

Manufacturer
Shenzhen Crastal Technology Co., Ltd., Shenzhen, China
In-house design
Roy Lu, Hao Xin, Wenjin Zhong
Web
www.buydeem.com

The K165 is a multifunctional, space-saving device on the basis of a tea maker for the purposes of preparing healthy drinks and food. It can be used for boiling, braising and steaming, depending on which accessory is attached. Control is via an easily understandable user interface with LCD display, by means of which temperature, timer function and programmes can be preset. A concealed NTC temperature sensor, its low-noise function as well as the use of glass and stainless steel contribute to a pleasant user experience.

Der K165 ist ein multifunktionales und platzsparendes Gerät auf Teekocher-Basis zur Zubereitung gesunder Getränke und Speisen. Dank seines durchdachten Zubehörs kann er je nach Auf- und Einsatz zum Kochen, Schmoren oder Dampfgaren genutzt werden. Die Steuerung erfolgt über eine gut verständliche Benutzeroberfläche mit LCD-Display, über die sich Temperatur, Timerfunktion und Programme einstellen lassen. Ein versteckter NTC-Temperatursensor, seine geräuscharme Funktion sowie der Einsatz von Glas und Edelstahl tragen zu einem angenehmen Benutzererlebnis bei.

Statement by the jury
This tea maker shows surprising multi-functionality. It features well-considered accessories as well as high-quality materials.

Begründung der Jury
Mit seiner überraschenden Multifunktionalität punktet dieser Teekocher. Er gefällt zudem mit durchdachtem Zubehör und der Verwendung hochwertiger Materialien.

BUYDEEM Teamaker K187
Multifunctional Tea Maker
Multifunktionaler Teekocher

Manufacturer
Shenzhen Crastal Technology Co., Ltd., Shenzhen, China
In-house design
Roy Lu, Hao Xin, Wenjin Zhong
Web
www.buydeem.com

The K187 multifunctional tea maker facilitates not only the preparation of tea but also steaming, boiling or braising of foods, as it comes with a wide range of accessories. All elements are made of stainless steel and tempered glass, giving the K187 a contemporary technical appearance. The operating panel with LCD colour display und symmetrically located knobs emphasises the hi-tech appeal and facilitates the selection between various programmes, such as the setting of temperature, timer and volume according to personal preferences.

Der multifunktionale Teekocher K187 ermöglicht nicht nur die Zubereitung von Tee, sondern in Kombination mit seinem umfangreichen Zubehör auch das Dampfgaren, Kochen oder Schmoren von Lebensmitteln. Korpus und Zubehör aus Edelstahl und gehärtetem Glas verleihen dem K187 ein zeitgemäßes, technisch wirkendes Erscheinungsbild. Die Bedienfläche mit LCD-Farbdisplay und symmetrisch positionierten Knöpfen unterstreicht den Hightech-Charakter und ermöglicht die Wahl zwischen verschiedenen Programmen sowie die Einstellung von Temperatur, Timer und Lautstärke nach persönlichen Präferenzen.

Statement by the jury
The K187 shows well-considered multifunctionality. Stainless steel and glass both contribute to its highly technical yet classic expression.

Begründung der Jury
Der K187 beeindruckt mit seiner durchdachten Multifunktionalität ebenso wie mit einem Erscheinungsbild, das durch den Einsatz von Edelstahl und Glas zugleich hochtechnisch und klassisch anmutet.

Temial
Tea Device
Teegerät

Manufacturer
Vorwerk Temial GmbH, Wuppertal, Germany
In-house design
Vorwerk Design
Web
www.temial.de

Temial is an intelligent tea device which makes traditional tea brewing especially simple by means of new technology. The device recognises the Temial organic tea varieties by scanning the code on the packaging. The user only needs to put the loose tea in the brewing jar and the device adjusts the brew automatically by setting the correct water temperature and the perfect brewing time. It also informs about the number of possible infusions and offers a waking-up function for very fine teas. Temial can also be controlled by an app.

Temial ist ein intelligentes Teegerät, das eine traditionelle Teezubereitung mithilfe neuer Technologien besonders einfach macht. Das Gerät erkennt die Temial-Bioteesorten per Scan eines auf der Verpackung aufgebrachten Codes. Der Nutzer gibt die losen Teeblätter in den Aufgussbehälter, und die Maschine passt den Aufgussvorgang automatisch an: Sie stellt die richtige Wassertemperatur sowie die perfekte Ziehzeit ein und zeigt die Anzahl der möglichen Aufgüsse an; für feinere Tees steht eine Aufweckfunktion zur Verfügung. Temial kann auch über eine App gesteuert werden.

Statement by the jury
The Temial combines traditional tea making with contemporary technologies. The system including the tea packages presents as particularly user friendly.

Begründung der Jury
Der Temial verbindet eine traditionelle Teezubereitung mit zeitgemäßen Technologien. Das System inklusive der Teeverpackungen ist auf eine besonders hohe Benutzerfreundlichkeit ausgerichtet.

AUTO Tea Maker
Teekocher

Manufacturer
Riviera & Bar, Mundolsheim, France
Top Electric Appliances Industrial Ltd., Hong Kong
In-house design
Top Electric Appliances Industrial Ltd. (Shilton Chong)
Web
www.riviera-et-bar.fr
www.top-ele.com.cn

AUTO Tea Maker is a fully automatic, programmable tea maker. It offers pre-settings for five different types of tea, for which the ideal brewing temperatures and drawing times are already set. The filled tea sieve sinks when the start button is pressed or at a pre-set time and lifts out of the tea automatically after the brewing time has expired. There is also a function for keeping the tea at the right temperature for one hour. Operation is via a one-touch button and an easily understandable user interface.

AUTO Tea Maker ist ein vollautomatischer, programmierbarer Teekocher. Er bietet Voreinstellungen für fünf verschiedene Teesorten, für die die idealen Brühtemperaturen und Ziehzeiten bereits hinterlegt sind. Das befüllte Teesieb senkt sich bei Drücken der Starttaste oder zu einer zuvor eingestellten festen Zeit automatisch herab und hebt sich nach Ablauf der Brühzeit wieder aus dem Tee heraus. Eine Warmhaltefunktion hält das Getränk eine Stunde lang auf Temperatur. Die Bedienung erfolgt mittels One-Touch-Taste und einer gut verständlichen Benutzeroberfläche.

Statement by the jury
This tea maker offers tea lovers who are short of time an uncomplicated and user-friendly method of making tea of various kinds under optimal brewing conditions.

Begründung der Jury
Dieser Teekocher bietet Teeliebhabern mit wenig Zeit eine unkomplizierte und benutzerfreundliche Möglichkeit, verschiedene Teesorten unter Einhaltung der optimalen Brühvoraussetzungen zuzubereiten.

Hourglass Tea Machine
Tea Maker
Teekocher

Manufacturer
Guangdong Xinbao Electrical Appliances Holdings Co., Ltd.,
Foshan, China
In-house design
Prof. Chen Long Hui, Prof. Yang Bin
Web
www.donlim.com

The design of the Hourglass Tea Machine breaks with tradition. Both the brewing vessel and the Gongdao pot are spherical and made of glass, imparting to the appliance its concise and elegant appearance. The user can follow all stages of the brewing process with all of his senses. When the tea has brewed for long enough, it flows through a filter and valve into a stylish teapot, ready to be served. Operation is simple and self-explaining.

Das Design der Hourglass Tea Machine bricht mit traditionellen Gestaltungsmustern in diesem Produktbereich. Sowohl das Aufbrühgefäß als auch die Gongdao-Kanne sind kugelförmig und aus Glas gefertigt, was dem Gerät sein prägnantes und elegantes Aussehen verleiht. Die Gestaltung ermöglicht es dem Nutzer zudem, sämtliche Schritte der Teezubereitung mit allen Sinnen zu verfolgen. Hat der Tee lange genug gezogen, fließt er durch einen Filter und ein Ventil in die Kanne und kann stilvoll serviert werden. Die Bedienung ist einfach und selbsterklärend.

Statement by the jury
The Hourglass Tea Machine impresses with an aesthetically attractive, very balanced design, which makes the appliance a real eye-catcher.

Begründung der Jury
Die Hourglass Tea Machine besticht mit einer ästhetisch reizvollen, sehr ausgewogenen Gestaltung, die die Maschine zum Blickfang macht.

BISTRO
Electric Milk Frother-Barista
Elektrischer Milchaufschäumer

Manufacturer
Bodum AG, Triengen, Switzerland
Design
Pi-Design AG, Triengen, Switzerland
Web
www.bodum.com

This electric milk frother offers various options for preparing milk – from frothing cold or warm milk to heating milk and preparing hot chocolate. The heating phase stops automatically once the temperature has reached 70 degrees Celsius. Operation is by a single button. When this lights up red, the milk is heated and if required frothed; a white light is for hot chocolate and blue is for cold frothing. Milk jug, whisk and lid are dishwasher-safe.

Dieser elektrische Milchaufschäumer bietet verschiedene Möglichkeiten zur Verarbeitung von Milch: Mit ihm lässt sich wahlweise kalte oder warme Milch aufschäumen, Milch erhitzen oder heiße Schokolade zubereiten. Die Erwärmungsphase wird automatisch gestoppt, wenn eine Temperatur von 70 Grad Celsius erreicht ist. Die Bedienung erfolgt über eine einzige Taste. Leuchtet diese Rot, wird die Milch erhitzt und, falls gewünscht, aufgeschäumt; weißes Licht steht für heiße Schokolade und blaues für kaltes Aufschäumen. Milchgefäß, Schneebesen und Deckel sind spülmaschinenfest.

Statement by the jury
With its one-button control and coloured lights, which show the selected mode, this milk frother of the Bistro collection is self-explanatory and thereby very user-friendly.

Begründung der Jury
Mit seiner Ein-Tasten-Bedienung und dem farbigen Licht, das den angewählten Modus anzeigt, ist dieser Milchaufschäumer der Bistro-Reihe selbsterklärend und dadurch sehr benutzerfreundlich.

201

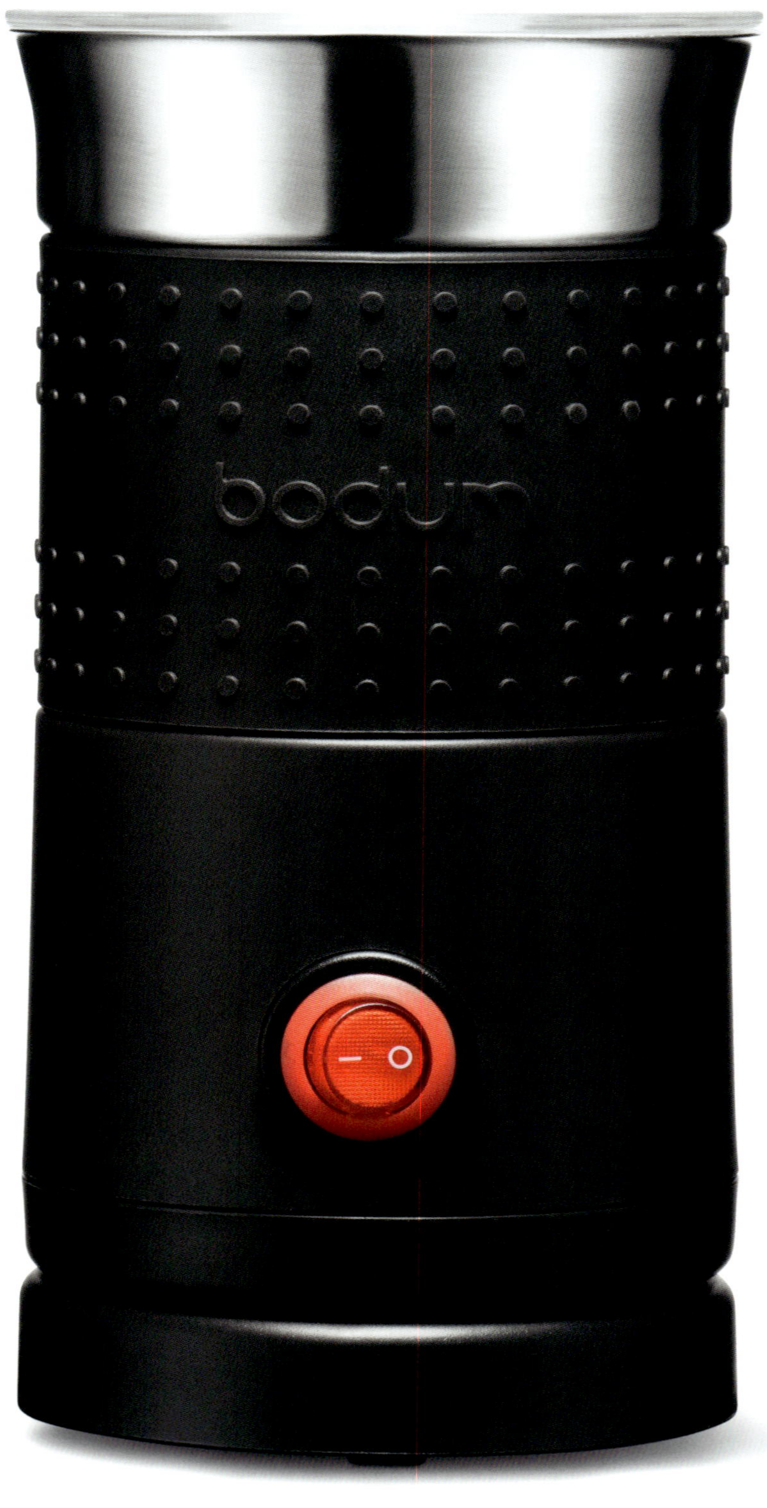
bodum

BISTRO
Electric Milk Frother
Elektrischer Milchaufschäumer

Manufacturer
Bodum AG, Triengen, Switzerland
Design
Pi-Design AG, Triengen, Switzerland
Web
www.bodum.com

With this electrical milk frother of the Bistro collection, milk can be heated and/or frothed. With the frothing function it produces finely structured, firm milk foam for various coffee specialities. It is also possible to simply heat up to 300 ml of milk. Once the milk has reached a temperature of 70 degrees Celsius the device stops automatically. If the milk jug is not taken from the base or the off switch operated, and the temperature falls below 50 degrees Celsius, the milk frother restarts the heating process.

Mit diesem elektrischen Milchaufschäumer der Bistro-Serie lässt sich Milch erhitzen und/oder aufschäumen. Mit der Aufschäumfunktion bereitet er fein strukturierter, festen Milchschaum für verschiedene Kaffeespezialitäten. Bis zu 300 ml Milch können auch einfach erwärmt werden. Wenn die Milch eine Temperatur von 70 Grad Celsius erreicht, stoppt das Gerät automatisch. Wird der Milchbehälter nicht von der Basis genommen oder der Ausschalter betätigt, und die Temperatur fällt unter 50 Grad Celsius, startet der Milchaufschäumer den Heizprozess erneut.

Statement by the jury
This milk frother gains merit with a clear design and easy use. Thanks to the knobbed surface it is also pleasant to the touch.

Begründung der Jury
Dieser Milchaufschäumer punktet mit einer klaren Gestaltung, ist mit seiner genoppten Oberfläche haptisch angenehm und zudem leicht zu bedienen.

Nespresso Barista
Milk Frother
Milchaufschäumer

Manufacturer
Nestlé Nespresso SA, Lausanne, Switzerland
In-house design
Web
www.nestle-nespresso.com

The Nespresso Barista milk frother enables the user to create different types of milk froth and diverse coffee specialities easily at home. All it needs is to pour the milk into a stainless-steel vessel, activate the wave-shaped whisk and choose the type of coffee for which the milk froth is needed. A dot matrix LED touchscreen displays the selection, while the induction system heats the milk. An app with recipes can also be used to save personal recipes on the device.

Statement by the jury
This milk frother is attractive with its calm, homogenous design. The solid stainless-steel jug adds further value.

Mit dem Milchaufschäumer Nespresso Barista lassen sich viele Arten von Milchschaum kreieren, um diverse Kaffeespezialitäten zu Hause zuzubereiten. Dafür wird die Milch in den Edelstahlbehälter gegeben, der wellenförmige Quirl eingesetzt und die Kaffeeart ausgewählt, für die der Milchschaum benötigt wird. Ein Punktmatrix-LED-Touchscreen zeigt die Auswahl an, während das Induktionssystem die Milch erwärmt. Eine App mit Rezepten kann auch genutzt werden, um personalisierte Rezepte auf dem Gerät zu speichern.

Begründung der Jury
Dieser Milchaufschäumer gefällt mit seiner ruhigen, homogenen Gestaltung. Der massive Edelstahlbehälter vermittelt eine hohe Wertigkeit.

Bamboo Dragonfly
Coffee Grinder
Kaffeemühle

Manufacturer
Hero, Beijing, China
In-house design
Zhen Xiaojing, Zhang Xiaoguang
Web
www.heromaker.com.cn

The hand-operated coffee grinder Bamboo Dragonfly combines a contemporary shape with traditional elements on the inside. The performance of the grinder is inspired by the Chinese toy of the same name, a rotating blade which flies high when previously spun. Inside the grinder these "dragonfly wings" grind the beans, a process which the user can watch from the outside. The grinder body consists of aluminium alloy, while the head of the turning grip is made of red wood.

Statement by the jury
Due to the choice of material and shape, this coffee grinder is truly a pleasure to hold. A beautiful detail is the visible grinding process involving the rotating "dragonfly wings".

Die handbetriebene Kaffeemühle Bamboo Dragonfly kombiniert eine zeitgemäße Formgebung mit traditionellen Elementen im Inneren. Die Funktionsweise der Mühle ist von dem gleichnamigen chinesischen Kinderspielzeug inspiriert, einem Rotorblatt, das hochfliegt, wenn es zuvor schnell gedreht wurde. Im Inneren der Mühle dienen diese „Libellenflügel" dem Mahlen der Bohnen, was der Nutzer von außen beobachten kann. Der Korpus der Mühle besteht aus einer Aluminiumlegierung, der Kurbelkopf aus rotem Holz.

Begründung der Jury
Dank ihrer Formen und Materialien liegt diese Kaffeemühle besonders angenehm in der Hand. Ein schönes Detail ist der sichtbare Mahlvorgang mithilfe der rotierenden „Libellenflügel".

Telve Duo
Turkish Coffee Maker
Türkische Kaffeemaschine

Manufacturer
Arçelik A.S., Istanbul, Turkey
In-house design
Asli Ökmen
Web
www.arcelik.com.tr

The coffee maker Telve Duo makes real Turkish coffee, in which the drink is served with the coffee grounds ("telve"). The modern design of the coffee maker integrates traditional elements in the form of curved surfaces on the body and pot. The innovative and directly accessible operating panel on the top of the appliance allows easy control. Telve Duo prepares coffee by means of induction technology directly in the metal jugs, thereby giving it the original taste.

Statement by the jury
Telve Duo skilfully combines traditional and modern design principles. It impresses with an appearance which radiates reserved elegance.

Die Kaffeemaschine Telve Duo bereitet echten türkischen Kaffee zu, der mit dem Kaffeesatz („Telve") serviert wird. Die moderne Gestaltung der Kaffeemaschine integriert auch traditionelle Elemente in Form von gewölbten Flächen an Gehäuse und Kanne. Das innovative und direkt zugängliche Bedienfeld an der Oberseite der Maschine ermöglicht eine einfache Steuerung. Telve Duo bereitet den Kaffee mithilfe von Induktionstechnik direkt in Metallkannen zu, was ihm seinen ursprünglichen Geschmack verleiht.

Begründung der Jury
Telve Duo verbindet sehr gekonnt Tradition und Moderne und besticht mit einem Erscheinungsbild, das eine zurückhaltende Eleganz ausstrahlt.

Smeg Drip Filter Coffee Machine (DCF01)
Filterkaffeemaschine

Manufacturer
Smeg S.p.A., Guastalla (Reggio Emilia), Italy
In-house design
Design
deepdesign, Milan, Italy
Web
www.smeg.com
www.deepdesign.it

This filter coffee machine is equipped with a simple and user-friendly operating panel, which gives the user the choice between two brew intensities. The brewing cycle can be pre-programmed by means of an auto-start function. The keep warm mode, a digital clock as well as a descaling alarm make operation even easier. The permanent filter with handle is simple to fill and clean. The water tank holds 1.4 litres, the equivalent of ten cups.

Statement by the jury
The Smeg Drip Filter Coffee Machine in the design of the 1950s draws attention with its strong colours and elegant lines and also gains merit with well-considered functionality.

Diese Filterkaffeemaschine ist mit einem einfachen und benutzerfreundlichen Bedienfeld ausgestattet, das dem Benutzer die Wahl zwischen zwei Brüh-Intensitätsstufen gewährt. Mit einer Autostart-Funktion lässt sich der Brühzyklus vorab programmieren. Eine Warmhaltefunktion, eine digitale Zeitschaltuhr sowie eine Entkalkungsanzeige erleichtern die Bedienung zusätzlich. Der Permanentfilter mit Griff ist einfach zu befüllen und zu reinigen, der Wassertank fasst 1,4 Liter, was zehn Tassen entspricht.

Begründung der Jury
Die Smeg Drip Coffee Machine im 1950er-Jahre-Design macht mit starken Farben und einer eleganten Linienführung auf sich aufmerksam und punktet zudem mit durchdachter Funktionalität.

WMF Lumero
Coffee Maker
Kaffeemaschine

Manufacturer
WMF Consumer Electric GmbH, Jettingen-Scheppach, Germany
Design
AHACKENBERG DESIGN, Prien am Chiemsee, Germany
Web
www.wmf.de
www.ahackenberg.com

The WMF Lumero achieves its purist appearance with geometric shapes and a housing of high-quality matte and polished stainless steel. When the machine is switched on, a surrounding LED ring integrated in the base visually elevates it from the worktop. The oval-shaped main body features an intuitive touch-screen user interface inclined at 45 degrees, facilitating ergonomic control of the machine from the front as well as from the side.

Statement by the jury
WMF Lumero catches the eye with its elegant appeal, while a light ring at the base adds an almost mystical touch. The operating panel is ergonomically placed, with high convenience in mind.

Ihr puristisches Erscheinungsbild erzielt die WMF Lumero mit geometrischen Grundkörpern und einem Gehäuse aus hochwertigem mattem und hochglänzendem Edelstahl. Ist die Maschine eingeschaltet, leuchtet ein im Sockel integriertes, umlaufendes LED-Band und hebt sie visuell von der Arbeitsfläche ab. In den ovalen Hauptkörper ist eine intuitive Touchscreen-Bedienoberfläche im 45-Grad-Winkel integriert, was eine ergonomische Bedienung der Maschine sowohl von vorne als auch von der Seite ermöglicht.

Begründung der Jury
Die WMF Lumero zieht mit ihrer eleganten und durch ein Leuchtband am Sockel fast mystisch wirkenden Anmutung die Blicke auf sich. Schön gelöst ist auch die ergonomische Positionierung des Bedienfelds.

Ninja CP307 Hot & Cold Brewing System
Tea and Coffee Maker
Tee- und Kaffeemaschine

Manufacturer
SharkNinja, Needham, Massachusetts, USA
In-house design
Colby Higgins, Dan Kestenbaum
Web
www.sharkninja.com

This machine enables the user to prepare hot or cold brew coffee and tea at the touch of a button. The device has a swivelling brew basket and automatically recognises the coffee or tea insert, displaying only the relevant brew options on a dynamic user interface. The integrated "Smart Scoop" measuring spoon makes choosing the precise dose of coffee grounds or tea leaves an easy task.

Statement by the jury
The Ninja CP307 Hot & Cold Brewing System combines complex functions with high user-friendliness in one compact appliance.

Mit dieser Maschine lässt sich auf Knopfdruck heiß oder kalt aufgebrühter Kaffee oder Tee zubereiten. Das Gerät hat einen schwenkbaren Siebträger und erkennt automatisch, ob dieser mit dem Kaffee- oder dem Teeeinsatz genutzt wird. Je nachdem werden nur die Kaffee- oder Tee-Brühoptionen auf der dynamischen Benutzeroberfläche eingeblendet. Ein dazugehöriger intelligenter Messlöffel („Smart Scoop") erleichtert das präzise Dosieren des Kaffeepulvers oder der Teeblätter.

Begründung der Jury
Das Ninja CP307 Hot & Cold Brewing System zeichnet sich dadurch aus, dass es eine komplexe Funktionalität mit hoher Benutzerfreundlichkeit auf kompakter Grundfläche vereint.

Infinissima
Capsule Coffee Maker
Kapsel-Kaffeemaschine

Manufacturer
Nescafé Dolce Gusto,
Lausanne, Switzerland
Design
Multiple SA (Pierre Struzka),
La Chaux-de-Fonds, Switzerland
Web
www.nestle.ch
www.multiple-design.ch

The Infinissima coffee maker attracts attention with its slender design and its form inspired by the symbol for eternity. Thanks to its easily filled, large 1.2-litre water tank, the height-adjustable drip-tray and a self-explanatory operation, various coffee specialities and drinks can be easily prepared. With its sculptural formal language, it blends in harmoniously with modern living environments.

Statement by the jury
This capsule coffee maker is an eye-catcher with its distinctive, captivating design and is also easy to operate.

Die Infinissima-Kaffeemaschine macht mit ihrer schlanken Gestaltung und der durch das Unendlichkeitssymbol inspirierten Form auf sich aufmerksam. Dank ihres leicht befüllbaren und extragroßen 1,2-Liter-Wassertanks, der höhenverstellbaren Tropfschale und einer selbsterklärenden Bedienung können verschiedene Kaffeespezialitäten und Getränke einfach zubereitet werden. Mit ihrer skulpturalen Formensprache fügt sie sich harmonisch in moderne Wohnumgebungen ein.

Begründung der Jury
Diese Kapsel-Kaffeemaschine ist mit ihrer markanten, aufmerksamkeitsstarken Gestaltung ein Blickfang und außerdem leicht bedienbar.

Breville Creatista Uno
Capsule Coffee Machine
Kapsel-Kaffeemaschine

Manufacturer
Breville, Sydney, Australia
In-house design
Web
www.breville.com

The Breville Creatista Uno simplifies the complex processes associated with traditional coffee making by means of its simple and intuitive One-Touch interface design. Driven by a Thermojet heater in combination with Nespresso coffee technology, this machine needs less than six seconds to prepare milk-based coffee recipes, whereby it automatically provides barista quality textured milk.

Statement by the jury
Its intuitive control by user interface and sophisticated functionality make the Breville Creatista Uno an uncomplicated coffee maker. The design presents as sturdy and is of high quality.

Die Breville Creatista Uno vereinfacht die komplexen Prozesse, die zur Zubereitung traditionellen Kaffees erforderlich sind, durch ihre einfache und intuitive Benutzeroberfläche mit One-Touch-Design. Angetrieben von einem Thermojet-Erhitzer und in Kombination mit Nespresso-Kaffeetechnologie braucht diese Maschine weniger als sechs Sekunden für die Zubereitung von Kaffee- und Milchkaffeespezialitäten, wobei sie automatisch die richtige Milchschaumstruktur bereitstellt.

Begründung der Jury
Ihre intuitiv nutzbare Oberfläche und ausgereifte Funktionalität machen die Breville Creatista Uno zu einer unkomplizierten Kaffeemaschine. Sie ist zudem robust und hochwertig gestaltet.

Carina/Easy
Capsule Coffee Machine
Kapsel-Kaffeemaschine

Manufacturer
Delica AG, Birsfelden, Switzerland
Design
2nd West (Michael Thurnherr,
Fabio Rutishauser, Jan Eugster),
Rapperswil, Switzerland
Web
www.delica.ch
www.2ndwest.ch

Carina/Easy is characterised by its architectural forms, the horizontal division of the body, its two-tone colour scheme and a soft, recessed handle. Operation is intuitive via three buttons, which can be programmed to the desired cup size. Thanks to a stand-by mode and a 15-second warm-up time, Carina/Easy is particularly energy-efficient. All plastic components are marked with material codes, unpainted and can easily be separated from each other, simplifying recycling. The capsules are aluminium-free.

Statement by the jury
This capsule coffee machine is characterised by a very distinct and concise design. Considerable thought went into sustainability aspects.

Carina/Easy ist durch ihre architektonische Formensprache, die horizontale Unterteilung des Korpus, ihre Zweifarbigkeit und eine weiche Griffmulde geprägt. Die Bedienung erfolgt intuitiv über drei Knöpfe, die auf die gewünschte Tassengröße programmierbar sind. Dank Stand-by-Modus und einer 15-sekündigen Aufwärmphase ist Carina/Easy stromsparend. Alle Kunststoffteile sind im Hinblick auf die Recycelbarkeit mit Materialkennzeichnungen versehen, unlackiert und trennbar montiert. Die Kapseln sind aluminiumfrei.

Begründung der Jury
Diese Kapsel-Kaffeemaschine zeichnet sich durch eine sehr klare und prägnante Gestaltung aus. Beeindruckend ist auch die Berücksichtigung von Nachhaltigkeitsaspekten im Designprozess.

TASSIMO MyWay
Multi Beverage System
Multigetränkesystem

Manufacturer
Robert Bosch Hausgeräte GmbH,
Munich, Germany
In-house design
Gregor Luippold, Katja Gnielka
Design
Jeff Miller Inc., New York, USA
Web
www.bsh-group.com
www.jeffmillerdesign.com

The Tassimo MyWay beverage system is inspired by barista culture and designed in a very user-friendly way. Beverage strength, cup size and temperature can be selected by gently touching the backlit sensor buttons and be set and saved individually as desired. Fully automated preparation of each drink is also possible. The device is available in red, black and white.

Statement by the jury
The Tassimo MyWay devices interpret the traditional coffee maker in an updated version. The many options for adapting drinks according to personal preference are impressive.

Die Gestaltung des Getränkesystems Tassimo MyWay ist von der Barista-Kultur inspiriert und auf eine hohe Benutzerfreundlichkeit ausgelegt. Getränkestärke, Tassengröße und Temperatur lassen sich durch eine sanfte Berührung der hinterleuchteten Sensortasten einfach auswählen und nach Belieben individuell anpassen und speichern. Eine vollautomatische Zubereitung des jeweiligen Getränks ist ebenso möglich. Die Maschine ist in den Farben Rot, Schwarz und Weiß erhältlich.

Begründung der Jury
Die Tassimo MyWay-Geräte interpretieren die traditionelle Kaffeemaschine sehr zeitgemäß. Beeindruckend sind die vielen Möglichkeiten, Getränke den persönlichen Vorlieben anzupassen.

Lavazza Idola
Espresso Maker
Espressomaschine

Manufacturer
Lavazza, Turin, Italy
In-house design
Florian Seidl
Web
www.lavazza.com

Organic forms and gentle curves impart on the Idola espresso machine its friendly impression. The exterior shell is made from one piece, reducing visible shut lines to a minimum. Idola features a touch-sensitive user interface with four selections as well as acoustic feedback. The large external tank is transparent and easily accessible. The drip tray has a solid metal grid, while the height of the cup rack is adjustable. Idola is quiet, achieves its operating temperature in 28 seconds and switches off automatically after nine minutes.

Statement by the jury
Idola convinces with precise engineering and a design in which great attention has been paid to attractively worked details.

Organische Formen und sanfte Kurven verleihen der Espressomaschine Idola ihre freundliche Ausstrahlung. Die äußere Hauptschale ist aus einem Guss, sodass sichtbare Fugen auf ein Minimum reduziert werden. Idola hat eine berührungsempfindliche Benutzeroberfläche mit vier Auswahloptionen und akustischem Feedback. Der große, externe Tank ist transparent und leicht zugänglich. Die Auffangschale hat ein solides Metallgitter und ist höhenverstellbar. Idola ist leise, erreicht in 28 Sekunden die Betriebstemperatur und schaltet sich nach neun Minuten automatisch ab.

Begründung der Jury
Idola überzeugt mit einer präzisen Fertigung und einer Gestaltung, bei der viel Wert auf schön ausgearbeitete Details gelegt wurde.

Lavazza Deséa
Espresso/Cappuccino Maker
Espresso-/Cappuccinomaschine

Manufacturer
Lavazza, Turin, Italy
In-house design
Florian Seidl
Web
www.lavazza.com

Deséa offers the requirements for easily preparing Italian coffee specialities such as espresso, cappuccino or latte macchiato in a compact machine. The touch operating panel is divided into a coffee and a milk zone, whereby temperature and milk foam settings can be personalised. The milk foam can be prepared directly in the glass cup, which is included in the package. The design of the machine is characterised by its distinct formal elements with surfaces which are just as clearly defined.

Statement by the jury
The clearly defined, distinctively designed operating panel of the Deséa is reminiscent of eyes and characterises the friendly overall impression of this high-quality coffee maker.

Deséa bietet in einer kompakten Maschine die Voraussetzungen, um italienische Kaffeespezialitäten wie Espresso, Cappuccino oder Latte Macchiato einfach zuzubereiten. Die Touch-Bedienfläche ist in einen Kaffee- und einen Milchbereich unterteilt, wobei sich Temperatur- und Milchschaumeinstellungen personalisieren lassen. Der Milchschaum kann direkt in der mitgelieferten Glastasse zubereitet werden. Das Design der Maschine ist durch klare formale Elemente mit ebenso klar definierten Flächen geprägt.

Begründung der Jury
Das klar definierte, markant gestaltete Bedienfeld der Deséa erinnert an Augen und prägt den freundlichen Gesamteindruck dieser hochwertigen Kaffeemaschine.

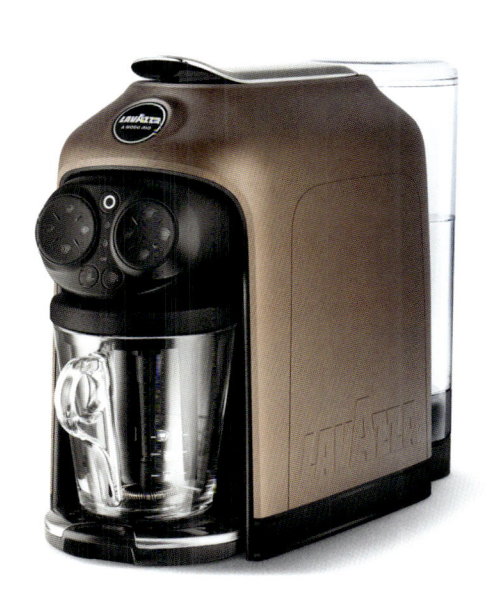

La Specialista
Espresso Maker
Espressomaschine

Manufacturer
De'Longhi Appliances, Treviso, Italy
In-house design
Francesco Fiorotto
Web
www.delonghi.com

La Specialista is a manual espresso maker which delivers convenient preparation of espresso-based drinks with consistent quality. An integrated coffee grinder with tamper system and other innovative functions hit the sweet spot between hands on coffee creativity and automated technology. La Specialista ensures a streamlined and personalised preparation process, providing a high degree of creativity and the satisfying feeling of self-brewed, authentic espresso.

La Specialista ist eine manuelle Espressomaschine, die es ermöglicht, Kaffeegetränke auf Espressobasis in gleichbleibender Qualität bequem selbst zuzubereiten. Eine integrierte Kaffeemühle mit Tamper-System und weitere innovative Funktionen verbinden eine eigenhändige und kreative Kaffeezubereitung mit automatisierten Prozessen. La Specialista ermöglicht einen effizienten und personalisierten Zubereitungsprozess und gewährleistet dabei ein Höchstmaß an Kreativität und das befriedigende Gefühl, authentischen Espresso selbst aufzubrühen.

Statement by the jury
The espresso machine La Specialista combines the sturdy appearance of traditional steel coffee makers with new technology for easy preparation of coffee specialities.

Begründung der Jury
Die Espressomaschine La Specialista verbindet das robuste Aussehen traditioneller Edelstahl-Kaffeemaschinen mit neuen Technologien zur einfachen Zubereitung der Kaffeespezialitäten.

BES878 Barista Pro
Espresso Maker
Espressomaschine

Manufacturer
Breville, Sydney, Australia
In-house design
Web
www.breville.com

This compact espresso maker with stainless-steel outer casing facilitates convenient and quick preparation of barista coffee. A conical grinder allows the choice of dose and grind size before delivering the freshly ground coffee directly into the Portafilter handle. The digitally controlled "ThermoJet" heating system heats the water precisely while a pre-brewing function with low pressure assures optimal espresso extraction as well as powerful steam for structured milk foam.

Statement by the jury
The Barista Pro impresses with its industrial aesthetics. Its innovative functions ensure high user-friendliness.

Diese kompakte Espressomaschine mit Edelstahlgehäuse ermöglicht dank innovativer Funktionen die bequeme und schnelle Zubereitung von Barista-Kaffee. Eine konische Mahlvorrichtung erlaubt die Wahl von Dosis und Mahlgrad und leitet das Kaffeepulver direkt in den Portafilter. Das digital gesteuerte Heizsystem „ThermoJet" erhitzt das Wasser präzise, und eine Vorbrühfunktion mit niedrigem Druck sorgt für eine optimale Espresso-Extraktion sowie starken Dampf für strukturierten Milchschaum.

Begründung der Jury
Die Barista Pro besticht durch ihre industrielle Ästhetik, die sich mit innovativen Funktionen zu einem gelungenen, bedienfreundlichen Produkt verbindet.

Breville Bambino Plus
Espresso Maker
Espressomaschine

Manufacturer
Breville, Sydney, Australia
In-house design
Web
www.breville.com

The Breville Bambino Plus, with a width of just 200 mm, is an extremely compact, espresso maker for households with little space. The espresso maker is driven by a Thermojet heater. It delivers coffee and perfectly textured micro-foam at the desired temperature and foam level in less than six seconds. The milk can also be textured manually for an authentic user experience.

Statement by the jury
Its stainless-steel housing imparts to this espresso maker a high-quality, sturdy appearance. The handling is as simply as it is speedy, ensuring a highly functional device.

Die Breville Bambino Plus ist mit einer Breite von 200 mm eine extrem kompakte Espressomaschine für Haushalte mit wenig Platz. Die Espressomaschine wird von einem Thermojet-Erhitzer angetrieben und bereitet in weniger als sechs Sekunden Kaffee und perfekt strukturierten Mikroschaum in der gewünschten Temperatur und Textur her. Für ein authentisches Nutzererlebnis kann die Texturierung der Milch auch manuell erfolgen.

Begründung der Jury
Ihr Edelstahlgehäuse verleiht dieser Espressomaschine ihr hochwertiges und zugleich robustes Aussehen. Funktional überzeugt sie durch eine einfache Handhabung und rasche Kaffeezubereitung.

WMF Lumero
Espresso Maker
Espressomaschine

Manufacturer
WMF Consumer Electric GmbH,
Jettingen-Scheppach, Germany
In-house design
Ernst Köhler
Web
www.wmf.de

The WMF Lumero is a very compact espresso machine with a clear, straightforward design. All functions are self-explanatory. The integrated portafilter, a pressure of 15 bar as well as hot water and frothing functions facilitate professional espresso and coffee making. The Ambient lighting concept creates a pleasant backlight when the machine is in use. All major housing and operating elements are made of Cromargan stainless steel.

Statement by the jury
This espresso maker is reduced to essentials in form and function. At the same time it offers everything necessary for professional coffee making.

Die WMF Lumero ist eine sehr kompakte Espressomaschine mit einer klaren, geradlinigen Gestaltung. Alle Funktionen sind selbsterklärend. Der integrierte Siebträger, ein Druck von 15 Bar sowie Heißwasser- und Aufschäumfunktionen ermöglichen eine professionelle Espresso- und Kaffeezubereitung. Das Lichtkonzept Ambient sorgt bei der Bedienung der Maschine für eine angenehme Hintergrundbeleuchtung. Die wichtigsten Gehäuse- und Bedienelemente sind aus dem Edelstahl Cromargan gefertigt.

Begründung der Jury
Diese Kaffeemaschine ist in Form und Funktion auf das Wesentliche reduziert und bietet dabei gleichzeitig alles, was für eine professionelle Kaffeezubereitung notwendig ist.

Nespresso Momento
Coffee Maker
Kaffeemaschine

Manufacturer
Nestlé Nespresso SA,
Lausanne, Switzerland
In-house design
Web
www.nestle-nespresso.com

Momento is a new, professional series of coffee makers, which was developed to meet the demands of modern offices with high coffee consumption. Its modern yet timeless design is a reference to the world of baristas but adapted to the professional environment. Prominent coffee heads and an elegant black-and-white touchscreen simplify interaction with the device – as does the absence of manual handles, steam pipes and multiple buttons.

Statement by the jury
The reduced and sturdy visual appearance of the Momento is characterised by the use of stainless steel for the housing. The machines further convince with their self-explanatory quality.

Momento ist eine neue, professionelle Nespresso-Maschinenserie, die entwickelt wurde, um den Anforderungen moderner Büros mit hohem Kaffeeverbrauch gerecht zu werden. Mit ihrer ebenso zeitgemäßen wie klassischen Gestaltung bezieht sie sich auf die Welt der Baristas, passt sich aber an das professionelle Umfeld an. Prominente Kaffeeköpfe, ein eleganter Schwarz-Weiß-Touchscreen sowie das Fehlen von Handgriffen, Dampfauslässen und Tasten vereinfachen die Interaktion mit der Maschine.

Begründung der Jury
Das gleichermaßen reduzierte wie robuste Erscheinungsbild der Momento ist durch die großflächige Verwendung von Edelstahl für das Gehäuse geprägt. Die Maschine überzeugt zudem mit einer hohen Selbsterklärungsqualität.

ENA 8 Signature Line
Automatic Coffee Machine
Kaffeevollautomat

Manufacturer
JURA Elektroapparate AG,
Niederbuchsiten, Switzerland
Design
Büttler Bosshard Industrial Designer,
Zürich, Switzerland
Web
www.jura.com
www.buettlerbosshard.ch

The ENA 8 Signature Line – Massive Aluminium combines traditional craftsmanship with state-of-the-art production technology. The result is an automatic coffee machine with a solid 3-mm-thick aluminium housing. The water tank is located at the side. With its cylindrical form and rhombus-shaped facets it is inspired by elegant crystal carafes. Operation of the one-cup machine is via a 2.8" TFT display with clearly defined operating panels at the front.

Statement by the jury
The automatic coffee machine delights with its high-quality aluminium housing and a minimalist front design, which contrasts with the filigree appearance of the water tank.

Die ENA 8 Signature Line – Massive Aluminium verbindet traditionelle Handwerkskunst mit modernster Fertigungstechnologie zu einem Kaffeevollautomaten mit einem soliden, 3 mm starken Aluminiumgehäuse. Der seitliche Wassertank ist zylindrisch, hat einen Schliff mit rautenförmigen Facetten und erinnert in Form und Struktur an eine elegante Kristallkaraffe. Die Bedienung des Eintassen-Vollautomaten erfolgt über ein 2,8"-TFT-Display mit klar definierten Bedienfeldern an der Frontseite.

Begründung der Jury
Dieser Kaffeevollautomat begeistert mit seinem hochwertigen Aluminiumgehäuse und einer minimalistischen Frontgestaltung, die durch den filigran anmutenden, eleganten Wassertank gekonnt kontrastiert wird.

ENA 8 Nordic White
Automatic Coffee Machine
Kaffeevollautomat

Manufacturer
JURA Elektroapparate AG,
Niederbuchsiten, Switzerland
Design
Büttler Bosshard Industrial Designer,
Zürich, Switzerland
Web
www.jura.com
www.buettlerbosshard.ch

A highly compact one-cup machine, the ENA 8 measures just 27.1 × 32.3 × 44.5 cm. By integrating new technologies it enables the user to prepare a large selection of coffee specialities. A special design feature is the cylindrical water tank, whose form is inspired by crystal carafes: rhombus-shaped facets refract the light and so produce a sparkle reminiscent of diamonds. A 2.8" TFT display and clearly defined operating panels offer simple operation.

Statement by the jury
This automatic coffee machine in Nordic White radiates minimalist elegance. This impression is emphasised by the clear graphics of the operating panel and the striking water tank.

Die mit 27,1 × 32,3 × 44,5 cm sehr kompakte ENA 8 integriert neue Technologien und ermöglicht es, eine große Auswahl an Kaffeespezialitäten zuzubereiten. Ein besonderes Designmerkmal des Eintassen-Vollautomaten ist sein zylindrischer Wassertank, dessen Form von Kristallkaraffen inspiriert ist. Durch die Lichtbrechung in den rautenförmigen Facetten entsteht ein Funkeln, das Gedanken an Diamanten weckt. Ein 2,8"-TFT-Display und klar definierte Bedienfelder ermöglichen eine einfache Handhabung.

Begründung der Jury
In der Farbe Nordic White strahlt dieser Kaffeevollautomat eine minimalistische Eleganz aus, die durch die klaren Grafiken der Bedienfläche und den prägnanten Wassertank noch verstärkt wird.

Faema E71E
Espresso Coffee Maker
Espresso-Kaffeemaschine

Manufacturer
Gruppo Cimbali S.p.A.,
Binasco (MI), Italy
Design
Italdesign, (Massimo Borrelli, Nicola Guelfo),
Moncalieri (TO), Italy
Web
www.faema.it
www.italdesign.it

Faema E71E espresso coffee machine has three independent groups to manage different coffee varieties, respecting the specific temperatures for optimal extraction. The hydraulic circuit with GTi control system guarantees management of the infusion times. An intuitive display for every group and the innovative steam wands ease baristas' interaction with the E71E.

Statement by the jury
The design of the E71E pays meticulous attention to details, as can be seen in the steam wands or the displays.

Die Espresso-Kaffeemaschine Faema E71E bietet drei separate Brühgruppen zur Zubereitung verschiedener Kaffeesorten, wobei die spezifischen Temperaturen für eine optimale Extraktion berücksichtigt werden. Zudem garantiert der Hydraulikkreislauf mit GTi-Steuerungssystem das Management der Infusionszeiten. Eine intuitive Anzeige für jede Gruppe und innovative Dampfdüsen erleichtern Baristas die Interaktion mit der E17E.

Begründung der Jury
Bei der E71E erkennt man an vielen Elementen wie den Dampfdüsen oder den Anzeigen, wie viel Aufmerksamkeit der präzisen Ausgestaltung auch kleiner Details geschenkt wurde.

Animo OptiMe
Fully Automatic Coffee Maker
Kaffeevollautomat

Manufacturer
Animo, Assen, Netherlands
Design
Pezy Group (Arif Veendijk),
Amsterdam, Netherlands
Web
www.animo.eu
www.pezygroup.com

The Animo OptiMe is a very compact, professional fully automatic coffee maker. It was developed especially for small and medium-sized businesses, offering a capacity of up to 125 cups a day. High flexibility is key here: the machine offers a user-friendly interface, various colours and housing panels, the option of personalising the settings via an app as well as accessories such as a milk cooler and a heater to warm the cups.

Statement by the jury
This fully automatic coffee maker offers a self-explanatory interface and many options for individualisation.

Der Animo OptiMe ist ein sehr kompakter, professioneller Kaffeevollautomat. Er wurde speziell für kleine und mittlere Unternehmen entwickelt und bietet eine Kapazität von bis zu 125 Tassen am Tag. Ein benutzerfreundliches Interface, diverse Gehäusefarben und -paneele, die Möglichkeit, die Maschine über eine App zu personalisieren sowie Zubehör wie ein Milchkühler und ein Tassenwärmer bieten hohe Flexibilität bei der Konfigurierung.

Begründung der Jury
Dieser Kaffeevollautomat überzeugt mit einem selbsterklärenden Interface und zahlreichen Möglichkeiten der Individualisierung.

CVA 7845
Built-in Coffee Maker
Einbaukaffeevollautomat

Manufacturer
Miele & Cie. KG, Gütersloh, Germany
In-house design
Web
www.miele.de

This fully automatic coffee maker is based on a new platform, for which all tanks and containers have been optimised with regard to ergonomics and functionality. When making coffee, the user can select beans from three separate interior containers and have them freshly grinded. Descaling and cleaning of the milk pipes and brewing unit are performed fully automatically by means of exchangeable cartridges. The illuminated pourer is controlled by sensor and adjusts by itself to the cup height. The milk holder can be inserted and removed at the front.

Statement by the jury
This fully automatic in-built coffee maker convinces as a visually attractive and functional product solution, well-considered in every detail.

Dieser Kaffeevollautomat basiert auf einer neuen Plattform, für die auch sämtliche Tanks und Behältnisse hinsichtlich Ergonomie und Funktionalität optimiert wurden. Bei der Kaffeezubereitung kann der Nutzer Bohnen aus drei separaten Innenbehältern wählen und frisch mahlen lassen. Entkalkung sowie die Reinigung von Milchleitungen und Brüheinheit erfolgen mithilfe von Wechselkartuschen vollautomatisch. Der beleuchtete Auslauf ist sensorgesteuert und passt sich selbstständig an die Tassenhöhe an. Das Milchgefäß kann von vorne aufgesteckt und wieder entnommen werden.

Begründung der Jury
Dieser Einbaukaffeevollautomat überzeugt als visuell ansprechende und funktional bis ins Detail durchdachte Produktlösung.

BOSCH accent | line carbon black
Built-in Appliance Range
Einbaugerätereihe

Manufacturer
Robert Bosch Hausgeräte GmbH,
Munich, Germany

In-house design
Robert Bosch Hausgeräte GmbH

Web
www.bsh-group.com

reddot award 2019
best of the best

New balance
The definition of the kitchen as a central living space has always been closely related to social developments. The design of the accent | line carbon black series is based on the increasing trend of a fusion between kitchen and living space. This range of kitchen appliances meets this trend with a reduced design, merged with impressively clear aesthetics. The simple design focuses on the essentials while conveying a sense of value and quality. Elegant and timeless, this range showcases a formal consistency that extends down to the last detail. Adopting a holistic approach, it defines a new balance between kitchen appliances and kitchen furniture. All appliances complement a given kitchen with their subtle presence and a silhouette marked by a fascinating interplay of light and shades. The quality of this range is also reflected in a user-friendly interface that interactively connects all individual elements. The appliances are equipped with an innovative sensor technology, which not only delivers a high degree of comfort, but also has the ability to independently recognise things and respond to changes. The integrated sensors thus ensure perfect food preparation, making cooking overall easier. In addition, integrated in the system, the Home Connect app allows sending recipes to the oven or taking a look into the fridge while the owner is on the go.

Neue Balance
Die Definition der Küche als Raum des Zusammenlebens steht in enger Beziehung zu den jeweiligen gesellschaftlichen Entwicklungen. Die Gestaltung der Serie accent | line carbon black orientiert sich am allgemeinen Trend der zunehmenden Verschmelzung mit dem Wohnraum. Diese Reihe von Küchengeräten begegnet dem mit einer gestalterischen Reduktion, wobei eine in ihrer Klarheit beeindruckende Ästhetik entstand. Die schlichte Formgebung lenkt den Blick auf das Wesentliche und vermittelt zugleich Wertigkeit und Qualität. Ebenso elegant wie zeitlos, zeigt diese Reihe eine formale Stringenz bis in die Details. Im Sinne eines ganzheitlichen Denkens wurde dabei eine neue Balance zwischen Küchengeräten und Küchenmöbeln geschaffen. Die Geräte ergänzen die Küche mit einer subtlen Präsenz und einer Silhouette, die durch das faszinierende Zusammenspiel von Licht und Schatten definiert wird. Die Qualität dieser Serie spiegelt sich zudem in einer alle Elemente interaktiv verbindenden, nutzerfreundlichen Bedienoberfläche wider. Die Geräte sind mit einer innovativen Sensortechnik ausgestattet, die ein hohes Maß an Komfort impliziert und die Fähigkeit hat, selbständig Dinge zu erkennen und auf Veränderungen zu reagieren. Die integrierten Sensoren sorgen so für eine perfekte Zubereitung und erleichtern das Kochen. Mittels der im System eingebundenen Home Connect-App können zudem etwa Rezepte an den Backofen gesendet werden oder der Nutzer schaut von unterwegs in seinen Kühlschrank.

Statement by the jury
The design of the accent | line carbon black range conveys elegance, which is further emphasised by the use of selected materials. All devices are characterised by careful attention to detail. An integral part of the form, the operation of the devices follows a modern and intelligent approach. Highly self-explanatory and of impressive logic, it promotes a variety of interactive user possibilities and sets new standards with its high level of comfort.

Begründung der Jury
Die Formensprache der Serie accent | line carbon black kommuniziert Eleganz, bekräftigt durch den Einsatz ausgesuchter Materialien. Alle Geräte zeichnet eine bis ins Detail ausgeführte Sorgfalt aus. Schlüssig in die Form integriert ist die zeitgemäße, intelligente Bedienung. In hohem Maße selbsterklärend und von bestechender Logik, bietet sie dem Nutzer vielfältige interaktive Möglichkeiten und setzt mit ihrem hohen Komfort neue Standards.

Designer portrait
See page 46
Siehe Seite 46

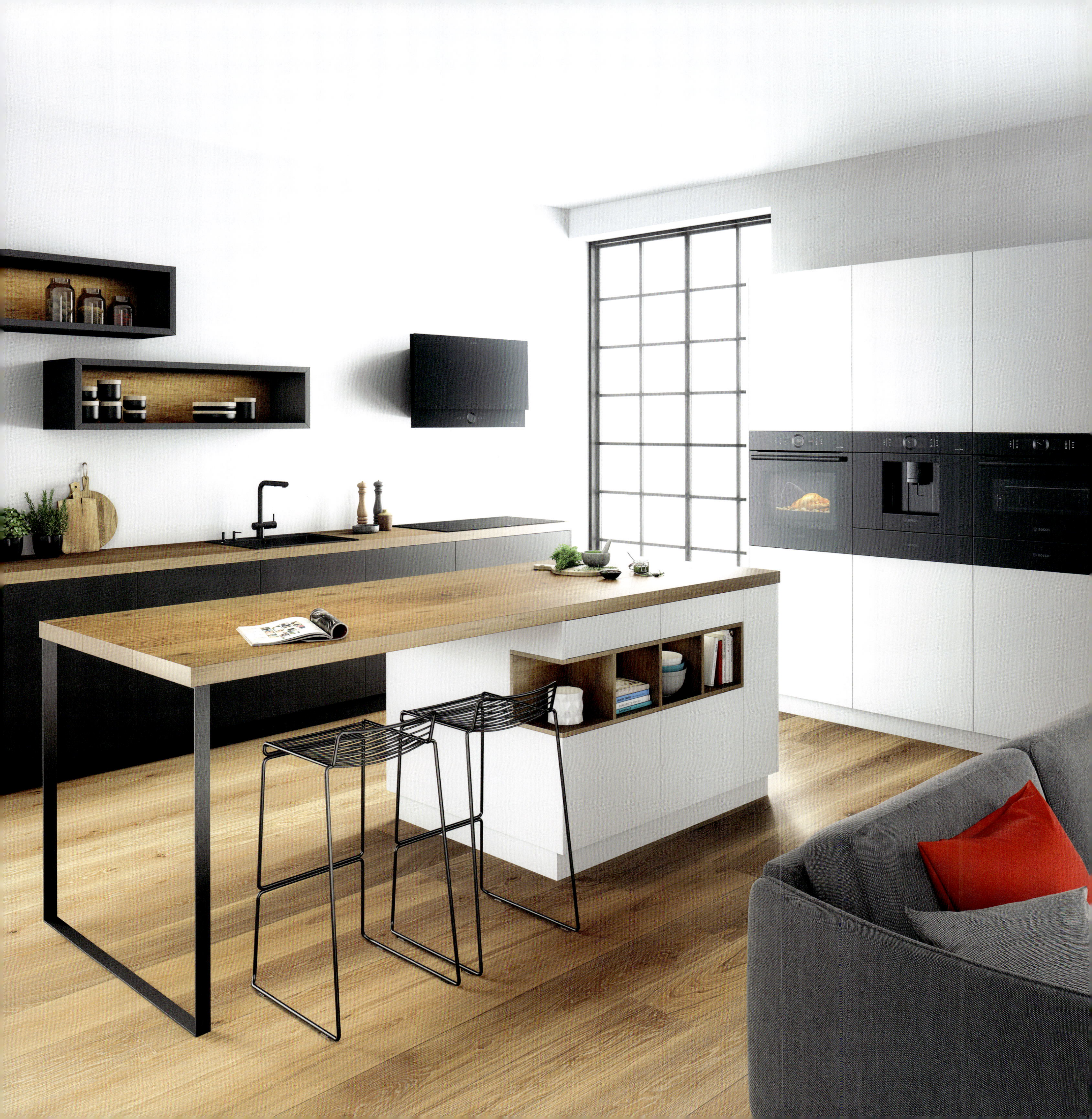

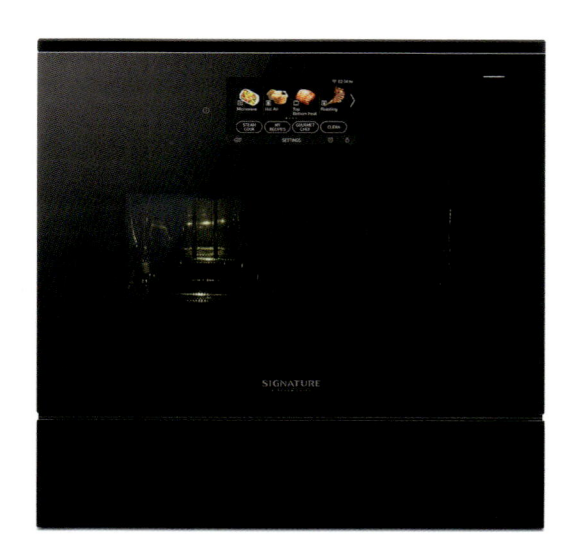

SIGNATURE Kitchen Suite
Built-in Kitchen Appliances
Einbauküchengeräte

Manufacturer
LG Electronics Inc., Seoul, South Korea
In-house design
Sooyeon Kim, Hangbok Lee,
Hanjin Jung, Yuna Jo, Sangwoo Kim
Web
www.lg.com

High-quality materials, precise engineering and intelligent technologies for a high degree of user-convenience characterise the appliances of the Signature Kitchen Suite. The series includes an oven, a fast-baking oven, an automatic coffee maker and a drawer for keeping items warm. The handle-free fronts with glass doors have a minimalist appeal; control is via a large 7" LCD colour display. LED illumination in the interior makes it easy to check on the food at a glance.

Statement by the jury
Precise manufacture and clear, minimalist front design indicate the high quality of the Signature Suite appliances. Intelligent functions and large displays make daily use easier.

Die Verwendung hochwertiger Materialien, eine präzise Verarbeitung und die Implementierung intelligenter Technologien für einen hohen Benutzerkomfort kennzeichnen die Geräte der Signature Kitchen Suite. Zu der Serie gehören ein Ofen, ein Schnellbackofen, ein Kaffeeautomat und eine Wärmeschublade. Die grifflosen Fronten mit Glastüren sind minimalistisch gehalten, die Steuerung erfolgt über ein großes 7"-LCD-Farbdisplay. LED-Beleuchtungen im Innenraum erleichtern die Überprüfung der Speisen mit bloßem Auge.

Begründung der Jury
Bei den Geräten der Signature Suite vermitteln eine präzise Fertigung und die klare, minimalistische Frontgestaltung hohe Qualität. Intelligente Funktionen und große Displays erleichtern den täglichen Gebrauch.

FINSMAKARE Combi Oven Microwave
Oven with Microwave
Backofen mit Mikrowelle

Manufacturer
IKEA of Sweden, Älmhult, Sweden
In-house design
Web
www.ikea.com

This appliance from the Finsmakare series is a combination of a microwave and a baking oven. Its clean front design is particularly eye-catching. A distinctive feature is the centrally located aluminium wheel, which stands out in colour and form from both the black glass door and operating panel. Furthermore, it offers an intuitive user experience, especially in combination with the touch-control operating panel, which only appears when switched on.

Statement by the jury
Due to its tidy operating panel with a central, pleasantly haptic wheel, this combination microwave presents as user-friendly. The homogenous front design is equally convincing.

Dieses Gerät der Finsmakare-Reihe ist eine Kombination aus Mikrowelle und Backofen und macht durch seine puristische Frontgestaltung auf sich aufmerksam. Markantes Gestaltungsmerkmal ist der zentral positionierte Aluminium-Drehknopf, der sich in Farbe und Form von der schwarzen Bedienblende sowie der ebenfalls schwarzen Glastür abhebt. Der Drehknopf bietet in Kombination mit dem Touch-Control-Bedienfeld, das nur in angeschaltetem Zustand zu sehen ist, ein intuitives Benutzererlebnis.

Begründung der Jury
Durch ihr aufgeräumtes Bedienpanel mit zentralem, haptisch angenehmem Drehknopf ist diese Kombi-Mikrowelle benutzerfreundlich. Zudem überzeugt die homogene Frontgestaltung.

FINSMAKARE Oven
Forced Air Oven
with Steam & Pyro
Heißluft-Backofen mit Dampf

Manufacturer
IKEA of Sweden, Älmhult, Sweden
In-house design
Web
www.ikea.com

This self-clean combination steam oven has a minimalist design, which is further emphasised by the deep black colour and black tinted glass. The door handle is made of solid aluminium with matte black powder coating and has a pleasant feel. The operating panel with a stainless-steel central double wheel is used to select from the menu and other settings, offering intuitive operation. The display is only visible when the oven is in operation.

Statement by the jury
With its deep black, minimalist front and solid aluminium handle, the Finsmakare steam oven has a high-quality, elegant appearance. The operating panel offers a pleasant experience for the user.

Dieser selbstreinigende Kombi-Dampfgarofen hat eine reduzierte Gestaltung, die durch die tiefschwarze Farbgebung und schwarz getöntes Glas im Türbereich betont wird. Der Türgriff besteht aus massivem Aluminium mit mattschwarzer Pulverbeschichtung und ist haptisch angenehm. Die Bedienfläche mit einem zentralen Doppel-Drehknopf aus Edelstahl, mit dem sich die Menüauswahl und andere Einstellungen vornehmen lassen, bietet ein intuitives Benutzererlebnis. Die Anzeige ist nur sichtbar, wenn der Ofen in Betrieb ist.

Begründung der Jury
Mit seiner tiefschwarzen, minimalistischen Front und dem massiven Aluminiumgriff wirkt der Finsmakare-Ofen hochwertig und elegant. Die Bedienfläche bietet mit ihrer klaren Gestaltung ein angenehmes Benutzererlebnis.

Dolce Stil Novo Oven (SFPR9604NR)
Backofen

Manufacturer
Smeg S.p.A., Guastalla (Reggio Emilia), Italy
In-house design
Web
www.smeg.com

These 90 cm wide, pyrolytic in-built ovens attract attention through their elegant and professional appearance. With a total capacity of 85 litres net, they offer space for several baking forms of various sizes and thus lend a high degree of flexibility. A circulating air system with three fans distributes the heat evenly and effectively, creating the perfect conditions for faster cooking.

Statement by the jury
The Dolce Stil Novo Oven impresses with its large cooking chamber. The elegant appearance blends harmoniously with modern living environments.

Diese 90 cm breiten, pyrolytischen Einbaubacköfen machen durch ihr elegantes und zugleich professionelles Erscheinungsbild auf sich aufmerksam. Mit einer Gesamtkapazität von 85 Litern Nettovolumen bieten sie Platz für mehrere Backformen unterschiedlicher Größe und damit ein hohes Maß an Flexibilität. Ein Umluftsystem mit drei Ventilatoren verteilt die Wärme gleichmäßig und effektiv und schafft damit die Voraussetzungen für schnelles Garen.

Begründung der Jury
Der Dolce Stil Novo Oven beeindruckt mit seinem großen Garraum und fügt sich mit seiner eleganten Gestaltung harmonisch in moderne Wohnwelten ein.

Electrolux Millenium Range
Built-in Kitchen Appliances
Einbauküchengeräte

Manufacturer
AB Electrolux, Stockholm, Sweden
In-house design
Web
www.electrolux.com

The Millennium built-in appliance range is characterised by its elegant mirror finish. A closer look reveals the attention to detail that has gone into this product. This includes the flush metal trim with discreet laser-etched branding, which is the result of a new technology for milling down the glass substrate beneath; the solid metal rotary knob with its capacitive touch feature and intuitive user interface; and the CNC-milled, solid metal handle.

Statement by the jury
The clear, homogenous design of the reflecting fronts imparts to the appliances of the Millennium Range their elegant impression. The precisely executed details, such as the handles, are particularly appealing.

Die Millennium-Einbaugeräteserie ist durch spiegelnde Oberflächen geprägt, was ihr ein elegantes Erscheinungsbild verleiht. Bei näherer Betrachtung fallen sorgfältig gearbeitete Details ins Auge, darunter die bündigen Metallzierleisten mit ihrem diskreten lasergeätzten Branding, welches das Ergebnis einer neuen Technik zum Abfräsen des Glassubstrats ist, ein massiver Metalldrehknopf mit kapazitiver Touch-Funktion und intuitiver Benutzeroberfläche sowie der CNC-gefräste Vollmetallgriff.

Begründung der Jury
Die klare, homogene Gestaltung der verspiegelten Fronten verleiht den Geräten der Millennium-Serie ihren eleganten Gesamteindruck. Schön gelöst sind präzise gearbeitete Details wie die Griffe.

Bauknecht Built-in Ovens – Class 9
Einbaubacköfen

Manufacturer
Whirlpool EMEA S.p.A., Pero (Milan), Italy
In-house design
Global Consumer Design EMEA, Biandronno (Varese), Italy
Web
www.whirlpool.eu
www.whirlpool.com

The contemporary, monolithic aesthetic of the ovens of the Bauknecht built-in suite is created by the use of dark glass, which contrasts strongly with the elegant stainless-steel band. The appliances make use of modern technology to ensure a user-friendly experience. A high-resolution, 3.5" TFT display guides through programmes, saves certain routines and suggests ideal settings. The appliances are also Wi-Fi enabled, which allows recipe settings to be downloaded and sent to the ovens.

Statement by the jury
The clear, highly contrasting design and the use of high-quality materials provide this built-in baking oven with a high-quality, elegant appearance.

Die zeitgemäße, monolithische Ästhetik der Backöfen der Bauknecht-Einbaugeräteserie wird durch die Verwendung von dunklem Glas erzeugt, das in starkem Kontrast zu einem eleganten Edelstahlband steht. Die Geräte nutzen moderne Technologien für eine hohe Benutzerfreundlichkeit. Ein hochauflösendes 3,5"-TFT-Display leitet durch die Programme, ermöglicht es, Routinen zu speichern und macht Vorschläge zu den idealen Einstellungen. Die Geräte sind Wi-Fi-fähig, sodass sich auch neue Rezepteinstellungen herunterladen und an die Öfen senden lassen.

Begründung der Jury
Die klare, kontrastreiche Gestaltung und der Einsatz hochwertiger Materialien verleihen diesen Einbaubacköfen ein sehr hochwertiges und elegantes Erscheinungsbild.

Gen7000 VitroLine
Built-in Kitchen Appliances
Einbauküchengeräte

Manufacturer
Miele & Cie. KG, Gütersloh, Germany
In-house design
Web
www.miele.de

As part of the Miele Generation7000, the VitroLine household appliance series is characterised by extensive glass fronts, which are available in obsidian black, brilliant white and graphite grey. The handles consist of a solid metal part, which surrounds a precisely ground glass element in the colour of the appliance. This ensures that they fit perfectly into the glass front. Control is by means of a large colour display with intuitive touch operation or via an app.

Statement by the jury
The VitroLine appliances impress by their equally high-quality as minimalist design and thus blend in with various kitchen environments.

Die Hausgeräteserie VitroLine, die zur Miele Generation7000 gehört, ist durch großflächige Glasfronten geprägt, die in den Glasfarben Obsidianschwarz, Brillantweiß und Graphitgrau hergestellt werden. Die Griffe bestehen aus einem massiven Metallteil, das den Abschluss eines präzise geschliffenen Glaselements bildet, wodurch sie sich harmonisch in die Front des Gerätes einfügen. Die Steuerung erfolgt über ein großes Farbdisplay mit intuitiver Touch-Bedienung oder über eine App.

Begründung der Jury
Die VitroLine-Geräte bestechen durch eine gleichermaßen hochwertige wie minimalistische Gestaltung und fügen sich damit in unterschiedliche Küchenumgebungen ein.

Gen7000 ArtLine
Built-in Kitchen Appliances
Einbauküchengeräte

Manufacturer
Miele & Cie. KG, Gütersloh, Germany
In-house design
Web
www.miele.de

The ArtLine range of household appliance is part of the Miele Generation7000. It was designed with special regard to open-plan kitchens and integration in the living environment. With its smooth glass front without handles the appliances blend in seamlessly with up-to-date living worlds. The doors open electrically at the touch of a finger. The ArtLine appliances are available in obsidian black, brilliant white and graphite grey. In the brilliant white version the black display background can be switched to white.

Statement by the jury
The reduced design of the ArtLine series with its purist, all-glass front emanates great elegance.

Die Hausgeräteserie ArtLine ist Teil der Miele Generation7000 und wurde insbesondere im Hinblick auf offene Küchen und die Integration ins Wohnumfeld gestaltet. Mit ihren glatten, grifflosen Glasfronten lassen sich die Geräte nahtlos in zeitgemäße Wohnwelten einfügen. Die Türen öffnen sich auf leichten Fingertipp elektrisch. Erhältlich sind die ArtLine-Geräte in Obsidianschwarz, Brillantweiß und Graphitgrau. Bei der brillantweißen Ausführung lässt sich der schwarze Displayhintergrund an die Korpusfarbe anpasssen.

Begründung der Jury
Die sehr reduziert gestaltete ArtLine-Serie mit einer puristischen Vollglasfront strahlt große Eleganz aus.

JZD50-Z6B
Pressure Steamer
Druckdampfgarer

Manufacturer
Vatti Corporation Limited,
Zhongshan, China
In-house design
Peng Chen, Xueliang Chen
Web
www.vatti.com.cn

By means of micro-pressure technology, the Z6B pressure steamer can raise the pressure inside to 550 kPa (5.5 bar) and the steam temperature to over 100 degrees Celsius. Consequently, the steam penetrates the food efficiently and assures that it remains fresh and tender. The corners of the aluminium handle are inclined and gently chamfered, to reduce collisions during normal use. The central part of the handle can be rotated 30 degrees to open and close the steam valve.

Statement by the jury
This pressure steam oven impresses with a balanced relationship between operating panel, three-part handle and glass door, imparting to it a calm, high-quality appearance.

Mithilfe von Mikrodrucktechnologie kann der Druckdampfgarer Z6B den Druck im Innenraum auf 550 kPa (5,5 bar) und die Temperatur auf 100 Grad Celsius erhöhen. Dadurch dringt der Dampf effizient in die Lebensmittel ein und sorgt dafür, dass sie frisch bleiben und zart werden. Die Ecken des Aluminiumgriffs sind abgeschrägt und sanft gerundet, um die Stoßgefahr zu reduzieren. Der mittlere Teil des Griffs lässt sich um 30 Grad drehen, um das Dampfventil zu öffnen und zu schließen.

Begründung der Jury
Dieser Druckdampfgarer besticht mit einem ausgewogenen Verhältnis von Bedienblende, dreiteiligem Griff und Glastür, was ihm ein ruhiges, wertiges Erscheinungsbild verleiht.

KZQC-40-C906
Combination Steam Oven
Kombidämpfer

Manufacturer
Hangzhou ROBAM Applicances Co., Ltd.,
Hangzhou, China
In-house design
Suping Zhong, Benqiang Zhao
Web
www.robam.com

This combination steam oven was designed bearing in mind the usually rather small kitchens in China: it combines the functions of a steam oven and a baking oven in one appliance. A noticeable design feature is the handle which consists of one haptic, attractive stainless-steel pipe, which is in strong visual contrast to the large black surface of the front. Operation is via a 5" TFT touch display, which offers over 50 recipes, as well as a pushbutton, which also serves to open the water tank.

Statement by the jury
An extended functionality, easy operation and a purist appearance characterise this combination steam oven. The round-shaped handle is particulary user-friendly.

Dieser Kombidämpfer wurde im Hinblick auf üblicherweise eher kleine Küchen in China konzipiert und verbindet die Funktionen eines Dampfgarers und eines Backofens in einem Gerät. Auffälliges Gestaltungsmerkmal ist der aus einem Edelstahlrohr bestehende, haptisch angenehme Griff, der in starkem visuellem Kontrast zur großflächigen Front aus Schwarzglas steht. Die Bedienung erfolgt über ein 5"-TFT-Touchdisplay, das Zugriff auf mehr als 50 Rezepte bietet, sowie über einen Tastknopf, der auch dem Öffnen des Wasserbehälters dient.

Begründung der Jury
Eine erweiterte Funktionalität, leichte Bedienbarkeit und ein puristisches Erscheinungsbild zeichnen diesen Kombidämpfer aus. Ein gelungenes Detail ist der rund geformte Griff.

meat°it
Cooking Probe
Bratenthermometer

Manufacturer
Mastrad, Paris, France
Design
2Lion (Jonathan Lion, Mathieu Lion), Paris, France
Web
www.mastrad-paris.fr
www.2lion.co

The meat°it cooking probe is completely wireless. The approximately 6 mm thick, pointed stainless-steel probe with black ceramic cap is equipped with two sensors. They precisely measure the core temperature of the meat as well as the speed of roasting and the residual cooking time. The probe connects via Bluetooth with a tablet or smartphone, where all information is clearly shown in an app. The thermometer has 24-hour battery life and is high temperature resistant: it withstands flare-up for up to three minutes.

Das Bratenthermometer meat°it ist völlig kabellos gestaltet. Der etwa 6 mm dicke, spitze Edelstahlstift mit schwarzer Keramikkappe ist mit zwei Sensoren ausgestattet, dank derer sich die Kerntemperatur von Fleisch ebenso wie die Gargeschwindigkeit und Restgarzeit präzise messen lassen. Via Bluetooth wird die Sonde mit dem Tablet oder Smartphone verbunden, wo alle Informationen in einer App übersichtlich angezeigt werden. Das Thermometer hat eine Akkulaufzeit von 24 Stunden und ist hitzebeständig – es widersteht Flammen bis zu drei Minuten lang.

Statement by the jury
meat°it combines a purist design and simple handling with intelligent technology, which tremendously eases pinpoint accuracy of meat roasting.

Begründung der Jury
meat°it verbindet eine puristische Gestaltung und einfache Handhabung mit intelligenter Technologie, die das punktgenaue Garen von Fleisch ungemein erleichtert.

BF-5 Smart Grill Thermometer
Grillthermometer

Manufacturer
Shenzhen Lankesun Intelligent Technology Co., Ltd.,
Shenzhen, China
Design
Shenzhen Zanidea Creative and Cultural Co., Ltd.,
Shenzhen, China
Web
www.szbfour.com
www.funblue.cn

The BF-5 Smart Grill Thermometer is an intelligent accessory which enables measurement of the grill temperature in real time. This is made possible by a probe which is connected to the device by metal wires, allowing the device to indicate the temperature in real time. The thermometer can be connected to the smartphone via Bluetooth. Users can enter the type of food and their preferences for grilling in the app. This warns when the temperature is reached, not reached or exceeded.

Das BF-5 Smart Grill Thermometer ist ein intelligentes Grillzubehör, mit dem die Grilltemperatur in Echtzeit erfasst wird. Ermöglicht wird dies durch eine Sonde, die über Metalldrähte mit dem Gerät verbunden ist, das wiederum die Temperatur in Echtzeit anzeigt. Das Thermometer kann via Bluetooth mit dem Smartphone verbunden werden. Nutzer können die Art des Grillguts und ihre Präferenzen für die Zubereitung in der App festlegen. Diese warnt, wenn die Temperatur erreicht, über- oder unterschritten wird.

Statement by the jury
In the purist design of the BF-5 Smart Grill Thermometer nothing distracts from the display, which indicates the most important information clearly and is easily to understand.

Begründung der Jury
Bei dem puristisch gestalteten BF-5 Smart Grill Thermometer lenkt nichts vom Display ab, das die wichtigsten Informationen klar verständlich anzeigt.

ACT.O
Combi Oven
Kombiofen

Manufacturer
Angelo Po, Carpi (Modena), Italy

Design
Studio Volpi (Massimo Battaglia),
Carnago (Varese), Italy

Web
www.angelopo.com
www.studiovolpi.com

reddot award 2019
best of the best

Flowing interaction

In busy professional kitchens, the form and functionality of an oven determine the working process significantly. The design of the ACT.O combi oven focuses on both a user-centred approach and the maxim of maintaining a clearly recognisable brand identity. The well-balanced style features sharp lines and an elegant-looking colour scheme that aims to convey a sense of robustness and reliability. A functionally sophisticated, boomerang-shaped handle facilitates opening the oven door even with full hands. Great convenience is provided by the large 10" touch display with its completely redesigned interface as well as the ergonomic knob, which has been integrated in such a way that chefs no longer have to shift the eyes from the display to the knob anymore. The entire control panel is detachable from the front side, allowing technical maintenance to be done as quickly and easily as possible. Furthermore, the panel is made of two different pieces of glass that can be personalised separately, making the work easier and more effective. The covers of core probe and accessory ports are detachable and magnetic. With its cleverly thought-out concept, the ACT.O combi oven offers the fascinating experience of smoothly flowing interaction during cooking.

Fließende Interaktion

In einer betriebsamen Profi-Küche bestimmt der Backofen durch seine Form und Funktionalität den Arbeitsprozess entscheidend mit. Bei der Gestaltung des Kombiofens ACT.O standen der Nutzer und die Maxime einer klar erkennbaren Markenidentität im Mittelpunkt. Seine ausgewogene Formensprache mit scharf geschnittenen Linien und einer elegant anmutenden Farbgebung zielt darauf ab, ein Gefühl von Robustheit und Verlässlichkeit zu vermitteln. Funktional durchdacht, ermöglicht ein bumerangförmiger Griff, die Ofentür auch mit vollen Händen zu öffnen. Viel Komfort bieten das große 10"-Touchdisplay mit seinem komplett überarbeiteten Interface und ein ergonomischer Drehknopf, der so integriert wurde, dass der Koch bei der Arbeit nicht mehr zwischen Display und Knopf hin- und herschauen muss. Das gesamte Bedienpanel kann zudem aus der Frontseite herausgenommen werden, um technische Wartungen möglichst rasch und einfach durchführen zu können. Das Panel ist darüber hinaus in zwei Glaselemente unterteilt, die sich einzeln personalisieren lassen, was die Arbeit einfacher und effektiver macht. Die Abdeckungen des Kerntemperaturfühlers und der sonstigen Anschlüsse sind abnehmbar und magnetisch. Mit einem klug durchdachten Konzept bietet der Kombiofen ACT.O das faszinierende Erlebnis einer fließenden, reibungslosen Interaktion während des Kochens.

Statement by the jury

The professional ACT.O oven fascinates with a user interface that has been carefully designed to the last detail. The highly functional control panel and the distinctive, ergonomically designed rotary knob offer a new, direct approach towards interaction. The entire interface is simple and highly self-explanatory. The combi oven promotes professionalism at first glance and lends efficiency and lightness to the work processes in professional kitchens.

Begründung der Jury

Der Profi-Backofen ACT.O begeistert durch seine sorgfältig bis ins Detail ausgearbeitete Bedienoberfläche. Das hochfunktionale Bedienpanel und der markante, ergonomisch geformte Drehknopf bieten eine neue, direkte Art der Interaktion. Das gesamte Interface ist einfach und in hohem Maße selbsterklärend. Dieser Kombiofen visualisiert seine Professionalität auf den ersten Blick und verleiht den Arbeitsabläufen in der Profi-Küche Effizienz und Leichtigkeit.

Designer portrait
See page 48
Siehe Seite 48

221

Skyline Frame
Ceiling Lift Hood
Deckenlifthaube

Manufacturer
berbel Ablufttechnik GmbH,
Rheine, Germany

Design
Studio Ambrozus,
Cologne, Germany

Web
www.berbel.de
www.studioambrozus.de

reddot award 2019
best of the best

Floating object
The design of the extractor hood is decisive for the entire appearance of a cooking area. The Skyline Frame ceiling lift hood exudes the appearance of an impressive geometric sculpture. Enhanced by a narrow, matte black frame made of 20 × 20 mm square tubes, it not only promotes an aesthetic of urban chic with modern loft characteristics, it also enriches kitchens with its well-thought-out functionality and versatility. Special shelf surfaces can be added at the sides, for instance, to hold spices, oil and vinegar. In addition, the hood can also serve as a diverse interior lighting object, featuring individually adjustable effect lighting concealed behind high-quality, grey smoked glass covers. The colder colour temperature setting emits a cool bluish tinge suitable for bright kitchens. The warmer colour temperature setting emits a soft copper-like appearance, providing a beautiful accent for kitchens in darker, earthy tones with wooden accessories. Skyline Frame is equipped with a powerful berbel system for effective fat separation, as well as a quiet EC fan motor to ensure clean air. The standard equipment includes the powerful berbel recirculation filter and a convenient lifting function. Suspended on sturdy, thin wires, the hood seems to be floating beneath the ceiling, permitting continuous and smooth height variation by remote control or via the smartphone app.

Schwebendes Objekt
Das Design einer Dunstabzugshaube prägt die Anmutung des Kochbereichs entscheidend mit. Die Deckenlifthaube Skyline Frame wirkt wie eine eindrucksvolle geometrische Skulptur. Gestaltet mit einem schmalen, mattschwarzen Rahmen aus Quadratrohren in den Maßen 20 × 20 mm, gibt sie dem Raum eine urbane Ausstrahlung und modernen Loftcharakter. Sie bereichert die Küche dabei mit ihrer gut durchdachten Funktionalität und Vielseitigkeit. So können in seitlich angeschlossene Regalflächen Gewürze, Öl und Essig eingestellt werden. Die Haube dient zudem als ein im jeweiligen Interieur variables Lichtobjekt. Hinter ihren Fronten aus grauem Rauchglas verbirgt sich eine individuell einstellbare Effektbeleuchtung. In der kälteren Einstellung der Farbtemperatur passt deren bläulich kühler Lichtverlauf gut zu hellen Küchen. Bei wärmerer Farbtemperatur zeigt sich das Licht sanfter mit einem kupferartigen Schein, was einen schönen Akzent für Küchen in dunkleren, erdigen Farbtönen mit Holzelementen schafft. Ausgestattet ist Skyline Frame mit dem leistungsstarken berbel Prinzip für eine effiziente Fettabscheidung, ein leiser EC-Lüftermotor hält die Luft rein. Die Deckenlifthaube verfügt zudem serienmäßig über einen leistungsfähigen berbel Umluftfilter und eine komfortable Liftfunktion. Aufgehängt an stabilen, feinen Seilen schwebt sie unter der Decke und lässt sich in der Höhe stufenlos einstellen, die Steuerung erfolgt per Fernbedienung oder per App über das Smartphone.

Statement by the jury
The Skyline Frame ceiling lift hood establishes a fascinating new aesthetic for the kitchen. Its clear geometric lines give it the appearance of an object floating in mid-air. Featuring high-quality craftsmanship down to the detail, it is inspiring both in material and in form. It is functionally well-thought-out and fits seamlessly into almost any given kitchen interior. The integrated effect lighting allows perfect individual customisation.

Begründung der Jury
Die Deckenlifthaube Skyline Frame etabliert eine faszinierend neue Ästhetik für die Küche. Ihre klare geometrische Linienführung verleiht ihr die Anmutung eines frei im Raum schwebenden Objekts. Handwerklich hochwertig auch im Detail verarbeitet, beeindruckt sie in Form und Materialität. Sie ist dabei funktional durchdacht und fügt sich nahtlos in das jeweilige Interieur ein. Die integrierte Effektbeleuchtung kann der Nutzer zudem perfekt individuell anpassen.

Designer portrait
See page 50
Siehe Seite 50

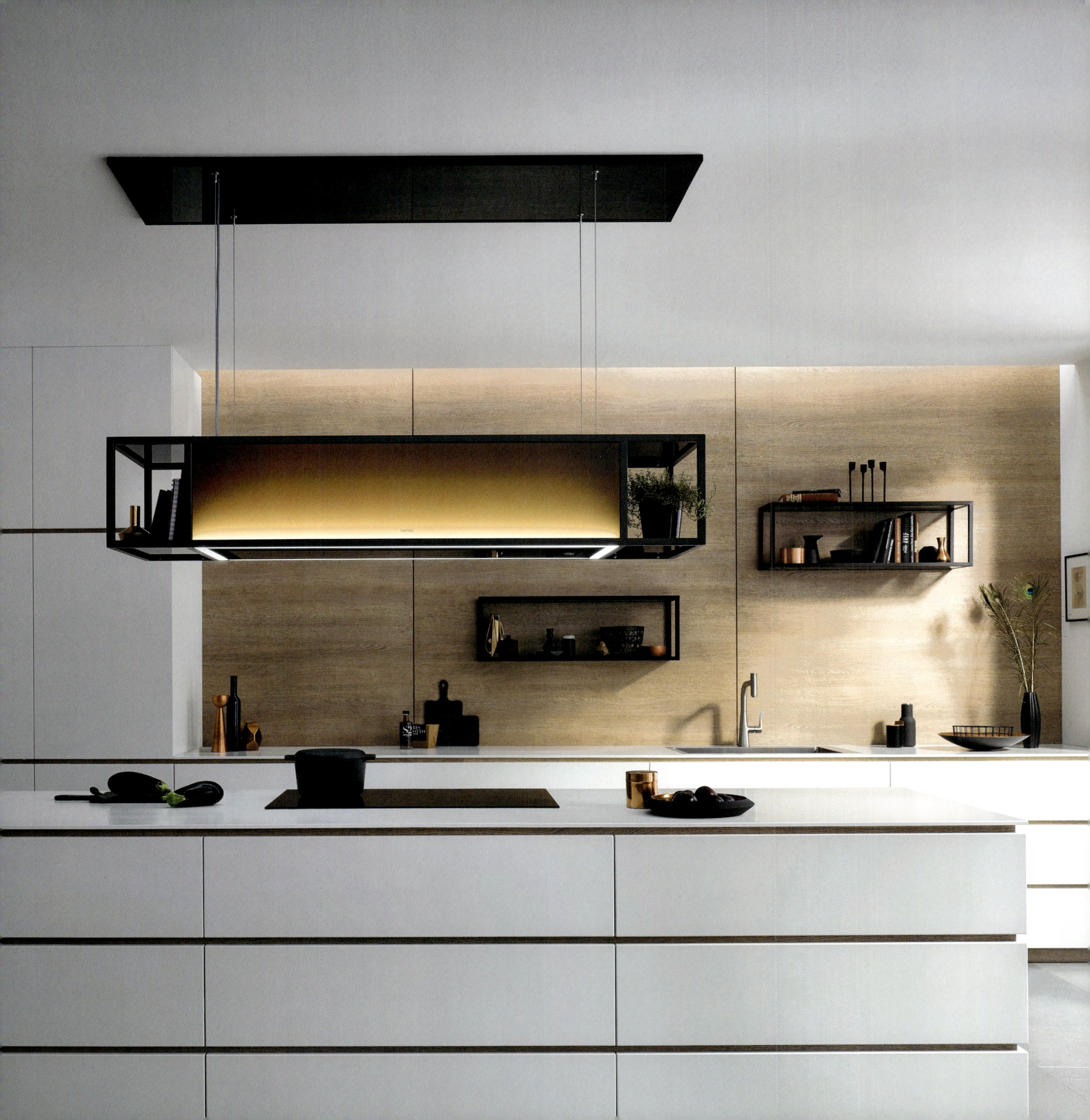

CXW-260-27X6
Range Hood
Dunstabzugshaube

Manufacturer
Hangzhou ROBAM Applicances Co., Ltd.,
Hangzhou, China
In-house design
Suping Zhong, Benqiang Zhao
Web
www.robam.com

The appearance of this automatic vapour extraction hood with side suction is characterised by a continuous glass plate, making it easy to clean. A particularly large extraction space increases the suction power. The integrated oil filter is made of stainless steel, which has been treated in a ten-step process. A nano-coating with oil guiding technology and the lotus effect support self-cleaning. By means of sensors the intelligent hood recognises smells and vapours and starts up automatically. It can also be controlled by gestures.

Statement by the jury
This extractor hood combines a minimalist design with complex suction technology and is also easy to clean.

Das Erscheinungsbild dieser automatischen Dunstabzugshaube mit seitlichem Abzug ist durch eine durchgängige und leicht zu reinigende Glasplatte geprägt. Ein besonders großer Abzugsraum verstärkt die Wirkung. Der integrierte Ölfilter ist aus Edelstahl gefertigt, der in zehn Arbeitsschritten behandelt wurde. Eine Nanobeschichtung mit Ölführungstechnologie und Lotuseffekt dient der Selbstreinigung. Mithilfe von Sensoren erkennt die intelligente Haube Gerüche und Dunst und startet automatisch. Die Bedienung kann auch über Gestensteuerung erfolgen.

Begründung der Jury
Diese Dunstabzugshaube verbindet eine minimalistische Gestaltung mit komplexer Absaugtechnologie und ist zudem besonders leicht zu reinigen.

FOKUSERA
Range Hood
Dunstabzugshaube

Manufacturer
IKEA of Sweden, Älmhult, Sweden
In-house design
Web
www.ikea.com

The Fokusera range hood combines a classical appearance with modern technology. Featuring soft, generous curves, the formal language is reminiscent of a traditional hearth furnace, an impression that is further emphasised by the matte black powder coating. However, the lower section of the hood with integrated user-interface feels decisively modern. The tactile operating elements such as the central rotary knob and toggle switch can be operated without looking at the operating panel.

Statement by the jury
This wall-mounted hood shows a robust, timeless appearance. Nice details are the tactile operating elements, which contribute to an immediate user experience.

Die Fokusera ist eine Dunstabzugshaube, die ein klassisches Erscheinungsbild mit moderner Technologie verbindet. Die Formensprache erinnert mit Kurven und großen Radien an einen traditionellen Herdofen, was durch die mattschwarze Pulverbeschichtung noch verstärkt wird. Die Unterseite der Haube mit integrierter Benutzeroberfläche wirkt hingegen sehr modern. Die taktilen Bedienelemente wie zentraler Drehknopf und Kippschalter lassen sich auch ohne Blick aufs Bedienfeld benutzen.

Begründung der Jury
Diese Wandhaube gefällt mit einem robusten, zeitlosen Erscheinungsbild. Ein schönes Detail sind die taktilen Bedienelemente, die zu einem unmittelbaren Benutzererlebnis beitragen.

Tower-Shaped Ventilator E662AHE
Range Hood
Dunstabzugshaube

Manufacturer
Vatti Corporation Limited,
Zhongshan, China
In-house design
Peng Chen, Xueliang Chen
Web
www.vatti.com.cn

The E662AHE range hood has been developed with the objective of ensuring that the user does not hit his head on the corner of the hood. The design concept "Curved Surface Angel" solves this problem by providing the E662AHE with sides which have rounded corners. For this, a seamless metal welding technology was used, making the hood appear as though it were made of one casting. "Smart Air Volume" technology recognises the air channel pressure automatically and adjusts the rotational speed of the DC motor accordingly.

Statement by the jury
The appearance of the range hood makes an impression of high precision and quality. A well-considered feature is the chamfered corners, which prevent painful collision with the hood.

Die Dunstabzugshaube E662AHE wurde mit dem Ziel entwickelt zu verhindern, dass Nutzer sich den Kopf an den Ecken der Haube stoßen. Das Designkonzept „Curved Surface Angel" löst dieses Problem, indem die E662AHE an den Seiten mit abgerundeten Ecken versehen wurde. Dafür kam eine nahtlose Metallschweißtechnologie zum Einsatz, die es ermöglicht, die Haube wie aus einem Guss erscheinen zu lassen. Eine „Smart Air Volume"-Technologie erkennt den Luftkanaldruck automatisch und passt die Drehzahl des DS-Motors an.

Begründung der Jury
Das Erscheinungsbild dieser Dunstabzugshaube vermittelt den Eindruck von hoher Präzision und Qualität. Ein durchdachtes Detail sind die abgeschrägten Ecken, die schmerzhafte Kollisionen mit der Haube verhindern.

Tower-Shaped Ventilator E636AH
Range Hood
Dunstabzugshaube

Manufacturer
Vatti Corporation Limited,
Zhongshan, China
In-house design
Peng Chen
Web
www.vatti.com.cn

The E636AH ventilator hood connects the extractor chamber with the outlet tower, so that they form one unit. The central filter is located further above and, together with the extractor chamber, generates a double negative pressure structure, which better captures the vapours and discharges them. This construction reduces the bends at the junction of the vapour cavity and the tower hood where the vapours must pass and makes cleaning easier. The black, hexagonal touch-operated user interface imparts to the hood a sculptural impression.

Statement by the jury
With its clear geometric design and distinctive operating interface, this tower-shaped hood is eye-catching. The innovative construction contributes to its high efficiency.

Die Kaminhaube E636AH verbindet die Abluftkammer und den Kamin, sodass sie eine Einheit bilden. Der zentrale Filter sitzt weiter oben und erzeugt zusammen mit der Abluftkammer eine doppelte Unterdruckstruktur, die die Dünste besser erfasst und abführt. Diese Konstruktion reduziert am Übergang von Abluftkammer und Kaminhaube die Ecken, um die die Luft fließen muss, und erleichtert die Reinigung. Die schwarze, hexagonale Touch-Bedienoberfläche verleiht der Haube eine skulpturale Wirkung.

Begründung der Jury
Mit ihrer klaren geometrischen Gestaltung und ihrer markanten Benutzeroberfläche zieht diese Dunstabzugshaube die Blicke auf sich. Ihre innovative Konstruktion trägt zu einer hohen Effizienz bei.

CXW-200-EM12TA
Updraft Range Hood
Dunstabzugshaube

Manufacturer
Ningbo Fotile Kitchen Ware Co., Ltd.,
Ningbo, China
Design
R&D Design Co., Ltd., Hangzhou, China
Web
www.fotile.com
www.rddesign.cc

The dominating design characteristics of this extraction hood are its distinctive lines and very precise engineering, which define the overall impression. In its construction, above all, great importance was put on simplification of use and ease of cleaning. The hood power adjusts automatically to the conditions and has an easily readable display. The user can operate it both via buttons and gestures.

Statement by the jury
Gesture control and sensors make operation of this vapour extraction hood convenient; its high-quality appearance is also appealing.

Dominante Gestaltungsmerkmale dieser Dunstabzugshaube sind ihre markante Linienführung und eine sehr präzise Verarbeitung, was den hochwertigen Gesamteindruck prägt. Bei der Konstruktion wurde vor allem Wert auf vereinfachte Arbeitsabläufe und eine leichte Reinigung gelegt. Die Leistung der Haube passt sich automatisch den Bedingungen an und wird gut sichtbar angezeigt. Die Bedienung durch den Benutzer ist sowohl mittels Tasten als auch Gesten möglich.

Begründung der Jury
Gestensteuerung und Sensoren machen die Bedienung dieser Dunstabzugshaube komfortabel, zudem gefällt sie mit einem hochwertigen Erscheinungsbild.

BORA Classic 2.0
Modular Cooktop Extractor System
Modulares Kochfeldabzugssystem

Manufacturer
BORA Vertriebs GmbH & Co KG, Niederndorf, Austria
Design
Phoenix Design GmbH + Co. KG, Stuttgart, Germany
Web
www.bora.com
www.phoenixdesign.com

BORA Classic 2.0 is a cooktop extractor system with modular cooktops and a central cooktop extractor. The intuitive "sControl+" operating panel centrally regulates the cooktop extractor and the cooktops, by a simple swipe of the finger up or down in the smooth hollow or a direct tap with the fingertip. With its minimalist, deep black and flush design the system harmonically integrates itself in the modern kitchen architecture. A broad collection of cooktops can be combined individually. Grease filter, grease drip pan and air inlet nozzle can be cleaned in the dishwasher.

BORA Classic 2.0 ist ein Kochfeldabzugssystem mit modularen Kochfeldern und zentralem Kochfeldabzug. Die intuitive Bedienung „sControl+" steuert zentral Kochfeldabzug und Kochfelder durch ein einfaches Auf- und Abbewegen des Fingers in einer geschliffenen Mulde oder durch direktes Antippen. Mit seinem minimalistischen, tiefschwarzen und flächenbündigen Design fügt sich das System harmonisch in die moderne Küchenarchitektur ein. Eine breite Auswahl an Kochfeldern kann individuell kombiniert werden. Fettfilter, Fettauffangwanne und Einströmdüse lassen sich in der Spülmaschine reinigen.

Statement by the jury
The BORA Classic 2.0 cooktop extractor system successfully combines a high degree of user-friendliness with sophisticated functionality and a reduced design.

Begründung der Jury
Das Kochfeldabzugssystem BORA Classic 2.0 verbindet auf gelungene Weise eine hohe Benutzerfreundlichkeit mit einer ausgereiften Funktionalität und einer reduzierten Gestaltung.

BORA Pure
Cooktop Extractor System
Kochfeldabzugssystem

Manufacturer
BORA Vertriebs GmbH & Co KG, Niederndorf, Austria
In-house design
Design
Imago Design GmbH, Gilching, Germany
Web
www.bora.com
www.imago-design.de

BORA Pure is a compact cooktop extractor system with an integrated cooktop extractor and a round inlet nozzle. Cooking vapours are effectively and quietly extracted downwards. The central touch-slide-operating panel "sControl" regulates the cooktop extractor and the cooking zones. All important functions are accessed by one tap. The cooktop and the cooktop extractor are flush designed, and the clear lines allow the compact system to be integrated into the modern kitchen architecture. Additional to the black version, the air inlet nozzle is available in five other colours.

BORA Pure ist ein kompaktes Kochfeldabzugssystem mit integriertem Kochfeldabzug und einer runden Einströmdüse. Kochdünste werden effektiv und leise nach unten abgesaugt. Die zentrale Touch-Slide-Bedienung „sControl" steuert Kochfeldabzug und Kochzonen. Alle wichtigen Bedienfunktionen sind über eine Berührung erreichbar. Kochfeld und Abzug sind flächenbündig und durch die klare Linienführung integriert sich das System in jede moderne Küchenarchitektur. Die Einströmdüse ist neben schwarz in fünf Farben erhältlich und ermöglicht so individuelle Farbakzente in der Küche.

Statement by the jury
This cooktop gains merit with its geometric forms, a very reserved design and its easily understandable user interface.

Begründung der Jury
Dieses Kochfeldabzugssystem punktet mit geometrischen Formen, einem sehr zurückgenommenen Design und einer gut verständlichen Benutzeroberfläche.

Fusion Hob
Cooktop Extractor System
Kochfeldabzugssystem

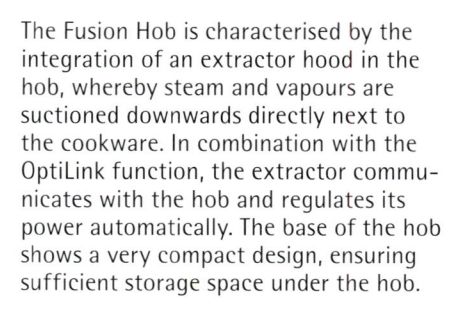

Manufacturer
V-ZUG AG, Zug, Switzerland
In-house design
Web
www.vzug.com

The Fusion Hob is characterised by the integration of an extractor hood in the hob, whereby steam and vapours are suctioned downwards directly next to the cookware. In combination with the OptiLink function, the extractor communicates with the hob and regulates its power automatically. The base of the hob shows a very compact design, ensuring sufficient storage space under the hob.

Statement by the jury
The combination of hob and extractor hood in one space-saving appliance pays off in everyday use. Intelligent functions make the cooking experience even more pleasurable.

Das Fusion Kochfeld ist dadurch gekennzeichnet, dass in das Kochfeld ein Dunstabzug integriert ist, wodurch Dämpfe und Dünste direkt neben dem Kochgeschirr nach unten abgesaugt werden. In Kombination mit der OptiLink-Funktion kommuniziert der Dunstabzug mit dem Kochfeld und reguliert seine Leistung automatisch. Der Unterbau des Kochfelds ist sehr kompakt gestaltet, sodass ausreichend Stauraum unterhalb der Kochstelle bleibt.

Begründung der Jury
Die Kombination von Kochfeld und Dunstabzug in einem platzsparend konstruierten Gerät macht sich im Küchenalltag bezahlt. Der Einsatz intelligenter Funktionen erleichtert das Kochen zusätzlich.

FullFlex
Induction Hob
Induktionskochfeld

Manufacturer
V-ZUG AG, Zug, Switzerland
In-house design
Web
www.vzug.com

The FullFlex induction hob offers great flexibility by abandoning the idea of specified cooking zones. By means of 48 inductors, it automatically detects the position and size of the respective cookware: up to six pots and pans can be placed simultaneously anywhere on the glass ceramic top. The hob offers a full-colour graphic display with a simple and intuitive operating concept, which can also display recipes.

Statement by the jury
By the use of innovative technology, this minimalist hob gives the user the greatest possible freedom when cooking.

Das Induktionskochfeld FullFlex bietet hohe Flexibilität, indem es auf vorgegebene Kochzonen verzichtet. Mithilfe von 48 Induktoren erkennt es jederzeit automatisch Position und Größe des Kochgeschirrs und ermöglicht es, bis zu sechs Pfannen und Töpfe beliebig auf der Glaskeramikplatte zu platzieren. Das Kochfeld verfügt zudem über ein vollfarbiges Grafikdisplay mit einem einfachen und intuitiven Bedienkonzept, auf dem sich auch Rezepte anzeigen lassen.

Begründung der Jury
Durch den Einsatz innovativer Technologie gewährt dieses minimalistische Kochfeld dem Benutzer größtmögliche Freiheit beim Kochen.

Jewell Premium
Gas Hob
Gaskochfeld

Manufacturer
Rinnai Korea, Incheon, South Korea
In-house design
Kevin Jeong, Yongjoon Joo
Web
www.rinnai.co.kr

The Jewell Premium gas hob is characterised by its 750 mm wide glass surface, an intuitive operating panel with semi-circular graphics ("touch-wheel") and cast-iron pan supports. It also integrates intelligent functions such as a timer and a water and rice cooking mode for each burner. Gleaming white LEDs are built into the toned-down silver glass base plate, emphasizing its elegant appearance. A dot-patterned graphic extends over the whole surface.

Statement by the jury
This gas hob conveys elegance and quality whilst also delivering a high degree of user-friendliness.

Das Jewell Premium Gaskochfeld ist durch seine 750 mm breite Glasoberfläche, ein intuitives Bedienfeld mit halbkreisförmiger Grafik („Touch-Wheel") und gusseiserne Topfträger gekennzeichnet. Es integriert zudem intelligente Funktionen wie Timer sowie Wasser- und Reis-Kochmodus für jede Kochstelle. In die mit einer abgetönten Silberfarbe hinterlegten Glasplatten sind weiß strahlende LEDs integriert, um die elegante Anmutung zu verstärken. Über die gesamte Oberfläche erstreckt sich ein geprägtes Punktmuster.

Begründung der Jury
Seine äußerst elegante und hochwertige Anmutung zeichnen dieses Gaskochfeld aus, das zudem eine hohe Benutzerfreundlichkeit bietet.

AEG SensePro
Induction Hob
Induktionskochfeld

Manufacturer
AB Electrolux, Stockholm, Sweden
In-house design
Web
www.electrolux.com

The SensePro induction hob was designed for professional demands and is equipped with sensor technology. A wireless and battery-free food probe in combination with a display on the touch-screen facilitate precise monitoring of the temperature and automatic adjustments as required. The design of the hob with its tactile dot pattern is minimalist, so that the focus is put on more efficiency in user interaction and on the food sensor.

Statement by the jury
Implementation of sensor technology in the SensePro hob leads to greater efficiency and user-friendliness. The seamlessly integrated, intuitive user interface is equally convincing.

Das SensePro-Induktionskochfeld wurde für professionelle Ansprüche konzipiert und mit Sensortechnologie ausgestattet. Ein kabel- und batterieloser Lebensmittelsensor ermöglicht in Kombination mit einer Anzeige auf dem Touchscreen die präzise Überwachung der Temperatur und passt diese bei Bedarf auch automatisch an. Die Gestaltung des Kochfelds mit taktilem Punktmuster ist minimalistisch, sodass der Fokus für mehr Effizienz auf der Benutzerinteraktion und dem Lebensmittelsensor liegt.

Begründung der Jury
Die Implementierung von Sensortechnologie führt beim SensePro-Kochfeld zu mehr Effizienz beim Kochen und hoher Bedienfreundlichkeit. Überzeugend ist auch die nahtlos integrierte, intuitive Benutzeroberfläche.

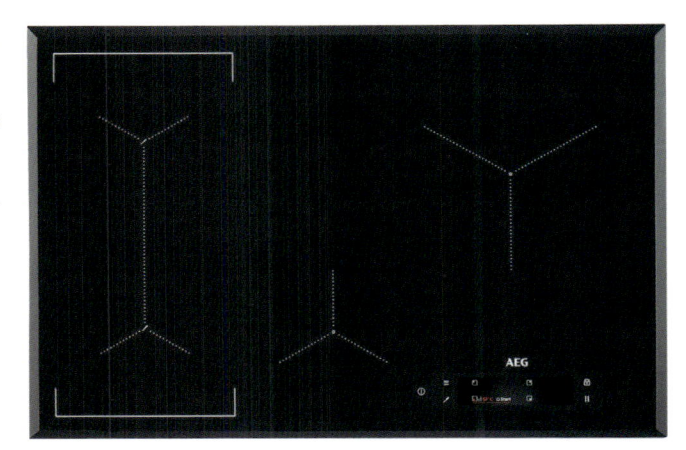

Simplicity 2.1
Induction Hob
Induktionskochfeld

Manufacturer
Gorenje, d.d., Velenje, Slovenia
In-house design
Matevž Popič, Urša Kovačič, Lidija Pritržnik, Uroš Bajt
Web
www.gorenjegroup.com

This induction hob of the Simplicity 2.1 collection incorporates sensor-supported process automation to simplify control. The large cooking surface has four separate heating elements with integrated sensors, which detect the position and size of the pots automatically and activate the control. Interactive graphics indicate the active heating zones and follow the pot movements. An unobtrusive pattern characterises the hob surface, protects it and separates the operating elements visually from the cooking area.

Statement by the jury
By the use of sensors, this hob adjusts automatically to the various user requirements and is very simple to operate.

Dieses Induktionskochfeld der Linie Simplicity 2.1 verfügt über eine sensorgestützte Prozessautomatisation, die die Steuerung vereinfacht. Das großflächige Kochfeld hat vier separate Heizelemente mit integrierten Sensoren, die Position und Größe der Töpfe automatisch erkennen und die Steuerung aktivieren. Interaktive Grafiken zeigen die aktiven Heizzonen an und folgen den Topfbewegungen. Ein dezentes Muster prägt die Kochfläche, schützt die Oberfläche und trennt die Bedienelemente visuell vom Kochfeld.

Begründung der Jury
Durch die Verwendung von Sensoren passt sich dieses Kochfeld automatisch den unterschiedlichen Nutzerbedürfnissen beim Kochen an und ist sehr einfach zu bedienen.

Easy Cook Hybrid Range
Induction Hobs
Induktionskochfelder

Manufacturer
SK magic, Seoul, South Korea
In-house design
Jeongeun Kim, Jongyoon Yu
Web
www.skmagic.com

When developing the Easy Cook Hybrid collection, particular focus was placed on simple operability. The rotary selection knobs at the front of the hob are elegantly designed and lie pleasantly in the hand, offering a user experience which is reminiscent of gas ovens. The power is indicated by clearly visible light points. They are easily noticable from a distance, enabling the user to check the status at a glance, even when busy with other things.

Bei der Entwicklung der Easy Cook Hybrid-Reihe lag ein besonderer Fokus auf einer einfachen Bedienbarkeit. Die Drehwahlknöpfe an der Vorderseite der Kochfelder sind elegant geformt und liegen angenehm in der Hand. Sie vermitteln beim Einstellen der Kochfelder ein Benutzererlebnis, das in seiner Unmittelbarkeit an die Bedienung eines Gasherds erinnert. Die Leistung wird durch deutlich sichtbare Lichtpunkte angezeigt, die auch aus der Distanz noch gut erkennbar sind, sodass der Status bei der Verrichtung anderer Tätigkeiten durch einen kurzen Blick überprüft werden kann.

Statement by the jury
This hob offers an immediate and intuitive user experience thanks to its rotary knobs and illuminated graphics.

Begründung der Jury
Dieses Kochfeld bietet mit seinen Drehknöpfen und seiner Leuchtgrafik ein unmittelbares und intuitives Benutzererlebnis.

Mi Induction Cooker
Induction Hob
Induktionskochfeld

Manufacturer
Xiaomi Inc., Beijing, China
In-house design
Web
www.mi.com

A round, black microcrystal plate and a shiny white housing characterise the minimalist appearance of the Mi Induction Cooker. The central rotary knob can be operated intuitively and integrates three functions: a LED display, a rotary switch and a press-button. There are also two buttons and nine light indicators for heat control. An app with pre-set recipes allows selection among a hundred cooking modes. A sensitive temperature sensor adjusts the power of the cooking plate automatically and avoids overheating and overflow.

Statement by the jury
This compact cooker is intuitive to operate and is attractive due to its minimalist and strongly contrasting design.

Eine runde, schwarze Mikrokristallplatte und ein weißes, glänzendes Gehäuse prägen das minimalistische Erscheinungsbild des Mi Induction Cooker. Der zentrale Drehknopf ist intuitiv zu bedienen und integriert drei Funktionen: eine LED-Anzeige, einen Drehschalter und eine Drucktaste. Hinzu kommen zwei Tasten und neun Lichtindikatoren für die Hitze. Eine App mit vorinstallierten Rezepten erlaubt die Wahl zwischen einhundert Kochmodi. Ein empfindlicher Temperaturfühler passt die Leistung des Kochfelds automatisch an und verhindert Überhitzung oder Überlaufen.

Begründung der Jury
Dieses kompakte Kochfeld ist intuitiv zu bedienen und gefällt mit seiner minimalistischen, auf starke Kontraste setzenden Gestaltung.

TOKIT Smart Induction Cooker Pro
Induction Hob
Induktionskochfeld

Manufacturer
Shanghai Chunmi Electronics Technology Co., Ltd., Shanghai, China
In-house design
Diego Kuo, Chung Kin Wong
Web
www.chunmi.com

The Tokit Smart Induction Cooker Pro is equipped with an innovative weighing system. This system can connect to an app, which offers over 100 cooking programmes and supports the user by controlling the time and the quantities of the ingredients to be added. With response from a sensitive temperature probe, it can automatically adjust cook time and output power. An intuitive rotary knob with OLED simulates the fine controlling of an oven.

Statement by the jury
By means of the interplay between an intelligent weighing system and an app, the clearly designed cooker helps users with little experience to make the cooking process easy.

Der Tokit Smart Induction Cooker Pro ist mit einem innovativen Wiegesystem ausgestattet. Dieses System kann mit einer App verbunden werden, die über hundert Kochprogramme bietet, und unterstützt den Nutzer beim Kochen, indem es den richtigen Zeitpunkt und die genaue Menge der hinzuzufügenden Zutaten steuert. Dank eines empfindlichen Temperaturfühlers können Garzeit und Leistung automatisch angepasst werden. Ein intuitiver Drehknopf mit OLED simuliert die Feinsteuerung eines Ofens.

Begründung der Jury
Durch das Zusammenspiel von intelligentem Wiegesystem und App erleichtert dieses klar gestaltete Kochfeld auch Nutzern mit wenig Erfahrung den Kochprozess.

COMFEE
Combi Microwave Oven
Kombi-Mikrowelle

Manufacturer
Guangdong Midea Kitchen Appliances Manufacturing Co., Ltd.,
Foshan, China
In-house design
Xiaowu Hu, Jia Zhang, Bangbin Hou, Wei Lu
Web
www.midea.com

Development of the Comfee combi microwave oven was based on studies of the lifestyle, behaviour and interests of a younger generation of Chinese. The result is an extremely compactly designed combination of microwave and baking oven, which occupies only a little space on the worktop. The operating panel is easily understood and facilitates presetting, for example, of the desired temperature for a drink.

Bei der Entwicklung der Kombi-Mikrowelle Comfee dienten Studien über das Leben, das Verhalten und die Interessen einer jungen Generation von Chinesen als Grundlage. Das Ergebnis ist eine extrem kompakt gestaltete Kombination aus Mikrowelle und Backofen, die nur wenig Raum auf der Arbeitsfläche in Anspruch nimmt. Das Bedienfeld ist leicht verständlich und ermöglicht es etwa, die gewünschte Temperatur für ein Getränk vorab einzustellen.

Statement by the jury
With its space-saving, contrasting design and extensive functionality, this combi-microwave oven is tailored to the demands of a young target group.

Begründung der Jury
Mit seiner platzsparenden, kontrastreichen Gestaltung und einer erweiterten Funktionalität ist diese Kombi-Mikrowelle passgenau auf die Ansprüche einer jungen Zielgruppe abgestimmt.

The Smart Oven Pizzaiolo
Electric Pizza Oven
Elektro-Pizzaofen

Manufacturer
Breville, Sydney, Australia
In-house design
Web
www.breville.com

The Smart Oven Pizzaiolo is a domestic counter-top oven capable of reaching 400 degrees Celsius. Combining this extreme heat with an innovative heater and reflector construction, brick oven-style pizza can be cooked in less than two minutes. The Incoloy heating elements have been developed with variable power intensities to bake the pizza crust evenly. Heat configuration and temperatures are controlled automatically as selected or set manually.

Statement by the jury
This sturdy, well-considered pizza oven makes it possible to bake brick oven pizza at home quickly and without much effort.

Der Smart Oven Pizzaiolo ist ein Pizzaofen für die heimische Küche, der bis zu 400 Grad Celsius erreicht. Durch die Kombination dieser extremen Hitze mit einer innovativen Erhitzer- und Reflektorkonstruktion kann Steinofenpizza in weniger als zwei Minuten zubereitet werden. Die Incoloy-Heizelemente wurden mit variabler Leistungsdichte entwickelt, um die Kruste der Pizza gleichmäßig zu rösten. Heizkonfigurationen und Temperaturen werden je nach Auswahl automatisch gesteuert oder manuell eingestellt.

Begründung der Jury
Dieser robust wirkende Pizzaofen macht es dank seiner durchdachten Funktionalität möglich, zu Hause schnell und ohne viel Aufwand Steinofenpizza zu backen.

Desktop Automatic Dough Mixer
Knetmaschine

Manufacturer
Bear Electric Appliance Co., Ltd., Foshan, China
In-house design
Caike Deng, Cancan Wang
Web
www.bears.com.cn

The objective when designing the Desktop Automatic Dough Mixer was to minimise the noise emission and vibration associated with automatic dough mixing. The result is a vertically designed kneading machine in which the kneading tool is driven from below instead of above. It is thus particularly powerful and at the same time emits less noise and less vibration. Furthermore, the bowl is easier to access and the machine better to operate.

Statement by the jury
Thanks to an altered construction, this kneading machine is compact and very functional, since it runs more smoothly and with improved mixing power.

Ziel bei der Konstruktion des Desktop Automatic Dough Mixer war es, die normalerweise mit dem automatischen Teigkneten verbundenen Geräuschemissionen und Vibrationen zu minimieren. Das Ergebnis ist eine vertikal ausgerichtete Knetmaschine, bei der der Antrieb der Knethaken von unten statt von oben erfolgt. Dadurch ist sie besonders leistungsstark und zugleich geräusch- und vibrationsarm. Zudem ist die Schüssel leichter erreichbar und die Maschine gut zu bedienen.

Begründung der Jury
Dank einer veränderten Bauweise ist diese Knetmaschine kompakt und sehr funktional, denn sie arbeitet ruhiger und mit verbesserter Rührkraft.

Hard Crust Bakery SD-ZP2000/SD-ZD2010/SD-ZF2010
Bread Maker
Brotbackautomat

Manufacturer
Panasonic Corporation, Kyoto, Japan
In-house design
Miki Kobayashi, Koji Yamaura
Web
www.panasonic.com

This bread maker combines a matte black body and metal lid with a rounded shape without sharp edges and corners. With this minimalist design, it fits unobtrusively into any kitchen space. The device bakes bread at high temperatures with a crispy crust. In order to provide for different preferences, a total of 18 styles of bread can be baked, among them brioche und gluten-free varieties.

Statement by the jury
Hard Crust Bakery shows a compact body, a user-friendly interface and a sophisticated functionality, which makes bread baking at home an easy task.

Dieser Brotbackautomat kombiniert ein mattschwarzes Gehäuse mit Metalldeckel mit einer abgerundeten, weichen Formgebung ohne scharfe Ecken und Kanten. Mit dieser minimalistischen Gestaltung fügt er sich dezent in jede Küchenumgebung ein. Das Gerät backt bei hohen Temperaturen Brot mit knuspriger Kruste. Um unterschiedlichen Vorlieben gerecht zu werden, können insgesamt 18 verschiedene Brotsorten gebacken werden, darunter Brioche und glutenfreie Varianten.

Begründung der Jury
Hard Crust Bakery punktet mit einem sachlichen, kompakten Gehäuse, einer bedienfreundlichen Gestaltung der Benutzeroberfläche und einer ausgereiften Funktionalität, die das Brotbacken zu Hause einfach macht.

Cosori Premium 5.8-Quart Air Fryer
CP158-AF
Heißluftfritteuse

Manufacturer
Arovast Corporation, Anaheim, California, USA
In-house design
Lin Yang
Web
www.cosori.com

An eye-catching design feature of this hot air fryer is its rectangular form. The brushed matte black housing incorporates high-quality metal elements, which also frame the user interface. A drawer which is removable from the front holds the food to be fried. The generously sized LED touch-panel displays time and temperature, with icons for controlling basic functions. There are eleven easily understandable pictogram buttons for selecting preset frying programmes.

Auffälliges Designmerkmal dieser Heißluftfritteuse ist ihre rechteckige Form. Das Gehäuse aus strukturiertem mattschwarzem Kunststoff hat wertige Akzente aus Metall, die auch die Benutzeroberfläche umrahmen. Eine nach vorne hin entnehmbare Schublade nimmt die zu frittierenden Lebensmittel auf. Die großzügige LED-Touch-Bedienfläche bietet neben Zeit- und Temperaturanzeige sowie Icons für die Steuerung der Grundfunktionen auch elf gut verständliche Piktogramm-Tasten für die Anwahl voreingestellter Frittierprogramme.

Statement by the jury
This hot air fryer facilitates the preparation of healthy food and delights with a tidy user interface, which is easy to understand due to the use of pictograms.

Begründung der Jury
Diese Heißluftfritteuse ermöglicht eine gesunde Nahrungszubereitung und begeistert mit einer aufgeräumten und durch die Verwendung von Piktogrammen intuitiv verständlichen Benutzeroberfläche.

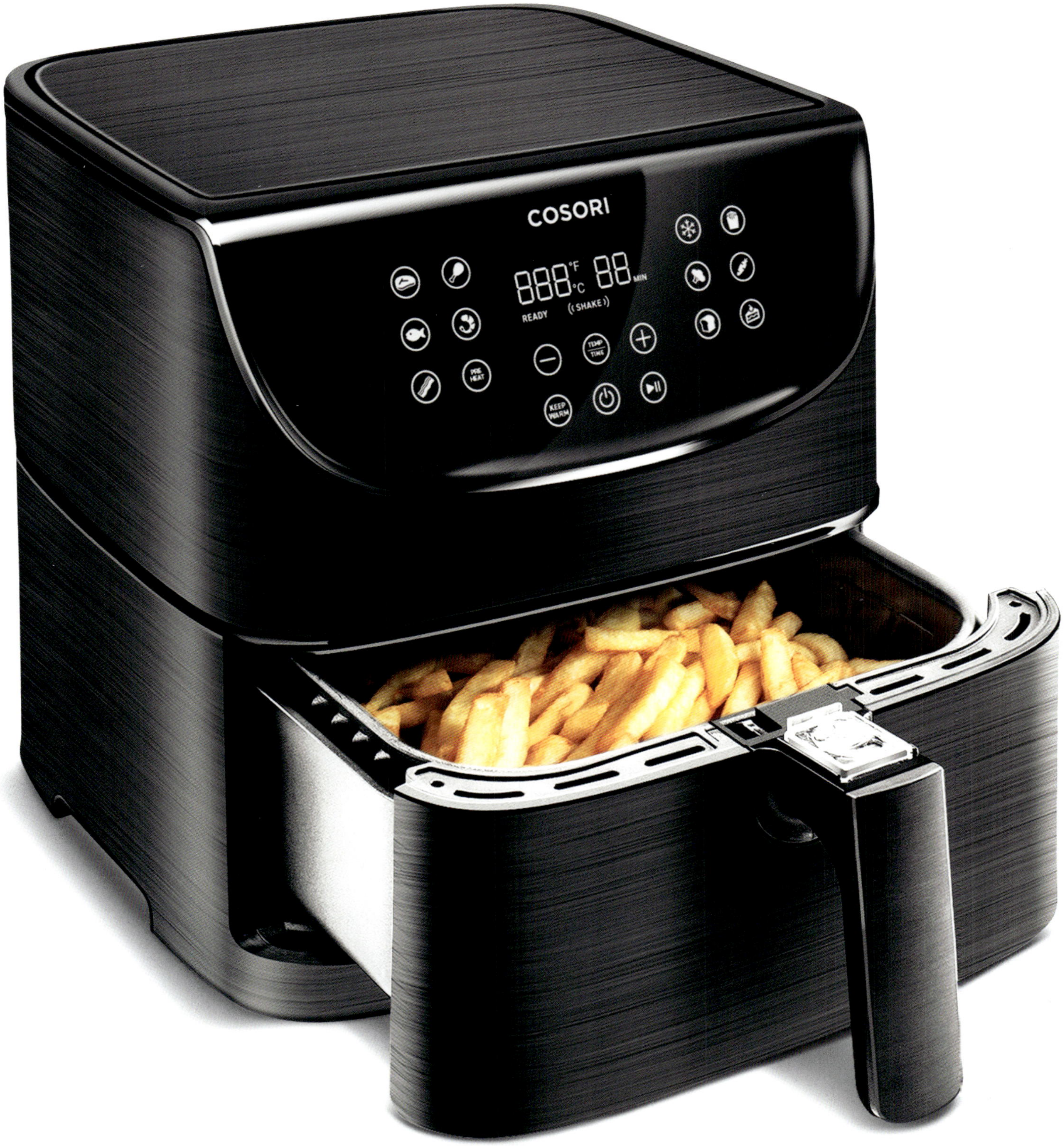
COSORI
READY
SHAKE
TEMP
TIME
PRE HEAT
KEEP WARM

SAHARA
Folding Dehydrator
Faltbarer Dehydrator

Manufacturer
Berkshire Innovations, Inc., Williamstown, Massachusetts, USA
In-house design
Warren Taylor, Michael Taylor
Design
AW Design International Ltd. (Albert Wan), Hong Kong
Antec Solutions Ltd. (W. L. Lau), Hong Kong
Web
www.brodandtaylor.com
www.awdesign.com.hk
Honourable Mention

The Sahara folding food dehydrator saves space by folding to one-third its size when not in use. It offers a large drying area of over 1 sqm and its digitally-controlled, 750 watt dual-heater design allows for large quantities of fruit and meat to be dried. The unit automatically switches to low-power mode for more efficient operation when food is partially dry or for lower temperatures when drying raw food.

Der Dehydrator Sahara zum Dörren von Lebensmitteln lässt sich bei Nichtgebrauch platzsparend auf ein Drittel seiner Größe zusammenfalten. Mit einem großen Trockenbereich von mehr als 1 qm und einem digital gesteuerten 750-Watt-Dual-Power-Heizsystem ermöglicht er das Trocknen großer Mengen Obst und Fleisch. Aus Effizienzgründen schaltet das Gerät automatisch auf niedrige Leistung um, wenn die Lebensmittel teilweise trocken sind oder rohe Lebensmittel bei geringer Temperatur gedörrt werden.

Statement by the jury
The folding ability of this dehydrator is a clever and space-saving solution.

Begründung der Jury
Die Zusammenfaltbarkeit dieses Dehydrators ist eine smarte und platzsparende Lösung.

Taji Type Electric Steam Boiler
Steam Pot
Dampfgarer

Manufacturer
Bear Electric Appliance Co., Ltd.,
Foshan, China
In-house design
Caike Deng, Cancan Wang
Web
www.bears.com.cn

The form of this steamer is taken from that of a Tajine, so that the original taste of the food cooked in it is preserved. In order to reduce loss of nutrients, the appliance combines a method which makes use of the distillation cycle with Tajine-style steam pressure cooking. By this means, the electric steam boiler also simplifies the preparation of traditional Chinese dishes and makes them healthier.

Statement by the jury
From a functional as well as a design viewpoint, the Taji Type Electric Steam Boiler combines contemporary technology with traditional methods of preparing food.

Die Form dieses Dampfgarers ist einer Tajine nachempfunden, um den ursprünglichen Geschmack und die Nährstoffe der darin gegarten Lebensmittel zu erhalten. In seinem Inneren kombiniert er eine Methode, die den Destillationszyklus nutzt, mit Dampfdruckkochen im Tajine-Stil, um den Nährstoffverlust zu reduzieren. Auf diese Weise vereinfacht der elektrische Dampfgarer auch die Zubereitung traditioneller chinesischer Speisen und macht sie gesünder.

Begründung der Jury
In funktionaler wie gestalterischer Hinsicht verbindet der Taji Type Electric Steam Boiler zeitgemäße Technologie mit einer traditionellen Methode der Essenszubereitung.

Tastier-Electric Food Steamer
Dampfgarer

Manufacturer
Bear Electric Appliance Co., Ltd.,
Foshan, China
In-house design
Caike Deng, Cancan Wang
Web
www.bears.com.cn

In contrast to a steam cooker with traditional form, this electric food steamer can be used in many different ways. Apart from steaming, it also allows users to prepare dishes like porridge or hotpots, as various cooking methods are available. The form of the steamer, including the base with horizontal operating panel, is rounded; the combination of steel pot and plastic outer shell imparts a distinctive appearance.

Statement by the jury
This compact steamer offers great flexibility for preparing various foods. Its appearance is just as elegant as it is friendly.

Anders als Dampfgarer mit traditioneller Formgebung bietet dieser Elektrodampfgarer vielfältige Einsatzmöglichkeiten, die über das herkömmliche Dämpfen von Speisen hinausgehen. So lassen sich mit diesem Gerät beispielsweise auch Porridge oder Hot Pots zubereiten. Je nach Zutat stehen unterschiedliche Kochmethoden zur Verfügung. Die Form des Dampfgarers inklusive seiner Basis mit horizontaler Bedienfläche ist gerundet, die Kombination aus Stahltopf und Kunststoffummantelung verleiht ihm sein markantes Aussehen.

Begründung der Jury
Eine hohe Flexibilität bei der Zubereitung unterschiedlichster Speisen bietet dieser kompakte Dampfgarer. Zudem gefällt er mit einem gleichermaßen eleganten wie freundlichen Erscheinungsbild.

Vermicular Musui-Kamado
Multicooker
Multifunktionskocher

Manufacturer
Aichi Dobby Ltd., Nagoya, Japan
In-house design
Tomoharu Hijikata, Mina Orihashi, Takayuki Fujita
Web
www.vermicular.jp

The Musui-Kamado combines the Musui, an enamelled cast-iron pot whose precision seal reflects Japanese craftsmanship, with the kamado. The kamado is a countertop induction burner inspired by the traditional Japanese stove. For perfect heat distribution and temperature control, Kamado uses a new heating technology. The innovative device supports various types of cooking such as roasting, searing, slow-cooking, braising, etc. For precise cooking, the temperature can be set between 30 and 95 degrees Celsius in one-degree increments.

Der Musui-Kamado kombiniert den Musui, einen emaillierten, gusseisernen Topf mit einer in japanischer Handwerkskunst gefertigten Präzisionsdichtung, mit der Kamado. Letztere ist eine Induktionsheizplatte, die einem traditionellen japanischen Herd nachempfunden ist. Für eine perfekte Wärmeverteilung und präzise Temperatursteuerung nutzt Kamado neue Heiztechnologie. Das innovative Gerät unterstützt unterschiedliche Gararten wie Braten, scharfes Anbraten, Langsamgaren, Schmoren etc. Für präzises Garen kann die Temperatur zwischen 30 und 95 Grad Celsius in 1-Grad-Schritten eingestellt werden.

Statement by the jury
The design of the Musui-Kamado combines traditional Japanese elements with new technologies which simplify cooking and offer a large range of cooking options.

Begründung der Jury
Der Musui-Kamado verbindet auf gelungene Weise traditionelle japanische Elemente mit neuen, das Kochen vereinfachenden Technologien und bietet eine große Bandbreite an Garmöglichkeiten.

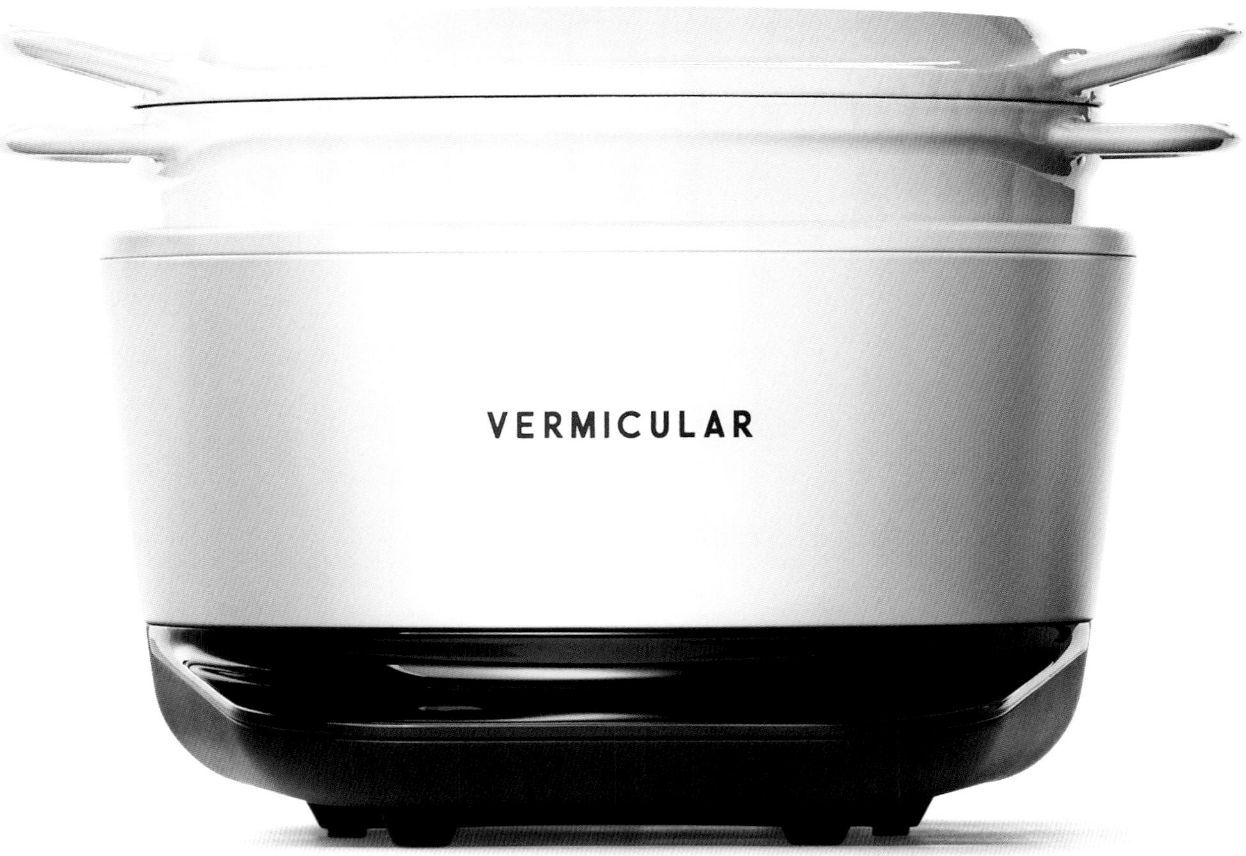
VERMICULAR

Excellent IH Cooker
Rice Cooker
Reiskocher

Manufacturer
Gree Electric Appliances, Inc. of Zhuhai, Zhuhai, China
In-house design
Jianming Tan, Sha Li, Nanfei Chen, Huanlong Wu, Jiahua Liu, Jiabao Feng, Yao Li, Yang Zhao, Jianfeng Lin, Wenbo Lu, Huijie Wang, Liangliang Cao, Sen Yang, Youmei Zhang, Hongyi Cheng, Shengsheng Liu, Yan Liu, Jinmei Feng, Shuaiwen Zhou, Xusheng Chen
Web
www.gree.com.cn

By the touch of a button, this intelligent rice cooker enables the user to prepare germinated brown rice, whose nutritional value is considerably higher than that of conventional rice. The brown rice germinates sufficiently within four hours, ready for cooking. The clear design of the rice cooker shows rounded upper elements on a square base. The housing is designed as seamlessly as possible to facilitate cleaning. The generous, immediately intelligible operating panel on the lid comes into sight only after touching. The device can also be controlled via an app.

Dieser intelligente Reiskocher ermöglicht es, auf Knopfdruck gekeimten Vollkornreis zu kochen, dessen Nährwert wesentlich höher ist als der von herkömmlichem Reis. Binnen vier Stunden hat der Vollkornreis ausreichend gekeimt, um gegart werden zu können. Die klare Gestaltung des Reiskochers ist im oberen Bereich von Kreisformen geprägt, der Boden ist viereckig. Das Gehäuse ist im Hinblick auf eine einfache Reinigung so nahtlos wie möglich konstruiert. Das großzügige, gut verständliche Bedienfeld auf dem Deckel wird erst bei Berührung sichtbar. Die Steuerung ist auch per App möglich.

Statement by the jury
The Excellent IH Cooker combines a healthy means of cooking rice with a well-balanced design.

Begründung der Jury
Der Excellent IH Cooker verbindet eine gesunde Art der Reiszubereitung mit einer ausgewogenen Gestaltung.

Simu Intelligent IH Rice Cooker
Reiskocher

Manufacturer
Gree Electric Appliances, Inc. of Zhuhai, Zhuhai, China
In-house design
Jianming Tan, Sha Li, Nanfei Chen, Huanlong Wu, Jiahua Liu, Xuxiang He, Yang Zhao, Jianfeng Lin, Jinmei Feng, Qinhong Chen, Liangliang Cao, Youmei Zhang, Hongyi Cheng, Shengsheng Liu, Jiabao Feng, Yan Liu, Shuaiwen Zhou, Xusheng Chen
Web
www.gree.com.cn

The appearance of this rice cooker is characterised by a shiny white body and golden decorative elements. Its display, with concise graphics, is concealed when switched off and becomes visible after touching the button. The intelligent induction rice cooker uses germinated rice technology (GABA method) by which means brown rice is first brought to germination, whereby the nutrition value is maximised and its GABA value (Gamma-aminobutyric acid) is increased by five times. An internal inner cover with honeycomb structure can be removed for easy cleaning.

Das Erscheinungsbild dieses Reiskochers ist durch einen glänzend weißen Korpus und goldene Dekorelemente geprägt. Sein Display mit prägnanter Grafik ist im ausgeschalteten Zustand verborgen und wird erst bei Berührung der Taste sichtbar. Der intelligente Induktionsreiskocher nutzt eine Reiskeimtechnologie (GABA-Methode), bei der Vollkornreis zunächst zum Keimen gebracht wird, wodurch der Nährwert maximiert wird und sein GABA-Wert (dt. Gamma-Aminobuttersäure-Wert) auf das Fünffache ansteigt. Eine Innenhülle mit wabenförmiger Struktur lässt sich für eine einfache Reinigung herausnehmen.

Statement by the jury
This rice cooker appears elegant with its white body and gold-coloured details. It integrates the GABA method, by which the rice is prepared in a healthy and more nutritional way.

Begründung der Jury
Sehr elegant wirkt dieser Reiskocher mit seinem weißen Korpus mit goldfarbenen Akzenten. Funktional punktet er mit der Integration der GABA-Methode, durch die der Reis gesünder und nahrhafter wird.

Steam Rice Cooker
Dampfreiskocher

Manufacturer
Joyoung, Hangzhou, China
In-house design
Lv Zheng, Sophia Lim
Web
www.joyoung.com

This Steam Rice Cooker permits the user to cook rice, vegetables, seafood, soups and other foods in an easy, healthy and nutritional way. The pot consists of two layers of stainless steel. It thus offers not only increased safety but also eases cleaning. Its form is inspired by tableware design, whereby the pot blends in harmoniously with the laid table. In addition to the stainless-steel pot, there are glass vessels which can be adopted as an alternative, depending on the type of food.

Dieser Dampfreiskocher ermöglicht es, auf einfache, gesunde und nährstofferhaltende Weise Reis, Gemüse, Meeresfrüchte, Suppen und andere Speisen zuzubereiten. Der Topf besteht aus zwei Lagen Edelstahl. Damit bietet er nicht nur erhöhte Sicherheit beim Gebrauch, sondern erleichtert auch die Reinigung. Seine Gestaltung ist von Tableware-Design inspiriert, wodurch sich der Topf auch harmonisch auf dem gedeckten Tisch einfügt. Zusätzlich zu dem Edelstahltopf gibt es auch Glasbehälter, die je nach Art des Lebensmittels alternativ eingesetzt werden können.

Statement by the jury
The Steam Rice Cooker attracts attention with a warm, non-technical appearance. The pot, with its ceramic-like appeal, can also be used as a serving dish.

Begründung der Jury
Der Steam Rice Cooker macht mit einem wenig technischen, warm anmutenden Erscheinungsbild auf sich aufmerksam. Ein besonders schöner Aspekt ist, dass sich der an Keramik erinnernde Topf auch als Serviergefäß nutzen lässt.

TOKIT Mini
Rice Cooker
Reiskocher

Manufacturer
Shanghai Chunmi Electronics
Technology Co., Ltd., Shanghai, China
In-house design
Diego Kuo, Baowen Zhao
Web
www.chunmi.com

The prominent design feature of the TOKIT Mini rice cooker is its rounded form, thanks to which it is very space-saving. The interactive operating panel is intuitive and self-explanatory. It blanks out all unnecessary visual information and guides the user through the process: the backlit touch-sensitive buttons light up or extinguish at every step. In combination with a smartphone app, the rice cooker offers over 100 cooking programmes for rice and other foods.

Statement by the jury
The TOKIT Mini delights with a particularly well understandable operating panel, which guides the user step-by-step through the preparation process.

Hervorstechendes Gestaltungsmerkmal des TOKIT Mini Reiskochers ist seine gerundete Form, dank derer er sehr platzsparend ist. Die interaktive Bedienfläche ist intuitiv und selbsterklärend. Sie blendet alle nicht benötigten visuellen Informationen aus und leitet den Nutzer durch den Prozess, indem die hinterleuchteten, berührungsempfindlichen Tasten bei jedem Schritt aufleuchten oder erlöschen. In Kombination mit einer Smartphone-App bietet der Reiskocher über 100 Kochprogramme für Reis und andere Gerichte.

Begründung der Jury
Der TOKIT Mini begeistert mit seiner besonders gut verständlichen und durchdachten Bedienoberfläche, die den Nutzer Schritt für Schritt durch den Zubereitungsprozess leitet.

TOKIT Smart IH
Rice Cooker
Reiskocher

Manufacturer
Shanghai Chunmi Electronics
Technology Co., Ltd., Shanghai, China
In-house design
Diego Kuo, Weihung Hung
Web
www.chunmi.com

The TOKIT Smart IH rice cooker combines a traditional kitchen appliance with contemporary, intelligent technology. It can, for example, be controlled via a smartphone app which offers over 800 recipes, among them stews, yoghurt and cakes. For each of these recipes a specific programme was developed, which is contained in the app and controls cooking time as well as induction power automatically. The user only needs to add the ingredients and press the start button.

Statement by the jury
By means of intelligent technologies and a high degree of automation, TOKIT Smart IH makes preparation of food particularly easy. It shows a homogeneous appearance and elaborated details.

Der Reiskocher TOKIT Smart IH verbindet ein traditionelles Küchengerät mit zeitgemäßer, intelligenter Technologie. Er kann beispielsweise über eine Smartphone-App gesteuert werden, die mehr als 800 Rezepte bereitstellt, darunter auch Eintöpfe, Joghurt oder Kuchen. Für jedes dieser Rezepte wurde wiederum ein spezifisches Garprogramm entwickelt, das in der App hinterlegt ist und Garzeit und Induktionsleistung automatisch steuert. Der Benutzer muss nur noch die Zutaten hinzufügen und die Starttaste drücken.

Begründung der Jury
Mithilfe intelligenter Technologien und einem hohen Grad an Automatisierung macht TOKIT Smart IH die Essenszubereitung besonders einfach. Er punktet zudem mit seinem die Details betonenden, homogenen Gesamtbild.

HC38 Low-sugar Electric Rice Cooker
Reiskocher

Manufacturer
Zhejiang Supor Electrical Appliances
Manufacturing, Hangzhou, China
In-house design
Cheng Kai, Cao Pu
Web
www.supor.com.cn

This rice cooker is able to reduce the sugar content of rice and was specially developed for diabetics and people with weight problems. The product can reduce the sugar content of rice by about 30 percent while preserving its nutrient contents thanks to a special cooking mechanism. An intelligent temperature control and a "benfu" pot assure that the rice retains its full flavour.

Statement by the jury
This rice cooker combines an elegant appearance with innovative features, supporting a healthier way to cook rice.

Dieser Reiskocher ist in der Lage, den Zuckergehalt von Reis zu reduzieren, und wurde speziell für Diabetiker und Menschen mit Gewichtsproblemen entwickelt. Das Produkt kann den Zuckergehalt von Reis um etwa 30 Prozent reduzieren und dabei dank eines speziellen Garmechanismus gleichzeitig die Nährstoffe bewahren. Eine intelligente Temperatursteuerung und der Einsatz eines Benfu-Topfs stellen sicher, dass der Reis während des Garens seinen vollen Geschmack beibehält.

Begründung der Jury
Eine innovative Funktionalität, die den Garprozess gesünder macht, verbindet sich bei diesem Reiskocher mit einem eleganten Erscheinungsbild.

DHZ4001XM
Rice Cooker
Reiskocher

Manufacturer
Foshan Shunde Midea Electrical
Heating Appliances, Foshan, China
In-house design
Hongtao Feng, Jie Ding,
Qianni Chen, Huanyi Zhao
Web
www.midea.com

This rice cooker draws attention with its elegant glass-and-metal housing. An insert for steaming allows for two different cooking processes to take place simultaneously, which saves time. A special induction technology and a titanium coated bottom with a structure promoting strong, bubbling boil ensure that the rice is evenly heated. Due to the interplay of temperature sensors and an intelligent electrode, the temperature is automatically measured and regulated.

Statement by the jury
The combination of innovative functionality and appealing design make this rice cooker a device which upgrades the kitchen.

Dieser Reiskocher macht mit einem eleganten Glas-Metall-Gehäuse auf sich aufmerksam. Zudem besticht seine innovative Funktionalität: Durch die Kombination mit einem Dampfeinsatz lassen sich zwei verschiedene Garvorgänge zeitsparend gleichzeitig durchführen. Eine spezielle Induktionstechnik und ein titanbeschichteter Boden mit einer Struktur, die für ein stark sprudelndes Kochen sorgt, stellen sicher, dass der Reis gleichmäßig erhitzt wird. Durch das Zusammenspiel von Temperatursensoren und einer intelligenten Elektrode wird die Temperatur automatisch erfasst und reguliert.

Begründung der Jury
Die Verbindung von innovativer Funktionsweise und ansprechender Gestaltung macht diesen Reiskocher zu einem Gerät, das eine Bereicherung für die Küche darstellt.

Schmieden
Rice Cooker
Reiskocher

Manufacturer
Guangdong Taigroo Electric
Technology Co., Ltd., Foshan, China
In-house design
Cocoon H, Chen Shu
Web
www.taigroo.com

Schmieden is a compact, fully automatic professional rice cooker. Utilizing technology, traditional preparation methods are replaced by a more contemporary way of cooking. Various cooking modes can be selected via a TFT display. Schmieden uses multi-stage induction heating technology, which adapts automatically to the food, thus also saving energy. A V-shaped interior container assures that the rice absorbs more water and tastes better.

Statement by the jury
The Schmieden rice cooker simplifies the process of cooking by use of new technologies. A reduced design and metallic appearance visualise its high efficiency.

Schmieden ist ein kompakter, vollautomatischer Profi-Reiskocher, der sich zugunsten einer zeitgemäßen, technologisch unterstützten Art des Reiskochens von traditionellen Zubereitungsmethoden löst. Über ein TFT-Display lassen sich verschiedene Kochmodi auswählen. Schmieden nutzt eine mehrstufige Induktionsheiztechnologie, die sich automatisch und energiesparend an die Gerichte anpasst. Ein V-förmiger Innenbehälter sorgt dafür, dass der Reis mehr Wasser aufnimmt und besser schmeckt.

Begründung der Jury
Der Reiskocher Schmieden vereinfacht den Prozess des Reiskochens durch den Einsatz neuer Technologien. Sein reduziertes, metallisches Erscheinungsbild visualisiert seine hohe Effizienz.

Multigrain Rice Cooker Avance Collection
Reiskocher

Manufacturer
Philips, Eindhoven, Netherlands
In-house design
Philips Design, Shanghai, China
Web
www.philips.com

The Philips Multigrain Rice Cooker uses "Hydro-penetration" technology to make cooking of various types of rice considerably quicker and easier, while also improving the taste. A 7" TFT colour display with a well-considered guide leads the user through the process. "Omni Spiral IH" technology precisely alternates the heat input, so that the rice is constantly in motion and all grains are cooked, while the enamel cast iron pot assures even distribution of the heat.

Statement by the jury
The Multigrain Rice Cooker impresses from an aesthetic viewpoint with an elegant appearance characterised by metal features. It also convinces with its sophisticated functionality.

Der Philips Multigrain-Reiskocher macht durch den Einsatz einer „Hydro-penetration"-Technologie das Kochen verschiedener Reissorten wesentlich einfacher und schneller, wobei zugleich der Geschmack verbessert wird. Ein 7"-TFT-Farbdisplay mit durchdachter Benutzerführung leitet durch den Prozess. Eine „Omni Spiral IH"-Technologie wechselt die Hitzezufuhr präzise, sodass der Reis in Bewegung bleibt und alle Körner gegart werden, während der emaillierte gusseiserne Topf für eine gleichmäßige Wärmeverteilung sorgt.

Begründung der Jury
Der Multigrain-Reiskocher besticht unter ästhetischen Gesichtspunkten mit einem eleganten, durch Metallakzente geprägten Erscheinungsbild und überzeugt auch mit seiner ausgereiften Funktionalität.

Fanxiaoer Rice Cooking Robot
Rice Cooker
Reiskocher

Manufacturer
Foshan Fanxiaoer Rice Cooking Robot Technology Co., Foshan, China
Design
LKKer Technology Co., Ltd.
(Luyao Zhuang, Li Ying, Wang Qiuchen), Beijing, China
Web
www.lkker.com

The Fanxiaoer Rice Cooking Robot combines the classic functions of a rice cooker with new technologies. It offers a high degree of automation, whereby rice preparation is made particularly simple. The device comprises a rice storage box with a capacity of 2.5 kg as well as an intelligent system for washing rice. When attached to the main water supply it can provide the correct quantity of rice itself, wash the rice and finally boil it. The rice cooker can also be controlled via an app.

Statement by the jury
This rice cooker performs preparation of rice mostly by itself, thanks to its sophisticated functionality. Operation is simple via display and app.

Der Fanxiaoer Rice Cooking Robot kombiniert klassische Funktionen eines Reiskochers mit neuen Technologien und bietet ein hohes Maß an Automation, wodurch die Zubereitung des Reises besonders einfach wird. Er verfügt über einen Reisspeicher mit einer Kapazität von 2,5 kg sowie ein intelligentes System zum Reiswaschen. An das Leitungssystem angeschlossen, kann er so die gewünschte Menge Reis selbst bereitstellen, den Reis waschen und anschließend kochen. Der Reiskocher lässt sich auch über eine App steuern.

Begründung der Jury
Dieser Reiskocher übernimmt die Reiszubereitung dank seiner ausgereiften Funktionalität weitestgehend selbst. Die Bedienung über Display und App ist einfach.

Smeg 4×4 Toaster (TSF03)

Manufacturer
Smeg S.p.A., Guastalla (Reggio Emilia), Italy
In-house design
Ilaria Bertelli
Design
deepdesign, Milan, Italy
Web
www.smeg.com
www.deepdesign.it

The distinctive appearance of the Smeg 4×4 toaster is characterised by its painted-steel body, chrome elements, back-lit buttons and two pairs of wide slots, with one operating button and a crumb tray each. The toaster, with a power of 2,000 watts, features slice centring technology with automatic pop-up, whereby the bread is toasted in a very short time and becomes crispy. Six browning levels, a hot, defrost and bagel function, sandwich tongs and a bun warmer make toasting easier.

Statement by the jury
The Smeg 4×4 Toaster convincingly combines high functionality with selected materials in classic retro design.

Das markante Erscheinungsbild des Smeg 4×4 Toasters ist geprägt durch sein Gehäuse aus lackiertem Stahl, Chromelemente, hinterleuchtete Knöpfe sowie zwei Paar breiter Schlitze, die jeweils über einen eigenen Bedienknopf und eine Krümelschublade verfügen. Der Toaster hat eine Leistung von 2.000 Watt sowie eine Selbstzentrierungs- und eine automatische Liftfunktion, wodurch das Brot in kürzester Zeit erhitzt und knusprig wird. Sechs Bräunungsstufen, Heiz-, Abtau- und Bagel-Modus, Sandwich-Zangen und Brötchenwärmer erleichtern das Toasten.

Begründung der Jury
Auf überzeugende Weise vereint der Smeg 4×4 Toaster hohe Funktionalität mit einer ausgesuchten Materialität in klassisch-elegantem Retrodesign.

Mesmerine Collection
Breakfast Collection
Frühstücksserie

Manufacturer
Kenwood Limited, Havant, United Kingdom
In-house design
Web
www.kenwoodworld.com

The Mesmerine collection combines an appealing appearance with high functionality. The housings of toasters and water kettles are decorated with a diamond pattern which is reminiscent of jewellery and yet is smooth, so that they are easily cleaned. Brightly polished metal elements add to the elegant impression and make the devices robust at the same time. The series is available in various fresh colours and can blend harmoniously in every kitchen.

Statement by the jury
The beautifully crafted and eye-catching design of the Mesmerine kitchen device collection is certain to attract attention in the kitchen.

Die Mesmerine-Kollektion verbindet ein ansprechendes Erscheinungsbild mit einer hohen Funktionalität. Die Gehäuse der Toaster und des Wasserkochers sind mit einem Diamantmuster versehen, das an Schmuckstücke erinnert. Die Oberfläche ist dennoch glatt und lässt sich leicht reinigen. Hochglanzpolierte Metallelemente ergänzen die elegante Anmutung und machen die Geräte gleichzeitig robust. Die Serie ist in verschiedenen frischen Farben erhältlich und fügt sich so in jede Küche harmonisch ein.

Begründung der Jury
Die schön verarbeiteten und aufmerksamkeitsstark gestalteten Küchengeräte der Mesmerine-Kollektion sind ein echter Blickfang in der Küche.

Changhong Egg Boiler ZDQ-812A
Eierkocher

Manufacturer
Changhong Meiling Co., Ltd., Hefei, China
In-house design
Design
Homwee Technology (Sichuan) Co., Ltd., Chengdu, China
Web
www.meiling.com
www.changhong.com

The egg boiler ZDQ-812A has been conceived with couples in mind: it can boil two eggs simultaneously. The device takes up little space because of its small size and is easy to stow away. Its shape is inspired by home accessories, resulting in it appearing less like a kitchen appliance and more like a beautifully designed object. A five-stage AI heating technology allows for even cooking and energy-saving operation. Slow-cooked onsen tomago are just as easily prepared as traditional soft-boiled or hard-boiled eggs.

Statement by the jury
With its soft lines and a compact housing, this egg boiler blends harmoniously in small kitchens.

Der Eierkocher ZDQ-812A wurde speziell für Paare konzipiert: Mit ihm lassen sich zwei Eier gleichzeitig kochen. Mit seiner geringen Größe nimmt er wenig Raum ein und lässt sich leicht verstauen. Seine Gestaltung ist von Wohnaccessoires inspiriert, wodurch er weniger wie ein Küchengerät als vielmehr wie ein stilvoll gestaltetes Deko-Objekt aussieht. Beim Kochen der Eier kommt eine fünfstufige, intelligente Heiztechnologie zum Einsatz, die gleichmäßig und energiesparend arbeitet. Auf diese Weise lassen sich langsam gegarte Onsen-Eier ebenso zubereiten wie weich oder hart gekochte Eier.

Begründung der Jury
Mit seiner weichen Linienführung und einem kompakten Gehäuse fügt sich dieser Eierkocher harmonisch in kleine Küchen ein.

HealthFriend Smart Juicer
Slow Juicer
Langsam-Entsafter

Manufacturer
NUC Electronics Co., Ltd., Daegu, South Korea
In-house design
Juhun Seo, Jieun Lee
Web
www.kuvings.com

The HealthFriend Smart Juicer is a high-quality slow juicer with an 82 mm inlet, which can also cope with whole fruits and longer-sized vegetables. Due to slow processing of the ingredients, the taste and nutrients remain preserved. The lid of the intake can be opened completely or partly according to the size of the fruit. The juicer has a function by means of which the user can analyse his body fat and acquire suggestions for juice recipes corresponding to the data.

Statement by the jury
With its solid base and translucent attachment, which allows insight into the juicing process, this slow juicer conveys its high efficiency.

Der HealthFriend Smart Juicer ist ein hochwertiger Langsam-Entsafter mit einem 82 mm weiten Einlass, der auch ganze Früchte und längeres Gemüse aufnehmen kann. Durch die langsame Verarbeitung der Zutaten bleiben Geschmack und Nährstoffe erhalten. Der Deckel am Einlass wird je nach Fruchtgröße ganz oder teilweise geöffnet. Der Entsafter hat eine Funktion, mit der der Nutzer sein Körperfett analysieren und sich individuell darauf abgestimmte Saftrezepte vorschlagen lassen kann.

Begründung der Jury
Mit seiner soliden Basis und einem durchsichtigen Aufsatz, der Einblick in den Entsaftungsprozess gewährt, vermittelt dieser Langsam-Entsafter seine hohe Leistungsfähigkeit.

Q15
Soymilk Maker
Sojamilch-Maschine

Manufacturer
Joyoung, Hangzhou, China
In-house design
Wang Lu, Li Yanchao, Zhang Yan
Web
www.joyoung.com

With the Q15 soymilk maker fresh soy milk can be made quickly and without complication. Thanks to its 700 to 1,300 ml capacity, it is also suitable for families. A surround stereo heating technology and motor power of 1,300 watt assure that the ingredients are fully boiled and pulped. Folding handles make handling convenient, with a large, interactive and easily understood operating panel further contributing to a pleasant user experience.

Statement by the jury
Q15 is a device which appeals in its functionality and appearance to a nutrition-conscious target group. With its well-considered construction it makes the daily soy milk production as easy as possible.

Mit der Sojamilch-Maschine Q15 lässt sich schnell und unkompliziert frische Sojamilch herstellen. Dank einer Kapazität von 700 bis 1.300 ml ist er auch für Familien geeignet. Eine dreidimensionale, umlaufende Stereo-Heiztechnologie und eine Motorleistung von 1.300 Watt stellen sicher, dass die Zutaten vollständig gekocht und zerkleinert werden. Klappgriffe erleichtern die Handhabung, während ein interaktives, leicht verständlich gestaltetes Bedienfeld für ein angenehmes Nutzererlebnis sorgt.

Begründung der Jury
Q15 ist ein Gerät, das sich in Funktionsweise und Aussehen an eine junge, ernährungsbewusste Zielgruppe richtet. Mit seiner durchdachten Konstruktion macht es die tägliche Sojamilchproduktion so einfach wie möglich.

Cubo Smart Blender
Standmixer

Manufacturer
Bianco Asia Ltd., Hong Kong
In-house design
Johnson Lee
Design
Innocenzo Rifino, Milan, Italy
Web
www.biancodipuro.com.hk
www.biancodipuroasia.com

Cubo is an intelligent blender with a special feature: a 5" LCD touch-display which can be tilted out to provide convenient operation and better visualising. Control is via tap, slide and scroll actions as is known from smartphones. The touch-panel offers access to over 60 recipes in seven categories and guides the user step-by-step through the preparation. The blender sends manufacturer data to the user via Wi-Fi, whereby software and recipe updates are regularly provided, along with tailor-made customer support.

Cubo ist ein intelligenter Standmixer, dessen Besonderheit ein 5"-LCD-Touchdisplay ist, das sich für eine bequemere Bedienung und bessere Sichtbarkeit ausklappen lässt. Die Steuerung erfolgt über Tap-, Slide- und Scroll-Gesten, wie sie vom Smartphone bekannt sind. Das Touch-Panel bietet Zugriff auf über 60 Rezepte in sieben Kategorien und leitet den Nutzer Schritt für Schritt durch die Zubereitung. Der Mixer übermittelt Herstellerdaten via Wi-Fi an den Nutzer, wodurch regelmäßige Software- und Rezepte-Updates ebenso ermöglicht werden wie ein passgenauer Kundensupport.

Statement by the jury
Intelligent functions and a tilt-out display, step-by-step instructions as well as a particularly user-friendly design are characteristics of the Cubo Smart Blender.

Begründung der Jury
Intelligente Funktionen und eine mit ausklappbarem Display und Schritt-für-Schritt-Anleitungen besonders benutzerfreundliche Gestaltung zeichnen den Cubo Smart Blender aus.

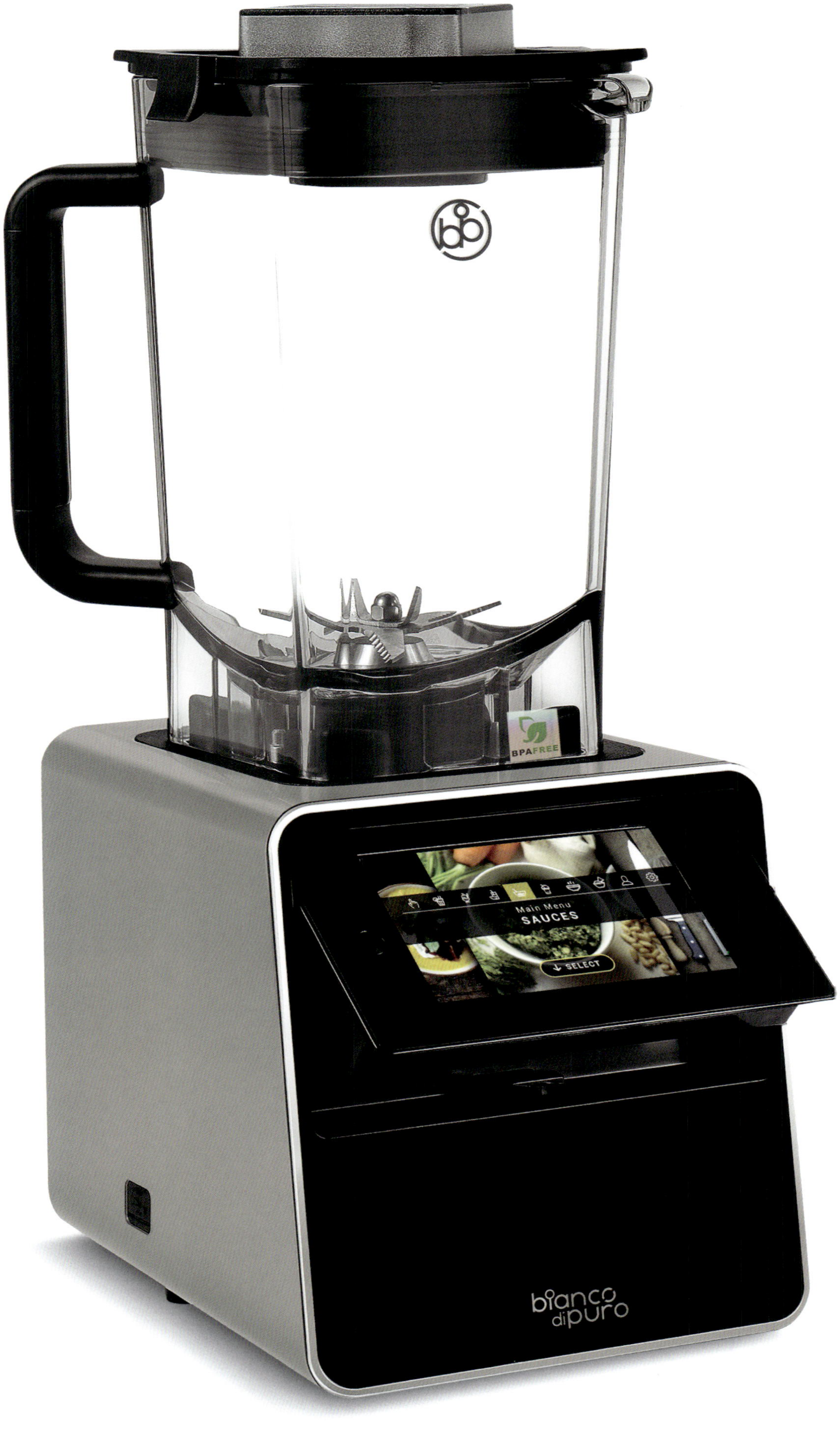
BPAFREE
Main Menu
SAUCES
SELECT
bianco
di puro

Silent HI-Speed Blender
Standmixer

Manufacturer
Zhejiang Supor Electrical Appliances
Manufacturing, Hangzhou, China
In-house design
Chen Jian, Yang Xue Jin
Web
www.supor.com.cn

The Silent HI-Speed Blender breaks open the cell walls efficiently while operating particularly quietly. Its noise level has been reduced to 72 decibels, so that the blender can be used at any time everywhere. By means of vacuum technology the fresh taste of foods as well as their nutrition value are retained. Intelligent temperature control and the bulbous mixer jug make preparation of food easy. The operating panel is divided into a section for hot and one for cold foods.

Statement by the jury
This blender is particularly quiet thanks to its soundproof shield. The display is divided into two different sections, adding further to the user-friendliness of the appliance.

Der Silent HI-Speed Blender bricht die Zellwände effizient auf und arbeitet dabei besonders leise. Sein Geräuschpegel wurde auf 72 Dezibel reduziert, sodass er jederzeit und überall genutzt werden kann. Mithilfe von Vakuumtechnologie wird zudem der frische Geschmack der Lebensmittel ebenso bewahrt wie ihre Nährstoffe. Eine intelligente Temperatursteuerung und der bauchige Mixbecher erleichtern die Essenszubereitung. Das Bedienfeld unterteilt sich in einen Bereich für heiße und einen für kalte Speisen.

Begründung der Jury
Dieser Standmixer punktet dank einer schalldichten Abschirmung mit einer besonders geräuscharmen Arbeitsweise. Sehr benutzerfreundlich ist zudem die Aufteilung des Displays in zwei Bereiche.

Silent Ultra-Blender Y35
Standmixer

Manufacturer
Joyoung, Hangzhou, China
In-house design
Binxiang Zhao, Pingping Wang, Yuan Fan
Web
www.joyoung.com

This blender offers purchasers in the manufacturer's online shop the possibility of uploading their own patterns and graphics and having them attached on the sides of the control panel. Thanks to a noise suppressing channel at the base, the high-performance blender operates quietly at 60 db. The base recognises automatically the various attachments for warm or cold food, soya milk or rice paste and adjusts the power accordingly.

Statement by the jury
The Silent Ultra-Blender Y35 offers a sophisticated, low-noise functionality. It can be personalised, which adds a further attractive feature.

Dieser Standmixer bietet Käufern die Möglichkeit, beim Kauf über die Website des Herstellers eigene Muster oder Grafiken hochzuladen und an den Seiten des Bedienfelds anbringen zu lassen. Dank eines geräuschreduzierenden Kanals an der Basis, arbeitet der leistungsstarke Mixer mit nur 60 dB. Die Basis identifiziert automatisch die verschiedenen Aufsätze für warme oder kalte Lebensmittel, Sojamilch oder Reispaste und passt die Leistung an.

Begründung der Jury
Der Silent Ultra-Blender Y35 bietet eine ausgereifte Funktionalität und arbeitet geräuscharm. Ein schönes Detail ist seine Personalisierbarkeit.

The Super Q™
Blender
Standmixer

Manufacturer
Breville, Sydney, Australia
In-house design
Design
Naked Image (Greg Upston),
Eumundi, Queensland, Australia
Web
www.breville.com

The Super Q high performance blender is driven by a 2,400-watt motor, with versatile cutting blades offering super slow stir to high speed milling. Drinks and food can be prepared in the two-litre jug, or in a takeaway blending cup. Thanks to pitcher recognition, blending time and speeds are automatically adjusted. Innovative fan and motor technology result in low-noise blending. The sturdy, seamless, stainless-steel design makes cleaning easy.

Statement by the jury
The Super Q is convincing as a high-performance and simultaneously quiet blender with a robust housing. A high degree of automation makes operation easy.

Der Hochleistungsmixer The Super Q arbeitet mit einem 2.400-Watt-Motor und vielfältig einsetzbaren Schneidmessern, die langsames Umrühren ebenso ermöglichen wie Hochgeschwindigkeitsmahlen. Getränke und Speisen lassen sich wahlweise im Zwei-Liter-Behälter oder einem To-go-Mixbecher zubereiten. Dank Mixbehältererkennung werden Mixzeit und Geschwindigkeiten automatisch angepasst. Eine innovative Lüfter- und Motortechnologie ermöglicht ein geräuscharmes Mixen. Das robuste, nahtlose Edelstahldesign erleichtert die Reinigung.

Begründung der Jury
The Super Q überzeugt als leistungsstarker und gleichzeitig leiser Mixer mit robustem Gehäuse. Ein hoher Grad an Automatisierung macht die Bedienung einfach.

Explore 7
Blender
Standmixer

Manufacturer
AB Electrolux, Stockholm, Sweden
In-house design
Web
www.electrolux.com

With its specific form and colour, the Explore 7 clearly targets the lifestyle segment. Particular attention was paid to ensure intuitive handling: the user interface incorporates well-considered graphics as well as light and sound elements. By means of PowerTilt technology, the blender grinds gently and precisely, so that freshness and nutrients remain intact. The low blending speed results in a lower temperature, whereby the taste is less impaired.

Statement by the jury
With elegant details such as a shiny metallic band, the Explore 7 appears very high in quality. It also delights with its user-friendliness and gentle processing of the ingredients.

Der Explore 7 ist ein Standmixer, der auf das Lifestyle-Segment abzielt, was in Form- wie Farbgebung zum Ausdruck kommt. Besonderer Wert wurde zudem auf eine intuitive Handhabung gelegt; dafür wurde die Benutzeroberfläche mit durchdachten Grafiken, Licht- und Tonelementen gestaltet. Mithilfe einer PowerTilt-Technologie zerkleinert der Mixer die Zutaten schonend und präzise, sodass Frische und Nährstoffe erhalten bleiben. Die geringe Schneidgeschwindigkeit resultiert in einer niedrigeren Temperatur, wodurch der Geschmack weniger beeinträchtigt wird.

Begründung der Jury
Mit eleganten Details wie einem umlaufenden, metallisch glänzenden Band wirkt der Explore 7 sehr hochwertig. Zudem begeistert er mit Benutzerfreundlichkeit und einer schonenden Verarbeitung der Zutaten.

Ninja Smart Screen Blender Duo (CT661V)
Vacuum Blender
Standmixer

Manufacturer
SharkNinja, Needham, Massachusetts, USA
In-house design
Martin Miller
Web
www.sharkninja.com

The Ninja Smart Screen Blender Duo with FreshVac technology works gently, so that vitamins, taste and colour of the blended drinks remain intact. The blender set comprises of a full-size pitcher and a single-serve to-go cup. Both use vacuum technology: the handheld FreshVac pump seals each vessel in seconds with a simple push of a button. The touchscreen displays vessel-specific programmes thanks to Smart Vessel Recognition.

Statement by the jury
This blender is equipped with innovative functions and shows great flexibility. Well-considered accessories such as the vacuum pump and takeaway cup provide real added value.

Der Ninja Smart Screen Blender Duo mit FreshVac-Technologie arbeitet schonend, sodass beim Pürieren Vitamine, Geschmack und Farbe der Getränke erhalten bleiben. Zu dem Mixer gehört neben dem großen Mixbecher auch ein Becher zum Mitnehmen; beide nutzen Vakuumtechnologie und lassen sich mithilfe der Hand-FreshVac-Pumpe auf Knopfdruck innerhalb von Sekunden luftdicht verschließen. Die Basis ist mit beiden Gefäßen kompatibel. Das Gerät erkennt den Aufsatz und blendet die entsprechenden Programme auf dem Display ein.

Begründung der Jury
Dank seiner innovativen Funktionsweise überzeugt dieser Standmixer mit hoher Flexibilität. Durchdachtes Zubehör wie die Vakuumpumpe und der To-go-Becher bilden einen echten Mehrwert.

Liantek Vacuum Blender
Standmixer

Manufacturer
Liantek Electrical Appliances (Shenzhen) Co., Ltd., Shenzhen, China
In-house design
Yao Yueqiang
Web
www.liantek.com

The Liantek Vacuum Blender uses vacuum technology which evacuates 80 percent of the air. By this means, oxidation of foods when blending is minimised, so that healthy and nutritious food and drinks can be prepared. The base, where the powerful motor is located, is conical in form and provides great efficiency and stability at every speed. Operation is uncomplicated via a rotary knob and two buttons.

Statement by the jury
The conical form of the base gives this blender its elegant impression and radiates technical efficiency, which it fulfils also from a functional viewpoint.

Der Liantek Vacuum Blender nutzt Vakuumtechnologie, die 80 Prozent der Luft heraussaugt. Dadurch wird die Oxidation der Lebensmittel beim Pürieren minimiert, sodass gesunde und nahrhafte Speisen und Getränke zubereitet werden können. Die Basis, in der ein leistungsstarker Motor untergebracht ist, ist konisch geformt und bietet hohe Effizienz und Standfestigkeit bei jeder Geschwindigkeitsstufe. Die Bedienung erfolgt unkompliziert anhand eines Drehknopfs und zweier Tasten.

Begründung der Jury
Die konische Form der Basis verleiht diesem Standmixer seine elegante Anmutung und strahlt eine technische Effizienz aus, der der Mixer auch in funktionaler Hinsicht gerecht wird.

BOSCH VitaMaxx
Vacuum-Blender
Vakuum-Standmixer

Manufacturer
Robert Bosch Hausgeräte GmbH, Munich, Germany
In-house design
Sascha Leng, Sonja Bürzle
Web
www.bsh-group.com

A brushed aluminium housing and a mixer jar of Tritan glass impart a high-quality impression to the vacuum blender. The vacuum arm elegantly braces the blender jar and the curved body of the base. The blender uses vacuum technology to process food by reducing oxidation with minimum loss of vitamins. Reusable, vacuum-sealed storage containers and a bottle for out and about help to diminish refuse. Clear text buttons and an LED process indicator make operation intuitive.

Ein gebürstetes Aluminiumgehäuse und ein Mixbecher aus Tritanglas verleihen dem Vakuum-Mixer VitaMaxx eine hochwertige Anmutung. Ein eleganter Vakuumarm fixiert den Mixbecher auf der sanft gerundeten Basis. Der Standmixer nutzt Vakuumtechnologie, um Lebensmittel durch reduzierte Oxidation bei minimalem Vitaminverlust zu verarbeiten. Wiederverwendbare, vakuumversiegelte Aufbewahrungsbehälter und eine Flasche für unterwegs helfen dabei, wenig Abfall zu erzeugen. Klartext-Tasten und LED-Prozessanzeige machen die Bedienung intuitiv.

Statement by the jury
The VitaMaxx, with its gentle way of processing food and the associated storage containers, offers a well-considered, sustainable and aesthetically convincing overall package.

Begründung der Jury
Der VitaMaxx bietet mit seiner schonenden Art der Lebensmittelverarbeitung und den zugehörigen Vorratsbehältnissen ein funktional durchdachtes, nachhaltiges und ästhetisch überzeugendes Gesamtpaket.

ProMix Hand Blender Viva Collection
Handmixer

Manufacturer
Philips, Eindhoven, Netherlands
In-house design
Philips Design, Shanghai, China
Web
www.philips.com

Included in this hand blender set are a few newly developed accessories which offer a good deal of flexibility when preparing and stocking healthy, home-made food; among them is a spiral cutter for vegetable noodles, a drinks bottle and soup vessel. A display which indicates the speed and other factors helps to process various ingredients intuitively with the corresponding accessory and the correct speed. With a one-click release knob, the accessories can be plugged in and out with one hand during use.

Statement by the jury
Thanks to the many sophisticated accessories, the compact hand blender set is multifunctional in its use and radiates sturdiness and quality.

Zu diesem Handmixer-Set gehören einige neu entwickelte Zubehörteile, die viel Flexibilität bei der Zubereitung und Bevorratung gesunder, hausgemachter Speisen bieten, darunter ein Spiralschneider für Gemüsenudeln, eine Trinkflasche und Suppenbehälter. Ein Display, das u. a. die Geschwindigkeit anzeigt, hilft dabei, intuitiv verschiedene Zutaten mit dem passenden Zubehörteil und der richtigen Geschwindigkeit zu verarbeiten. Mit einem Ein-Klick-Entriegelungsknopf können Zubehörteile während des Gebrauchs einhändig aufgesetzt und abgenommen werden.

Begründung der Jury
Das kompakte Handmixer-Set ist dank der vielen ausgereiften Zubehörteile multifunktional einsetzbar und strahlt Robustheit und Qualität aus.

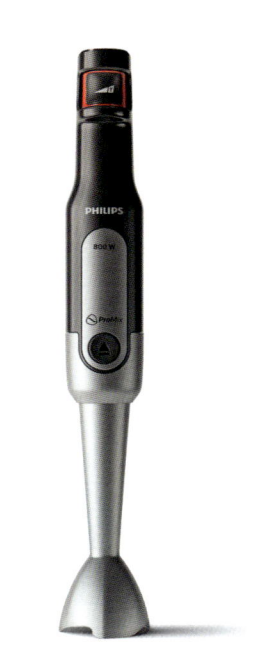

17PIN JuStar Cup
Portable Juicer
Handmixer

Manufacturer
Beijing 17PIN Network Technology Co., Ltd., Beijing, China
In-house design
Hongjun Wang, Deqing Yin
Web
https://youpin.mi.com

The 17PIN JuStar Cup is a hand mixer whose drive and cutting unit are integrated into the cap. This way the outer appearance remains undisturbed and the cup lies nicely in the hand. A safety switch is located under the sealing ring, which ensures that the mixing process cannot be started when the cap is open. With a weight of just 475 grams, the device is very light. It can purée up to 15 times when fully charged.

Statement by the jury
This compact hand mixer serves as a cup with a purée function. It is very light and therefore suitable for use when out and about.

Der 17PIN JuStar Cup ist ein Handmixer, dessen Antrieb und Schneideeinheit in die Kappe integriert sind. Durch den Einbau des Mixers in den Deckel stört nichts das äußere Erscheinungsbild, und der Becher liegt gut in der Hand. Ein unter dem Dichtring liegender Sicherheitsschalter verhindert, dass der Mixvorgang bei offenem Deckel gestartet werden kann. Mit einem Gewicht von 475 Gramm ist der Handmixer sehr leicht. Vollständig aufgeladen kann das Gerät bis zu 15 Mal pürieren.

Begründung der Jury
Dieser Handmixer vereint auf kleinem Raum Trinkgefäß mit Pürierfunktion, ist sehr leicht und eignet sich damit perfekt für den Einsatz unterwegs.

Coravin Model Eleven
Wine Preservation System
Weinkonservierungssystem

Manufacturer
Coravin, Burlington, Massachusetts, USA
In-house design
Web
www.coravin.com

With this innovative wine conserving system, wine from partially used bottles is still preserved for weeks, months, or even years. For this, the product is placed on top of the bottle and its needle pushed through the cork. A green light ring then indicates that the wine is ready to be served. As the wine is poured from the bottle, it is replaced with argon, an inert gas used by winemakers. Model Eleven can be controlled via Bluetooth with the corresponding app.

Statement by the jury
Coravin Model Eleven combines complex functionality with simple, intuitive handling.

Mit diesem innovativen Weinkonservierungssystem lässt sich Wein aus angebrochenen Flaschen auch nach Wochen, Monaten oder sogar Jahren noch trinken. Dazu wird das Produkt zunächst auf die Flasche gesetzt und seine Nadel durch den Korken gedrückt. Ein grüner Leuchtring zeigt an, dass der Wein ausgeschenkt werden kann. Der Wein fließt bei Neigung der Flasche automatisch heraus, und die entnommene Menge wird mit dem Schutzgas Argon aufgefüllt. Model Eleven kann via Bluetooth mit der dazugehörigen App verbunden werden.

Begründung der Jury
Coravin Model Eleven verbindet eine komplexe Funktionalität mit einer einfachen, intuitiven Handhabung.

Bosch Aqua 7100 P
Water Purifier
Wasseraufbereiter

Manufacturer
Bosch Thermotechnology (Beijing) Co., Ltd.,
Beijing, China
Design
Bosch Thermotechnik GmbH
(Fabian Kollmann), Wernau, Germany
Bosch Thermotechnology (Shanghai) Co., Ltd.
(Xuefei Liu), Shanghai, China
Web
www.bosch-climate.cn
www.bosch-thermotechnik.de

The Bosch Aqua 7100 P is an elegant water dispenser with reverse osmosis water treatment, which blends in discretely with any kitchen environment. The user-friendly touch-control interface, the simple filter replacement without tools as well as the fast heating element provide efficiency and convenience. The interface supplies information on water quality and status of the filters. The desired water temperature can be selected and frequently used settings, e.g. for tea or baby food, can be stored by the device as favourites.

Statement by the jury
With its slender and clear design, the Bosch Aqua 7100 P makes an elegant impression. Its user-friendliness, which is exemplified by tool-free filter replacement, is equally convincing.

Der Bosch Aqua 7100 P ist ein eleganter Wasserspender mit Umkehrosmose-Wasseraufbereitung, der sich dezent in jedes Küchenumfeld einfügt. Das benutzerfreundliche Touch-Bedienfeld, der einfache werkzeuglose Filterwechsel sowie das schnelle Heizelement bieten Effizienz und Komfort. Das Interface informiert über die Wasserqualität sowie den Zustand der Filter. Die gewünschte Wassertemperatur lässt sich auswählen und oft genutzte Einstellungen, z. B. für Tee oder Babynahrung, können als Favoriten gespeichert werden.

Begründung der Jury
Mit seiner schlanken und klaren Gestaltung hinterlässt der Bosch Aqua 7100 P einen eleganten Eindruck. Überzeugend ist auch seine Benutzerfreundlichkeit, die sich etwa im werkzeuglosen Filterwechsel manifestiert.

LG Slim Stand Water Purifier (S2)
Water Purifier and Dispenser
Wasseraufbereiter und -spender

Manufacturer
LG Electronics Inc., Seoul, South Korea
In-house design
Kyukwan Choi, Hyoungwon Roh,
Najung Cho, Sookyeong Kang
Web
www.lg.com

In the design and construction of the S2 Slim water purifier emphasis was placed on intuitive operability and compact size to facilitate installation in small business premises. The S2 Slim offers space under the water output to place a tray and fill several bottles or drink vessels at the same time. The slightly longer outlet spouts indicate to the user exactly where the drinking water will be discharged. A removable drip tray makes cleaning easier.

Statement by the jury
Its space-saving construction, its discreet appearance and well-considered user-friendly functionality allow the S2 Slim water purifier to blend well into business premises.

Bei der Konstruktion und Gestaltung des S2 Slim-Wasseraufbereiters lag der Fokus auf einer intuitiven Bedienbarkeit und einer kompakten Größe, damit er platzsparend in Geschäftsräumen aufgestellt werden kann. Der S2 Slim bietet unterhalb der Wasserauslasse Platz, um ein Tablett abzustellen und so auch mehrere Flaschen oder Trinkgefäße auf einmal zu befüllen. Leicht nach unten hin verlängerte Ausflussrohre signalisieren dem Benutzer, wo genau das Trinkwasser austreten wird. Eine abnehmbare Auffangschale erleichtert die Reinigung.

Begründung der Jury
Seine platzsparende Bauweise, sein dezentes Erscheinungsbild und eine durchdachte, benutzerfreundliche Funktionsweise führen dazu, dass sich der S2 Slim Wasseraufbereiter gut in Geschäftsräume einfügt.

CIROO Series (CHP-7300R, CHP-6310L)
Water Purifier
Wasseraufbereiter

Manufacturer
Coway, Seoul, South Korea
In-house design
Nari Lee, Soyeon Lee
Web
www.coway.com

The water purifier of the Ciroo series supplies not only hot, lukewarm or cold water but also water at a precise temperature, as is needed, for example, for making baby milk or coffee. The series comprises a basic and a premium model, which displays detailed information on water quantity and temperature. The premium model also enables height adjustment of the output tap. Both models allow easy removal of the tap for cleaning to prevent contamination.

Statement by the jury
Both the premium and the basic model of the Ciroo series impress with their high functionality and user-friendliness.

Die Wasseraufbereiter der Ciroo-Serie liefern sowohl warmes, lauwarmes oder kaltes Wasser als auch Wasser mit einer spezifischen Temperatur, wie es etwa für die Zubereitung von Tee, Babymilch oder Kaffee gebraucht wird. Zur Serie gehören ein Basis- und ein Premiummodell, das detaillierte Informationen zu Wassermenge und -temperatur anzeigt. Beim Premiummodell kann zudem die Höhe des Auslaufs eingestellt werden. Bei beiden Modellen lässt sich der kontaminationsanfällige Auslass leicht abnehmen und reinigen.

Begründung der Jury
Sowohl das Premium- als auch das Basismodell der Ciroo-Serie beeindrucken mit einer hohen Funktionalität und Bedienfreundlichkeit.

Newtro Ambient
Water Purifier
Wasseraufbereiter

Manufacturer
Bodyfriend Co., Ltd., Seoul, South Korea
In-house design
Myong Kyu Kim, Il Soo Yeom
Web
www.bodyfriend.co.kr

The Newtro Ambient is a water purifier which combines contemporary aesthetics with retro elements, as can be observed in the interplay of high-gloss chromium and matte silver. The elegant water purifier is also easy to handle and presents a user-friendly design. The space-saving filter element integrates three different filter technologies and can be replaced via a door at the front of the device in an unproblematic way.

Statement by the jury
The purist appearance of the Newtro Ambient is inspired by retro design. It combines a high-quality, space-saving construction with easy operability.

Der Newtro Ambient ist ein Wasseraufbereiter, der eine zeitgemäße Ästhetik mit Retro-Elementen kombiniert, wie am Zusammenspiel von hochglänzendem Chrom und mattem Silber ersichtlich wird. Der elegante Wasseraufbereiter ist mit seiner einfachen Handhabung zudem sehr benutzerfreundlich gestaltet. Das platzsparend konstruierte Filterelement integriert drei verschiedene Filtertechniken und lässt sich unproblematisch über eine Tür an der Vorderseite des Geräts austauschen.

Begründung der Jury
Ein puristisches, vom Design der Vergangenheit inspiriertes Erscheinungsbild verbindet der Newtro Ambient mit einer platzsparenden Konstruktion und leichter Bedienbarkeit.

G20
Water Dispenser
Wasserspender

Manufacturer
Midea Kitchen & Water Heater
Appliance Division, Foshan, China
In-house design
Li Jianping, Chen Shishi, Wu Feipeng
Design
Kurz Kurz Design China
(Xiong Hao, Kong Chengxiang, Chen Xin,
Zhang Shenrong, Guo Ziyuan),
Foshan, China
Web
www.midea.com
www.kkdesign.cn

G20 is a water dispenser with a compact refrigerator in the bottom section. The bright housing with a wood grain finish at the front gives the appliance a striking appearance. The water dispenser is connected directly to the main water supply and uses a water treatment unit to provide drinking water. It is operated by means of a button which offers the option of cold, warm and hot water as well as ice cubes.

Statement by the jury
With its wood optics and gentle curves, this water dispenser conveys an elegant, high-quality appeal. It easily blends in with various environments.

G20 ist ein Wasserspender mit einem kompakten Kühlschrank im unteren Bereich. Das helle Gehäuse mit Holzmaserung an der Vorderseite verleiht dem Gerät ein prägnantes Aussehen. Der Wasserspender ist direkt an das Leitungssystem angeschlossen und nutzt einen Wasseraufbereiter, um Trinkwasser zu liefern. Die Bedienung erfolgt komfortabel über einen Knopf, der die Wahl zwischen kaltem, warmem und heißem Wasser sowie Eiswürfeln ermöglicht.

Begründung der Jury
Dieser Wasserspender hat durch den Einsatz der Holzoptik und seine weichen Rundungen eine elegante und wertige Anmutung, durch die er sich gut in verschiedene Umgebungen integrieren lässt.

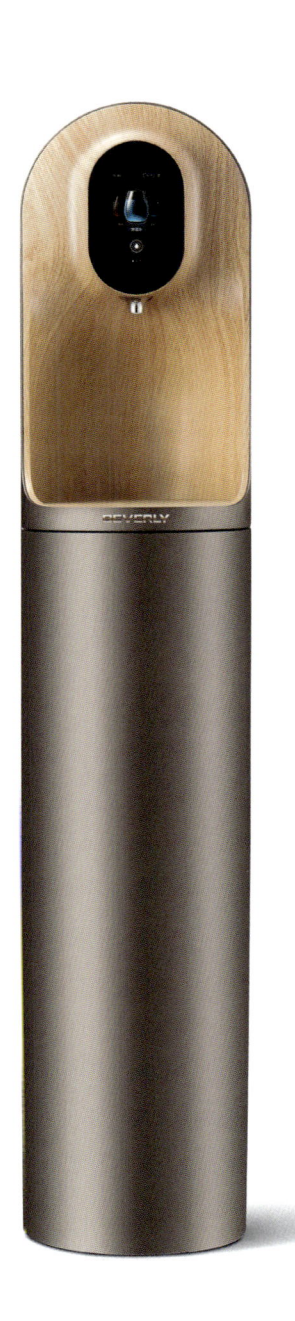

Large-Flow 400-Gallon Water Purifier
Wasseraufbereiter

Manufacturer
Gree Electric Appliances, Inc. of Zhuhai, Zhuhai, China
In-house design
Jianming Tan, Sha Li, Nanfei Chen, Huanlong Wu, Jiahua Liu, Jianfeng Lin, Yang Zhao, Min Zhang, Xusheng Chen, Youmei Zhang, Qi Xi, Yu Zhang, Shengsheng Liu, Shuaiwen Zhou, Jiabao Feng, Yan Liu, Jinmei Feng
Web
www.gree.com.cn

This under-counter water purifier has a high flow capacity of 400 gallons (approximately 1,500 litres). In the interior the water is purified with an adsorptive front panel and double filter. The design makes filter changing easy. A light ring in the lower body section indicates the status and flashes red in case of error. The life expectancy of the filter can be checked on a mobile by an app.

Dieser Untertisch-Wasserfilter hat mit 400 Gallonen (ca. 1.500 Litern) eine hohe Durchflusskapazität. Im Inneren wird das Wasser mit einem adsorptiven Frontelement und Doppelfiltern gereinigt. Der Filterwechsel ist so ausgelegt, dass er einfach durchgeführt werden kann. Ein Leuchtring im unteren Bereich des Korpus zeigt den Status an und blinkt rot, wenn ein Fehler auftritt. Über eine App lässt sich die Lebensdauer der Filter auch mobil überprüfen.

Statement by the jury
The clean design of this water purifier imparts a visual expression to its function and places the light display at the centre of attention.

Begründung der Jury
Die puristische Gestaltung dieses Wasseraufbereiters verleiht seiner reinigenden Funktion visuellen Ausdruck und rückt die Leuchtanzeige in den Mittelpunkt der Aufmerksamkeit.

The Waterfall
Water Purifier
Wasseraufbereiter

Manufacturer
KEMFLO (Nanjing) Enviromental
Technology Co., Ltd., Nanjing, China
In-house design
Eugene Lin
Web
www.kemflo.net

The Waterfall, designed for small to medium-sized households, is a water purifier for installation under the sink. It is fitted directly to the mains water and cleans it by reverse osmosis. While being treated, the water flows downwards as in a waterfall. A drop-shaped element treated with acrylic is integrated in the top of the device, clearly indicating the status of the purifying process. The motor comes separately, which saves space and eases configuration. The rotary filter cartridges are energy-saving and user-friendly.

The Waterfall ist ein Wasseraufbereiter zur Installation unter der Spüle, der für kleine und mittlere Haushalte konzipiert wurde. Das Gerät ist direkt an das Leitungswasser angeschlossen und reinigt es mithilfe von Umkehrosmose. Wie bei einem Wasserfall fließt das Wasser bei der Reinigung nach unten. In die Oberseite des Geräts ist ein mit Acryl behandeltes, tropfenförmiges Element integriert, auf dem der Status gut sichtbar angezeigt wird. Ein externer Motor spart Platz und erleichtert die Konfiguration. Die Drehfilterpatronen sind energiesparend und benutzerfreundlich.

Statement by the jury
With its gentle curves, this well-considered and user-friendly water purifier makes a supple visual impression. Furthermore, the user interface is very clearly designed.

Begründung der Jury
Das Gehäuse dieses sehr durchdacht und benutzerfreundlich gestalteten Wasseraufbereiters wirkt mit seinen sanften Kurven weich. Die Bedienoberfläche ist zudem sehr übersichtlich gestaltet.

Waterdrop Reverse Osmosis (RO) Water Filtration System
Wasseraufbereiter

Manufacturer
Qingdao Ecopure Filter Co., Ltd.,
Qingdao, China
Hong Kong Ecoaqua Co., Ltd.,
Hong Kong
In-house design
Qingdao Ecopure Filter Co., Ltd.
(Aiden Zhang)
Hong Kong Ecoaqua Co., Ltd.
Web
www.water-filter.com

Waterdrop is an intelligent water filtration system, which works by reverse osmosis. It is equipped with a variety of sensors to record the quality, capacity and pressure of the water. The slender white appliance is attached directly to the main water supply and removes a majority of impurities with a filtration speed of 1.05 litres per minute. The filter can be changed with one single turn. An LED display indicates the status.

Statement by the jury
With its space-saving design, white body and discreet appearance, Waterdrop imparts an impression of freshness and purity.

Waterdrop ist ein intelligentes Wasserfiltersystem, das mit Umkehrosmose arbeitet und mit einer Vielzahl von Sensoren ausgestattet ist, die Wasserqualität, -kapazität sowie -druck erfassen. Das schlanke weiße Gerät ist direkt an das Leitungssystem angeschlossen, und das Leitungswasser wird mit einer Filtrationsgeschwindigkeit von 1,05 Litern/Minute von einem Großteil aller Verunreinigungen befreit. Der Filter lässt sich mit einer einzigen Drehung austauschen. Ein LED-Display zeigt den Status an.

Begründung der Jury
Mit seinem platzsparend konstruierten weißen Korpus und seinem unaufdringlichen Erscheinungsbild vermittelt Waterdrop den Eindruck von Frische und Reinheit.

RO Water Purifier
Wasseraufbereiter

Manufacturer
Clean Best (Shenzhen) Technology Co., Ltd.,
Shenzhen, China
In-house design
Yuecheng Huang, Junji Yang
Web
www.clbst.com.cn

This matte white reverse-osmosis water purifier is designed with elegantly rounded edges. An integrated waterway board and a glued, printed circuit board effectively protect from the risk of a water leakage and increase the service life. The filter head features triple filtration (PP cotton, active charcoal, RO membrane) and, thanks to a snap-on construction, is easy to replace. A light display indicates the status of the filter in green, yellow and red.

Statement by the jury
This water purifier uses several filter technologies and is thereby particularly efficient. Its matte white housing symbolises purity.

Dieser mattweiße Umkehrosmose-Wasserfilter ist mit elegant abgerundeten Kanten gestaltet. Eine integrierte Wasserstraßenplatine und eine geklebte Leiterplatte reduzieren wirksam das Risiko eines Wasseraustritts und erhöhen die Lebensdauer. Das Filterelement arbeitet mit Dreifachfiltration (PP-Baumwolle, Aktivkohle, RO-Membran) und lässt sich dank einer Schnappkonstruktion einfach austauschen. Eine Leuchtanzeige zeigt mit den Farben Grün, Gelb und Rot den Status des Filters an.

Begründung der Jury
Dieser Wasseraufbereiter nutzt mehrere Filtriertechniken und ist dadurch besonders effizient. Sein mattweißes Gehäuse symbolisiert Reinheit.

BRITA mypure pro
Water Filtration System
Wasserfiltersystem

Manufacturer
BRITA GmbH, Taunusstein, Germany
Design
Pearl Creative, Storti&Rummel GbR,
Ludwigsburg, Germany
Web
www.brita.de
www.pearlcreative.com

The BRITA mypure pro family is a water filter system with an innovative, four-stage filtration for installation under the sink. It filters particles, bacteria and other impurities from the water without removing important minerals. The filtration process itself relies solely on the water pressure: neither an electric pump nor an additional tank are necessary. Thanks to the direct filtration, 100 per cent of the incoming water is filtered and no waste water is produced.

Statement by the jury
This contemporary water filter system fits in any kitchen thanks to its compact dimensions. It also delights with a well-considered, user-friendly design which allows for easy changing of the capsules.

Die BRITA mypure Pro-Filterfamilie ist ein Wasserfiltersystem zur Installation unter der Spüle mit einer innovativen Vier-Stufen-Filtration. Es filtert Partikel, Viren, Bakterien und weitere Schadstoffe aus dem Wasser, während es einen Großteil der für den Menschen wichtigen Mineralien im Wasser belässt. Der Filtrationsprozess selbst läuft allein über den Wasserdruck, eine elektrische Pumpe ist ebenso wenig erforderlich wie ein zusätzlicher Tank. Dank der Direktfiltration werden 100 Prozent des Wassers gefiltert und kein untrinkbares Abwasser produziert.

Begründung der Jury
Dieses zeitgemäße, puristische Wasserfiltersystem passt dank kompakter Maße in jede Küche. Es begeistert zudem mit einer durchdachten, benutzerfreundlichen Gestaltung, die den Wechsel der Kartuschen sehr einfach macht.

Bosch Aqua 3000/5600/6600 P
Water Purifier
Wasseraufbereiter

Manufacturer
Bosch Thermotechnology (Beijing) Co., Ltd.,
Beijing, China
Design
Bosch Thermotechnik GmbH
(Fabian Kollmann), Wernau, Germany
Bosch Thermotechnology (Shanghai) Co., Ltd.
(Xuefei Liu), Shanghai, China
Web
www.bosch-climate.cn
www.bosch-thermotechnik.de

The Bosch Aqua water purifier collection for under the sink combines an elegant housing with simple installation, handling and cleaning. Supported by a colour TFT display (Aqua 6600 P) not only the water quality is displayed but also the status and lifetime of each individual filter. Furthermore, a colour LED ring indicates the water quality directly at the tap, without the need to open the under-sink case. The filter can be replaced easily and quickly.

Statement by the jury
These water purifiers are designed with a high degree of user-friendliness. Their clear, timeless shape and their high-grade materiality indicate their quality.

Die Bosch Aqua Wasseraufbereiter-Serie für den Unterbau kombiniert ein elegantes Gehäuse mit einer einfachen Installation, Nutzung und Reinigung. Unterstützt durch ein Farb-TFT-Display (Aqua 6600 P) werden nicht nur die Wasserqualität, sondern auch Zustand und Lebensdauer jedes einzelnen Filters angezeigt. Darüber hinaus gibt ein farbiger LED-Ring direkt an der Zapfstelle über die Wasserqualität Auskunft, ohne dass der Unterschrank geöffnet werden muss. Der Filter kann einfach und schnell gewechselt werden.

Begründung der Jury
Diese Wasseraufbereiter sind in jedem Detail auf hohe Benutzerfreundlichkeit ausgerichtet. Ihr klares, zeitloses Design und ihre hochwertige Materialität vermitteln zudem ihre hohe Qualität.

WP400
Water Purifier
Wasseraufbereiter

Manufacturer
Olansi Healthcare Co., Ltd.,
Guangzhou, China
In-house design
Dong Wen Li, Wei Peng
Web
www.gzolans.com

The appearance of the WP400 water purifier is characterised by a cylindrical housing. This form is based on the Chinese cosmology concept of the "upper circle and lower square". The result is a water purifier with a geometric body and an easily understandable button operation. Light displays indicate the status of the device and the filter in three colours. By means of its vertical construction, the WP400 is space-saving and at the same time copes with the purification of large volumes of water.

Statement by the jury
The WP400 water purifier gains merit with its cylindrical basic form, which imparts the impression of harmony. With its lights, it also indicates its status in an intuitively understandable way.

Das Erscheinungsbild des Wasseraufbereiters WP400 ist durch seine zylindrische Gehäuseform geprägt. Dieser Formgebung liegt das chinesische Kosmologiekonzept vom „runden Oben und quadratischen Unten" zugrunde. Das Resultat ist ein Wasserreiniger mit geometrischem Korpus und einer gut verständlichen Tastenbedienung. Leuchtanzeigen signalisieren mit drei Farben den Geräte- und Filterstatus. Durch seine vertikale Konstruktion ist der WP400 platzsparend, gleichzeitig bewältigt er die Reinigung großer Wassermengen.

Begründung der Jury
Der Wasseraufbereiter WP400 punktet mit seiner zylindrischen Grundform, die den Eindruck von Harmonie vermittelt. Mit seinen Leuchten kommuniziert er zudem intuitiv verständlich seinen Status.

Phyn Plus
Smart Water Assistant and Shutoff
Intelligenter Wassermanager
und Sicherheitsabsperrventil

Manufacturer
Uponor GmbH, Hassfurt, Germany
Phyn LLC, Torrance, California, USA
Design
Ritual Creative Inc. (Thorben Neu),
Los Angeles, California, USA
Web
www.uponor.com
www.phyn.com

Phyn Plus is an intelligent smart water assistant which protects the home from leaks, diagnoses issues with plumbing and gives powerful insights into water use. By using patented, high-definition pressure wave analysis and machine learning it alerts the user via SMS or App immediately when a leak is detected, mitigates costly damage through automatic water shut-off and teaches the homeowner about the water use.

Statement by the jury
Thanks to its well-considered functionality, the Phyn Plus water sensor system considerably eases monitoring of the water supply.

Phyn Plus ist ein intelligenter Wassermanager, der Wohnhäuser vor Leckagen schützt, Unregelmäßigkeiten in der Trinkwasser-Installation erkennt und wertvolle Einblicke in den Wasserverbrauch gibt. Mithilfe patentierter, hochempfindlicher Ultraschallsensoren und maschinellen Lernens informiert das System den Nutzer sofort per SMS oder App, wenn eine undichte Stelle entdeckt wird. Durch automatisches Abschalten der Wasserzufuhr werden kostspielige Schäden vermieden und der Hausbesitzer behält den Wasserverbrauch im Blick.

Begründung der Jury
Dank seiner durchdachten Funktionalität erleichtert das Wassersensorsystem Phyn Plus die Überwachung der Wasserversorgung erheblich.

Cayenne Semi-Pro Kitchen Faucet
Küchenarmatur

Manufacturer
American Standard,
Piscataway, New Jersey, USA
In-house design
Web
www.americanstandard.com

The appearance of the Cayenne kitchen tap is characterised by a clear, geometric form. The single lever tap with a high spout has a particularly flexible, close spiral spring design for easy use as well as a multifunctional jet with one-touch flow or spray function. With the help of the "Dock-Tite" holding system, the pull-down spray head can be attached to the spout, thus providing reliable and convenient handling.

Statement by the jury
With its functional design, this kitchen tap makes a very professional impression, fulfilling the associated expectations when in use.

Das Aussehen der Küchenarmatur Cayenne ist durch eine klare, geometrische Formgebung geprägt. Die Einhebelarmatur mit hohem Auslauf verfügt über ein besonders flexibles, enges Spiralfederdesign für eine einfache Anwendung sowie eine Multifunktionsdüse mit One-Touch-Strahl oder Brausefunktion. Mithilfe des Haltesystems „Dock-Tite" lässt sich der ausziehbare Brausekopf magnetisch am Auslauf befestigen und ermöglicht so eine zuverlässige und komfortable Handhabung.

Begründung der Jury
Diese Küchenarmatur wirkt mit ihrer sachlichen Gestaltung sehr professionell und vermag die damit einhergehende Erwartungshaltung auch im Gebrauch zu erfüllen.

Instant Heating Kitchen Faucet
Küchenarmatur

Manufacturer
Easo, Xiamen, China
In-house design
Liumei Yang
Web
www.easo.cn

In this tap, the heating system for warm water is integrated directly into the body. This helps saving water and energy, since the hot water starts to flow from the outlet after only three seconds, without having to be kept warm or first flowing cold. Control is via a lever which, by turning it back, switches to hot water mode. The tap has two spray functions; the spray head is held by a magnet at the arm and is easily detached.

Statement by the jury
This kitchen tap convinces with its sophisticated functionality which makes it possible for water to be heated quickly, thereby saving energy.

Bei dieser Armatur wurde das Heizsystem für Warmwasser direkt in den Korpus integriert. Dadurch unterstützt sie das Einsparen von Wasser und Energie, denn das heiße Wasser fließt bereits nach drei Sekunden aus dem Auslass, ohne dass es zuvor warmgehalten werden oder kaltes Wasser zunächst abfließen muss. Die Steuerung erfolgt über einen Hebel, der beim Zurückdrücken in den Heißwassermodus schaltet. Die Armatur hat zwei Brausefunktionen, der Brausekopf wird durch einen Magneten am Arm fixiert und kann leicht gelöst werden.

Begründung der Jury
Diese Küchenarmatur überzeugt mit ihrer ausgereiften Funktionalität, die es ermöglicht, Wasser rasch zu erhitzen und dabei Energie einzusparen.

Kitchen Faucet with Water Purity Filter
Filter Tap
Filter-Armatur

Manufacturer
Zhejiang Ballee Sanitary Wares
Technology Co., Ltd., Wenzhou, China
In-house design
Shili Shi
Web
www.andeb.cn

With its filter element situated on the outside rather than inside the device, this kitchen tap with water treatment function presents as striking and unique. Furthermore, the filter element is easily replaced and also very effective. The water treatment system absorbs chemical substances and removes solid particles and impurities such as heavy metals and bacteria from the water.

Statement by the jury
This filter tap combines a minimalist design with high functionality and easy handling.

Bereits auf den ersten Blick unterscheidet sich diese Küchenarmatur mit Wasseraufbereitungsfunktion von anderen dadurch, dass das Filterelement nicht in die Armatur integriert ist, sondern eine gut sichtbare, äußere Ergänzung darstellt. Dies hat den Vorteil, dass es einfach auszutauschen und zudem sehr leistungsstark ist. Der Wasseraufbereiter absorbiert chemische Substanzen und befreit das Wasser von festen Partikeln und Schadstoffen wie Schwermetallen und Bakterien.

Begründung der Jury
Diese Filterarmatur verbindet eine minimalistische Gestaltung mit hoher Funktionalität und einer einfachen Handhabung.

Tanaro 316 Diamond
Kitchen Tap
Küchenarmatur

Manufacturer
Bradano, Plouescat, France
In-house design
Machiel Quadt
Web
www.bradano.fr

The appearance of this stainless-steel tap with a black coloured hose is as clean as it is elegant: The operating elements, the temperature control button with a diamond cut and the water control are integrated into the body of the tap, allowing a minimalist design with functionality. The hygienic silicon hose can be rotated 360 degrees and is easily detached from the body. All steel parts of this tap are made of stainless steel 316.

Statement by the jury
The Tanaro 316 Diamond tap convinces with its timeless design, which makes a particularly purist impression by integrating the operating elements into the stainless steel tap body.

Das Erscheinungsbild dieser Edelstahlarmatur mit schwarzem Silikonschlauch ist gleichermaßen klar wie elegant: Die Steuerungselemente, die Temperatursteuertaste mit Diamantschliff und die Einhebel-Wassersteuerung sind in den Armaturenkorpus integriert, was in einem minimalistischen, funktionalen Design mündet. Der hygienische Silikonschlauch kann um 360 Grad gedreht werden und lässt sich leicht von der Basis lösen. Alle Stahlelemente der Armatur sind aus Edelstahl 316 gefertigt.

Begründung der Jury
Die Armatur Tanaro 316 Diamond überzeugt mit ihrem zeitlosen Design, das durch die Integration der Bedienelemente in den Edelstahlzylinder besonders puristisch anmutet.

Fino Diamond
Kitchen Tap
Küchenarmatur

Manufacturer
Bradano, Plouescat, France
In-house design
Machiel Quadt
Web
www.bradano.fr

The characteristic design features of the Fino Diamond stainless steel tap are its diamond cut temperature control button and single lever water control, both aesthetically integrated in the tap body. The "Straight Mix" ceramic cartridge assures precise control of both flow rate and temperature with one hand. Once installed the faucet can easily be removed from the base creating access behind the sink and allow windows to open inwards.

Statement by the jury
The Fino Diamond tap gains merit with its clean design, in which the operating elements seamlessly blend with the body, yet are at the same time easy to access.

Charakteristische Konstruktionsmerkmale der Edelstahlarmatur Fino Diamond sind ihr Diamond-Cut-Temperaturkontrollknopf sowie die Einhebel-Wassersteuerung, die visuell in den Armaturenkörper integriert sind. Die „Straight Mix"-Keramikkartusche gewährleistet die präzise Kontrolle von Durchflussmenge und Temperatur mit einer Hand. Einmal installiert lässt sich die Armatur leicht von der Basis abnehmen, sodass der Platz hinter der Spüle erreichbar ist und sich Fenster nach innen öffnen lassen.

Begründung der Jury
Die Armatur Fino Diamond punktet mit ihrer reduzierten Gestaltung, bei der die Bedienelemente weitgehend mit dem Korpus verschmelzen, gleichzeitig jedoch gut erreichbar sind.

Dixon
Filter Taps
Filterarmaturen

Manufacturer
Bravat, Guangzhcu, China
In-house design
Zhengtie Yu, Xing Xie, Caiyun Huang
Web
www.bravat.com

The user must first lend a hand before drinking water can flow from the Dixon series filter tap. The special feature of the tap is that it is delivered with a straight pipe to keep the package small. In order to use the tap, it is first bent to the desired radius. Dixon consists of an anti-bacterial copper pipe with a silicon coating, and is available in various colours.

Statement by the jury
The basic design concept of these filter taps helps to save packaging material. It allows for personalisation, as each tap must first be formed according to the individual wish of the user.

Bei der Filterarmaturenserie Dixon gilt es zunächst selbst Hand anzulegen, bevor das Trinkwasser fließen kann: Die Besonderheit der Armatur besteht darin, dass sie zur Reduzierung der Verpackungsgröße mit geradem Rohr geliefert wird. Damit sie genutzt werden kann, wird dieses vom Nutzer erst im gewünschten Radius gebogen. Dixon besteht aus einem antibakteriellen Kupferrohr, das mit einer in verschiedenen Farben erhältlichen Silikonschicht ummantelt ist.

Begründung der Jury
Das diesen Filterarmaturen zugrunde liegende Gestaltungkonzept hilft dabei, Verpackungsmüll einzusparen. Es ermöglicht eine besondere Art der Individualisierung, da jede Armatur zunächst vom Nutzer in die gewünschte Form gebracht wird.

SmartControl Zedra
Kitchen Tap
Küchenarmatur

Manufacturer
Grohe AG, Düsseldorf, Germany
In-house design
Web
www.grohe.com

The body of the SmartControl Zedra kitchen tap is characterised by a conical base and clear lines, which are not interrupted by noticeable operating elements, thanks to the counter-sunk smart control elements integrated in the tap. The SmartControl valve provides separation of water flow and temperature and is located at the front of the spout, ensuring the water flow can be started and stopped by a simple push. The pull-out spout offers various spray functions.

Der Korpus der Armatur SmartControl Zedra ist durch eine konische Basis und eine klare Linienführung geprägt, die dank des flächenbündig in die Armatur integrierten SmartControl-Elements nicht durch auffällige Bedienelemente unterbrochen wird. Das Kontrollventil „SmartControl" erlaubt eine Trennung der Steuerung von Wasserfluss und Temperatur und ist an der Vorderseite des Auslaufs positioniert, sodass der Wasserstrahl durch Drücken des Ventils gestartet und gestoppt werden kann. Der herausziehbare Auslauf bietet verschiedene Brausefunktionen.

Statement by the jury
Zedra combines contemporary elegance with a high degree of operating convenience, which is simplified due to the innovative SmartControl elements.

Begründung der Jury
Zedra verbindet zeitgemäße Eleganz mit einem hohen Bedienkomfort, der durch das innovative SmartControl-Element vereinfacht wird.

SmartControl Minta
Kitchen Tap
Küchenarmatur

Manufacturer
Grohe AG, Düsseldorf, Germany
In-house design
Web
www.grohe.com

This kitchen tap features the new valve technology "SmartControl", with an integrated control valve situated at the front of the tap. The water flow is regulated by simply pushing the valve by hand or lower arm. This is not only hygienic, but also allows for a particularly clean design, as there is no need for an operating lever.

Statement by the jury
The Minta tap shows an extremely reduced form, which is emphasised by the high L-shaped spout. With its intuitive design, it is also very user-friendly.

Bei dieser Küchenarmatur sorgt die Integration der neuen Ventiltechnologie „SmartControl" für ein besonders puristisches Erscheinungsbild, da auf Bedienhebel komplett verzichtet werden konnte. Die Interaktion mit dem Wasser erfolgt stattdessen über ein Steuerventil, das so in die Armaturenfront eingelassen ist, dass die Kontrolle des Wasserflusses allein durch Drücken mit der Hand oder dem Unterarm möglich ist, was die Bedienung besonders hygienisch macht.

Begründung der Jury
Die Armatur Minta punktet mit einer äußerst reduzierten Formgebung, die durch den hohen L-förmigen Auslauf noch betont wird. Funktional überzeugt sie mit intuitiver Bedienbarkeit.

SmartControl Essence
Kitchen Tap
Küchenarmatur

Manufacturer
Grohe AG, Düsseldorf, Germany
In-house design
Web
www.grohe.com

With its elegant, minimalist appearance, the SmartControl Essence tap blends harmoniously with a variety of kitchen environments. Thanks to the innovative SmartControl valve, operation is particularly intuitive and hygienic. The extractable spout can be swivelled manually by up to 140 degrees and thus offers great flexibility.

Statement by the jury
The SmartControl Essence tap combines a well-considered function concept and easy operation with a purist, elegant design.

Mit ihrem eleganten, minimalistischen Erscheinungsbild fügt sich die Armatur SmartControl Essence harmonisch in unterschiedliche Küchenumgebungen ein. Die Bedienung ist dank des innovativen SmartControl-Ventils besonders intuitiv und hygienisch. Die Armatur besitzt einen herausziehbaren Auslauf, lässt sich um bis zu 140 Grad schwenken und bietet dadurch eine hohe Flexibilität.

Begründung der Jury
Die Armatur SmartControl Essence verbindet ein durchdachtes Funktionskonzept und eine einfache Bedienung mit einer puristisch-eleganten Gestaltung.

Ozone
Kitchen Tap
Küchenarmatur

Manufacturer
Xiamen Solex High-Tech Industries Co., Ltd.,
Xiamen, China
In-house design
Zhida Chen, Shenghua Li
Web
www.solex.com.cn

The Ozone kitchen tap combines normal water function with a mode for ozonisation: the disinfecting of hands and food through ozone dissolved in water. Control of the mains water supply is by means of a lever. A button ("Electronica Touch Switch"), located on the opposite side of the tap, is used to switch to ozone water. Just one touch is sufficient to start and stop the disinfection process.

Die Küchenarmatur Ozone kombiniert eine normale Wasserfunktion mit einem Modus zur Ozonisierung. Bei dieser Methode wird Ozon in Wasser gelöst, das anschließend der Desinfektion von Händen und Lebensmitteln dient. Die Steuerung des Leitungswassers erfolgt über einen Hebel. Eine auf der gegenüberliegenden Seite der Armatur angebrachte Taste („Electronica Touch Switch") dient der Umstellung auf Ozonwasser. Eine Berührung reicht aus, um den Desinfektionsvorgang zu starten und wieder zu stoppen.

Statement by the jury
In its organically formed body, Ozone effectively combines the water and disinfection functions. Two separate regulators facilitate the simple switching between modes.

Begründung der Jury
Ozone verbindet in ihrem organisch geformten Korpus auf gelungene Weise Wasser- und Desinfektionsfunktion. Zwei unterschiedliche Regler ermöglichen ein einfaches Umschalten zwischen den Modi.

Switchover
Kitchen Tap
Küchenarmatur

Manufacturer
Xiamen Solex High-Tech Industries Co., Ltd.,
Xiamen, China
In-house design
Zhida Chen, Xiaodong Liao
Web
www.solex.com.cn

The Switchover kitchen tap uses a new technology that allows users to easily and comfortably switch between water stream and spray function. With its slender form and pure lines it blends in discreetly with every kitchen environment.

Statement by the jury
This kitchen tap is pleasing with its classical, linear appearance and is characterised by a particularly high user-friendliness.

Die Armatur Switchover nutzt eine neue Sprühumschalttechnologie, die es Nutzern erlaubt, ihren Bedürfnissen entsprechend unkompliziert zwischen Wasserstrahl und Brausefunktion hin und her zu schalten. Mit ihrer schlanken Form und einer puristischen Linienführung fügt sie sich dezent in jede Küchenumgebung ein.

Begründung der Jury
Diese Küchenarmatur gefällt mit ihrer klassischen, geradlinigen Erscheinung und zeichnet sich durch eine besonders hohe Benutzerfreundlichkeit aus.

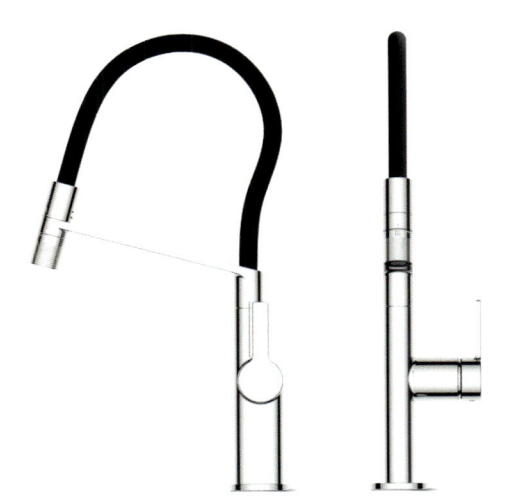

Nimble
Kitchen Tap
Küchenarmatur

Manufacturer
Xiamen Lota International Co., Ltd.,
Xiamen, China
In-house design
Yonghuang Li, Yongqiang He, Chuanbao Zhu
Web
www.xmlota.com

The principal innovation of this kitchen tap is an integrated handle mechanism, making it easier to select between regular water flow and filtered water. Light pressure on the mains water control lever activates an electric button, which allows the change from filtered water as well as pre-setting the volume of water required. Filtered and unfiltered water use different paths in order to prevent cross-contamination.

Statement by the jury
Its innovative, ergonomically designed handle mechanism makes the Nimble kitchen tap especially easy to operate and user-friendly.

Die Hauptinnovation dieser Küchenarmatur ist ein integrierter Griffmechanismus, der die Auswahl zwischen regulärem Wasserfluss und filtriertem Wasser erleichtert. Am mechanischen Hebel zur Steuerung des Leitungswassers kann durch leichtes Drücken eine elektronische Taste aktiviert werden, die die Umstellung auf Filterwasser sowie die Festlegung eines bestimmten Wasservolumens erlaubt. Gefiltertes und ungefiltertes Wasser nutzen unterschiedliche Wasserwege, um eine Kreuzkontamination zu verhindern.

Begründung der Jury
Ihr innovativer, ergonomisch gestalteter Griffmechanismus macht die Küchenarmatur Nimble besonders leicht handhabbar und benutzerfreundlich.

Flex
Kitchen Tap
Küchenarmatur

Manufacturer
Xiamen Lota International Co., Ltd.,
Xiamen, China
In-house design
Yongqiang He, Yuanxin Wang,
Yonghuang Li, Chuanbao Zhu
Web
www.xmlota.com

From a design as well as a functional viewpoint, the Flex kitchen tap is characterised by the freely folding docking arm of the spray head. Thanks to this arm the user can set the spout to any desired position. The head is held in place by a magnet and is easily released. The tap can be adjusted as required for a full flow or for aerated water, for example for washing fruit or vegetables.

Statement by the jury
The Flex kitchen tap gains merit with its functional and elegant design. Further pleasant features are its foldable holder which provides flexibility.

Gestalterisch wie funktional ist die Küchenarmatur Flex durch eine frei klappbare Halterung des Brausekopfs geprägt. Dank dieses Arms kann der Benutzer den Auslass in jeder gewünschten Position fixieren. Der Kopf wird durch einen Magneten gehalten und lässt sich leicht lösen. Die Armatur kann je nach Bedarf so eingestellt werden, dass sie einen vollen Strahl oder mit Luft angereichertes Wasser abgibt, etwa zum Abbrausen von Obst und Gemüse.

Begründung der Jury
Die Küchenarmatur Flex punktet mit einer funktionalen und formschönen Gestaltung. Darüber hinaus gefällt die durch eine klappbare Halterung erzielte Flexibilität.

In-Spout Filtration Kitchen Mixer (All in One Filtration Faucet Type AJ/AK)
Kitchen Tap
Küchenarmatur

Manufacturer
LIXIL Corporation, Tokyo, Japan
In-house design
Yoshihiko Ando
Web
www.lixil.com

This single lever mixer tap with features such as a built-in water filter, a retractable outlet and a switch for measured water flow offers a well-considered functionality. To save space, an innovative small high-performance filter with finely granulated active carbon powder is directly integrated into the outlet, meaning a separate drinking water tap and under-sink filter is no longer required. The control between filtered and mains water, as well as the water stream and spray flow functions, is conveniently located at the spout.

Diese Einhebel-Mischbatterie bietet mit Eigenschaften wie einem eingebauten Wasserfilter, einem herausziehbaren Auslauf und einem Schalter für die dosierte Wasserabgabe eine durchdachte Funktionalität. Ein innovativer kleiner Hochleistungsfilter mit fein granuliertem Aktivkohlepulver ist platzsparend direkt in den Auslauf integriert, sodass weder ein separater Trinkwasserhahn noch ein Untertischfilter erforderlich sind. Das Umschalten zwischen Filter- und Leitungswasser sowie Strahl- und Brausefunktion erfolgt komfortabel am Auslass.

Statement by the jury
This tap in classically simple design is convincing in its space-saving construction, which is accomplished by integrating the filter into the output pipe.

Begründung der Jury
Bei dieser klassisch-schlicht gestalteten Armatur überzeugt ihr platzsparender Aufbau, der durch die Integration des Filters in das Auslassrohr ermöglicht wurde.

VITAL Capsule Filter Taps
Filter Tap Series
Filter-Armaturenserie

Manufacturer
Franke Küchentechnik AG, Franke
Kitchen Systems, Aarburg, Switzerland
In-house design
Web
www.franke.com

The Vital tap collection is fitted with a separate outlet for filtered water. The water is cleaned by guiding it through a compactly designed, highly effective capsule filter system, which combines active carbon with a high-tech membrane and by this means removes impurities and bacteria. The space-saving filter capsules can clean about 500 litres of water. Afterwards they can be easily exchanged.

Statement by the jury
This filter tap series gains merit with a simple operating concept and its very practical appearance, which is characterised by precise lines.

Die Vital-Armaturenserie ist mit einem separaten Auslass für gefiltertes Wasser ausgestattet. Das Wasser wird zur Reinigung durch ein kompakt gestaltetes, hocheffektives Kapselfiltersystem geleitet, das Aktivkohle mit einer Hightech-Membran kombiniert und auf diese Weise Schadstoffe und Bakterien entfernt. Mit einer der platzsparenden Filterkapseln können etwa 500 Liter Wasser gereinigt werden; danach lässt sich die Kapsel einfach austauschen.

Begründung der Jury
Diese Filter-Armaturenserie punktet mit einem einfachen Bedienkonzept und ihrem sehr sachlichen Erscheinungsbild, das durch eine präzise Linienführung geprägt ist.

Kubus 2
Kitchen Sink
Spülbecken

Manufacturer
Franke Küchentechnik AG, Franke
Kitchen Systems, Aarburg, Switzerland
In-house design
Web
www.franke.com

The Kubus 2 kitchen sink has a linear design whereby it is counter-sunk in the worktop. Thus, it harmonically blends in with every surface. With the corresponding accessories such as a wooden chopping board or a dish drainer, the worktop can quickly be extended so as to make use of the space over the sink. An additional accessory shelf incorporated in the sink offers room for a second work level.

Statement by the jury
With its accessories which can be located at two levels, this clearly designed sink becomes a flexibly usable workplace.

Das geradlinig gestaltete Spülbecken Kubus 2 ist so konzipiert, dass es in die Arbeitsfläche eingelassen wird und sich dadurch harmonisch in jede Oberfläche einfügt. Mit dem passenden Zubehör wie Holzschneidebrett oder Abtropfvorrichtung kann die Arbeitsfläche durch die Nutzung des Raums über der Spüle mit wenigen Handgriffen vergrößert werden. Eine zusätzliche, in das Spülbecken eingearbeitete Zubehörleiste bietet Halt für eine zweite Arbeitsebene.

Begründung der Jury
Mit ihrem Zubehör, das sich auf zwei Ebenen platzieren lässt, wird diese klar gestaltete Spüle zu einem flexibel nutzbaren Arbeitsplatz.

Stainless Steel Step
Kitchen Sink
Spüle

Manufacturer
Ningbo Mengo Kitchen Equipment Co., Ltd.,
Ningbo, China
Design
Ningbo Morgen Industry Design Co., Ltd.,
Ningbo, China
Web
www.mensarjor.com
www.morgendesign.com

This stainless-steel sink can quickly and easily transform into a work surface. For this purpose, for example, a cutting board and other items such as a draining sieve or waste container are placed on the rods located on both sides of the sink. The items can be pushed aside, allowing the remaining sink surface to be easily accessed. The board has a drain for liquids and two differently designed sides, which can be selected according to the required kitchen task.

Statement by the jury
Thanks to a well-considered and space-saving design solution, this kitchen sink can easily transform into a flexible and multifunctional kitchen worktop.

Schienen auf beiden Seiten des Spülbeckens ermöglichen es, diese Edelstahlspüle schnell und einfach in eine Arbeitsfläche umzuwandeln. Zu diesem Zweck können beispielsweise ein Schneidebrett sowie andere Einsätze wie Sieb oder Abfallbehälter auf die Schienen gesetzt und leicht verschoben werden, wobei die restliche Spülfläche gut erreichbar bleibt. Das Brett hat einen Abfluss für Flüssigkeit und zwei unterschiedlich gestaltete Seiten, zwischen denen je nach zu verrichtender Küchenarbeit gewählt werden kann.

Begründung der Jury
Dank einer durchdachten und platzsparenden Gestaltungslösung kann sich dieses Spülbecken leicht in eine flexible und multifunktionale Küchenarbeitsfläche verwandeln.

Quick Select Dishwasher
Geschirrspüler

Manufacturer
AB Electrolux, Stockholm, Sweden
In-house design
Web
www.electrolux.com

The Quick Select dishwasher series offers a novel type of dishwasher control: the user simply selects the desired running time of the rinse cycle by means of the central slide on the user interface. A display, the "Ecometer", then indicates the energy consumption for the time chosen and thus gradually leads the user to always choose the most efficient and sustainable cycle.

Statement by the jury
This dishwasher allows for the flexible selection of running time via a sliding regulator in a very intuitive and user-friendly way.

Die Quick Select Geschirrspüler-Serie bietet eine neue Art der Spülmaschinensteuerung: Der Benutzer wählt über den zentralen Schieberegler im Bedienfeld einfach die gewünschte Laufzeit des Spülgangs. Ein Display („Ecometer") zeigt daraufhin den Energieverbrauch für die gewählte Zeit an und bringt den Nutzer so nach und nach dazu, immer die effizienteste und nachhaltigste Wahl für jeden Spülgang zu treffen.

Begründung der Jury
Bei dieser Spülmaschine ist die flexible Wahl der Laufzeit über einen Schieberegler mit direkter Rückmeldung zum Energieverbrauch sehr intuitiv und benutzerfreundlich.

G7000 Series Semi-Integrated (G7915 SCi)
Dishwasher
Geschirrspüler

Manufacturer
Miele & Cie. KG, Gütersloh, Germany
In-house design
Web
www.miele.de

This semi-integrated dishwasher with generous M-Touch colour display uses the innovative automatic dispensing system "AutoDos": a rotating container, the PowerDisk, holds a specifically developed powder granulate, which it dispenses at the right time in the right quantity. With their clear structure the new FlexLine baskets offer a good overview and great convenience. The 3D-Multiflex cutlery drawer also provides space for small dishes.

Statement by the jury
Integration of an automatic dosing system and the well-considered operating panel of this dishwasher assure a high degree of user-friendliness.

Dieser halbintegrierte Geschirrspüler mit großzügigem M-Touch-Farbdisplay nutzt die innovative automatische Dosierungsfunktion „AutoDos". Dabei wird ein eigens entwickeltes Pulvergranulat in einem rotierenden Behälter, der PowerDisk, vorgehalten und während des Programms in der exakt benötigten Menge und zum richtigen Zeitpunkt abgegeben. Die neuen FlexLine-Körbe bieten durch eine klare Gliederung einen guten Überblick und hohen Komfort. Die 3D-Multiflex-Besteckschublade bietet auch Platz für kleine Geschirrteile.

Begründung der Jury
Die Integration eines Autodosierungssystems und die durchdacht gestaltete Bedienblende sorgen bei diesem Geschirrspüler für eine hohe Benutzerfreundlichkeit.

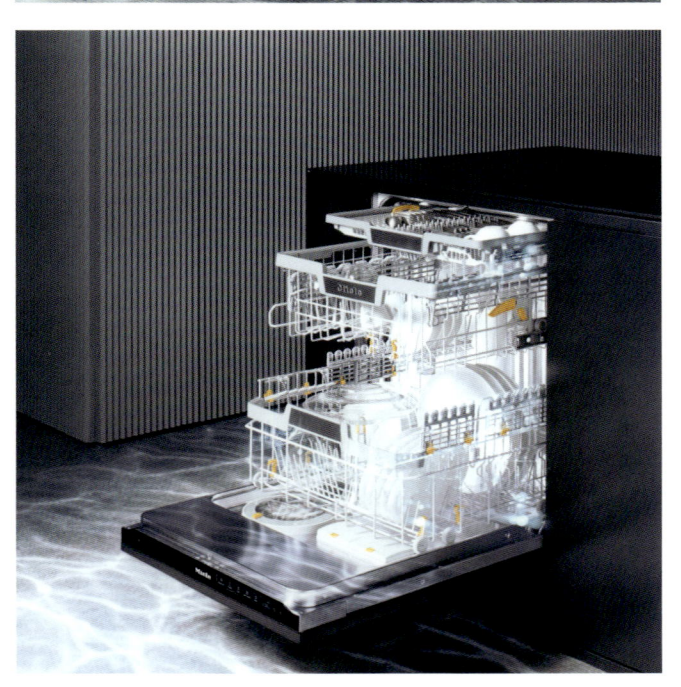

G7000 Series Fully-Integrated (G7965 ScVi)
Dishwasher
Geschirrspüler

Manufacturer
Miele & Cie. KG, Gütersloh, Germany
In-house design
Web
www.miele.de

This fully integrated dishwasher, which opens automatically when knocked on twice, blends seamlessly in handle-free kitchens. The "M Touch Vi" display with illuminated logo is integrated in the black operating panel and can be controlled quickly, easily and intuitively by tapping or wiping. The new "AutoDos" system with the PowerDisk – filled with cleaning granulate and situated inside the door – always dispenses the right amount of detergent. Furthermore, the baskets and cutlery drawer are optimised, so that they can be loaded easily and flexibly.

Statement by the jury
This dishwasher impresses with its intuitive operation and, thanks to newly designed and clearly structured baskets, offers flexibility and convenience of loading and unloading.

Als vollintegrierter Geschirrspüler fügt sich dieses Gerät nahtlos in grifflose Küchen ein, denn es öffnet sich auf zweimaliges Klopfen hin automatisch. Per „M Touch Vi"-Display, das in die schwarze Bedienblende mit leuchtendem Logo integriert ist, lässt sich der Geschirrspüler dann schnell, einfach und intuitiv über direktes Tippen oder Wischen steuern. Die neue Funktion „AutoDos" ermöglicht es, eine mit Reinigungsgranulat gefüllte PowerDisk an der Türinnenseite einzusetzen, die dann selbstständig die richtige Menge an Spülmittel abgibt. Zudem sind Körbe und Besteckschublade optimiert, sodass sie sich einfach und flexibel befüllen lassen.

Begründung der Jury
Dieser Geschirrspüler besticht mit einer intuitiven Bedienung und bietet dank neu gestalteter, klar gegliederter Körbe auch beim Be- und Entladen viel Flexibilität und Komfort.

NP-TZ100
Dishwasher
Geschirrspüler

Manufacturer
Panasonic Corporation, Kyoto, Japan
In-house design
Tomohiro Shigeura
Web
www.panasonic.com

The design of the NP-TZ100 is based on the idea of creating a dishwasher which combines dish washing with dish storage in one product. The result is a compact, minimalist designed cabinet to be placed on the worktop. When stored in the cabinet, the dishes are sterilised and deodorised or – by activating the washing process – cleaned. A touch-sensitive door makes access easy, while operation is intuitive.

Statement by the jury
The NP-TZ100 skilfully combines a purist exterior and a space-saving construction with multifunctionality in the interior.

Das Gestaltungskonzept des Geschirrspülers NP-TZ100 basiert auf der Idee, einen Spülschrank zu kreieren, der die Reinigung von Geschirr mit dessen Aufbewahrung in einem Produkt kombiniert. Das Ergebnis ist ein kompakter, minimalistisch gestalteter Schrank, der auf der Arbeitsfläche Platz findet. Das Geschirr wird bei der Lagerung im Schrank sterilisiert und desodoriert oder – bei Aktivierung des Spülgangs – gesäubert. Eine berührungsempfindliche Tür erleichtert den Zugriff, die Bedienung ist intuitiv.

Begründung der Jury
Der NP-TZ100 verbindet auf gekonnte Weise ein puristisches Äußeres und eine platzsparende Bauweise mit Multifunktionalität im Inneren.

Sterilizer ZTD100-H10
Sterilisator

Manufacturer
Vatti Corporation Limited, Zhongshan, China
In-house design
Peng Chen, Xin Shao
Web
www.vatti.com.cn
Honourable Mention

The H10 Steriliser for the Chinese market uses two technologies for quick and safe sterilisation: high-temperature sterilisation and "UVC-LED" sterilisation. The latter shortens sterilisation time by 50 percent and has the advantage that no ozone odour escapes, ideal for baby articles and plastic dishes. The stainless-steel handle is flush-fitted at the front. The operating panel is inclined at 12 degrees to provide better reading and easier operation.

Statement by the jury
The extremely purist design with strong contrasts between metal and black glass surfaces imparts to the H10 steriliser its original appearance.

Der Sterilisator H10 für den chinesischen Markt nutzt zwei Technologien für eine schnelle und sichere Sterilisation: die Hochtemperatursterilisation und die „UVC-LED"-Sterilisation. Letztere verkürzt die Sterilisationsdauer um 50 Prozent und hat den Vorteil, dass kein Ozongeruch auftritt, was sie für Säuglingsartikel und Plastikgeschirr prädestiniert. Die Front mit eingelassenem Griff ist aus Edelstahl gefertigt. Das Bedienfeld ist um 12 Grad geneigt, um sich besser lesen und bedienen zu lassen.

Begründung der Jury
Eine äußerst puristische Gestaltung mit starken Kontrasten zwischen Metall- und schwarzen Glasflächen verleiht dem Sterilisator H10 sein eigenständiges Erscheinungsbild.

D7 Integrated Dishwasher
Geschirrspüler

Manufacturer
Zhejiang Marssenger Kitchenware Co., Ltd., Haining, China
In-house design
Zhou Zhangling, Li Xiaozhu
Web
www.marssenger.com

This multifunctional combination makes optimal use of space in the kitchen by combining dishwasher, crushing of food residues, cleaning of fruit, sink and bottom cabinet in one product. The dishwasher cleans by means of innovative technologies for very thorough removal of food residues. A slender, inclined operating panel makes operation simple. The seamlessly welded sink and a tap with glass inlay emphasise the overall impression of high quality. The modular construction facilitates the maintenance processes.

Dieses multifunktionale Ensemble nutzt den Raum in Küchen optimal aus, indem es Spülmaschine, Zerkleinerung von Speiseresten, Reinigung von Früchten, Spüle und Unterschrank in einem Produkt kombiniert. Der Geschirrspüler reinigt mithilfe innovativer Technologien zur Entfernung von Lebensmittelrückständen sehr gründlich. Ein schlankes, geneigtes Bedienpanel ermöglicht eine einfache Bedienung. Das nahtlos geschweißte Spülbecken und eine Armatur mit Glas-Inlay unterstreichen den hochwertigen Gesamteindruck. Der modulare Aufbau erleichtert die Wartungsprozesse.

Statement by the jury
D7 Integrated Dishwasher combines many functions in a compact space, whereby the workflow becomes more efficient and convenient. The product also displays high quality.

Begründung der Jury
D7 Integrated Dishwasher vereint viele Funktionen auf kompaktem Raum, wodurch die Arbeitsabläufe effizienter und komfortabler werden. Das Ensemble strahlt zudem Hochwertigkeit aus.

271

CORA
Compact Kitchen
Kompaktküche

Manufacturer
3B S.p.A., Salgareda (Treviso), Italy
Design
Emidio Corbetta Design, Conegliano (Treviso), Italy
Web
www.3bspa.com
www.emidiocorbetta.it

The Cora compact kitchen integrates basic kitchen elements such as cooker, storage room, sink and dishwasher in the smallest space. It is therefore particularly space-saving, functional and efficient and can be installed to add a small kitchen facility to rooms which are used for other purposes. Due to its innovative design and high-quality workmanship, Cora is a room element on its own; however, it also blends well with every environment.

Die Kompaktküche Cora integriert grundlegende Küchenelemente wie Kochstelle, Stauraum, Spülbecken und Spülmaschine auf kleinstem Raum. Dadurch ist sie besonders platzsparend, funktional und effizient. Als solches kann sie anderweitig genutzte Räume um einen kleinen Küchenbereich ergänzen. Durch ihre innovative Gestaltung und ihre hochwertige Ausführung steht Cora als Raumelement für sich, fügt sich jedoch zugleich in jedes Umfeld harmonisch ein.

Statement by the jury
Cora is designed with great care, employing high-quality materials. It convinces as a kitchen element which, thanks to its compactness and multifunctionality, is diversely adaptable.

Begründung der Jury
Cora ist mit viel Aufmerksamkeit und unter Einsatz hochwertiger Materialien gestaltet. Sie überzeugt als Küchenelement, das dank seiner Kompaktheit und seiner Multifunktionalität vielseitig einsetzbar ist.

ATON
Light Shelf
Beleuchtetes Wandregal

Manufacturer
AKD Design GmbH, Modal Concept,
Hüllhorst, Germany
Design
byform design (Felix Schmidt, Kristina Meyer,
Thorsten Rosenstengel), Bielefeld, Germany
Web
www.modal-concept.de
www.byform.de

Consistent architectural lines and high functionality characterise the Aton light shelf. The light rail can be used in kitchens as well as in bathrooms, living rooms and offices. Due to its modularity, it allows for a wide range of different configurations. High-quality wooden boxes and organisation elements can be simply positioned and shifted. At the same time, Aton serves as wall illumination, providing ambient upward lighting while also illuminating surfaces below it.

Statement by the jury
The Aton light shelf impresses due to its purist aesthetics. From a functional viewpoint, the versatile individual alignment possibilities are particularly convincing.

Eine konsequent architektonische Linienführung und hohe Funktionalität kennzeichnen das Lichtregal Aton. Die Lichtreling lässt sich sowohl in der Küche als auch in Wohn- und Arbeitsräumen sowie im Bad einsetzen und bietet durch ihre Modularität großen Gestaltungsspielraum. Die hochwertig ausgeführten Holzboxen und Ordnungselemente können einfach platziert und verschoben werden. Aton dient zugleich der Wandillumination: Nach oben wird Ambientebeleuchtung abgegeben, auch darunter liegende Flächen lassen sich beleuchten.

Begründung der Jury
Das Lichtregal Aton besticht durch seine puristische Ästhetik und überzeugt in funktionaler Hinsicht durch vielseitige individuelle Ausgestaltungsmöglichkeiten.

Wave
Drawer Organizer Set
Schubladeneinsatz-Set

Manufacturer
Kuhn Rikon AG, Rikon, Switzerland
Design
BIG-GAME, Lausanne, Switzerland
Web
www.kuhnrikon.ch
www.big-game.ch

The Wave six-part drawer organiser set was designed for kitchen and desk drawers. The various modules can be fitted perfectly together for this purpose. The set consists of a knife holder as well as an organising set with two large, two small and a medium-sized unit. The undulating base simplifies the removal of the utensils. The stackable modules are suitable for drawers with a minimum height of six centimetres.

Statement by the jury
With its well-considered design and very precise engineering, Wave serves as a flexible organising system for drawers.

Das sechsteilige Schubladeneinsatz-Set Wave dient der Organisation in Küchen- und Schreibtischschubladen. Die verschiedenen Module können zu diesem Zweck passgenau zusammengesetzt werden. Das Set besteht aus einem Messerhalter, jeweils zwei großen und zwei kleinen sowie einem mittleren Organisationseinsatz. Der wellenförmige Boden vereinfacht das Herausnehmen der Utensilien. Die Module eignen sich für Schubladen mit einer Mindesthöhe von sechs Zentimetern und sind stapelbar.

Begründung der Jury
Mit seiner durchdachten Gestaltung sowie einer sehr genauen Fertigung dient Wave als flexibles Ordnungssystem für Schubladen.

Cox Work®
Utensil Box
Utensilienbox

Manufacturer
Naber GmbH, Nordhorn, Germany
Vauth-Sagel Systemtechnik GmbH & Co. KG,
Brakel-Erkeln, Germany
Design
Bureau Kilian Schindler, Karlsruhe, Germany
Web
www.naber.com
www.vauth-sagel.de
www.kilianschindler.com

This modular utensil box, made of ABS plastic, has been designed to store kitchen utensils, office supplies, tools, sewing kits, toys or gardening equipment. The base is a sturdy container with an integrated carrying handle and features U- and V-shaped dividers as well as a tray for small parts, which can all be securely locked into place. In addition, the items to be stowed can be held in place by crossed rubber bands. Cox Work is available in four harmoniously coordinated colours for individual combination.

Statement by the jury
Thanks to its sophisticated functionality, this utensil box provides flexible usage options, complemented by a persuasive, trend-oriented colour scheme.

Diese modulare, aus ABS-Kunststoff gefertigte Utensilienbox wurde zur Aufbewahrung von Küchenartikeln, Büroartikeln, Werkzeug, Nähzeug, Spielzeug, Gartenwerkzeug etc. konzipiert. Die Basis bildet eine stabile Box mit integriertem Tragegriff, in der u- und v-förmige Trennstege sowie eine Schale für Kleinteile sicher arretiert werden. Zudem lassen sich die zu verstauenden Utensilien durch gekreuzte Gummibänder fixieren. Cox Work ist in vier aufeinander abgestimmten Farbkombinationen erhältlich, die individuell zusammengestellt werden können.

Begründung der Jury
Aufgrund ihrer ausgereiften Funktionalität bietet diese Utensilienbox flexible Nutzungsmöglichkeiten, darüber hinaus überzeugt die trendorientierte Farbgebung.

LG SIGNATURE Bottom Freezer
Refrigerator
Kühlschrank

Manufacturer
LG Electronics Inc.,
Seoul, South Korea

In-house design
Seonil Yu, Kyukwan Choi,
Daesung Lee, Yong Kim,
Hyun Choi

Web
www.lg.com

reddot award 2019
best of the best

In line with the times
Since refrigerators are an important part of everyday life, they are always a direct expression of the spirit of the times. In developing the LG SIGNATURE Bottom Freezer, the design identity of the French Door model of the series has been retained and further developed to impressive effect in terms of functionality and ergonomics. While the rails of the wine cellar shelves are in general fixed on the inside of the refrigerator, the shelf design of this model has combined the cantilever and the under-rail. This delivers flexibility to users by allowing individual layouts. A central aspect of the aesthetics is the use of high-quality wood materials for the wine bottle shelf part, paired with aluminium on the shelf front. This creates a sense of visual unity with the elegant-looking metal finished exterior of the refrigerator. Responding to the high demands of wine connoisseurs, the upper refrigerator deck features separate temperature controls for the red wine, white wine and champagne zones. Also highly convenient is the drawer with automatic lift function applied to the lower deck, eliminating the need for users to bend down when using it. In addition, the refrigerator also impresses with an automatic door-opening function, as well as a sophisticated lighting concept. As with the French Door model, when tapping on the refrigerator door pane, the knock-on function activates the lighting and allows a view into the interior without users having to open the door.

Design für den Zeitgeist
Da er ein wichtiger Teil des täglichen Lebens ist, ist der Kühlschrank stets auch ein direkter Ausdruck des jeweiligen Zeitgeistes. Bei der Konzeption des LG SIGNATURE Bottom Freezer wurde das Design des French-Door-Modells der Serie beibehalten und in Funktionalität und Ergonomie beeindruckend weiterentwickelt. Sind etwa üblicherweise die Schienen der Regalfächer an der Innenseite eines Weinkühlschranks befestigt, wurden hier der Ausleger und die Unterschiene kombiniert gestaltet. Dies bietet dem Nutzer Flexibilität und ermöglicht ein individuelles Anordnen. Ein zentraler Aspekt der Ästhetik ist die Gestaltung der Weinregalfächer mit den hochwertigen Materialien Holz sowie Aluminium auf der Vorderseite. Dies schafft eine visuelle Einheit mit dem elegant anmutenden Metallfinish des Kühlschranks. Den hohen Ansprüchen von Weinkennern entsprechend, ist für den oberen Bereich eine jeweils separate Temperaturregelung der Rotwein-, Weißwein- und Champagnerzonen möglich. Sehr komfortabel ist auch die Gestaltung des unteren Bereichs mit einem Schubfach, welches sich automatisch anhebt, damit man sich nicht bücken muss. Der Kühlschrank beeindruckt zudem mit einer automatischen Türöffnen-Funktion und einem ausgefeilten Beleuchtungskonzept. Wie beim French-Door-Modell aktiviert die Knock-on-Funktion durch Klopfen an die Scheibe der Kühlschranktür die Beleuchtung und erlaubt einen Blick ins Innere, ohne die Tür öffnen zu müssen.

Statement by the jury
The LG SIGNATURE Bottom Freezer achieves an impressive combination of functionality, aesthetics and convenience. It boasts a sophisticated design, an innovative lighting concept as well as highly practical functions including its sensor-controlled door-opening mechanism. The wine refrigerator delivers perfectly designed ergonomics and conveys exclusivity through the use of high-quality materials. Generating its own design idiom, it enriches almost any environment.

Begründung der Jury
Dem LG SIGNATURE Bottom Freezer gelingt eine eindrucksvolle Kombination aus Komfort, Ästhetik und Funktionalität. Er verfügt über eine sehr durchdachte Ausstattung, ein innovatives Beleuchtungskonzept sowie praktische Features wie etwa eine sensorgesteuerte Türöffnen-Funktion. Der Weinkühlschrank ist ergonomisch perfekt gestaltet und vermittelt durch seine hochwertigen Materialien Exklusivität. Eine eigene Formensprache generierend, bereichert er so das Ambiente.

Designer portrait
See page 52
Siehe Seite 52

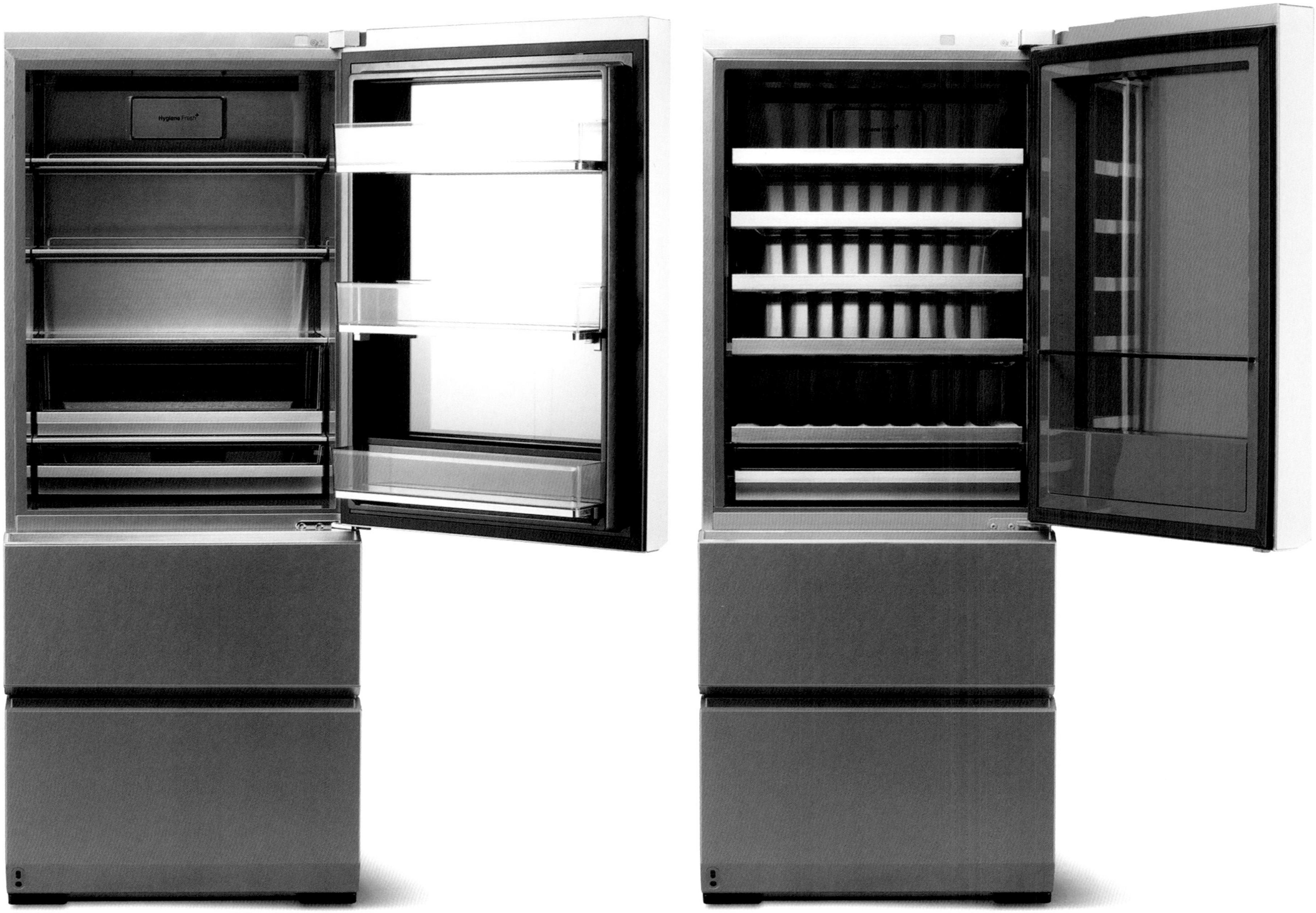

LG Bottom Freezer (V+)
Fridge-Freezer
Kühl-Gefrier-Kombination

Manufacturer
LG Electronics Inc., Seoul, South Korea
In-house design
Kyukwan Choi, Sanghun Kim,
Seungjin Yoon, Jinhee Park
Web
www.lg.com

This fridge-freezer is so designed that when integrated in the kitchen front, it juts out as little as possible. For a homogenous appearance, metallic materials and concealed touch displays are used. Metal is also used in the interior, in drawers, at the back and for the ceiling, where cold air is discharged to improve the cooling power. The interior components are kept as plain and clear as possible to create the impression of simplicity and spaciousness.

Statement by the jury
The Bottom Freezer V+ convinces with a design which facilitates its harmonious and discreet integration in the kitchen front.

Dieses Kühlgerät ist so gestaltet, dass es bei der Integration in die Küchenfront so wenig wie möglich hervorragt. Für ein homogenes Erscheinungsbild wurden metallische Materialien und versteckte Touchdisplays verwendet. Metall kommt im Innenraum auch an Einschüben, an der Rückwand und an der Decke zum Einsatz, an der kalte Luft abgelassen wird, um die Kühlleistung zu verbessern. Das Innenleben ist so einfach und klar wie möglich gehalten, um den Eindruck von Schlichtheit und Geräumigkeit hervorzurufen.

Begründung der Jury
Der Bottom Freezer V+ überzeugt mit einer Gestaltung, die es ermöglicht, ihn harmonisch und dezent in die Küchenfront einzubinden.

LG Bottom Freezer (Universe)
Fridge-Freezer
Kühl-Gefrier-Kombination

Manufacturer
LG Electronics Inc., Seoul, South Korea
In-house design
Kyukwan Choi, Sanghun Kim,
Seungjin Yoon, Jinhee Park, Junghyun Joo
Web
www.lg.com

Its metallic exterior and a concealed touch display give this fridge-freezer a minimalist and simultaneously luxurious impression. In the design special attention was paid to simple operability – for example, a metal handle which increases the convenience. The inner rear panel and the ceiling outlet, where cold air is discharged, are designed to visualise the high cooling power, using shiny metallic surfaces.

Statement by the jury
The widespread use of metal, both in the body and the interior, characterise the high-quality overall impression of this fridge-freezer combination.

Sein metallisches Äußeres und ein verborgenes Touch-Display verleihen dieser Kühl-Gefrier-Kombination eine minimalistische und zugleich luxuriöse Anmutung. Besonderer Wert wurde bei der Gestaltung auch auf eine einfache Bedienbarkeit gelegt – so erhöht etwa ein markanter Metallgriff den Komfort. Die hintere Innenwand und der Deckenauslass, an dem kalte Luft austritt, sind durch den Einsatz metallisch glänzender Flächen so gestaltet, dass sie die hohe Kühlleistung visualisieren.

Begründung der Jury
Die großflächige Verwendung von Metall sowohl am Korpus als auch im Innenraum prägt den hochwertigen Gesamteindruck dieser Kühl-Gefrier-Kombination.

LG InstaView Door-in-Door Refrigerator (Next-8)
Kühlschrank

Manufacturer
LG Electronics Inc., Seoul, South Korea
In-house design
Kyukwan Choi, Sanghun Kim,
Inseon Yeo, Yezo Yun
Web
www.lg.com

The striking feature of the InstaView refrigerator is its door: with a "KnockOn" gesture its window in the right upper side becomes transparent, revealing the so-called "Magic Space" behind. The user can thus locate the desired food before opening the door and thereby reduce the cooling loss by up to 47 percent. This especially simplifies access to the foods or drinks that are used most frequently. With another "KnockOn" gesture the door will turn opaque again.

Statement by the jury
From a functional viewpoint and with regard to energy saving, the door of the InstaView offers real added value and is at the same time a distinctive design element. The interaction of the user with the appliance is also convincing.

Hervorstechendes Merkmal des Kühlschranks InstaView ist seine Tür: Mit der Geste „KnockOn" wird deren Fenster im rechten oberen Viertel transparent und gibt den Blick auf den „Magic Space" dahinter frei. Dadurch kann der Nutzer schon vor dem Öffnen der Tür sehen, wo sich das gewünschte Lebensmittel befindet, und den Kühlluftverlust um bis zu 47 Prozent reduzieren. Vor allem der Zugriff auf häufig verwendete Lebensmittel oder Getränke wird damit erleichtert. Per neuerlichem „KnockOn" wird das Fenster wieder opak.

Begründung der Jury
Die Tür des InstaView bietet in funktionaler Hinsicht und mit Blick aufs Energiesparen einen echten Mehrwert und ist zugleich ein markantes Gestaltungselement. Überzeugend ist auch die intuitive Interaktion des Nutzers mit dem Gerät.

Midea 718WGPZV Cross Four-Door Refrigerator
Kühlschrank

Manufacturer
Hefei Midea Refrigerator Co., Ltd., Hefei, China
In-house design
Web
www.midea.com

This four-door French door refrigerator offers numerous intelligent functions to simplify everyday food management. It reminds the user of the expiry dates of the cooled items or when to take medication and also provides the possibility to order food online. The front is coated with metallic glass which has a particular depth effect resulting from UV light treatment. In one of the upper doors a slightly tilted 23.6" TFT colour display is integrated. The doors are opened with electric support.

Dieser viertürige French-Door-Kühlschrank bietet zahlreiche intelligente Funktionen, die das Lebensmittelmanagement im Alltag einfacher machen. Dazu gehören Erinnerungen zur Haltbarkeit der Kühlgüter oder zur Medikamenteneinnahme ebenso wie die Online-Bestellung von Lebensmitteln. Die Front ist mit einem metallischen Glas beschichtet, das durch eine UV-Licht-Behandlung eine besondere Tiefenwirkung entfaltet. In eine der oberen Türen ist ein leicht geneigtes 23,6"-TFT-Farbdisplay integriert. Die Türen haben eine elektrische Öffnungsunterstützung.

Statement by the jury
The front design of this fridge is characterised by its high formal quality and pleasant materiality. With its large display and many additional functions it enhances operating convenience.

Begründung der Jury
Die Frontgestaltung dieses Kühlschranks zeichnet sich durch eine hohe formale Qualität und schöne Materialität aus. Mit seinem großen Display und vielen Zusatzfunktionen erhöht er zudem den Bedienkomfort.

Whirlpool W Collection 4 Doors Fridge-Freezer
Kühl-Gefrier-Kombination

Manufacturer
Whirlpool EMEA S.p.A., Pero (Milan), Italy
In-house design
Global Consumer Design EMEA, Biandronno (Varese), Italy
Web
www.whirlpool.eu
www.whirlpool.com

The W Collection 4 Doors Fridge-Freezer is characterised by its polished aluminium blade, an elegant, full-width black interface and an integrated pocket handle. Opening the doors reveals the panoramic interior and expansive view of the appliance. The fridge-freezer makes use of "6TH SENSE Technology", including smart sensors that monitor conditions to optimise food preservation. The fridge is illuminated by a large LED panel placed in the ceiling that casts a homogeneous light inside the cavity.

Statement by the jury
This fridge-freezer combination attracts attention with its high-quality front design. The interior is convincing with its use of intelligent technology as well as pleasant lighting.

Der W Collection 4 Doors Fridge-Freezer ist durch eine Front aus poliertem Aluminium, eine elegante schwarze Bedienoberfläche, die sich über die gesamte Breite erstreckt, sowie eine integrierte Griffleiste geprägt. Beim Öffnen der Türen wird ein weiter Blick ins Geräteinnere und auf das Panorama-Innenleben freigegeben. Die Kühl-Gefrier-Kombination nutzt die „6TH-SENSE-Technologie", bei der die Lagerbedingungen mit intelligenten Sensoren permanent kontrolliert und optimiert werden. Ein großes Decken-LED-Panel sorgt für eine homogene Ausleuchtung des Innenraums.

Begründung der Jury
Mit ihrer hochwertigen Frontgestaltung macht diese Kühl-Gefrier-Kombination auf sich aufmerksam. Im Inneren überzeugt der Einsatz intelligenter Technologie ebenso wie die angenehme Beleuchtung.

Siemens Ceramic Fridge
Kühlschrank

Manufacturer
BSH Home Appliances (China) Co., Ltd., Nanjing, China
In-house design
Christoph Becke, Max Eicher, Christine Rieder, Marco Lärm, Maximilian Bauer, Klaus Försterling, Yao Xingen, Zeng Rong, Xu Fenglin
Web
www.bsh-group.com

The monolithic appearance of this fridge is characterised by use of a special ceramic at the front. The innovative material is manufactured from carefully selected clay, stone and sandy soil and is particularly pure. By this means it became possible to upgrade the entire front with a single, very thin ceramic layer. This front design is inspired by architecture and appeals to the user's senses by its particular haptics.

Statement by the jury
Innovative use of materials in the front design characterise this refrigerator and impart in it an autonomous appearance as well as a pleasant haptic.

Das monolithische Erscheinungsbild dieses Kühlschranks ist durch den Einsatz einer Spezialkeramik an der Front geprägt. Das innovative Material ist aus sorgfältig ausgewähltem Ton-, Stein- und Sandboden hergestellt und besonders rein. Dadurch wurde es möglich, die gesamte Vorderseite mit einer einzigen, sehr dünnen Keramikschicht zu veredeln. Diese Frontgestaltung ist von der Architektur inspiriert und spricht durch ihre besondere Haptik und Struktur die Sinne des Nutzers an.

Begründung der Jury
Ein innovativer Materialeinsatz in der Frontgestaltung zeichnet diesen Kühlschrank aus und verleiht ihm sein eigenständiges Aussehen sowie eine angenehme Haptik.

MasterCool Series
Cooling Appliances Side-by-Side Combination
Kältegeräte
Side-By-Side-Kombination

Manufacturer
Miele & Cie. KG, Gütersloh, Germany
In-house design
Web
www.miele.de

The purist appearance of the appliances of the MasterCool range is characterised by clear horizontal lines, use of high-quality materials and bright LED illumination. The drawers offer the ideal climate for foods. The motorised door opening aid, easy-to-clean door racks and glass shelves with overflow protection provide convenient attributes. The wooden rack in the wine cabinet can be adjusted to the bottles' diameter, while the dark front strips can be inscribed with a chalk pencil. The user also has the option of five different light moods.

Statement by the jury
This combination of wine cabinet and fridge delights with its well-considered interior organisation, pleasant details and clean design.

Das puristische Aussehen der Geräte der MasterCool-Baureihe ist geprägt durch eine klare horizontale Linienführung, den Einsatz hochwertiger Materialien und eine helle LED-Beleuchtung. Die Schubladen liefern das ideale Klima für Lebensmittel. Die motorische Türöffnungshilfe, leicht zu reinigende Türabsteller und Glasböden mit Überlaufschutz bieten Komfort. Die Holzroste im Weinschrank lassen sich an die Flaschen anpassen. Die dunklen Frontleisten sind mit Kreidestift beschreibbar. Der Nutzer hat zudem die Wahl zwischen fünf verschiedenen Lichtstimmungen.

Begründung der Jury
Mit einer durchdachten Innenraumorganisation und schönen Detaillösungen begeistert diese puristisch gestaltete Wein-Kühlschrank-Kombination.

Bosch Ceramic Fridge
Kühlschrank

Manufacturer
BSH Home Appliances (China) Co., Ltd., Nanjing, China
In-house design
Ralph Staud, Thomas Tischer, Andreas Kessler, Philipp Kleinlein, Yao Xingen, Wang Kai, Xu Fenglin, Ji Yun, Mi Dawei
Web
www.bsh-group.com

The front of this fridge is covered with a thin ceramic coating, which gives the appliance a very autonomous appearance. The ceramic material consists of certificated clay, stone and sandy soil to ensure an even, level surface without inclusions. The result is a naturally appealing surface with a pleasant feel and in a timeless, clear design.

Statement by the jury
With its unusual ceramic front, this fridge is eye-catching and makes a classical yet modern impression.

Die Front dieses Kühlschranks ist mit einer dünnen Keramikoberfläche beschichtet, die dem Gerät ein sehr eigenständiges Erscheinungsbild verleiht. Das Keramikmaterial setzt sich aus zertifiziertem Ton-, Stein- und Sandboden zusammen, um eine gleichmäßige, ebene Fläche ohne Einschlüsse zu gewährleisten. Das Ergebnis ist eine natürlich anmutende, haptisch angenehme Oberfläche in zeitlos-klarem Design.

Begründung der Jury
Mit seiner ungewöhnlichen Keramikfront zieht dieser Kühlschrank die Blicke auf sich und wirkt klassisch und zeitgemäß zugleich.

Dishwasher Refrigerator
Kühlschrank-Geschirrspüler-Kombination

Manufacturer
Haier Group, Qingdao, China
Design
Haier Innovation Design Center (Fei Zhaojun, Yi Zuowei, Zhou Shu, Feng Zhiqun, Liu Haibo), Qingdao, China
Web
www.haier.com

This combination of refrigerator and dishwasher has been specially developed for Chinese kitchens, which have severely limited space. So far, dishwashers are not the norm in China, and this combination appliance offers the possibility of integrating a dishwasher within the fridge platform as a space-saving solution in any existing kitchen. The French door refrigerator in the upper half is easily accessible; the dishwasher has room in a spacious drawer and can be loaded conveniently.

Diese Kombination aus Kühlschrank und Geschirrspüler wurde speziell im Hinblick auf räumlich eng begrenzte chinesische Küchen entwickelt. Geschirrspüler sind in China bislang noch nicht so verbreitet, und dieses Kombigerät bietet die Möglichkeit, einen Geschirrspüler innerhalb der Kühlschrankgrundfläche platzsparend in die vorhandene Küche zu integrieren. Der French-Door-Kühlschrank in der oberen Hälfte ist gut erreichbar, der Geschirrspüler findet in einer geräumigen Schublade Platz und lässt sich bequem befüllen.

Statement by the jury
At first glance, the combination of dishwasher and refrigerator in one appliance seems surprising. However, it offers an aesthetic and functional solution for lack of space in Chinese kitchens.

Begründung der Jury
Die auf den ersten Blick überraschende Kombination von Geschirrspüler und Kühlschrank in einem Gerät bietet eine ästhetisch wie funktional gelungene Lösung für das Platzproblem in chinesischen Küchen.

REF-609
Refrigerator
Kühlschrank

Manufacturer
Haier Group, Qingdao, China
Design
Haier Innovation Design Center (Ma Lifeng, Zhang Limei, Jiang Chunhui, Bao Changliang, Liu Mingjun, Wei Xiaobo), Qingdao, China
Web
www.haier.com

This fridge-freezer combination of the Casarte collection can be flexibly integrated into the kitchen front. A dynamic, three-stage cooling technology for separate temperature regulation is employed in the interior. Thanks to its separation into humid zone, dry zone and a zone with infrared supported constant temperature, the appliance complies with the various demands for food storage. The slightly arched doors can be fully opened to 90 degrees; operation is via a vertical all-in-one display.

Diese Kühl-Gefrier-Kombination der Casarte-Linie lässt sich flexibel in die Küchenfront integrieren. Im Inneren kommt eine dynamische dreistufige Kühltechnologie für die separate Temperaturregelung ihrer drei Kühlbereiche zum Einsatz. Dank der Unterteilung in Feuchtzone, Trockenzone und einen Bereich mit Infrarot-gestützter konstanter Temperatur wird das Gerät unterschiedlichen Anforderungen an die Lagerung von Lebensmitteln gerecht. Die leicht gewölbten Türen lassen sich im 90-Grad-Winkel vollständig öffnen, die Bedienung erfolgt über ein vertikales All-in-One-Display.

Statement by the jury
The slightly arched doors of this refrigerator are indicative of the size of the interior, which is sensibly divided and equipped with up-to-date technology.

Begründung der Jury
Bei diesem Kühlgerät kommuniziert die leichte Außenwölbung der Türen die Größe des Innenraums. Dieser ist zudem sinnvoll unterteilt und mit zeitgemäßer Technologie ausgestattet.

Casarte 420 F+ Refrigerator
Kühlschrank

Manufacturer
Haier Group, Qingdao, China
Design
Haier Innovation Design Center (Wan Lulu, Zhang Limei, Jiang Chunhui, Kang Jingru, Dou Zhendong), Qingdao, China
Web
www.haier.com

This refrigerator for the Chinese market unites the large-space interior of a French door fridge with the possibility of separate storage of different foods, such as offered by a multi-door fridge. Thanks to a reduced body depth and doors which can open 90 degrees, it is space-saving, in spite of its interior volume with various cool and freezer zones. With its coloured glass front, it appeals to the target group of younger families. An infrared function regulates the temperature automatically by means of air input.

Dieser Kühlschrank für den chinesischen Markt vereint das große Raumangebot eines French-Door-Kühlschranks mit der Möglichkeit einer getrennten Lagerung unterschiedlicher Lebensmittel, wie sie ein Multitür-Kühlschrank bietet. Dank einer reduzierten Korpustiefe und Türen, die sich im 90-Grad-Winkel öffnen, ist er trotz seines Innenraumvolumens mit verschiedenen Kühl- und Gefrierzonen platzsparend. Mit seiner Front aus Colorglas richtet er sich an die Zielgruppe jüngerer Familien. Eine Infrarot-Konstanttemperatur-Funktion reguliert die Temperatur mithilfe von Luftzufuhr automatisch.

Statement by the jury
This fridge-freezer combination for young families convinces with its generously dimensioned storage space, which is divided into various climatic and freezer zones.

Begründung der Jury
Mit beeindruckend großzügigem Stauraum, der in verschiedene Klima- und Gefrierzonen unterteilt ist, überzeugt diese Kühl-Gefrier-Kombination für junge Familien.

REF-551
Refrigerator
Kühlschrank

Manufacturer
Haier Group, Qingdao, China
Design
Haier Innovation Design Center (Zhang Limei, Jiang Chunhui, Bao Changliang, Lu Yue), Qingdao, China
Web
www.haier.com

The design of this fridge-freezer of the Casarte collection has been optimised as to flexibly integrate in various kitchen environments. Even when it is located in the corner, the doors and drawers of this appliance can be fully opened. The operating element is integrated in a transparent panel and, thanks to a sensor, lights up dimly when someone approaches. Use of modern technology assures precise, automatic control. A separate compartment is available for storing baby food.

Die Gestaltung dieser Kühl-Gefrier-Kombination der Casarte-Reihe ist im Hinblick auf eine flexible Integration in verschiedene Küchenumgebungen optimiert. Türen und Schubladen lassen sich vollständig öffnen, selbst wenn das Gerät in der Ecke platziert wird. Die Bedienoberfläche ist in eine transparente Blende integriert und leuchtet dank eines Sensors sanft auf, wenn sich jemand nähert. Der Einsatz zeitgemäßer Technologien sorgt für eine präzise automatische Temperatursteuerung. Ein separates Fach ist speziell auf die Aufbewahrung von Babynahrung ausgerichtet.

Statement by the jury
With a high-quality and tidy interior and exterior design, this fridge-freezer communicates efficiency and blends in well with a modern kitchen environment.

Begründung der Jury
Mit einer hochwertigen und aufgeräumten Interieur- wie Exterieurgestaltung kommuniziert diese Kühl-Gefrier-Kombination Effizienz und fügt sich gut ins moderne Küchenumfeld ein.

REF-549
Refrigerator
Kühlschrank

Manufacturer
Haier Group, Qingdao, China
Design
Haier Innovation Design Center (Meng Xiangbo, Li Xia, Jiang Chunhui, Li Pengtao), Qingdao, China
Web
www.haier.com

A particularly slim housing is the striking feature of this fridge-freezer combination and assures more storage capacity. By means of extrusion technology the waist-high handle has pleasant haptics and is durable. The doors can be opened to 90 degrees and offer convenient access to the interior, allowing the fridge to be installed directly next to a wall. Drawers for dry and humid zones are self-sliding, making handling easier.

Ein besonders dünnes Gehäuse ist das hervorstechende Merkmal dieser Kühl-Gefrier-Kombination und sorgt für mehr Lagerkapazität. Durch den Einsatz von Extrusionstechnik ist der Aluminiumgriff auf Taillenhöhe haptisch angenehm und strapazierfähig. Die sich im Winkel von 90 Grad öffnenden Türen bieten komfortablen Zugriff auf das Innere und ermöglichen es gleichzeitig, den Kühlschrank direkt neben einer Wand aufzustellen. Trocken- und Feuchtzonen-Schubfächer haben einen Selbsteinzug, was die Handhabung komfortabel macht.

Statement by the jury
The REF-549 gains merit with a body construction which takes up little space, so that the volume of the fridge interior can be maximised.

Begründung der Jury
Der REF-549 punktet mit einer sehr wenig Platz in Anspruch nehmenden Korpuskonstruktion, durch die das Volumen des Kühlschrankinnenraums maximiert werden konnte.

REF-506
Refrigerator
Kühlschrank

Manufacturer
Haier Group, Qingdao, China
Design
Haier Innovation Design Center (Sui Xinyuan, Jiang Chunhui, Li Xia, Wang Zhenhao, Zhang Xiaoyue, Hu Minhui), Qingdao, China
Web
www.haier.com

This product is an innovative refrigerator with French 4-door operation, whereby the entire interior has a special fresh-holding function. Separate compartments offer high storage capacity; dry and humid zone drawers are self-closing and preserve foods particularly effectively. The especially wide construction of the air inlet at the back prevents direct airflow to the cooled items and keeps them fresh for longer.

Dieses Produkt ist ein innovativer viertüriger French-Door-Kühlschrank, bei dem der gesamte Innenraum eine besondere Frischhaltefunktion erfüllt. Separierte Fächer bieten eine hohe Lagerkapazität, Trocken- und Feuchtzonen-Schubladen sind selbstschließend und konservieren mithilfe passiver Sauerstoffkontrolle Lebensmittel besonders effektiv. Die breite Konstruktion der Luftzufuhr an der Rückwand verhindert, dass das Kühlgut direktem Luftzug ausgesetzt ist, und hält es so länger frisch.

Statement by the jury
Thanks to its sophisticated functionality and the division in various cooling zones, food in this refrigerator is stored with special care.

Begründung der Jury
Dank seiner ausgefeilten Funktionalität und der Unterteilung in verschiedene Klimazonen lagern Lebensmittel in diesem Kühlschrank besonders schonend.

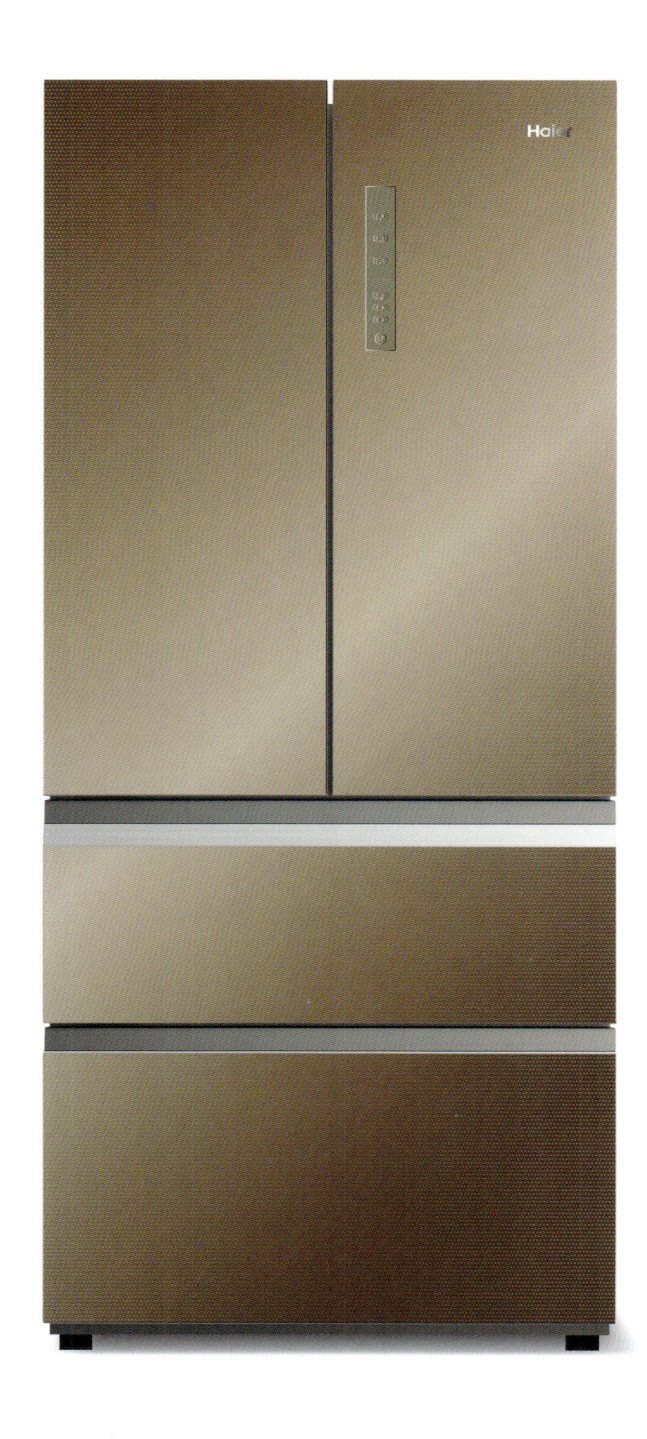

CHiQ BCD-482WQ3M
Fridge-Freezer
Kühl-Gefrier-Kombination

Manufacturer
Changhong Meiling Co., Ltd., Hefei, China
In-house design
Design
Homwee Technology (Sichuan) Co., Ltd., Chengdu, China
Web
www.meiling.com
www.changhong.com

Its thin-wall technology makes this fridge-freezer combination stand out: the walls of the box body show a thickness of merely 39 mm, while the doors are just 45 mm thick. The insulating foam layer is 30 percent thinner than in usual fridges, meaning that the space utilisation rate is increased by 15 per cent. An innovative preservation technology extends the storage time by reducing enzyme activity; it also limits damage to the cell membrane.

Statement by the jury
This fridge-freezer features an innovative construction with thin-walled housing, resulting in a considerable increase of the interior space.

Das Besondere an dieser Kühl-Gefrier-Kombination ist ihre Konstruktion mit einem extrem dünnwandigen Korpus (39 mm) und Türen, die eine Stärke von nur 45 mm aufweisen. Die Dicke der Isolierschaumschicht ist 30 Prozent geringer als bei üblichen Kühlschränken, wodurch sich die Nutzfläche um 15 Prozent vergrößert. Eine innovative Konservierungstechnologie verlängert den Lagerzeitraum durch eine Verminderung der Enzymaktivität; auch Beschädigungen der Zellmembran wird vorgebeugt.

Begründung der Jury
Eine innovative Konstruktion mit geringerer Gehäusedicke mündet bei dieser Kühl-Gefrier-Kombination in ein größeres Platzangebot im Innenraum.

CHiQ BCD-656WQ3M
Fridge-Freezer
Kühl-Gefrier-Kombination

Manufacturer
Changhong Meiling Co., Ltd., Hefei, China
In-house design
Design
Homwee Technology (Sichuan) Co., Ltd., Chengdu, China
Web
www.meiling.com
www.changhong.com

This fridge-freezer with its innovative six-door design combines a French-door fridge above with two cooling drawers in the middle and a French-door freezer below. Thus, it offers three zones whose temperature can be controlled variably and independently from each other. Doors and body are particularly thin, having a thickness of 45 and 39 mm respectively, maximising the space in the interior. Storage boxes and drawers structure the interior in a sensible way.

Statement by the jury
The double-French-door construction of the fridge-freezer makes access to the cooled contents extremely convenient. The interior is generous and well organised.

Diese Kühl-Gefrier-Kombination mit einem innovativen Sechs-Tür-Design kombiniert einen French-Door-Kühlschrank oben mit zwei Kälteschubladen in der Mitte und einem French-Door-Gefrierschrank unten. Damit bietet sie drei unabhängig voneinander variabel temperierbare Zonen. Türen und Korpus sind mit einer Dicke von 45 bzw. 39 mm besonders dünn, was die Fläche im Innenraum maximiert. Aufbewahrungsboxen und Einschübe strukturieren das Innere sinnvoll.

Begründung der Jury
Die Doppel-French-Door-Bauweise dieser Kühl-Gefrier-Kombination macht den Zugang zum Kühlgut äußerst komfortabel. Die Innenraumgestaltung ist großzügig und übersichtlich.

CHiQ BCD-681WQ3S
Fridge-Freezer
Kühl-Gefrier-Kombination

Manufacturer
Changhong Meiling Co., Ltd., Hefei, China
In-house design
Design
Homwee Technology (Sichuan) Co., Ltd., Chengdu, China
Web
www.meiling.com
www.changhong.com

Thanks to its particularly thin-walled body, this four-door fridge-freezer offers four spacious compartments. These compartments are each divided in order to meet the requirements of the user and to facilitate professional storage of various foods. Organising elements such as a closed storage box for prepared food or a storage box and roomy vegetable compartment with integrated temperature control further contribute to the user-friendliness of the appliance.

Statement by the jury
A very well-considered organisation of the interior with a great deal of accessories for storage of particular food categories characterise this four-door fridge-freezer.

Diese viertürige Kühl-Gefrier-Kombination bietet durch einen besonders dünnwandig gestalteten Korpus vier große Räume. Diese Räume sind ihrerseits so unterteilt, dass sie den Bedürfnissen des Benutzers gerecht werden und eine professionelle Lagerung unterschiedlicher Lebensmittel ermöglichen. Dafür wurden Organisationselemente wie eine geschlossene Aufbewahrungsbox für zubereitete Nahrung oder eine Aufbewahrungsbox und ein geräumiges Gemüsefach mit Temperaturregelung integriert.

Begründung der Jury
Eine sehr durchdachte Organisation des Innenraums mit viel Zubehör zur Lagerung spezieller Lebensmittelgruppen zeichnet diese viertürige Kühl-Gefrier-Kombination aus.

BC/BD-200WEGU1
Freezer
Gefriertruhe

Manufacturer
Haier Group, Qingdao, China
Design
Haier Innovation Design Center (Jiang Xiaoxia, Sun Ke, Wan Lulu, Jiang Chunhui, Yu Dong, Xie Yugang), Qingdao, China
Web
www.haier.com

This freezer of full-colour crystal glass uses a four-dimensional air-cooling technology and thus solves the problem of ice formation. A waterfall air supply combines the air-cooled, frost-free technology with a 360-degree air supply, freezes evenly with a large volume of air, locks up the cell moisture quickly and assures freezing and preservation at cell level. An antibacterial coating ensures hygienic storage. Blue light in the area of the stable aluminium handles indicates the high cooling power.

Diese Gefriertruhe aus vollfarbigem Kristallglas nutzt eine vierdimensionale Luftkühltechnik und löst damit das Problem der Eisbildung. Eine Wasserfall-Luftversorgung kombiniert die luftgekühlte, frostfreie Technologie mit einer 360-Grad-Luftzufuhr, friert bei großem Luftvolumen gleichmäßig ein, schließt die Zellfeuchtigkeit schnell ein und sorgt für Gefrieren und Konservieren auf Zellebene. Eine antibakterielle Beschichtung stellt die hygienische Lagerung sicher. Blaues Licht im Bereich der stabilen Aluminiumgriffe kommuniziert die hohe Kühlleistung.

Statement by the jury
The clear, practical appearance and the blue illumination visualise the high efficiency of this freezer. By including new technology, it becomes very functional.

Begründung der Jury
Das klare, sachliche Erscheinungsbild und eine blaue Beleuchtung visualisieren bei dieser Kühltruhe ihre hohe Effizienz. Durch die Einbindung neuer Technologien ist sie sehr funktional.

REF-405
Refrigerator
Kühlschrank

Manufacturer
Haier Group, Qingdao, China
Design
Haier Innovation Design Center (Cheng Yongli, Jiang Chunhui, Huang Zeping, Gao Rongna, Huang Yi), Qingdao, China
Web
www.haier.com

The appearance of this four-door refrigerator is characterised by an aluminium frame construction with rounded corners and edges. The rounded edges are the result of a special aluminium bending process. Thanks to laser ink printing, the pattern on the bright glass seems to change colour when seen from different angles and impart to the refrigerator its distinctive appearance. The interior space stretches across the entire fridge width; two differing, separate drawer types in the freezing chamber make organisation of the food items easy and prevent odours from mixing.

Das Erscheinungsbild dieses viertürigen Kühlschranks ist durch eine Aluminiumrahmenkonstruktion mit abgerundeten Ecken und Kanten geprägt. Letztere wurden durch ein spezielles Aluminiumbiegeverfahren ermöglicht und verleihen dem Kühlschrank in Kombination mit der hellen, changierenden Glasfront sein markantes Aussehen. Der Innenraum zieht sich über die gesamte Kühlschrankbreite. Zwei unterschiedliche, separierte Schubladentypen im Gefrierfach erleichtern die Organisation des Kühlguts und verhindern eine Geruchsvermischung.

Statement by the jury
With gentle lines, well-balanced proportions and an unusual colour, this refrigerator looks very harmonic. Its interior convinces with its highly functional divisions.

Begründung der Jury
Mit sanften Linien, ausgewogenen Proportionen und seiner ungewöhnlichen Farbgebung vermittelt dieser Kühlschrank Ruhe und Harmonie. Im Inneren überzeugt er mit seiner hochfunktionalen Aufteilung.

Ice Bar LC-258WU1
Kühlschrank

Manufacturer
Haier Group, Qingdao, China
Design
Haier Innovation Design Center (Wang Shupeng, Yu Zhaoting, Wan Lulu, Jiang Chunhui, Sun Ke, Yan Hongyan, Wu Xiaoli, Chen Jun), Qingdao, China
Web
www.haier.com

This refrigerator was designed for standing in the living room. It has three separate zones. The top serves to store shared items such as fruit, snacks or drinks; the middle section offers space for various bar utensils. In the lower section, which can be used for private storage, there are several drawers with their own temperature and humidity controls to store, for example, tea or wine. A 360-degree air curtain inside reduces air change, so that fast and even cooling is assured. The functions can also be controlled via app, thanks to a Wi-Fi module.

Dieser Kühlschrank wurde speziell für das Wohnzimmer konzipiert. Er hat drei voneinander getrennte Bereiche. Der obere dient der Aufbewahrung gemeinsam genutzter Lebensmittel wie Obst, Snacks oder Getränken; der mittlere bietet Platz für verschiedene Barutensilien. Im unteren Bereich, der als privater Stauraum genutzt werden kann, gibt es mehrere Schubladen mit unabhängiger Temperatur- und Luftfeuchtigkeitskontrolle, etwa für die Lagerung von Tee oder Wein. Ein 360-Grad-Luftschleier im Inneren reduziert den Luftaustausch, sodass eine schnelle und gleichmäßige Kühlung erreicht wird. Eine Steuerung der Funktionen ist dank WiFi-Moduls auch per App möglich.

Statement by the jury
A linear, clear appearance characterises this multifunctional fridge, which provides various cooling zones and is thus flexible in use.

Begründung der Jury
Ein sehr geradliniges, klares Erscheinungsbild zeichnet dieses multifunktionale Kühlgerät aus, das verschiedene Kühlzonen beherbergt und damit flexibel nutzbar ist.

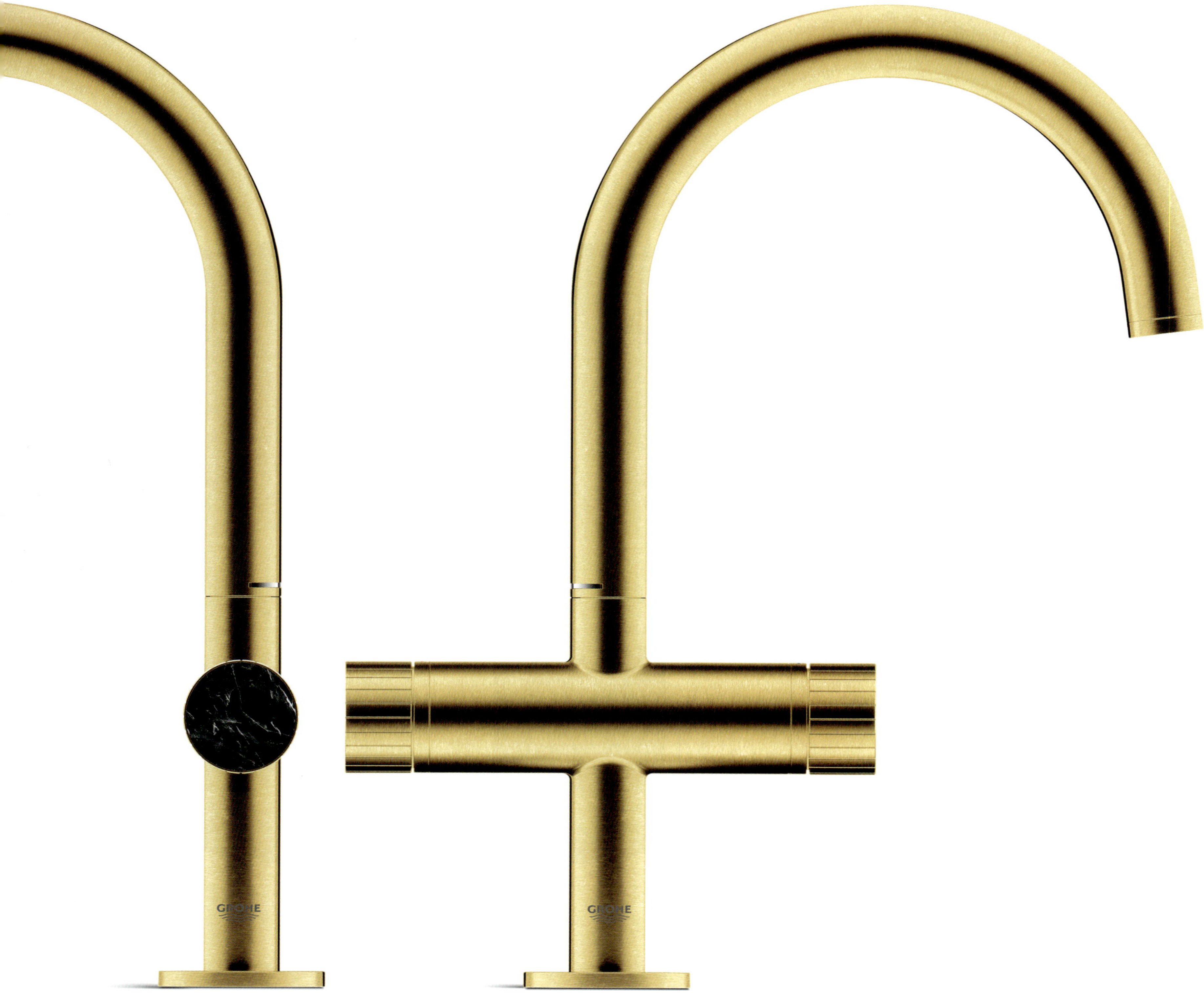
GROHE
GROHE

Bathrooms and sanitary equipm
Bad und Sanitär

Bathroom furniture
Basin mixers
Bathroom series
Shower heads
Shower systems
Showers
Single lever mixers
Toilets and accessories
Two-handle fittings
Wash basins

Badmöbel
Badserien
Duschen
Duschköpfe
Duschsysteme
Einhebelmischer
Waschtischbatterien
Waschtische
WCs und WC-Zubehör
Zweigriffarmaturen

Ruy Ohtake by Roca
Washbasin
Waschtisch

Manufacturer
Roca Brasil,
Jundiaí, Brazil

Design
Ruy Ohtake,
São Paulo, Brazil

Web
www.br.roca.com

reddot award 2019
best of the best

Designing the unexpected
Nature is abundant in shapes and patterns that are fascinating in their simplicity and perfection. The design of the Ruy Ohtake by Roca collection is inspired by such phenomena as the curved lines of waves, the ever-changing line of the horizon, as well as one of the purest forms, the egg. "I really like the curved element because it's harder than a straight line," the designer and architect Ruy Ohtake reflects about his design. He chose the shape of the curve, because it is not fixed in its course; rather, it is unpredictable and can be perceived differently by various observers depending on their viewing angle. Specifically, the design of this collection is also aimed at embodying the complex sensations and intimacy that every person associates with a washbasin in daily use: in the morning, people go to the bathroom, wash their hands, wash their face and brush their teeth, starting the day thinking about what they did yesterday or what they are going to do today. "These minutes are very beautiful and important," the designer says. And therefore, the washbasin has to be appealing and designed to be something special. Moreover, the subtle design also reflects the basic function of a washbasin, namely to collect the water. The guiding design principle here has been the relationship that the water has to the edge of the basin – leading to a curved edge of soft and elegant appearance.

Gestaltung des Unvorhersehbaren
In der Natur finden sich Formen und Linien, die durch ihre Einfachheit und Perfektion faszinieren. Die Kollektion Ruy Ohtake by Roca wurde in ihrer Gestaltung von solchen Phänomenen, wie der Kurvenform der Wellen, der sich stetig verändernden Linie des Horizonts und einer der reinsten Formen, dem Ei, inspiriert. „Ich mag eben das geschwungene Element, weil es schwieriger ist als eine gerade Linie", stellt der Designer und Architekt Ruy Ohtake zu seinem Entwurf fest. Er wählte die Form der Kurve, weil diese in ihrem Verlauf nicht festgelegt, unvorhersehbar ist und beim Betrachter je nach Perspektive unterschiedlich wahrgenommen werden kann. Die Gestaltung dieser Kollektion sollte außerdem die komplexen Empfindungen und die Intimität verkörpern, die jeder Mensch täglich mit dem Waschtisch verbindet. Man geht morgens ins Badezimmer, wäscht sich die Hände, das Gesicht, putzt sich die Zähne und beginnt den Tag damit, darüber nachzudenken, was man gestern gemacht hat oder an diesem neuen Tag gleich tun wird. „Diese Minuten sind sehr schön und wichtig", so Ruy Ohtake, und gerade deshalb muss der Waschtisch ansprechend gestaltet und etwas Besonderes sein. Die feinsinnige Formgebung spiegelt auch die zentrale funktionale Aufgabe wider, das Wasser zu versammeln. Gestaltungsleitend war dabei die Beziehung, die das Wasser zum Beckenrand hat – die wellenförmige Kante ist entsprechend weich und elegant ausgeführt.

Statement by the jury
Exploring the possibilities of form, Ruy Ohtake by Roca has emerged as a refreshingly different washbasin. His filigree ceramic bowl fascinates with its organically curved, sensual-looking silhouette – technology, functionality and aesthetics come together in a symbiotic way. The design impressively uses the form here to visualise the fragile lightness of the material.

Begründung der Jury
Die Möglichkeiten der Form auslotend, entstand mit Ruy Ohtake by Roca ein erfrischend andersartiger Waschtisch. Seine filigrane Keramikschale fasziniert mit ihrer organisch geschwungenen, sinnlich anmutenden Silhouette. Technologie, Funktionalität und Ästhetik vereinen sich auf symbiotische Weise miteinander. Eindrucksvoll nutzt Design hier die Form, um die fragile Leichtigkeit des Materials zu visualisieren.

Designer portrait
See page 54
Siehe Seite 54

WATERFOIL
All in one LAV for public bathroom
All-in-one-Waschtisch für öffentliche Toiletten

Manufacturer
Kohler Company
In-house design
Kohler Design Studio
Web
www.kohler.com

WATERFOIL is a technically sophisticated solution for hand washing in public places. Faucet, soap dispenser and dryer are fully integrated into the basin. The entire washing process takes place within the washbasin bowl, keeping the immediate environment clean and dry. The organic shape and the water outlet, which is inspired by water flowing in nature, give users the sensation of dipping their hands into a river for cleaning. The operation is intuitive, thanks to a user interface with self-explanatory icons subtly embedded in the edge.

Statement by the jury
The WATERFOIL washbasin takes hand cleaning in public spaces to a higher level, combining contemporary technology with restrained aesthetics.

WATERFOIL ist eine technisch ausgereifte Lösung für die Handreinigung in öffentlichen Räumen. Wasserhahn, Seifenspender und Trockner sind vollständig in das Becken integriert. Der gesamte Waschvorgang findet unterhalb der Waschtischoberfläche statt, sodass die unmittelbare Umgebung sauber und trocken bleibt. Die organische Form und der von natürlichen Wasserläufen inspirierte Wasseraustritt vermitteln dem Nutzer das Gefühl, die Hände zur Reinigung in einen Fluss zu tauchen. Die Bedienung erfolgt intuitiv über eine dezent im Rand eingelassene Benutzeroberfläche mit selbsterklärenden Icons.

Begründung der Jury
Der Waschtisch WATERFOIL hebt die Handreinigung in öffentlichen Räumen auf ein höheres Niveau, indem er zeitgemäße Technologie mit zurückhaltender Ästhetik verbindet.

BetteCraft
Washbasin
Waschtisch

Manufacturer
Bette GmbH & Co. KG, Delbrück, Germany
Design
Produktdesign Tesseraux+Partner, Potsdam, Germany
Web
www.bette.de
www.tesserauxundpartner.de

The BetteCraft washbasin combines clear lines and a filigree design language with solid materials. The basin made of titanium steel is handcrafted and glazed in an elaborate process. Its thin walls taper towards the top, lending the generous shape a delicate and organic appearance. The washbasin bowl can be freely placed on consoles or support plates, permitting flexible combinations and individual bathroom arrangements, regardless of conventional standard dimensions.

Statement by the jury
The contrast of solid material and filigree shapes has been skilfully merged into a high-quality washbasin bowl of aesthetic appeal that can complement different bathroom facilities.

Der Waschtisch BetteCraft verbindet eine klare Linienführung und filigrane Formensprache mit solider Materialität. Die Schale besteht aus Titanstahl und wird in einem aufwendigen Verfahren handgefertigt und glasiert. Ihre dünnen Wände verjüngen sich nach oben hin. Der großzügigen Form verleiht das eine organische und zarte Anmutung. Die Waschtisch-Schale kann frei auf Konsolen oder Trägerplatten platziert werden, was unabhängig von gängigen Standardmaßen flexible Kombinationen und eine individuelle Badgestaltung möglich macht.

Begründung der Jury
Der Gegensatz von filigranen Formen und solidem Material vereint sich ästhetisch gekonnt zu einer hochwertigen Waschtisch-Schale, die unterschiedliche Badeinrichtungen ergänzen kann.

Amelie
Washbasin
Waschtisch

Manufacturer
Eumar Santehnika OÜ, Tallinn, Estonia
In-house design
Arkadi Berman
Web
www.eumardesign.com

The Amelie washbasin harmoniously balances straight lines and gently rounded forms. Slightly rounded edges lend the rectangular basic shape a softer appearance, while the drain is almost invisibly integrated into the basin. The raised rim prevents water from spilling over. Visually separated from the wet area, the slightly lowered centre console provides a generous shelf surface for toiletries or accessories. Towel openings that harmoniously blend into the design concept can be optionally added.

Statement by the jury
The Amelie washbasin impresses with a well-balanced interplay of angular and round shapes, as well as high practicability.

Der Waschtisch Amelie bringt gerade Linien und sanfte Rundungen harmonisch in Einklang. Leicht abgerundete Kanten verleihen der rechteckig gehaltenen Grundform eine weiche Anmutung und der Abfluss ist nahezu unsichtbar in das Becken integriert. Der hochgezogene Rand verhindert das Überlaufen von Wasser. Optisch vom Nassbereich getrennt, gibt die etwas abgesenkte Abstellfläche Accessoires und Toilettenartikeln ausreichend Raum. Optional können Handtuchöffnungen ergänzt werden, die sich stimmig in das Gestaltungskonzept einfügen.

Begründung der Jury
Der Waschtisch Amelie beeindruckt mit einem ausgewogenen Zusammenspiel eckiger und runder Formen sowie hoher Praktikabilität.

Collaro
Surface-Mounted Washbasins
Aufsatzwaschtische

Manufacturer
Villeroy & Boch AG, Mettlach, Germany
Design
volume3 design (Bernd Schriefer), Stuttgart, Germany
Web
www.villeroy-boch.com
www.volume3-design.de

The basic concept of the Collaro surface-mounted washbasins is based on four geometric shapes combined to form two variants. The TitanCeram models are available in an oval shape with a round inner basin or as a rectangular version with a square inner basin. The recessed tap bench features a slim edging, offering splash and anti-slip protection. In addition to the glossy white finish, the surfaces are also available in matt Stone White.

Statement by the jury
Collaro stands out with a sophisticated interplay of geometric shapes, which make for two stylish models of self-sufficient appearance.

Das Grundkonzept der Aufsatzwaschtische Collaro basiert auf vier geometrischen Formen, die in zwei Varianten zusammengeführt werden. Die aus TitanCeram gefertigten Modelle gibt es in ovaler Form mit rundem Innenbecken oder als rechteckige Version mit quadratischer Innenvariante. Eine abgesenkte Hahnlochbank fungiert jeweils als Spritz- und Anti-Rutsch-Schutz und geht in eine schmale Umrandung über. Die Oberflächen sind in glänzendem Weiß gehalten, aber auch in mattem Stone White erhältlich.

Begründung der Jury
Collaro besticht mit dem raffinierten Spiel geometrischer Formen, das zwei stilvolle Varianten mit eigenständigem Erscheinungsbild entstehen lässt.

Geberit ONE
Complete Bathroom Solution
Komplettbadlösung

Manufacturer
Geberit International AG, Jona, Switzerland
Design
Christoph Behling Design Ltd.,
London, United Kingdom
Web
www.geberit.com

The Geberit ONE bathroom solution uses the advantages of pre-wall installation. Technical components are integrated into the wall, allowing the design to take centre stage. The timeless appearance harmonises with different styles, while at the same time reducing the cleaning effort. The toilet features TurboFlush technology. Seat ring and lid can be easily removed and cleaned separately. The wall-mounted fittings are precisely tailored to match the inner geometry of the washbasins, ensuring that the entire washbasin is rinsed clean.

Die Badlösung Geberit ONE nutzt die Vorteile der Vorwandinstallation. Technische Komponenten werden in die Wand integriert, das Design rückt in den Fokus. Die zeitlose Optik harmoniert mit unterschiedlichen Stilen und sorgt zugleich für einen reduzierten Reinigungsaufwand. Das WC verfügt über eine TurboFlush-Spülung, Sitzring und Deckel lassen sich zudem leicht entfernen und separat säubern. Die in der Wand angebrachten Armaturen sind exakt auf die Innengeometrie der Waschtische abgestimmt, sodass die Becken vollständig ausgespült werden.

Statement by the jury
Geberit ONE impressively translates complex sanitary technology and timeless design into comprehensive, user-oriented solutions for the modern bathroom.

Begründung der Jury
Eindrucksvoll überführt Geberit ONE komplexe Sanitärtechnik und zeitloses Design in umfassende, nutzerorientierte Lösungen für das moderne Bad.

source
Bathroom Furniture Collection
Badezimmer-Kollektion

Manufacturer
talsee AG, Hochdorf, Switzerland
In-house design
Mark Wunderlin
Design
tale Designstudio GmbH, Münchenstein/Basel, Switzerland
Web
www.talsee.ch
www.tale.ch

The concept of the "source" collection has been inspired by nature: the bathroom furniture also responds to external conditions and, in interaction with them, develops an individual character. The sculptural, straightforwardly designed elements introduce structure and order into the bathroom design. Versatile in combination, they emerge as shelves, steps and seating surfaces. Protrusions, slight recesses and partially open mirror cabinets all create space for personal accessories, decorative items or plants.

Bei der Konzeption der Kollektion source stand die Natur Pate: Auch die Badmöbel richten sich nach den äußeren Gegebenheiten und entwickeln im Zusammenspiel mit diesen ihren individuellen Charakter. Die skulptural anmutenden, schnörkellos gestalteten Elemente bringen Struktur und Ordnung in die Badgestaltung. Vielseitig kombinierbar, fügen sie sich zu Ablagen, Stufen und Sitzflächen zusammen. Vorsprünge, leichte Vertiefungen und zum Teil offen gestaltete Spiegelschränke schaffen Platz für persönliche Accessoires, Dekoratives und Pflanzen.

Statement by the jury
The "source" bathroom collection has been consistently modelled on the adaptability of nature. With its timeless and functionally-oriented design, it offers a harmonious solution for modern bathrooms.

Begründung der Jury
Die Anpassungsfähigkeit der Natur greift die Badezimmer-Kollektion source konsequent auf. Mit der zeitlosen und auf Funktionalität ausgerichteten Gestaltung bietet sie eine harmonische Lösung für das moderne Bad.

VIGOUR vogue asymmetric bathtub
Bathtub
Badewanne

Manufacturer
VIGOUR GmbH, Berlin, Germany
Design
Michael Stein Design, Velbert, Germany
Web
www.vigour.de
www.michaelsteindesign.de

With its asymmetric design, the Vigour vogue free-standing bathtub brings a new aesthetic to the bathroom while also considering functional aspects. Expanding towards the top, the body provides sufficient space for two people, while keeping the necessary amount of water and the space required in the bathroom as low as possible. The bathtub is composed of two acrylic parts to form a homogeneous unit. It features soft surfaces and gently rounded edges that not only project a sense of elegant lightness, but also meet the users' need for ergonomics. Weight was reduced using a hollow shell construction.

Mit ihrer asymmetrischen Gestaltung bringt die frei stehende Wanne aus der Designlinie vogue von Vigour eine neue Ästhetik ins Bad und berücksichtigt zugleich funktionale Aspekte. Der sich nach oben erweiternde Korpus bietet ausreichend Platz für zwei Personen, gleichzeitig werden die benötigte Wassermenge und der Platzbedarf im Bad so gering wie möglich gehalten. Weiche Flächen und sanft abgerundete Kanten verleihen der aus zwei Acrylteilen homogen zusammengefügten Badewanne eine elegante Leichtigkeit und kommen dem Bedürfnis der Nutzer nach Ergonomie entgegen. Hohlkammern in ihrem Inneren reduzieren das Gewicht.

Statement by the jury
The Vigour vogue bathtub convinces with an elegant appearance. Its soft shapes and gentle curves ensure a comfortable and ergonomic lying position.

Begründung der Jury
Die Badewanne aus der Designlinie vogue von Vigour überzeugt durch ein elegantes Erscheinungsbild. Ihre weichen Formen und die sanfte Kurvenführung gewährleisten ein ergonomisches, bequemes Liegen.

XSquare
Bathroom furniture series
Badmöbelserie

Manufacturer
Duravit AG, Hornberg, Germany
Design
studio KMJ GmbH, Zürich, Switzerland
Web
www.duravit.de
www.kurtmerkijr.com

The XSquare bathroom furniture is attuned in style and design to the contemporary DuraSquare washbasins. The defining feature of the series is a quarter-circle chrome profile, framing the furniture elements on the sides and lending them a distinctive autonomy. In the floor-standing model, the accentuated frame seamlessly transitions into the base frame. XSquare is focused on furnishing bathrooms with a holistic approach: in combination with bathtubs, toilets and fittings, the range offers high-quality furnishing solutions for an elegant ambience.

Die Badmöbel XSquare sind in Stil und Design auf die modernen DuraSquare-Waschtische abgestimmt. Prägendes Gestaltungsmerkmal der Serie ist ein Viertelkreisprofil in Chrom, das die Möbelelemente seitlich einrahmt und ihnen markante Eigenständigkeit verleiht. Bei der bodenstehenden Variante geht der akzentuierte Rahmen nahtlos in das Fußgestell über. XSquare ist auf die ganzheitliche Ausstattung von Bädern ausgerichtet: In Kombination mit Wannen, WCs und Armaturen bietet die Serie hochwertige Einrichtungslösungen für ein elegantes Ambiente.

Statement by the jury
The XSquare bathroom furniture series inspires with a pronounced sense of style. Versatile combinations open up additional scope for creativity in planning and design.

Begründung der Jury
Die Badmöbelserie XSquare begeistert mit ausgeprägtem Stilbewusstsein. Vielseitige Kombinationen eröffnen der planerischen Kreativität zusätzliche Spielräume.

Solo
Bathtub and Washbasin
Badewanne und Waschbecken

Manufacturer
RAVAK a.s., Pribram, Czech Republic
Design
Nosal Design Studio (Kryštof Nosál), Cernosice, Czech Republic
Web
www.ravak.com
www.nosaldesign.cz

The Solo free-standing bathtub dominates bathrooms with its minimalist, yet distinctive design. The rectangular base expands into a generous oval tub body. This effective interplay of forms lends it visual independence and achieves volume, while also ensuring the stable stand of the bathtub. The corresponding washbasin is made of cast marble and continues the sovereign style of the series on a small scale. In this way, both elements form an aesthetically balanced unit.

Die frei stehende Badewanne Solo dominiert das Bad mit ihrem minimalistischen und zugleich einprägsamen Design. Die rechteckige Grundfläche erweitert sich zu einem großzügigen ovalen Wannenkörper. Dieses wirkungsvolle Formenspiel kreiert visuelle Unabhängigkeit, schafft Volumen und sorgt zudem für den stabilen Stand der Wanne. Das zugehörige Waschbecken ist aus Gussmarmor gefertigt und greift den souveränen Stil der Serie im Kleinen schlüssig auf. Auf diese Weise bilden beide Elemente eine ästhetisch ausbalancierte Einheit.

Statement by the jury
The Solo series effectively combines rectangular and oval shapes. The characteristic design of the bathtub and washbasin succeeds in setting modern accents in the bathroom.

Begründung der Jury
Rechteckige und ovale Formen werden in der Serie Solo wirkungsvoll zusammengeführt. Die charakteristische Gestaltung von Wanne und Waschbecken setzt moderne Akzente im Bad.

SX I AX Series I Shower Enclosure
Shower Enclosure
Duschkabine

Manufacturer
Blue Sanitary Ware, Foshan, China
In-house Design
Blue Sanitary Design Team Germany
(Prof. Günter Horntrich), Cologne, Germany
Web
www.bluesanitary.com

The SX I AX Series I shower enclosure combines a filigree form language with high functionality. It features a characteristic matte black frame with fittings and profiles that are unobtrusively integrated into the design. A magnetic bar concealed in the door frame closes the shower unit precisely and securely, while the flush-mounted connections contribute to easy cleaning. The handle reaches almost to the floor, effectively continuing the formal appearance.

Statement by the jury
The shower enclosure impresses with a modern, consistent design that places great importance on user-friendliness.

Die Duschkabine SX I AX Series I Shower Enclosure vereint eine filigrane Formensprache mit hoher Funktionalität. Charakteristisches Merkmal ist der in mattem Schwarz gehaltene Rahmen, dessen Beschläge und Profile unaufdringlich in die Gestaltung integriert sind. Eine im Türrahmen verborgene Magnetleiste verschließt die Duschkabine sicher und passgenau, die flächenbündigen Anschlüsse schaffen zudem gute Voraussetzungen für eine einfache Reinigung. Der Handgriff reicht nahezu bis zum Boden und führt das formale Erscheinungsbild wirkungsvoll weiter.

Begründung der Jury
Die Duschkabine besticht mit einer modernen, stringenten Formgebung, die hohen Wert auf Benutzerfreundlichkeit legt.

DN Series I Comfort Close
Shower Enclosure
Duschkabine

Manufacturer
Blue Sanitary Ware, Foshan, China
In-house Design
Blue Sanitary Design Team Germany
(Prof. Günter Horntrich), Cologne, Germany
Web
www.bluesanitary.com

Clear lines and a focus on the essential characterise the shower enclosure of the DN Series I Comfort Close shower enclosure. The slim profile frame lends it a distinctive lightness. The hinge embedded in the frame, as well as a stabiliser bar, support the static equilibrium of the construction. No handle is necessary to open the shower enclosure, since the glass door protrudes slightly and can be easily grasped and moved. A patented mechanism controls the smooth closing of the door with the aid of a gas-pressure spring.

Statement by the jury
The sophisticated locking system of the shower enclosure forms the basis of a memorable, handleless design that offers added value in terms of aesthetics and functionality.

Eine klare Linienführung und die Konzentration auf das Wesentliche prägen die Duschkabine der DN Serie I Comfort Close. Der dünne Profilrahmen verleiht ihr eine auffällige Leichtigkeit. Dabei unterstützt das im Rahmen verbaute Scharnier ebenso wie die Stabilisierungsstange die Statik der Konstruktion. Zum Öffnen der Duschkabine ist kein Griff notwendig, denn die Glastür steht leicht über und lässt sich gut greifen und bewegen. Ein patentierter Mechanismus steuert mithilfe einer Gasdruckfeder das sanft-kontrollierte Schließen der Tür.

Begründung der Jury
Das ausgeklügelte Schließsystem der Duschkabine ist Basis einer einprägsamen, grifflosen Gestaltung, die einen ästhetischen und funktionalen Mehrwert bietet.

Visign for More 201
Push Plate
WC-Betätigungsplatte

Manufacturer
Viega Supply Chain GmbH & Co. KG,
Attendorn, Germany
Design
ARTEFAKT design, Darmstadt, Germany
Web
www.viega.de
www.artefakt.de

Flowing lines characterise the design of this toilet push plate. As if from a sheet of paper, the two flush keys rise from the flat surface of the activation plate and run towards each other. Visign for More 201 has been cut from thin stainless steel, stamped and bent, offering a visual, as well as tactile experience. At night, a subtly integrated lighting provides orientation and facilitates flushing. The surface is available in the three finishes of brushed stainless steel, as well as white or black grey lacquered.

Statement by the jury
The Visign for More 201 toilet push plate convinces with a high-quality appearance that is both outstanding and timeless in its aesthetic appeal.

Fließende Linien charakterisieren die Gestaltung dieser WC-Betätigungsplatte. Wie aus einem Blatt Papier erheben sich die federnden Spültasten aus der flachen Platte und laufen aufeinander zu. Aus dünnem Edelstahl gestanzt, geprägt und gebogen, bietet Visign for More 201 ein visuelles und zugleich haptisches Erlebnis. In der Nacht sorgt eine dezent integrierte Beleuchtung für Orientierung und erleichtert die Benutzung der Spülung. Die Oberfläche ist in den drei Varianten Edelstahl gebürstet, Weiß und Schwarzgrau lackiert verfügbar.

Begründung der Jury
Die WC-Betätigungsplatte Visign for More 201 überzeugt durch ein hochwertiges Erscheinungsbild, das von einer ausgefallenen und zugleich zeitlosen Ästhetik geprägt ist.

Public Line
Bathroom Series
Badserie

Manufacturer
JOMOO Kitchen & Bath Co., Ltd.,
Fujian, China
In-house design
Johann Dück, Yunwei Zhu, Daniel Dirks
Web
www.jomoo.com.cn

The Public Line bathroom series is particularly well-thought-out: the washbasin, toilet and urinal are designed to offer added value to users, cleaning staff and installers alike. The design is simple and straightforward. Thanks to this restrained appearance, the series easily adapts to different public spaces such as schools, train stations and hotels. The flat washbasin mixer in combination with the strikingly deep washbasin prevents water splashes. The water tap features an integrated soap dispenser.

Die Badserie Public Line ist besonders durchdacht: Waschbecken, WC und Urinal sind so konzipiert, dass sie Anwendern, Reinigungspersonal und Installateuren gleichermaßen einen Mehrwert bieten. Die Gestaltung ist schnörkellos und geradlinig gehalten. Dank dieses zurückhaltenden Erscheinungsbildes passt sich die Serie unterschiedlichen öffentlichen Räumen wie Schulen, Bahnhöfen und Hotels an. Der flache Waschtischmischer verhindert in Kombination mit dem auffallend tiefen Waschbecken störende Wasserspritzer. Im Hahn ist ein Seifenspender integriert.

Statement by the jury
The Public Line bathroom series sets new standards in the design of public toilets. An appealing design that combines high user-friendliness and functionality.

Begründung der Jury
Die Badserie Public Line setzt bei der Gestaltung öffentlicher Toiletten neue Maßstäbe. Das attraktive Design geht einher mit hoher Nutzerfreundlichkeit und Funktionalität.

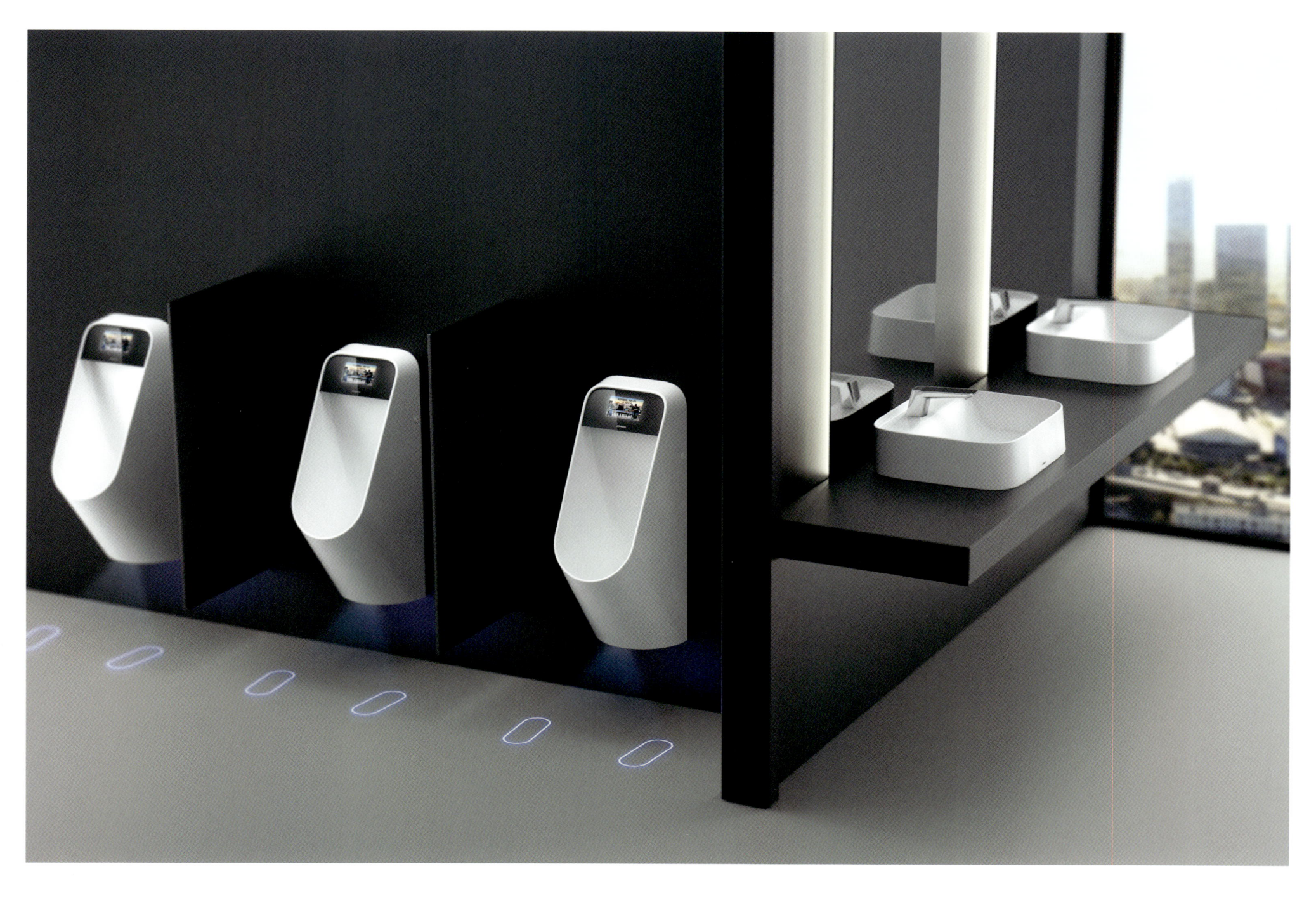

DXV AT200 LS SpaLet Integrated Bidet Toilet
Shower Toilet
Dusch-WC

Manufacturer
DXV, Piscataway, New Jersey, USA
In-house design
Jean-Jacques L'Henaff, Kibok Song
Web
www.dxv.com

Minimalist in design, the AT200 LS SpaLet shower toilet provides a variety of user-friendly functions that are easy to operate via remote control. The two-nozzle water-spray system with integrated air dryer ensures gentle cleansing, while the seat heating provides additional comfort. The Room Refresh deodorizer, which utilizes modern Plasmacluster ion technology, frees the air in the room and the inside of the toilet bowl of unpleasant odours.

Statement by the jury
With modern cleansing functions, the AT200 LS SpaLet shower toilet fullfils high requirements for cleanliness and hygiene. Its simple design is also convincing in terms of aesthetics.

Minimalistisch in der Formgebung, verfügt das Dusch-WC AT200 LS SpaLet über eine Vielzahl nutzerfreundlicher Funktionen, die sich bequem per Fernbedienung steuern lassen. Das zweistrahlige Wassersprühsystem mit integriertem Lufttrockner sorgt für eine sanfte Reinigung, während die Sitzheizung zusätzlichen Komfort ermöglicht. Mithilfe des Room Refresh Deodorizers, der mit moderner Plasmacluster-Ionentechnologie arbeitet, werden die Raumluft sowie das Innere des Toilettenbeckens von störenden Gerüchen befreit.

Begründung der Jury
Mit modernen Reinigungsfunktionen erfüllt das Dusch-WC AT200 LS SpaLet hohe Anforderungen an Sauberkeit und Hygiene. Durch seine schlichte Gestaltung überzeugt es auch in ästhetischer Hinsicht.

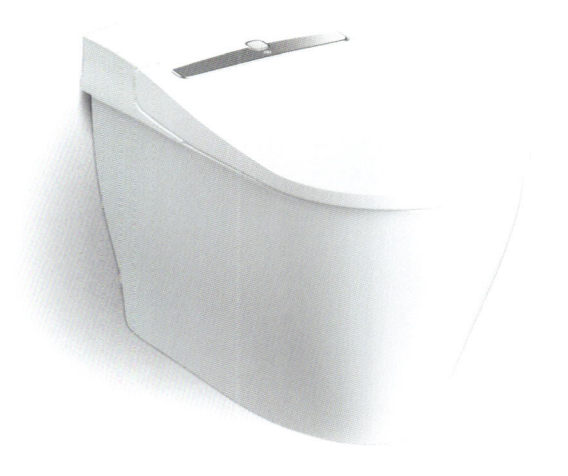

Geberit AquaClean Sela
Shower Toilet
Dusch-WC

Manufacturer
Geberit International AG, Jona, Switzerland
Design
Christoph Behling Design Ltd.,
London, United Kingdom
Web
www.geberit.com

The WC AquaClean Sela shower toilet is characterised by simple, intuitive functions. Its patented WhirlSpray shower technology ensures gentle and thorough cleansing. Thanks to the newly developed continuous flow heater, hot water is instantly available and remains at a constant temperature throughout the entire spray process. The innovative TurboFlush flush technology is based on an asymmetrical rimless WC ceramic appliance which enables the flushing-out process to be particularly thorough and quiet. Another useful feature is the small orientation light that guides users at night.

Statement by the jury
The clear, elegant appearance of the AquaClean Sela shower toilet is paired with innovative technology that meets the highest standards for ease of use and hygiene.

Intuitiv steuerbare Funktionen zeichnen das Dusch-WC AquaClean Sela aus. Seine patentierte WhirlSpray-Duschtechnologie bewirkt eine schonende und gründliche Reinigung. Warmes Wasser steht dank des neu entwickelten Durchlauferhitzers, der die Wassertemperatur die gesamte Nutzungsdauer hindurch konstant hält, schnell zur Verfügung. Die innovative TurboFlush-Spültechnik basiert auf einer asymmetrischen spülrandlosen WC-Keramik, die eine besonders gründliche und leise Ausspülung ermöglicht. Hilfreich ist das kleine Licht, das dem Nutzer nachts Orientierung bietet.

Begründung der Jury
Das klare, elegante Erscheinungsbild des Dusch-WCs AquaClean Sela geht einher mit einer innovativen Technologie, die hohen Ansprüchen an Bedienkomfort und Hygiene gerecht wird.

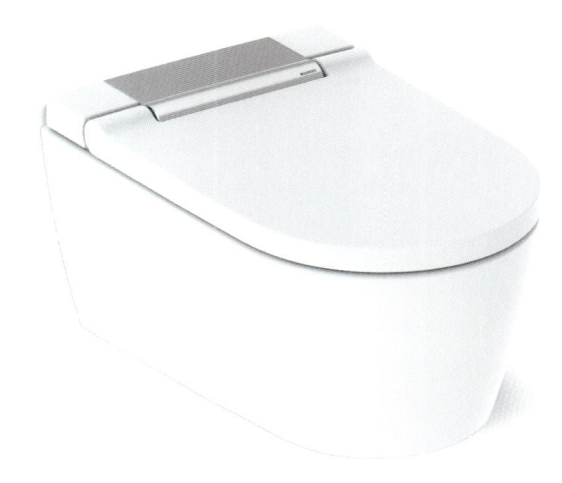

LaPreva P3
Shower Toilet
Dusch-WC

Manufacturer
LaPreva AG, Diepoldsau, Switzerland
Design
Vetica Group, Lucerne, Switzerland
Web
www.lapreva.com
www.vetica-group.com

The LaPreva P3 shower toilet impresses with a design that showcases reduction. Its restrained appearance unobtrusively blends into any bathroom environment. With up to 3.5 litres of water per minute, the integrated shower jet ensures a pleasant feeling of cleanliness. For hygienic reasons, the shower toilet does without a flushing rim. In addition, the automatic descaling function as well as the removable seat and lid unit allow for residue-free cleaning of the shower toilet, which can be operated via a multifunctional button or via the LaPreva app.

Statement by the jury
LaPreva P3 blends a stylish, unobtrusive design with a high level of user-friendliness and practical functions.

Das Dusch-WC LaPreva P3 überzeugt mit einer Gestaltung, die durch Reduktion ins Auge fällt. Seine zurückhaltende Optik fügt sich unaufdringlich in jedes Badambiente ein. Mit bis zu 3,5 Litern Wasser pro Minute sorgt der integrierte Duschstrahl für ein angenehmes Reinheitsgefühl. Auf einen Spülrand wurde aus hygienischen Gründen verzichtet. Zudem ermöglichen die automatische Entkalkungsfunktion sowie die abnehmbare Sitz-Deckel-Einheit eine rückstandslose Reinigung des Dusch-WCs, das sich über einen Multifunktionsknopf oder via LaPreva-App bedienen lässt.

Begründung der Jury
LaPreva P3 kombiniert eine stilvolle, zurückgenomme Formgebung mit hoher Nutzerfreundlichkeit und praktischen Funktionen.

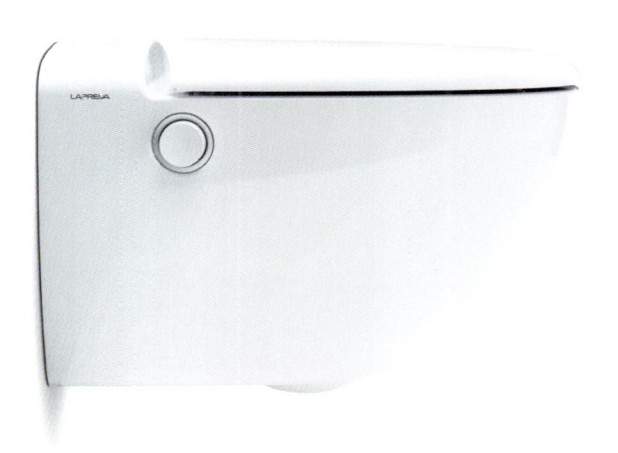

AXOR Edge
Washbasin Tap
Waschtischarmatur

Manufacturer
Hansgrohe SE,
Schiltach, Germany

Design
Studio Massaud
(Jean-Marie Massaud),
Paris, France

Web
www.axor-design.com
www.massaud.com

reddot award 2019
best of the best

Precision of form
The cubic shape, discovered as a formal element by the avant-gardists in the 20th century, has played an important role in both art and design, and it has also been instrumental in the development of AXOR Edge. As a "luxurious symbiosis of geometric bodies and ultra-precision", this collection of basin taps exudes a solid yet at the same time refined appearance. The complex production of the taps makes use of a diamond tool, as commonly used in the laser and aerospace industries, for precision-milling chamfers that meet at an exact angle of 45 degrees. The otherwise smooth and bump-free surfaces facilitate a perfect reflection of light. The highly refined structural details of the fittings are achieved by faceting the surface of solid brass blocks to micrometre precision with the diamond tool. The faceting is done line by line in several steps to create highly precise pyramid shapes that showcase a fascinating play of light and shadow. In addition, these elegant washbasin taps also allow for customisation in different ways, with a huge selection of refined FinishPlus surfaces to choose from. A special PVD (physical vapour deposition) process is used to apply an additional metal layer. This high-tech process lends the surface more resistance and longevity, but above all, colour and brilliance.

Die Präzision der Form
Die von den Avantgardisten im 20. Jahrhundert als Gestaltungselement entdeckte Form des Kubus spielt eine wichtige Rolle in Kunst und Design. Sie war auch bestimmend für die Entwicklung von AXOR Edge. Als „luxuriöse Symbiose aus geometrischen Körpern und Ultrapräzision" zeigt diese Kollektion von Waschtischarmaturen eine massive und zugleich filigrane Anmutung. Die aufwendige Herstellung erfolgt unter Einsatz eines Diamantwerkzeugs, wie es in der Raumfahrt- und Laserindustrie verwendet wird. Exakt im Winkel von 45 Grad gefräste Fasen treffen dabei punktgenau aufeinander. Mit einer Oberfläche ohne Unebenheiten wird so eine perfekte Reflexion des Lichts ermöglicht. Sehr feine Strukturdetails erhalten die Waschtischarmaturen dadurch, dass mit der Diamantiermaschine mikrometergenau die Oberfläche des massiven Messingblocks der Armatur facettiert wird. Die Fertigung geschieht Linie für Linie in mehreren Schritten, bis präzise Pyramidenstümpfe entstehen, die ein faszinierendes Spiel von Licht und Schatten wiedergeben. Diese eleganten Waschtischarmaturen können zudem auf unterschiedliche Weise individualisiert werden. Dafür steht eine große Auswahl an edlen FinishPlus-Oberflächen zur Verfügung. In einem speziellen PVD-Verfahren (Physical Vapour Deposition) wird dabei eine zusätzliche Metallschicht aufgebracht. Dieses Hightech-Verfahren verleiht der Oberfläche mehr Widerstandskraft und Langlebigkeit, aber vor allem auch Brillanz und Farbigkeit.

Statement by the jury
The AXOR Edge product family conveys a strong sense of luxury and exclusivity. With their high-precision cubic geometry, these basin taps adopt a timeless and universal appearance, while the finely crafted structural elements lend them a new kind of elegance. The design merges a strong, expressive formal presence with the path-breaking approach of making the taps blend into their respective interior environment through customisable material and surface treatment options.

Begründung der Jury
Die Produktfamilie AXOR Edge vermittelt das Gefühl von Luxus und Exklusivität. Mit ihrer hochpräzisen kubischen Geometrie wirken diese Waschtischarmaturen zeitlos und universell. Fein gearbeitete Strukturelemente verleihen ihnen eine neue Art von Eleganz. In ihrer Gestaltung vereint sich eine aussagekräftige, starke Formgebung mit dem zukunftsweisenden Ansatz, sie durch eine individuell wählbare Material- und Oberflächenbehandlung dem jeweiligen Interieur anzupassen.

Designer portrait
See page 56
Siehe Seite 56

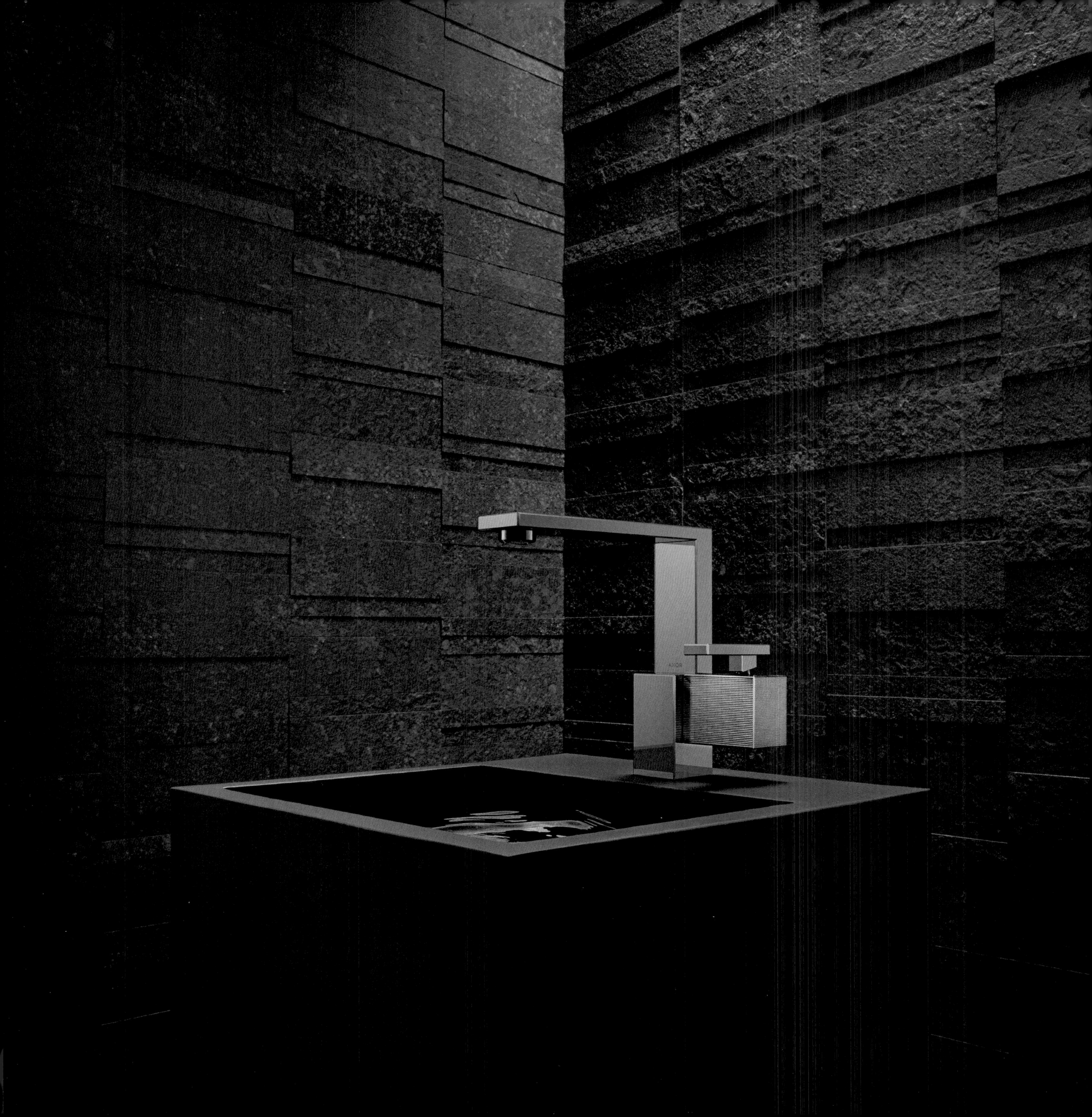

XPOSH Faucet
Basin Mixer
Waschtischmischer

Manufacturer
The Siam Sanitary Fittings Co., Ltd.,
Pathum Thani, Thailand
In-house design
COTTO Design Team
Web
www.cotto.com/en

The XPOSH basin mixer is characterised by distinctive lines, lending the fitting its sculptural look and elegant appeal. Particular attention was paid to the design of the lever, which is ergonomically sophisticated and ensures great ease of use. When the tap is turned on, cold water flows first in order to conserve energy, thanks to the integrated Cold Start Cartridge function. Slightly turning the lever to the left adjusts the water temperature as needed.

Statement by the jury
The design idiom of XPOSH ensures a high recognition value. The basin mixer promotes both premium quality and timeless elegance.

Den Waschtischmischer XPOSH zeichnet eine markante Linienführung aus, die der Armatur ihre skulpturale Anmutung und elegante Wirkung verleiht. Besonderes Augenmerk wurde auf die Gestaltung des Reglers gelegt, der ergonomisch durchdacht ist und hohen Bedienkomfort bietet. Wird der Hahn aufgedreht, fließt aufgrund der integrierten Funktion „Cold Start Cartridge" zuerst kaltes Wasser, um Energie zu sparen. Leichte Drehbewegungen des Reglers nach links passen die Wassertemperatur dem Bedarf an.

Begründung der Jury
Die Formensprache von XPOSH hat einen hohen Wiedererkennungswert. Der Waschtischmischer strahlt zeitlose Eleganz und Hochwertigkeit aus.

Apex
Basin Mixer
Waschtischmischer

Manufacturer
JOMOO Kitchen & Bath Co., Ltd.,
Fujian, China
In-house design
Lichuan Wu, Faxiang Wu, Li Jiang,
Xiaoming Lv, Jiqiao Lin, Yihui Fu
Web
www.jomoo.com.cn

Inspired by waves, the eye-catching feature of the Apex series is the handle design. Thanks to a fine texture reminiscent of water drops, the controls of the basin mixers provide a secure grip, while at the same time creating an expressive contrast to the reduced design of the tap and spout. The matte black colour underlines the modern appeal of the collection, which includes basin mixers in different heights as well as shower and bath accessories.

Statement by the jury
Featuring high-quality craftsmanship, the Apex collection impresses with its elegant aesthetics based on the skilful combination of straight forms and soft lines.

Das von Wellen inspirierte Griffdesign ist der besondere Blickfang der Serie Apex. Dank einer feinen, an Wassertropfen erinnernden Struktur lassen sich die Regler der Waschtischmischer sicher fassen. Zugleich entsteht ein ausdrucksstarker Gegensatz zur reduzierten Gestaltung von Hahn und Auslauf. Die mattschwarze Farbgebung unterstreicht die moderne Wirkung der Kollektion, die Waschtischmischer in unterschiedlichen Höhen sowie Dusch- und Badzubehör umfasst.

Begründung der Jury
Die hochwertig verarbeitete Kollektion Apex begeistert mit einer eleganten Ästhetik, die auf der gekonnten Verbindung gerader Formen und weicher Linien beruht.

X-Joy
Basin Mixer
Waschtischmischer

Manufacturer
AM PM Europe GmbH, Berlin, Germany
Design
GP designpartners gmbh
(Christoph Pauschitz), Vienna, Austria
Web
www.ampm-germany.com
www.gp.co.at

The visually dominant design element of the X-Joy basin mixer is the asymmetrically raised lever. This ergonomically well-thought-out design ensures comfortable handling and precise adjustment of the desired water flow and temperature. The smooth, cylindrically shaped body of the faucet forms an obtuse angle, allowing for easy cleaning.

Statement by the jury
X-Joy impresses with a clear appearance, and not only proves to be an all-rounder in any environment, but also convinces with intuitive usability.

Ein asymmetrisch zum Auslauf aufragender Hebel bildet die visuell dominierende Komponente des Waschtischmischers X-Joy. Diese ergonomisch durchdachte Gestaltung gewährleistet die komfortable Handhabung sowie die präzise Einstellung der gewünschten Wassermenge und -temperatur. Der glatte, zylindrisch geformte Korpus der Armatur beschreibt einen stumpfen Winkel, wodurch eine mühelose Reinigung ermöglicht wird.

Begründung der Jury
X-Joy beeindruckt durch ein klares Erscheinungsbild, das sich als Allrounder in jeder Umgebung erweist und mit intuitiver Bedienbarkeit überzeugt.

The New Classic Faucet Series
Basin Mixer
Waschtischmischer

Manufacturer
Laufen Bathrooms AG, Laufen, Switzerland
Design
Studio Marcel Wanders,
Amsterdam, Netherlands
Web
www.laufen.com
www.marcelwanders.com

The New Classic is a reinterpretation of a design classic. The basin mixer collection creates a harmonious balance between form innovation and archetypes. Flowing lines, rounded edges and cylindrically shaped base bodies have emerged to form elegant contemporary fixtures that can feature prominently in both classic and modern bathroom environments. Their characteristic element is the soft, ring-shaped groove in the base, which the design picks up again below the handle.

Statement by the jury
The design of these basin mixers meets high aesthetic demands. The New Classic thus offers stylish solutions for both modern and classic bathrooms.

The New Classic interpretiert einen Design-Klassiker neu. Die Waschtischmischer-Kollektion schafft dabei eine ausgewogene Balance zwischen Forminnovation und Archetyp. Fließende Linien, zylindrisch geformte Grundkörper und abgerundete Ecken lassen zeitgemäße, elegante Armaturen entstehen, die klassische und moderne Bäder gleichermaßen ausdrucksstark in Szene setzen. Charakteristisch ist die weiche, ringförmige Einkerbung am Sockel, die unterhalb des Griffs ein weiteres Mal aufgenommen wird.

Begründung der Jury
Die Formgebung dieser Waschtischmischer wird hohen ästhetischen Anforderungen gerecht. The New Classic bietet damit stilvolle Lösungen für das moderne und klassische Bad.

BRIM
Bathroom Tap Collection
Armaturen-Kollektion

Manufacturer
Zucchetti Rubinetteria S.p.A.,
Gozzano (Novara), Italy
Design
Palomba Serafini Associati,
Milan, Italy
Web
www.zucchettikos.it
www.palombaserafini.com

The BRIM collection is the result of an intensive development process focusing on shapes and their effect. The series merges opposing geometries into a balanced unity. The proportions of this tap collection are based on square and round basic shapes, visually blending with each other thanks to rounded edges, harmonious lines and smooth glossy surfaces. The mixers are available in different models to complement classic as well as modern bathroom interiors with their timeless appearance.

Statement by the jury
The BRIM collection impresses with the sophisticated combination of geometric shapes that are fused into a stylish, modern design.

Die Kollektion BRIM ist das Ergebnis eines intensiven Entwicklungsprozesses, in dem Formen und ihre Wirkung im Zentrum standen. Gegensätzliche Geometrien verbinden sich in der Serie zu einer ausgewogenen Einheit. Die Proportionen dieser Armaturen-Kollektion basieren auf quadratischen und runden Grundformen, die dank abgerundeter Kanten, harmonischer Linienführung und sanft glänzender Flächen visuell miteinander verschmelzen. Die Armaturen sind in verschiedenen Varianten verfügbar und komplettieren das klassische wie das moderne Badinterieur mit ihrem zeitlosen Erscheinungsbild.

Begründung der Jury
Die Kollektion BRIM überzeugt mit der raffinierten Verbindung geometrischer Formen, die sich zu einem stilvollen, modernen Design zusammenfügen.

ZA series lavatory faucet
Basin Mixer
Waschtischmischer

Manufacturer
Toto Ltd., Fukuoka, Japan
In-house design
Keishi Tomiya
Web
www.toto.com

Delicate lines and gentle shapes characterise the basin mixers of the ZA series. The organically designed handle tapers to the front and, through its slightly asymmetrical positioning, stands out from the spout, which has a particularly slim form, thanks to modern welding technology. The contrasting surface design of polished and brushed metal underlines an aesthetic of virtual weightlessness and at the same time lends the fitting a pleasant feel. The wide range of available surface finishes and colour options is highly user-friendly.

Feine Linien und sanfte Formen zeichnen die Waschtischmischer der Serie ZA aus. Der organisch gestaltete Griff verjüngt sich nach vorne hin und hebt sich durch die leicht asymmetrische Positionierung vom Auslauf ab, der mithilfe moderner Schweißtechnik besonders schlank geformt werden kann. Die kontrastierende Oberflächengestaltung aus poliertem und gebürstetem Metall unterstreicht die schwerelose Ästhetik und verleiht der Armatur zugleich eine angenehme Haptik. Sehr nutzerfreundlich ist die breite Palette an Oberflächenausführungs- und Farbvarianten.

Statement by the jury
The washbasin mixer of the ZA series distinguishes itself with their high aesthetic standard. In particular, the sophisticated handle design stands out.

Begründung der Jury
Die Waschtischmischer der Serie ZA ragen mit einem hohen ästhetischen Anspruch heraus. Besonders einprägsam ist das ausgereifte Griffdesign.

GM series lavatory faucet
Basin Mixer
Waschtischmischer

Manufacturer
Toto Ltd., Fukuoka, Japan
In-house design
Web
www.toto.com

The design of the GM basin mixer series shows influences from traditional Japanese architecture. Curved lines and rounded edges characterise the design. The elegant form language with the arch-shaped spout exudes a unique presence. The slim, slightly curved handle, running parallel to the spout, is easy to grasp and intuitive to use. Available in three heights and in different colours, the mixers can adapt to different bathroom interiors.

Die Gestaltung der Waschtischmischer-Serie GM zeigt Einflüsse aus der traditionellen japanischen Architektur. Geschwungene Linien und abgerundete Kanten prägen das Design. Die elegante Formgebung mit dem bogenförmigen Auslauf verleiht der Armatur Präsenz. Parallel zu diesem verläuft der schlanke, leicht gewölbte Hebel, der sich angenehm greifen und intuitiv bedienen lässt. Die Armaturen sind in drei Höhen sowie verschiedenen Farben erhältlich und passen sich so unterschiedlichen Badstilen an.

Statement by the jury
This product family impresses with its characteristic form language, while at the same time exhibiting high versatility, which benefits individual user needs.

Begründung der Jury
Die Produktfamilie beeindruckt mit ihrer charakteristischen Formgebung und weist zugleich hohe Variabilität auf, was individuellen Nutzerbedürfnissen zugutekommt.

GC series lavatory faucet
Basin Mixer
Waschtischmischer

Manufacturer
Toto Ltd., Fukuoka, Japan
In-house design
Web
www.toto.com

The design of these basin mixers reinterprets the classic column shape, using variations of straight and curved contours. A delicate horizontal line marks the transition from the base to the rectangular faucet. Similar to the spout, the tip of the handle points downwards. The V-shaped recess at the back is a merger of design and functionality. The lever fits easily in the hand and the newly developed valve allows for precise flow control. The mixers of the collection are available in three different heights.

Das Design dieser Waschtischmischer interpretiert die klassische Säulenform neu und variiert gerade und geschwungene Konturen. Eine feine horizontale Linie markiert den Übergang vom Sockel in den rechteckigen Korpus. Wie der Auslauf ist auch der Griff am Ende nach unten gerichtet. Seine keilförmige Aussparung hinten vereint Formgebung und Funktionalität. Der Hebel liegt gut in der Hand und das neu entwickelte Ventil ermöglicht eine präzise Durchflusskontrolle. Die Armaturen der Kollektion sind in drei verschiedenen Höhen verfügbar.

Statement by the jury
The GC collection skilfully transforms classic shapes into a timeless design and convinces with its practicality.

Begründung der Jury
Die Kollektion GC transformiert klassische Formen gekonnt in eine zeitlose Gestaltung und überzeugt durch ihre Praktikabilität.

GE series lavatory faucet
Basin Mixer
Waschtischmischer

Manufacturer
Toto Ltd., Fukuoka, Japan
In-house design
Web
www.toto.com

The sharp edges and clear shapes of the GE basin mixer are a reference to traditional Japanese forging techniques. The visually dominant V-shaped spout tapers towards the front, almost reminiscent of a sharp knife blade. Spout and lever continue this distinctive design feature. The polyhedral base of the mixer offers a special refinement: depending on the viewing angle, it constantly reveals new facets of the basin mixers.

Die scharfen Kanten und klaren Formen der Waschtischmischer GE verweisen auf traditionelle japanische Schmiedetechniken. Visuell dominierende Komponente ist der V-förmige Korpus, der nach vorne hin spitz zuläuft und so an eine scharfe Messerklinge erinnert. Auch Auslauf und Regler greifen das markante Gestaltungsmerkmal auf. Die polyedrische Grundform der Armatur wartet noch mit einer besonderen Finesse auf: Je nach Blickwinkel des Betrachters kommen immer wieder neue Facetten der Waschtischmischer zur Geltung.

Statement by the jury
The GE basin mixers are visually impressive with their unusual design that effectively blends tradition and modernity.

Begründung der Jury
Optisch imponieren die Waschtischmischer GE mit ihrer ausgefallenen Gestaltung, die Tradition und Moderne wirkungsvoll vereint.

Liquid
Basin Mixer & Accessories
Waschtischmischer & Zubehör

Manufacturer
Corona, Colceramica, Bogotá, Colombia
In-house design
Corona Design Team (Nicolas Ochoa,
Juan Mesa, Maria Isabel Toro, Andres Lopez)
Design
GRO design, Eindhoven, Netherlands
Web
www.corona.com.co
www.grodesign.com

The design of the Liquid basin mixer and accessories collection plays with the concept of superficial tension. Its soft shapes harmoniously converge like flowing water. The smooth surfaces capture light and reflect it like a water surface, an effect that lends Liquid a timeless appearance. In addition, the virtually seamless surface and the concealed water outlet integrated into the spout of the washbasin mixer permit easy cleaning of the fitting. With its rounded edges, the handle fits quite comfortably in the hand.

Die Gestaltung der Armaturen- und Zubehörkollektion Liquid spielt mit der Oberflächenspannung. Wie fließendes Wasser laufen die weichen Formen harmonisch ineinander. Die glatten Oberflächen fangen das Licht ein und reflektieren es einer Wasseroberfläche gleich. Ein Effekt, der Liquid eine zeitlose Anmutung verleiht. Die weitgehend nahtlose Oberfläche und der unsichtbar in den Auslauf des Waschtischmischers integrierte Auslass erlauben eine mühelose Reinigung der Armatur. Mit seinen abgerundeten Kanten liegt der Hebel angenehm in der Hand.

Statement by the jury
Liquid impresses with a design idea that has been consistently implemented. The different elements harmonise very well with each other, and can be individually combined.

Begründung der Jury
Liquid gefällt mit einer Gestaltungsidee, die konsequent umgesetzt wird. Die verschiedenen Elemente harmonieren sehr gut miteinander und lassen sich schlüssig kombinieren.

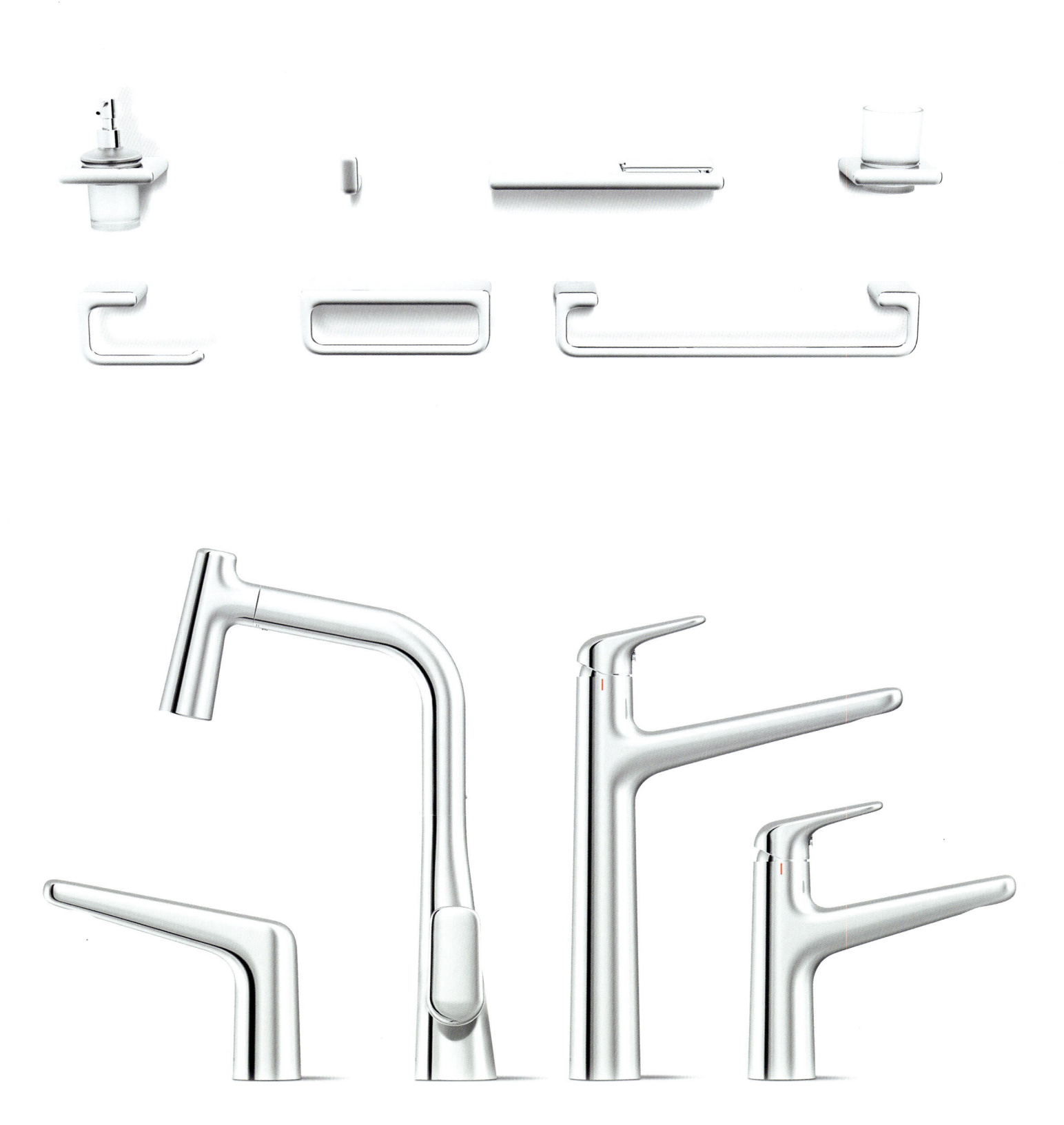

Cranes
Basin Mixer
Waschtischmischer

Manufacturer
Rifeng Enterprise Group Co., Ltd.,
Foshan, China
In-house design
Jianying Huang, Jiangming Peng,
Xiaobing Yang, Donghong Xiao,
Zhengbing Qu, Qingyun Ai,
Jincui Zhan, Puhua Zhong
Web
www.rifeng.com.cn

The design of this basin mixer is inspired by cranes, which are used in the construction of high-rise buildings. Modelled on their straightforward, sleek lines, Cranes translates this into a timeless design that conveys durability and blends harmoniously into modern ambience. Positioned in parallel to the spout of the basin mixer, the slim lever is moved upwards for continuous adjustments of water flow and temperature.

Statement by the jury
Cranes shows a highly dynamic design. The unusual positioning of the lever blends smoothly into the design concept and is highly functional.

Inspirationsquelle für die Gestaltung dieser Armatur waren Kräne, die beim Bau von Hochhäusern zum Einsatz kommen. Cranes übernimmt die geradlinige, schlanke Linienführung der Vorbilder und übersetzt diese in ein zeitloses Design, das Langlebigkeit ausstrahlt und sich harmonisch in ein modernes Ambiente einfügt. Der schmale, parallel zum Auslauf ausgerichtete Hebel des Waschtischmischers wird nach oben bewegt und ermöglicht so eine stufenlose Regulierung von Wasserfluss und -temperatur.

Begründung der Jury
Cranes besticht durch sein dynamisches Design. Die ungewöhnliche Positionierung des Reglers fügt sich stimmig in das Gestaltungskonzept ein und ist zudem sehr funktional.

Ma ya
Basin Mixer
Waschtischmischer

Manufacturer
KEFAN Houseware & Furnishings Intelligent Manufacturing Co., Ltd., Foshan, China
Design
Rifeng Enterprise Group Co., Ltd.
(Jianying Huang, Jiangming Peng,
Xiaozhou Qiu, Xiaobing Yang,
Zhengbing Qu, Qingyun Ai, Jincui Zhan,
Puhua Zhong), Foshan, China
Web
www.kefan-china.com
www.rifeng.com.cn

The lever and outlet of this washbasin mixer are dominated by hollow oval shapes that lend the Ma ya its characteristic appearance. Its surface showcases two colours to underline its sophisticated appearance: The high-contrast combination of matte black and glossy copper gives the mixer an elegant, yet simultaneously modern appeal. Thanks to the distinctive opening, the lever can be easily grasped, enabling comfortable water and temperature adjustments.

Statement by the jury
Ma ya impresses with its characteristic openings, lending the washbasin mixer a geometric elegance while also fulfilling a functional purpose.

Hebel und Auslauf dieses Waschtischmischers werden von ovalen Aussparungen dominiert, die Ma ya sein charakteristisches Äußeres verleihen. Seine Oberfläche ist in zwei Farben gehalten, wodurch das raffinierte Erscheinungsbild noch unterstrichen wird: Die kontrastreiche Kombination aus mattem Schwarz und glänzendem Kupfer wirkt elegant und modern zugleich. Dank der ausgeprägten Öffnung ist der Hebel gut zu greifen, was eine bequeme Wasser- und Temperaturregulierung erlaubt.

Begründung der Jury
Ma ya imponiert mit charakteristischen Aussparungen, die dem Waschtischmischer geometrische Eleganz verleihen und zugleich einen funktionalen Zweck erfüllen.

Smart ring faucet
Basin Mixer
Waschtischmischer

Manufacturer
Rifeng Enterprise Group Co., Ltd.,
Foshan, China
In-house design
Jianying Huang, Jiangming Peng,
Xiaobing Yang, Donghong Xiao,
Zhengbing Qu, Qingyun Ai,
Jincui Zhan, Puhua Zhong
Web
www.rifeng.com.cn

The Smart ring breaks with the common appearance of basin mixers, as the slim faucet flows into an oval, ring-shaped outlet that integrates three functions in one unit: a waterfall mode, hand disinfection via UV light, and a warm air hand dryer. Water flow and temperature are easily adjusted via the mixing lever on the faucet. Controlled by a push button on the top of the outlet, the two complementary modes round off the comfortable 3-in-1 hand cleaning

Statement by the jury
Smart ring basin mixer translates useroriented features into a highly distinctive design that lends bathrooms an individual style.

Die Armatur Smart ring bricht mit der für Waschtischmischer gängigen Optik, denn der schlanke Hahn mündet in einen ovalen, ringförmigen Auslauf, der gleich drei Funktionen in sich vereint: einen Wasserfallmodus, eine Handdesinfektion via UV-Licht und einen Handtrockner, der mit Warmluft arbeitet. Wasserfluss und Temperatur lassen sich über den Mischhebel an der Armatur leicht einstellen. Die beiden ergänzenden Modi runden die komfortable 3-in-1-Handreinigung ab und werden über einen Druckknopf am Auslauf gesteuert.

Begründung der Jury
Der Waschtischmischer Smart ring faucet überführt nutzerorientierte Funktionen in ein unverwechselbares Design, das im Bad eigene Akzente setzt.

Acme
Basin Mixer
Waschtischmischer

Manufacturer
Xiamen Lota International Co., Ltd.,
Xiamen, China
In-house design
Yonghuang Li, Yongqiang He, Chuanbao Zhu
Web
www.xmlota.com

The outstanding feature of this basin mixer is its exceptionally flat appearance, with a thickness of only 5 mm at the thinnest point. Characterised by straight lines, the corpus merges into the spout at a right angle. A side-positioned lever, which is easy to grasp and operate, elaborates the design concept. Rotating the lever to the front turns on the water and adjusts the temperature.

Statement by the jury
Featuring a clear operating structure and restrained design, Acme creates an appealing clarity, both functionally and visually.

Hervorstechendes Merkmal des Waschtischmischers ist sein außergewöhnlich flaches Erscheinungsbild mit einer Materialstärke von lediglich 5 mm an der dünnsten Stelle. Der von geraden Linien gekennzeichnete Korpus geht im rechten Winkel in den Auslauf über. Ein seitlich angebrachter Regler, der sicher zu fassen und einfach zu bedienen ist, führt das Gestaltungskonzept fort. Mit einer Drehbewegung nach vorn hin wird der Hahn geöffnet und die Wassertemperatur reguliert.

Begründung der Jury
Acme schafft durch seine klare Bedienstruktur und die zurückhaltende Formgebung funktionell und optisch eine ansprechende Klarheit.

Plus 3-hole deck mount
Basin Tap
Waschtischarmatur

Manufacturer
Grohe AG, Düsseldorf, Germany
In-house design
Web
www.grohe.com

The Plus 3-hole basin tap merges round and square shapes into an expressive design. The front of the fitting is dominated by straight lines and compact surfaces, while at the back, the controls follow gentle curves, lending the mixer an elegant appeal. The harmoniously coordinated appearance of this line is complemented by practical functions, including a swivel spout, which contribute to a convincing product solution.

Statement by the jury
The basin tap impresses with its original appearance, which at the same time meets high requirements for practicability.

Runde und quadratische Formen verbinden sich in der Waschtischarmatur Plus 3-Loch zu einem ausdrucksstarken Design. Beim Blick auf die Front der Armatur dominieren gerade Linien und kompakte Flächen. Nach hinten verlaufen die Regler in sanften Bögen, die dem Erscheinungsbild zusätzlich eine elegante Anmutung verleihen. Ergänzt wird die gut abgestimmte Optik der Linie durch praktische Funktionen wie einen schwenkbaren Auslauf, die zu einer überzeugenden Produktlösung beitragen.

Begründung der Jury
Die Armatur imponiert mit ihrem originellen Erscheinungsbild, das zugleich hohen Anforderungen an Praktikabilität gerecht wird.

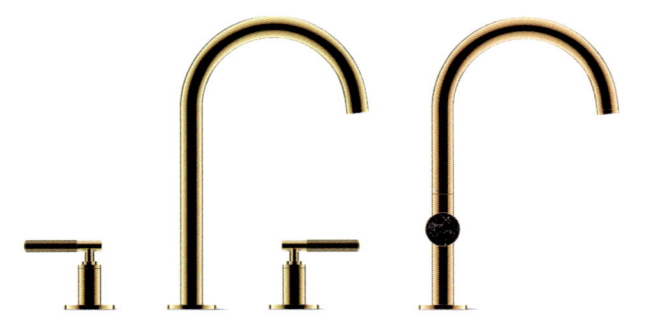

Atrio Private Collection
Bathroom Tap Collection
Armaturen-Kollektion

Manufacturer
Grohe AG, Düsseldorf, Germany
In-house design
Web
www.grohe.com

The Atrio Private Collection relies on individuality. The wide range of levers, material inserts and colours allows a finely tuned personalisation of bathroom interiors. The product collection meets the demands of different styles: the design aesthetic ranges from minimalist to classic, while at the same time remaining true to the series' basic design features. Clear lines and round shapes characterise the timeless appearance.

Statement by the jury
Atrio Private stands out with its versatility and meets the need for individual bathroom furnishings in terms of functionality and visual appeal.

Die Badarmaturen der Atrio Private Collection setzen auf Individualität. Das breite Spektrum an Hebeln, Materialeinsätzen und Farben ermöglicht eine fein abgestimmte Personalisierung der Badeinrichtung. Die Produktfamilie wird dabei unterschiedlichen Stilen gerecht: Die Designästhetik reicht von minimalistisch bis klassisch, zugleich bleibt die Serie ihren gestalterischen Grundmerkmalen treu. Eine klare Linienführung und runde Formen prägen das zeitlose Erscheinungsbild.

Begründung der Jury
Atrio Private besticht mit Variabilität und kommt dem Bedürfnis nach individueller Badeinrichtung optisch wie funktional entgegen.

Atrio ICON 3D
Basin Tap
Waschtischarmatur

Manufacturer
Grohe AG, Düsseldorf, Germany
In-house design
Web
www.grohe.com

The Atrio ICON 3D is a reinterpretation of the existing Atrio collection while exploring and pushing the limits of 3D metal printing. The basin tap combines modern technology, craftsmanship and minimalist design. The appearance is reduced to the essentials and clearly stands out from conventional fitting design. The body is remarkably flat, merging seamlessly into the spout and extending in a high arc over the basin. The control elements also showcase restrained design and thanks to their flat grip area are comfortable to use.

Atrio ICON 3D ist eine Neuinterpretation der bestehenden Atrio-Kollektion und lotet die Möglichkeiten des 3D-Metalldrucks aus. Die Waschtischarmatur verbindet moderne Technik, Handwerk und minimalistisches Design. Das Erscheinungsbild ist auf das Wesentliche reduziert und hebt sich deutlich von der gängigen Gestaltung von Armaturen ab. Der Korpus ist auffallend flach geformt, geht nahtlos in den Auslauf über und erstreckt sich in hohem Bogen über das Becken. Zurückhaltend im Design sind auch die Regler, die mit ihrer flachen Griffffläche angenehm zu handhaben sind.

Statement by the jury
Manufactured with innovative, pioneering technology, Atrio ICON 3D impresses with a design that is both sophisticated and aesthetically appealing.

Begründung der Jury
Hergestellt mit innovativer, zukunftsorientierter Technologie beeindruckt Atrio ICON 3D mit einem ebenso anspruchsvollen wie ästhetischen Design.

Plus 2-hole wall mount
Basin Tap
Waschtischarmatur

Manufacturer
Grohe AG, Düsseldorf, Germany
In-house design
Web
www.grohe.com

The characteristic element of this basin tap is the arched shape. Its square rosettes, with which the fitting is mounted on the wall, create a bold contrast to the round lines. The eye-catching lever also implements this interplay of forms in a functionally sophisticated manner. Its half-round body merges into a downward-facing handle that provides a secure grip. Further user-oriented details of this line include the swivel spout and extendable spray head.

Statement by the jury
Its high-contrast form language lends Plus 2-hole a self-confident, extraordinary appearance, which is complemented by user-oriented functions.

Die Bogenform ist das charakteristische Element dieser Waschtischarmatur. In wirkungsvollem Kontrast zu den runden Linien stehen die quadratischen Rosetten, mit denen die Armatur an der Wand montiert wird. Besonderer Blickfang ist der Regler, der das Formenspiel auch funktional ausgeklügelt umsetzt. Sein halbrunder Korpus geht in einen nach unten ragenden Griff über, der sicher zu fassen ist. Weitere anwenderorientierte Details dieser Linie sind der schwenkbare Auslauf und der ausziehbare Sprühkopf.

Begründung der Jury
Seine kontrastreiche Formgebung verleiht Plus 2-Loch eine selbstbewusste, außergewöhnliche Anmutung, die durch nutzerorientierte Funktionen durchdacht ergänzt wird.

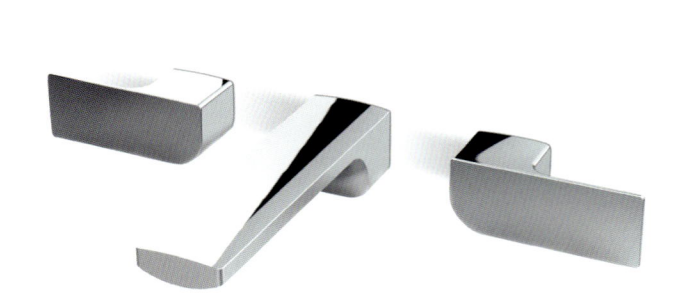

JUSTIME Arch 2
Basin Faucet
Wall-Mounted Basin Mixer
Waschtischmischer für die Wandmontage

Manufacturer
Shengtai Brassware Co., Ltd., Changhua, Taiwan
In-house design
Justime Design Team
Web
www.justime.com

Arch 2 is the design interpretation of a traditional Chinese wisdom. With squares standing for sincerity and circles symbolising intelligence, this basin mixer embodies a harmonious design combination that symbolises wisdom. The basic square shape of the body and controls is rounded off by gentle curves, while straight and curved lines flow into one another. Particularly eye-catching features are the handles of slightly asymmetrical shape, as they evenly frame the spout and further emphasise the independent appearance of the fitting.

Statement by the jury
The Arch 2 washbasin mixer stands out with an aesthetically balanced design that integrates equally well into both classic and modern facilities.

Arch 2 ist die gestalterische Interpretation einer traditionellen chinesischen Weisheit: Quadrate, die für Aufrichtigkeit stehen, und Kreise, Zeichen für Intelligenz, gehen im Design des Waschtischmischers eine harmonische Verbindung ein, die Weisheit symbolisiert. Dabei runden Kurven die quadratische Grundform von Korpus und Reglern ab, gerade und geschwungene Linien fließen ineinander. Besonders ins Auge fallen die leicht asymmetrisch geformten Griffe, die den Auslauf gleichmäßig einrahmen und die eigenständige Optik der Armatur auf diese Weise zusätzlich unterstreichen.

Begründung der Jury
Der Waschtischmischer Arch 2 punktet mit einer ästhetisch ausgewogenen Gestaltung, die sich in klassische und moderne Einrichtungen gleichermaßen integriert.

JUSTIME Pan 2
Wall-Mounted Basin Mixer
Waschtischmischer für die Wandmontage

Manufacturer
Shengtai Brassware Co., Ltd., Changhua, Taiwan
In-house design
Justime Design Team
Web
www.justime.com

The Pan 2 basin mixer is characterised by a reduced design language that adapts particularly well to modern bathroom environments. The slightly rounded spout is flanked by two horizontal regulators on the sides, ensuring an ergonomically comfortable operation. They rest firmly in the hand, and serve to regulate the intensity of the water flow and temperature via slight up and down movements. The basin mixer is easy to install accurately: Even after installation, adjustments of up to 25 mm are possible.

Statement by the jury
Pan 2 impresses with timelessly elegant aesthetics. The design of the spout and levers is harmoniously aligned.

Kennzeichen des Waschtischmischers Pan 2 ist seine reduzierte Formensprache, die sich besonders in moderne Badumgebungen stimmig einfügt. Der leicht abgerundete Hahn wird seitlich von zwei waagrecht stehenden Reglern flankiert, die für eine ergonomisch komfortable Bedienbarkeit sorgen. Sie liegen sicher in der Hand und regulieren Strahlstärke und Temperatur über leichte Bewegungen nach oben und unten. Der Waschtischmischer lässt sich einfach und exakt installieren: Auch nach der Montage ist eine Justierung von bis zu 25 mm möglich.

Begründung der Jury
Pan 2 besticht durch zeitlos elegante Ästhetik. Auslauf und Regler sind in ihrer Formgebung harmonisch aufeinander abgestimmt.

JUSTIME Yes 2 Basin Mixer
Two-Handle Basin Mixer
Zweihebel-Waschtischmischer

Manufacturer
Shengtai Brassware Co., Ltd.,
Changhua, Taiwan
In-house design
Justime Design Team
Web
www.justime.com

The eye-catching feature of the Yes 2 basin mixer is its Y-shaped design. At the water outlet, the cylindrical body merges into two regulators diverging in opposite directions. Their handles contain small hollows that provide for convenient operation. Flow rate and temperature are controlled separately: The lower handle is used to start the water flow and regulate the flow rate, while the upward-pointing counterpart adjusts the hot and cold water settings.

Statement by the jury
Yes 2 convinces with an overall consistent design – merging an appealing language of form with the user-oriented handling.

Augenfälliges Merkmal des Waschtischmischers Yes 2 ist seine Y-förmige Gestalt. Der zylindrische Korpus geht am Wasserauslauf in zwei Regler über, die in entgegengesetzte Richtungen auseinanderstreben. In ihre Griffe sind kleine Mulden eingearbeitet, die eine angenehme Bedienung erlauben. Durchflussmenge und Temperatur werden separat geregelt: Über den unteren Griff wird der Wasserfluss gestartet und die Strahlstärke reguliert. Sein nach oben ausgerichtetes Pendant steuert die Warm- und Kaltwassereinstellungen.

Begründung der Jury
Bei Yes 2 besticht die rundum schlüssige Gestaltung – von der attraktiven Formgebung bis hin zur nutzerorientierten Handhabung.

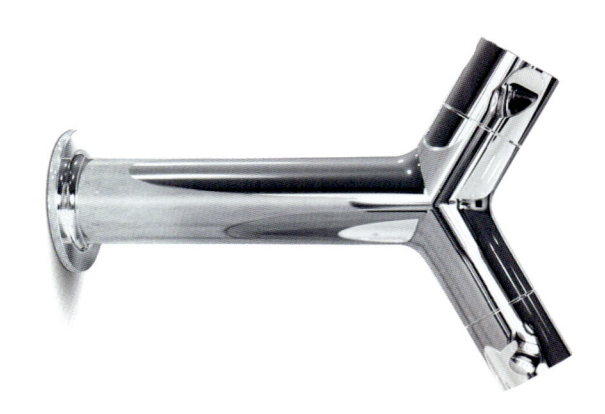

Levoir™
Wall-Mounted Basin Mixer
Wandmontierter Waschtischmischer

Manufacturer
Brizo, Indianapolis, Indiana, USA
In-house design
Celine Garland
Web
www.brizo.com

The Levoir Single-Handle Wall Mount Lavatory Faucet is inspired by the slender proportions and graceful forms seen in classic British automobile design. A truly sophisticated and eye-catching feature, the cross-shaped handle not only sets visual accents, but also convinces in terms of ergonomics. The faucet is available in five different finishes, from polished chrome to a luxurious golden colour.

Statement by the jury
The basin mixer impresses with a compact language of form reduced to clear lines. Its versatility is remarkably user-friendly.

Der Levoir Einhebelmischer für die Wandmontage ist inspiriert von den schlanken Proportionen und anmutigen Formen des klassischen britischen Automobildesigns. Blickfang ist der raffiniert gestaltete, kreuzförmige Griff, der optisch Akzente setzt und zugleich in ergonomischer Hinsicht überzeugt. Die Oberflächen sind in fünf verschiedenen Varianten verfügbar, von poliertem Chrom bis hin zum luxuriösen Goldton.

Begründung der Jury
Der Waschtischmischer beeindruckt durch eine auf klare Linien reduzierte, kompakte Formensprache. Seine Variabilität ist ausgesprochen anwenderfreundlich.

Auto foaming hand wash
Soap Dispenser
Seifenspender

Manufacturer
Beijing Jiangxinxiaozhen e-business Co., Ltd.,
Beijing, China
In-house design
Changying Xu, Jin Li, Gushun Su

The development of this soap dispenser, which is reminiscent of a faucet, focused on hygienic hand cleaning. Its 21-cm-high, cylindrical shape blends into any environment and fits on washbasins of different sizes. The automatic soap dispenser offers hands-free operation, preventing the spread of pathogens among the users. When the liquid soap is used up, the empty container can be replaced in a few simple steps.

Statement by the jury
This soap dispenser is a practical tool for daily, hygienic hand cleaning and convinces by a successful interplay of form and function.

Die hygienische Handreinigung stand bei der Entwicklung dieses Seifenspenders im Fokus, der in seiner Optik an einen Wasserhahn angelehnt ist. Seine 21 cm hohe, zylindrische Form fügt sich gut in jedes Ambiente ein und findet auf Waschbecken unterschiedlicher Größe Platz. Der automatische Seifenspender funktioniert berührungslos, was einer Verbreitung von Krankheitserregern unter den Nutzern entgegenwirkt. Ist die Flüssigseife aufgebraucht, lässt sich der leere Behälter mit wenigen Handgriffen gegen einen neuen austauschen.

Begründung der Jury
Dieser Seifenspender ist ein praktisches Tool für die tägliche, hygienische Handreinigung und überzeugt mit einem gelungenen Zusammenspiel von Form und Funktion.

Black Line
Bathroom Tap Collection
Badarmaturen-Kollektion

Manufacturer
Grohe AG, Düsseldorf, Germany

In-house design
Grohe AG

Web
www.grohe.com

reddot award 2019
best of the best

Visionary form
Especially in the planning of open architectural living concepts, all design details must be closely considered and finely crafted to achieve a harmonious overall unity. To address this trend in demands, the goal has been to provide a sophisticated range of colours and finishes for the interior design in contemporary bath and kitchen environments. Purist and clean in their aesthetics, the fittings give versatile freedom of choice to express individuality through the combination of the design lines and exclusive colours. The Black Line bathroom collection focuses on the user experience, as well as a harmonious balance of aesthetics and functionality. The resulting elegant design language corresponds to the innovative material and its properties. The Black Line offers fascinating possibilities for putting individual visions of the perfect interior into reality. Based on a subtle concept, the collection matches well with both high-contrast interiors and tone-on-tone dark interiors, ranging from plain and low-contrast interiors to colourful high-contrast homes. The Black Line and ten additional premium colours and finishes have been created to allow consumers to optimally express and realise their own interior design ideas.

Visionäre Form
Insbesondere bei der Planung offener architektonischer Wohnkonzepte müssen für ein stimmiges Gesamtbild alle gestalterischen Details miteinbezogen werden. Um diesem Trend zu begegnen, war es das Ziel, eine ausgereifte Palette von Farben und Materialoberflächen für die Innenraumgestaltung in zeitgemäßen Bad- und Küchenumgebungen bereitzustellen. Die in ihrer Ästhetik puristisch klaren Armaturen geben durch die Kombination ihrer Designlinien und exklusiven Farben vielfältige gestalterische Freiheiten. Bei der Badezimmerkollektion Black Line stand das Nutzererlebnis im Mittelpunkt sowie eine ausgewogene Balance von Ästhetik und Funktionalität. Die daraus resultierende elegante Formensprache geht einher mit innovativen Materialeigenschaften. Black Line bietet faszinierende Realisierungsmöglichkeiten für die Vision vom perfekten Interieur. Durch ihre feinsinnige Konzeption passt sie ebenso in Umgebungen mit hohem Kontrast wie in dunkle Ton-in-Ton-Umgebungen, die Einsatzmöglichkeiten reichen von einfarbigen bis hin zu bunten Interieurs. Die Kollektion Black Line sowie zehn weitere exklusive Farben und Oberflächen erlauben es, die Ideen der Planenden für ihr Interior Design optimal umzusetzen.

Statement by the jury
This elegant series is characterised by an impressively consistent design language. With its highly integrated design, the Black Line creates a new aesthetic for bathroom environments, defined by a perfectly coordinated overall appearance. Both the interplay of high contrasts and the available choice among the fine tone-on-tone interiors are fascinating. Highly functional and durable, this collection communicates its high quality at first glance.

Begründung der Jury
Diese elegante Serie zeichnet sich durch eine beeindruckend konsistente Formensprache aus. Black Line kreiert dank einer hochintegrativen Gestaltung eine neue Ästhetik für Badumgebungen mit einem perfekt aufeinander abgestimmten Erscheinungsbild. Dabei kann sowohl das Spiel der Kontraste faszinieren wie auch die mögliche Wahl edler Ton-in-Ton-Interieurs. Hochfunktional und langlebig, kommuniziert diese Kollektion auf den ersten Blick ihre hohe Qualität.

Designer portrait
See page 58
Siehe Seite 58

319

Rainfinity
Showerpipes, Overhead and Hand Showers
Showerpipes, Kopf- und Handbrausen

Manufacturer
Hansgrohe SE,
Schiltach, Germany

Design
Phoenix Design GmbH + Co. KG,
Stuttgart, Germany

Web
www.hansgrohe.com
www.phoenixdesign.com

reddot award 2019
best of the best

Allocating well-being
The daily shower signifies a break from everyday routine. The design of Rainfinity has been created to offer corresponding scenarios for these moments. This shower collection, which also includes shelves and a separate flush-mounted control, boasts versatile functionality. The concept goes hand in hand with intuitive operation and a sense of comfort that ensures an intense showering experience, offering wellness benefits. The overhead shower, for example, has an innovative wall connection, featuring an adjustable angle and replacing the traditional shower arm. Furthermore, the shoulder jet serves to shower the body, without necessarily causing the face and hair to get wet. The special jet types are aimed at enhancing the showering pleasure, such as the microfine PowderRain jet, the curved jet discs of which feature newly arranged outlet openings to diffuse the water at different intensities. The design with its clear and reduced forms allows a seamless integration of the fittings into modern bathroom interiors. The matte and subtly structured surfaces are pleasant to the touch and, together with the curved shape of the jet disc, create a warm, homely feeling. Last but not least, Rainfinity showcases a highly contemporary surface colour, with the matte white of the showers creating a noble-looking contrast to the graphite-coloured jet discs.

Orte des Wohlfühlens
Die tägliche Dusche bedeutet stets ein Innehalten vom Alltag. Durch die Gestaltung von Rainfinity werden für solche Momente entsprechende Szenarien geschaffen. Diese Brausenkollektion, zu der auch Ablagen und eine separate Unterputzsteuerung gehören, bietet eine vielseitige Funktionalität. Das Konzept geht einher mit einer intuitiven Bedienung und einem Komfort, der für ein intensives Duscherlebnis mit Wellness-Charakter sorgt. So verfügt die Kopfbrause über einen innovativen Wandanschluss, der sich im Winkel verstellen lässt und den traditionellen Brausearm ersetzt. Mit der Schulterbrause wiederum wird der Körper benetzt, ohne dass dabei zwangsläufig Gesicht und Haare nass werden. Besondere Strahlarten erhöhen den Duschgenuss, wie etwa die mikrofeine Strahlart PowderRain, bei der das Wasser unterschiedlich intensiv aus den gewölbten, mit neu angeordneten Austrittsöffnungen versehenen Strahlscheiben gelenkt wird. Die Gestaltung mit klaren und reduzierten Formen erlaubt eine nahtlose Integration der Armaturen in moderne Interieurs. Die matten und dezent strukturierten Oberflächen sind haptisch angenehm und erzeugen zusammen mit der gewölbten Form der Strahlscheibe ein warmes, wohnliches Gefühl. Rainfinity ist zudem mit einer zeitgemäßen Oberflächenfarbigkeit gestaltet. Das matte Weiß der Brausen steht dabei in einem edel anmutenden Kontrast zu den graphitfarben ausgeführten Strahlscheiben.

Statement by the jury
The Rainfinity shower collection inspires with its clear lines and excellent quality. Its subtle design interprets well-known geometries in an exciting manner, projecting a new use of forms. Paired with smart and functional solutions, the collection has emerged as a novel approach towards showering. Based on innovations such as the PowderRain jet type, which offers intuitive control, the bath turns into an inspiring place of well-being.

Begründung der Jury
Die Brausenkollektion Rainfinity begeistert durch klare Linien und eine exquisite Qualität. Ihre feinsinnige Gestaltung interpretiert bekannte Geometrien auf spannende Weise und bringt dabei eine neue Formensprache hervor. Mit cleveren und funktionalen Lösungen kreiert sie eine besondere Art des Duschens. Auf der Basis von Innovationen wie der intuitiv steuerbaren Strahlart PowderRain wird das Bad zu einem inspirierenden Wellness-Ort.

Designer portrait
See page 60
Siehe Seite 60

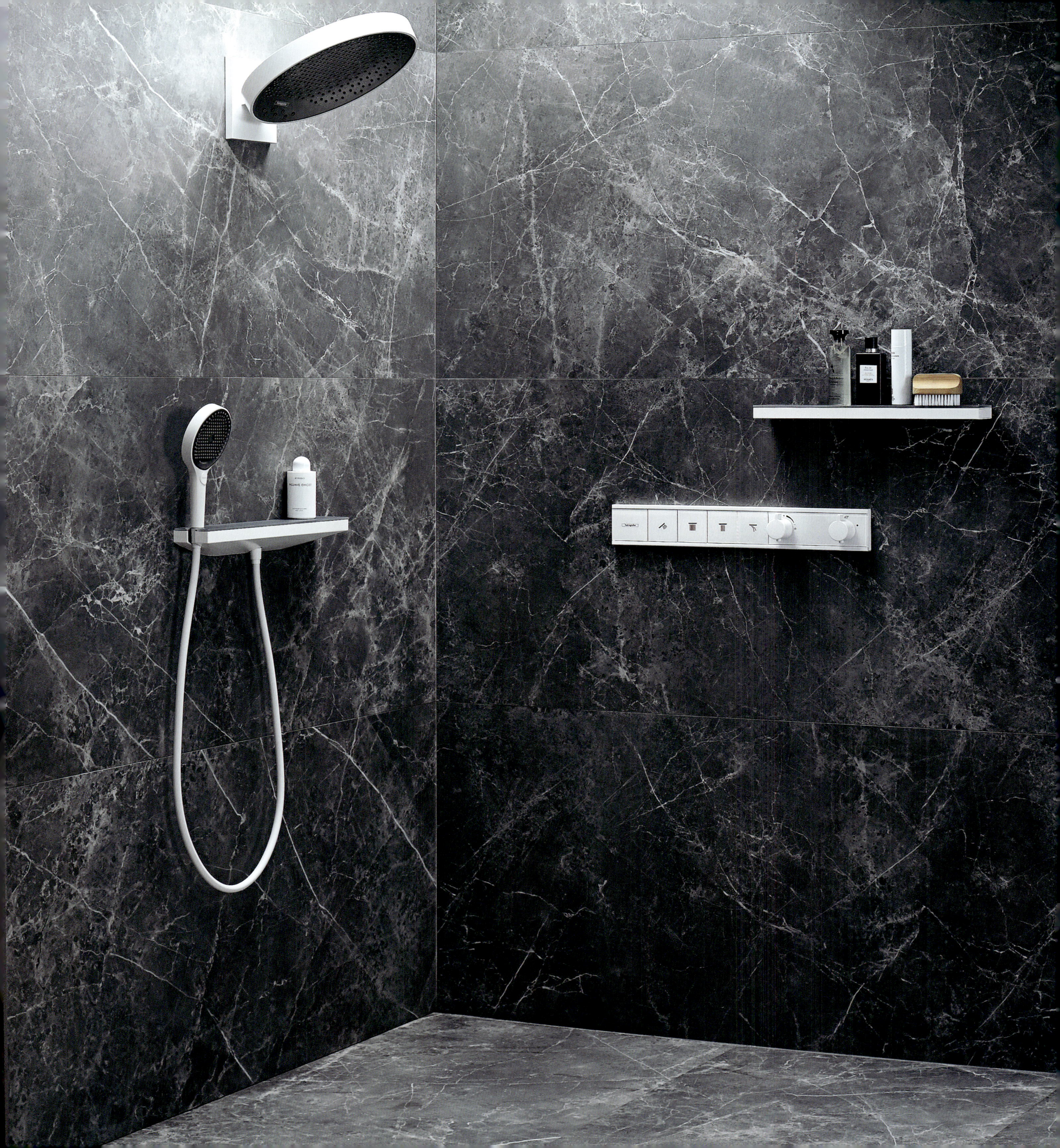

Maxim
Head Shower
Kopfbrause

Manufacturer
Kohler Mira, Cheltenham, United Kingdom
In-house design
Kohler Mira Design Team
Web
www.kohlermira.co.uk

The appearance of the Maxim overhead shower is defined by distinctive design elements and a sleek profile. The pattern on the discreetly white spray area is inspired by the movement of water, achieving a unique, dynamic aesthetics. At the same time, the arrangement of the nozzles delivers a fine water spray, which in combination with the centrally placed focused spray, constitutes an extraordinary rain shower. The interplay of the different spray types is also visually impressive, consistently rounding off the showering comfort.

Ihr schlankes Profil und eingängige Designelemente machen das Erscheinungsbild der Kopfbrause Maxim aus. Das Muster der dezent in Weiß gehaltenen Sprühfläche ist Wellenbewegungen nachempfunden, wodurch eine unverwechselbare, dynamische Ästhetik erreicht wird. Gleichzeitig ermöglicht die Anordnung der Düsen einen feinen Wasserfluss, der in Kombination mit dem mittig platzierten, gebündelten Strahl eine außergewöhnliche Regendusche bildet. Das Zusammenspiel der Strahlarten ist zudem auch visuell beeindruckend und rundet den Duschkomfort stimmig ab.

Statement by the jury
The concept of the Maxim overhead shower has been consistently thought through. Its premium workmanship and timeless aesthetics as well as high quality of use are fascinating.

Begründung der Jury
Die Konzeption der Kopfbrause Maxim ist konsequent durchdacht. Die hochwertige Ausführung, zeitlose Ästhetik und hohe Gebrauchsqualität begeistern.

SMOOTH
Head Shower
Kopfbrause

Manufacturer
JOMOO Kitchen & Bath Co., Ltd.,
Fujian, China
In-house design
Yanping Luo, Kunpeng Huang,
Hua Feng, Jianxiang Xiao, Zhaoping Zheng
Web
www.jomoo.com.cn

Its flowing language of forms, lends SMOOTH an elegant, stylish appearance. The sleek head shower features an automatic descaling function. Underneath the generously dimensioned spray surface, each spray nozzle is equipped with a flexible tip. When the shower is in operation, these are automatically lifted by the water pressure to immediately remove any dirt and lime deposits.

Statement by the jury
Thanks to the well-balanced combination of a subtle design language and advanced technology, the SMOOTH head shower provides extraordinary user-friendliness.

Ihre fließende Formensprache verleiht SMOOTH eine elegante, stilvolle Anmutung. Die flach gestaltete Kopfbrause verfügt über eine automatische Entkalkungsfunktion. Unterhalb der großzügig dimensionierten Sprühfläche ist jede einzelne Düse mit einer flexiblen Spitze versehen. Ist die Dusche in Betrieb, werden diese durch den Wasserdruck automatisch angehoben, um etwaige Schmutz- und Kalkablagerungen sofort wieder zu entfernen.

Begründung der Jury
Durch die ausgewogene Verbindung von dezenter Formensprache und fortschrittlicher Technologie beweist die Kopfbrause SMOOTH außergewöhnliche Anwenderfreundlichkeit.

micro-droplets showerhead
Head Shower
Kopfbrause

Manufacturer
Xiamen Oshince Technology Co., Ltd.,
Xiamen, China
In-house design
Deqing Yang, Quansen Hu
Web
www.goloy.com

This shower head distinguishes itself from conventional models with a highly minimalist design and unusual copper-coloured finish. The flat, disc-shaped design offers a generous spray area with openings of only 0.3 mm in diameter. These nozzles provide a particularly soft water flow that gently surrounds the user, promoting a relaxing spa experience.

Statement by the jury
This exceptionally designed shower head embodies a timeless elegance. The shower technology is paired with a pronounced user comfort.

Diese Kopfbrause unterscheidet sich in ihrem sehr minimalistischen Design und der ausgefallenen kupferfarbenen Ausführung von gängigen Modellen. Ihre flache, scheibenförmige Gestaltung schafft eine großzügige Sprayfläche, die mit Öffnungen von nur 0,3 mm Durchmesser versehen ist. Diese Düsen sorgen für einen besonders weichen Wasserfluss, der den Benutzer sanft umhüllt und an ein wohltuendes Spa-Erlebnis erinnert.

Begründung der Jury
Diese außergewöhnlich gestaltete Kopfbrause verkörpert zeitlose Eleganz. Ihre Brausetechnologie geht einher mit einem ausgeprägten Nutzerkomfort.

Rainshower 310
Digital Shower System
Digitales Duschsystem

Manufacturer
Grohe AG, Düsseldorf, Germany
In-house design
Web
www.grohe.com

The Rainshower 310 digital shower system merges design and technology. The round, timelessly and elegantly formed controller includes all control functions. The three available spray types can be regulated by pushing the respective symbols indicated on the digital controller. Once a spray is activated, users immediately receive tactile feedback. The design of the shower system eliminates the need for complex in-wall mounting, which significantly simplifies installation and commissioning.

Das digitale Duschsystem Rainshower 310 vereint Design und Technologie. Dabei umfasst das runde, zeitlos-elegant gestaltete Bedienelement sämtliche Steuerungsfunktionen. Die drei zur Verfügung stehenden Strahlarten lassen sich über Drücken des entsprechenden Symbols, mit dem die digitalen Regler gekennzeichnet sind, steuern. Sobald eine Strahlart aktiviert ist, erhält der Nutzer umgehend ein haptisches Feedback. Bei der Konzeption des Duschsystems wurde auf aufwendige Unterputzinstallationen verzichtet, wodurch die Montage und Inbetriebnahme deutlich vereinfacht wird.

Statement by the jury
The Rainshower 310 digital shower system, with its state-of-the-art control solution, promotes a contemporary showering experience and high utility value.

Begründung der Jury
Das digitale Duschsystem Rainshower 310 ermöglicht mit seiner modernen Steuerungslösung ein zeitgemäßes Duscherlebnis und erzielt einen hohen Gebrauchswert.

Euphoria SmartControl 310 Chrome
Shower System
Duschsystem

Manufacturer
Grohe AG, Düsseldorf, Germany
In-house design
Web
www.grohe.com

Characterised by a slim design and compact dimensions, the shower system embodies a space-saving solution that easily integrates into smaller bathrooms. The shower head is generously sized with a diameter of 310 mm, and is available in a round and a square design, ensuring relaxing shower experiences. The operation is simple and self-explanatory: at the touch of a button, the spray type is selected, and then the water flow adjusted with a turn of the knob.

Statement by the jury
The Euphoria SmartControl 310 Chrome shower system fascinates with its minimalist design, which has been convincingly attuned to deliver user-oriented functions.

Eine schlanke Gestaltung und kompakte Abmessungen zeichnen das Duschsystem aus, das auch in kleineren Bädern platzsparend integriert werden kann. Großzügig dimensioniert ist die Duschbrause mit einem Durchmesser von 310 mm, die – in quadratischer oder runder Ausführung – für ein entspannendes Duschen sorgt. Die Bedienung ist einfach und selbsterklärend: Per Knopfdruck wird die Strahlart gewählt, mit einer Drehung des Reglers kann anschließend der Wasserdurchfluss gesteuert werden.

Begründung der Jury
Das Duschsystem Euphoria SmartControl 310 Chrome begeistert mit einem minimalistischen Design, das überzeugend mit anwenderorientierten Funktionen in Einklang gebracht wird.

Euphoria SmartControl 310 Hard Graphite
Shower System
Duschsystem

Manufacturer
Grohe AG, Düsseldorf, Germany
In-house design
Web
www.grohe.com

With its dark grey surfaces, the Euphoria SmartControl 310 Hard Graphite shower system skilfully showcases modern bathroom design. The rotary knobs with simple symbols on the thermostat front ensure intuitive operation. Thanks to the integrated push-and-turn technology, water flow, spray intensity and temperature can be conveniently and precisely controlled. Directly positioned above the control element, the EasyReach shower shelf provides a convenient storage space for cosmetics.

Statement by the jury
Euphoria SmartControl 310 Hard Graphite fascinates with an unusual, elegant surface design that meets the high standards of modern bathroom ambience.

Mit seinen dunkelgrauen Oberflächen setzt das Duschsystem Euphoria SmartControl 310 Hard Graphite das moderne Bad gekonnt in Szene. Für eine intuitive Bedienbarkeit sorgen die mit einfachen Symbolen versehenen Drehregler an der Front des Thermostats. Dank der integrierten Push-and-Turn-Technologie lassen sich Wasserfluss, Strahlstärke und Temperatur komfortabel und präzise regeln. Direkt über dem Bedienelement ist die Duschablage EasyReach angebracht, auf der Kosmetika platziert werden können.

Begründung der Jury
Euphoria SmartControl 310 Hard Graphite fasziniert mit einer ausgefallenen, eleganten Oberflächengestaltung, die hohen Ansprüchen an ein modernes Badambiente gerecht wird.

EasySET Shower System
Shower System
Duschsystem

Manufacturer
American Standard, Singapore
In-house design
American Standard In-House Design Team
Web
www.lixil.com.sg

Form and function go hand in hand in the EasySET shower system. Its modern, clearly structured appearance is complemented by a variety of user-friendly functions. The EasyGlide holder allows users to adjust the height of the hand shower with only one hand. The spray mode can be selected at the touch of a button, while the desired amount of water is adjusted by turning the dials around the buttons. A colour indicator shows which jet type is in operation.

Statement by the jury
The EasySET shower system is functionally sophisticated, meeting high individual user demands.

Form und Funktion gehen bei dem Duschsystem EasySET Hand in Hand. Sein modernes, klar strukturiertes Erscheinungsbild wird durch viele nutzerfreundliche Funktionen ergänzt. Die Höhe der Handbrause lässt sich über den EasyGlide-Halter mit nur einer Hand nach Wunsch variieren. Per Knopfdruck kann die Strahlart ausgewählt und die gewünschte Wassermenge mit einer Drehung des Reglers eingestellt werden. Ein Farbindikator zeigt an, welche Strahlart in Betrieb ist.

Begründung der Jury
Das Duschsystem EasySET ist funktional ausgeklügelt und wird hohen individuellen Nutzeranforderungen gerecht.

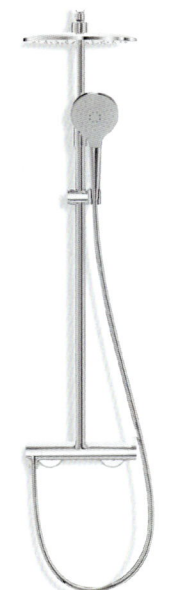

Meka
Shower System
Duschsystem

Manufacturer
JOMOO Kitchen & Bath Co., Ltd.,
Fujian, China
In-house design
Gang Chen, Lichuan Wu, Zhipeng Zheng, Wenqiang Zheng, Xiaoming Lv, Zhihuai Hong
Web
www.jomoo.com.cn

Meka combines user comfort and contemporary design with high versatility. A storage shelf – available in chrome, wood or stone finish – can be installed above the slim thermostat to customise the shower system and make it blend harmoniously into different bathroom interiors. An optional digital temperature display complements the user-oriented functions. Two push buttons, integrated into the side of the rotary knob, enable switching between the hand and overhead shower.

Statement by the jury
The Meka shower system places user needs centre stage, and fulfils the demand for customisable bathroom designs with its versatility.

Meka verbindet Nutzerkomfort und zeitgemäßes Design mit hoher Variabilität. Oberhalb des schlanken Thermostats lässt sich eine Ablagefläche anbringen, die – wahlweise in Chrom, Holz- oder Steinoptik – das Duschsystem individualisiert und stimmig in unterschiedliche Badeinrichtungen einfügt. Bei Bedarf ergänzt eine digitale Temperaturanzeige die nutzerorientierten Funktionen. Seitlich im Drehregler integrierte Knöpfe steuern den Wechsel zwischen Hand- und Kopfbrause.

Begründung der Jury
Das Duschsystem Meka stellt die Nutzerbedürfnisse in den Mittelpunkt und erfüllt mit seiner Variabilität den Wunsch nach individuell gestalteten Bädern.

POPOO
Shower System
Duschsystem

Manufacturer
Guangdong Lehua Intelligent Sanitary Ware Co., Ltd., Foshan, China
Design
Shijiazhuang Yiqi Technology Co., Ltd. (Chen Jianquan, Lin Jie, Cai Zengyi, Lin Kai, Zhang Yu, Zhang Mi, Huang Kunsong, Liu Yibing, Xu Lujiang), Shijiazhuang, China
Jinjiang Yiqi Technology Co., Ltd.,
Jinjiang, China
Web
www.arrowsanitary.com.cn
www.yiqitech.cn

Clear contours and geometric shapes give the POPOO shower system a contemporary look. The flat and level surface of the wall-fixed overhead shower continues in the shower rod, while the thermostat creatively picks up on the round shape of the overhead shower. Water flow and temperature are controlled by a rotary knob that is recessed in the side of the fitting and emerges upon a slight push. Only then the shower can be put into operation, a lock function that reliably prevents scalding.

Statement by the jury
POPOO impresses with a sophisticated design. The combination of distinctive and soft shapes lends it a gentle yet precise appearance.

Klare Konturen und geometrische Formen verleihen dem Duschsystem POPOO eine zeitgemäße Anmutung. Die plane Fläche der fest installierten Kopfbrause setzt sich in der Duschstange fort, während der Thermostat gestalterisch die runde Form der Kopfbrause aufnimmt. Wasserfluss und -temperatur werden über einen Drehknopf geregelt, der seitlich in der Armatur versenkt ist und auf leichten Druck hervortritt. Erst dann kann die Dusche in Betrieb genommen werden. Dieser Sperrmodus beugt Verbrühungen zuverlässig vor.

Begründung der Jury
POPOO beeindruckt durch eine ausgereifte Gestaltung. Die Kombination markanter und weicher Formen vermittelt einen sanften und zugleich präzisen Eindruck.

Croma E 280 Showerpipe
Shower System
Duschsystem

Manufacturer
Hansgrohe SE, Schiltach, Germany
Design
Phoenix Design GmbH + Co. KG,
Stuttgart, Germany
Web
www.hansgrohe.com
www.phoenixdesign.com

Croma E 280 harmonises with both rounded and angular bathroom elements, and thus easily adapts to a variety of interior styles. The shower system is defined by its generously dimensioned overhead shower, which features a SoftCube design combining straight edges and gently rounded corners. Its extra-soft RainAir shower function makes showering especially enjoyable for children as well. In addition, the corresponding hand shower offers the three spray modes of SoftRain, IntenseRain and Massage.

Statement by the jury
The design of Croma E 280 is aesthetically sophisticated. The shower system can be harmoniously integrated into any bathroom interior.

Croma E 280 harmoniert mit runden sowie eckigen Badelementen und passt somit zu einer Vielzahl von Einrichtungsstilen. Das Duschsystem wird geprägt von der großzügig dimensionierten Kopfbrause, die in ihrem SoftCube-Design gerade Kanten und sanft abgerundete Ecken zusammenführt. Ihre üppig-weiche Duschfunktion RainAir macht das Duschen auch für Kinder besonders angenehm. Die zugehörige Handbrause verfügt zudem über die drei Strahlarten SoftRain, IntenseRain und Massage.

Begründung der Jury
Die Formgebung von Croma E 280 ist ästhetisch ausgereift. Das Duschsystem lässt sich harmonisch in jede Badeinrichtung integrieren.

JUSTIME Nature
Built-In Bath/Shower Mixers
Unterputz Bad- und Duschsystem

Manufacturer
Shengtai Brassware Co., Ltd.,
Changhua, Taiwan
In-house design
Justime Design Team
Web
www.justime.com

The design of this bath and shower system was inspired by nature. Marked by soft lines, gentle contours and an interplay of shapes, the disordered, organic growth of meristem or plant tissue is clearly reflected in the design of "Nature". The hand showers of this bath system feature a cylindrical shape while the spout tapers conically, lending it its organic appearance. "Nature" is also easy to install, thanks to a movable cartridge. And even after the installation of the valve, the position can be adjusted by up to 10 mm.

Statement by the jury
The "Nature" bath and shower system merges different shapes in an extremely harmonious way. The installation effort is minimal and user-friendly.

Die Natur war Inspirationsquelle bei der Konzeption dieses Bad- und Duschsystems. Das ungeordnete Wachstum des Pflanzengewebes Meristem spiegelt sich in der Gestaltung von Nature wider, das von weichen Linien, sanften Konturen und einem Spiel mit Formen geprägt ist. Die Handbrausen sind zylindrisch geformt, der Auslauf des Badsystems läuft konisch zu, was ihm eine organische Anmutung verleiht. Dank einer beweglichen Kartusche lässt sich Nature leicht installieren. Auch nach der Montage des Ventils kann die Position um bis zu 10 mm variiert werden.

Begründung der Jury
In dem Bad- und Duschsystem Nature sind unterschiedliche Formen äußerst stimmig kombiniert. Der Installationsaufwand ist gering und anwenderfreundlich.

JUSTIME Yes 2
Shower Mixers
Duschsystem

Manufacturer
Shengtai Brassware Co., Ltd.,
Changhua, Taiwan
In-house design
Justime Design Team
Web
www.justime.com

Hand shower, thermostat and controls of the JUSTIME Yes 2 feature a cylindrical shape. This lends the shower system an extravagant and puristic appearance that also delivers a high degree of user-friendliness. The Y-shaped controls are intuitive to use, while smooth recesses in the handles ensure a secure grip during operation. The necessary technology has been skilfully integrated into the shower system. The cartridge is located in front of the wall, and together with the simplified structure of the valve facilitates maintenance.

Statement by the jury
The unusual, minimalist appearance of the JUSTIME Yes 2 shower system creates a modern aesthetic in bathrooms. Operating it is highly intuitive.

Handbrause, Thermostat und Regler von JUSTIME Yes 2 sind zylindrisch geformt. Das verleiht dem Duschsystem ein extravagantes, puristisches Äußeres, das zudem hohe Nutzerfreundlichkeit mit sich bringt. Die wie ein „Y" gestalteten Regler sind intuitiv zu bedienen, sanfte Vertiefungen in den Griffen sorgen für sicheren Halt bei der Bedienung. Die notwendige Technik wurde geschickt in das Duschsystem integriert. Die Kartusche liegt vor der Wand, was die Wartung zusammen mit dem einfach konzipierten Ventil erleichtert.

Begründung der Jury
Das ausgefallene, minimalistische Erscheinungsbild des Duschsystems JUSTIME Yes 2 erzeugt eine moderne Ästhetik im Bad. Seine Bedienung erschließt sich dem Nutzer intuitiv.

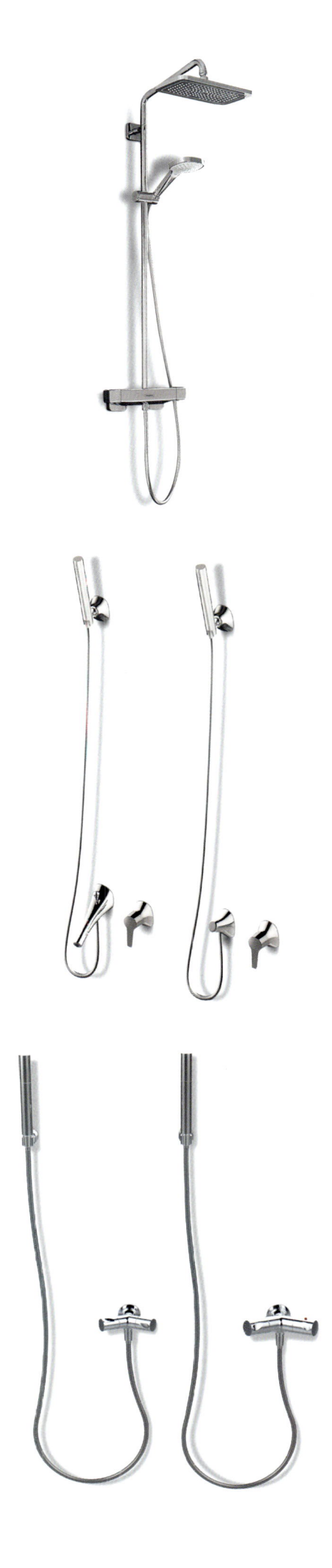

Ultra-Simplified Liquid silicone hand shower
Hand Shower
Handbrause

Manufacturer
Hangzhou Qingguxiaoxiang
Technology Co., Ltd., Hangzhou, China
Design
AUG Shenzhen Industrial Design Co., Ltd.
(Gao Fanyu, Zhang Wei), Shenzhen, China
Web
www.augid.com.cn

The design objective of the Liquid hand shower was to merge aesthetics and sustainability. The use of environmentally friendly, pollutant-free materials has therefore been placed centre stage in its conception. The white, narrow-rimmed spray surface is made of non-toxic, food-grade silica gel. The small nozzles with a diameter of only 0.4 mm ensure a particularly soft, fine water flow.

Statement by the jury
With its clear design, the Liquid hand shower embodies timeless elegance and also scores with high user-friendliness.

Ästhetik und Nachhaltigkeit zu vereinen, war das Ziel der Gestaltung bei der Handbrause Liquid. Die Verwendung umweltfreundlicher, schadstofffreier Materialien stand daher im Mittelpunkt der Konzeption. Die weiß gehaltene Sprühfläche mit schmalem Rand besteht aus ungiftigem Silicagel in Lebensmittelqualität. Die kleinen, einen Durchmesser von lediglich 0,4 mm aufweisenden Düsen sorgen für einen besonders weichen, feinen Wasserfluss.

Begründung der Jury
Die Handbrause Liquid verkörpert aufgrund ihrer klaren Gestaltung zeitlose Eleganz und punktet zudem mit hoher Nutzerfreundlichkeit.

Spirit V2.0
Hand Shower
Handbrause

Manufacturer
AM PM Europe GmbH, Berlin, Germany
Design
GP designpartners gmbh
(Christoph Pauschitz), Vienna, Austria
Web
www.ampm-germany.com
www.gp.co.at

The Spirit V2.0 hand shower combines three spray modes into a shower head that is marked by harmonious lines. A pushbutton positioned between handle and shower changes the natural spray into the revitalising EnerJet or the relaxing Spray+Massage function. The individual nozzles are designed to form soft transitions to the all-white spray surface, lending the hand shower particularly good hygiene properties.

Statement by the jury
Spirit V2.0 convinces with a user-oriented design. The design language is restrained, yet at the same time sets effective accents.

Die Handbrause Spirit V2.0 vereint drei Strahlarten in dem von einer harmonischen Linienführung gekennzeichneten Kopf. Die zwischen Griff und Brause positionierte Drucktaste regelt den Wechsel vom natürlichen Spray zur vitalisierenden EnerJet- oder zur entspannenden Spray+Massage-Funktion. Die einzelnen Düsen sind so konzipiert, dass weiche Übergänge zu der ganz in Weiß gehaltenen Strahlfläche entstehen – so zeigt die Handbrause besonders gute Hygieneeigenschaften.

Begründung der Jury
Spirit V2.0 überzeugt mit einer nutzerorientierten Gestaltung. Die Formensprache ist zurückhaltend und setzt zugleich wirkungsvolle Akzente.

Cloud
Shower System
Duschsystem

Manufacturer
Xiamen Clease Industries Co., Ltd.,
Xiamen, China
In-house design
Zhida Chen, Xian Lin
Web
www.solex.cn

"Cloud" merges overhead shower, mixer and hand shower into a consistently designed unit. The main design feature of the shower system are the all-black spray surfaces that set visual accents and, thanks to a circular arrangement of the nozzles, can create eight different spray types – from the gentle "Silk Spray" to the rain shower. The smooth, sleek surface structure is easy to clean. In addition, a sophisticated self-cleaning function keeps the nozzles clear and prevents limescale accumulation.

Statement by the jury
The "Cloud" shower system appeals with a reduced appearance, which focuses on functionality and user-friendliness.

Cloud vereint Kopfbrause, Mischer und Handbrause zu einer schlüssig gestalteten Einheit. Gestalterisches Hauptmerkmal des Duschsystems sind die ganz in Schwarz gehaltenen Sprühflächen, die optisch Akzente setzen und mit ihren kreisförmig angeordneten Düsen acht verschiedene Strahlarten entstehen lassen – vom sanften „Silkspray" bis zur Regendusche. Die glatte, geschmeidige Oberflächenstruktur lässt sich leicht säubern. Zudem hält eine ausgeklügelte Selbstreinigungsfunktion die Düsen durchlässig und verhindert Kalkablagerungen.

Begründung der Jury
Das Duschsystem Cloud gefällt mit einem reduzierten Erscheinungsbild, das Funktionalität und Benutzerfreundlichkeit in den Fokus rückt.

Ecostat E WAP CoolContact
Bathtub Thermostat with CoolContact
Wannenthermostat mit CoolContact

Manufacturer
Hansgrohe SE, Schiltach, Germany
Design
Phoenix Design GmbH + Co. KG, Stuttgart, Germany
Web
www.hansgrohe.com
www.phoenixdesign.com

Distinctive contours lend the Ecostat E WAP bathtub thermostat a modern appeal. The rosettes are positioned almost invisibly behind the thermostat, supporting a clear design style. The innovative CoolContact cooling technology and the integrated SafetyStop ensure a safe bathing experience, as they prevent the thermostat housing from heating up and ensure that the water from the shower is pleasantly tempered and not too hot.

Statement by the jury
Ecostat E WAP fascinates with an overall well-balanced concept that harmoniously merges modern aesthetics with user-friendly functionality.

Markante Konturen verleihen dem Wannenthermostat Ecostat E WAP eine moderne Anmutung. Die Rosetten sind nahezu unsichtbar hinter dem Thermostat positioniert, wodurch der klare Gestaltungsstil unterstützt wird. Für ein sicheres Badeerlebnis sorgen die innovative Kühltechnologie CoolContact und der integrierte SafetyStop. Diese verhindern das Aufheizen des Thermostatgehäuses und gewährleisten, dass das Wasser angenehm temperiert und nicht zu heiß aus der Brause kommt.

Begründung der Jury
Ecostat E WAP begeistert mit einem ausgewogenen Gesamtkonzept, das moderne Ästhetik und anwenderfreundliche Funktionalität überzeugend in Einklang bringt.

Vienna
Shower System
Duschsystem

Manufacturer
Bravat, Guangzhou, China
In-house design
Yuxing Zheng, Jianan Ji, Wanfeng Wu
Web
www.bravat.com

The core element of the Vienna shower system is its user-friendly push-button technology. Seamlessly integrated into the control element, two buttons direct the water flow into either the overhead or the hand shower. Finely-drawn symbols, positioned quite visibly above the push-buttons, ensure easy handling. The water intensity is adjusted by a separate, pivoting lever, that opens at a 90-degree angle and enables continuous, precise regulation of the water flow.

Statement by the jury
The Vienna shower system places the needs of users at centre stage and fascinates with intuitive usability.

Herzstück des Duschsystems Vienna ist die benutzerfreundliche Druckknopftechnologie. Über zwei nahtlos in das Bedienelement integrierte Tasten wird der Wasserfluss in die Kopf- oder die Handbrause gelenkt. Fein gezeichnete Symbole, die gut sichtbar oberhalb der Drucktasten angebracht sind, gewährleisten eine einfache Handhabung. Die Strahlstärke wird über einen separaten, schwenkbaren Regler gesteuert, der sich im 90-Grad-Winkel öffnet und eine stufenlose, genaue Regulierung der Wassermenge zulässt.

Begründung der Jury
Das Duschsystem Vienna stellt die Bedürfnisse der Nutzer in den Mittelpunkt und beeindruckt mit intuitiver Bedienbarkeit.

X-Joy
Single-Lever Bath and Shower Mixer
Einhebel-Wannenarmatur/-Brausearmatur

Manufacturer
AM PM Europe GmbH, Berlin, Germany
Design
GP designpartners gmbh (Christoph Pauschitz), Vienna, Austria
Web
www.ampm-germany.com
www.gp.co.at

X-Joy merges round shapes, clear contours and gently rounded edges to form a timelessly designed bath and shower mixer that harmoniously complements various interior design styles in bathrooms. The distinctively shaped, upward-pointing lever provides a pleasant feel and enables safe and easy operation. The water flow and temperature can be continuously adjusted and regulated.

Statement by the jury
The skilful interplay of geometric shapes lends X-Joy a dynamic aesthetic. The bath and shower mixer blends well into almost any ambience.

Runde Formen, klare Konturen und sanft abgerundete Kanten fügen sich in X-Joy zu einer zeitlos gestalteten Wannen- und Brausearmatur, die verschiedene Einrichtungsstile im Bad stimmig ergänzt. Der markant geformte, nach oben zeigende Griff bietet eine angenehme Haptik und ermöglicht die sichere und einfache Bedienbarkeit. Wasserfluss und Temperatur lassen sich stufenlos einstellen und regulieren.

Begründung der Jury
Das gekonnte Spiel mit geometrischen Formen verleiht X-Joy eine dynamische Ästhetik. Die Wannen- und Brausearmatur fügt sich gut in nahezu jedes Ambiente ein.

Architectural lighting	Arbeitsleuchten
Built-in lighting	Architekturleuchten
Ceiling lighting	Außenleuchten
Decorative lighting	Deckenleuchten
Desk lamps	Dekorationsleuchten
Downlights	Downlights
Dynamic lighting	Dynamisches Licht
Floodlighting	Einbauleuchten
Floor lamps	Fluter
Hanging lamps	Hängeleuchten
Light bulbs and tubes	Leuchtmittel
Mobile lighting	Mobile Leuchten
Outdoor lamps	Outdoor-Leuchten
Outdoor lighting	Pendelleuchten
Pendant luminaires	Retailleuchten
Retail lighting	Schreibtischleuchten
Solar-powered lamps	Solarleuchten
Special-purpose lamps	Spezialleuchten
Spotlights	Stehleuchten
Table lamps	Strahler
Torches	Taschenlampen
Wall lamps	Tischleuchten
Work lighting	Wandleuchten

Lighting and lamps
Licht und Leuchten

Aperture Circles
Pendant Luminaire
Pendelleuchte

Manufacturer
Fluxwerx Illumination Inc.,
Surrey, British Columbia, Canada

In-house design
Fluxwerx Illumination Inc.

Web
www.fluxwerx.com

reddot award 2019
best of the best

Fascinating openness
The idea of guiding light playfully through invisible apertures to add more aesthetic appeal to the interior of a house is an idea that dates all the way back to antiquity. Available in two different pattern models, Aperture is a linear LED pendant luminaire featuring a fascinating open aperture design. Aperture Circles consists of a series of circular cellular voids that allow clear views through the luminaire to the architecture. The minimalist design of this luminaire delivers an outstanding optical and energy performance. Its anodised architectural grade extruded aluminium components are precision-machined and factory-installed for a perfect fit. Aperture does not require any electrical connections at the fixture joints and can be installed as an independent pendant or as a continuous lighting system with virtually seamless transitions. It delivers highly advanced functionality and energy efficiency. Its innovative ocular anidolic optic technology provides a precisely controlled batwing light distribution with no view of the LED point source, which makes it integrate easily with modern architectural designs. The luminaire's wide-angle indirect distribution option allows for greater on-centre spacing with a uniform, luminous ceiling plane for maximum illumination efficiency and lower energy density.

Faszinierende Offenheit
Die Lenkung und das Spiel mit dem Licht wurde bereits in der Antike für die Ästhetisierung von Räumen genutzt, indem man es durch unsichtbare Schächte ins Innere des Hauses führte. Aperture ist eine in zwei verschiedenen Varianten erhältliche lineare LED-Pendelleuchte mit einer faszinierend offenen Konstruktionsweise. Aperture Circles besteht aus einer Reihe zellenartiger kreisförmiger Hohlräume, durch die hindurch man einen freien Blick auf die Architektur hat. Diese minimalistisch gestaltete Leuchte bietet eine hervorragende optische und energetische Leistung. Ihre aus eloxiertem Aluminium stranggepressten Bauteile in architektonischer Qualität sind präzise gefertigt und werksseitig für eine perfekte Passform vormontiert. Aperture erfordert keine zusätzlichen elektrischen Anschlüsse an den Verbindungsstellen und kann als einzelne Pendelleuchte oder als kontinuierliches Lichtsystem mit nahezu nahtlosen Übergängen installiert werden. Sie bietet eine hochentwickelte Funktionalität und Energieeffizienz. Ausgestattet mit einer innovativen anidolischen Okularoptik-Technologie ermöglicht sie eine präzis kontrollierte Batwing-Lichtverteilung ohne Sicht auf die LED-Punktquelle und integriert sich so gut in zeitgemäße Architektur. Die optionale Ausführung mit indirekter Weitwinkelverteilung erlaubt einen größeren Mittenabstand für eine gleichmäßig helle Deckenebene, bei gleichzeitig maximaler Ausleuchtung und geringerer Energiedichte.

Statement by the jury
With its unusual open design structure, this linear LED pendant luminaire captivates the viewer. With its minimalist lines and invisibly integrated light sources, the luminaire presents itself as an object full of meaning. Based on meticulous attention to design details, it projects technological precision embodied in a lighting solution of almost poetic appeal. This luminaire offers an outstanding optical performance and high energy efficiency.

Begründung der Jury
Mit ihrer ungewöhnlichen Art der Gestaltung zieht diese lineare LED-Pendelleuchte den Betrachter in ihren Bann. Ihre minimalistische Linienführung mit unsichtbar integrierten Lichtquellen macht sie zu einem aussagekräftigen Objekt. Mittels einer exakten Detaillierung wird hier technologische Präzision mit einer geradezu poetisch anmutenden Lichtlösung kombiniert. Diese Leuchte bietet dabei eine hervorragende optische Leistung und hohe Energieeffizienz.

Designer portrait
See page 62
Siehe Seite 62

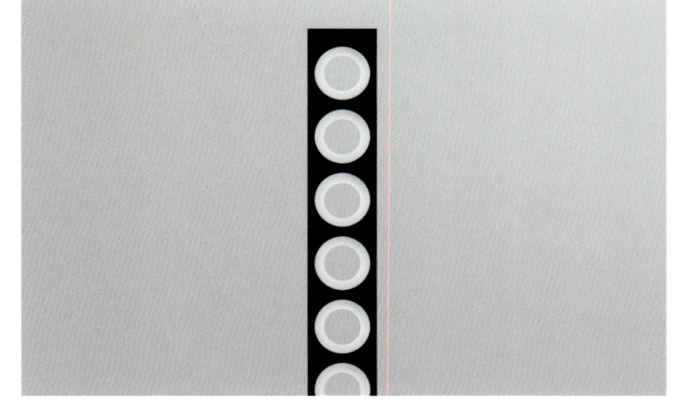

333

Aperture Squares
Pendant Luminaire
Pendelleuchte

Manufacturer
Fluxwerx Illumination Inc.,
Surrey, British Columbia, Canada
In-house design
Web
www.fluxwerx.com

Aperture Squares is a linear pendant luminaire featuring a unique open aperture with a series of square, cellular voids. It can be installed as an independent pendant or as a continuous lighting system with virtually seamless runs. Its integral ocular Anidolic optic technology provides a precisely controlled batwing distribution with no view of the LED point source. Combining performance, aesthetics and value, the luminaire opens up opportunities for a wide range of applications.

Statement by the jury
Thanks to its geometric design language, the glare-free Aperture Squares pendant luminaire achieves an overall architectural appearance.

Aperture Squares ist eine lineare Pendelleuchte, deren offene Blenden in Form von quadratischen Zellhohlräumen charakteristisch gestaltet sind. Sie kann entweder einzeln oder als kontinuierliches System in einer scheinbar nahtlosen Leuchtenreihe installiert werden. Ihre anidolische Optik sorgt für eine gleichmäßige Lichtstärkenverteilung ohne sichtbare LED-Punktquelle. Mit der Kombination von Leistung, Ästhetik und Nutzen eröffnet die Leuchte Möglichkeiten für vielseitige Anwendungen.

Begründung der Jury
Aufgrund ihrer geometrischen Linienführung erreicht die blendfreie Pendelleuchte Aperture Squares ein architektonisch anmutendes Gesamtbild.

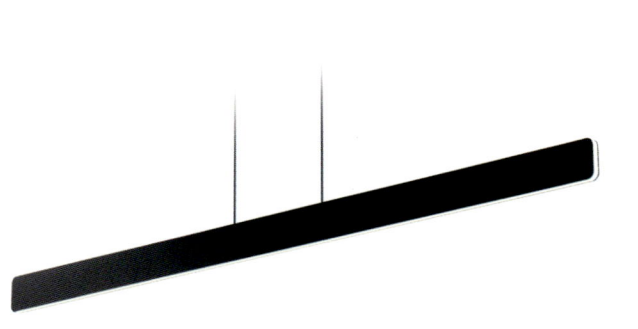

Sub
Pendant Luminaire
Pendelleuchte

Manufacturer
Koncept, Monrovia, California, USA
In-house design
Edmund Ng, Kenneth Ng
Web
www.koncept.com

A continuous line of LED lights wraps around the entire profile of this pendant luminaire, offering 360 degrees light emission. Sub serves as a direct task light as well as providing indirect ambient lighting. The minimalist body, made of matte polished aluminium, is distinctively slim and the suspension discreetly conceals the power supply. The luminaire is compatible with ELV wall dimmers and suitable for contemporary homes as well as public areas.

Statement by the jury
Following a minimalist design approach, the Sub pendant luminaire showcases linear aesthetics, underlining its high degree of functionality.

Eine durchgehende Reihe von LEDs umschließt das gesamte Profil dieser Pendelleuchte und bietet somit eine 360-Grad-Lichtemission. Sub dient daher sowohl der direkten Arbeitsplatzbeleuchtung als auch der indirekten Raumbeleuchtung. Das minimalistische Gehäuse aus mattpoliertem Aluminium ist auffallend flach, wobei die Aufhängung die Stromversorgung dezent verbirgt. Die Pendelleuchte ist mit ELV-Wanddimmern kompatibel und eignet sich für zeitgemäße Wohnungen sowie öffentliche Bereiche.

Begründung der Jury
Einem minimalistischen Gestaltungsansatz folgend, zeigt die Pendelleuchte Sub eine lineare Ästhetik, die eine hohe Funktionalität untermalt.

MUSE LIGHT
Pendant Luminaire
Pendelleuchte

Manufacturer
XAL GmbH, Graz, Austria
In-house design
Web
www.xal.com

This pendant luminaire has been developed to have a positive impact on lighting conditions and acoustics in offices. The double-walled body of the luminaire consists of self-supporting polyester fleece with sound-absorbing properties. Available in felt grey, anthracite, indigo blue and light blue, the lamp creates positive visual effects. MUSE LIGHT is height-adjustable without tools. The glare-free pendant light can be dimmed and combined with additional sound-reducing elements.

Statement by the jury
A highly self-reliant design language characterises this pendant lamp, which also impresses with its multi-functionality.

Um die Beleuchtung und die Akustik in Büroräumen positiv zu beeinflussen, wurde diese Pendelleuchte entwickelt. Der doppelwandige Leuchtenkörper besteht aus einem selbsttragenden Polyester-Vlies mit schallabsorbierenden Eigenschaften. Wahlweise in Filzgrau, Anthrazit, Indigoblau oder Hellblau erhältlich, setzt die Leuchte visuelle Akzente. MUSE LIGHT ist werkzeuglos höhenverstellbar. Die blendfreie Pendelleuchte lässt sich dimmen und mit zusätzlichen schallreduzierenden Elementen kombinieren.

Begründung der Jury
Eine höchst eigenständige Formensprache zeichnet diese Pendelleuchte aus. Darüber hinaus beeindruckt ihre Multifunktionalität.

One-And-Only
Pendant Luminaire
Pendelleuchte

Manufacturer
Delta Light N.V., Wevelgem, Belgium
In-house design
Web
www.deltalight.com

The objective in the design of One-And-Only was to create a linear luminaire profile which catches the eye even with the power switched off. The cross-shaped profile of the distinctive body allows up to five lines of light: three for direct and two for indirect illumination above bar counters, reception desks or conference tables. In addition to other models, the lamp is available with anodised metal sides in gold champagne colour and black end caps.

Statement by the jury
Thanks to its distinctive profile design, the pendant luminaire sets architectural accents in public spaces, offering versatile illumination.

Zielführende Prämisse bei der Gestaltung von One-And-Only war es, ein lineares Leuchtenprofil zu schaffen, das auch im ausgeschalteten Modus Aufmerksamkeit weckt. Das kreuzförmige Profil des prägnanten Gehäuses ermöglicht bis zu fünf Lichtlinien: drei für eine direkte und zwei für eine indirekte Beleuchtung von Tresen, Empfangstheken oder Konferenztischen. Neben weiteren Ausführungen ist die Leuchte mit eloxierten Metallseiten im Farbton Gold Champagne sowie schwarzen Endkappen erhältlich.

Begründung der Jury
Dank ihrer prägnanten Profilgestaltung setzt die Pendelleuchte architektonische Akzente in öffentlichen Räumen und bietet eine vielseitige Beleuchtung.

Philips Ledalite Eyeline
Pendant Luminaire
Pendelleuchte

Manufacturer
Signify, Langley, British Columbia, Canada
In-house design
Signify Design Team,
Burlington, Massachusetts, USA
Web
www.signify.com

The Eyeline pendant luminaire has been developed to make a bold statement in any architectural scenario while, at the same time, offering high application flexibility. Thin, modular panels merge to create a linear lighting solution by combining direct and indirect light. Gently curved ends emphasise the gap between the rectangular modules, creating smooth transitions. The glare-free, yet powerful LEDs allow large row spacing.

Statement by the jury
As an expression of a sophisticated design concept, this pendant luminaire is characterised by its contemporary aesthetics and high level of lighting comfort.

Um in unterschiedlichen architektonischen Szenarien ein Zeichen zu setzen und zugleich eine hohe Anwendungsflexibilität zu bieten, wurde die Pendelleuchte Eyeline entwickelt. Flache, modulare Paneele vereinen sich zu einer linearen Beleuchtungslösung, die direktes mit indirektem Licht kombiniert. Sanft gerundete Enden betonen den Spalt zwischen den rechteckigen Modulen und sorgen so für einen ausgewogenen Übergang. Die blendfreien und dennoch leistungsstarken LEDs machen einen großen Reihenabstand möglich.

Begründung der Jury
Als Ausdruck eines durchdachten Gestaltungskonzepts zeichnet sich diese Pendelleuchte durch ihre zeitgemäße Ästhetik und ihren hohen Beleuchtungskomfort aus.

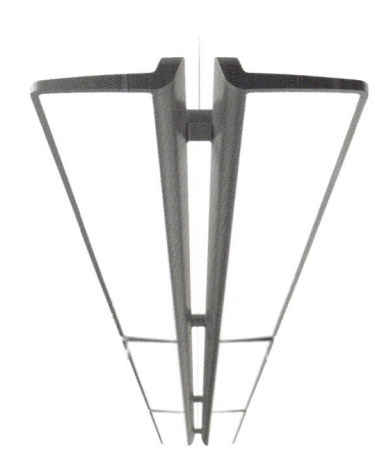

SMALL LINE
Pendant Luminaire
Pendelleuchte

Manufacturer
Performance in Lighting S.p.A.,
Colognola ai Colli (Verona), Italy
In-house design
Design
Büro Sommer, Zapfendorf, Germany
Web
www.performanceinlighting.com
www.buero-sommer.de

SMALL LINE consists of three LED-equipped aluminium profiles joined to form a slim, translucent pendant luminaire. The suspension, which has no visible power cord, lends the luminaire an elegant appearance. Developed for use in offices, the luminaire is available in different versions: with individual lenses for optimal light distribution or with high-gloss reflectors for maximum efficiency. Both provide both glare-free direct light and pleasant indirect room lighting.

Statement by the jury
The characteristic overall appearance of this pendant luminaire is marked by clear lines. Moreover, the luminaire provides convincing functionality.

SMALL LINE besteht aus drei LED-bestückten Aluminiumprofilen, die sich zu einer schmalen, lichtdurchlässigen Pendelleuchte vereinen. Eine Aufhängung ohne sichtbare Stromversorgung verleiht der Leuchte Eleganz. Die für den Einsatz im Büro konzipierte Leuchte wird in unterschiedlichen Ausführungen angeboten: mit einzelnen Linsen für eine optimale Streuung des Lichts oder hochglänzenden Reflektoren für maximale Effizienz. Beide bieten sowohl blendfreies Direktlicht als auch eine angenehme indirekte Raumbeleuchtung.

Begründung der Jury
Eine klare Linienführung prägt das charakteristische Gesamtbild dieser Pendelleuchte, die zudem eine überzeugende Funktionalität bietet.

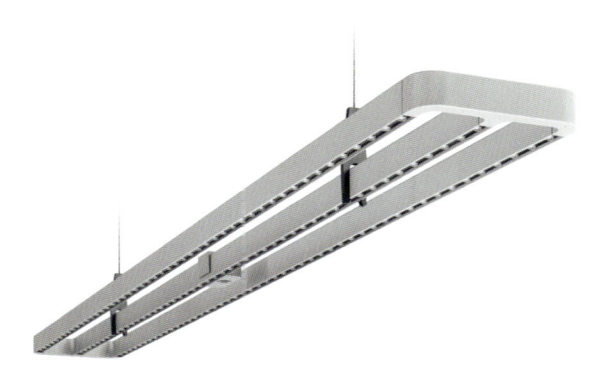

Art
Pendant Luminaire
Pendelleuchte

Manufacturer
Arkoslight, Ribarroja del Turia, Spain
In-house design
Rubén Saldaña Acle
Web
www.arkoslight.com

Art is a minimalist pendant luminaire which allows for a versatile range of arrangements: while it exudes a rather sober look as a single lamp, it reveals a distinctive sculptural effect when it is arranged in an ensemble. Its flexibility makes it suitable for both the subtle illumination of a table as well as for serving as a gentle, indirect ambient light. Each pendant lamp consists of three cylindrical luminaires held together by slim connecting bars. The discreet cable routing enhances the floating character of the light-weight pendant luminaire.

Art ist eine minimalistische Pendelleuchte, die eine flexible Bandbreite an Kompositionen erlaubt: Während sie als einzelne Leuchte eher nüchtern wirkt, entfaltet sie als Leuchten-Ensemble eine auffallend skulpturale Wirkung. Ihre Vielseitigkeit ermöglicht sowohl eine dezente Beleuchtung von Tischen als auch eine sanfte, indirekte Raumbeleuchtung. Jede Pendelleuchte besteht aus drei zylindrischen Leuchtkörpern, die durch schmale Zwischenstücke miteinander verbunden sind. Die dezente Kabelführung unterstützt den schwebenden Charakter der leicht anmutenden Pendelleuchte.

Statement by the jury
The Art pendant luminaire fascinates with its clear geometric design, which exudes an appearance which is both simple and distinctive.

Begründung der Jury
Die Pendelleuchte Art begeistert aufgrund ihrer klaren geometrischen Gestaltung, die gleichermaßen schlicht und charakteristisch erscheint.

Hugo Architectural System
Pendant Luminaire
Pendelleuchte

Manufacturer
Slamp S.p.A., Pomezia (Rome), Italy
In-house design
Web
www.slamp.com

The Hugo Architectural System provides versatile lighting solutions for both private and public places. With its elegant linear design, it is suitable for installations with several lights, freely arranged in different orientations and heights. Two to seven pendant luminaires can be connected to one power source, using flexible cables. A patented synthetic polymer provides a soft, wide room light. The system is in line with the UNI EN 12464-1:2011 standard.

Das Hugo Architectural System erlaubt eine vielfältige Raumbeleuchtung, sowohl im privaten als auch im öffentlichen Bereich. Mit seiner eleganten Linienführung eignet es sich für Lichtinstallationen, bei denen mehrere Leuchten in unterschiedlichen Ausrichtungen und Höhen angeordnet werden. An einem Stromanschluss können jeweils zwei bis sieben Pendelleuchten installiert werden, wozu sich deren Anschlusskabel flexibel biegen lassen. Patentiertes Technopolymer sorgt für weiches, breitflächiges Raumlicht. Das System entspricht der Norm UNI EN 12464-1: 2011.

Statement by the jury
In combination with an architecturally appealing design, the creative arrangement of these pendant luminaires catches the eye.

Begründung der Jury
In Kombination mit einer architektonisch anmutenden Gestaltung erweckt die kreative Anordnung dieser Pendelleuchten die Aufmerksamkeit der Betrachter.

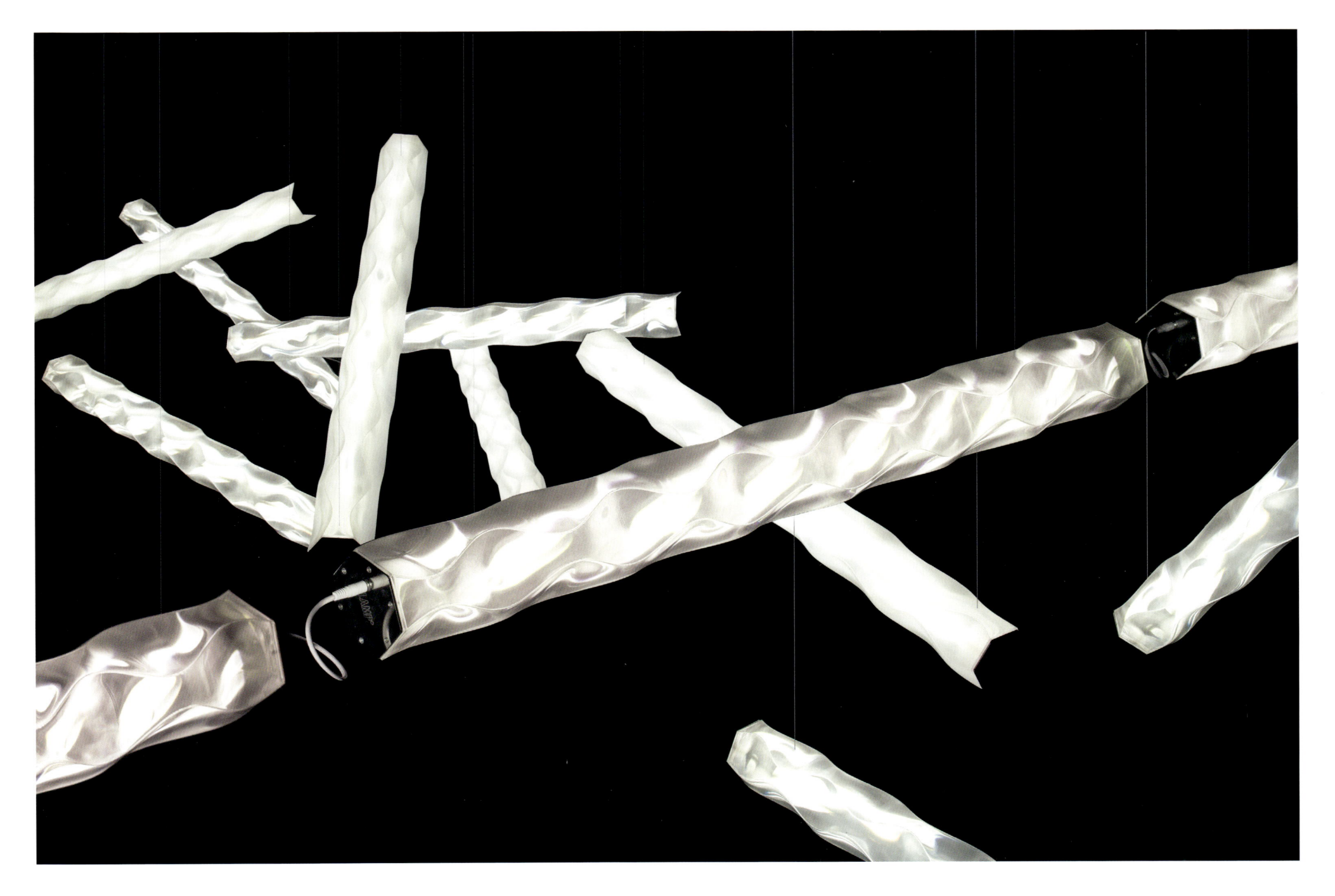

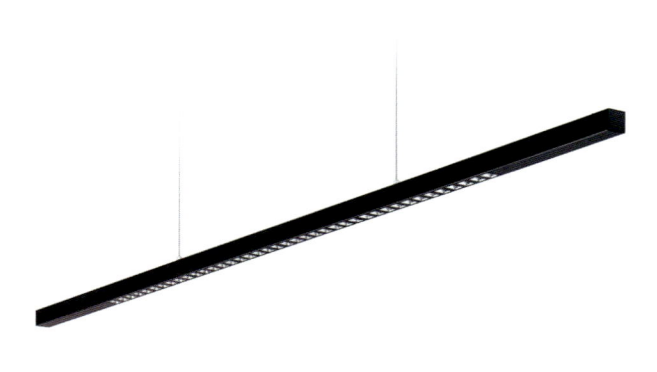

LINETIK
Pendant Luminaire
Pendelleuchte

Manufacturer
Zumtobel Lighting GmbH,
Dornbirn, Austria
Design
F Mark Ltd., Gamlingay,
Cambridgeshire, United Kingdom
Luke Smith-Wightman,
London/Brighton, United Kingdom
Web
www.zumtobel.com
www.fmark.co.uk
www.lukesmith-wightman.com

With a cross section of 25 × 25 mm, LINETIK is a filigree, linear pendant luminaire for the commercial sector. The individually controllable, direct and indirect light components allow a flexible adaptation to the respective lighting requirements. Complying with EN 12464, the luminaire creates a comfortable balance between room and workplace lighting. Thanks to its formal reduction, it blends harmoniously into different architectures and is also available in various colour combinations.

Statement by the jury
Following a consistent design and equipped with advanced technology, this pendant luminaire discreetly blends into the interior.

Mit einem Querschnitt von 25 × 25 mm ist LINETIK eine filigrane, lineare Pendelleuchte für den Objektbereich. Die individuell steuerbaren Direkt- und Indirektlichtanteile ermöglichen eine flexible Anpassung an den jeweiligen Beleuchtungsbedarf. Unter Berücksichtigung der DIN EN 12464 bietet die Leuchte eine komfortable Balance zwischen Raum- und Arbeitsplatzbeleuchtung. Dank ihrer formalen Reduktion fügt sie sich harmonisch in die Architektur ein, zudem ist sie in diversen Farbkonstellationen erhältlich.

Begründung der Jury
Einer konsequenten Linienführung folgend und mit einer hochentwickelten Technologie ausgestattet, fügt sich diese Pendelleuchte dezent ins Interieur ein.

CLARIS evolution
Pendant Luminaire
Pendelleuchte

Manufacturer
Zumtobel Lighting GmbH,
Dornbirn, Austria
Design
a·g Licht GbR (Klaus Adolph),
Bonn, Germany
Web
www.zumtobel.com
www.aglicht.de

With a width of 128 mm and a visible height of only 26 mm, this pendant luminaire appears particularly light and slim. CLARIS evolution is available in 24 colour combinations, allowing a harmonious integration into the interior. Its lighting effect can be influenced by a choice of glossy or matt reflectors. The combination of double-sided LED printed circuit board, light chamber, micro-prismatic optics and free-form reflector provides workplaces with light which always conforms to EN 12464.

Statement by the jury
Due to its high functionality and versatility, this pendant luminaire offers a convincing practical value, especially in the commercial sector.

Mit ihrer Breite von 128 mm und einer sichtbaren Höhe von nur 26 mm wirkt diese Pendelleuchte besonders leicht und flach. CLARIS evolution ist in 24 Farbkombinationen erhältlich und ermöglicht so eine stimmige Integration ins Interieur. Ihre Lichtwirkung lässt sich durch die Auswahl von glänzenden oder matten Reflektoren beeinflussen. Eine Kombination aus doppelseitig bestückter LED-Platine, Lichtkammer, Mikroprismen-Optik und Freiformreflektor beleuchtet Arbeitsplätze gemäß DIN EN 12464.

Begründung der Jury
Dank ihrer hohen Funktionalität und Variabilität bietet diese Pendelleuchte einen überzeugenden Gebrauchswert, insbesondere im Objektbereich.

TEELA
Pendant Luminaire
Pendelleuchte

Manufacturer
Zumtobel Lighting GmbH,
Dornbirn, Austria
Design
Delugan Meissl Associated Architects,
Vienna, Austria
Web
www.zumtobel.com
www.dmaa.at

TEELA is a multifaceted pendant luminaire with diffused and accentuated light components. Their spotlights can be controlled regardless of the diffuse component and adjusted continuously by 10 degrees in all directions. The luminaire can be controlled either via Bluetooth and smartphone app or conventionally, while the adjustable tunableWhite diffuse light allows the generation of lighting moods. The lamp is enveloped by a flexible knitted fabric and available in three sizes and two colour versions.

Statement by the jury
With its characteristic contours and sophisticated functionality, this pendant luminaire offers particularly versatile lighting options.

TEELA ist eine facettenreiche Pendelleuchte mit einem diffusen sowie einem akzentuierten Lichtanteil. Ihre Spotlights lassen sich unabhängig vom Diffusanteil steuern und können um 10 Grad stufenlos in jeder Richtung justiert werden. Die Leuchte kann wahlweise via Bluetooth und Smartphone-App oder konventionell gesteuert werden, wobei das über tunableWhite regulierbare Diffuslicht die Generierung von Lichtstimmungen erlaubt. Die Leuchte ist von flexiblem Strickgewebe umhüllt sowie in drei Größen und zwei Farbvarianten erhältlich.

Begründung der Jury
Mit ihren charakteristischen Konturen und ihrer ausgereiften Funktionalität bietet diese Pendelleuchte besonders vielseitige Beleuchtungsmöglichkeiten.

Verner
Pendant Luminaire
Pendelleuchte

Manufacturer
Eureka Lighting, Montreal, Canada
In-house design
Eureka Lighting Design Team
Web
www.eurekalighting.com

Verner is a minimalist pendant luminaire which combines considerable light output with geometric aesthetics. It has been designed for high ceilings and open spaces where only little attention is to be directed towards the ceiling. The cone-shaped lampshade ensures that the glare-free light is directed downwards, intentionally avoiding the indirect illumination of the ceiling. The standard version of the LED light source reaches 2,400 Lumens while the high output model delivers over 4,200 Lumens.

Statement by the jury
Clear lines, adopting a traditional design idiom, emphasise the high light output of this pendant luminaire.

Verner ist eine minimalistische Pendelleuchte, die eine beträchtliche Lichtleistung mit geometrischer Ästhetik verbindet. Sie wurde für hohe Räume und offene Bereiche konzipiert, wo nur wenig Aufmerksamkeit zur Decke gelenkt werden soll. Der kegelförmige Schirm richtet das blendfreie Licht gezielt nach unten, wobei auf eine indirekte Deckenbeleuchtung bewusst verzichtet wird. Die LED-Lichtquelle erreicht in der Standardausführung 2.400 Lumen und über 4.200 Lumen in der lichtstarken Ausführung.

Begründung der Jury
Eine klare Linienführung, die eine traditionelle Formensprache aufgreift, betont die hohe Beleuchtungsleistung dieser Pendelleuchte.

Biba
Pendant Luminaire
Pendelleuchte

Manufacturer
Intra Lighting,
Sempeter pri Gorici, Slovenia
Design
Wilsonic Design, Trzin, Slovenia
Web
www.intra-lighting.com
www.wilsonicdesign.com

Showcasing a compact contour, this pendant luminaire is reminiscent of a water drop. The small-scale body invites an effective arrangement of several lights. Nevertheless, even individually installed luminaires are powerful enough to illuminate a reception desk or a table. Biba fits into the minimalist ambiences of contemporary restaurants, hotel lobbies, urban store concepts and private spaces. The substantial weight of the aluminium pendant luminaire ensures that the power cable is pulled taut.

Statement by the jury
Well-balanced proportions and high-quality materials underline the simple elegance of the miniaturised design of the Biba pendant luminaire.

Mit ihrer kompakten Kontur erinnert diese Pendelleuchte an einen Wassertropfen. Der kleinformatige Korpus bietet ein wirkungsvolles Arrangement mehrerer Leuchten an. Dennoch ist auch eine einzelne Leuchte wirkungsstark genug, um eine Empfangstheke oder einen Tisch auszuleuchten. Biba passt zum minimalistischen Ambiente von zeitgemäßen Restaurants, Hotellobbys, urbanen Store-Konzepten oder privaten Räumen. Das substantielle Gewicht der Pendelleuchte aus Aluminium sorgt dafür, dass das Stromkabel straff gespannt ist.

Begründung der Jury
Ausgewogene Proportionen und hochwertige Materialien untermalen die schlichte Eleganz der miniaturisiert gestalteten Pendelleuchte Biba.

Philips deco LED giant
Pendant Luminaires
Pendelleuchten

Manufacturer
Signify, Shanghai, China
In-house design
Signify Design Team
Web
www.signify.com

The deco LED giant pendant luminaires are reminiscent of traditional incandescent bulbs and delivers a soft, evenly distributed light. The warm white or orange glow from the triple spiral LED filament creates a relaxing lighting mood for sociable places in homes, such as the dining area. The interplay of double-walled glass bodies with their purist suspension exudes the nostalgic charm of the past. The luminaires are available in three models with different contours.

Statement by the jury
Thanks to their visual presence and homely light quality, these pendant luminaires are a fascinating contemporary product solution.

Die Pendelleuchten deco LED giant erinnern an traditionelle Glühbirnen und liefern ein weiches, gleichmäßiges Licht. Das warmweiße oder orangefarbene Leuchten des dreifach spiralförmigen LED-Fadens vermittelt eine entspannende Lichtstimmung für gesellige Wohnbereiche wie Esstische. Das Zusammenspiel doppelwandiger Glaskörper mit einer puristisch anmutenden Aufhängung vermittelt den nostalgischen Charme vergangener Zeiten. Die Leuchten sind in drei unterschiedlichen Konturen erhältlich.

Begründung der Jury
Dank ihrer visuellen Präsenz und ihrer wohnlich anmutenden Lichtqualität faszinieren diese Pendelleuchten als zeitgemäße Produktlösung.

Sero
Pendant Luminaire
Pendelleuchte

Manufacturer
Nulite Lighting, Denver, USA
In-house design
Web
www.nulite-lighting.com

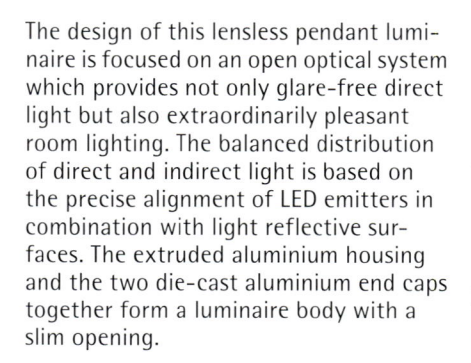

The design of this lensless pendant luminaire is focused on an open optical system which provides not only glare-free direct light but also extraordinarily pleasant room lighting. The balanced distribution of direct and indirect light is based on the precise alignment of LED emitters in combination with light reflective surfaces. The extruded aluminium housing and the two die-cast aluminium end caps together form a luminaire body with a slim opening.

Statement by the jury
With its gently rounded contours, the Sero pendant luminaire exudes an appealing elegance. Moreover, it also offers a high level of lighting comfort.

Bei dieser linsenlosen Pendelleuchte steht ein offenes optisches System im Mittelpunkt der Gestaltung, das neben einem blendfreien Direktlicht eine angenehme Raumbeleuchtung ermöglicht. Die ausgewogene Verteilung von direktem und indirektem Licht beruht auf einer präzisen LED-Ausrichtung in Kombination mit lichtreflektierenden Oberflächen. Das Gehäuse aus stranggepresstem Aluminium bildet in Verbindung mit zwei Endkappen aus Aluminiumdruckguss ein Leuchtenkorpus mit schmaler Öffnung.

Begründung der Jury
Mit ihren sanft gerundeten Konturen vermittelt Sero eine ansprechende Eleganz. Die Pendelleuchte bietet darüber hinaus einen hohen Beleuchtungskomfort.

Philips Hue Ensis
Pendant Luminaire
Pendelleuchte

Manufacturer
Signify, Eindhoven, Netherlands
In-house design
Signify Design Team
Web
www.signify.com

The Hue Ensis pendant luminaire combines scene-setting indirect lighting with a warm white direct light for dining tables or workstations. Following a minimalist design approach, the slim luminaire delivers both up- and down-lighting. Its two LED light strips can be separately controlled via the Hue app, offering a wide choice of colour shades, a light output of up to 6,000 lumens and a colour temperature of up to 6,500 kelvins.

Statement by the jury
This pendant luminaire blends sophisticated lighting technology with an appealing design. In addition, Hue Ensis also offers a high degree of user-friendliness.

Der Pendelleuchte Hue Ensis kombiniert eine stimmungsvolle indirekte Raumbeleuchtung mit einer direkten, warmweißen Esstisch- oder Arbeitsplatzbeleuchtung. Einem minimalistischen Gestaltungsansatz folgend, strahlt die schmale Leuchte das Licht sowohl nach oben als auch nach unten hin ab. Die beiden LED-Leuchtstreifen lassen sich separat über die Hue App steuern. Dabei besteht die Auswahl zwischen unzähligen Farbnuancen, einer Lichtleistung bis zu 6.000 Lumen sowie einer Farbtemperatur von bis zu 6.500 Kelvin.

Begründung der Jury
Eine raffinierte Lichttechnik trifft bei dieser Pendelleuchte auf eine ansprechende Gestaltung. Hue Ensis bietet zudem einen hohen Bedienkomfort.

PIVOT
Lighting System
Lichtsystem

Manufacturer
XAL GmbH, Graz, Austria
In-house design
Web
www.xal.com

PIVOT is a cylindrical light insert made of black anodised aluminium and satined plastic polymer which provides homogeneous illumination. Thanks to its magnetic mount and locking mechanism, it can be installed and moved without tools and thus offers a high degree of flexibility. The lighting system is suitable for mounting in two MOVE IT 25 / 25 S profiles as well as in one profile in axial arrangement. The bracket can be rotated by 360 degrees. The integrated technology offers high efficiency and good colour rendering.

Statement by the jury
As an artistically ambitious product solution, PIVOT exudes a strong visual presence which offers fascinating flexibility.

PIVOT ist ein zylindrischer Lichteinsatz aus schwarz eloxiertem Aluminium und satiniertem Kunststoff, der für eine homogene Ausleuchtung sorgt. Dank Magnethalterung und Verriegelung ist er werkzeuglos einsetz- und verschiebbar und bietet somit ein hohes Maß an Flexibilität. Das Lichtsystem kann in zwei MOVE IT 25 / 25 S Profile sowie in Axialanordnung in ein Profil eingesetzt werden. Die Halterung ist um 360 Grad drehbar. Die integrierte Technologie bietet eine hohe Effizienz und eine gute Farbwiedergabe.

Begründung der Jury
Als künstlerisch ambitionierte Produktlösung erreicht PIVOT eine visuelle Präsenz und bietet eine faszinierende Gestaltungsfreiheit.

Space B
Pendant Luminaire
Pendelleuchte

Manufacturer
Nordlux A/S, Aalborg, Denmark
Design
Bønnelycke Arkitekter ApS, Aarhus, Denmark
Web
www.nordlux.com
www.bonnelycke.com

The design concept of Space B followed the objective of creating a pendant luminaire reduced to the essentials. Its tubular contour opens downwards to form a luminaire body, which confines the light angle to the sides. A discreet, laterally placed switch allows intuitive operation. The pendant luminaire offers a choice between 2,200, and 2,700 as well as 3,000 kelvins, which allows setting the lighting mood to satisfy different illumination requirements.

Statement by the jury
Thanks to its unconventional form, this user-friendly pendant luminaire projects highly distinctive aesthetics.

Das Gestaltungskonzept von Space B folgte der Zielsetzung, eine auf das Wesentliche reduzierte Pendelleuchte zu kreieren. Ihre röhrenförmige Kontur öffnet sich nach unten zu einem Leuchtenkorpus, der den Lichtwinkel seitlich begrenzt. Ein seitlich dezent platzierter Schalter ermöglicht eine intuitive Bedienung. Die Pendelleuchte bietet die Auswahl zwischen 2.200, 2.700 und 3.000 Kelvin, wodurch die Lichtstimmung auf unterschiedliche Beleuchtungsanforderungen abgestimmt werden kann.

Begründung der Jury
Dank ihrer unkonventionellen Form zeigt diese bedienfreundliche Pendelleuchte eine unverwechselbare Ästhetik.

Q LED
Pendant Luminaire
Pendelleuchte

Manufacturer
Nowodworski sp.j., Czestochowa, Poland
In-house design
Lukasz Jaworski
Web
www.nowodvorski.com

Q LED is a pendant luminaire with an asymmetric cover which produces different illumination angles. Since on one side the angle is wider than on the other side, the area below is illuminated wider than on the opposite side. Thus, the pendant luminaire is particularly well suited, for instance, for the targeted illumination of reception desks. Available in white or black, the luminaire has been designed as a product solution for offices and public areas.

Statement by the jury
This purist pendant luminaire owes its high degree of lighting comfort to the consistent implementation of an astounding design idea.

Q LED ist eine Pendelleuchte, deren asymmetrische Abdeckung unterschiedliche Beleuchtungswinkel entstehen lässt. Da der Winkel auf der einen Seite größer als auf der anderen ist, wird der darunterliegende Bereich breitflächiger beleuchtet als auf der gegenüberliegenden Seite. Somit empfiehlt sich die Pendelleuchte u. a. zur gezielten Beleuchtung von Empfangstheken. Die in Weiß oder Schwarz erhältliche Leuchte wurde als Produktlösung für Büros oder öffentliche Bereiche konzipiert.

Begründung der Jury
Der stringenten Umsetzung einer verblüffenden Gestaltungsidee verdankt diese puristische Pendelleuchte ein hohes Maß an Beleuchtungskomfort.

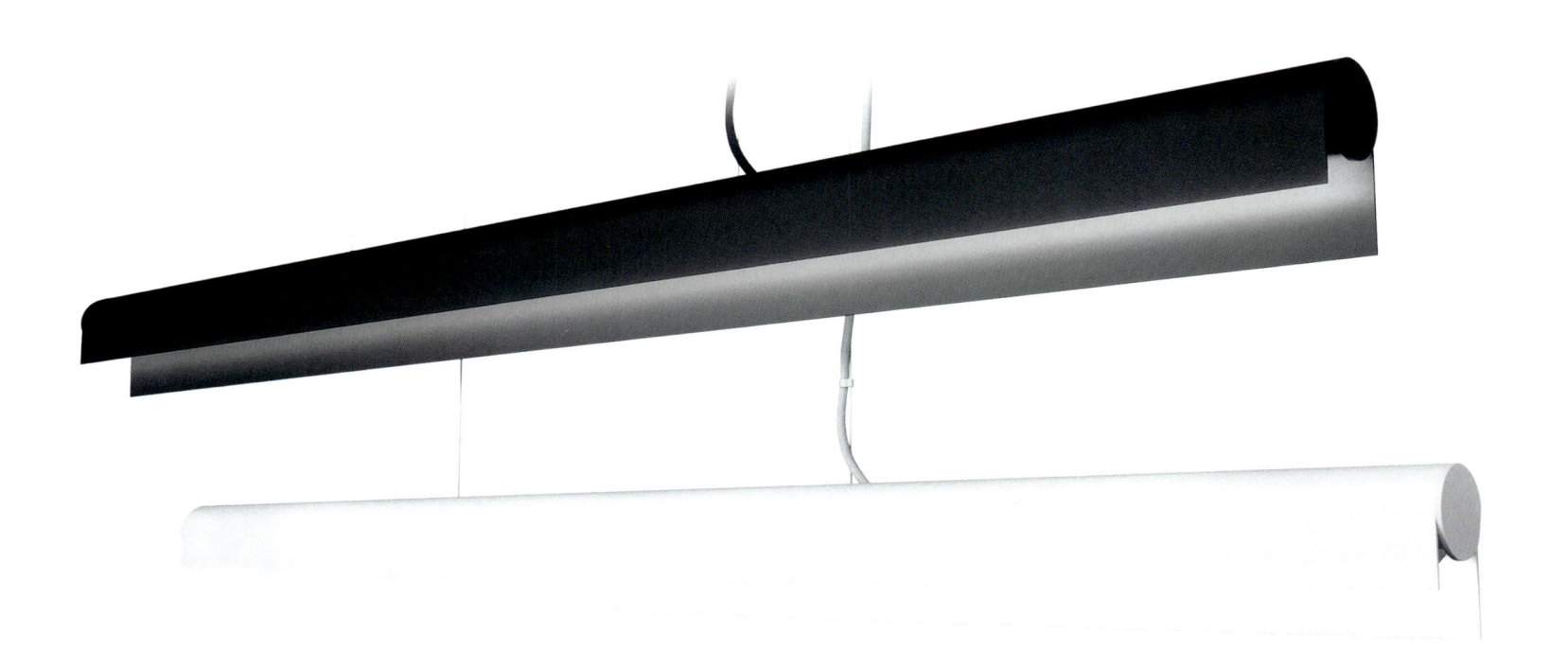

Dawn
Pendant Luminaire
Pendelleuchte

Manufacturer
Intra Lighting,
Sempeter pri Gorici, Slovenia
Design
Lorenzo Truant, Venice, Italy
Web
www.intra-lighting.com

As implied by the product name, the design of this pendant luminaire was inspired by the dawn. For this reason, the light source is not positioned in the centre but at the edge of the luminaire, from where it emits a smooth and even glow modelled on early morning light. Design details, such as the curved contour of the lampshade, its opaque luminous surface and the distinctive cable routing, attract attention.

Statement by the jury
With a keen sense for details, this product design yields self-reliant aesthetics. In addition, Dawn provides a highly appealing lighting effect.

Wie ihr Produktname andeutet, wurde die Gestaltung dieser Pendelleuchte von der Morgendämmerung inspiriert. Aus diesem Grund ist die Lichtquelle nicht mittig, sondern am Rand der Leuchte platziert, von wo aus sie ein sanftes und gleichmäßiges Schimmern abgibt, das dem Licht des frühen Morgens nachempfunden ist. Gestaltungsdetails wie die geschwungene Kontur des Leuchtenschirms, dessen blickdichte Leuchtfläche sowie die auffällige Kabelführung ziehen die Aufmerksamkeit auf sich.

Begründung der Jury
Mit viel Gespür für Details erzielt diese Produktgestaltung eine eigenständige Ästhetik. Dawn bietet zudem einen höchst ansprechenden Beleuchtungseffekt.

Philips GreenPerform Highbay Elite
Highbay Lighting
Hallenbeleuchtung

Manufacturer
Signify, Shanghai, China
In-house design
Signify Design Team
Web
www.signify.com

The GreenPerform Highbay Elite has been completely redesigned: together with a compact driver, the newly developed, circular LED board ensures better thermal management. This is made possible by a reduced profile, which dispenses with the fin structures of previous models. Furthermore, its low weight also facilitates easy installation. A strong black-silver contrast adds a premium feel to the luminaire, while the body conveys robustness.

Statement by the jury
With its contemporary design, the GreenPerform Highbay Elite emphasises the effectiveness of a high-performance lighting solution.

Die Hallenbeleuchtung GreenPerform Highbay Elite wurde komplett überarbeitet: Zusammen mit einem kompakt konstruierten Treiber sorgt die neu entwickelte, kreisförmige LED-Platine für ein besseres Wärmemanagement. Ermöglicht wird dies durch ein reduziertes Leuchtenprofil, das auf die Rippenstrukturen früherer Modelle verzichtet. Das geringe Gewicht erleichtert zudem die Installation. Ein starker Schwarz-Silber-Kontrast verleiht der Leuchte Wertigkeit, während der Korpus Robustheit vermittelt.

Begründung der Jury
Eine zeitgemäße Formensprache betont bei GreenPerform Highbay Elite die Effektivität einer leistungsstarken Hallenbeleuchtungslösung.

O Zero
Pendant Luminaire
Pendelleuchten

Manufacturer
BUZAO, Foshan, China
In-house design
Web
www.buzao.me

O Zero is an aluminium pendant luminaire manufactured in a traditional sand casting process, which lends its surface a grainy, natural look. While only the edges are ground after the casting process, the rest of the luminaire's body remains untreated. The lamp is available in two models, which can flexibly be combined to meet the lighting requirements in restaurants, offices or other public places.

Statement by the jury
The O Zero merges a distinctive design language with a material quality which lends these pendant luminaires a unique a character.

O Zero ist eine Pendelleuchte aus Aluminium, die im traditionellen Sandgussverfahren gefertigt wird. Dieses Verfahren lässt eine körnige, natürlich wirkende Oberfläche entstehen. Nach dem Guss werden nur die Kanten geschliffen, der Rest bleibt unbehandelt. Die Leuchte ist in zwei Varianten erhältlich. Beide können flexibel miteinander kombiniert werden, um so den Beleuchtungsanforderungen von Restaurants, Büros oder anderen öffentlichen Räumen zu entsprechen.

Begründung der Jury
Bei der O Zero trifft eine prägnante Formensprache auf eine Materialbeschaffenheit, die diesen Pendelleuchten einen unverwechselbaren Charakter verleiht.

Derby
Pendant Luminaire
Pendelleuchte

Manufacturer
Linea Light Group,
Castelminio di Resana (Treviso), Italy
In-house design
Mirco Crosatto
Web
www.linealight.com

Derby is a lighting fixture which combines a sound-absorbing body with a high-grade LED light source. The curved shape of the large pendant luminaire frames a narrow LED light bar. Using special diffused and dark light optics, it offers glare-free lighting according to UGR regulations. The luminaire is particularly suitable to illuminate tables in public areas, where it pleasantly subdues the background noise.

Statement by the jury
This pendant luminaire offers a high utility value by providing both glare-free lighting and the reduction of ambient noise.

Derby kombiniert einen schallabsorbierenden Leuchtenkörper mit einer hochwertigen LED-Lichtquelle. Die geschwungene Form der großflächigen Pendelleuchte umrahmt eine schmale LED-Lichtleiste. Aufgrund einer diffusen Optik sowie einer speziellen Darklight-Optik bietet sie eine blendfreie Beleuchtung nach geltenden UGR-Bestimmungen. Die Leuchte eignet sich insbesondere für eine Tischbeleuchtung in öffentlichen Bereichen, wo sie in ihrem Umkreis für eine angenehm gedämpfte Geräuschkulisse sorgt.

Begründung der Jury
Diese Pendelleuchte bietet einen hohen Gebrauchswert, indem sie eine blendfreie Beleuchtung bietet und zudem die Umgebungsgeräusche mindert.

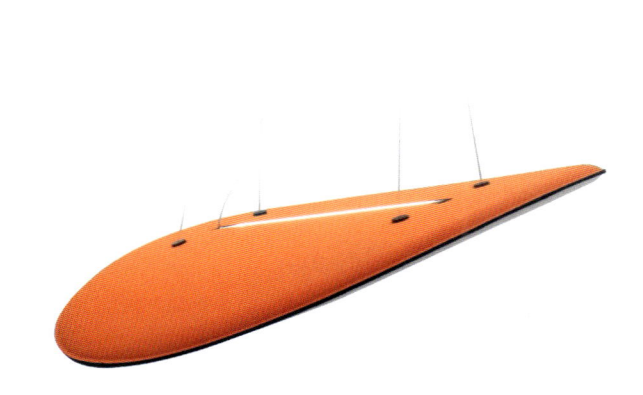

Demì
Pendant Luminaire
Pendelleuchte

Manufacturer
Linea Light Group,
Castelminio di Resana (Treviso), Italy
In-house design
Mirco Crosatto
Web
www.linealight.com

Demì places a plastic polymer lampshade centre stage. Looking completely transparent when the light is turned off, the shape of the luminaire only comes to live when it is illuminated. This effect is enhanced by laser micro-incisions, diverting the light beams on two sides. This allows a diffuse, glare-free and screen-compatible lighting which complies with UGR regulations. The LED light source is placed in the centrally positioned white-painted aluminium ring.

Statement by the jury
Thanks to its sophisticated surface design, Demì impresses as a visually appealing pendant luminaire delivering pleasant illumination.

Bei Demì steht ein Leuchtenschirm aus Kunststoff im gestalterischen Fokus: Da dieser unbeleuchtet vollkommen transparent ist, tritt seine Form erst im beleuchteten Zustand zutage. Unterstützt wird dieser Effekt durch Laser-Mikroeinschnitte, die Lichtstrahlen zweiseitig ableiten. Dies ermöglicht eine diffuse, blendfreie und bildschirmgerechte Beleuchtung innerhalb der UGR-Bestimmungen. Die LED-Lichtquelle befindet sich im mittig platzierten, weiß lackierten Aluminiumring.

Begründung der Jury
Dank ihrer raffinierten Oberflächengestaltung begeistert Demì als visuell reizvolle Pendelleuchte, die zudem eine angenehme Beleuchtung bietet.

MATRIX
Pendant Luminaire
Pendelleuchte

Manufacturer
Peters Design GmbH, Rinteln, Germany
In-house design
Moritz Peters
Design
Kardorff Ingenieure Lichtplanung GmbH
(Prof. Volker von Kardorff, Stephan Müller),
Berlin, Germany
Web
www.petersdesign.de
www.kardorff.de

This ring-shaped pendant luminaire creates a surprising light structure: when switched on, the unobtrusively designed outer surface of the lamp shows a brightly shining 3D groove structure. In combination with innovative lighting technology, the room illumination attracts a high level of attention. Matrix is available in several standard sizes. In addition, it can be tailored in shape, size, colour and lighting technology to the needs of individual construction projects.

Statement by the jury
Showcasing a distinctive lighting effect, the Matrix pendant luminaire convinces as a characteristic room illumination in the commercial sector.

Diese ringförmige Pendelleuchte ermöglicht eine überraschende Lichtstruktur: Im eingeschalteten Modus zeigt die dezent gestaltete Außenfläche der Leuchte eine Rillenstruktur, die im 3D-Effekt hell leuchtet. Verbunden mit einer innovativen Lichttechnik weckt die Raumbeleuchtung ein hohes Maß an Aufmerksamkeit. Matrix ist in mehreren Standardgrößen erhältlich. Zudem kann sie in Form, Größe, Farbe und Lichttechnik auf den Bedarf einzelner Bauprojekte abgestimmt werden.

Begründung der Jury
Mit ihrem unverwechselbaren Lichteffekt überzeugt die Pendelleuchte Matrix als charakteristische Raumbeleuchtung im Objektbereich.

Qbini
Ceiling Lighting
Deckenleuchten

Manufacturer
Modular Lighting Instruments, Pits NV,
Roeselare, Belgium
Design
Florent Coirier, Paris, France
Web
www.supermodular.com
www.florentcoirier.fr

Qbini – the product name is a portmanteau blending the words cubic and mini – offers a miniaturised LED lighting solution for living rooms, hospitality venues and boutiques. The modular design allows the realisation of diverse concepts: the ceiling light is available in a variety of frames, shapes, colours and accessories and combines this selection with high-quality technology. Different lamp configurations complement the concept.

Statement by the jury
This ceiling lighting is characterised by high versatility. Each configuration precisely adapts to its respective environment.

Qbini – der Produktname ist ein zusammengefügtes Kunstwort aus „cubic" und „mini" – bietet eine miniaturisierte LED-Beleuchtungslösung für Wohnräume, Gastronomiebetriebe und Verkaufsräume. Der modulare Aufbau ermöglicht die Umsetzung vielfältiger Beleuchtungskonzepte: Die Deckenleuchte ist in einer Vielzahl von Formen, Rahmen, Farben und Zubehör erhältlich und kombiniert diese Auswahl mit einer hochwertigen Lichttechnik. Unterschiedliche Lampenkonfigurationen runden das Konzept ab.

Begründung der Jury
Ein hohes Maß an Variabilität zeichnet diese Deckenleuchten aus, wobei sich ihre Ausführungen exakt dem jeweiligen Umfeld anpassen lassen.

White Line SLOT
Ceiling Lighting
Deckenleuchten

Manufacturer
PVD Concept, Kapellen, Belgium
In-house design
Patrik van Daele
Web
www.pvdconcept.be

This ceiling lighting is equipped with a novel 10 mm LED reflector, its chip offering the choice between the colour temperatures of 2,700, 3,000 and 4,000 kelvins. The housing has been designed to conceal the reflectors, which are fixed on the inside, and efficiently cool the LED modules. White Line SLOT is available in various models, allowing surface and recessed as well as trimless mounting.

Statement by the jury
Thanks to its innovative LED reflectors, this particularly slim ceiling lighting is impressive as a discreet and efficient product solution.

Diese Deckenleuchten sind mit einem neuartigen 10-mm-LED-Reflektor ausgestattet, dessen Chip die Wahl zwischen den Farbtemperaturen 2.700, 3.000 und 4.000 Kelvin bietet. Das Gehäuse ist so konstruiert, dass die darin fixierten Reflektoren nicht sichtbar sind und die LED-Module darüber hinaus effizient gekühlt werden. White Line SLOT ist in mehreren Versionen erhältlich, die sowohl eine Aufputz- als auch eine Unterputz-Montage sowie eine randlose Montage erlauben.

Begründung der Jury
Dank ihrer innovativen LED-Reflektoren beeindrucken diese besonders schmalen Deckenleuchten als dezente und zugleich effektive Produktlösung.

Aura Collection
Ceiling Lighting
Deckenleuchten

Manufacturer
Kriskadecor, Montblanc, Spain
Design
Yonoh Studio, Valencia, Spain
Web
www.kriskadecor.com
www.yonoh.es

The Aura collection was developed especially for large rooms. The appealing sculptural quality of the ceiling lights is based on anodized metal chains, which are arranged in tubular structures allowing asymmetric installations, with those tubular metal chain structures overlapping. From the opal glass diffusers, which are mounted on the ceiling, the light travels along the chains and gradually vanishes, generating a characteristic aura effect.

Die Aura-Kollektion wurde speziell für große Räume entwickelt. Die reizvolle skulpturale Qualität der Deckenleuchten basiert auf eloxierten Metallketten, die zu röhrenförmigen Gebilden arrangiert werden. Deren flexible Anordnung erlaubt u. a. asymmetrische Installationen, wobei sich die Metallketten-Röhren überlappen. Von den an der Decke montierten Diffusoren aus Opalglas wandert das Licht die Ketten entlang und schwächt sich dabei allmählich ab, wodurch ein typischer Aura-Effekt entsteht.

Statement by the jury
Thanks to the consistent implementation of a creative design idea, the Aura collection projects a highly appealing, self-reliant overall appearance.

Begründung der Jury
Dank der stringenten Umsetzung einer kreativen Gestaltungsidee erreicht die Aura-Kollektion ein sehr ansprechendes, eigenständiges Gesamtbild.

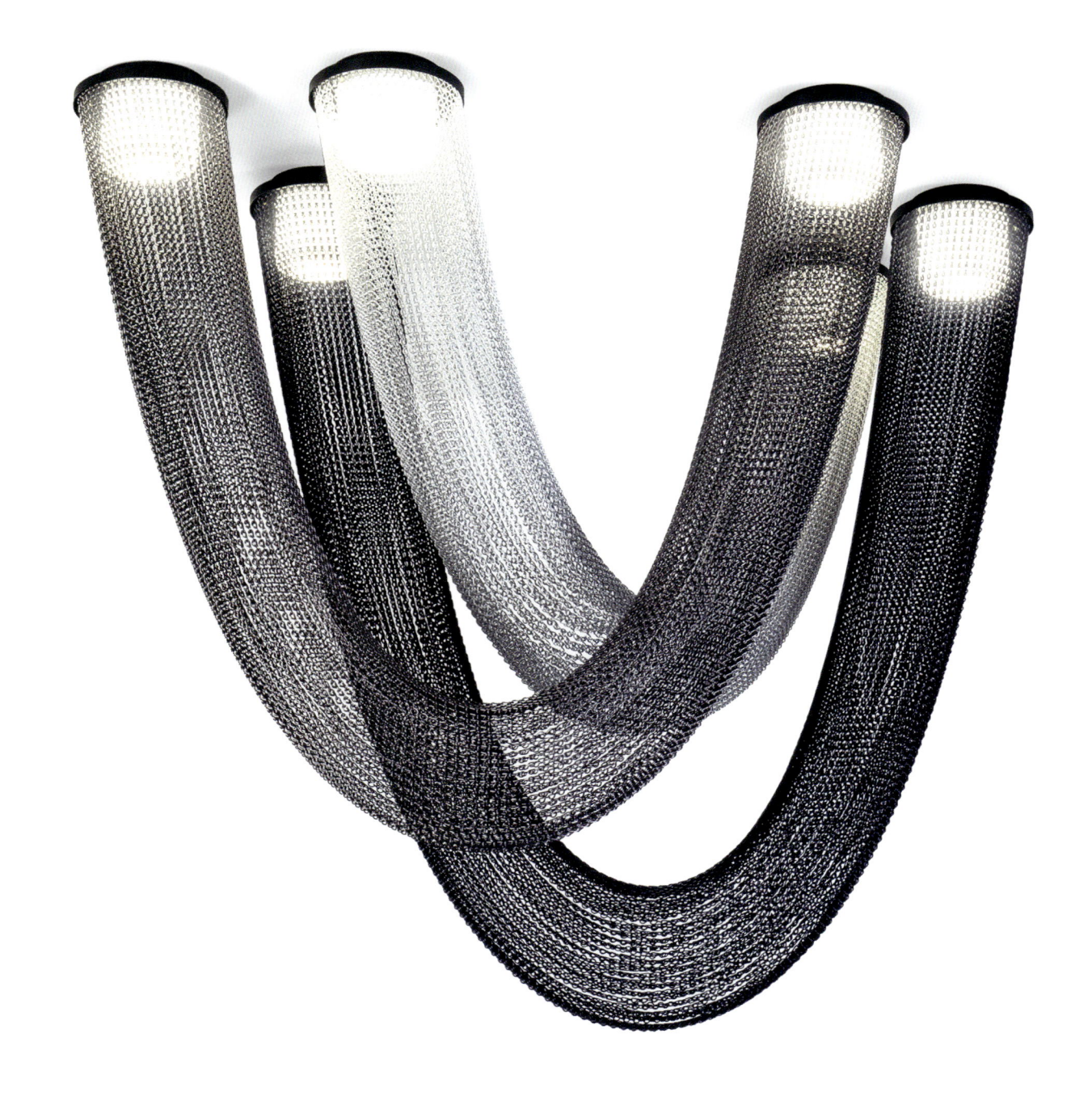

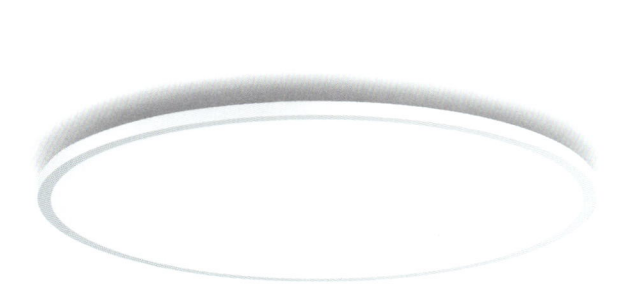

TASK round
Ceiling Light
Deckenleuchte

Manufacturer
XAL GmbH, Graz, Austria
In-house design
Web
www.xal.com

This discreet ceiling light is characterised by a round aluminium body with a low-profile design of only 15 mm. Its powder-coated surface is optionally available in black or white. The slim frame accommodates contemporary technology, with efficient LEDs delivering a high light intensity. The perforated reflector creates a balance between direct and indirect light output. Anti-glare prisms ensure comfortable workplace illumination.

Statement by the jury
With its high degree of lighting comfort, TASK round not only satisfies high user demands, it also projects an appealing minimalist design language.

Diese dezente Deckenleuchte wird von einem runden Leuchtenkorpus aus Aluminium mit einer flachen Bauform von nur 15 mm geprägt. Ihre pulverbeschichtete Oberfläche ist optional in Weiß oder Schwarz erhältlich. Hinter dem flachen Rahmenprofil verbirgt sich eine zeitgemäße Lichttechnik, wobei effiziente LEDs eine hohe Lichtstärke erreichen. Durch den perforierten Reflektor entsteht ein ausgewogenes Verhältnis zwischen direktem und indirektem Lichtanteil. Entblendungsprismen sorgen für eine bildschirmtaugliche Beleuchtung.

Begründung der Jury
Mit ihrem hohen Maß an Beleuchtungskomfort erfüllt TASK round gehobene Ansprüche, zudem gefällt die minimalistische Formensprache.

AVA
Ceiling Light
Deckenleuchte

Manufacturer
Licht+Raum AG, Ittigen, Switzerland
In-house design
Sandro Roth
Web
www.lichtraum.ch

AVA combines the aesthetic of an illuminated disc with the warm qualities of a textile lampshade. In order to facilitate installation, the ceiling light is equipped with a patented click system, allowing the simple attachment of the lampshade to the housing as well as an easy replacement. The 420 mm wide and 103 mm high luminaire has an energy efficiency class of A+ and its Chintz fabric shade is available in 77 different colours.

Statement by the jury
This timeless, elegant ceiling light impresses with a high-quality material mix and a wide range of available colours.

AVA verbindet die Ästhetik einer beleuchteten Scheibe mit der wohnlichen Ausstrahlung eines textilen Lampenschirms. Um die Montage zu erleichtern, ist die Deckenleuchte mit einem patentierten Click-System ausgestattet. Dadurch lässt sich der Schirm unkompliziert am Gehäuse anbringen und ebenso einfach austauschen. Der Chintz-Stoffschirm ist in 77 unterschiedlichen Farben erhältlich. Die 420 mm breite und 103 mm hohe Leuchte hat die Energieeffizienzklasse A+.

Begründung der Jury
Diese zeitlos-elegante Deckenleuchte begeistert durch einen hochwertigen Materialmix und eine breit gefächerte Farbpalette.

Triona
Lamp Series
Leuchtenserie

Manufacturer
RZB Rudolf Zimmermann, Bamberg GmbH, Bamberg, Germany
In-house design
Web
www.rzb.de

Triona is a lamp series which includes ceiling, wall and pendant luminaires. By featuring tunable white technology, it creates a room lighting which is perceived as highly pleasant. Thanks to their lateral light emission, the luminaires provide an even, glare-free light and come also with an additional indirect light output. Triona is available in three diameters, three colours and various diffuser designs, including a model made of fine Murano glass, which reaches a UGR value of less than 19.

Triona ist eine Leuchtenserie, die sowohl Decken- und Wand- als auch Pendelleuchten umfasst. Ausgestattet mit einer Tunable-White-Technologie, bietet sie eine als angenehm empfundene Raumbeleuchtung. Aufgrund einer seitlichen Lichteinkopplung spenden die Leuchten ein gleichmäßiges blendfreies Licht und sind auch als Version mit zusätzlichem indirektem Lichtaustritt verfügbar. Triona ist in drei Durchmessern, drei Farben sowie verschiedenen Diffusor-Ausführungen erhältlich. Darunter auch eine Version aus edlem Muranoglas, die einen UGR-Wert von unter 19 erreicht.

Statement by the jury
The Triona lamp series merges a characteristic design language with sophisticated lighting technology to satisfy high user demands.

Begründung der Jury
Bei Triona trifft eine charakteristische Formensprache auf eine raffinierte Lichttechnik, die gehobenen Ansprüchen entspricht.

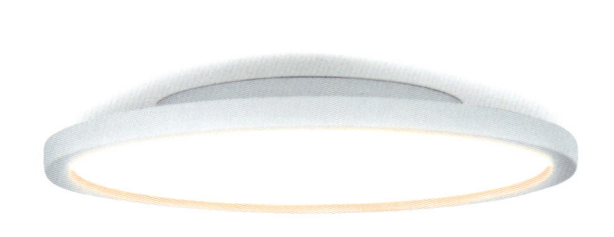

Philips Hue Aurelle
Panel Lights
Flächenleuchten

Manufacturer
Signify, Eindhoven, Netherlands
In-house design
Signify Design Team
Web
www.signify.com

Hue Aurelle is a user-friendly panel light which illuminates rooms evenly and is available in several shapes. Users can choose from a wide range of programmes via voice or smart device control, which allows to adjust the lighting seamlessly in colour temperature and control the dimming as well as it is also possible to set a light schedule, use automatic geofencing detection etc. Thanks to its low thickness, the luminaire is also suitable for rooms with low ceilings.

Statement by the jury
A clear, geometric design line meets sophisticated lighting technology in these purist panel lights.

Hue Aurelle ist eine bedienungsfreundliche Flächenleuchte, die Räume ansprechend gleichmäßig ausleuchtet und in mehreren Formen erhältlich ist. Die Nutzer können über eine Sprach- oder Gerätesteuerung eine Auswahl aus breit gefächerten Beleuchtungsprogrammen treffen. So lässt sich die Beleuchtung durch nahtlose Farbtemperatur- und Dimmer-Regelung, Lichtplanerstellung, automatische Geofencing-Erkennung etc. anpassen. Dank ihrer geringen Aufbauhöhe eignet sich die Leuchte auch für Räume mit niedrigen Decken.

Begründung der Jury
Bei dieser puristisch anmutenden Flächenleuchte trifft eine klare, geometrische Linienführung auf eine bis ins Detail durchdachte Beleuchtungstechnik.

Oyamo
Surface-Mounted Luminaire
Anbauleuchte

Manufacturer
Trilux GmbH & Co. KG, Arnsberg, Germany
Design
Berrel Berrel Kräutler AG, Basel, Switzerland
Web
www.trilux.com
www.bbk-architekten.ch

The ring-shaped, surface-mounted luminaire has been designed for the stylish illumination of prestigious areas and is suitable for wall and ceiling mounting. Its spatial contour catches the eye while its homogeneous light creates a pleasant atmosphere. With its direct and indirect, glare-free light, the Oyamo achieves high lighting quality and a lighting effect for well-being. The attractive surface-mounted luminaire can be dimmed digitally.

Statement by the jury
Blending harmoniously into public spaces, the Oyamo surface-mounted luminaire owes its elegance to its organic design language.

Die ringförmige Anbauleuchte dient der stilvollen Beleuchtung repräsentativer Bereiche und eignet sich zur Wand- und Deckenmontage. Dank ihrer räumlich wirkenden Kontur zieht sie die Blicke auf sich, während ihr homogenes Licht ein angenehmes Ambiente schafft. Mit ihrer direkten und indirekten, blendfreien Beleuchtung erreicht die Oyamo eine hohe Lichtqualität und schafft eine Lichtwirkung zum Wohlfühlen. Die attraktive Anbauleuchte lässt sich digital dimmen.

Begründung der Jury
Einer organisch anmutenden Formensprache verdankt die Anbauleuchte Oyamo eine Eleganz, die sich harmonisch in öffentliche Bereiche einfügt.

VIOR
Ceiling Lighting
Deckenleuchte

Manufacturer
Ribag Licht AG, Safenwil, Switzerland
In-house design
Web
www.ribag.com

VIOR offers both: brilliant direct and soft ceiling lighting, using only a single point light source. The ceiling luminaire uses the technology of a specially developed micro-facet reflector. The complex surface geometry disperses the indirect component of the light evenly and free of shadows across the ceiling. The glare-free direct light is guided through lenses in beam angles of optionally 40, 50, or 60 degrees. The transparent housing blends discreetly into any interior.

Statement by the jury
As a result of a consistent product development, VIOR convinces as an aesthetically appealing and functionally sophisticated ceiling light.

VIOR bietet mit nur einer Punktlichtquelle sowohl ein brillantes Direktlicht als auch eine sanfte Deckenbeleuchtung. Dabei nutzt die Deckenleuchte die Lichtlenkungstechnik eines eigens entwickelten Mikrofacetten-Reflektors. Dessen komplexe Oberflächengeometrie verteilt den indirekten Lichtanteil schattenfrei und gleichmäßig über die Decke. Der blendfreie Direktlichtanteil wird durch Linsen optional in Abstrahlungswinkel von 40, 50 oder 60 Grad gelenkt. Das transparente Gehäuse fügt sich dezent ins Interieur ein.

Begründung der Jury
Als Ergebnis einer bis ins Detail stimmigen Produktentwicklung überzeugt VIOR als ästhetisch reizvolle und funktional ausgereifte Deckenleuchte.

TUBIC
Surface-Mounted Ceiling Luminaires
Deckenanbauleuchten

Manufacturer
Brumberg Leuchten GmbH & Co. KG, Sundern, Germany
In-house design
Web
www.brumberg.com

The TUBIC surface-mounted ceiling luminaires have been developed under the premise of creating a harmonious room ambience and blend well into different areas of application. When switched on, a fascinating lighting effect creates the impression of the luminaries floating in mid-air under the ceiling. The surface-mounted ceiling luminaires are available in different sizes and equipped with powerful, energy-efficient LEDs.

Statement by the jury
Thanks to a design idiom that has been reduced to the essentials, the TUBIC surface-mounted ceiling luminaires achieve a highly self-sufficient appearance.

Die TUBIC Deckenanbauleuchten wurden unter der Prämisse eines harmonischen Raumbilds entwickelt und fügen sich gut in unterschiedliche Nutzungsbereiche ein. Im eingeschalteten Modus erweckt ein faszinierender Lichteffekt den Eindruck, als würde die Leuchte unter der Decke schweben. Die Deckenanbauleuchten sind in unterschiedlichen Größen erhältlich und mit einer leistungsstarken, energieeffizienten LED ausgestattet.

Begründung der Jury
Dank einer aufs Wesentliche reduzierten Formensprache erzielen die TUBIC Deckenanbauleuchten ein höchst eigenständiges Gesamtbild.

CATCH
Downlight Series
Deckenleuchten-Serie

Manufacturer
Simes S.p.A., Corte Franca (Brescia), Italy
In-house design
Web
www.simes.com

CATCH is a range of weatherproof downlights designed for outdoor installation. Depending on the number of integrated LEDs, the luminaires are available in square or rectangular housings of different sizes. Their high ease of use is based on the fact, that the optical bases can be tilted at various angles. Thanks to their innovative lighting system, the downlights enable the realisation of versatile, glare-free illumination concepts.

Statement by the jury
Using contemporary technology, this timeless downlight series offers a high degree of lighting comfort.

CATCH ist eine Serie von wetterfesten Deckeneinbauleuchten, die für eine Installation im Außenbereich entwickelt wurden. Abhängig von der Anzahl der integrierten LEDs sind die Leuchten in quadratischen oder rechteckigen Gehäusen von unterschiedlicher Größe erhältlich. Ihr hoher Bedienkomfort beruht darauf, dass die Lichtträger in verschiedenen Winkeln gekippt werden können. Aufgrund ihres innovativen Lichtsystems ermöglichen die Deckeneinbauleuchten die Umsetzung vielseitiger, blendfreier Beleuchtungskonzepte.

Begründung der Jury
Unter Einsatz einer zeitgemäßen Technik bietet diese zeitlos anmutende Deckeneinbauleuchten-Serie ein hohes Maß an Beleuchtungskomfort.

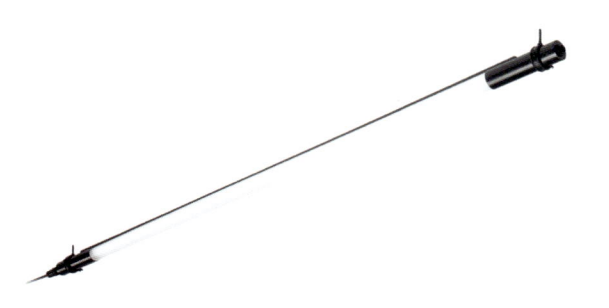

So-Tube
Ceiling Lighting
Deckenleuchte

Manufacturer
Trilux GmbH & Co. KG,
Arnsberg, Germany
Design
jack be nimble (Sophia Klees),
Berlin, Germany
Web
www.trilux.com
www.jackbenimble.de

This unconventional ceiling light has been designed to provide a trend-oriented lighting solution for refurbished industrial buildings and their typical roof structures. The tubular So-Tube combines industrial charm with power LED technology, paired with a variety of mounting options. The purist lines of the luminaire blend easily into the unique atmosphere of industrial halls, offering lighting designers a high degree of creative freedom.

Statement by the jury
Thanks to its various mounting options, the ceiling light convinces as a sophisticated product development. Its luminous intensity lends it a strong sense of concision.

Diese unkonventionelle Deckenleuchte wurde entwickelt, um eine trendorientierte Lichtlösung für sanierte Industriehallen und deren typische Dachkonstruktionen zu bieten. Die röhrenförmige So-Tube vereint industriellen Charme mit einer leistungsfähigen LED-Technologie. Dank vielfältiger Montagevarianten fügt sich die puristische Linienführung der Leuchte in die besondere Atmosphäre sanierter Industriehallen ein und bietet Lichtplanern einen hohen Gestaltungsspielraum.

Begründung der Jury
Dank vielseitiger Montagemöglichkeiten überzeugt die Deckenleuchte als durchdachte Produktentwicklung. Ihre Lichtstärke verleiht ihr Prägnanz.

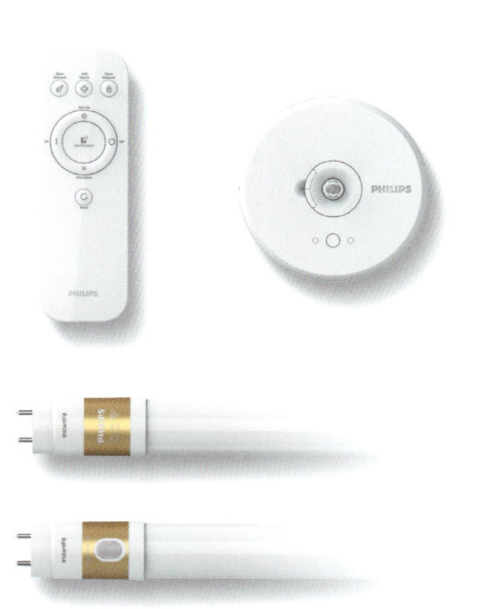

Philips MasterConnect LED Tube
LED Tubes Series
LED-Röhrenserie

Manufacturer
Signify, Shanghai, China
In-house design
Signify Design Team
Web
www.signify.com

The MasterConnect LED tube series enables contemporary lighting including intelligent control. Wireless occupancy and environmental sensors trigger automatic responses, such as dynamically turning lights on and off or dimming them. Significant energy savings compared to conventional fluorescent tubes are the result. Moreover, it is easy to put the 2.4 GHz wireless mesh network technology into operation and reliably connect it to various control devices.

Statement by the jury
As an energy-saving product solution, this LED tube series offers a remarkable utility value, offering a particularly convincing ease of use.

Die MasterConnect LED-Röhrenserie ermöglicht eine zeitgemäße Beleuchtung inklusive intelligenter Steuerung. Drahtlose Präsenz- und Umgebungssensoren lösen automatische Reaktionen aus, um das Licht dynamisch ein- und auszuschalten oder abzudimmen. Auf diese Weise lässt sich im Vergleich zu herkömmlichen Leuchtstoffröhren eine deutliche Energieeinsparung erzielen. Die 2,4 GHz drahtlose Mesh-Netzwerktechnologie lässt sich einfach in Betrieb nehmen und integriert sich zuverlässig in unterschiedliche Steuerungsgeräte.

Begründung der Jury
Als energiesparsame Produktlösung bietet diese LED-Röhrenserie einen bemerkenswerten Gebrauchswert, wobei insbesondere der Bedienkomfort überzeugt.

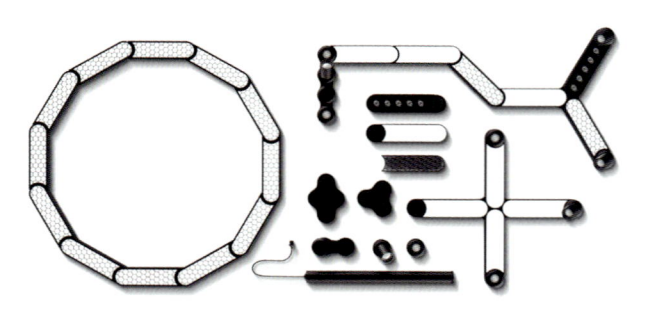

HANS 2.0
Lighting System
Lichtsystem

Manufacturer
Romney Opto-electronic Systems Technology (Guangdong) Co., Ltd.,
Zhongshan, China
In-house design
Yinshui Peng
Design
Guangzhou Alighting IOT & Technology Co., Ltd., Guangzhou, China
Shenzhen Dizan Technology Co., Ltd., Shenzhen, China
Web
www.romney-lighting.com
www.alighting.com
www.rui-d.com

HANS 2.0 is an optimised lighting system and its modules are connected in a chain-like construction. Using a patented connection mechanism, the system enables flexible light installations which can illuminate ring-shaped, spiral-shaped or honeycomb-shaped areas in rooms. The system currently comprises seven lighting modules for individually tailored use, from area lighting to adjustable spotlighting. It can be installed like pendent luminaires or surface-mounted ceiling luminaires.

Statement by the jury
Thanks to its remarkable structure, this lighting system promotes a versatile, emotionally appealing lighting of interiors.

HANS 2.0 ist optimiertes Lichtsystem, dessen Module kettenartig miteinander verbunden sind. Unter Einsatz einer patentierten Verbindungsmechanik erlaubt das System flexible Lichtinstallationen, die unter anderem ring-, spiral- oder wabenförmig bestimmte Bereiche im Raum ausleuchten. Das System umfasst derzeit sieben Beleuchtungsmodule, die von der Flächenbeleuchtung bis zum verstellbaren Spotlight gezielt eingesetzt werden können. Es lässt sich hängend sowie als Aufbauleuchte direkt unter die Decke installieren.

Begründung der Jury
Dank seiner bemerkenswerten Struktur erlaubt dieses Lichtsystem eine vielseitige, emotional ansprechende Beleuchtung von Innenräumen.

KALO
Surface-Mounted Spotlight
Aufbaustrahler

Manufacturer
Oktalite Lichttechnik GmbH,
Cologne, Germany
In-house design
Web
www.oktalite.com

Designed for versatile use in retail areas, this surface-mounted spotlight adapts to different requirements: featuring six white light colours as well as special light colours suitable for fresh food areas, KALO ensures attractive product presentations. The LED luminous flux reaches up to 4,000 lumens. The miniaturised housing can be equipped with five exchangeable reflectors without the need of tools. With a balanced centre of gravity, it facilitates a focused light alignment.

Statement by the jury
As a highly functional product solution, the miniaturised surface-mounted spotlight projects the convincing illumination of sales areas.

Konzipiert für einen vielseitigen Einsatz in Verkaufsräumen lässt sich dieser Aufbaustrahler an unterschiedliche Anforderungen anpassen: Mit sechs Weißlichtfarben sowie sämtlichen Speziallichtfarben für den Frischebereich dient KALO einer ansprechenden Warenpräsentation. Der LED-Lichtstrom erreicht bis zu 4.000 Lumen. Das miniaturisierte Gehäuse lässt sich werkzeuglos mit fünf auswechselbaren Reflektoren ausstatten. Es hat einen austarierten Schwerpunkt und erleichtert so die gezielte Lichtausrichtung.

Begründung der Jury
Als hochfunktionale Produktlösung ermöglicht der miniaturisiert gestaltete Aufbaustrahler eine überzeugende Beleuchtung von Verkaufsflächen.

GRADO TWIN
Track Mounted Spotlight
Aufbaustrahler

Manufacturer
Oktalite Lichttechnik GmbH,
Cologne, Germany
In-house design
Web
www.oktalite.com

The GRADO TWIN track mounted spotlight ensures, with its two luminaire heads, a focused illumination of goods in supermarkets. In order to illuminate the entire height of a shelf, the luminaire heads can be tilted by 110 degrees to either side. Equipped with a glare-suppressed rectangular reflector and thanks to their well-balanced light distribution, they offer great visual comfort. The double spotlight allows installations with a reduced number of luminaires in the shop, thus supporting an unobtrusive ceiling appearance.

Statement by the jury
This track-mounted spotlight merges a functionality which has been tailored to the retail sector with a clear, purposeful design idiom.

Der Aufbaustrahler GRADO TWIN sorgt mit seinen beiden Leuchtenköpfen für eine gezielte Warenausleuchtung in Supermärkten. Um die gesamte Höhe eines Regals zu beleuchten, lassen sich die Leuchtenköpfe zu beiden Seiten um 110 Grad schwenken. Sie sind mit einem entblendeten Wannenreflektor ausgestattet und bieten durch eine ausgewogene Lichtverteilung einen hohen Sehkomfort. Der Doppelstrahler macht eine reduzierte Anzahl von Leuchten im Geschäft möglich und unterstützt somit ein dezentes Deckenbild.

Begründung der Jury
Eine auf den Retailbereich abgestimmte Funktionalität vereint sich bei diesem Aufbaustrahler mit einer klaren, zweckgerichteten Formensprache.

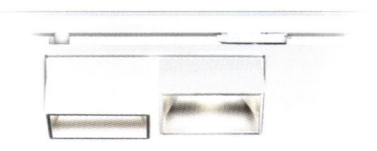

MINITRACK
Spotlight System
Strahlersystem

Manufacturer
SELF Electronics Co., Ltd., Ningbo, China
In-house design
Web
www.self-electronics.com

MINITRACK is a spotlight system which satisfies the sophisticated lighting requirements expected in a wide range of sales and exhibition spaces. The spotlights are lightweight and have a compact design that allows them to be discreetly mounted into display cases. The corresponding lighting track of the system can be tailored to the respective room layout. The system comprises different spots as well as linear and surface flood lights for individual, suitable arrangements.

Statement by the jury
As a technically sophisticated and compact product solution, this spotlight system enables effective illumination even in narrow spaces.

MINITRACK ist ein Strahlersystem, welches die gehobenen Beleuchtungsanforderungen unterschiedlichster Verkaufs- und Ausstellungräume erfüllt. Die Strahler sind leicht und so kompakt konstruiert, dass sie auch dezent in Vitrinen montiert werden können. Die zum System gehörende Lichtschiene kann auf die jeweilige Raumsituation zugeschnitten werden. Das System umfasst unterschiedliche Spot-, Linear- und Flächenstrahler, die bedarfsgerecht miteinander kombiniert werden können.

Begründung der Jury
Als technisch ausgereifte und kompakte Produktlösung ermöglicht dieses Strahlersystem selbst auf engstem Raum eine wirkungsvolle Ausleuchtung.

Flying Saucer
Retail Lighting
Retailleuchte

Manufacturer
NVC Lighting Technology Corporation, Huizhou, China
In-house design
Xiaosong Hong, Shin Inho,
Rong Xiang, Hua Hu, Weijian Wu
Web
www.nvc-lighting.com.cn

Flying Saucer has been developed for retail premises and its indirect light is tailored to the requirements of commercially used spaces. The bright yet glare-free spotlights direct the attention to the product display, creating a pleasant mood in the sales room. Available in different colours, the lights feature a remarkably flat construction. Their heat sink weighs only 155 grams and makes use of a novel heat pipe technology to dissipate heat. The rough surface of the precision-machined metal case is anodised to enhance protection.

Flying Saucer ist eine Retailleuchte, deren indirektes Licht auf die Anforderungen kommerziell genutzter Räume abgestimmt ist. Die lichtstarken und dennoch blendfreien Strahler lenken die Aufmerksamkeit auf die Produktauslage und schaffen eine angenehme Lichtstimmung im Verkaufsraum. Die in unterschiedlichen Farben erhältlichen Leuchten sind auffallend flach konstruiert. Ihr Kühlkörper wiegt nur 155 Gramm und nutzt eine neuartige Wärmerohrtechnologie zum Ableiten der Hitze. Die raue Oberfläche des präzise gefertigten Metallgehäuses wird zum Schutz eloxiert.

Statement by the jury
Thanks to its sophisticated functionality and high light output, Flying Saucer convinces with effective accent illumination in sales rooms.

Begründung der Jury
Aufgrund ihrer durchdachten Funktionalität und hohen Lichtleistung überzeugt diese Retailleuchte als wirkungsvolle Akzentbeleuchtung in Verkaufsräumen.

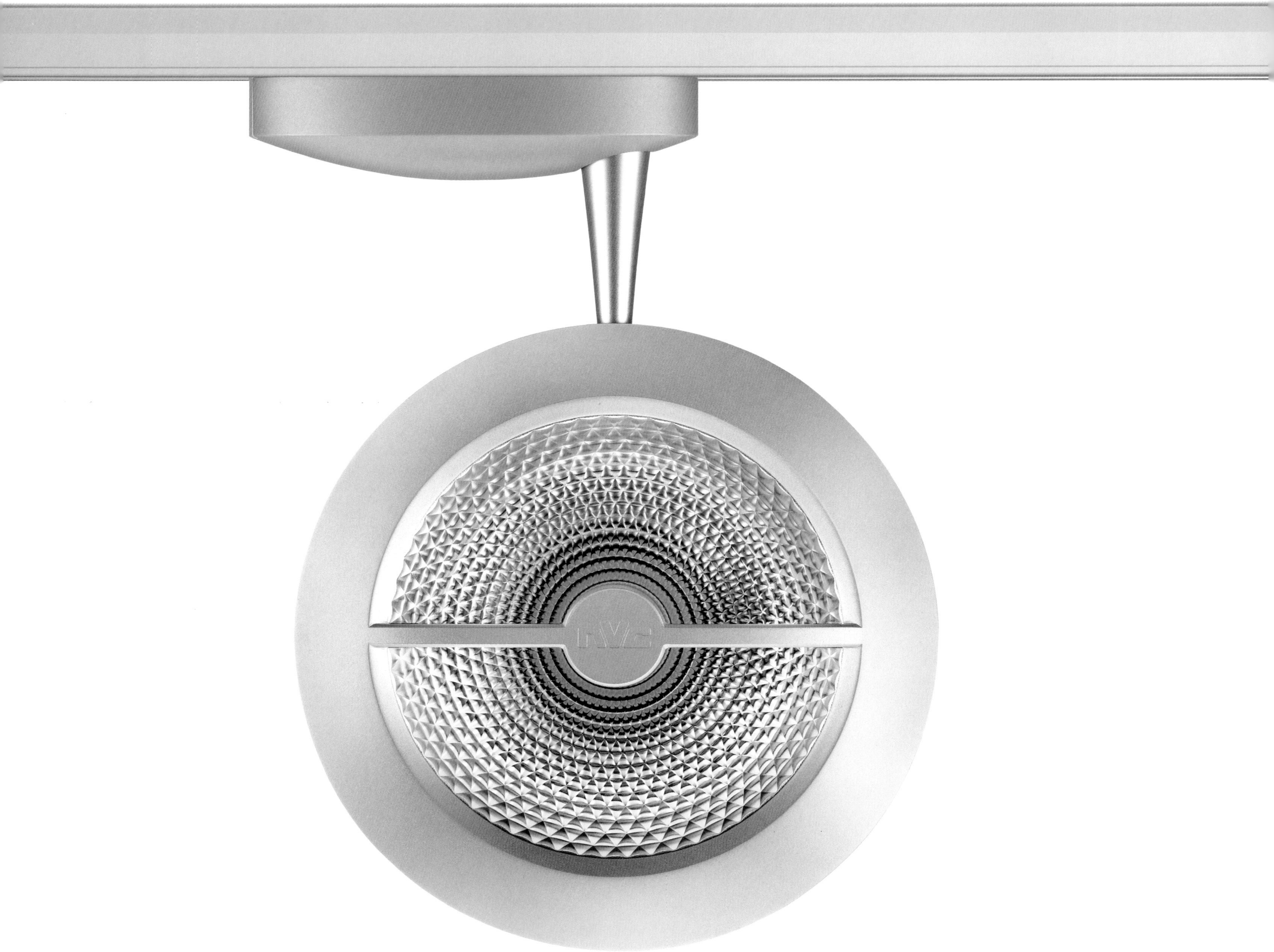

Chameleon
Spotlight Series
Strahlerserie

Manufacturer
Opple Lighting Co., Ltd., Shanghai, China
In-house design
Web
www.opple.com

Chameleon is a versatile spotlight series, the modular design of which allows flexible configuration. It offers, among other things, a choice of six different anti-glare devices. An integrated sensor allows the precise adjustment of the desired light colour from the RGB space. The series is complemented by a variety of accessories and the housing of the spotlights is available in different colours to make them match their respective environment.

Statement by the jury
Thanks to its versatility and well thought-out functionality, the Chameleon spotlight series provides an enhanced lighting comfort.

Chameleon ist eine vielseitige Strahlerserie, deren modularen Aufbau eine variable Ausstattung erlaubt. Unter anderem stehen sechs unterschiedliche Blendschutzvorrichtungen zur Auswahl. Ein integrierter Farbsensor ermöglicht eine präzise Einstellung der gewünschten Lichtfarbe aus dem RGB-Farbraum. Eine Vielzahl an Zubehör rundet die Strahlerserie ab, zudem ist das Strahlergehäuse passend zur jeweiligen Umgebung in verschiedenen Farbvarianten erhältlich.

Begründung der Jury
Dank einer bis ins Detail durchdachten Funktionalität bietet die variable Strahlerserie Chameleon einen gehobenen Beleuchtungskomfort.

Cubie
Spotlight System
Strahler-System

Manufacturer
Acofusion Lighting, Guandong, China
In-house design
Web
www.acofusion.com

The Cubie spotlight system can be adapted to the respective interior by simply exchanging the side panel of the transformer. The panel is available in four different finishes. The spotlight system itself comes in black or white. Cubie has been designed for the illumination of sales and exhibition areas and, thanks to its improved LED technology, offers various lighting options. The different spots can easily be mounted without the use of tools.

Statement by the jury
Due to its flexibility, this spotlight system integrates into different interiors. In addition, Cubie also offers convincing functionality.

Das Strahler-System Cubie lässt sich an die jeweilige Raumausstattung anpassen, indem die Seitenverkleidung des Trafos einfach ausgetauscht wird. Diese Verkleidung ist in vier unterschiedlichen Dekors erhältlich. Zudem wird das Strahler-System in Schwarz oder Weiß angeboten. Konzipiert für die Beleuchtung von Verkaufs- und Ausstellungsbereichen, bietet Cubie aufgrund seiner verbesserten LED-Ausstattung diverse Beleuchtungsmöglichkeiten. Die unterschiedlichen Spots lassen sich werkzeuglos montieren.

Begründung der Jury
Dank seiner Variabilität passt dieses Strahler-System zu unterschiedlichen Interieurs. Darüber hinaus bietet Cubie eine überzeugende Funktionalität.

Philips PerfectBeam gen.2
Spot Series
Strahlerserie

Manufacturer
Signify, Eindhoven, Netherlands
In-house design
Signify Design Team
Web
www.signify.com

PerfectBeam gen.2 is a spot series especially developed for accent illumination in museums. Its light quality and beam flexibility offer numerous options to shape light. A zoom mechanism ranging from 7 to 55 degrees combines with exchangeable round and linear front lenses to enable a wide range of effects which cater for changing exhibitions or last-minute adjustments to the lighting design. The precisely designed body of the spotlight is inspired by professional cameras and conveys a high-quality standard.

Statement by the jury
With a design focus on functionality, this spot series offers convincing lighting flexibility at a professional level.

PerfectBeam gen.2 ist eine Strahlerserie, die speziell zur Akzentbeleuchtung in Museen entwickelt wurde. Ihre Lichtqualität und Flexibilität bieten zahlreiche Möglichkeiten der Lichtgestaltung: Ein Zoommechanismus von 7 bis 55 Grad sowie austauschbare runde und lineare Frontlinsen erlauben eine Vielzahl von Lichteffekten für wechselnde Ausstellungen oder Beleuchtungswünsche. Der präzise gestaltete, von professionellen Kameras inspirierte Strahler-Korpus vermittelt einen hohen Qualitätsanspruch.

Begründung der Jury
Mit einem gestalterischen Fokus auf Funktionalität bietet diese Strahlerserie eine überzeugende Beleuchtungsflexibilität auf professionellem Niveau.

Philips High Lumen Master
LED Spot Series
LED-Lampenserie

Manufacturer
Signify, Shanghai, China
In-house design
Signify Design Team
Web
www.signify.com

High Lumen Master is an LED spot series with a high colour rendering which resembles that of halogen lamps. Its light temperature is therefore perceived to be pleasant and homely. Thanks to their longevity and efficiency, the luminaires minimise operating and maintenance costs. They can easily replace most halogen lights since they are compatible. Available in different sizes and colours, they blend unobtrusively into existing ceiling lamps.

Statement by the jury
This LED spot series meets current consumer demands in terms of energy savings and individual configurations.

High Lumen Master ist eine LED-Lampenserie, deren hohe Farbwiedergabe der des Halogenlichts ähnelt. Ihre Lichttemperatur wird entsprechend als angenehm und wohnlich empfunden. Aufgrund ihrer Langlebigkeit und Effizienz minimieren die Lampen die Betriebs- und Wartungskosten. Sie sind mit den meisten Halogenleuchten kompatibel, sodass ein Austausch in diesen Fällen problemlos möglich ist. Erhältlich in unterschiedlichen Größen und Farben, fügen sich die Lampen unauffällig in bestehende Deckenleuchten ein.

Begründung der Jury
Diese LED-Lampenserie entspricht den aktuellen Ansprüchen der Verbraucher hinsichtlich der Energieersparnis sowie der individuellen Konfiguration.

NUT
Spotlight Series
Strahlerserie

Manufacturer
Opple Lighting Co., Ltd., Shanghai, China
In-house design
Web
www.opple.com

These water- and dust-proof spotlights come in three different sizes, each of them with a different number of LEDs. The innovative integration of those high-performance LEDs ensures even heat dissipation while height-adjustable lenses provide three different illumination angles in all models of this spotlight series. Different bases and matching accessories are available for flexible mounting.

Statement by the jury
In this spotlight series, a purist vocabulary of form and a compact housing design pair up with a sophisticated technical configuration.

Diese wasser- und staubdichten Strahler sind in drei unterschiedlichen Größen erhältlich, die sich hinsichtlich ihrer LED-Anzahl unterscheiden. Eine innovative Integration leistungsstarker LEDs ermöglicht eine gleichmäßige Ableitung der Wärme. Mithilfe von höhenverstellbaren Linsen lassen sich bei allen Varianten dieser Strahlerserie drei unterschiedliche Beleuchtungswinkel einstellen. Zur variablen Befestigung stehen unterschiedliche Sockel und passendes Zubehör zur Verfügung.

Begründung der Jury
Eine puristische Formensprache und kompakte Gehäusegestaltung gehen bei dieser Strahlerserie mit einer raffinierten technischen Ausstattung einher.

Stage Round Spot
Spotlight
Strahler

Manufacturer
Simes S.p.A., Corte Franca (Brescia), Italy
Design
Holscher Design, Copenhagen, Denmark
Web
www.simes.com
www.holscherdesign.com

Following the style of the manufacturer's same-named luminaire series, the Stage Round Spot showcases a special grid at the back. In addition, the spotlight is characterised by its flexible light orientation at different angles as well as its sophisticated aesthetics. Although the size of the luminaire has been reduced to a minimum, it offers a comfortable lighting quality, the intensity of which can be adjusted as required.

Statement by the jury
This spotlight is characterised by a high degree of functionality while its characteristic design vocabulary lends the body an enhanced aesthetic appeal.

In formaler Anlehnung an die gleichnamige Leuchtenserie des Herstellers zeigt der Stage Round Spot ein spezifisches Raster an seiner Rückseite. Zudem ist der Strahler gekennzeichnet von der flexiblen Lichtausrichtung in verschiedenen Winkeln sowie einer anspruchsvollen Ästhetik. Obwohl seine Größe auf ein Minimum reduziert wurde, bietet der Strahler eine komfortable Beleuchtungsqualität und eine bedarfsgerechte Lichtstärke.

Begründung der Jury
Ein hohes Maß an Funktionalität zeichnet diesen Strahler aus, wobei der Korpus aufgrund seiner charakteristischen Formensprache gefällt.

Over-all
Ground Spot
Bodenstrahler

Manufacturer
Simes S.p.A., Corte Franca (Brescia), Italy
In-house design
Web
www.simes.com

Over-all is a ground spot and its flat polypropylene base plate is directly attached to the surface without an in-ground fixture. With a focus on well-balanced proportions, the design of the luminaire has been reduced to the essentials. Its remarkably flat housing is fixed without visible screws. The spot is suitable for a variety of applications and can be used to illuminate trees and shrubbery just as effectively as the facades of buildings.

Statement by the jury
As a product solution which is easy to install, the ground spot impresses with its design language and lighting options.

Over-all ist ein Bodenstrahler, dessen flache Bodenplatte aus Polypropylen direkt auf den jeweilen Bodenbelag montiert wird, ohne dafür eine Einbauvorrichtung zu benötigen. Unter der Prämisse ausgewogener Proportionen entstand ein aufs Wesentliche reduzierter Leuchtenkörper. Sein auffallend flaches Gehäuse wird ohne sichtbare Schrauben befestigt. Der Bodenstrahler eignet sich für unterschiedliche Anwendungsbereiche, er beleuchtet Bäume und Sträucher gleichermaßen wirkungsvoll wie Häuserfassaden.

Begründung der Jury
Als komfortabel zu installierende Produktlösung überzeugt der Bodenstrahler hinsichtlich seiner Formensprache sowie seiner Beleuchtungsoptionen.

MANGO
Spotlight
Strahler

Manufacturer
Opple Lighting Co., Ltd., Shanghai, China
In-house design
Web
www.opple.com

This spotlight features an unusual cooling system. It has a cubic structure and offers an optimised heat dissipation surface. Inspired by diced mango pulp, it integrates square LED carriers. In their entirety, they achieve a maximum surface area for the effective cooling of the spotlight. Thus, the weight and materials used are significantly reduced. In addition, the cooling system marks the overall appearance of the spotlight and simplifies its handling.

Statement by the jury
With its innovative cooling system, this compactly designed spotlight achieves a convincingly high efficiency.

Dieser Strahler verfügt über ein ungewöhnliches Kühlsystem, dessen würfelförmige Struktur eine optimierte Wärmeableitfläche bietet. Inspiriert von kleingewürfeltem Mango-Fruchtfleisch wurden quadratische LED-Träger integriert. In ihrer Gesamtheit erreichen sie eine größtmögliche Oberfläche zur effektiven Kühlung des Strahlers. Somit konnten dessen Gewicht und Materialverbrauch deutlich reduziert werden. Darüber hinaus prägt das Kühlsystem das Gesamtbild des Strahlers und vereinfacht seine Handhabung.

Begründung der Jury
Mit seinem innovativen Kühlsystem erreicht dieser kompakt konstruierte Strahler eine überzeugend hohe Effektivität.

Philips Hue Lily White & Color Ambiance
Outdoor Spotlight Set
Außenstrahler-Set

Manufacturer
Signify, Eindhoven, Netherlands
In-house design
Signify Design Team
Web
www.signify.com

Hue Lily White & Color Ambiance comprises a set of three outdoor spotlights which illuminate gardens in all kinds of colours. Through a combination of diffuse and focused light, they are ideal for highlighting individual plants and for illuminating balconies or terraces. The spotlights can be controlled from anywhere via smartphone. Low-voltage cables securely connect the components while a range of accessories allows for easy positioning.

Statement by the jury
The overall appearance of this outdoor spotlight set is marked by a design geared towards functionality. In addition, they allow versatile lighting effects.

Hue Lily White & Color Ambiance umfasst ein Set von drei Außenstrahlern, mit denen sich Gärten in allen erdenklichen Farben illuminieren lassen. Durch die Kombination von diffusem und fokussiertem Licht eignen sich die Strahler zur Hervorhebung einzelner Pflanzen sowie zur Beleuchtung von Balkonen oder Terrassen. Dazu können die Strahler ortsunabhängig über das Smartphone gesteuert werden. Niederspannungskabel verbinden die Komponenten auf sichere Weise, während eine Reihe von Zubehörteilen eine einfache Platzierung ermöglicht.

Begründung der Jury
Eine auf Funktionalität ausgerichtete Gestaltung prägt das Gesamtbild des Außenstrahler-Sets. Zudem ermöglichen sie variantenreiche Beleuchtungseffekte.

Philips Hue Lucca
Outdoor Luminaire Range
Außenleuchten-Serie

Manufacturer
Signify, Eindhoven, Netherlands
In-house design
Signify Design Team
Web
www.signify.com

Hue Lucca is a series of robust yet elegant outdoor luminaires which emit a warm white light. The characteristic round louvres prevent direct glare and protect the housing from damage. Their sophisticated attachment ensures that they do not affect the natural distribution of the light. Due to the high light output, the dimmable wall and bollard luminaires are suitable for security as well as accent lighting in the garden.

Statement by the jury
This powerful outdoor luminaire series showcases a highly distinctive appearance, which is characterised by a mix of high-contrast materials.

Hue Lucca ist eine Serie robuster und dennoch eleganter Außenleuchten, die ein warmweißes Licht ausstrahlen. Charakteristische Rundblenden verhindern eine Direktblendung und schützen das Gehäuse vor Beschädigungen. Durch eine geschickte Befestigung der Lamellen wird sichergestellt, dass die gleichmäßige Lichtstreuung nicht beeinträchtigt wird. Aufgrund ihrer hohen Lichtleistung eignen sich die dimmbaren Wand- und Pollerleuchten als Sicherheitsbeleuchtung sowie als Akzentbeleuchtung im Garten.

Begründung der Jury
Diese lichtstarke Außenleuchten-Serie zeigt eine unverwechselbare Anmutung, die von einem Mix kontrastreicher Materialien geprägt ist.

223
Outdoor Wall Lamp
Outdoor-Wandleuchte

Manufacturer
Ningbo Royalux Lighting Co., Ltd.,
Ningbo, China
Design
J&W Design Ltd. (Jackie Luo,
Wilfried Buelacher), Hong Kong
Web
www.royalux.cn
www.buelacher-luo.design

Inspired by wall mirrors, the 223 outdoor wall lamp shows a distinctive aesthetic appeal. Its circular contour enables uniform light distribution with a high ratio of indirect light. The wall lamp produces a pleasant warm illumination of 3,000 kelvins. In addition, it is equipped with an integrated motion detector, with a detection range of six to ten metres and a detection angle of 120 degrees.

Inspiriert von einem Wandspiegel zeigt die Outdoor-Wandleuchte der Serie 223 eine unverwechselbare Ästhetik. Ihre kreisrunde Kontur ermöglicht eine gleichmäßige Lichtverteilung mit einem hohen Anteil an indirektem Licht. Die Wandleuchte erzeugt eine als angenehm empfundene Beleuchtung von 3.000 Kelvin. Zudem ist sie mit einem integrierten Bewegungsmelder ausgestattet, der einen Erfassungsbereich von sechs bis zehn Metern und einen Erfassungswinkel von 120 Grad abdeckt.

Statement by the jury
This outdoor wall lamp quotes a familiar design language. It convinces as a multifunctional and emotionally appealing product solution.

Begründung der Jury
Diese Outdoor-Wandleuchte zitiert eine vertraute Formensprache. Sie überzeugt als multifunktionale und emotional ansprechende Produktlösung.

359

CUBA
Wall Lamp
Wandleuchte

Manufacturer
Ningbo Utec Electric Co., Ltd.,
Yuyao, Zhejiang, China
In-house design
Web
www.lutec.com

CUBA is a wall lamp for outdoor use and its upper and lower lamp head can be aligned flexibly. In order to achieve this, both modules are independently rotatable – counterclockwise by 260 degrees and clockwise by 90 degrees. A material mix of die-cast aluminium and unbreakable synthetics ensures weather resistance. The luminaire is suitable for vertical as well as horizontal wall mounting and illuminates facades with 500 lumens for each lamp head.

CUBA ist eine Wandleuchte für den Außenbereich, deren oberer und unterer Leuchtenkopf flexibel ausgerichtet werden können. Dazu sind beide Module unabhängig voneinander drehbar – zum einen gegen den Uhrzeigersinn um 260 Grad und zum anderen im Uhrzeigersinn um 90 Grad. Eine Fertigung aus Aluminiumdruckguss und bruchsicherem Kunststoff sorgt für Wetterfestigkeit. Die Leuchte eignet sich sowohl für eine vertikale als auch eine horizontale Wandmontage und beleuchtet Hausfassaden mit 500 Lumen pro Leuchtenkopf.

Statement by the jury
This rotatable wall lamp offers a high degree of flexibility, while its geometric lines possess an architectural quality.

Begründung der Jury
Ein hohes Maß an Flexibilität bietet diese drehbare Wandleuchte, wobei die geometrische Linienführung eine architektonische Qualität erreicht.

dia
Outdoor Wall Lamp
Außenwandleuchte

Manufacturer
IP44 Schmalhorst GmbH & Co. KG,
Rheda-Wiedenbrück, Germany
Design
Sebastian David Büscher,
Gütersloh, Germany
Web
www.ip44.de
www.sebastian-buescher.de

As a modern interpretation of a classic lantern, dia combines a die-cast powder-coated frame with a grey-tinted blown glass body, which holds a reflecting acrylic rod that appears to be floating. Featuring the optimised IvyLight technology, the outdoor wall lamp, which is equipped with 230V power LEDs, achieves 6 watts at 88 lumens system performance. It is available in anthracite and deep black, and can optionally be controlled with a dimmer.

Statement by the jury
The dia outdoor wall lamp features an appealing design language and impresses with its sophisticated lighting technology.

Als zeitgemäße Interpretation einer klassischen Laterne kombiniert dia einen pulverbeschichteten Aluminiumguss-Rahmen mit einem Körper aus grau getöntem, mundgeblasenem Glas. In diesem scheint ein reflektierender Acrylstab zu schweben. Ausgestattet mit der optimierten IvyLight-Technologie, erreicht die Außenwandleuchte mit ihrer 230-Volt-Power-LED eine Systemleistung von 6 Watt mit 88 Lumen. Sie ist in Anthrazit und einem satten Schwarz erhältlich und kann optional mit einem Dimmer betrieben werden.

Begründung der Jury
Die Außenwandleuchte dia zeigt eine ansprechende Formensprache und überzeugt aufgrund ihrer raffinierten Beleuchtungstechnik.

FACET Collection
Outdoor Wall Lamp
Outdoor-Wandleuchte

Manufacturer
Hong Kong L.C.Z Group Limited,
Zhongshan, China
Design
Design Studio Lars Vejen
for LIGHT-POINT A/S, Copenhagen, Denmark
Web
www.larsvejen.dk
www.light-point.com

The idea behind the design of the FACET Collection was to create a lamp with a reduced and functional design language. Combining an asymmetrically extruded profile with a square back, this wall luminaire spreads light over the wall in a visually appealing manner. Made of aluminium, it intelligently merges industrial objectivity with handcrafted details. They are manufactured in two sizes, both of them available in black or white.

Statement by the jury
The FACET Collection convinces with its asymmetric lines of sculptural appeal. Furthermore, the light distribution helps to create characteristic room atmospheres.

Die zielführende Gestaltungsidee für die FACET Collection war es, eine reduzierte und funktionale Formensprache zu schaffen. Die Kombination eines asymmetrisch geschnittenen Strangpressprofils mit einer quadratischen Rückseite lässt eine Wandleuchte entstehen, deren Licht sich visuell reizvoll über die Wand verteilt. Die Leuchte aus Aluminium vereint auf intelligente Weise industrielle Sachlichkeit mit handwerklich ausgearbeiteten Details. Sie wird in zwei Größen sowie in Schwarz oder Weiß gefertigt.

Begründung der Jury
Die FACET Collection überzeugt mit einer asymmetrischen Linienführung, die skulptural anmutet. Auch das Lichtbild erreicht ein charakteristisches Ambiente.

LANTERN Collection
Outdoor Lamps
Outdoor-Leuchtenserie

Manufacturer
Hong Kong L.C.Z Group Limited,
Zhongshan, China
Design
Light-Point A/S (Marie Dam Holsting),
Copenhagen, Denmark
Web
www.light-point.com

The design of the LANTERN Collection is based on the contemporary interpretation of a classic lantern. Rectangular glass panels framed by black lacquered aluminium combine to form a cuboid. The indirect LED source creates an interplay of geometric areas of light and shades, lending the collection an architectural appeal. The series includes wall, bollard and portable lights, all of which are available in different sizes.

Statement by the jury
Featuring geometric lines, this timeless outdoor lamp series projects an emotionally appealing overall image.

Die Gestaltung der LANTERN Collection beruht auf der zeitgemäßen Interpretation einer klassischen Laterne. Rechteckige, von schwarz lackiertem Aluminium gerahmte Glasscheiben fügen sich dabei zu einem Quader. Die indirekte LED-Quelle erzeugt ein Wechselspiel aus geometrischen Licht- und Schattenflächen, was der Kollektion einen architektonischen Reiz verleiht. Die Serie umfasst eine Wand-, eine Poller- sowie eine tragbare Leuchte, die allesamt in verschiedenen Größen erhältlich sind.

Begründung der Jury
Mit ihrer geometrischen Linienführung lässt diese zeitlose Outdoor-Leuchtenserie ein emotional ansprechendes Gesamtbild entstehen.

Sonnenglas Mini
Solar Lantern
Solarlaterne

Manufacturer
Sonnenglas GmbH, Abstatt, Germany
In-house design
Sonnenglas Design Team
Web
www.sonnenglas.net

Sonnenglas Mini has been developed for areas without electricity in South Africa and is produced by hand in Johannesburg. Equipped with specially coated solar cells, the lantern can be used for up to 20 hours. Thanks to its intelligent electronics, it monitors the surrounding brightness and automatically switches off at sunrise. In order to ensure a long-life cycle, a plug-in system allows for the regular replacement of all individual components. The lantern can be charged via USB port.

Das Sonnenglas Mini wurde für Südafrikas Gegenden ohne ausreichende Stromversorgung entwickelt und wird von Hand in Johannesburg gefertigt. Dank spezialbeschichteter Solarzellen leuchtet die Solarlaterne bis zu 20 Stunden. Mithilfe einer intelligenten Elektronik überwacht sie die Umgebungshelligkeit und schaltet sich bei Sonnenaufgang automatisch ab. Im Sinne eines langen Lebenszyklus sorgen Stecksysteme dafür, dass die Einzelkomponenten fortwährend erneuerbar sind. Die Laterne kann auch über einen USB-Anschluss aufgeladen werden.

Statement by the jury
Equipped with intelligent technology and robust solar cells, this lantern convinces as a socially and ecologically sound product solution.

Begründung der Jury
Ausgestattet mit einer intelligenten Technologie und unter Verwendung robuster Solarzellen überzeugt diese Solarlaterne als sozial und ökologisch sinnvolle Produktlösung.

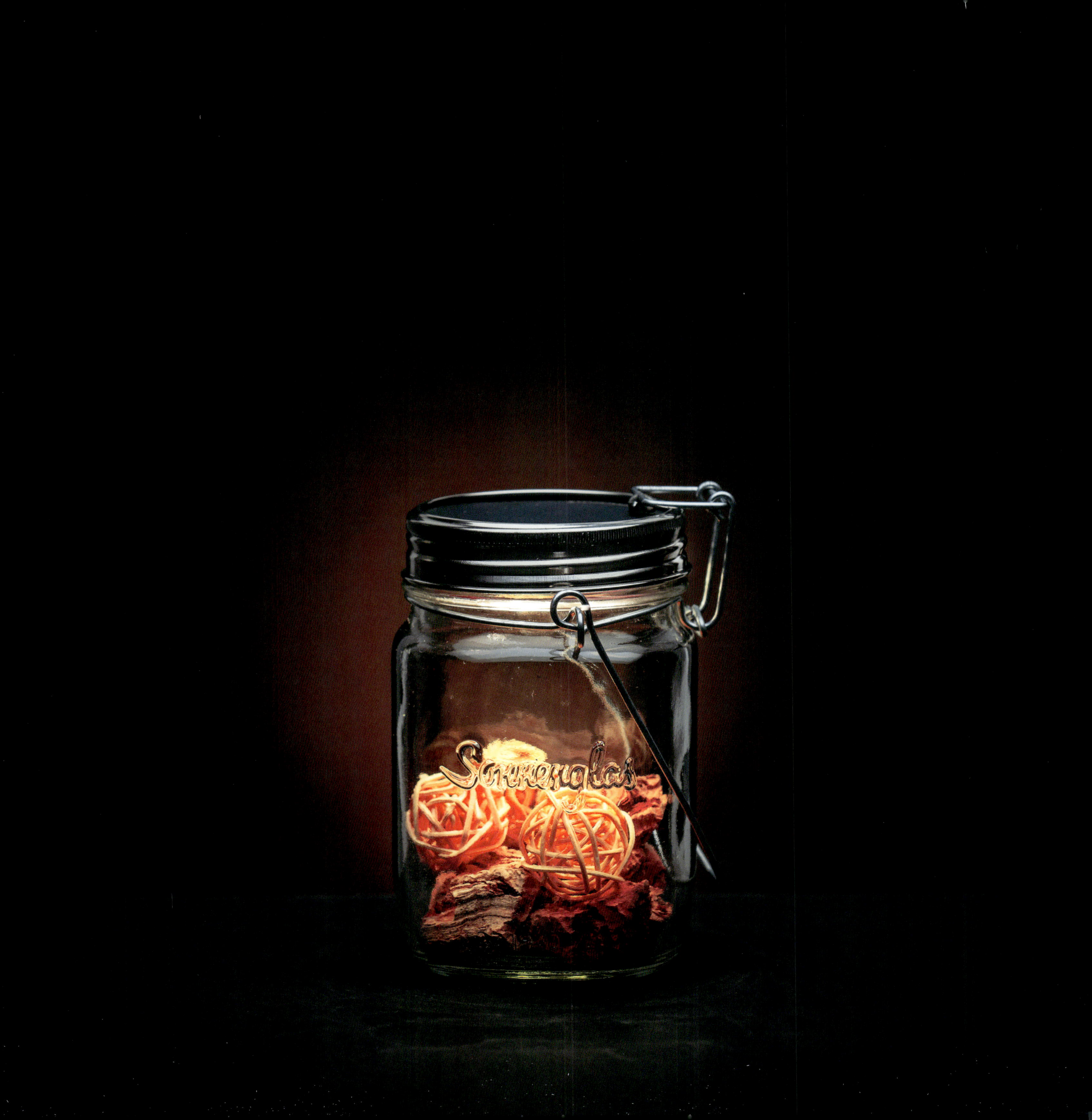
Sonnenglas

ANI LAMP
Mobile Lamp
Tragbare Leuchte

Manufacturer
blomus GmbH, Sundern, Germany
Design
kaschkasch
(Florian Kallus, Sebastian Schneider),
Cologne, Germany
Web
www.blomus.com
www.kaschkasch.com

Inspired by a street light, the mobile ANI LAMP offers versatile use: it can be put up on a stand, hung on a rope or placed on a table. The light cone can be changed by simply turning the lampshade and the luminaire is operated by briefly touching the rings of it. This allows users to select between two brightness levels and switch the light on and off. A charging cradle and a USB Cable are used for the recharging of the lamp.

Statement by the jury
The modular concept of this portable luminaire promotes versatile use. Its distinctive, yet familiar-looking design idiom is emotionally appealing.

Inspiriert von einer Straßenlaterne entstand diese tragbare Leuchte, die variabel nutzbar ist: ANI LAMP kann auf einen Standfuß gesetzt, an ein Seil gehängt oder auf einen Tisch gestellt werden. Durch einfaches Umdrehen des Lampenschirms verändert sich der Lichtkegel. Bedient wird die Leuchte durch ein kurzes Berühren der Ringe auf dem Lampenschirm. So lassen sich zwei Helligkeitsstufen sowie das Ein- und Ausschalten der Leuchte steuern. Zum Wiederaufladen dient eine Ladeschale mit USB-Kabel.

Begründung der Jury
Aufgrund ihrer modularen Konstruktion erlaubt diese tragbare Leuchte einen vielseitigen Einsatz. Ihre vertraute Formensprache spricht emotional an.

321-MODULAR
Outdoor Lamp Series
Outdoor-Leuchtenserie

Manufacturer
Ningbo Royalux Lighting Co., Ltd.,
Ningbo, China
Design
J&W Design Ltd.
(Jackie Luo, Wilfried Buelacher),
Hong Kong
Web
www.royalux.cn
www.buelacher-luo.design

The weatherproof wall and bollard luminaires of the 321-MODULAR outdoor lamp series follow a design approach of clearly defined structures and lines. The powder-coated aluminium body in graphite grey, for example, exudes a minimalist look. The slim, swivelling lamp head comes with high-quality LEDs, providing a pleasant and sufficiently bright light. All luminaires in the series can optionally be equipped with a motion detector, a movable solar module or both.

Statement by the jury
The reduced design language of this outdoor lamp series conveys the contemporary look and comfort of a focused garden lighting.

Die wetterfesten Wand- und Pollerleuchten der Outdoor-Leuchtenserie 321-MODULAR folgen einem Gestaltungsansatz mit klar definierten Strukturen und Linien. So wirkt der pulverbeschichtete Aluminiumkörper in Graphitgrau minimalistisch. Der flache, schwenkbare Lampenkopf ist mit hochwertigen LEDs ausgestattet und sorgt für eine angenehme und ausreichend helle Beleuchtung. Alle Leuchten der Serie können optional mit einem Bewegungsmelder, einem beweglichen Solarmodul oder beidem ausgestattet werden.

Begründung der Jury
Eine reduzierte Formensprache vermittelt bei dieser Outdoor-Leuchtenserie den zeitgemäßen Komfort einer fokussierten Gartenbeleuchtung.

235
Outdoor Lamp Series
Outdoor-Leuchtenserie

Manufacturer
Ningbo Royalux Lighting Co., Ltd.,
Ningbo, China
Design
J&W Design Ltd.
(Jackie Luo, Wilfried Buelacher),
Hong Kong
Web
www.royalux.cn
www.buelacher-luo.design

The wall and bollard lamps of this outdoor lighting series are characterised by geometric lines. Their mix of materials creates a distinctive contrast between the bright concrete base and the black aluminium body. The filigree body of the lamp features an elegant appeal and directs the view to the luminaire's head. All lamps in this series can optionally be equipped with a motion detector.

Statement by the jury
High-quality materials in combination with a minimalist design lend the 235 outdoor lamp series a characteristic overall appearance.

Eine geometrische Linienführung kennzeichnet die Wand- und Pollerleuchten dieser Outdoor-Leuchtenserie. Ihr Materialmix lässt einen prägnanten Kontrast zwischen dem hellen Betonsockel und dem schwarzen Aluminiumkörper entstehen. Der filigran anmutende Leuchtenkörper wirkt elegant und lenkt den Blick zum Leuchtenkopf. Sämtliche Leuchten dieser Serie können bei Bedarf mit einem Bewegungsmelder ausgestattet werden.

Begründung der Jury
Hochwertige Materialien in Kombination mit einer minimalistischen Gestaltung verleihen der Outdoor-Leuchtenserie 235 ein charakteristisches Gesamtbild.

Philips Hue Outdoor Lightstrip
Philips Hue Outdoor-Lichtleiste

Manufacturer
Signify, Eindhoven, Netherlands
In-house design
Signify Design Team
Web
www.signify.com

In a visually effective way, the Hue Outdoor Lightstrip can be used to differentiate individual garden areas and illuminate them in numerous colour shades. The compact strip can be flexibly bent to emphasise the contours of flower beds, terraces, facades and fences. Thanks to its matte finish, it offers a perfectly even, all-around glow. The subtle light strip is waterproof and connects to the power supply via safe low volt cables.

Statement by the jury
The Hue Outdoor Lightstrip convinces as a consistently thought-out product solution. It offers fascinating possibilities for accent lighting in the garden.

Auf visuell wirkungsvolle Weise lassen sich einzelne Gartenbereiche mithilfe der Hue Outdoor-Lichtleiste voneinander abgrenzen und in zahlreichen Farbnuancen illuminieren. Die kompakte Leiste lässt sich flexibel verbiegen, um so die Konturen von Beeten, Terrassen, Fassaden oder Zäunen zu betonen. Aufgrund ihrer matten Oberflächenbeschichtung bietet die Leiste ein rundum gleichmäßiges Leuchten. Die dezente Lichtleiste ist wasserdicht und wird über sichere Niederspannungskabel ans Stromnetz angeschlossen.

Begründung der Jury
Die Hue Outdoor-Lichtleiste überzeugt als stringent durchdachte Produktlösung. Sie bietet faszinierende Möglichkeiten zur Akzentbeleuchtung im Garten.

Ren
Bollard Light Series
Pollerleuchten-Serie

Manufacturer
DW Windsor, Hoddesdon,
Hertfordshire, United Kingdom
In-house design
Design
Fine Science,
Brighton, United Kingdom
Web
www.dwwindsor.com
www.finescience.net

This bollard light series is designed to provide a variety of lighting options through a flat-screen optical system. While the Performance model offers a horizontal light distribution in combination with a strong forward and lateral ground illumination, the Performance-Plus model allows a vertical light distribution with an added area of diffused light to improve facial recognition. Ren is available in three different height options, two widths and in a variety of colour finishes.

Statement by the jury
As a product solution for both the private and the public sector, the Ren bollard lights series is characterised by a wide illuminant spectrum.

Diese Pollerleuchten-Serie wurde entwickelt, um mithilfe eines optischen Flachbildschirm-Systems eine Vielzahl von Beleuchtungsoptionen zu ermöglichen. Während die Performance-Version eine horizontale Lichtverteilung zur flächigen Bodenausleuchtung bietet, erlaubt die Performance-Plus-Variante eine vertikale Lichtverteilung inklusive Streulichtfläche, die der besseren Personenwahrnehmung dient. Ren ist in drei verschiedenen Höhen und zwei Breiten sowie in verschiedenen Farbausführungen erhältlich.

Begründung der Jury
Als Produktlösung für den privaten wie den öffentlichen Bereich zeichnet sich die Pollerleuchten-Serie Ren durch ihr breites Beleuchtungsspektrum aus.

SLV Malu
Outdoor Lamp Series
Außenleuchten-Serie

Manufacturer
SLV GmbH, Übach-Palenberg, Germany
In-house design
Philippe Stephant
Web
www.slv.com

Alongside wall and ceiling lights, the Malu outdoor lamp series also includes floor lights of class A++ energy efficiency. The matte black surfaces of the luminaires are made of powder-coated aluminium, lending them a high-quality appeal. Thanks to the extraordinary light heads, the integrated LEDs achieve a particularly wide light distribution and uniform illumination. Complying with IP55 protection class, the reliable luminaires are suitable for outdoor use.

Statement by the jury
Based on a classic design language, this outdoor lamp series achieves a harmonious interplay of functionality and materiality.

Die Außenleuchten-Serie Malu umfasst neben Decken- und Wandleuchten auch Standleuchten der Energieeffizienzklasse A++. Um eine hohe Wertigkeit zu vermitteln, bestehen die mattschwarzen Oberflächen der Leuchten aus pulverbeschichtetem Aluminium. Aufgrund der außergewöhnlichen Leuchtenköpfe erreichen die integrierten LEDs eine besonders breite Lichtverteilung und eine gleichmäßige Ausleuchtung. Die Leuchten eignen sich gemäß der Schutzart-Klassifizierung IP55 zuverlässig für den Außenbereich.

Begründung der Jury
In Anlehnung an eine klassische Formensprache gelingt bei dieser Außenleuchten-Serie ein stimmiges Zusammenspiel von Funktionalität und Materialität.

Work Light
Arbeitsleuchte

Manufacturer
Ningbo Bright Electric Co., Ltd.,
Ningbo, China
In-house design
Wang Yinpeng
Web
www.nb-bright.com

This work light has been developed to provide wide-range illumination for night-time outdoor work or car repairs. Its concept picks up on typical aspects of car design; Thus, the front panel of the light is reminiscent of a radiator grille. The high light output of 3,500 lumens can be set to seven brightness levels. The large capacity battery with 4,000 mAh achieves a long runtime and also allows for the charging of mobile phones. An app provides convenient control from a distance.

Statement by the jury
The compact work light surprises with an unusual design language and impresses with its high lighting efficiency.

Um nächtliche Außenarbeiten oder Autoreparaturen großflächig zu beleuchten, wurde diese Arbeitsleuchte entwickelt. Ihre Gestaltung greift typische Aspekte des Autodesigns auf; so erinnert die Frontblende der Leuchte an einen Kühlergrill. Die hohe Lichtleistung von 3.500 Lumen lässt sich in sieben Helligkeitsstufen einstellen. Das Großraum-Akku mit 4.000 mAh erreicht eine lange Laufzeit und erlaubt auch das Aufladen von Mobiltelefonen. Die APP-Steuerung ermöglicht eine komfortable Regelung aus der Ferne.

Begründung der Jury
Die kompakt konstruierte Arbeitsleuchte überrascht mit einer ungewöhnlichen Formensprache und überzeugt mit einer hohen Beleuchtungseffektivität.

Cameo ZENIT® B200
Outdoor Wash Light
Outdoor-Scheinwerfer

Manufacturer
Adam Hall GmbH, Neu-Anspach, Germany
In-house design
Web
www.cameolight.com/ZENITB200

This battery-powered outdoor wash light offers a highly intense luminous flux of 6,600 lumens. It is IP65-rated for permanent outdoor use, featuring convection cooling which ensures silent operation. Additional diffusers with different beam angles can be attached magnetically. The OLED display features four touch-sensitive panels for easy configuration while the compact housing, made of die-cast aluminium components, provides stability.

Statement by the jury
This battery-powered outdoor wash light is characterised by sophisticated functionality and impresses with its luminous intensity and ease of use.

Dieser batteriebetriebene Outdoor-Scheinwerfer bietet mit einem Lichtstrom von 6.600 Lumen eine hohe Lichtstärke. Er ist IP65-klassifiziert und für einen dauerhaften Außeneinsatz geeignet, seine Konvektionskühlung arbeitet geräuschlos. Zusätzliche Diffusoren mit unterschiedlichen Abstrahlwinkeln lassen sich magnetisch anbringen. Das OLED-Display verfügt über vier berührungsempfindliche Bedienfelder zur einfachen Konfiguration. Das kompakte Gehäuse aus Aluminium-Druckgussteilen ist standfest.

Begründung der Jury
Eine ausgereifte Funktionalität zeichnet diesen batteriebetriebenen Outdoor-Scheinwerfer aus, der zudem mit Lichtstärke und Bedienkomfort punktet.

Handheld Work Light
Tragbare Arbeitsleuchte

Manufacturer
AEC Lighting Solutions Co., Ltd., Shanghai, China
In-house design
Aixia Bian
Web
www.aeclight-reel.com

This portable work light has been designed for professional use and provides a light output of up to 1,000 lumens. The front chip-on-board LEDs can be continuously dimmed while the powerful LED on the top serves as a spotlight. The slim aluminium housing is dust and water resistant. A fan, integrated in the back, provides effective cooling. The back also features a multi-functional clip which serves as a magnetic wall mount and convenient stand.

Diese tragbare Arbeitsleuchte wurde für eine professionelle Anwendung konzipiert und liefert eine Lichtleistung von bis zu 1.000 Lumen. Die vorderen Chip-on-Board-LEDs lassen sich stufenlos dimmen, die leistungsstarke LED an der Oberseite dient als Strahler. Das flache Aluminiumgehäuse ist staub- und wasserdicht. Ein auf der Rückseite integrierter Lüfter erreicht eine effektive Kühlung. Auf der Rückseite befindet sich zudem ein Multifunktionsclip zur magnetischen Wandbefestigung sowie zum Aufstellen der Leuchte.

Statement by the jury
In this handheld work light, a high degree of functionality meets convincing product features such as a compact and robust construction.

Begründung der Jury
Ein hohes Maß an Funktionalität trifft bei dieser tragbaren Arbeitsleuchte auf überzeugende Produkteigenschaften wie Handlichkeit und Robustheit.

N9-LUMENA2
LED Lantern
LED-Leuchte

Manufacturer
Onankorea, Busan, South Korea
In-house design
Joonghun Jin, Sebin Park, Sungchoon Ha
Web
www.nnine.com

N9-LUMENA2 is an LED lantern for outdoors. It is suitable to be used on camping sites as well as in open terrain, for example with a backpack. The compact product has suspension devices such as a magnetic hook and can thus be attached to angles, poles, tarpaulins or tents, for example. With its anodised finish, the lantern is aesthetically pleasing and also very stabil and durable. It is waterproof and dustproof to IP67 and easy to handle thanks to its light weight.

N9-LUMENA2 ist eine LED-Leuchte für den Außenbereich. Sie lässt sich ebenso auf dem Campingplatz wie im freien Gelände, etwa unterwegs mit dem Rucksack, verwenden. Das kompakte Produkt verfügt über Aufhängevorrichtungen wie einen Magnethaken und kann so etwa an Winkeln, Stangen, Planen oder Zelten angebracht werden. Mit ihrem eloxierten Finish ist die Laterne ästhetisch gestaltet und zudem sehr stabil und haltbar. Sie ist wasserdicht und staubdicht gemäß IP67 und lässt sich dank ihres geringen Gewichts leicht handhaben.

Statement by the jury
The LED lantern N9-LUMENA2 conveys reliability and robustness and impresses with functionality designed for practical use.

Begründung der Jury
Die LED-Leuchte N9-LUMENA2 vermittelt Zuverlässigkeit und Robustheit und gefällt mit einer praxisbezogen gestalteten Funktionalität.

GPDesign PSR51
LED Torch
LED-Taschenlampe

Manufacturer
GPI International Limited, Hong Kong
In-house design
Simon Davies
Web
www.gpbatteries.com

The GPDesign PSR51 torch can be recharged and features a slim, robust design. It is IPX8 water proof and also equipped with a multi-coloured dual tail switch. The carefully designed user interface integrates a series of comfortable functions. The centrally located rubber switch and the steel switch at the end of the torch offer different light modes. The ribbed finish on the head gives the user a secure grip to rotate it and select one of four colours (white, red, blue or green). A lockout function prevents accidental power-up.

Die wiederaufladbare Taschenlampe GPDesign PSR51 zeigt eine schlanke, robuste Formgebung. Sie ist IPX8 wasserdicht und mit einem mehrfarbigen Doppelheckschalter ausgestattet. Ihre sorgfältig gestaltete Benutzeroberfläche integriert komfortable Funktionen: Der zentral angeordnete Gummischalter sowie ein Stahlschalter am hinteren Ende bieten mehrere Leuchtmodi. Die gerippte Oberfläche am Kopf ermöglicht einen sicheren Griff, um ihn zu drehen und zwischen vier Farben (Weiß, Rot, Blau oder Grün) zu wählen. Eine Sperrfunktion verhindert ein versehentliches Einschalten.

Statement by the jury
The PSR51 torch skilfully combines a design geared towards stability and quality with a sophisticated range of functions.

Begründung der Jury
Gekonnt verbindet sich in der Taschenlampe PSR51 eine auf Stabilität und Wertigkeit ausgerichtete Gestaltung mit einem ausgereiften Funktionsumfang.

Dawn to Dusk
Table and Floor Lamp
Tisch- und Stehleuchte

Manufacturer
Haberdashery,
London, United Kingdom

In-house design
Nathanael Hunt, Thomas Turner

Web
www.haberdashery.com

reddot award 2019
best of the best

Staging light moods

The position of the sun in the course of a day has an influence on both the physical well-being of people and their individual moods. The design of the Dawn to Dusk table and floor lamp has been inspired by the ambience of the rising and setting sun, bathing interiors into a fascinating spectacle of changing light. The lamp is operated by manually sliding the head up and down the stand, as well as rotating it through 360 degrees. In doing so, the light gradually changes from the off-state at the bottom of the stand into an intense red to orange and peach and then into warm white and finally a colour temperature of 2,700 kelvins. For simulating twilight and other lighting situations, the luminaire can be pointed forwards into the room or be used to flood colour up a wall, creating a range of different moods in a given environment. A special effect has been added in that, even when pointed away, there is a halo of light still visible. The red light has an element of distinctively refined pink, giving it a subtle quality with added health benefits. The orange range allows for both intense hues as well as soft peach tones. The colour range is achieved by three sets of LED arrays which are blended to deliver a highly natural colour palette. By creating a physical interaction between the lamp and its users, Dawn to Dusk promotes a strong understanding of the importance of colour temperature on the body's natural circadian rhythms.

Stimmungsvoll inszeniert

Der Stand der Sonne im Tagesverlauf beeinflusst die Physis wie auch die individuellen Stimmungen des Menschen. Die Gestaltung der Leuchte Dawn to Dusk ist vom Ambiente der aufgehenden und untergehenden Sonne inspiriert und bietet im Interieur ein faszinierendes Schauspiel des Lichtwechsels. Bedient wird sie durch ein einfaches manuelles Verschieben des Leuchtenkopfes auf ihrem Standfuß, wobei auch eine Drehung um 360 Grad möglich ist. Das Licht ändert sich dabei vom ausgeschalteten Zustand am unteren Rand des Ständers über ein intensives Rot zu Orange und Pfirsich und schließlich in warmes Weiß bis hin zu einer Farbtemperatur von 2.700 Kelvin. Für eine Simulation der Dämmerung oder anderer Lichtsituationen kann die Leuchte nach vorne in das Zimmer gerichtet werden oder eine Wand in Farbe tauchen und so unterschiedliche Stimmungen erzeugen. Ein besonderer Effekt ist, dass, auch wenn die Lichtquelle abgewendet ist, immer noch ein Lichtkranz erkennbar bleibt. Das rote Licht enthält zudem Anteile eines nuancierten Rosatons, was für eine subtile Qualität mit zusätzlichen gesundheitlichen Vorteilen sorgt. Der orangene Bereich ermöglicht intensive Farbtöne ebenso wie weiche Pfirsichtöne. Die Farbpalette wird durch drei LED-Arrays erreicht, die sich zu einem sehr natürlichen Spektrum zusammenfügen. In der Interaktion zwischen Leuchte und Nutzer erlaubt Dawn to Dusk ein intensives Verständnis der Bedeutung der Farbtemperatur für die zirkadianen Rhythmen des Körpers.

Statement by the jury

Imitating the natural progression of the sun and thus daylight, Dawn to Dusk creates sensuous lighting scenarios, enhanced by the lamp's impressive iconic silhouette. The luminaire is suitable as both a table and floor lamp and impresses with a self-explanatory functionality that allows changing the light setting in an intuitive manner. The natural appeal of the lamp completes the analogy to the course of the sun without an app or computer in a stimulating way.

Begründung der Jury

Den natürlichen Verlauf des Tageslichts imitierend, kreiert Dawn to Dusk stimmungsvolle Lichtszenarien, wobei ihre Form eine eindrucksvolle ikonische Silhouette zeigt. Die Leuchte kann als Tisch- oder Stehleuchte verwendet werden und begeistert mit einer sich sofort erklärenden Funktionalität, die einen intuitiven Wechsel des Lichts ermöglicht. Belebend vollzieht sie ihre selbstverständlich wirkende Analogie des Sonnenverlaufs ohne App oder Computer.

Designer portrait
See page 64
Siehe Seite 64

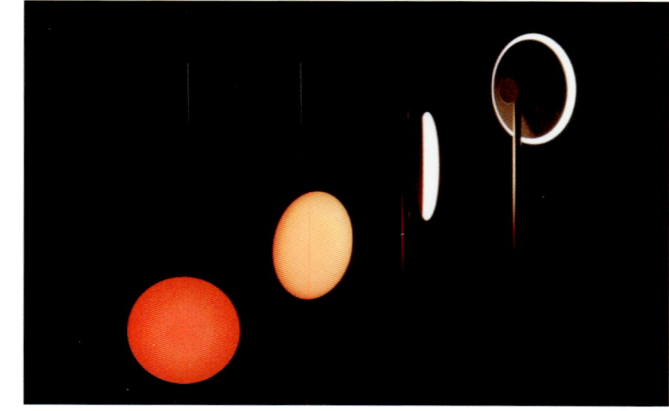

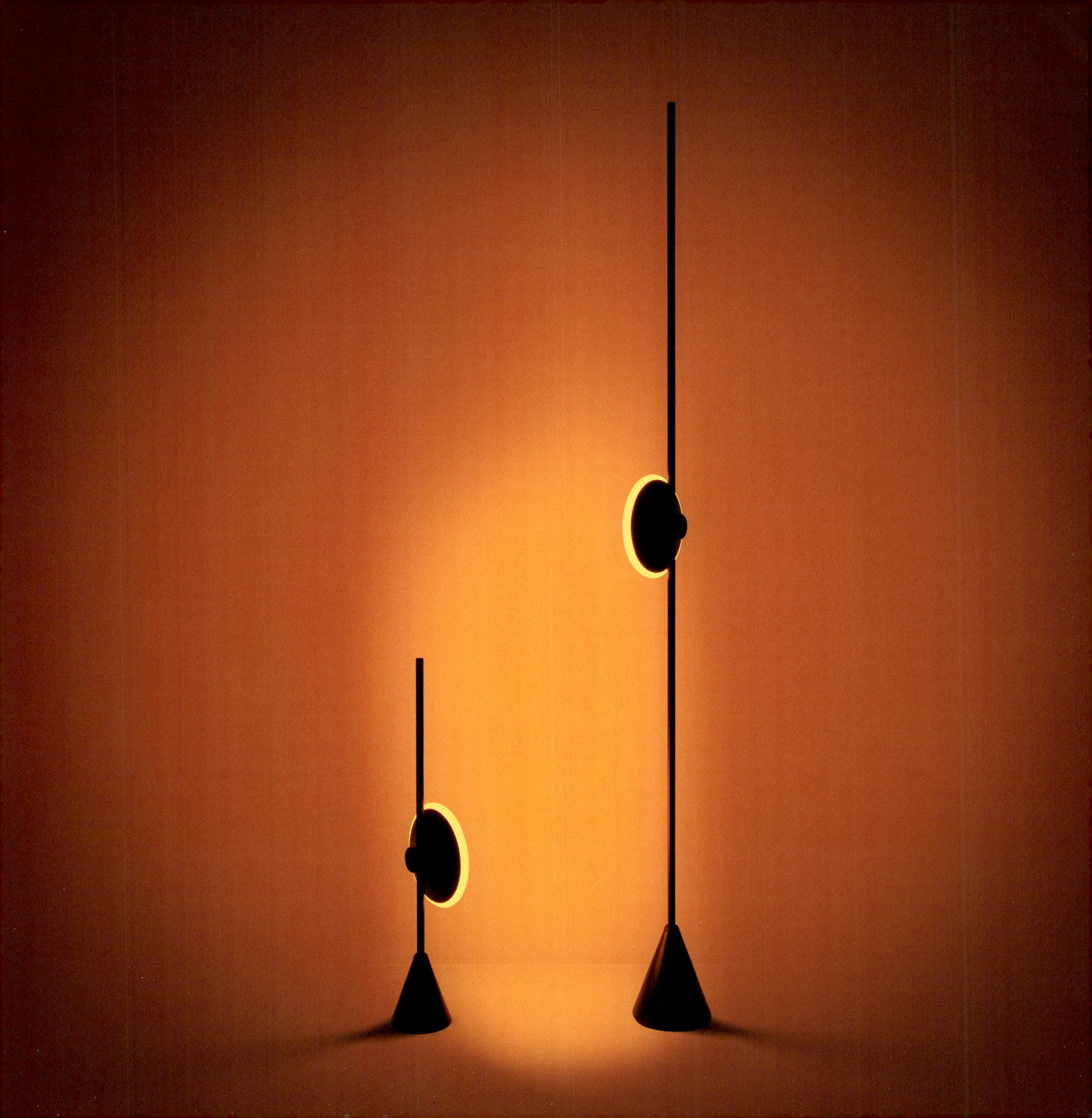

Desk Lamp
Schreibtischleuchte

Manufacturer
Miniso Hong Kong Limited,
Guangzhou, China
In-house design
Qupeng Li, Tingbin Wu
Web
www.miniso.com

This desk lamp can just be folded for space-saving storage after use. This is made possible by a flexible lamp arm, which is lowered into the recess of the base like a spiral. In this way, the luminaire head merges with the round foot to form a compact, 30 mm thick housing. When unfolded, the desk lamp can be individually adjusted to specifically illuminate surfaces.

Statement by the jury
This desk lamp surprises with its highly flexible structure, which also allows for extremely space-saving storage.

Um nach dem Gebrauch platzsparend verstaut zu werden, lässt sich diese Schreibtischleuchte einfach zusammenklappen. Möglich wird dies durch einen flexiblen Leuchtenarm, der spiralförmig in die obere Aussparung des Standfußes eingedreht wird. Der auf diese Weise abgesenkte Leuchtenkopf verbindet sich mit dem runden Fuß zu einem kompakten, 30 mm hohen Gehäuse. In aufgerichtetem Zustand kann die Schreibtischleuchte individuell auf die zu beleuchtende Fläche ausgerichtet werden.

Begründung der Jury
Diese Schreibtischleuchte überrascht durch ihre hochflexible Struktur, die eine äußerst platzsparende Aufbewahrung erlaubt.

Yeelight Prime
Desk Lamp
Schreibtischleuchte

Manufacturer
Qingdao Yeelink Information
Technology Co., Ltd., Qingdao, China
In-house design
Web
www.yeelight.com

Equipped with 50 LEDs, this desk lamp provides eye-friendly lighting with a low level of blue light and a high colour rendering index of 90. The integrated Wi-Fi module supports convenient app control while the touch panel allows continuous dimming. With a diameter of 160 mm, the base only takes up little space. The concealed rotation axle design allows for the flexible alignment of the lamp head.

Statement by the jury
This desk lamp not only offers contemporary lighting comfort, it also impresses with its geometric design language.

Diese mit 50 LEDs ausgestattete Schreibtischleuchte bietet eine augenfreundliche Beleuchtung mit einem geringen Blaulichtanteil und einem hohen Farbwiedergabeindex von Ra 90. Das integrierte Wi-Fi-Modul unterstützt eine komfortable App-Steuerung, zudem erlaubt die Touch-Bedienung ein stufenloses Dimmen. Mit einem Durchmesser von 160 mm nimmt die Sockelkonstruktion nur wenig Stellfläche in Anspruch. Die verdeckt gestaltete Rotationsachse erlaubt eine flexible Ausrichtung des Leuchtenkopfs.

Begründung der Jury
Diese Schreibtischleuchte bietet zeitgemäßen Beleuchtungskomfort und überzeugt zudem durch ihre geometrische Formensprache.

Multi-Way
Desk Lamp
Schreibtischleuchte

Manufacturer
Concept 7, Shanghai, China
In-house design
Web
www.spointdesign.com

Multi-Way is a desk lamp with a timeless design, offering a variety of illumination angles. Three hidden pivot joints allow for the flexible alignment of the head, the arm and the base of the lamp. The light intensity is individually adjustable via the touch control panel on the lamp head. The concave, bevel design of the LED panel reduces the glare of the light to a minimum. In addition, the lamp delivers a flicker-free light quality for working, reading or relaxing.

Statement by the jury
As an expression of a sophisticated design concept, this desk lamp stands out with its balanced proportions and ease of use.

Multi-Way ist eine zeitlos gestaltete Schreibtischleuchte, die eine Vielzahl von Beleuchtungswinkeln ermöglicht. Drei versteckt integrierte Drehgelenke erlauben eine flexible Ausrichtung von Leuchtenkopf, -arm und -fuß. Die Lichtintensität lässt sich über das Touch-Bedienfeld am Leuchtenkopf individuell einstellen. Die konkave Fasen-Gestaltung des LED-Panels reduziert die blendenden Lichtanteile auf ein Minimum. Zudem bietet die Leuchte eine flackerfreie Lichtqualität zum Arbeiten, Lesen oder Entspannen.

Begründung der Jury
Als Ausdruck eines durchdachten Gestaltungskonzepts fällt diese Schreibtischleuchte durch ihren Bedienkomfort und ausgewogene Proportionen auf.

LightStrip
Table Lamp
Tischleuchte

Manufacturer
Shanghai Allocacoc Industrial
Design Co., Ltd., Shanghai, China
In-house design
Zexin He, Shuaishuai Wang
Web
www.allocacoc.com

This table lamp allows interactive control: in order to turn it on, the arm of the lamp is pivoted up and then adjusted as needed. The 360-degree rotatable arm offers a wide range of illumination angles. The light can be dimmed via touch control. Thanks to its modular design, up to three LightStrips can be combined. The luminaire can be flexibly used on desks as well as conference or bedside tables.

Statement by the jury
With its innovative ease of use, this table lamp fulfils high standards and impresses with its clear, contemporary design.

Diese Tischleuchte ermöglicht eine interaktive Steuerung: Um sie einzuschalten, wird der Leuchtenarm nach oben geschwenkt und bedarfsgerecht ausgerichtet. Der um 360 Grad drehbarer Arm bietet ein breites Spektrum an Beleuchtungswinkeln. Das Licht lässt sich über einen Touch-Regler dimmen. Aufgrund ihres modularen Aufbaus können bis zu drei LightStrips miteinander kombiniert werden. Die Leuchte kann flexibel auf Schreibtischen, Konferenztischen oder auch Nachttischen eingesetzt werden.

Begründung der Jury
Mit ihrem innovativen Bedienkomfort erfüllt diese Tischleuchte gehobene Ansprüche und begeistert durch eine klare, zeitgemäße Linienführung.

Mi
Desk Lamp
Schreibtischleuchte

Manufacturer
Xiaomi Inc., Beijing, China
In-house design
Web
www.mi.com

Mi is a minimalist desk lamp which provides eye-friendly lighting for working and reading. The product concept is completed by flicker-free light output, a high colour rendering index of more than 90 CRI as well as flexibly adjustable colour temperatures. Equipped with three joints, the luminaire can be adjusted to different scenarios in height and angle. A corresponding smartphone app and voice control ensure convenient operation.

Statement by the jury
This desk lamp combines sophisticated technology with minimalist lines, exuding a timeless and elegant appeal.

Mi ist eine minimalistisch anmutende Schreibtischleuchte, die eine augenschonende Beleuchtung zum Arbeiten und Lesen bietet. Ihre flackerfreie Lichtstärke, ein hoher Farbwiedergabeindex von über 90 CRI sowie eine flexibel einstellbare Farbtemperatur runden das Produktkonzept ab. Die mit drei Gelenken ausgestattete Leuchte lässt sich in Höhe und Leuchtwinkel an unterschiedliche Situationen anpassen. Eine begleitende Smartphone-App sowie eine Sprachsteuerung ermöglichen eine komfortable Bedienung.

Begründung der Jury
Bei dieser Schreibtischleuchte vereint sich eine ausgereifte Technik mit einer auf das Wesentliche reduzierten Linienführung, die zeitlos-elegant wirkt.

ROOMOR
Table Lamp
Tischleuchte

Manufacturer
Wever & Ducré BVBA, Kortrijk, Belgium
In-house design
Web
www.weverducre.com

Inspired by the style of the 1920s, the ROOMOR table lamp is based on a modular structure and thus available in different designs and colours. Its versatility makes it suitable, for example, as a desk lighting or a table lamp in hotel lobbies. Individual components, such as the lampshade, can be exchanged in a few simple steps. Various shade forms are available in either brushed aluminium or finely textured felt.

Statement by the jury
With a nostalgic design, the ROOMOR table lamp successfully implements a well thought-through modular concept.

Die vom Stil der 1920er-Jahre inspirierte Tischleuchte folgt einem modularen Aufbau. Daher ist ROOMOR in unterschiedlichen Ausführungen und Farben erhältlich. In ihrer Wandelbarkeit eignet sie sich beispielsweise zur Schreibtischbeleuchtung sowie als Tischleuchte in einer Hotellobby. Einzelne Bestandteile wie der Leuchtenschirm lassen sich mit wenigen Handgriffen austauschen. Diverse Schirmformen sind entweder aus gebürstetem Aluminium oder aus fein strukturiertem Filz gefertigt.

Begründung der Jury
Bei der nostalgisch gestalteten Tischleuchte ROOMOR gelingt die Umsetzung eines gut durchdachten modularen Konzepts.

giro
Table Light
Tischleuchte

Manufacturer
Mawa Design Licht- und Wohnideen GmbH,
Michendorf, Germany
Design
Serge Cornelissen BVBA
(Robert Cornelissen, Serge Cornelissen),
Kortrijk, Belgium
Web
www.mawa-design.de
www.sergecornelissen.com

This three-piece table light consists of two inversely oriented, truncated cones which are pierced by a round rod, made of either brass or stainless steel. The rod is tiltable by 24 and the lampshade pivotable by 120 degrees, both individually adjustable. An energy-efficient LED provides glare-free illumination with 11 watts, a colour temperature of 2,700 kelvins and a luminous flux of 1,400 lumens. Switching and dimming is controlled by a flush-integrated metal switch in the base of the lamp. A memory function serves to save the last selected brightness setting.

Die dreiteilige Tischleuchte besteht aus zwei zueinander gerichteten Kegelschnitten, durchdrungen von einem Rundstab aus Messing oder Edelstahl. Stab und Leuchtenschirm lassen sich separat einstellen: Der Leuchtenschirm ist um 120 Grad schwenkbar und der Stab um 24 Grad neigbar. Die energieeffiziente LED bietet eine blendfreie Ausleuchtung mit 11 Watt, einer Farbtemperatur von 2.700 Kelvin und einem Lichtstrom von 1.400 Lumen. Geschaltet und gedimmt wird über einen flächenbündig integrierten Metalltaster im Leuchtenfuß. Eine Speicherfunktion behält die zuletzt gewählte Helligkeit bei.

Statement by the jury
The emotionally appealing giro table light showcases an astounding design which facilitates individual adjustments of the lampshade.

Begründung der Jury
Die emotional ansprechende Tischleuchte giro zeigt eine verblüffende Konstruktion, die zur individuellen Ausrichtung des Lampenschirms auffordert.

INVITING
Desk Lamp
Schreibtischleuchte

Manufacturer
Faro Barcelona, Barcelona, Spain
Design
Bohman Folenius, Gothenburg, Sweden
Web
www.faro.es
www.bohmanfolenius.com

The INVITING desk lamp allows users to set the illumination as needed. The luminaire head can be adjusted both in its horizontal and vertical axis. The light can also be dimmed infinitely: sliding the round control element forwards or backwards alters the intensity, while rotating the control element changes the colour temperature. The desk lamp is available in different colour shades and allows for flexible positioning on a desk or bedside table by means of either a foot or clamping fixture.

Die Schreibtischleuchte INVITING lädt Nutzer dazu ein, das Licht bedarfsgerecht einzustellen. Ihr Leuchtenkopf ist sowohl in seiner horizontalen als auch in seiner vertikalen Achse verstellbar. Zudem lässt sich das Licht stufenlos dimmen: Durch das Vor- und Zurückschieben des runden Bedienelements wird die Intensität des Lichts eingestellt, durch das Drehen des Bedienelements lässt sich die Farbtemperatur verändern. Die Tischleuchte ist in mehreren Farben erhältlich und erlaubt per Standfuß oder Klemmvorrichtung eine flexible Positionierung an Schreibtisch oder Nachttisch.

Statement by the jury
Boasting a high level of user-friendliness and a distinctive design language, the INVITING desk lamp impresses as a sophisticated product solution.

Begründung der Jury
Mit ihrem hohen Maß an Bedienkomfort und einer prägnanten Formensprache punktet die Schreibtischleuchte INVITING als durchdachte Produktlösung.

IKEA SVALLET
Work Lamp
Arbeitsleuchte

Manufacturer
IKEA of Sweden, Älmhult, Sweden
In-house design
Henrik Preutz
Web
www.ikea.com

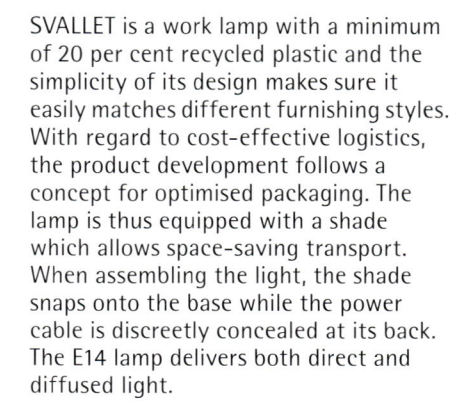

SVALLET is a work lamp with a minimum of 20 per cent recycled plastic and the simplicity of its design makes sure it easily matches different furnishing styles. With regard to cost-effective logistics, the product development follows a concept for optimised packaging. The lamp is thus equipped with a shade which allows space-saving transport. When assembling the light, the shade snaps onto the base while the power cable is discreetly concealed at its back. The E14 lamp delivers both direct and diffused light.

Statement by the jury
Under the premise of space-saving packaging and resource-saving production, SVALLET has achieved a self-sufficient aesthetic.

SVALLET ist eine Schreibtischleuchte aus mindestens 20 Prozent recyceltem Kunststoff, deren schlichte Gestaltung zu unterschiedlichen Einrichtungsstilen passt. Im Hinblick auf eine kostengünstige Logistik, folgt diese Produktentwicklung einem verpackungsoptimierten Produktkonzept: Somit ist die Leuchte mit einem Schirm ausgestattet, der sich platzsparend transportieren lässt. Beim Aufbauen schnappt der Schirm auf den Standfuß, auf dessen Rückseite das Stromkabel dezent verdeckt wird. Die E14-Lampe liefert sowohl direktes als auch diffuses Licht.

Begründung der Jury
Unter der Prämisse einer platzsparenden Verpackung und einer ressourcenschonenden Fertigung erreicht SVALLET eine eigenständige Ästhetik.

Little KONG
Ambient Lamp Series
Ambient-Leuchtenserie

Manufacturer
Above Lights (HK) Limited, Shenzhen, China
In-house design
Guogang Peng, Zhifu You
Design
Shenzhen Dizan Technology Co., Ltd.
(Yan Wang, Qixing He, Xiaotong Long),
Shenzhen, China
Web
www.abovelights.co
www.rui-d.com

Little KONG is an ambient lamp series which can be turned on and off via gestures. The LED chips, concealed at the top of the metal post, illuminate a transparent lampshade, which, without a visible light source, appears surprisingly empty. It can be manufactured in different textures as well as according to individual design ideas. The light series comprises table lamps, floor lamps, suspended luminaires and wall lights. In addition, the table lamp offers a wireless charging function for mobile phones.

Statement by the jury
Due to the consistent implementation of a sophisticated design idea, this ambient lighting series adopts a highly self-reliant, overall appearance.

Little KONG ist eine Ambient-Leuchtenserie, die sich über Gesten ein- und ausschalten lässt. Die oben im Metallmast versteckten LED-Chips illuminieren einen transparenten Leuchtenschirm, der ohne sichtbares Leuchtmittel überraschend leer erscheint. Er kann in verschiedenen Texturen sowie nach individuellen Vorstellungen gefertigt werden. Die Leuchtenserie umfasst Tisch-, Steh-, Hänge- und Wandleuchten, wobei die Tischleuchte eine drahtlose Ladefunktion für Mobiltelefone bietet.

Begründung der Jury
Aufgrund der stringenten Umsetzung einer raffinierten Gestaltungsidee zeichnet sich diese Ambient-Leuchtenserie durch ein höchst eigenständiges Gesamtbild aus.

nord
Table Lamps
Tischleuchte

Manufacturer
Lumini, São Paulo, Brazil
In-house design
Fernando Prado
Web
www.lumini.com.br

With a colour temperature of 2,400 kelvins and a high colour rendering index, the nord table lamp is particularly well suited to create atmospheric lighting. It is available in two versions, which differ in size and material. While the smaller model has a solid base made of Brazilian Freijó hardwood, the base of the larger model is made of Tauari. The unbleached linen lampshade encloses a reflector which is available in sand grey or brass.

Statement by the jury
This aesthetic table lamp follows a traditional design idiom and scores with natural materials.

Die Tischleuchte nord dient mit einer Farbtemperatur von 2.400 Kelvin und einem hohen Farbwiedergabeindex vor allem der stimmungsvollen Beleuchtung. Sie ist in zwei Varianten erhältlich, die sich hinsichtlich ihrer Größe und Materialien unterscheiden: Während die kleinere Variante einen Massivholzsockel aus dem brasilianischen Hartholz Freijó aufweist, ist der Sockel der größeren aus Tauari gefertigt. Der Leuchtenschirm aus ungebleichtem Leinen umschließt einen Reflektor, der in Sandgrau oder messingfarben erhältlich ist.

Begründung der Jury
Diese ästhetische Tischleuchte folgt einer traditionellen Formensprache und punktet mit natürlichen Materialien.

Yeelight Bedside Lamp
Yeelight Nachttischleuchte

Manufacturer
Qingdao Yeelink Information
Technology Co., Ltd., Qingdao, China
In-house design
Web
www.yeelight.com

This LED bedside lamp allows versatile lighting scenarios which can be controlled via mobile app. An integrated Wi-Fi module, which connects to the smartphone, allows not only the adjustment of colour temperature, RGB light colour and brightness, but also scheduled on and off switching, among other things. In addition, the luminaire body offers a convenient touch operation area. The minimalist LED lamp provides users with a choice of different light modes.

Statement by the jury
With its balanced proportions and harmonious contours, this bedside lamp exudes an overall elegant appearance which blends discreetly into the interior.

Diese LED-Nachttischleuchte erlaubt vielfältige Beleuchtungsszenarien, die sich per App mobil steuern lassen. Ein integriertes WiFi-Modul, das sich mit dem jeweiligen Smartphone verbindet, erlaubt neben der Anpassung von Farbtemperatur, RGB-Lichtfarbe und Helligkeit u. a. auch ein zeitlich festgelegtes Ein- und Ausschalten. Zudem bietet der Leuchtenkorpus einen komfortablen Touch-Bedienbereich. Die minimalistisch anmutende LED-Leuchte stellt den Nutzern verschiedene Lichtmodi zur Auswahl.

Begründung der Jury
Mit ausgewogenen Proportionen und harmonischen Konturen lässt diese Nachttischleuchte ein elegantes Gesamtbild entstehen, das sich dezent ins Interieur einfügt.

Table Lamp
Tischleuchte

Manufacturer
Shenzhen Aukey E-Business Co., Ltd.,
Shenzhen, China
In-house design
Zhihua Wang
Web
www.aukey.com

This elegant table lamp with touch control creates a warm white light temperature. Its even, diffused light is easy on the eyes and good for reading or relaxing. The light is easily switched on and off by touching the surface of the metal top. In addition, the brightness can be infinitely adjusted to individual lighting needs. Thanks to its memory function, the most recent setting is automatically activated the next time the lamp is switched on.

Statement by the jury
This table lamp distinguishes itself with a high degree of operating and lighting comfort, and blends harmoniously into a variety of interiors.

Diese elegante Tischleuchte mit Touch Control erzeugt eine warmweiße Lichttemperatur. Ihr gleichmäßiges, diffuses Licht ist angenehm für die Augen und eignet sich gut zum Lesen oder Entspannen. Durch das Berühren der oberen Metallfläche lässt sich die Leuchte bequem an- und ausschalten. Zudem kann die Helligkeit stufenlos an die individuellen Beleuchtungsbedürfnisse angepasst werden. Aufgrund ihrer Speicherfunktion wird die zuletzt vorgenommene Einstellung beim nächsten Einschalten automatisch aktiviert.

Begründung der Jury
Ein hohes Maß an Bedien- und Beleuchtungskomfort zeichnet diese Tischleuchte aus. Sie fügt sich harmonisch in unterschiedliche Interieurs ein.

Mi 2
Bedside Lamp
Nachttischleuchte

Manufacturer
Qingdao Yeelink Information
Technology Co., Ltd., Qingdao, China
Design
Xiaomi Inc., Beijing, China
Web
www.yeelight.com
www.mi.com

The bedside lamp Mi 2 uses high-quality LEDs, a special colour mixing technique and a double-walled lampshade to provide particularly pleasant illumination. An intuitive control bar allows the infinite adjustment of the brightness. In addition, the light can be set via an app or voice control. The brightness spectrum from 2 to 400 lumens fulfils lighting requirements for different uses, such as reading, falling asleep or waking up.

Statement by the jury
This bedside lamp impresses with a remarkable ease of use. In addition, it showcases a simple elegance which matches different interiors.

Die Nachttischleuchte Mi 2 setzt hochwertige LEDs, eine spezielle Farbmischtechnik sowie einen doppelwandigen Leuchtenschirm ein, um eine besonders angenehme Beleuchtung zu bieten. Über eine intuitive Steuerungsleiste lässt sich die Helligkeit stufenlos regeln, zudem kann die Leuchte per App oder Sprachassistenten eingestellt werden. Das Helligkeitsspektrum von 2 bis 400 Lumen erfüllt unterschiedliche Beleuchtungsbedürfnisse zum Lesen, Einschlafen und Aufwachen.

Begründung der Jury
Mit einem bemerkenswerten Bedienkomfort begeistert diese Nachttischleuchte. Zudem zeigt sie eine schlichte Eleganz, die zu diversen Interieurs passt.

Table Lamp
Tischleuchte

Manufacturer
Shunde Guoxin Electric Ind Co., Ltd of Foshan, Foshan, China
In-house design
Hongrong Huang, Yujiong Huang
Web
www.gxdiffuser.com

This table lamp combines a traditional design language with contemporary functionality. A discreetly integrated power button also allows for the comfortable control of the lamp, for example the adjustment of the colour temperature and brightness through a slight touch. In addition, the table lamp features gesture control, which allows to turn it on and off without physical contact. Another option is an app control, which completes the product concept.

Statement by the jury
A remarkable ease of use characterises this table lamp. The natural materials exude an emotional appeal.

Diese Tischleuchte verbindet eine traditionell anmutende Formensprache mit einer zeitgemäßen Funktionalität. Ein dezent integrierter Einschaltknopf ermöglicht die komfortable Steuerung der Leuchte, auch die Farbtemperatur und Helligkeit des Lichts lassen sich durch eine leichte Berührung des Knopfs einstellen. Zudem bietet die Tischleuchte eine Gestensteuerung, wodurch ein berührungsfreies Ein- und Ausschalten möglich ist. Als weitere Option rundet eine App-Steuerung das Produktkonzept ab.

Begründung der Jury
Ein bemerkenswerter Bedienkomfort zeichnet diese Tischleuchte aus. Ihre natürlich anmutenden Materialien sprechen die Betrachter emotional an.

Oplàmp
Table Lamp
Tischleuchte

Manufacturer
Sapiens Design, Cesano Maderno, Italy
In-house design
Gloria Gianatti, Alessandro Mattia
Web
www.sapiensdesign.it

The Oplàmp table lamp consists of a solid oak base holding an LED light source and a removable ceramic body. Designed in the form of three cones fused in the middle, the body can be positioned on the base of the lamp in three different orientations. Each position provides its own lighting effects through various light angles, facing upwards or downwards. Oplàmp is made by hand in Italy.

Statement by the jury
Based upon an unconventional design idea, this table lamp achieves an overall distinctive appearance for producing changing lighting moods.

Die Tischleuchte Oplàmp besteht aus einem massiven Eichenfuß, auf dem eine LED-Lichtquelle platziert ist, und einem abnehmbaren Keramikkörper. Dieser ist in Form dreier an der Basis miteinander verschmolzener Kegel gestaltet und kann in drei unterschiedlichen Ausrichtungen auf dem Fuß positioniert werden. Jede Position ermöglicht eigene Beleuchtungseffekte durch unterschiedliche Lichtwinkel, die nach oben oder nach unten geneigt sind. Oplàmp wird von Hand in Italien gefertigt.

Begründung der Jury
Einer unkonventionellen Gestaltungsidee folgend, erreicht diese Tischleuchte ein unverwechselbares Gesamtbild und ermöglicht variable Lichtstimmungen.

O-Bao
Mobile Night Light
Mobiles Nachtlicht

Manufacturer
Opple Lighting Co., Ltd., Shanghai, China
In-house design
Web
www.opple.com

This mobile night light has been designed to protect the highly sensitive eyes of babies. If light is too bright, it could damage a baby's retina. O-Bao therefore uses an OLED source, shaped like a luminous thin-film element. It emits a uniform area-type light of low brightness which is gentle on the eye. The organic LED produces a continuous light spectrum with a low amount of blue light. The lamp, which is equipped with a convenient handle, is simply placed onto a wireless station for charging.

Statement by the jury
O-Bao convinces as a responsible product solution, adjusting the lighting comfort of the OLED night light to baby eyes.

Dieses mobile Nachtlicht wurde entwickelt, um die besonders empfindlichen Augen von Säuglingen zu schützen. Da ein zu helles Licht deren Netzhaut schädigen könnte, nutzt O-Bao eine augenschonende OLED-Lichtquelle in Form eines leuchtenden Dünnschichtelements, die ein dämmriges Flächenlicht abgibt. Die organische Leuchtdiode erzeugt ein kontinuierliches Lichtspektrum mit geringem Blauanteil. Zum Aufladen wird das mit einem handlichen Griff ausgestattete Nachtlicht einfach auf die kabellose Ladestation gestellt.

Begründung der Jury
O-Bao überzeugt als eine verantwortungsvolle Produktlösung, indem der OLED-Beleuchtungskomfort des Nachtlichts auf Baby-Augen abgestimmt ist.

Philips Hue Adore
Mirror Light
Spiegelleuchte

Manufacturer
Signify, Eindhoven, Netherlands
In-house design
Signify Design Team
Web
www.signify.com

Hue Adore is a mirror light which immerses bathrooms either in an invigorating or in a relaxing light. Flush-mounted behind a round mirror, the luminaire easily blends into different furnishing styles. In addition, it is also intuitive to control. The indirect illumination is designed to create good lighting conditions in the bathroom without any disturbing shadows. Made from high-quality materials, Hue Adore meets the requirements for a moisture-proof luminaire.

Statement by the jury
As an expression of a well thought out design concept, this mirror light stands out with its simple elegance and high level of lighting comfort.

Hue Adore ist eine Spiegelleuchte, die das Badezimmer in eine energetisierende oder eine entspannende Lichtstimmung taucht. Die flächenbündig hinter dem runden Spiegel integrierte Leuchte passt zu unterschiedlichen Einrichtungsstilen. Sie lässt sich zudem komfortabel steuern. Die indirekte Beleuchtung ist so konzipiert, dass im Bad gute Lichtverhältnisse herrschen, ohne dabei störende Schatten entstehen zu lassen. Hergestellt aus hochwertigen Materialien, erfüllt Hue Adore die Anforderungen an eine Feuchtraumleuchte.

Begründung der Jury
Als Ausdruck eines durchdachten Gestaltungskonzepts fällt diese Spiegelleuchte durch ihre schlichte Eleganz und ihren hohen Beleuchtungskomfort auf.

Philips Hue Liane
Wall Lamp
Wandleuchte

Manufacturer
Signify, Eindhoven, Netherlands
In-house design
Signify Design Team
Web
www.signify.com

The Hue Liane wall lamp allows the atmospheric illumination of living rooms in countless colour shades and offers various lighting programmes. In addition, it can be synchronised with music the user is listening to or the sound of a movie the user is watching. Its slim silhouette lends the lamp a contemporary appearance. Its indirect light creates an appealing ambience for living spaces. It can be conveniently controlled via smartphone, which invites users to select the right lighting mood for different situations.

Statement by the jury
Following a contemporary design approach, this wall light achieves a sculptural appearance and impresses as an aesthetic light source.

Die Wandleuchte Hue Liane erlaubt eine stimmungsvolle Wohnraumbeleuchtung in unzähligen Farbnuancen und bietet verschiedene Lichtprogramme. Darüber hinaus lässt sie sich mit Musik oder Filmsound synchronisieren. Ihre schlanke Silhouette verleiht der Leuchte eine zeitgemäße Anmutung. Das indirekte Licht setzt Wohnräume ansprechend in Szene. Die komfortable Steuerung über das Smartphone motiviert dazu, die richtige Lichtstimmung für jeden Moment auszuwählen.

Begründung der Jury
Als Ergebnis eines zeitgemäßen Gestaltungskonzepts erreicht diese Wandleuchte eine skulpturale Anmutung und überzeugt als ästhetische Lichtquelle.

Philips Hue Play
Light Bar Series
Lichtbalken-Serie

Manufacturer
Signify, Eindhoven, Netherlands
In-house design
Signify Design Team
Web
www.signify.com

The Hue Play light bar series has been designed in particular to provide appealing background illumination when watching TV. The light bars can either be simply set up horizontally or mounted flexibly with two TV mounts, allowing an indirect lighting behind the TV. The unobtrusive V-shaped design avoids any unnecessary detail and provides multiple benefits, ranging from reduced glare to flexible cable fitting and easy installation.

Statement by the jury
Thanks to its flexible applications, the Hue Play light bar series encourages the creative realisation of individual lighting ideas.

Um insbesondere die Hintergrundbeleuchtung beim Fernsehen ansprechend zu gestalten, wurde die Lichtbalken-Serie Hue Play entworfen. Die Lichtbalken lassen sich einfach horizontal aufstellen oder flexibel befestigen: Zwei TV-Halterungen ermöglichen eine indirekte Beleuchtung hinter dem Fernseher. Die dezente, V-förmige Gestaltung verzichtet auf unnötige Details und bietet von der Blendungsbegrenzung über die flexible Kabelverschraubung bis hin zur einfachen Installation diverse Vorteile.

Begründung der Jury
Aufgrund ihrer flexiblen Verwendungsmöglichkeiten motiviert die Lichtbalken-Serie Hue Play zur kreativen Umsetzung individueller Beleuchtungsideen.

Pluck
Floor Lamp Series
Stehleuchten-Serie

Manufacturer
SONNEMAN – A Way of Light,
Larchmont, New York, USA
In-house design
Robert Sonneman
Web
www.sonnemanawayoflight.com

For more freedom of movement, the luminaires of the Pluck Floor Lamp series have been equipped with a long tube. The puck-shaped lamp head is held by a magnet at the end of the height-adjustable arc. The flexible design allows to adjust the LED light source as required. Its innovative lamp lens comprises four layers of film diffusion, including a textured bottom layer which creates evenly-distributed and glare-free lighting. The four-point touch activation and a slide dimmer located on the lamp head allow for easy control.

Um mehr Bewegungsfreiheit zu bieten, wurde die Stehleuchten-Serie Pluck mit einem hochaufragenden Leuchtenarm versehen. Am Ende des höhenverstellbaren Bogens wird der puckförmige Leuchtenkopf von einem Magneten gehalten. Die Flexibilität dieser Konstruktion ermöglicht eine bedarfsgerechte Positionierung der LED-Lichtquelle. Ihre innovative Lampenlinse umfasst vier Schichten, darunter eine strukturierte Basisfolie, die für eine gleichmäßige und blendfreie Beleuchtung sorgt. Eine Vierpunkt-Touch-Aktivierung sowie ein Schiebedimmer am Leuchtenkopf erlauben eine bequeme Steuerung.

Statement by the jury
Pluck impresses with a filigree silhouette. It is the curved contour of the lamp's tube in particular which projects an elegant appearance.

Begründung der Jury
Pluck begeistert mit einer filigranen Silhouette. Insbesondere die geschwungene Kontur des Leuchtenarms lässt eine elegante Anmutung entstehen.

Space B
Floor Lamp
Stehleuchte

Manufacturer
Nordlux A/S,
Aalborg, Denmark
Design
Bønnelycke Arkitekter ApS,
Aarhus, Denmark
Web
www.nordlux.com
www.bonnelycke.com

This sculptural floor lamp can be flexibly tilted to all sides to achieve versatile alignments of the light beam. For indirect room lighting, it can be placed directly in front of a wall. In this way, the emitting indirect light creates a decorative lighting effect. The floor lamp is available in black and white. In order to suit different scenarios, users have a choice of various colour temperatures.

Statement by the jury
With its versatility and flexibility, this simply designed floor lamp fascinates as a multi-faceted lighting solution.

Diese skulptural anmutende Stehleuchte lässt sich flexibel zu allen Seiten neigen, um den Lichtstrahl variabel auszurichten. Wenn eine indirekte Raumbeleuchtung gewünscht ist, kann die Leuchte direkt vor der Wand platziert werden. So lässt das abstrahlende, indirekte Licht einen dekorativen Beleuchtungseffekt entstehen. Die Stehleuchte ist in Schwarz und Weiß erhältlich. Passend zu unterschiedlichen Situationen können verschiedene Farbtemperaturen eingestellt werden.

Begründung der Jury
Mit ihrer Variabilität und Flexibilität begeistert diese schlicht gestaltete Stehleuchte als vielseitige Beleuchtungslösung.

HARI
Floor Lamp
Stehleuchte

Manufacturer
FLUA Lighting Co., Ltd.,
Jiangmen, China
In-house design
James Luk
Web
www.flua.com

This floor lamp has been designed to flexibly meet different lighting needs. Thus, HARI is equally well suited for dining rooms, living rooms and work spaces, and can serve, for example, as a reading lamp or desk lighting. The diffuser profile accommodates a line of LEDs, providing remarkably surprisingly good illumination. Its slim shape lends the floor lamp a distinctive visual appeal.

Statement by the jury
With timeless elegance, the floor lamp blends into different interiors and fascinates with its filigree arch.

Diese Stehleuchte wurde entworfen, um auf flexible Weise unterschiedliche Beleuchtungsbedürfnisse erfüllen zu können. Somit kann HARI gleichermaßen im Esszimmer wie im Wohn- oder Arbeitsraum eingesetzt werden, zum Beispiel als Leselampe oder Schreibtischbeleuchtung. Das Diffusorprofil nimmt eine Reihe von LEDs auf und sorgt damit für eine überraschend gute Beleuchtung. Seine schlanke Form verleiht der Stehleuchte ihren visuellen Reiz.

Begründung der Jury
Zeitlos-elegant fügt sich die Stehleuchte in unterschiedliche Interieurs ein und gefällt mit ihrem filigranen Bogen.

fina
Floor Lamp
Stehleuchte

Manufacturer
Lumini, São Paulo, Brazil
In-house design
Fernando Prado
Web
www.lumini.com.br

The design concept of this floor lamp followed the objective to create an efficient and, at the same time, comfortable indirect light without causing ambient lighting. Due to an intelligent dimming system, users can individually control the light intensity. The LED module offers a colour temperature of 2,500 kelvins and a high colour rendering index. fina is made of aluminium and available in different colours. With its clear lines, it blends harmoniously into private as well as public areas.

Statement by the jury
Formally reduced to the essential, the fina floor lamp achieves a simple aesthetic. In addition, it convinces with its high lighting comfort.

Das Gestaltungskonzept dieser Stehleuchte folgte dem Ziel, ein effizientes und zugleich komfortables indirektes Licht ohne Umgebungsbeleuchtung zu erzeugen. Dank eines intelligenten Dimmersystems können die Nutzer die Lichtintensität individuell steuern. Das LED-Modul bietet eine Farbtemperatur von 2.500 Kelvin und einen hohen Farbwiedergabeindex. Fina ist aus Aluminium gefertigt und in verschiedenen Farben erhältlich. Mit ihrer klaren Linienführung fügt sie sich harmonisch in private wie öffentliche Bereiche ein.

Begründung der Jury
Formal reduziert auf das Wesentliche, erreicht die Stehleuchte fina eine schlichte Ästhetik. Darüber hinaus überzeugt sie mit ihrem hohen Beleuchtungskomfort.

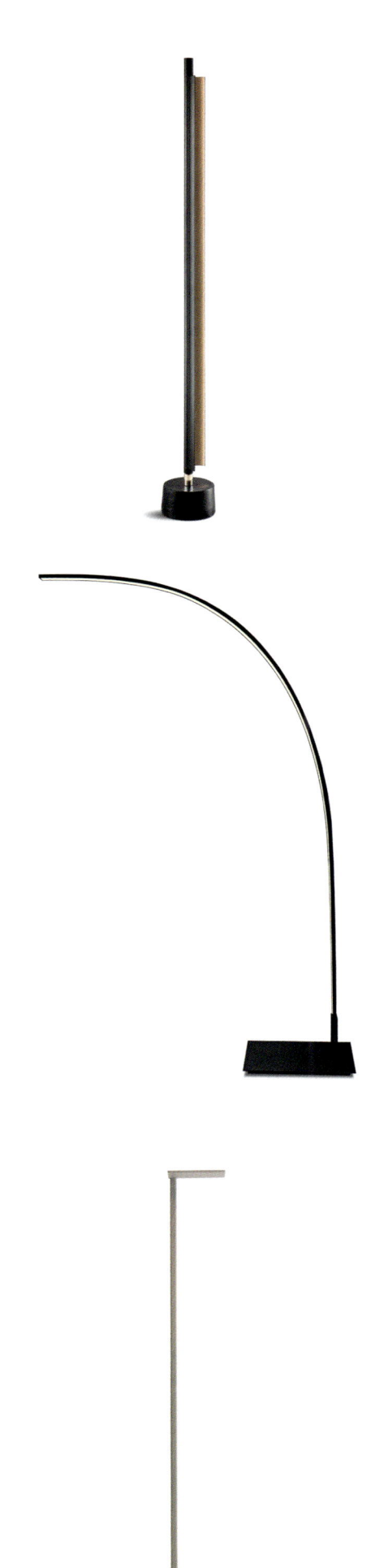

Building elements	Bauelemente
City and landscape planning	Laternen
Park benches	Parkbänke
Street furniture	Städte- und Landschaftsbau
Street lanterns	Stadtmobiliar
Street luminaires	Straßenleuchten
Temporary architecture	Temporäre Architektur

Urban design and public spaces
Urban Design und öffentlicher Raum

Arpino OXS Design Line
Urban Furniture
Stadtmobiliar

Manufacturer
Arpino,
Luanda, Angola; Porto, Portugal

In-house design
Carlos Pereira

Web
www.arpino-design.com

reddot award 2019
best of the best

Elements of communal living
As a part of globalisation, metropolises around the globe have moved closer to each other in terms of their aesthetic look. The Arpino OXS urban furniture line aims to face the challenges of the new global city, imagining it as a place of autonomy, community and connectivity. Its design is inspired by a notion of what it means to inhabit common spaces that are used day and night and which accommodate and include all cultures. The line therefore offers a variety of different products, including elegant urban lighting and wayfinders, airy pergolas and multimedia kiosks, as well as tree guards, bins, benches and bollards. The individual elements of the design line all share the same concept of modular and neutral forms that are highly adaptable to different spaces, ranging from housing estates and public plazas to schools and shopping malls. They project a sleek, zinc-free range of steel pieces that have been designed specifically for contemporary urban spaces and which are available in stainless steel or powder-coated steel. The powder-coated steel models are closer to the nature with an earth tone colour palette that ranges from deep red, green or bronze to grey, blue and black. The products of this series combine functionality, flexibility and minimal, inclusive design aesthetics, making them blend harmoniously into urban surroundings.

Elemente des Zusammenlebens
Im Zuge der Globalisierung nähern sich auch die Metropolen der Welt in ihrer Ästhetik einander an. Das Arpino OXS-Stadtmobiliar will sich den Herausforderungen der neuen globalen Stadt stellen und diese als einen Ort der Autonomie, Gemeinschaft und Vernetzung visualisieren. Seine Gestaltung orientiert sich an einer Vorstellung von Straßenmöbeln, die bei Tag und bei Nacht in öffentlichen Räumen genutzt werden und alle Kulturen einbeziehen sollen. Diese Serie bietet dafür eine vielseitige Produktpalette und umfasst eine elegante Stadtbeleuchtung sowie Wegweiser, luftige Pergolen und Multimedia-Kioske, außerdem Baumschutzgitter, Abfalleimer, Bänke und Poller. Das die einzelnen Elemente verbindende Konzept sind neutrale und modulare Formen, die sich sehr gut an unterschiedliche Räume wie Wohnanlagen und öffentliche Plätze bis hin zu Schulen und Einkaufszentren anpassen lassen. Als schlanke, zinkfreie Stahlteile wurden alle Elemente der Serie für zeitgenössische urbane Räume entwickelt und sind in den Ausführungen Edelstahl oder pulverbeschichteter Stahl erhältlich. Die Variante des pulverbeschichteten Stahls ist mit einer erdfarbenen Palette von Dunkelrot, Grün, Bronze bis Grau, Blau oder Schwarz der Natur angenähert. Die Funktionalität, Flexibilität und minimale, umfassende Gestaltungsästhetik dieser Serie verbinden sich so nahtlos mit der städtischen Umgebung.

Statement by the jury
With its elegant and sculptural appearance, this urban furniture lends public spaces a highly appealing character. It is based on an innovative design vocabulary that harmoniously unites all elements, resulting in a uniform aesthetics. With its nuanced colour scheme and a modularity that can be expanded at any time, it provides city planners with a lot of freedom in envisioning the city of the future.

Begründung der Jury
Mit seiner eleganten wie skulpturalen Anmutung verleiht dieses Stadtmobiliar dem öffentlichen Bereich einen sehr ansprechenden Charakter. Es basiert auf einer innovativen, alle Elemente stimmig miteinander verbindenden Formensprache, wodurch eine einheitliche Ästhetik erzielt wird. Durch seine beliebig erweiterbare Modularität und seine nuancierte Farbgebung bietet es Planern viel Freiheit für ihre Visionen von der Stadt der Zukunft.

Designer portrait
See page 66
Siehe Seite 66

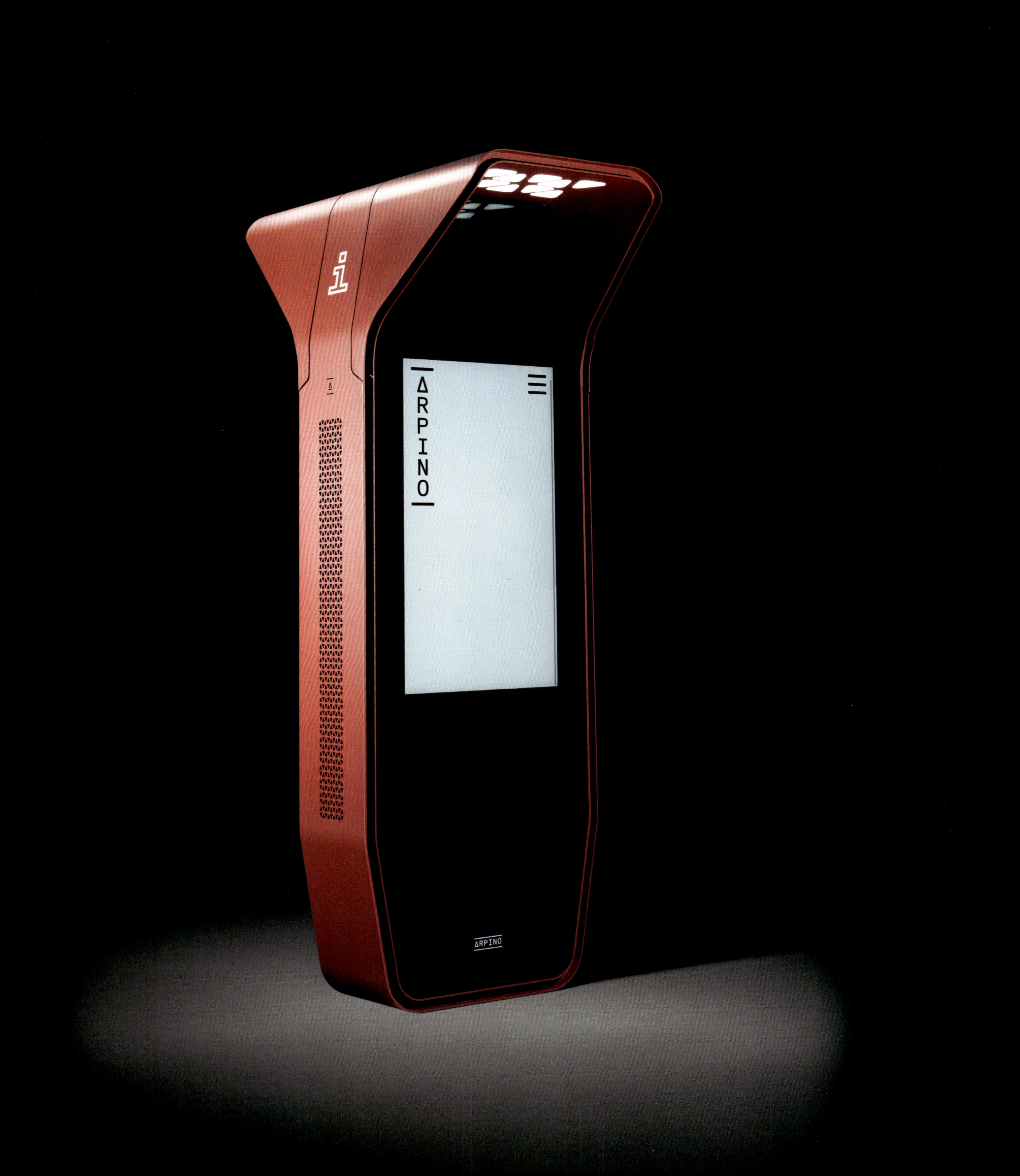
i
ΔRPINO
ΔRPINO

Pixel
Park Bench
Bank

Manufacturer
mmcite 1 a.s., Bilovice, Czech Republic
In-house design
Design
David Karasek, Bilovice, Czech Republic
Eduard Herrmann, Prague, Czech Republic
Matej Coufal, Prague, Czech Republic
Web
www.mmcite.com

Pixel is a functional piece of seating for public spaces and consists of square modules that can be arranged in groups. In addition, the orientation of the wooden slats out of which the seats are made can be varied to give the impression of a playful mosaic. Both symmetrical and irregular patterns can be created. Furthermore, the contrast of natural wood nuances and coloured surfaces opens up possibilities for experimentation. The seating also comes with accessories such as backrests, tables and flowerpots.

Pixel ist ein funktionales Sitzmöbel für den öffentlichen Raum, das aus quadratischen Modulen besteht. Diese lassen sich zu Gruppen arrangieren. Dabei kann die Ausrichtung der Holzlamellen, aus denen die Sitzfläche besteht, variiert werden, sodass der Eindruck eines verspielten Mosaiks entsteht. Es lassen sich symmetrische, aber auch unregelmäßige Muster kreieren. Zudem kann mit den natürlichen Farbnuancen des Holzes oder aber mit farbigen Oberflächen experimentiert werden. Ergänzen lässt sich das Sitzmobiliar durch Rückenlehnen, Tische und Blumentöpfe.

Statement by the jury
The refined design of the modular park bench Pixel is many-sided in its focus. In addition, the modern appearance is attractive.

Begründung der Jury
Die raffinierte Gestaltung des modularen Sitzmobiliars Pixel ist auf Vielseitigkeit ausgerichtet. Zudem gefällt das modern anmutende Erscheinungsbild.

ALBROAD 23NP
Lounge Seating
Sitzmöbel

Manufacturer
Okamura Corporation, Yokohama, Japan
In-house design
Hiroshi Saotome
Web
www.okamura.jp

Albroad 23NP provides very comfortable seating for public spaces such as airports. The rounded form of the seat avoids pressure on the thighs and helps create a comfortable sitting position. The seat is firm, but pleasantly soft to the touch and mounted on a metal support with slim legs, thus almost giving the impression of floating. The height of the seat can be adjusted to make it easier for the user to stand up. Optional extras are side tables and power points whose cables are integrated directly into the floor.

Als ein Sitzmöbel für öffentliche Räume wie z. B. Flughäfen bietet Albroad 23NP hohen Komfort. Seine geschwungene Bauweise, die druckmindernd auf Oberschenkel wirkt, unterstützt eine bequeme Sitzhaltung. Die Schale ist fest, fühlt sich aber dennoch angenehm soft an. Montiert ist sie auf einem Metallträger mit schlanken Beinen, was einen beinahe schwebenden Eindruck erzeugt. Die Sitzhöhe lässt sich verstellen und ermöglicht so ein leichtes Aufstehen. Optional sind Seitentische sowie Steckdosen, deren Leitungskanal direkt in den Boden integriert wird, erhältlich.

Statement by the jury
The clever design of the Albroad 23NP lounge seating delights through its high level of comfort, user-friendliness and a refined appearance.

Begründung der Jury
Die clevere Gestaltung des Sitzmöbels Albroad 23NP punktet mit hohem Komfort, nutzerfreundlichen Eigenschaften und einem edlen Erscheinungsbild.

Prague Street Furniture
Bins
Abfalleimer

Client
City of Prague, Czech Republic

Design
Olgoj Chorchoj Studio
(Aleš Kachlík, Prof. Michal Froněk,
Prof. Jan Němeček),
Prague, Czech Republic

Web
www.praha.eu
www.olgojchorchoj.cz
www.iprpraha.cz

reddot award 2019
best of the best

Marks of distinction
Much like the city of Paris, for instance, which is always associated with ornate art nouveau railings and lanterns, the perception of any public space or living environment is equally shaped by the distinctive mark of its urban furniture. The series of street furniture for the city of Prague intentionally follows the maxim of not thoroughly harmonising individual elements in terms of shape to lend them a strong sense of self-sufficiency. This is based on the idea that insisting too much on formal harmony leads to more problems than benefits in real situations, since in reality individual objects generally function more in the context of other, already existing, but formally different elements. The elements of this street furniture are, however, visually linked by material, design and colour principles. The graceful looking bins of the range captivate through their elegant, moderate appearance and intentionally "uncertain period-setting". Eminently functional in everyday city life, they are available in a hanging or free-standing version, and the series is to be extended in the future. They are very durable, and a rough surface design protects them reliably against graffiti and fly-posters. Their clear morphology is based on the geometric shapes of a circle and an oval. This results in a highly balanced aesthetic appeal, which facilitates easy installation of the objects in different architectural contexts.

Prägende Eindrücke
So wie etwa die Stadt Paris stets mit ihren kunstvollen Geländern und Laternen aus der Zeit des Jugendstils in Verbindung gebracht wird, prägt das Stadtmobiliar in hohem Maße die Lebenswelt und Wahrnehmung eines Ortes. Die Serie von Straßenmöbeln für die Stadt Prag folgt bewusst der Maxime, die einzelnen Elemente gestalterisch nicht zu vereinheitlichen, sondern ihnen Eigenständigkeit zu verleihen. Dem liegt die Überlegung zugrunde, dass ein übermäßiges Festhalten an formaler Einheitlichkeit in der Realität zu mehr Problemen als Vorteilen führt, da die einzelnen Objekte immer im Kontext von anderen, bereits existierenden, formal unterschiedlichen Elementen stehen. Visuell sind die Elemente der Serie dennoch durch Material-, Farb- und Formgebung miteinander verbunden. Die grazil anmutenden Abfalleimer der Serie bestechen durch ihr elegantes, zurückhaltendes Erscheinungsbild und eine absichtlich „zeitlose Zeitnähe". Im Stadtalltag überaus funktional, sind sie erhältlich in einer hängenden sowie einer freistehenden Version, wobei die Serie in der Zukunft noch erweitert werden soll. Sie sind sehr langlebig, und eine raue Oberflächengestaltung schützt sie zuverlässig vor Graffitis und wildem Plakatieren. Ihr klares Design basiert auf den geometrischen Formen des Kreises und des Ovals. Dies führt zu einer sehr ausgewogenen Ästhetik, welche problemlos die Aufstellung in verschiedensten architektonischen Kontexten ermöglicht.

Statement by the jury
The design of the bins for the Prague street furniture series masters the art of reduction and simplicity. As integrative yet formally independent components of the series, they showcase extremely elegant lines and an excellent construction. Highly robust and durable, they are perfect for outdoor installation. These bins are of exceptionally high quality, which enhances and coalesces into their surroundings.

Begründung der Jury
Die Gestaltung der Abfalleimer aus der Serie von Stadtmobiliar für die Stadt Prag beherrscht die Kunst der Reduktion und Einfachheit. Als integrative und doch formal selbständige Bestandteile der Serie zeigen sie überaus elegante Linien und eine exzellente Konstruktion. Für den Einsatz im Freien sind sie dabei sehr stabil und langlebig. Diese Abfalleimer weisen eine außerordentlich hohe Qualität auf, die sich auf die Umgebung überträgt und sie aufwertet.

Designer portrait
See page 68
Siehe Seite 68

389

Bamboo Pavilion
Bambuspavillon

Client
Taichung Real Estate Development Association, Taichung, Taiwan
Design
Zuo Studio, Taichung, Taiwan
Web
www.yuansen-design.com/zuo

As one of the theme pavilions in the Taiwan World Flora Exposition, this bamboo pavilion corresponds to the global trend of reducing the carbon footprint. Its design emulates the Central Mountain Range on Taiwan Island. At the same time, the building symbolises a seed as a sign for sustainability and eternal growth. Its appearance, with its network of bamboo and the use of traditional methods of wall construction, mirrors far-eastern authenticity. The pavilion invites visitors to linger and take time to relax, but also offers facilities for exhibitions and cultural events.

Als einer der Themenpavillons der Taiwan World Flora Exposition entspricht dieser Bambuspavillon dem globalen Trend der Reduzierung des CO_2-Fußabdrucks. Seine Gestaltung ahmt die Form des Taiwanischen Zentralgebirges nach. Zudem symbolisiert sie einen Samen als Symbol für Nachhaltigkeit und ewiges Wachstum. Sein Aussehen spiegelt mit seinen Bambusgeflechten und dem Einsatz traditioneller Maurertechniken fernöstliche Authentizität wider. Der Pavillon lädt zum Verweilen und Ausruhen ein, bietet aber auch Raum für Ausstellungen und kulturelle Darbietungen.

Statement by the jury
The design of this bamboo pavilion combines sustainability with both an artistic attitude and traditionally minded aesthetics in an impressive manner.

Begründung der Jury
Auf beeindruckende Weise vereint die Gestaltung dieses Bambuspavillons eine nachhaltige Bauweise mit einer sowohl kunstvollen wie traditionsbewussten Ästhetik.

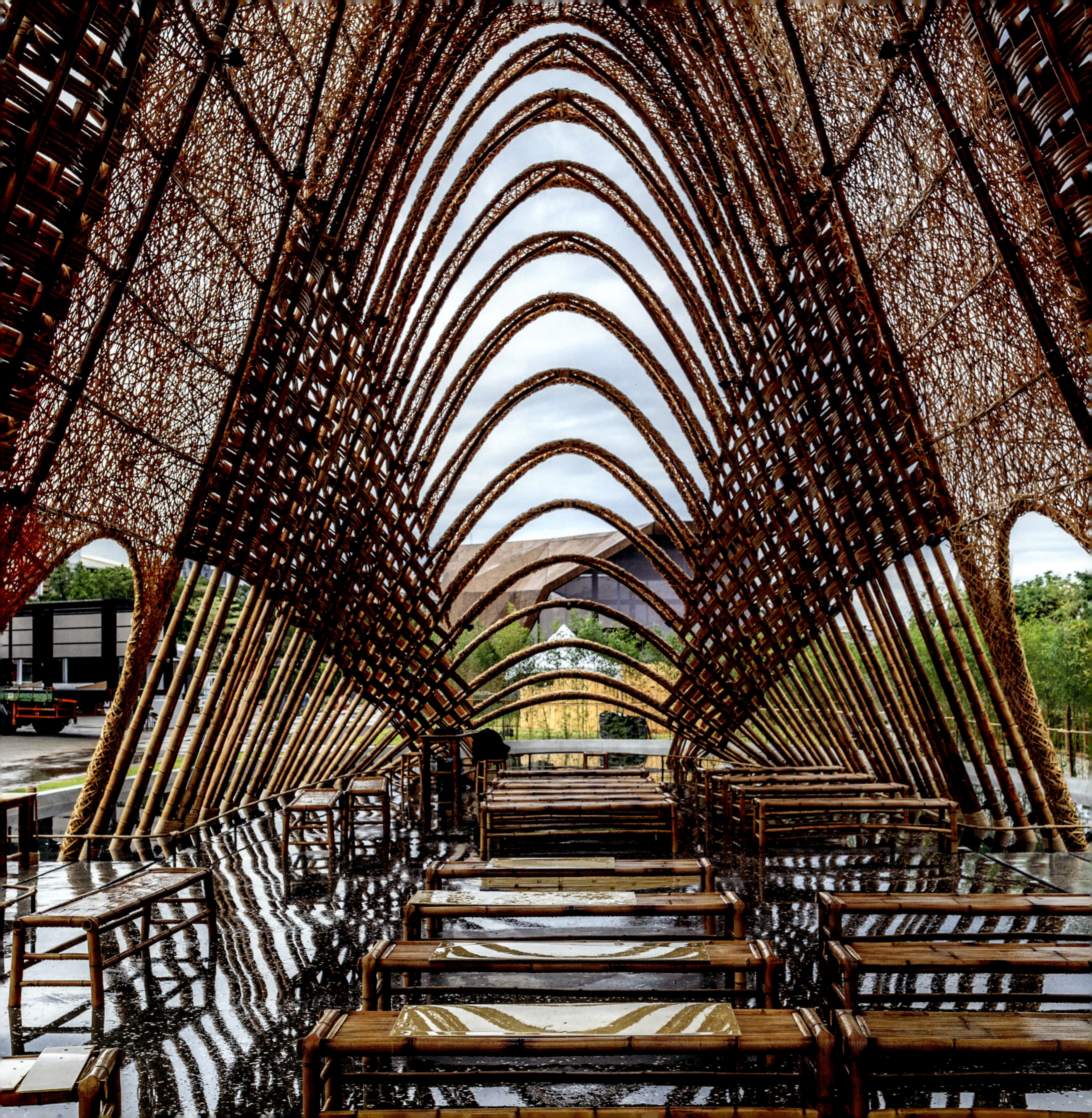

Morning Glory
Shelter
Unterstand

Manufacturer
Samsung C&T Corporation, Resort Group,
Landscape Business (Everscape), Yongin, South Korea
In-house design
Sooncheol Baek, Youngwoo Seo
Web
http://rnc.samsungcnt.com

The design of the Morning Glory shelter was inspired by the flower of the same name. The resemblance is strengthened by decoration with a petal motif to create an unmistakable appearance. The use of high-pressure laminate gives the shelter a harmonic, sweeping form. The circular roof is seamlessly linked to the central column and offers generous protection from the elements. Models with various heights and colours may be placed together to form an eye-catching group.

Die Formgebung des Unterstands Morning Glory (Prachtwinde) ist von dem Aussehen der gleichnamigen Blume inspiriert. Die Verzierung mit einem Blütenblattmuster verstärkt die Ähnlichkeit und erzeugt gleichzeitig ein unverwechselbares Erscheinungsbild. Dank der Verwendung von Hochdrucklaminat weist der Unterstand eine harmonisch geschwungene Linienführung auf. Die kreisrunde Bedachung geht dabei nahtlos in die mittig platzierte Säule über und bietet so großzügigen Schutz. Mehrere in Höhe und Farbe variierende Modelle lassen sich zu einer aufmerksamkeitsstarken Gruppe arrangieren.

Statement by the jury
With its sweeping form and harmonious charisma, the Morning Glory shelter is a real eye-catcher in a public area.

Begründung der Jury
Mit seiner fließenden Linienführung und seiner harmonischen Ausstrahlung ist der Unterstand Morning Glory ein Hingucker im öffentlichen Raum.

Allium Pergola
Pavilion
Pavillon

Manufacturer
Samsung C&T Corporation, Resort Group,
Landscape Business (Everscape), Yongin, South Korea
In-house design
Sooncheol Baek, Youngwoo Seo
Web
http://rnc.samsungcnt.com

This small pavilion takes its name from the root shape of bulbous plants and is an eye-catcher in public spaces. Allium Pergola emulates this shape in an artistic way. The form is made possible by the use of high-pressure laminate that can be bent in the required way. Inside, the circular seating invites passers-by to stop and rest awhile. In the centre, organically shaped wooden columns complete the impression of a bulbous plant, but also serve as a possible support for plants such as vines.

Ein Zwiebelgewächs (allium) ist Namenspate für diesen Pavillon, der im öffentlichen Raum aufmerksamkeitsstarke Akzente setzt. Allium Pergola ahmt dessen runde Form kunstvoll nach. Ermöglicht wird dies durch die Verwendung von Hochdrucklaminat, das sich entsprechend biegen lässt. Im Inneren des Pavillons befindet sich eine gerundet gestaltete Bank, die zum Verweilen einlädt. Organisch anmutende Holzsäulen im Zentrum vervollständigen einerseits die Anmutung eines Zwiebelgewächses, dienen andererseits aber auch als Rankhilfe, beispielsweise für Weinreben.

Statement by the jury
With its organic form language and seemingly natural appearance, this pavilion skilfully draws attention to itself in an urban environment.

Begründung der Jury
Mit seiner organischen Formensprache und natürlichen Anmutung zieht dieser Pavillon im urbanen Umfeld gekonnt die Blicke auf sich.

Quik-Turn™ Radius Coupling
Drainage Channel
Entwässerungsrinne

Manufacturer
NDS, Member of Norma Group,
Woodland Hills, California, USA
In-house design
David Rusch, Dan Nourian
Web
www.norma-watermanagement.com

This drainage channel allows a deflection of up to six degrees between its single segments, thus allowing them to create continuous bends and curves. Thanks to the flexible design, they can fit the sweeping curves of swimming pools, paths or running tracks. Several Quik-Turn elements can be used together for particularly tight radiuses. The durable drainage channel possesses solid material properties, it can neither tear nor break.

Statement by the jury
High flexibility and the use of long-lasting materials are in the focus of the cleverly thought-out design of this robust drainage channel.

Diese Entwässerungsrinne ermöglicht eine Auslenkung von bis zu sechs Grad zwischen ihren einzelnen Segmenten, wodurch mühelos fortlaufende Bögen und Kurven realisiert werden können. Mit ihrem flexiblen Design kann sie sich so gut der geschwungenen Linienführung von Swimmingpools, Spazierwegen oder Laufstrecken anpassen. Um besonders enge Radien zu ermöglichen, lassen sich mehrere Quik-Turn-Elemente miteinander verbinden. Die widerstandsfähige Entwässerungsrinne verfügt über solide Materialeigenschaften, sie kann weder reißen noch brechen.

Begründung der Jury
Ein hohes Maß an Flexibilität und ein langlebiger Materialeinsatz stehen im Fokus der klug durchdachten Gestaltung dieser robusten Entwässerungsrinne.

Prisma
Grating for Heavy Loads
Schwerlastrost

Manufacturer
Richard Brink GmbH & Co. KG,
Schloß Holte-Stukenbrock, Germany
In-house design
Magnus Brock
Web
www.richard-brink.de

Prisma is a cast-iron grating for covering drainage channels that are subjected to heavy loads. Aside from its functionality, it offers an appropriate appearance for an urban environment. The homogenous surface has a fine structure of interwoven facets that reflect the light in a variety of ways. The locking device is placed on a second level to avoid disturbance of impression given by the continuous pattern. A high-quality cataphoretic coating in anthracite grey completes the overall appearance.

Statement by the jury
The contemporary design of the Prisma grating for heavy loads impresses with a harmonious appearance that skilfully adds interesting aspects to urban landscapes.

Prisma ist ein gusseiserner Schwerlastrost zur Abdeckung von Linienentwässerungen, der neben seiner technischen Funktionalität auch ein ansprechendes Aussehen im urbanen Umfeld bietet. Seine feinteilige und homogene Oberfläche mit den ineinander verwobenen facettierten Flächen bricht das Licht immer wieder neu. Die Verriegelungstechnik befindet sich auf einer zweiten Ebene, damit der optische Gesamteindruck des fortlaufenden Musters nicht unterbrochen wird. Eine hochwertige kathodische Tauchlackierung in Anthrazitgrau rundet das edle Erscheinungsbild ab.

Begründung der Jury
Die zeitgemäße Gestaltung des Schwerlastrostes Prisma überzeugt mit einem harmonischen Erscheinungsbild, das im Stadtbild gekonnt Akzente setzt.

U-Cara
Wall System
Wandsystem

Manufacturer
Unilock, Toronto, Canada
In-house design
Ray Rodenburgh, Scott Swierad
Web
www.unilock.com

U-Cara is a two-component wall system that can be used to create retaining walls, garden planters, barbecue tables or water features. The system features interchangeable fascia panels which are available in many different colours and surface textures that can be combined together in different designs. This allows the creation of landscape gardens that complement the buildings they surround. The various elements come in a size that makes them easy to lift and position where they are needed.

Statement by the jury
A high level of variability and flexibility allowing for the design of a wide range of landscape and garden designs are the characteristic features of the U-Cara wall system.

U-Cara ist ein aus zwei Komponenten bestehendes Wandsystem, mit dem sich Stützmauern, Pflanzgefäße, Grilltische oder Wasserspiele realisieren lassen. Das System verfügt über austauschbare Frontblenden, die in vielen verschiedenen Farben und Oberflächenstrukturen erhältlich sind und die miteinander zu verschiedenen Dessins kombiniert werden können. Auf diese Weise lassen sich Landschaftsgärten gestalten, die die von ihnen umgebenen Gebäude komplementieren. Die einzelnen Bauelemente haben eine komfortable Größe und lassen sich einfach anheben und verbauen.

Begründung der Jury
Große Variabilität und Flexibilität, die viel Raum für eine individuelle Landschafts- und Gartengestaltung lassen, zeichnen das Wandsystem U-Cara aus.

SCADA VZ5
Lawn Ornament
Rasenornament

Manufacturer
Godelmann GmbH & Co. KG,
Fensterbach, Germany
Design
Rain(a)Way (Fien Dekker),
Eindhoven, Netherlands
Web
www.godelmann.de
www.rainaway.nl

The SCADA VZ5 concrete lawn ornament combines a tendril-like pattern with ecologically useful features. The spaces in the paving stones may be filled with grit or a mixture of humus, sand and grit to allow grass or other plants to ornament the lawn. Thus, 30 per cent of the surface remains porous. The paving stones are 30 × 30 × 12 cm in size and can carry axle weights up to ten tons. This makes them suitable for the construction of parking spaces and fire-brigade access routes that feature infiltration capabilities.

Statement by the jury
The design of the SCADA VZ5 lawn ornament meets high demands in aesthetic quality and is at the same time attractive due to its ecological features.

Das Beton-Rasenornament SCADA VZ5 kombiniert mit seinen Rankenmustern ein fantasievolles Erscheinungsbild mit ökologisch sinnvollen Eigenschaften. Die Hohlräume des Pflastersteins können mit Splitt oder einer Mischung aus Humus, Sand und Splitt gefüllt werden, um die Ornamente mit Rasen oder Kräutern zu begrünen. Auf diese Weise bleibt die Oberfläche zu 30 Prozent unversiegelt. Die 30 × 30 × 12 cm großen, mit bis zu zehn Tonnen Achslast belastbaren Pflastersteine eignen sich beispielsweise gut für den Bau versickerungsfähiger Parkplätze und Feuerwehrzufahrten.

Begründung der Jury
Die Gestaltung des Rasenornaments SCADA VZ5 erfüllt hohe Ansprüche an ästhetische Qualität. Zudem gefallen seine umweltfreundlichen Eigenschaften.

Mingata
LED Street Light Series
LED-Straßenleuchten-Serie

Manufacturer
RZB Rudolf Zimmermann, Bamberg GmbH,
Bamberg, Germany
In-house design
Mathias Mößle
Web
www.rzb.de

The Mingata street light series is suitable for mounting on the sides and top of lamp posts. The lights are powerful and equipped with high-quality, mostly replaceable components that are designed to have a long life with sustainability in mind. Thanks to efficient thermal management, they need no visible cooling ribs. The flat top can be opened for easy installation and maintenance. The lights come already prepared for LEDs and Zhaga standard management systems and are therefore reliable for planning – also with respect to the Smart City concept.

Die zur Mastansatz- und Mastaufsatzmontage geeignete Straßenleuchten-Serie Mingata ist leistungsstark und mit ihren hochwertigen, größtenteils austauschbaren Komponenten auf Langlebigkeit und Nachhaltigkeit ausgerichtet. Dank eines effizienten Thermomanagements kommt sie ohne sichtbare Kühlrippen aus. Das plan gestaltete Leuchtenoberteil lässt sich zur werkzeugfreien Montage und Wartung aufklappen. Durch die werkseitige Vorbereitung für LEDs und Managementsysteme nach Zhaga-Standard ist die Leuchte planungssicher – auch im Hinblick auf das Konzept Smart City.

Statement by the jury
The design of the Mingata street light series is made impressive by its user-friendliness and, at the same time, by its functionality based on sustainability.

Begründung der Jury
Die Gestaltung der Straßenleuchten-Serie Mingata beeindruckt mit einer anwenderfreundlichen, dabei gleichzeitig auf Nachhaltigkeit bedachten Funktionalität.

Philips SmartBright Road
LED Street Light
LED-Straßenleuchte

Manufacturer
Signify, Eindhoven, Netherlands
In-house design
Signify Design Team
Web
www.signify.com

The Philips SmartBright Road street light is very compact and slim with a side thickness of only 2 cm. It demonstrates high thermal efficiency, a consciously simple design and a "light only" concept that focuses on a high level of light output. Thanks to this design concept, the use of material is kept to a minimum. The newly developed driver-on-board solution reduces the weight of these LED lights, something that is an advantage in both the delivery and installation.

Statement by the jury
The design of the slim shaped Philips SmartBright Road street light focuses on what is most important, an efficient light output.

Die Straßenleuchte Philips SmartBright Road ist sehr kompakt und schlank konstruiert und weist eine Seitenstärke von lediglich 2 cm auf. Sie zeichnet sich durch hohe thermische Effizienz, ein bewusst einfaches Design und ein „Nur Licht"-Konzept, das den Fokus auf eine hohe Lichtleistung richtet, aus. Dank dieses Gestaltungskonzepts lässt sich der Materialverbrauch reduzieren. Die neu entwickelte Driver-on-board-Lösung verringert zudem das Gewicht dieser LED-Leuchte, was sowohl die Auslieferung als auch die Installation erleichtert.

Begründung der Jury
Die Gestaltung der schlank gebauten Straßenleuchte Philips SmartBright Road ist mit einer effizienten Lichtausbeute auf das Wesentliche ausgerichtet.

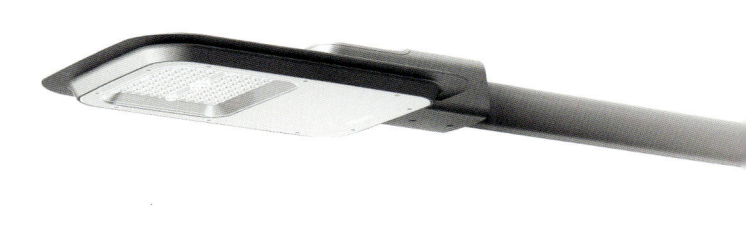

Philips RoadCharm
LED Street Light
LED-Straßenleuchte

Manufacturer
Signify, Eindhoven, Netherlands
In-house design
Signify Design Team
Web
www.signify.com

Philips RoadCharm is a modern, powerful street light whose design features soft flowing lines and a clean, smooth surface. Its technically updated layout enables the LED module to be placed directly in the die-cast housing. One advantage is that this solves technical problems and the other is that it makes the light slimmer and lighter. The reduced weight means that its installation is easier and also makes it safer by reducing the risk of damage from outdoor conditions.

Statement by the jury
The stylish construction of the Philips RoadCharm street light gives it a refined appearance which enables it to blend well into public places.

Philips RoadCharm ist eine moderne, leistungsstarke Straßenleuchte, deren Gestaltung eine sanft geschwungene Linienführung sowie eine klar anmutende Oberfläche aufweist. Ihr technisch modifizierter Aufbau ermöglicht es, das LED-Modul direkt auf dem Druckgussgehäuse zu platzieren. Dies löst einerseits thermische Probleme und macht andererseits die Leuchte schlanker und leichter. Das geringere Gewicht vereinfacht wiederum die Installation und sorgt zudem für Sicherheit, da das Risiko von Schäden durch Außenbedingungen reduziert wird.

Begründung der Jury
Dank ihrer stilvollen Konstruktion weist die Straßenleuchte Philips RoadCharm ein edles Aussehen auf, mit dem sie sich gut im öffentlichen Raum einfügt.

The jury 2019
International orientation and objectivity
Internationalität und Objektivität

The jurors of the Red Dot Award: Product Design
All members of the Red Dot Award: Product Design jury are appointed on the basis of independence and impartiality. They are independent designers, academics in design faculties, representatives of international design institutions, and design journalists.

The jury is international in its composition, which changes every year. These conditions assure a maximum of objectivity. The members of this year's jury are presented in alphabetical order on the following pages.

Die Juroren des Red Dot Award: Product Design
In die Jury des Red Dot Award: Product Design wird als Mitglied nur berufen, wer völlig unabhängig und unparteiisch ist. Dies sind selbständig arbeitende Designer, Hochschullehrer der Designfakultäten, Repräsentanten internationaler Designinstitutionen und Designfachjournalisten.

Die Jury ist international besetzt und wechselt in jedem Jahr ihre Zusammensetzung. Unter diesen Voraussetzungen ist ein Höchstmaß an Objektivität gewährleistet. Auf den folgenden Seiten werden die Jurymitglieder des diesjährigen Wettbewerbs in alphabetischer Reihenfolge vorgestellt.

David Andersen
Denmark
Dänemark

David Andersen, born in 1978, graduated from Glasgow School of Art and the Fashion Design Academy in 2003. Until 2014, he developed designs for ready-to-wear clothes, shoes, perfume, underwear and home wear and emerged as a fashion designer working as chief designer at Dreams by Isabell Kristensen as well as designing couture for the royal Danish family, celebrities, artists etc. under his own name. In 2007, he debuted his collection "David Andersen". He has received many awards and grants for his designs, e.g. a grant from the National Art Foundation. David Andersen is also known for his development of sustainable clothing with his collection, Zero Waste, and has received several awards for his work on ecology and sustainable productions. David Andersen has changed his job as Vice President for Design at Rosendahl Design Group and is now working for the fur giant, KC FUR in China, as Design Director. Furthermore, David Andersen is a guest lecturer at different schools and colleges.

David Andersen, 1978 geboren, studierte an der Glasgow School of Art und der Fashion Design Academy, wo er 2003 sein Examen machte. Bis 2014 fertigte er Entwürfe für Konfektionsware, Schuhe, Parfüm, Unterwäsche und Homewear. Daraus entwickelte sich eine Karriere als Modedesigner und er begann, bei Dreams von Isabell Kristensen als Chefdesigner zu arbeiten sowie unter seinem eigenen Namen Couture für die dänische Königsfamilie, Prominente, Künstler etc. zu entwerfen. Im Jahr 2007 stellte er erstmals seine eigene „David Andersen"-Kollektion vor. Für seine Entwürfe erhielt er bereits viele Auszeichnungen und Fördergelder, darunter ein Stipendium der National Art Foundation (Nationale Kunststiftung). David Andersen hat sich auch mit „Zero Waste", einer Kollektion nachhaltiger Kleidung, einen Namen gemacht, und mehrere Auszeichnungen für seine Arbeit im Bereich von Umwelt und nachhaltiger Produktion erhalten. David Andersen hat seine ehemalige Stelle als Vizepräsident für Design bei der Rosendahl Design Group aufgegeben und ist jetzt Design Director für den riesigen Pelzkonzern KC Fur in China. Darüber hinaus ist er Gastdozent an verschiedenen Schulen und Hochschulen.

01–02
Designs of David Andersen's sustainable "Zero Waste" collection
Entwürfe aus David Andersens nachhaltiger Kollektion „Zero Waste"

01

02

"The most important thing is to be true to oneself. Never compromise unless it is a necessity."

„Das Wichtigste ist, sich selbst treu zu bleiben. Niemals Kompromisse eingehen, es sei denn, es ist absolut notwendig."

What can people surprise you with in your role as fashion designer?
Most people think that being a fashion designer is glamour, red runner and lots of parties. The fashion industry is filled with glamour, but you have to create it yourself and that is hard work.

What, in your opinion, makes for good design?
Good design must be able to stand for itself and, at the same time, do something good for the person who will carry it. The design becomes interesting when there is a good story behind and through the choice of materials, shape and colour.

What, currently, stands out especially in the fashion industry?
An incredible amount is happening. In recent years, we have worked hard to create a more sustainable approach to the way we work with our clothing. In a short time, there has been tremendous development in sustainable fashion, which is incredibly interesting to be a part of, and to work every day to do better.

Womit können Menschen Sie in Ihrer Rolle als Modedesigner überraschen?
Die meisten Menschen glauben, dass das Leben eines Modedesigners aus Glamour, roten Teppichen und vielen Partys besteht. Die Modeindustrie ist voller Glamour, doch muss man ihn selbst schaffen und das erfordert harte Arbeit.

Was macht Ihrer Meinung nach gutes Design aus?
Gutes Design muss sowohl für sich alleine funktionieren als auch für denjenigen, der es trägt, etwas Gutes tun. Design wird interessant, wenn es im Hintergrund eine gute Story gibt – und auch durch die Wahl von Materialien, Form und Farbe.

Was ist gerade besonders auffallend in der Modeindustrie?
Es geschieht wahnsinnig viel. In den letzten Jahren haben wir hart gearbeitet, um einen nachhaltigeren Ansatz für unsere Arbeit in der Modebranche zu etablieren. In relativ kurzer Zeit hat es im Bereich nachhaltiger Mode eine enorme Entwicklung gegeben. Es ist sehr interessant, Teil davon zu sein und jeden Tag zu versuchen, besser zu werden.

Prof. Masayo Ave
Japan/Germany
Japan/Deutschland

Professor Masayo Ave is the founder of the design studio MasayoAve creation and SED.Lab, Sensory Experience Design Laboratory in Berlin. The Japanese designer merges culture and disciplines and brings to bear her expertise in her sensory-based innovative design works and also in the field of design education. A graduate in architecture from Hosei University in Japan, her design career began in Milan in the early 1990s. Taking a sensorial and imaginative approach to basic design principles, her focus on material exploration and experimental design development brought her critical fame and many international design awards. In the early 2000s, Masayo Ave also became involved in the field of design education and was appointed a professor at University of Arts in Berlin, the Estonian Academy of Arts and recently at Berlin International University of Applied Sciences. As a prominent designer-teacher, she has also been dedicating her career to developing a new design education programme for children and young people that encompasses sensory-based design experiences.

Professor Masayo Ave ist Gründerin des Designstudios MasayoAve creation und des SED.Lab, einem Labor für sensorische Designforschung in Berlin. Die japanische Designerin verschmilzt Kultur mit Wissenschaftsfächern und bringt ihre Fachkenntnisse in ihre innovativen, auf Sensorik basierenden Gestaltungsprojekte ein, ebenso wie auf dem Gebiet der Designausbildung. Nach einem Architekturabschluss an der Hosei University in Japan begann sie ihre Designkarriere in Mailand in den frühen 1990er Jahren. Maßgebende Designgrundlagen ging sie mit einem sensorischen und ideenreichen Konzept an. Ihre Ausrichtung auf Rohstoffforschung und experimentelle Designentwicklung hatte das Lob der Kritiker und viele internationale Designauszeichnungen zur Folge. In den frühen 2000er Jahren fing Masayo Ave an, sich auch mit der Designausbildung zu beschäftigen, und wurde zur Professorin an der Universität der Künste in Berlin sowie an der Estländischen Kunstakademie und unlängst an der Berlin International University of Applied Sciences ernannt. Als prominente Designerin und Lehrerin hat sie sich im Laufe ihrer Karriere für die Entwicklung eines neuen Designausbildungsprogramms für Kinder und Jugendliche eingesetzt, das auch auf Sensorik basierende Designerlebnisse beinhaltet.

01 GENESI
Table light with a cover made from a washable open-cell polyester and a body in chromed steel, launched in her own collection "MasayoAve creation", 1998

Tischleuchte mit einem Lampenschirm aus waschbarem, offenporigem Polyester und einem Körper aus verchromtem Stahl, erschienen in ihrer eigenen Kollektion „MasayoAve creation", 1998

01

"My advice for young designers is to observe details of their everyday living environment with a scientific designer's eye. The answer exists there and is waiting to be discovered."

„Mein Ratschlag für junge Designer ist, die Details des täglichen Lebens mit einem wissenschaftlichen Designerauge zu betrachten. Die Antwort ist dort zu finden und wartet nur darauf, entdeckt zu werden."

How did you get into design?
By being imaginative and curious about the potential of industrial materials in relation to lifestyle culture.

What does the "MasayoAve creation" design studio stand for?
It is a cross-disciplinary platform where design projects and sensory experiences interconnect.

What, to date, has been the most exciting project of your career?
Each moment in the past projects was unforgettably exciting, but I may say the newest sensory experience design project which I am now working on is the most exciting one.

Where do you find inspiration?
Learning the fundamentals of design is to get a comprehensive understanding of one's own living environment through perceptive senses. The everyday discoveries of tiny details in nature have inspired me a lot.

Wie sind Sie zum Design gekommen?
Indem ich dem Potenzial für industrielle Materialien in Bezug auf unsere Lebenskultur mit Phantasie und Neugierde begegnet bin.

Wofür steht das Designstudio „MasayoAve creation"?
Es ist eine interdisziplinäre Plattform, die Designprojekte mit sensorischen Erlebnissen verbindet.

Was war Ihr bisher spannendstes Projekt?
Jeder Moment vergangener Projekte war unvergesslich spannend, doch kann ich sagen, dass das neueste Designprojekt für sensorische Erlebnisse, an dem ich gerade arbeite, das spannendste ist.

Woher nehmen Sie Ihre Inspiration?
Wenn man die Grundlagen der Gestaltung lernt, erwirbt man mithilfe seiner sinnlichen Wahrnehmung auch ein grundlegendes Verständnis seines Lebensraums. Die täglichen Entdeckungen kleinster Details in der Natur haben mich sehr inspiriert.

Martin Beeh
Germany
Deutschland

Martin Beeh is a graduate in Industrial Design from the Darmstadt University of Applied Sciences in Germany and the ENSCI-Les Ateliers, Paris, and completed a postgraduate course in business administration. In 1995, he became design coordinator at Décathlon in Lille/France, in 1997 senior designer at Electrolux Industrial Design Center Nuremberg and Stockholm and furthermore became design manager at Electrolux Industrial Design Center Pordenone/Italy, in 2001. He is a laureate of several design awards as well as founder and director of the renowned student design competition "Electrolux Design Lab". In the year 2006, he became general manager of the German office of the material library Material ConneXion in Cologne. Three years later, he founded the design office beeh_innovation. Martin Beeh lectured at the Folkwang University of the Arts in Essen, the University of Applied Sciences Schwäbisch Gmünd and the University of Applied Sciences Hamm-Lippstadt and was professor for design management at the University of Applied Sciences Ostwestfalen-Lippe in Lemgo from 2012 to 2015. He has furthermore developed the conference format "materials.cologne" as a dialogue platform for materials, design and innovation.

Martin Beeh absolvierte ein Studium in Industriedesign an der Fachhochschule Darmstadt und an der ENSCI-Les Ateliers, Paris, sowie ein Aufbaustudium der Betriebswirtschaft. 1995 wurde er Designkoordinator bei Décathlon in Lille/Frankreich, 1997 Senior Designer im Electrolux Industrial Design Center Nürnberg und Stockholm sowie 2001 Design Manager im Electrolux Industrial Design Center Pordenone/Italien. Er ist Gewinner diverser Designpreise und gründete und leitete den renommierten Designwettbewerb für Studierende, das „Electrolux Design Lab". Im Jahr 2006 wurde er General Manager der deutschen Niederlassung der Materialbibliothek „Material ConneXion" in Köln. Drei Jahre später gründete Martin Beeh das Designbüro beeh_innovation. Martin Beeh hatte Lehraufträge an der Folkwang Universität der Künste in Essen, an der Hochschule für Gestaltung Schwäbisch Gmünd und an der Hochschule Hamm-Lippstadt und war von 2012 bis 2015 Professor für Designmanagement an der Hochschule Ostwestfalen-Lippe in Lemgo. Darüber hinaus entwickelte er das Konferenzformat „materials.cologne" als Plattform für den Dialog zwischen Material, Design und Innovation.

01
Key visual of the
materials.cologne –
the conference for
design and innovation 2019
Initiative and project
management: beeh_innovation
Design: Büro Freiheit
Keyvisual der
materials.cologne –
Die Konferenz für
Design und Innovation 2019
Initiative und Projektleitung:
beeh_innovation
Design: Büro Freiheit

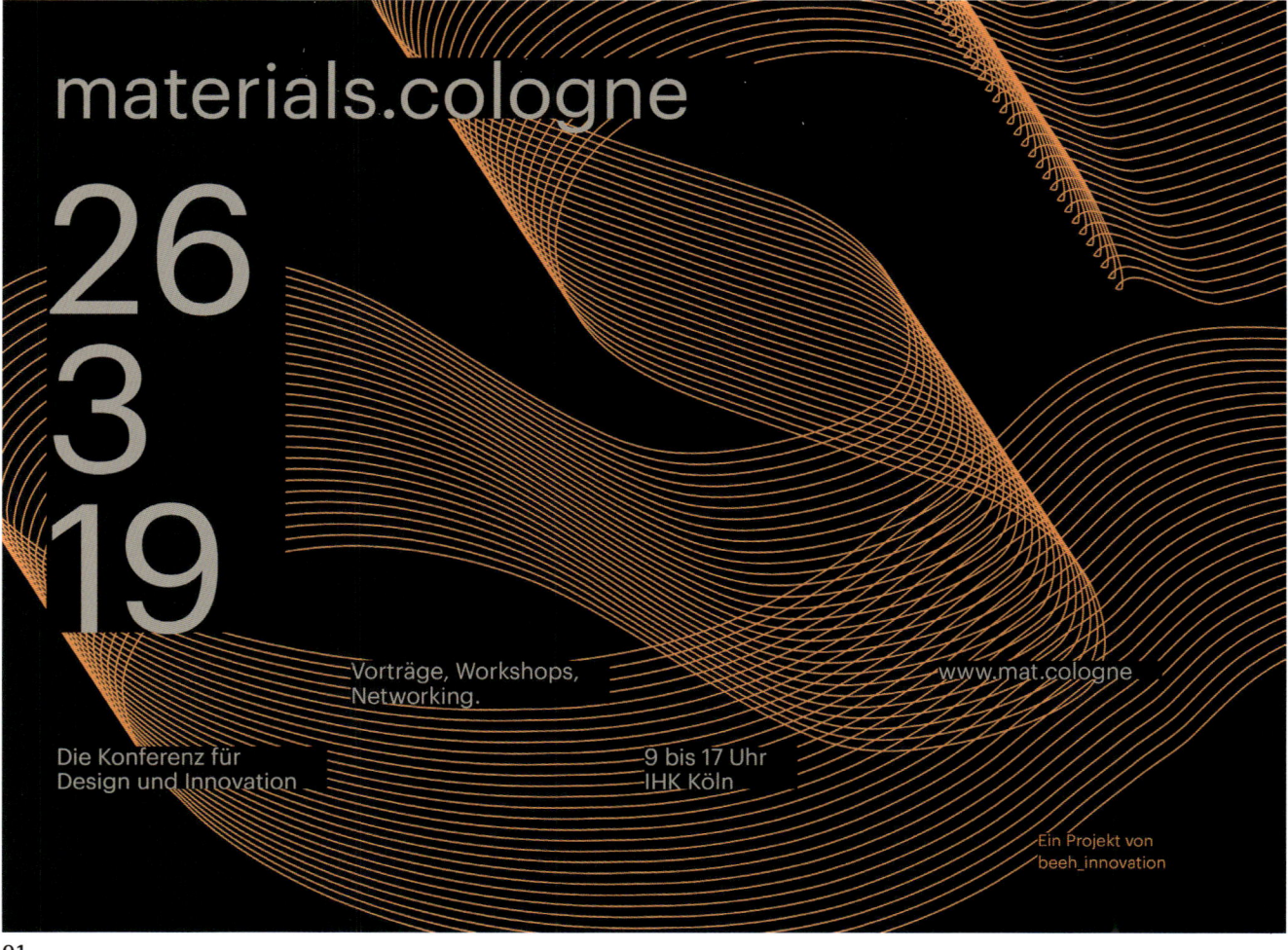

01

"Good design is as little 'visual noise' as possible: if the product comes up with a convincing solution and is easy and intuitive to use."

„Gutes Design ist so wenig ‚weißes Rauschen' wie möglich: wenn das Produkt eine überzeugende Lösung bietet und einfach und intuitiv zu benutzen ist."

With what can a product surprise you?
As a designer, design manager and design juror I evaluate if a product gives an original, human, effective and sustainable solution to an identified problem. If the product is also nice to look at and to work with, it is a good product. To make it really a pleasant surprise, the product should have more benefits and functions then you might first think.

What inspires you?
I had the chance to intensively research the design process of Ray and Charles Eames. Curiosity, experiment, a strong purpose, profoundness, patience combined with a thinking from sketch to production to user, are part of a "total design process" – together with all crafts from others that we need to integrate to create value-adding products.

Which innovations will in future influence our everyday life?
Sustainability is first, smart digital integration second. We will use and share products, not own them.

Womit kann Sie ein Produkt überraschen?
Als Designer, Designmanager und Designjuror beurteile ich ein Produkt danach, ob es eine originelle, menschliche, wirksame und nachhaltige Lösung für ein bestimmtes Problem bietet. Wenn es auch noch gut aussieht und angenehm zu handhaben ist, ist es ein gutes Produkt. Eine wirklich positive Überraschung ist es, wenn es mehr Vorteile und Funktionalitäten bietet, als man zuerst denkt.

Was inspiriert Sie?
Ich habe die Chance gehabt, den Designprozess von Ray und Charles Eames intensiv zu erforschen. Neugierde, Experimentierfreude, Zielstrebigkeit, Tiefe und Geduld, verbunden mit einem Prozess, der von der Skizze über die Herstellung bis zum Verbraucher durchdacht ist, sind Teil eines „kompletten Designprozesses" – genauso wie das Handwerk aller Beteiligten, das wir in den Prozess einfließen lassen müssen, um ein Produkt mit Mehrwert zu schaffen.

Welche Innovationen werden künftig unseren Alltag prägen?
An erster Stelle Nachhaltigkeit, dann die intelligente digitale Integration. Wir werden Produkte gemeinsam benutzen, statt sie zu besitzen.

Gordon Bruce
USA

Gordon Bruce is the owner of Gordon Bruce Design LLC and has been a design consultant for 45 years working with many multinational corporations in Europe, Asia and the USA. He has worked on a wide range of products, interiors and vehicles – from aeroplanes to computers to medical equipment to furniture. From 1991 to 1994, Gordon Bruce was a consulting vice president for the Art Center College of Design's Kyoto programme and, from 1995 to 1999, chairman of Product Design for the Innovative Design Lab of Samsung (IDS) in Seoul, Korea. In 2003, he played a crucial role in helping to establish Porsche Design's North American office. For many years, he served as head design consultant for Lenovo's Innovative Design Center (IDC) in Beijing. He recently worked with Bühler, in Switzerland, and Huawei Technologies Co., Ltd., in China. Gordon Bruce is a visiting professor at several universities in the USA and China. He has been an author for Phaidon Press, London and has written for several international design magazines. He has several products in various permanent design collections such as with MoMA, in New York City. Gordon Bruce recently received Art Center College of Design's "Lifetime Achievement Award".

Gordon Bruce ist Inhaber der Gordon Bruce Design LLC und seit mittlerweile 45 Jahren als Designberater für zahlreiche multinationale Unternehmen in Europa, Asien und den USA tätig. Er arbeitete bereits an einer Reihe von Produkten, Inneneinrichtungen und Fahrzeugen – von Flugzeugen über Computer bis hin zu medizinischem Equipment und Möbeln. Von 1991 bis 1994 war Gordon Bruce beratender Vizepräsident des Kioto-Programms am Art Center College of Design sowie von 1995 bis 1999 Vorsitzender für Produktdesign beim Innovative Design Lab of Samsung (IDS) in Seoul, Korea. Im Jahr 2003 war er wesentlich daran beteiligt, das Büro von Porsche Design in Nordamerika zu errichten. Über viele Jahre war er leitender Designberater für Lenovos Innovative Design Center (IDC) in Beijing. In letzter Zeit arbeitete er für Bühler, Schweiz, und für Huawei Technologies Co., Ltd. in China. Gordon Bruce ist Gastprofessor an zahlreichen Universitäten in den USA und in China. Er war auch als Buchautor für Phaidon Press in London und als Verfasser von Artikeln für diverse internationale Designmagazine aktiv. Einige seiner Produkte werden in verschiedenen Dauerausstellungen gezeigt, unter anderem im MoMA in New York. Kürzlich erhielt Gordon Bruce vom Art Center College of Design den Lifetime Achievement Award.

01
Recreational High-Bypass Turbofan Bi-Plane
Design concept for Industrial Design Magazine, 1984
Freizeit-Hochbypass-Mantelstromtriebwerk-Doppeldecker
Designkonzept für Industrial Design Magazine, 1984

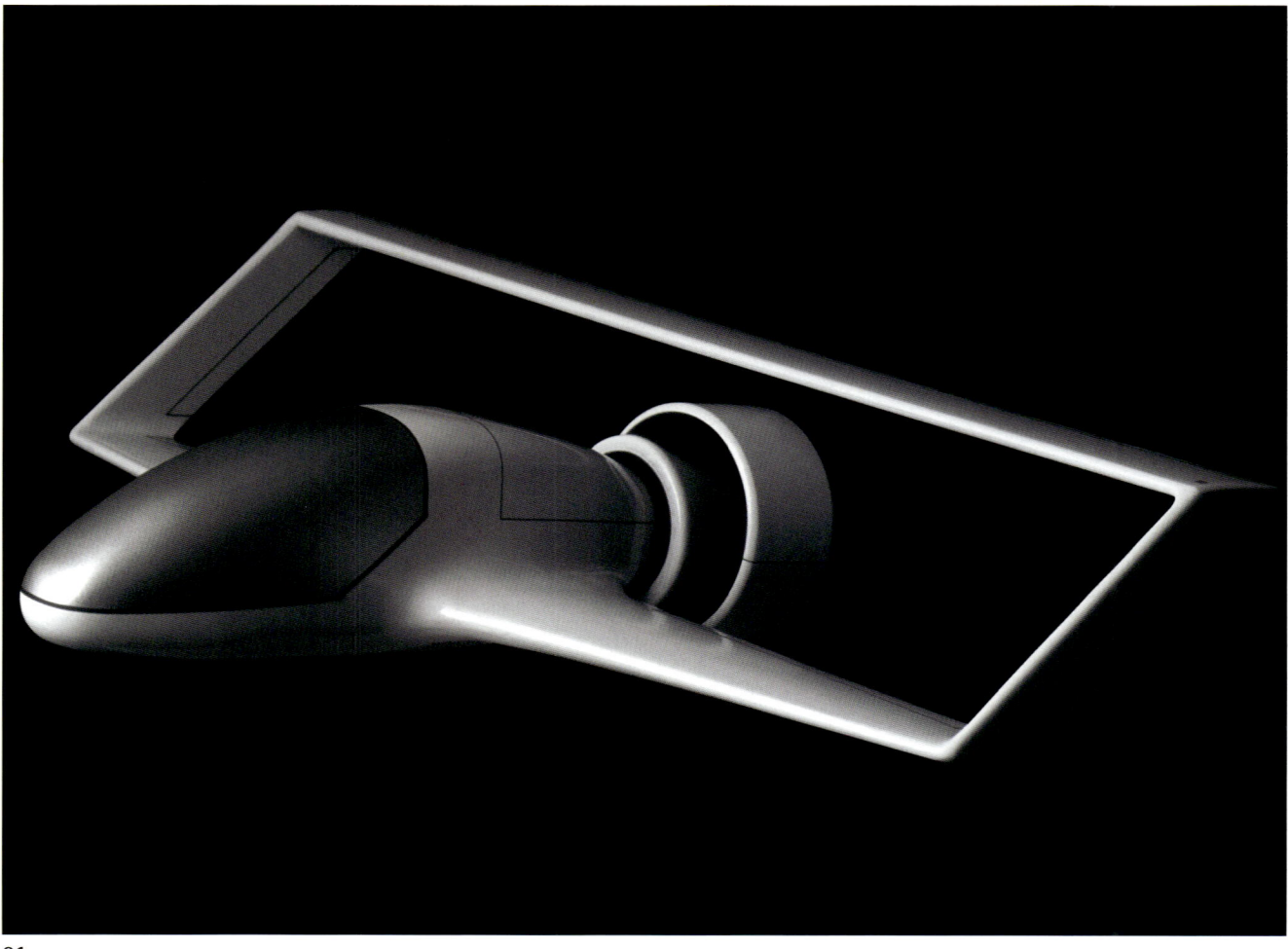

01

"Seeing design beyond professional practices, business strategies, and fashion statements, young designers need to advance their own heightened sense of design mindfulness, because design is a way of thinking about all one does in life."

„Junge Designer sollten bei Design an mehr als die berufliche Praxis, Geschäftsstrategien und Modestatements denken und einen gesteigerten Sinn für Designachtsamkeit entwickeln, da Design eine Geisteshaltung ist, mit der man alles betrachtet, was man im Leben tut."

To what do you attach particular importance when judging products?
The basis for my design judgement is similar to that of a three-legged stool where all supports need to be strong. The first leg is why is a design relevant? If this aspect is unique and pertinent to resolving problems, it brings credibility to the design idea. The second one concerns how the design conforms to the user. This gives credence to the design idea. The third leg is whether the product represents the true character of the designer or the company and embodies a design spirit, attitude and philosophy that gives it a distinctive quality.

What direction would you like product design to take in future?
There are many benefits to be gained from the products we use, as in the areas of health, safety, productivity or ecology. However, they can embody unanticipated hidden dangers as well. Just look at the downside of our civility due to the effects from smart phones and gaming upon minds and behaviour. So, future design professions need to eliminate any of the bad hidden within the good in our products.

Worauf legen Sie bei der Bewertung von Produkten besonderen Wert?
Die Basis für mein Designurteil ähnelt der Struktur eines dreibeinigen Hockers, bei dem alle drei Beine stark sein müssen. Das erste Bein ist, ob eine Gestaltung relevant ist. Wenn dieser Aspekt einzigartig und zweckdienlich ein Problem löst, ist die Designidee glaubwürdig. Das zweite Bein betrifft die Art, in der die Gestaltung auf den Nutzer eingeht. Das gibt der Designidee Überzeugungskraft. Das dritte Bein ist, ob das Produkt die wahre Natur des Designers oder des Unternehmens darstellt und den Geist, die Einstellung und die Philosophie des Designs verkörpert. Das gibt ihm eine unverkennbare Qualität.

Was wünschen Sie sich für die Zukunft des Produktdesigns?
Die Produkte, die wir benutzen, liefern uns viele Vorteile, so wie in den Bereichen Gesundheit, Sicherheit, Produktivität oder Ökologie. Allerdings können sie auch unerwartete Gefahren mit sich bringen. Nehmen Sie nur mal den Rückgang an Höflichkeit aufgrund des negativen Effekts, den Smartphones und Computerspiele auf unseren Verstand und unser Verhalten haben. Zukünftige Designberufe werden daher all das Schlechte, das in dem Guten unserer Produkte versteckt ist, beseitigen müssen.

Gisbert L. Brunner
Germany
Deutschland

Gisbert L. Brunner, born in 1947, has been working on watches, pendulum clocks and other precision timepieces since 1964. During the quartz clock crisis of the 1970s, his love for the apparently dying-out mechanical timepieces grew. His passion as a hobby collector eventually led to the first newspaper articles in the early 1980s and later to the by now more than 20 books on the topic. Amongst others, Brunner works for magazines such as Chronos, Chronos Japan, Ganz Europa, Handelszeitung, Prestige, Terra Mater, GQ and ZEIT Magazin. He also shares his expertise on Focus Online. Together with a partner, he founded the Internet platform www.uhrenkosmos.com in 2018. After the successful Watch Book I (2015) and Watch Book II (2016), the teNeues publishing house published the Watch Book Rolex, written by Gisbert L. Brunner, in June 2017. The book has appeared in German, English and French and has already been reprinted several times due to high international demand.

Gisbert L. Brunner, Jahrgang 1947, beschäftigt sich seit 1964 mit Armbanduhren, Pendeluhren und anderen Präzisionszeitmessern. Während der Quarzuhren-Krise in den 1970er Jahren wuchs seine Liebe zu den anscheinend aussterbenden mechanischen Zeitmessern. Ein leidenschaftliches Sammelhobby führte ab den frühen 1980er Jahren zu ersten Zeitschriftenartikeln und inzwischen mehr als 20 Büchern über dieses Metier. Brunner ist u. a. für Magazine wie Chronos, Chronos Japan, Ganz Europa, Handelszeitung, Prestige, Terra Mater, GQ und ZEIT Magazin tätig. Darüber hinaus stellt er seine Expertise Focus Online zur Verfügung. 2018 gründete er zusammen mit einem Partner die Internet-Plattform www.uhrenkosmos.com. Nach den erfolgreichen Publikationen Watch Book I (2015) und Watch Book II (2016) publizierte der teNeues Verlag im Juni 2017 das wiederum von Gisbert L. Brunner verfasste Watch Book Rolex in den Sprachen Deutsch, Englisch und Französisch. Aufgrund der hohen internationalen Nachfrage musste es schon mehrfach nachgedruckt werden.

**01 THE WATCH BOOK –
COMPENDIUM**
Published by teNeues, 2019
Erschienen bei teNeues, 2019

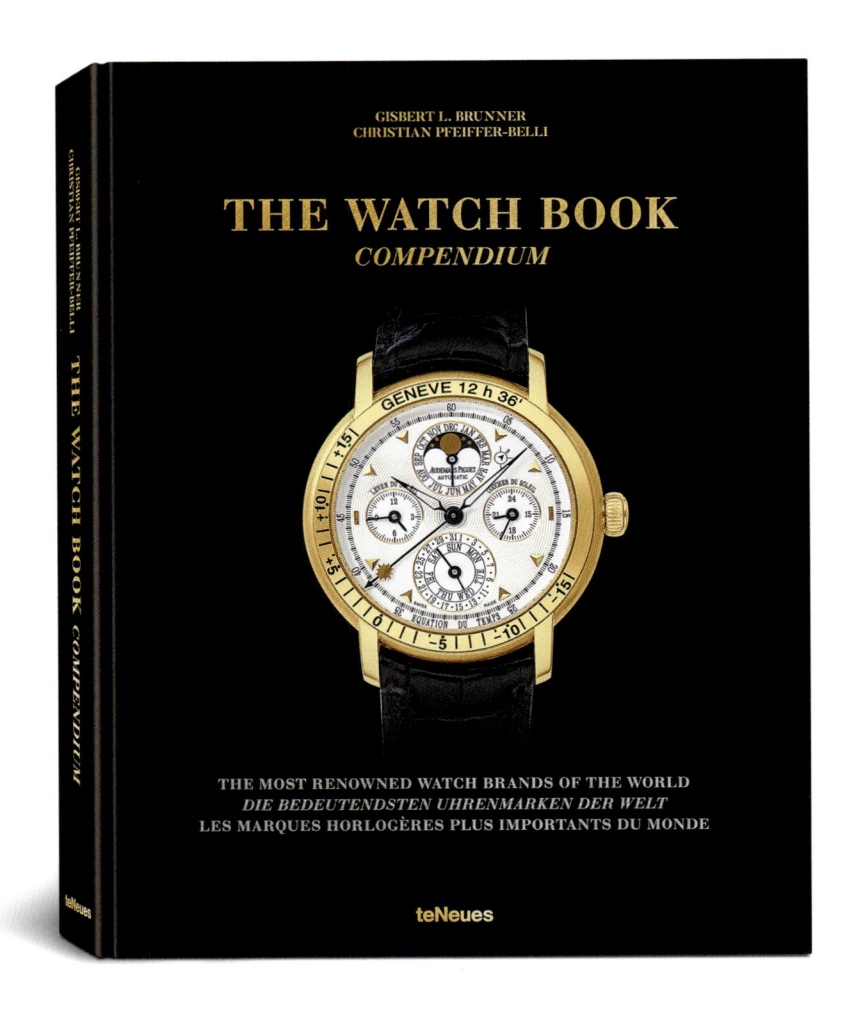

01

"The most exciting trends in the world of watches at the moment are coloured watch faces, smartwatches, bronze casings and a retro look."

„Die spannendsten Trends der Uhrenbranche sind aktuell farbige Zifferblätter, Smartwatches, Bronzegehäuse und Retrolook."

What does a watch have to offer in order to persuade you of its merits?
Naturally, it must look good, have a harmonious design and the correct signature as well as show real watchmaking quality or be truly original.

Where will the watch industry be ten years from now?
That's something nobody can really predict with any certainty as the middle and long-term impact of smartwatches is not yet clear at the moment. But one thing is sure, the traditional mechanical watch will survive.

What is the hallmark of good design?
In good, considered design, it is almost inevitable that form follows function. It is not ostentatious, but appeals instead with a classical, more reserved appearance. Nevertheless, it attracts attention. A significant aspect, where applicable, is ease of use.

How do you proceed when evaluating products?
Step by step. Firstly by screening a watch, then by examining all aspects in detail as well as its tactile properties.

Was muss eine Uhr mitbringen, um Sie zu überzeugen?
Sie muss natürlich gut aussehen, ein stimmiges Design und die richtige Signatur besitzen sowie uhrmacherische Qualität vorweisen oder besonders originell sein.

Wo wird die Uhrenbranche in zehn Jahren stehen?
Das kann niemand mit letzter Sicherheit vorhersagen, weil die mittel- und langfristigen Auswirkungen der Smartwatch momentan noch nicht absehbar sind. Aber die gute alte Mechanik wird sicher überleben.

Was kennzeichnet gutes Design?
Bei gutem, durchdachtem Design folgt die Form beinahe zwangsläufig der Funktion. Es wirkt nicht vordergründig, sondern besticht durch klassischen, eher zurückhaltenden Auftritt. Trotzdem weckt es die Aufmerksamkeit des Betrachters. Ein maßgeblicher Aspekt ist, sofern gegeben, eine intuitive Bedienbarkeit.

Wie gehen Sie bei der Bewertung von Produkten vor?
Schrittweise. Erst Screening, dann Begutachtung der Uhr aus allen Perspektiven inklusive aller Details sowie Prüfung der Haptik.

Rüdiger Bucher
Germany
Deutschland

Rüdiger Bucher, born in 1967, graduated in political science from Philipps-Universität Marburg and completed the postgraduate study course "Interdisciplinary studies on France" in Freiburg, Germany. Since 1995, he has been in charge of "Scriptum. Die Zeitschrift für Schreibkultur" (Scriptum. The magazine for writing culture) at the Verlagsgruppe Ebner Ulm publishing house where he became editorial manager of Chronos, the leading German-language special interest magazine for wrist watches in 1999. As chief editor since 2005, he has positioned Chronos internationally with subsidiary magazines and licensed editions in China, Korea, Japan and Poland. At the same time, Rüdiger Bucher established a successful corporate publishing department for Chronos. Since 2014, he has been editorial director and, in addition to Chronos, is also in charge of the sister magazines "Uhren-Magazin" (Watch Magazine), "Klassik Uhren" (Classic Watches) and the New York-based "WatchTime". Rüdiger Bucher lectures as an expert for mechanical wrist watches and is a sought-after interview partner for various media.

Rüdiger Bucher, geboren 1967, absolvierte ein Studium in Politikwissenschaft an der Philipps-Universität Marburg und das Aufbaustudium „Interdisziplinäre Frankreich-Studien" in Freiburg. Ab 1995 betreute er beim Ebner Verlag Ulm fünf Jahre lang „Scriptum. Die Zeitschrift für Schreibkultur", bevor er im selben Verlag 1999 Redaktionsleiter von „Chronos", dem führenden deutschsprachigen Special-Interest-Magazin für Armbanduhren wurde. Ab 2005 Chefredakteur, hat sich Chronos seitdem mit Tochtermagazinen und Lizenzausgaben in China, Korea, Japan und Polen international aufgestellt. Gleichzeitig baute Rüdiger Bucher für Chronos einen erfolgreichen Corporate-Publishing-Bereich auf. Seit 2014 verantwortet er als Redaktionsdirektor neben Chronos auch die Schwestermagazine „Uhren-Magazin", „Klassik Uhren" sowie die in New York beheimatete „WatchTime". Als Experte für mechanische Armbanduhren hält Rüdiger Bucher Vorträge und ist ein gefragter Interviewpartner für verschiedene Medien.

01
Chronos is available around the globe with different magazine issues and special supplements.
Mit verschiedenen Ausgaben und Sonderheften ist Chronos rund um den Globus vertreten.

01

"Good design should ensure that appearance and tactile properties evoke positive emotions and also reflect the unique characteristics of the brand."

„Gutes Design sollte optisch wie haptisch positive Emotionen hervorrufen und zugleich die besonderen Eigenheiten der Marke verkörpern."

What fascinates you about watches?
The fact that they manage to show the time with a precision of 99.99 per cent – often completely by mechanical means. Also, that the technology and design history of major brands, which are often over 150 years old, is encapsulated in such a small space.

What three qualities must a watch have in order to persuade you of its merits?
It must evoke strong emotions, be instantly recognisable, and easy and fast to read.

Where will the watch industry be five years from now?
There will be increased digitalisation and online selling will be much more established. Brands will be even more important, and, at the same time, need to keep reinventing themselves.

How do you proceed when evaluating products?
I check whether the design is new and unique, if the proportions are correct and if it is pleasant to wear. I also establish whether the design gets across the idea behind the watch and its function.

Was begeistert Sie an Uhren?
Dass sie es – oft mit rein mechanischen Mitteln – schaffen, die Zeit mit einer Präzision von 99,99 Prozent anzuzeigen. Und dass sich auf so kleinem Raum die Technik- und Designgeschichte großer, oft 150 Jahre alter Marken widerspiegelt.

Welche drei Eigenschaften muss eine Uhr mitbringen, um Sie zu überzeugen?
Sie muss starke Gefühle evozieren, unverwechselbar sowie gut und schnell ablesbar sein.

Wo wird die Uhrenbranche in fünf Jahren stehen?
Sie wird noch mehr digitalisiert und der Onlinehandel deutlich stärker etabliert sein. Marken werden noch wichtiger und müssen sich gleichzeitig immer wieder neu erfinden.

Wie gehen Sie bei der Bewertung von Produkten vor?
Ich prüfe, ob das Design neu und einzigartig ist, ob die Proportionen der Uhr stimmen und wie es sich mit der Haptik verhält. Ich untersuche, ob und wie das Design die Idee, die hinter der Uhr und ihrer Funktion steht, zur Geltung bringt.

Prof. Jun Cai
China

Jun Cai is professor at the Academy of Arts & Design, and director of the Design Management Research Lab at Tsinghua University in Beijing. He is also external reviewer for the Aalto University and Design School of Hong Kong Polytechnic University. Professor Cai has focused on research for design strategy and design management since the 1990s. Through exploration of design-driven business innovation and user-centred design thinking by theoretical and practical research, he was a consultant for more than 60 projects for among others Motorola, Nokia, LG, Boeing, Lenovo, Coway, Fiyta and Aftershockz. Furthermore, he has published papers and publications on design research, design strategy and design management.

Jun Cai ist Professor an der Academy of Arts & Design sowie Direktor des Design Management Research Lab an der Tsinghua University in Beijing. Er ist zudem externer Referent der Aalto University und der Designschule der Polytechnic University in Hongkong. Bereits seit den 1990er Jahren konzentriert sich Professor Cai auf die Forschung in den Bereichen Designstrategie und Designmanagement. Aufgrund seiner Erforschung von designorientierter Geschäftsinnovation und benutzerzentriertem Designdenken durch theoretische und praktische Forschung war er in mehr als 60 Projekten beratend tätig, unter anderem für Motorola, Nokia, LG, Boeing, Lenovo, Coway, Fiyta und Aftershockz. Außerdem hat er bereits Abhandlungen und Veröffentlichungen über Designforschung, Designstrategie und Designmanagement verfasst.

01 Dust of Galaxy
Lighting design
Leuchtendesign

01

"The quality of design improves the core competence of a company from market differentiation to brand recognition."
„Die Designqualität verbessert die Kernkompetenz eines Unternehmens, angefangen bei der Marktdifferenzierung bis hin zum Markenbekanntheitsgrad."

You are a professor at the Academy of Arts & Design. What advice do you give your students for their future career?
Be creative and have space in your heart for love and empathy. Be sensitive to changes in nature and always concerned with environment. A designer should have the responsibility not only to bring the beauty to the world, but also to protect our home planet.

What do you find most enjoyable about your work as a jury member?
It is exciting to see the progress of design and to witness change. I am always inspired by the work of talented designers, by their creative innovation and unique imagination.

What does a product have to offer in order to surprise you?
An experience far beyond function and an external shape that touches me inside. A really good product can be a reliable partner that only emerges when you need it.

Sie sind Professor an der Academy of Arts & Design. Welchen Rat geben Sie Ihren Studenten für ihre zukünftige Karriere?
Seid kreativ und habt in euerm Herzen Platz für Liebe und Empathie. Nehmt die Veränderungen in der Natur mit Sensibilität wahr und kümmert euch um die Umwelt. Ein Designer hat nicht nur die Aufgabe, Schönes zur Welt zu bringen, sondern ist auch für den Schutz unseres Planeten verantwortlich.

Was macht Ihnen an Ihrer Arbeit als Juror am meisten Spaß?
Es ist aufregend, den Fortschritt und die Veränderung im Design beobachten zu können. Mich inspiriert immer wieder die Arbeit der talentierten Designer, ihre kreativen Neuerungen und einzigartige Phantasie.

Was muss ein Produkt mitbringen, um Sie zu überraschen?
Ein Erlebnis, das über die Funktion hinausgeht, und eine äußere Form, die mich im Innersten berührt. Ein wirklich gutes Produkt kann ein verlässlicher Partner sein, der nur dann erscheint, wenn er gebraucht wird.

Vivian Wai-kwan Cheng
Hong Kong
Hongkong

On leaving the Kee Hong Kong Design Institute after 19 years of educational service, Vivian Cheng founded "Vivian Design" in 2014 to provide consultancy services and promote her own art in jewellery and glass. She graduated with a BA in industrial design from the Hong Kong Polytechnic University and was awarded a special prize in the Young Designers of the Year award hosted by the Federation of Hong Kong Industries in 1987, and the Governor's Award for Industry: Consumer Product Design in 1989, after joining Lambda Industrial Limited as the head of the product design team. In 1995 she finished her master's degree and joined the Vocational Training Council, teaching product design, and later became responsible for, among others, establishing an international network with design-related organisations and schools. Vivian Cheng was the International Liaison Manager at the Hong Kong Design Institute (HKDI), member of the Board of Directors of the Hong Kong Design Centre (HKDC) from 2002 to 2004, and was board member of the World Design Organization (formerly Icsid) from 2013 to 2017. Furthermore, she has been a panel member for various adjudication boards of the government and various NGOs.

Nach 19 Jahren im Lehrbetrieb verließ Vivian Cheng 2014 das Hong Kong Design Institute und gründete „Vivian Design", um Beratungsdienste anzubieten und ihre eigene Schmuck- und Glaskunst weiterzuentwickeln. 1987 machte sie ihren BA in Industriedesign an der Hong Kong Polytechnic University. Im selben Jahr erhielt sie einen Sonderpreis im Wettbewerb „Young Designers of the Year", veranstaltet von der Federation of Hong Kong Industries, sowie 1989 den Governor's Award for Industry: Consumer Product Design, nachdem sie bei Lambda Industrial Limited als Leiterin des Produktdesign-Teams angefangen hatte. 1995 beendete sie ihren Masterstudiengang und wechselte zum Vocational Training Council, wo sie Produktdesign unterrichtete und später u. a. für den Aufbau eines internationalen Netzwerks mit Organisationen und Schulen im Designbereich verantwortlich war. Vivian Cheng war International Liaison Manager am Hong Kong Design Institute (HKDI), Vorstandsmitglied des Hong Kong Design Centre (HKDC) von 2002 bis 2004 sowie Gremiumsmitglied der World Design Organization (ehemals Icsid) von 2013 bis 2017. Außerdem war sie Mitglied verschiedener Bewertungsgremien der Regierung und vieler Nichtregierungsorganisationen.

01 FIRE
Casting in Shibuichi (metal alloy)
Shibuichi-Guss (Metalllegierung)

02 AIR
Casting in silver
Silberguss

01

02

"A piece of jewellery must have value in emotion and design values, besides being well produced, well crafted and perfect inside out."

„Ein Schmuckstück muss eine Wertigkeit an Emotionen und Designwerten ausdrücken und natürlich auch hervorragend gemacht, gut ausgearbeitet und rundum perfekt sein."

What trends have caught your attention in the fashion industry?
Its currently biggest challenge is making its products sustainable. How to retain the product values and make them last over time are the biggest difficulties the fashion industry is encountering.

What do you appreciate about the evaluation process at Red Dot?
The evaluation process is very fair and the jury is given full autonomy while judging the products. Design is well respected during the course of judging and if the jury should have any doubt at all, no decision will be made until all is cleared.

What experience has had a long-term impact on your career?
The design process is never a linear equation to find a solution, but a multi-directional and there are thousands of ways to reach the destination. As such, it makes me understand that there is always another way to create an answer.

Welche Trends können Sie in der Modebranche ausmachen?
Zurzeit liegt die größte Herausforderung für die Modebranche darin, die Produkte nachhaltig zu gestalten, ihre Produktwerte zu bewahren und sicherzustellen, dass sie sich langfristig bewähren. Das sind die größten Schwierigkeiten, die die Branche überwinden muss.

Was schätzen Sie am Evaluationsprozess bei Red Dot?
Der Evaluationsprozess ist sehr fair und die Jury hat während der Bewertung der Produkte vollkommene Freiheit. Design wird während der Jurierung sehr ernst genommen. Sollte ein Juror irgendeinen Zweifel haben, wird keine Entscheidung getroffen, bis nicht alle einverstanden sind.

Welche Erfahrung prägte Ihre Karriere nachhaltig?
Der Designprozess ist keine lineare Gleichung, mit der man eine Lösung findet, sondern ein Mehrwegprozess. Denn es gibt tausend verschiedene Wege, mit denen man ans Ziel kommen kann. Ich habe gelernt, dass es immer auch einen anderen Weg gibt, um eine Antwort zu finden.

Mårten Claesson
Sweden
Schweden

Mårten Claesson was born in Lidingö, Sweden, in 1970. After studying at the Vasa Technical College in Stockholm in the department of construction engineering and at the Parsons School of Design in New York in the departments of architecture and product design, he graduated in 1994 with an MFA degree from Konstfack, the University College of Arts, Crafts and Design in Stockholm. He is co-founder of the Swedish design partnership Claesson Koivisto Rune, which is multidisciplinary in the classic Scandinavian way and which pursues the practice of both architecture and design. Mårten Claesson is also a writer and lecturer in the field of architecture and design.

Mårten Claesson wurde 1970 in Lidingö, Schweden, geboren. Nachdem er am Vasa Technical College in Stockholm im Fachbereich Bautechnik und an der Parsons School of Design in New York im Fachbereich Architektur und Produktdesign studiert hatte, schloss er 1994 sein Studium mit einem MFA-Abschluss der Konstfack, der Universität für Kunst, Handwerk und Design in Stockholm, ab. Er ist Mitgründer der schwedischen Design-Sozietät „Claesson Koivisto Rune", die im klassisch-skandinavischen Sinne multidisziplinär in Architektur und Design arbeitet. Mårten Claesson ist darüber hinaus als Autor und Dozent tätig.

01
Zander K Hotel in
Bergen, Norway

01

"Good teamwork is flat, without hierarchy. And with a work outcome that is greater than the sum of the individuals' capacity."

„Gute Teamarbeit ist flach, ohne Hierarchie. Und das Ergebnis der Arbeit ist stärker als die Summe der individuellen Fähigkeiten."

What does a product have to offer in order to persuade you of its merits?
The product should be designed in such a way that its use becomes self-explanatory, with sound and ecological materials, in an overall quality. But above all the design has to evoke a sense of beauty.

What will the house of the future look like?
At present, the individual expression is back but many times only as a kind of pick-your-style in the marketplace. I hope to see a more genuine architecture, focusing on the essentials: spatiality and honest materials.

In 2019, Bauhaus celebrates its 100th anniversary. To what extent has this school of design influenced your work?
I read the history of Bauhaus before attending design university. When I had studied for just one year, I travelled to Dessau (and stayed in one of the studio flats) together with my two new friends, today my partners Eero Koivisto and Ola Rune. So, I guess to call Bauhaus formative would be almost an understatement.

Was muss ein Produkt mitbringen, um Sie zu überzeugen?
Das Produkt sollte so gestaltet sein, dass seine Nutzung offensichtlich ist. Es sollte aus soliden, ökologischen Materialien bestehen und rundum von einer hohen Qualität sein. Vor allem aber sollte das Design eine Empfindung von Schönheit hervorrufen.

Wie sieht das Haus der Zukunft aus?
Zurzeit erlebt die individuelle Ausdrucksform ein Comeback, doch häufig nur als eine aus dem Marktangebot gewählte Stilrichtung. Ich hoffe, dass wir mehr authentische Architektur sehen werden, die ihr Augenmerk auf das Wesentliche richtet: Räumlichkeit und ehrliche Materialien.

Das Bauhaus feiert 2019 sein 100-Jahr-Jubiläum. Inwieweit hat die Designschule Ihre Arbeit beeinflusst?
Ich habe die Geschichte des Bauhauses gelesen, bevor ich an der Universität Design studierte. Nach dem ersten Studienjahr reiste ich zusammen mit zwei neuen Freunden nach Dessau (und wohnte mit ihnen in einer der 1-Zimmer-Wohnungen). Heute sind das meine Partner, Eero Koivisto und Ola Rune. Bauhaus als nachhaltig prägend zu bezeichnen, wäre daher wohl untertrieben.

Vincent Créance
France
Frankreich

After graduating from the Ecole Supérieure de Design Industriel, Vincent Créance began his career in 1985 at the Plan Créatif agency where he became design director in 1990 and developed numerous products for high-tech and consumer markets. In 1996, he joined Alcatel as Design Director for all phone activities on an international level. In 1999, he became Vice President Brand in charge of industrial design, user experience and communications for the Mobile Phones BU. In 2004, Vincent Créance advanced to the position of Design and Corporate Communications Director of the Franco-Chinese joint-venture TCL & Alcatel Mobile Phones. In 2006, he became president and CEO of MBD Design, one of the major design agencies in France, providing design solutions in transport design and product design. Then, in 2017 he created the Design Center of the Université Paris-Saclay, bringing together 14 famous French engineering schools and research institutes, with the mission to promote design in this new ecosystem. Créance is a member of the board of directors of APCI (Agency for the Promotion of Industrial Creation), and of ENSCI (National College of Industrial Creation), and a member of the Design Strategic Advisory Board for Paris Region and for Strate College.

Vincent Créance begann seine Laufbahn nach seinem Abschluss an der Ecole Supérieure de Design Industriel 1985 bei der Agentur Plan Créatif. Hier stieg er 1990 zum Design Director auf und entwickelte zahlreiche Produkte für den Hightech- und Verbrauchermarkt. 1996 ging er als Design Director für sämtliche Telefonaktivitäten auf internationaler Ebene zu Alcatel und wurde 1999 Vice President Brand, zuständig für Industriedesign, User Experience sowie die gesamte Kommunikation für den Geschäftsbereich „Mobile Phones". 2004 avancierte Vincent Créance zum Design and Corporate Communications Director des französisch-chinesischen Zusammenschlusses TCL & Alcatel Mobile Phones. 2006 wurde er Präsident und CEO von MBD Design, einer der wichtigsten Designagenturen in Frankreich, und entwickelte Designlösungen für Transport- und Produktdesign. Im Jahr 2017 gründete er das Centre de Design der Université Paris-Saclay und vereinte 14 berühmte französische Ingenieurschulen und Forschungsinstitute in dem Bestreben, Design in diesem neuen Ökosystem zu fördern. Créance ist Vorstandsmitglied von APCI (Agency for the Promotion of Industrial Creation) und von ENSCI (National College of Industrial Design) sowie Mitglied im wissenschaftlichen Designbeirat der Region Paris und des Strate College.

01
Tram for Reims Tramway, France
The Alstom tram shows five different joyful and bubbly colours. This one in yellow has a unique design for the city of Champagne, which subliminally evokes a champagne flute.
Straßenbahn für Reims Tramway, Frankreich
Die Alstom-Straßenbahn gibt es in fünf verschiedenen freudigen und lebendigen Farbtönen. Diese Bahn in Gelb trägt ein einzigartiges Design für die Stadt Champagne, das unterschwellig an eine Champagnerflöte erinnert.

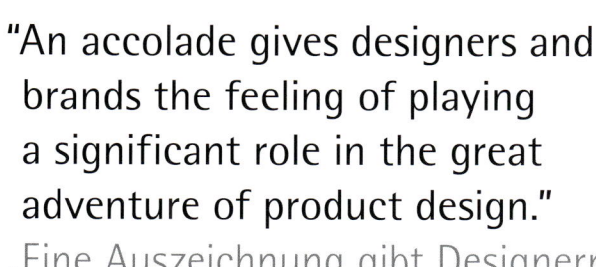

01

"An accolade gives designers and brands the feeling of playing a significant role in the great adventure of product design."

„Eine Auszeichnung gibt Designern und Marken das Gefühl, in dem großen Abenteuer des Produktdesigns eine bedeutende Rolle zu spielen."

What typifies the evaluation process at Red Dot?
The jurors come from a wide mix of continents: more than a globalised international point of view, this offers a multicultural judgement. I also very much appreciate that the independence of us jurors is not just a phrase but a precious asset.

Does a well-designed product make elaborate communication design redundant?
A brand is like an opera bringing together singers, musicians, director, scenographer, etc. – each of them must serve the same dramaturgy in harmony. When all of them resonate together, it becomes magical. Design as one of the most important communication tools must be outstanding to hold its rank in the structure.

What can consumers expect from products today?
To improve our everyday life, while preserving our future. In other words, it mostly means useful, simple and attractive products, creating respectful jobs for people, and preserving our resources.

Was macht den Evaluierungsprozess bei Red Dot aus?
Die Juroren kommen von den verschiedensten Kontinenten. Zusätzlich zu einer globalisierten, internationalen Sichtweise bedeutet das ein multikulturelles Urteil. Ich schätze außerdem ungemein, dass unsere Unabhängigkeit als Juroren nicht nur eine Phrase, sondern ein kostbares Gut ist.

Macht ein gut gestaltetes Produkt ausgeklügeltes Kommunikationsdesign überflüssig?
Eine Marke ist wie eine Oper, die Sänger, Musiker, den Intendanten, den Szenografen usw. zusammenbringt – in Eintracht muss jeder von ihnen der gleichen Dramaturgie dienen. Wenn alle harmonieren, wird es magisch. Design als eines der wichtigsten Kommunikationsinstrumente muss hervorragend sein, um in der Struktur seine Stelle bewahren zu können.

Was darf ein Konsument heutzutage von Produkten erwarten?
Dass sie den Alltag verbessern und gleichzeitig die Zukunft bewahren. Mit anderen Worten meine ich damit hauptsächlich Produkte, die nützlich, einfach und attraktiv sind, wertschätzende Arbeitsplätze für Menschen schaffen und unsere Ressourcen schonen.

Martin Darbyshire
Great Britain
Großbritannien

Martin Darbyshire founded tangerine in 1989 and under his stewardship it has developed into a global strategic design consultancy that creates award-winning solutions for internationally recognised brands such as LG, Samsung, Hyundai, Toyota, Nikon, Huawei, Virgin Australia and Cepsa. Before founding tangerine, he worked for Moggridge Associates and then in San Francisco at ID TWO (now IDEO). A design leader on the international stage, Martin Darbyshire combines his work for tangerine with a worldwide programme of keynote speeches and activities promoting the importance of design. He has served as UKT&I Ambassador for the UK Creative Industries and two terms as a board member of the World Design Organization (formerly Icsid). He was also formerly a visiting professor at Central Saint Martins. Martin Darbyshire is a trustee of the UK Design Council and a juror at the Red Dot Award and Contemporary Good Design. Moreover, the UK Creative Industries Council recognised his global export success awarding him the CIC International Award 2016.

Martin Darbyshire gründete tangerine 1989. Unter seiner Leitung entwickelte sich das Büro zu einem globalen strategischen Designberatungsunternehmen, das preisgekrönte Lösungen für weltweit anerkannte Marken wie LG, Samsung, Hyundai, Toyota, Nikon, Huawei, Virgin Australia und Cepsa entwickelt. Zuvor arbeitete er für Moggridge Associates und dann in San Francisco bei ID TWO (heute IDEO). Als ein weltweit führender Designer verbindet Martin Darbyshire seine Arbeit für tangerine mit einem globalen Programm von Keynote-Referaten und -Aktivitäten, um den bedeutenden Beitrag von Design hervorzuheben. Martin Darbyshire war für das Ministerium für Handel und Investition des Vereinigten Königreichs Botschafter des Bereichs Kreativindustrie und für zwei Amtszeiten Gremiumsmitglied der World Design Organization (ehemals Icsid). Er war zudem Gastdozent an der Central Saint Martins. Martin Darbyshire ist Kurator des UK Design Council sowie Juror des Red Dot Awards und von Contemporary Good Design. Darüber hinaus wurde er für seinen weltweiten Exporterfolg vom UK Creative Industries Council mit dem CIC International Award 2016 ausgezeichnet.

01
Gulf Air cabin
A total re-brand and new customer experience designed for the flag carrier of the Kingdom of Bahrain
Gulf-Air-Kabine
Kompletter Markenrelaunch und ein neues Kundenerlebnis, gestaltet für die Fluggesellschaft des Königreichs Bahrain

01

"Good design needs to be groundbreaking, effective and appealing."

„Gutes Design muss bahnbrechend, wirksam und ansprechend sein."

How do you proceed when evaluating products?
It's always a balance of physically experiencing something on the day and comparing it to one's present experience of comparable things. Listening to the points of view across the judges to reach a unified viewpoint is also an important step.

With what can a designer surprise you?
Achieving something really new and meaningful in a crowded market.

Where do you expect the design industry to be ten years from now?
Better understood and more appreciated.

Which three qualities do you value in a customer?
Open-mindedness. Objectivity. Curiosity.

Wie gehen Sie bei der Bewertung der Produkte vor?
Es ist immer ein Balanceakt zwischen der greifbaren physischen Erfahrung eines Produkts an dem Tag und den Erfahrungen, die man mit vergleichbaren Produkten gesammelt hat. Ein weiterer wichtiger Schritt ist es, auch die Meinungen der anderen Juroren zu erwägen, um dann einen vereinten Standpunkt zu finden.

Womit kann ein Designer Sie überraschen?
Indem er in einem überfüllten Markt etwas wirklich Neues und Sinnhaftes schafft.

Wo sehen Sie die Designbranche in zehn Jahren?
Besser verstanden und mehr geschätzt.

Welche drei Eigenschaften schätzen Sie an einem Kunden?
Aufgeschlossenheit. Objektivität. Neugier.

Katrin de Louw
Germany
Deutschland

Katrin de Louw studied interior design at Detmold School for Architecture and Interior Design. Since 1997, she has been working as an independent interior designer and design manager in the furniture industry and for manufacturers of materials. In 2006, she instigated the "servicepoint A30" trend and event forum in East Westphalia, thereby setting up a nationally leading network of material manufacturers and suppliers to the furniture industry, that discusses innovative trends in furniture and interior design and provides information on topics that are of interest to the industry. Katrin de Louw's agency "TRENDFILTER – Designzukunft für Möbel und Materialien" (future of design of furniture and materials) advises global players from industry, trade and the retail sector including Abet Laminati, BASF, Continental Group, Europlac, Koelnmesse, SURTECO GROUP, Swiss Krono Group, Westag & Getalit and and Windmöller Flooring. She is recognised as the leading trend expert for furniture, interiors and materials in German-speaking countries. She also works as a freelance author and provides comprehensive design consulting services together with her team of interior, product and graphic designers as well as marketing professionals.

Katrin de Louw studierte Innenarchitektur an der Detmolder Schule für Architektur und Innenarchitektur. Seit 1997 ist sie als selbständige Innenarchitektin und Designmanagerin der Möbelindustrie und für Materialhersteller tätig. 2006 initiierte sie mit dem Trend- und Eventforum „servicepoint A30" in Ostwestfalen das bundesweit führende Netzwerk von Materialherstellern und Möbelzulieferern, das innovative Trends im Möbel- und Raumdesign diskutiert und über branchenrelevante Themen informiert. Mit ihrem Büro „TRENDFILTER – Designzukunft für Möbel und Materialien" berät Katrin de Louw Global Player aus Industrie, Handwerk und Handel, darunter Abet Laminati, BASF, Continental Group, Europlac, Koelnmesse, SURTECO GROUP, Swiss Krono Group, Westag & Getalit und Windmöller Flooring. Sie gilt als führende Trendexpertin für Möbel, Inneneinrichtungen und Materialien im deutschsprachigen Raum, ist freie Autorin und bietet zusammen mit ihrem Team aus Innenarchitekten, Produkt- und Grafikdesignern sowie Marketingexperten umfassendes Design Consulting an.

01
New works with new materials in the spotlight: a branch of the Swiss Krono Group on the Kurfürstendamm in Berlin
Neues Arbeiten mit neuen Materialien im Fokus: die Dependance der Swiss Krono Group am Berliner Kurfürstendamm

01

"Materials transport emotions, because a virtual impulse cannot yet replace the experience of touch. Haptics are therefore increasingly important and will, in future, be a critical factor in the success of a product."

„Materialien sind emotionale Träger, denn haptische Erlebnisse sind mit virtuellen Impulsen noch nicht vergleichbar. Die Haptik wird also immer wichtiger und ist zukünftig mitentscheidend für den Erfolg eines Produkts."

What future innovations do you expect to see in materials and surfaces?
Particularly the combination of high-tech with sustainability will, in future, lead to ideas for new materials, their processing and uses. Waste products will also increasingly be seen as a source of raw materials. In general, more and more materials will become part of the cradle-to-cradle cycle.

Could you describe your typical day at TRENDFILTER?
Happy and varied. We have so many different projects related to materials and interior design that nothing is routine. Trend research and design consultation for national and international companies form an important part of that work, but we also carry out special exhibitions, industry events, workshops, presentations and publishing activities.

What material trends are noticeable in the furniture industry?
Aside from sustainable materials, there is a trend to use completely new materials. It is up to industry to explore fresh avenues not only in the choice of materials and their processing, but also in how they can be recycled in the future.

Welche Neuheiten erwarten Sie künftig im Bereich der Materialien und Oberflächen?
Insbesondere die Verknüpfung von Hightech und Nachhaltigkeit wird zukünftig neue Ideen für Materialien, deren Verarbeitung und Einsatzmöglichkeiten auf den Markt bringen. Auch Abfälle werden zunehmend als Rohstoffquelle wahrgenommen und generell gelangen Materialien stärker in den Cradle-to-Cradle-Kreislauf.

Wie sieht Ihr Alltag bei TRENDFILTER aus?
Fröhlich und bunt. Wir haben so viele unterschiedliche Projekte rund um das Thema „Material und Inneneinrichtung", dass nichts zur Gewohnheit wird. Dabei sind Trendrecherche und Design Consulting für nationale und internationale Unternehmen eine wichtige Säule. Aber auch Sonderschauen, Branchenevents, Workshops, Vorträge und Autorentätigkeiten gehören dazu.

Welche Materialtrends gibt es in der Möbelindustrie?
Neben dem Trend zu nachhaltigen Materialien gibt es den zu ganz neuen Materialien. Hier ist es an der Industrie, neue Wege zu gehen – sowohl bei der Materialwahl und deren Verarbeitung als auch dabei, wie Materialien zukünftig recycelt werden können.

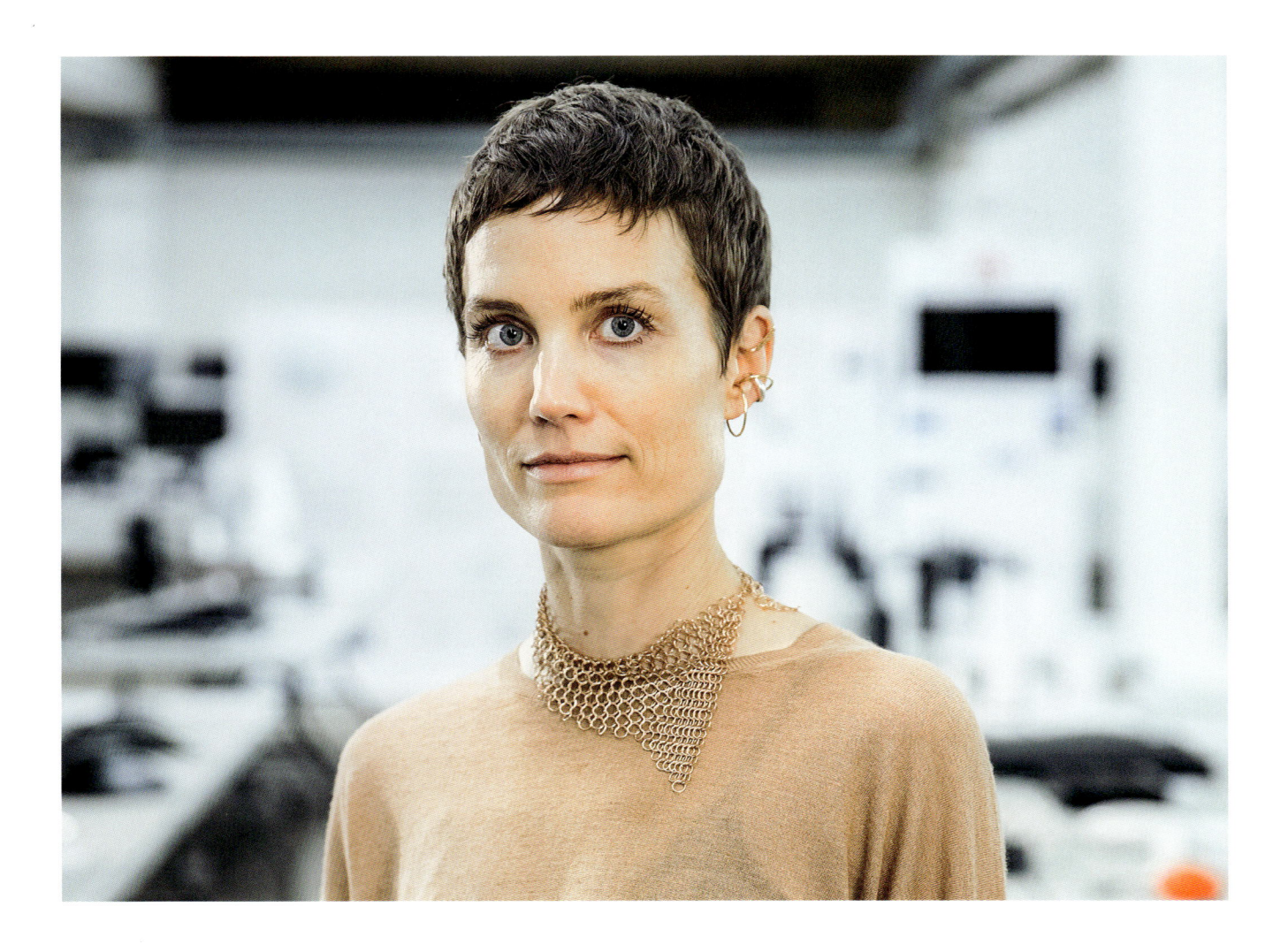

Saskia Diez
Germany
Deutschland

After a stay in Paris in 1996, Saskia Diez began training in Germany as a goldsmith which she completed in 2000 as the local state winner. In 2001, she began studying industrial design, but at the same time worked for Christian Haas, where she designed lighting, china or paper products, as well as for Rosenthal and Konstantin Grcic. She started working under her own name in 2005 and, amongst others, designed trade fair stands for different companies before returning to jewellery work. In 2007/08, she set up her own label. Her aim was to explore the very notion of jewellery from invisible jewellery (perfume) to new ways of wearing jewellery, the use of new materials – also for handbags, sunglasses, nail varnish, etc. Saskia Diez works together with designers, companies, brands and artists including Arita Porzellan, e15, Pan and the Dreams, Uslu Airlines, Netaporter, Bevza, Kismet, Geza Schön, Mirko Borsche, Gym Yilmaz, Hermès, Viu, Stählemühle and the Julia Stoschek Collection.

Nach einem Aufenthalt in Paris 1996 begann Saskia Diez eine Ausbildung zur Goldschmiedin, die sie 2000 als Landessiegerin abschloss. 2001 nahm sie ein Studium in Industriedesign auf und arbeitete parallel bei Christian Haas, wo sie Leuchten, Geschirr oder Papeterie entwarf, bei Rosenthal und Konstantin Grcic. 2005 begann sie, unter eigenem Namen tätig zu werden, und entwarf unter anderem Messeauftritte für diverse Firmen, bevor sie zum Schmuck zurückkehrte und 2007/08 ihr eigenes Label gründete. Ihre Intention ist es, den Schmuckbegriff von unsichtbarem Schmuck (Parfum) über neue Arten, Schmuck zu tragen, bis hin zu neuen Materialien, auch für Taschen, Sonnenbrillen, Nagellack etc., auszuloten. Saskia Diez arbeitet mit Designern, Unternehmen, Marken und Künstlern zusammen, darunter Arita Porzellan, e15, Pan and the Dreams, Uslu Airlines, Netaporter, Bevza, Kismet, Geza Schön, Mirko Borsche, Gym Yilmaz, Hermès, Viu, Stählemühle sowie Julia Stoschek Collection.

01 Gold ME
Sunglasses, chained, 2016
These glasses come without edges or frame and were cut from a single piece of nylon. They were developed in cooperation with the glasses company VIU and made in Italy. The nylon makes them flexible, stable, lightweight and comfortable to wear. All metal parts of the shades have been gold-plated. The glasses themselves are lightly veiled with a gold dust finish.
Sonnenbrille mit Kette, 2016
Diese Brille hat keine Ränder und keinen Rahmen. Sie wurde aus einem einzigen Stück geschnitten, in Zusammenarbeit mit der Brillenfirma VIU entwickelt und in Italien hergestellt. Das Nylon-Material macht sie sehr flexibel, stabil, leicht und bequem zu tragen. Alle Metallteile der Brille sind vergoldet. Die Brillengläser wurden mit einem leichten Schleier aus Goldstaub versehen.

01

"What I find fascinating about jewellery is that it allows me to get very close to people. Jewellery is almost always charged with memories, life stories, love or even sorrow. It can be used to express a good deal, to strengthen oneself, adorn oneself, prepare oneself."

„An Schmuck fasziniert mich, dass ich Menschen damit sehr nahekomme. Schmuck ist fast immer aufgeladen mit Erinnerungen, Lebensgeschichten, Liebe oder auch Trauer. Mit Schmuck kann man sehr viel ausdrücken, sich stärken, schmücken, rüsten."

What jewellery do you personally like wearing?
I mostly wear a kind of "basic kit" for several months without a break: a pair of ear cuffs, rings, bracelets. Things, that I don't even take off when I go to bed. And depending on whether I am going out, how I feel, how decked out I want to be or on the occasion, I may add earrings or a necklace. I particularly like ear jewellery. It frames the face, is always visible, no matter how busy the party may be.

What distinguishes your design "signature"?
I always try to see things with a fresh pair of eyes, to extend the notion of jewellery and to push boundaries. So, it is always exciting to try out new materials or techniques. What is very important to me is that my jewellery must be wearable. It is more low-key than loud, but always distinct. I like working on a single idea, focusing on it and reducing it until I reach a point when the essence emerges.

With what can a designer surprise you?
With quirkiness, consistency, personality, intelligence.

Welchen Schmuck tragen Sie selbst gerne?
Meistens trage ich eine Art Grundausstattung mehrere Monate ununterbrochen: ein Paar Ear Cuffs, Ringe, Armreifen. Dinge, die ich dann auch zum Schlafen nicht mehr ablege. Und je nachdem, ob ich ausgehe, wie ich mich fühle, wie sehr ich geschmückt sein will oder was der Anlass ist, kommen dann noch Ohrringe oder eine Kette dazu. Ohrschmuck mag ich besonders gerne, er rahmt das Gesicht, ist immer sichtbar, egal, wie voll die Party ist.

Was kennzeichnet Ihre gestalterische Handschrift?
Ich versuche immer wieder, Dinge neu zu sehen, den Schmuckbegriff auszuweiten und Grenzen zu verschieben. So bleibt es für mich spannend, neue Materialien oder Techniken auszuprobieren. Sehr wichtig ist mir dabei: Mein Schmuck ist tragbar. Er ist eher leise als laut, aber immer klar. Ich arbeite gerne an einer einzelnen Idee, stelle sie in den Mittelpunkt und reduziere um sie herum so lange, bis sich deren Essenz herauskristallisiert.

Wie kann ein Designer Sie überraschen?
Mit Eigenheit, Schlüssigkeit, Persönlichkeit, Intelligenz.

Stefan Eckstein
Germany
Deutschland

Stefan Eckstein is the founder and CEO of ECKSTEIN DESIGN in Munich. The studio focuses on industrial, interaction and corporate industrial design. Stefan Eckstein studied industrial design at the Muthesius Academy of Fine Arts and Design in Kiel and ergonomics at the Anthropological Institute of the University of Kiel, Germany. Together with his design team, he has received many design awards in national and international competitions. Today, Stefan Eckstein is recognised as a renowned designer for industrial design. In line with his principle, "reduction to the essential leads to a better result", he has developed a user-driven approach to innovation, called "agile design development". It combines innovative concept- and development methods in a structured thought process. Stefan Eckstein has served on numerous international juries, has been a member of the Association of German Industrial Designers (VDID) for 25 years and was elected president of the Association in 2012. Under his management, the VDID CODEX was developed. Today, it serves as a model for the ethical values of the profession of industrial designers.

Stefan Eckstein ist Gründer und Geschäftsführer von ECKSTEIN DESIGN, einem Studio für Industriedesign, Interaction Design und Corporate Industrial Design in München. Er studierte Industrial Design an der Kieler Muthesius-Hochschule und Ergonomie am Anthropologischen Institut der Christian-Albrechts-Universität zu Kiel. Zusammen mit seinem Designteam erhielt er zahlreiche Auszeichnungen. Heute gehört Stefan Eckstein zu den renommierten Designern im Bereich des Industrial Designs. Gemäß seiner Philosophie „Reduzierung auf das Wesentliche führt zu einem besseren Ergebnis" entwickelte er eine nutzerorientierte Innovationsmethode, die „Agile Designentwicklung". In einem besonders strukturierten Denkprozess werden dabei innovative Konzept- und Entwicklungsphasen miteinander verbunden. Stefan Eckstein ist international als Juror tätig, seit über 25 Jahren Mitglied im Verband Deutscher Industrie Designer (VDID) und seit 2012 Präsident des Verbandes. Der VDID CODEX wurde unter seiner Leitung entwickelt und steht heute als Leitbild für die ethischen Werte des Berufsstandes.

01 METRAHIT IM XTRA
A digital multimeter is a technical hand-held measuring instrument used to monitor electrical devices in areas such as industry, communication technology, labs or outdoors. A special new feature is a replaceable battery pack which increases the operational readiness of the equipment through a reserve of charged batteries.
For GOSSEN METRAWATT, 2018.

Ein Digitalmultimeter ist ein technisches Handmessgerät für die Prüfung stromführender Geräte im professionellen Bereich wie Industrie, Kommunikationstechnik und Labor oder im Außenbereich. Besonderes Novum ist der wechselbare Akkupack, der die Einsatzbereitschaft des Geräts durch Vorhalten mehrerer geladener Akkus erhöht.
Für GOSSEN METRAWATT, 2018.

01

"Industrial design refers to the design of products, systems and an interactive product world. It makes sense of things and renders them efficient and understandable."

„Industriedesign ist die Gestaltung von Produkten, Systemen und der interaktiven Produktwelt. Es gibt den Dingen Sinn und macht sie effizient und verständlich."

Why does a back to basics approach lead to a better final result?
The term "reduction" has Latin origins. It comes from the verb "reducere" and means to lead back or bring back. In the context of the question it is today generally used to imply "limit to the essentials". This means the design focuses on usability, function and aesthetics. The clarity gained by this approach deliberately draws the attention of users to the essential features of a product or system and gives them a better designed product.

What is "agile design development"?
Agile design development is a user-oriented innovation method with a pared down structure. It links a structured iterative process to short concept and development phases in a team environment. The customer is always an important element of the design process. In this way, internal and external expertise are brought together.

Warum führt die Reduzierung auf das Wesentliche zu einem besseren Ergebnis?
Der Begriff „Reduktion" hat seinen Ursprung im Lateinischen. Er kommt von „reducere" und bedeutet „zurückführen". Im heutigen Gebrauch ist jedoch eher die Begrenzung auf das Wesentliche als Kernaussage gemeint. Auf diese Weise wird über die Gestaltung mehr Aufmerksamkeit auf Usability, Funktion und Ästhetik gerichtet. Durch die so gewonnene Überschaubarkeit wird der User auf das Wesentliche eines Produkts oder Systems gelenkt und bewusst geführt und bekommt so ein besser gestaltetes Produkt.

Was ist „Agile Designentwicklung"?
Agile Designentwicklung ist eine nutzenorientierte Innovationsmethode mit schlanker Struktur. Sie verbindet einen strukturierten Iterationsprozess mit kurzen Konzept- und Entwicklungsphasen im Team. Der Kunde ist dabei stets ein wichtiger Teil des Designprozesses, und so werden interne und externe Kompetenzen gebündelt.

Robin Edman
Sweden
Schweden

In 2017, Robin Edman founded the Robin Edman Innovation company and has since been working as an independent design consultant. He was previously, from 2001 onwards chief executive of SVID, the Swedish Industrial Design Foundation. After studying industrial design at Rhode Island School of Design, he joined AB Electrolux Global Design in 1981 and parallel to this started his own design consultancy. In 1989, Robin Edman joined Electrolux North America as vice president of Industrial Design for Frigidaire and in 1997, moved back to Stockholm as vice president of Electrolux Global Design. Throughout his entire career he has worked towards promoting a better understanding of users, their needs and the importance of design in society at large. His engagement in design-related activities is reflected in the numerous international jury appointments, speaking engagements, advisory council and board positions he has held. Robin Edman served on the board of the World Design Organization (formerly Icsid) from 2003 to 2007, the last term as treasurer. From 2015 to 2017, he has been the president of BEDA (Bureau of European Design Associations).

Robin Edman gründete 2017 das Unternehmen „Robin Edman Innovation" und ist seitdem selbständig als Designberater tätig. Zuvor war er seit 2001 Firmenchef der SVID, der Swedish Industrial Design Foundation. Nach einem Industriedesign-Studium an der Rhode Island School of Design kam er 1981 zu AB Electrolux Global Design und startete parallel seine eigene Unternehmensberatung für Design. 1989 wechselte Edman zu Electrolux North America als Vizepräsident für Industrial Design für Frigidaire und kehrte 1997 als Vizepräsident von Electrolux Global Design nach Stockholm zurück. Während seiner gesamten Karriere setzte er sich für ein besseres Verständnis für Nutzer und ihre Bedürfnisse ebenso ein wie für die Bedeutung von Design in der Gesellschaft insgesamt. Sein Engagement in designbezogenen Aktivitäten spiegelt sich in zahlreichen Jurierungsberufungen sowie in Rednerverpflichtungen und Positionen in Gremien sowie Beratungsausschüssen wider. Von 2003 bis 2007 war Robin Edman Mitglied im Vorstand der World Design Organization (ehemals Icsid), in der letzten Amtsperiode als Schatzmeister. Von 2015 bis 2017 war er Präsident von BEDA (Bureau of European Design Associations).

01
The company re:innovation specialises in design-driven innovation in supporting management in businesses and the public sector to grow, become more efficient and better serve their customers. Presently working with start-ups to multinationals.

Das Unternehmen re:innovation ist auf gestaltungsorientierte Innovation spezialisiert, die Führungskräfte von Unternehmen und staatlichen Behörden dabei unterstützt, zu expandieren, wirtschaftlicher zu werden und ihre Kunden besser zu versorgen. Aktuell arbeitet re:innovation sowohl mit Start-ups als auch mit multinationalen Konzernen zusammen.

re:innovation

01

"Design as a driver of societal and cultural change has the power to transform human behaviour and can radically change the way we perceive, execute and develop our products, services and systems."

„Design als Träger gesellschaftlichen und kulturellen Wandels hat die Kraft, menschliches Verhalten zu verändern, und verwandelt auch die Art, wie wir unsere Produkte, Dienstleistungen und Systeme sehen, erschaffen und entwickeln."

Please name three features of good design:
Good design consists of the integration of functional, emotional and social utilities. A product, service, process or strategy needs to include all three: the way it works, how do I feel about using it and what do other people say. Not until all three get together in a sustainable way, is it good design.

How important is user friendliness in a product?
Extremely important! Without a focus on the users and the way the products are perceived, used and discarded of, a product will never reach its full potential and achieve success.

To what extent do well designed products make our everyday life easier?
To a very high extent! A product that fulfils human desires and caters to the functional, emotional and societal needs will deliver at its best without hardly being noticed. The best designed products deliver way beyond expectations – in a way as if it was the most natural thing in the world.

Bitte nennen Sie drei Merkmale guten Designs:
Gutes Design besteht aus der Integration funktionaler, emotionaler und sozialer Leistungen. Ein Produkt – wie auch eine Dienstleistung, ein Prozess oder eine Strategie – muss alle drei einbeziehen: wie das Produkt funktioniert, wie ich mich fühle, wenn ich das Produkt verwende, und was andere Leute darüber sagen. Erst wenn alle drei nachhaltig im Einklang sind, ist es gutes Design.

Wie wichtig ist die Benutzerfreundlichkeit eines Produktes?
Extrem wichtig! Wenn Nutzer und die Art, in der Produkte gesehen, verwendet und entsorgt werden, nicht im Mittelpunkt stehen, wird ein Produkt nie sein ganzes Potenzial ausschöpfen und Erfolg erzielen.

Inwieweit erleichtern gut gestaltete Produkte unseren Alltag?
Enorm! Ein Produkt, das die Sehnsüchte von Menschen erfüllt und auf ihre funktionalen, emotionalen und sozialen Bedürfnisse eingeht, leistet sein Bestes, wenn es kaum bemerkt wird. Die am besten gestalteten Produkte liefern weit mehr als erwartet – fast so, als sei es das Natürlichste der Welt.

Prof. Lutz Fügener
Germany
Deutschland

Professor Lutz Fügener began his studies at the Technical University Dresden, where he completed a foundation course in mechanical engineering. He then transferred to the Burg Giebichenstein University of Art and Design in Halle/Saale, Germany, where he obtained a degree in industrial design in 1995. In the same year, he became junior partner of Fisch & Vogel Design in Berlin. Since then, the firm (today called "studioFT") has increasingly specialised in transportation design. Two years after joining the firm, Lutz Fügener became senior partner and co-owner. In 2000, he was appointed as Professor of Transportation Design/3D Design by Pforzheim University and there chairs the prestigious BA degree course in transportation design. Lutz Fügener is also active as an author and journalist for a number of different daily newspapers, weekly magazines and periodicals, as well as blogs in which he writes on mobility-related design topics.

Professor Lutz Fügener absolvierte ein Grundstudium in Maschinenbau an der Technischen Universität Dresden und nahm daraufhin ein Studium für Industrial Design an der Hochschule für Kunst und Design, Burg Giebichenstein, in Halle an der Saale auf. Sein Diplom machte er im Jahr 1995. Im selben Jahr wurde er Juniorpartner von Fisch & Vogel Design in Berlin. Seit dieser Zeit spezialisierte sich das Büro (heute „studioFT") mehr und mehr auf den Bereich „Transportation Design". Zwei Jahre nach seinem Einstieg wurde Lutz Fügener Seniorpartner und gleichberechtigter Mitinhaber des Büros. Im Jahr 2000 wurde er von der Hochschule Pforzheim auf eine Professur für Transportation Design/3D-Gestaltung berufen und ist Leiter des renommierten BA-Studiengangs für Fahrzeugdesign. Lutz Fügener ist als Autor und Journalist für verschiedene Tageszeitungen, Wochenmagazine, Periodika und Blogs tätig und schreibt über Themen des Designs im Zusammenhang mit Mobilität.

01 BEE
An autonomous vehicle for Continental
Ein autonomes Fahrzeug für Continental

01

"In the future, automotive designers must address a wider set of issues and focus more intensely on other areas in the design world where they can intersect such as User Experience Design (UX) and fields dominated by engineering."

„Fahrzeugdesigner müssen sich in Zukunft thematisch breiter aufstellen und Schnittstellen zu designinternen Bereichen wie User-Experience-Design (UX) sowie vom Ingenieurwesen bestimmten Feldern intensivieren."

With what can a car surprise you?
As cars are so complex, there are many different ways. The spectrum ranges from successful, aesthetic proportions to the outstanding design of form and material through to an obvious, functionally convincing overall concept.

What challenges will automotive designers have to deal with in future?
The attempted global commercialisation of cars is currently challenged by the increasingly heterogeneous development of the markets. While the impact of production, distribution and use of cars on the environment has led to tremendous pressure in Europe, the largest international market in the Far East is clamouring for larger vehicles such as SUVs. Another challenge is the automation of cars which is taking fundamentally different approaches in the USA, Europe and China. Predictions for future car purchase behaviour also pose a major challenge, not least for designers. New ways of using vehicles require different cars. Emotional aspects of driving are also under debate and are increasingly shifting to the topic of personal mobility.

Womit kann ein Auto Sie überraschen?
Dank seiner Komplexität auf sehr verschiedene Art und Weise. Das Spektrum reicht von gelungenen, ästhetischen Proportionen über eine hohe Gestaltungsqualität in Form und Material bis zum sinnfälligen, funktional überzeugenden Gesamtkonzept.

Welche Herausforderungen müssen Automobildesigner künftig meistern?
Gegen die möglichst weltweite Vermarktung von Automobilen steht derzeit eine zunehmend heterogene Entwicklung der Märkte. Während hierzulande der Druck in Bezug auf die Auswirkungen von Herstellung, Verteilung und Nutzung auf die Umwelt groß ist, verlangt der größte internationale Markt in Fernost eher voluminöse Automobile im SUV-Format. Dazu kommt die Automatisierung des Fahrens, die in USA, Europa und China grundlegend andere Ansätze zeigt. Auch Prognosen zum Verhalten künftiger Fahrzeugkäufer stellen nicht zuletzt Designer vor große Herausforderungen. Neue Nutzungskonzepte verlangen andere Fahrzeuge. Emotionale Aspekte des Fahrens stehen zur Debatte bzw. verlagern sich zunehmend in Bereiche der individuellen Mobilität.

Hideshi Hamaguchi
USA/Japan

Hideshi Hamaguchi graduated with a Bachelor of Science in chemical engineering from Kyoto University. Starting his career with Panasonic in Japan, Hamaguchi later became director of the New Business Planning Group at Panasonic Electric Works, Ltd. and then executive vice president of Panasonic Electric Works Laboratory of America, Inc. In 1993, he developed Japan's first corporate Intranet and also led the concept development for the first USB flash drive. Hideshi Hamaguchi has over 15 years of experience in defining strategies and decision-making, as well as in concept development for various industries and businesses. As Executive Fellow at Ziba Design and CEO at monogoto, he is today considered a leading mind in creative concept and strategy development on both sides of the Pacific and is involved in almost every project this renowned business consultancy takes on. For clients such as FedEx, Polycom and M-System he has led the development of several award-winning products.

Hideshi Hamaguchi graduierte als Bachelor of Science in Chemical Engineering an der Kyoto University. Seine Karriere begann er bei Panasonic in Japan, wo er später zum Direktor der New Business Planning Group von Panasonic Electric Works, Ltd. und zum Executive Vice President von Panasonic Electric Works Laboratory of America, Inc. aufstieg. 1993 entwickelte er Japans erstes Firmen-Intranet und übernahm zudem die Leitung der Konzeptentwicklung des ersten USB-Laufwerks. Hideshi Hamaguchi verfügt über mehr als 15 Jahre Erfahrung in der Konzeptentwicklung sowie Strategie- und Entscheidungsfindung in unterschiedlichen Industrien und Unternehmen. Als Executive Fellow bei Ziba Design und CEO bei monogoto wird er heute als führender Kopf in der kreativen Konzept- und Strategieentwicklung auf beiden Seiten des Pazifiks angesehen und ist in nahezu jedes Projekt der renommierten Unternehmensberatung involviert. Für Kunden wie FedEx, Polycom und M-System leitete er etliche ausgezeichnete Projekte.

01 Cintiq 24HD
for Wacom, 2012
für Wacom, 2012

01

"Innovation I would define as unprecedented, controversial, yet achievable."
„Ich würde Innovation als etwas noch nie Dagewesenes, Kontroverses, jedoch Erreichbares definieren."

What inspired you to create the USB stick?
Rather than the problem itself, I was inspired by the biases of professionals trying to solve the problem on effective data storage.

What was the most important moment of your career to date?
I feel like I am inspired by every single detail around me, every day. The sensitivity towards these perpetual inspirations took me here where I am today.

With what can a designer surprise you?
With a sense of unease which has been carefully designed for viewers to feel in an unexpected way.

What do you pay particular attention to when evaluating products?
I look for beautiful intentions behind each design.

Was inspirierte Sie zum USB-Stick?
Eher als das Problem an sich inspirierten mich die Vorurteile der Fachleute, die versuchten, das Problem der effektiven Datenspeicherung zu lösen.

Was war der bedeutendste Moment Ihrer bisherigen Karriere?
Ich habe den Eindruck, dass jedes noch so kleine Detail in meiner Umgebung mich inspiriert – jeden Tag. Die Sensibilität für diese ständigen Inspirationen hat mich dorthin gebracht, wo ich heute bin.

Womit kann ein Designer Sie überraschen?
Mit einem Gefühl der Unruhe, das vom Designer bewusst hervorgerufen wird, damit Betrachter das Produkt auf unerwartete Weise erleben.

Worauf achten Sie bei der Bewertung von Produkten?
Ich suche bei jedem Design nach den schönen Absichten, die hinter der Gestaltung stecken.

Prof. Renke He
China

Professor Renke He, born in 1958, studied civil engineering and architecture at Hunan University in China. From 1987 to 1988, he was a visiting scholar at the Industrial Design Department of the Royal Danish Academy of Fine Arts in Copenhagen and, from 1998 to 1999, at North Carolina State University's School of Design. Renke He is dean and professor of the School of Design at Hunan University and is also director of the Chinese Industrial Design Education Committee. Currently, he holds the position of vice chair of the China Industrial Design Association.

Professor Renke He wurde 1958 geboren und studierte an der Hunan University in China Bauingenieurwesen und Architektur. Von 1987 bis 1988 war er als Gastprofessor für Industrial Design an der Royal Danish Academy of Fine Arts in Kopenhagen tätig, und von 1998 bis 1999 hatte er eine Gastprofessur an der School of Design der North Carolina State University inne. Renke He ist Dekan und Professor an der Hunan University, School of Design, sowie Direktor des Chinese Industrial Design Education Committee. Er ist derzeit zudem stellvertretender Vorsitzender der China Industrial Design Association.

01
Scarf design with traditional Dong minority brocade patterns for the New Channel Design & Social Innovation Programme.
Design: School of Design of Hunan University, China.

Schaldesign mit traditionellen Brokatmustern der Dong-Minderheit für das New Channel Design & Social Innovation Programme.
Gestaltung: Designschule der Hunan-Universität, China.

01

"For the young generation of designers global warming and sustainable development will be real challenges and responsibilities."

„Für die jüngere Designergeneration sind der Klimawandel und eine nachhaltige Entwicklung die wirklichen Herausforderungen und Aufgabenbereiche."

What qualities must a well-designed product have?
High functionality, a well-designed human-machine relationship, eco-friendliness and aesthetic attractiveness.

What do you pay particular attention to when evaluating products?
In our digital age, technology becomes more and more complicated in many product designs. Interactive design is the key issue when evaluating products. Good interactive design makes for a good user experience – the most important value of design.

What would the ideal design apprenticeship look like, in your opinion?
Learning by doing is a long tradition in the design profession. Practice makes perfect is still an important rule in design education. In my opinion, the ideal design apprenticeship is a platform or system which encourages students to join design teams in design studios or companies in order to practice real projects under the guidance of skilled designers.

Welche Qualitäten muss ein gut gestaltetes Produkt aufweisen?
Eine hohe Funktionalität, eine gut gestaltete Schnittstelle zwischen Mensch und Maschine, Umweltfreundlichkeit und ästhetischen Reiz.

Worauf legen Sie bei der Bewertung von Produkten besonderen Wert?
In unserem digitalen Zeitalter wird die Technik in vielen Produktdesigns immer komplizierter. Die interaktive Gestaltung ist bei der Bewertung von Produkten der zentrale Punkt. Eine gute interaktive Gestaltung führt zu einem guten Nutzererlebnis – der wichtigste Beitrag von Design.

Wie sähe die ideale Designlehre für Sie aus?
„Learning by Doing" hat in der Designbranche schon lange Tradition. Die wichtige Regel „Übung macht den Meister" gilt in der Designausbildung auch heute noch. Meiner Meinung nach ist die ideale Designlehre eine Plattform oder ein System, das Studenten anregt, Teil eines Designteams in einem Designstudio oder einem Unternehmen zu werden, damit sie wirkliche Projekte unter der Anleitung sachkundiger Designer ausführen können.

Prof.
Carlos Hinrichsen
Chile

Professor Carlos Hinrichsen graduated as an industrial designer in Chile in 1982 and earned his master's degree in engineering in Japan in 1991. Currently, he is Vice-Chancellor of Academic Affairs of INACAP Polytechnic and University, the largest in the country. At present, Chile is in transition from an efficiency-based towards an innovation-based economy where INACAP contributes with actions and initiatives to achieve this important aim for the country, mixing research, innovation, business, design and engineering spheres. From 2007 to 2009, Carlos Hinrichsen was president of the World Design Organization (formerly Icsid) and currently serves as senator within the organisation. In 2010, he was honoured with the distinction "Commander of the Order of the Lion of Finland". From 2014 to 2016, he was dean of the Faculty of Business, Engineering and Digital Arts at the Gabriela Mistral University in Santiago and from 2016 to 2017, he was the Senior Managing Coordinator of Engineering Design in the School of Engineering in the P. Universidad Católica de Chile. For more than three decades he has led interdisciplinary teams to enable corporations, educational and other institutions to gain leadership and competitive positioning.

Professor Carlos Hinrichsen machte 1982 seinen Abschluss in Industriedesign in Chile und erhielt 1991 seinen Master der Ingenieurwissenschaft in Japan. Aktuell ist er Rektor für Studienangelegenheiten an der INACAP Fachhochschule und Universität, der größten im Land. Zurzeit befindet sich Chile im Übergang von einer effizienzbasierten zu einer innovationsbasierten Wirtschaft, in der INACAP mit Maßnahmen und Initiativen dazu beiträgt, dieses wichtige Landesziel durch eine Mischung aus Forschung, Innovation, Handel, Design und Ingenieurwesen zu erreichen. Von 2007 bis 2009 war Carlos Hinrichsen Präsident der World Design Organization (ehemals Icsid) und dient heute als Senator innerhalb der Organisation. 2010 wurde er mit der Auszeichnung „Commander of the Order of the Lion of Finland" geehrt. Von 2014 bis 2016 war er Dekan der Fakultät für Handel, Ingenieurwesen und Digitale Künste an der Gabriela-Mistral-Universität in Santiago und von 2016 bis 2017 leitender geschäftsführender Koordinator für Engineering Design an der P. Universidad Católica de Chile. Seit mehr als drei Jahrzehnten leitet er interdisziplinäre Teams, um Unternehmen, Bildungsinstituten und anderen Organisationen zu helfen, eine marktführende und starke Wettbewerbsposition zu erlangen.

01
The INACAP Polytechnic and University is a learning ecosystem with technology-based study programmes, distributed in 26 campuses throughout Chile. In this scenario, the Fablab INACAP is part of the largest network of rapid prototyping labs in the country, promoting interdisciplinarity and active learning with a focus on innovation, entrepreneurship, applied research and development.

Die Universität INACAP ist ein lernendes Ökosystem mit technologiegestützten Studiengängen, die auf 26 Campus-Standorten in ganz Chile angeboten werden. In dieser Konstellation ist Fablab INACAP Teil des größten Netzwerks an Rapid-Prototyping-Laboratorien im Land und fördert Interdisziplinarität sowie aktives Lernen mit einem Schwerpunkt auf Innovation, Unternehmergeist, angewandter Forschung und Entwicklung.

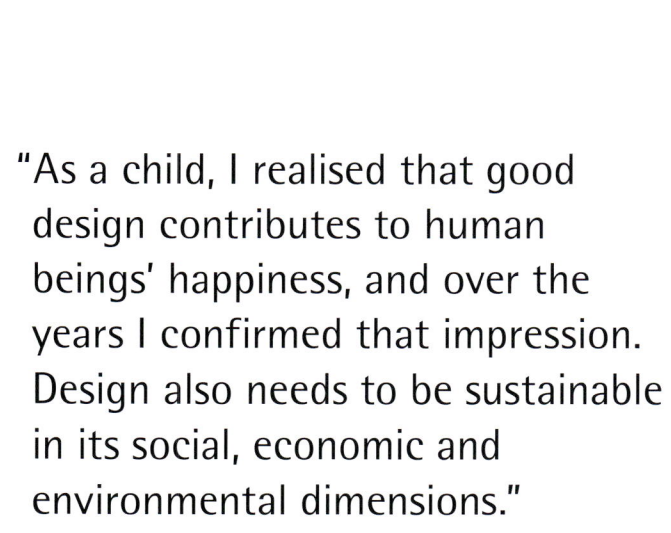

01

"As a child, I realised that good design contributes to human beings' happiness, and over the years I confirmed that impression. Design also needs to be sustainable in its social, economic and environmental dimensions."

„Als Kind habe ich festgestellt, dass gutes Design zum Glücksgefühl der Menschen beitragen kann. Mit den Jahren hat sich dieser Eindruck bestätigt. Design muss allerdings ebenfalls aus sozialer, wirtschaftlicher und ökologischer Sicht nachhaltig sein."

What do you pay particular attention to when evaluating products?
I focus on the unique or particular way of responding to the needs and requirements of end users, as well as how this product responds to what we know today as a circular economy. Besides, I try to recognise the relationship between design and quality, and identify which of the products fit their purpose best.

What trends have you noticed in the design industry?
In a world where new technologies are modelling, transforming the industry, business and society in which we live every day, I see trends as an effort by design solutions at the level of products, services or experiences to capture value in these changing processes, and as a means of adding value for multiple users with new requirements and changing demands, who now expect an almost instantaneous response, due to the changes and speed of response generated by the impact of the digital transformation.

Worauf legen Sie bei der Bewertung von Produkten besonderen Wert?
Ich achte auf die einzigartige oder besondere Art und Weise, wie ein Produkt auf die Bedürfnisse und Anforderungen der Benutzer eingeht, und auf das, was wir heute als Kreislaufwirtschaft bezeichnen. Außerdem versuche ich, das Verhältnis von Gestaltung zu Qualität zu erkennen und zu erfassen, welche Produkte ihren Zweck am besten erfüllen.

Welche Trends können Sie in der Designbranche identifizieren?
In einer Welt, in der neue Technologien die Industrie, den Handel und die Gesellschaft, in der wir jeden Tag leben, formen und umwandeln, sehe ich Trends als einen Versuch an, aus diesen Änderungsprozessen mithilfe von Designlösungen in der Form von Produkten, Dienstleistungen und Erlebnissen Wert zu schöpfen. Sie bieten ebenfalls einen Mehrwert für eine Vielzahl von Nutzern mit neuen Anforderungen und wechselnden Bedürfnissen, die aufgrund der durch die digitale Transformation verursachten Veränderungen und Reaktionsgeschwindigkeit eine fast sofortige Reaktion erwarten.

Simon Husslein
Germany/Switzerland
Deutschland/Schweiz

Simon Husslein was born in Werneck, Germany, in 1976 and studied industrial design from 1995 to 2000 at Darmstadt University of Applied Sciences. From 2000 to 2005, he worked closely with his mentor and friend Hannes Wettstein at Wettstein's studio in Zurich. From 2005 to 2007, he completed a master's degree in Design Products at the London Royal College of Art. Subsequently, he led a number of projects in London and Shanghai and lectured at Shanghai's Tongji University. Between 2008 and 2014, he put his mark on a large number of projects at the Studio Hannes Wettstein in Zurich where he was creative director and member of the executive committee. In 2015, he founded the Atelier Simon Husslein. Simon Husslein develops products, furniture, installations and spatial design. Since 2017, he has been professor of interior architecture at Geneva School of Art and Design, HEAD – Geneva, Switzerland.

Simon Husslein, geboren 1976 in Werneck, Deutschland, studierte von 1995 bis 2000 Industrial Design an der Fachhochschule Darmstadt. Von 2000 bis 2005 arbeitete er eng mit seinem Mentor und Freund Hannes Wettstein in dessen Zürcher Studio zusammen. Von 2005 bis 2007 absolvierte er ein Masterstudium in Design Products am Royal College of Art in London. Danach betreute er eigene Projekte in London und Shanghai und unterrichtete an der Tongji University in Shanghai. Zwischen 2008 und 2014 prägte er als Creative Director und Mitglied der Geschäftsleitung eine Vielzahl der Projekte des Studios Hannes Wettstein in Zürich. 2015 gründete er das Atelier Simon Husslein. Simon Husslein entwickelt Produkte, Möbel, Installationen und Raumgestaltungen. Seit 2017 ist er Professor für Interior Architecture an der Geneva School of Art and Design, HEAD – Genf, Schweiz.

01 Minimatik
Wristwatch for NOMOS Glashütte/SA Roland Schwertner KG
Armbanduhr für NOMOS Glashütte/SA Roland Schwertner KG

01

"If good design is the result of a meticulous design process, then it stands a much better chance of maintaining its position in the market for a very long time."

„Gutes Design als Resultat eines sorgfältigen Designprozesses erhöht die Chance signifikant, dass sich ein Produkt überdurchschnittlich lange in seinem Marktumfeld behaupten kann."

What do you pay particular attention to when evaluating products?
A watch has many different features that must add up and make a whole. In the case of a new model, one of the questions that arises concerns the authenticity of the concept. In general, I pay a good deal of attention to the use of detailing. How has the transition between the strap and the body of the watch been managed? Does the design of the casing harmonise with the surface treatment? Do the various elements have a common design typology? Only when the design is consistent and well implemented in all aspects is it worth an award.

What distinguishes your design "signature"?
Precision, emotion and the pursuit of the archetype.

What matters when it comes to teamwork?
If the mix of personalities is right, the team can achieve great things.

Worauf legen Sie bei der Bewertung von Produkten besonderen Wert?
Bei einer Uhr gibt es sehr viele unterschiedliche Aspekte, die als Ganzes stimmen müssen. Bei einer Neukreation stellt sich beispielsweise die Frage der Authentizität des Entwurfs. Generell achte ich sehr auf den Umgang mit Details: Wie verläuft der Übergang zwischen Bandanschluss und Gehäuse? Wurde die Gehäusegestaltung mit der Veredelungstechnologie der Oberflächen schlüssig abgestimmt? Haben die verschiedenen Elemente eine gemeinsame Gestaltungstypologie? Nur wenn das Design auf allen Ebenen konsequent und gut umgesetzt wurde, verdient es eine Auszeichnung.

Was kennzeichnet Ihre gestalterische Handschrift?
Präzision, Emotionalität und die Suche nach dem Archetypus.

Worauf kommt es bei Teamarbeit an?
Wenn die Mischung aus Persönlichkeiten stimmt, kann im Team Großes erreicht werden.

Qiong Er Jiang
China

Qiong Er Jiang, founder of lifestyle brand SHANG XIA, is an internationally renowned designer. After many years studying in Europe, she brings a cosmopolitan approach and multi-cultural experience to her designs. As artistic director and CEO of SHANG XIA, she combines traditional crafts with contemporary design. Her works received wide acclaim and distinguished design awards at national and international level, being collected by world-class museums like British Museum, Musée Guimet and Musée des Arts Décoratifs. In 2011, Forbes named Qiong Er Jiang as one of the 25 most influential Chinese in "Global Fashion and Lifestyle". Furthermore, she was honoured several times in recognition of her contribution to the cultural exchange between China and France.

Qiong Er Jiang, Gründerin der Lifestyle-Marke SHANG XIA, ist eine international renommierte Designerin. Nachdem sie mehrere Jahre in Europa studiert hat, verfolgt sie bei ihren Entwürfen einen weltoffenen und multikulturellen Ansatz. Als Artistic Director und CEO von SHANG XIA kombiniert sie traditionelles Handwerk mit zeitgenössischem Design. Ihre Arbeiten haben sowohl auf nationaler als auch auf internationaler Ebene große Anerkennung und angesehene Auszeichnungen erhalten. Außerdem werden sie in Museen von Weltrang wie dem British Museum, dem Musée Guimet und dem Musée des Arts Décoratifs gesammelt. 2011 zählte Forbes Qiong Er Jiang zu den 25 einflussreichsten Chinesen im Bereich „Global Fashion und Lifestyle". Darüber hinaus wurde sie mehrere Male für ihren Beitrag zum kulturellen Austausch zwischen China und Frankreich geehrt.

01 GARDEN
Round Box in red Bo Luo lacquer with gold inlay. The red and gold lidded box is inspired by the traditional Chinese Cuan Pan vessel sets, signifying happiness and completeness.

Runde Schachtel mit roter Bo-Luo-Lackarbeit und goldenen Intarsien. Die Schachtel mit dem rot-goldenen Deckel wurde von den traditionellen chinesischen Cuan-Pan-Gefäße-Sets inspiriert und symbolisiert Glück und Vollkommenheit.

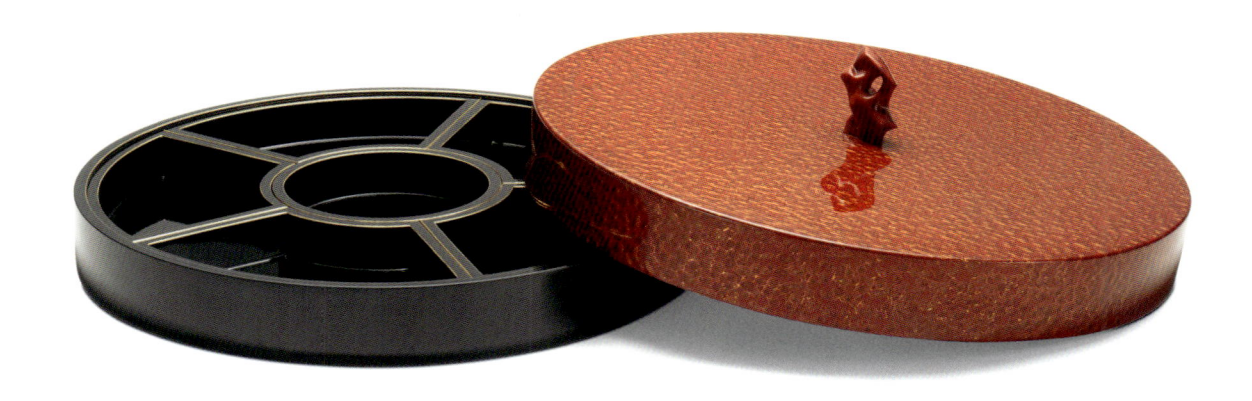

01

"My experience in Europe offered me the chance to see my own culture from another angle. The opportunity to twist my views in this unique way offered a positive influence in the creations of my designs."

„Meine Erfahrungen in Europa haben mir erlaubt, meine eigene Kultur aus einer anderen Perspektive zu sehen. Diese Gelegenheit, meine Sichtweise auf so eine einzigartige Weise umzustellen, hat sich positiv auf mein gestalterisches Schaffen ausgewirkt."

What does a product have to offer in order to surprise you?
Emotion, emotion and emotion. Of course, the emotion can come from the material of the product, craftsmanship, design concept, or cultural background story. And it may even come from all of these things combined!

What distinguishes your design "signature"?
My design encapsulates an encounter, or a dialogue, between: tradition and modernity, craft and technology, functionality and emotion, past and future. There is true emotion put into and captured through my designs.

Why is the cultural exchange between different nations valuable?
From my understanding, though the nations are different, the culture is fundamentally the same: it's about love and beauty. The cultural exchange can be conveyed through expression and style to portray "beauty", while feeling and understanding this allows for deeper "emotion". The diversity of these translations enriches our lives and makes it meaningful.

Was muss ein Produkt mitbringen, um Sie zu überzeugen?
Emotion, Emotion und noch mal Emotion! Selbstverständlich kann diese Emotion von dem Material des Produkts, seiner Handwerkskunst, dem Gestaltungskonzept oder dem kulturellen Hintergrund ausgehen. Es kann sogar eine Verschmelzung aller dieser Quellen sein.

Was kennzeichnet Ihre gestalterische Handschrift?
Mein Design bringt eine Begegnung, einen Dialog zwischen Tradition und Moderne, Handwerk und Technik, Funktionalität und Gefühl, Vergangenheit und Zukunft auf den Punkt. In meinen Gestaltungen steckt ehrliche Emotion.

Warum ist der kulturelle Austausch zwischen verschiedenen Nationen wichtig?
Nach meiner Auffassung unterscheiden sich Nationen zwar, doch ist die Kultur prinzipiell die gleiche: Es geht immer um Liebe und Schönheit. Der kulturelle Austausch kann durch eine Stilrichtung und eine Ausdrucksform, die „Schönheit" darstellt, vermittelt werden. Wenn man das versteht und spürt, ist das „emotionale Erlebnis" stärker. Die Vielfalt dieser Interpretationen bereichert unser Leben und gibt ihm Bedeutung.

Prof. Cheng-Neng Kuan
Taiwan

In 1980, Professor Cheng-Neng Kuan earned a master's degree in Industrial Design (MID) from the Pratt Institute in New York. He is currently a chair professor and served as the vice president of Shih-Chien University, Taipei, Taiwan, from 2008 to 2017. With the aim of developing a more advanced design curriculum in Taiwan, he founded the Department of Industrial Design, in 1992. He served as department chair until 1999. Moreover, Cheng-Neng Kuan founded the School of Design in 1997 and had served as the dean from 1997 to 2004 and as the founding director of the Graduate Institute of Industrial Design from 1998 to 2007. He had also held the position of the 16th chairman of the board of China Industrial Designers Association (CIDA), Taiwan. His fields of expertise include design strategy and management as well as design theory and creation. Having published various books on design and over 180 research papers and articles, he is an active member of design juries in his home country and internationally. He is a consultant to major enterprises on product development and design strategy.

1980 erwarb Professor Cheng-Neng Kuan einen Masterabschluss in Industriedesign (MID) am Pratt Institute in New York. Derzeit ist er Lehrstuhl-Professor und war von 2008 bis 2017 Vizepräsident der Shih-Chien University in Taipeh, Taiwan. 1992 gründete er mit dem Ziel, einen erweiterten Designlehrplan zu entwickeln, das Department of Industrial Design in Taiwan. Bis 1999 war Cheng-Neng Kuan Vorsitzender des Instituts. Darüber hinaus gründete er 1997 die School of Design, deren Dekan er von 1997 bis 2004 war. Von 1998 bis 2007 war er Gründungsdirektor des Graduate Institute of Industrial Design. Zudem war er der 16. Vorstandsvorsitzende der China Industrial Designers Association (CIDA) in Taiwan. Seine Fachgebiete umfassen Designstrategie, -management, -theorie und -kreation. Neben der Veröffentlichung verschiedener Bücher über Design und von mehr als 180 Forschungsarbeiten und Artikeln ist er aktives Mitglied von Designjurys in seiner Heimat sowie auf internationaler Ebene. Zudem ist er als Berater für Großunternehmen im Bereich Produktentwicklung und Designstrategie tätig.

01 Plier
A piece of furniture for an open space, designed by Lin-Huei Hwang, can be transformed into a screen panel or bar table. This project was selected as a winner of Taiwan's Young Pin Design Award 2017.
Ein Möbelstück für ein Freigelände, von Lin-Huei Hwang gestaltet. Es kann als eine Leinwand oder als ein Bartisch verwendet werden. Dieses Projekt wurde zu einem Gewinner des Young Pin Design Award 2017 in Taiwan gekürt.

01

"Good design needs to bring inspiring emotional satisfaction right to the target users."

„Gutes Design muss seiner Zielgruppe direkte, inspirierende und emotionale Befriedigung bieten."

With what can a product surprise you?
A composition of concept and language that seems unfamiliar to me yet opens up a new design horizon.

How do you proceed when evaluating products?
By seeing and thinking if the first impression offers design reasons that convince me of its excellence.

What message would you like to give your students for their future career?
Keep exploring the messages of lifestyle changes, and use your design to give it a specific meaning.

What challenges will designers have to meet in future?
Facing unprecedented ecological crisis, we designers have to rethink the spirit of brands with regard to human welfare.

Womit kann ein Produkt Sie überraschen?
Mit einer Kombination aus Konzept und Formensprache, die mir unbekannt ist und mir einen neuen Designhorizont eröffnet.

Wie gehen Sie bei der Bewertung der Produkte vor?
Indem ich sehe und überlege, ob der erste Eindruck Gründe für das Design liefert, die mich von seiner Vortrefflichkeit überzeugen.

Welche Botschaft möchten Sie Ihren Studenten mit auf den Weg geben?
Weiterhin die Botschaften aufzuspüren, die aus den Veränderungen im Lebensstil hervorgehen, und ihren Gestaltungskonzepten eine bestimmte Bedeutung zu verleihen.

Welchen Herausforderungen müssen sich Designer künftig stellen?
In Anbetracht der beispiellosen ökologischen Krise müssen wir Designer den Sinn von Marken in Bezug auf das Gemeinwohl überdenken.

Steve Leung
Hong Kong
Hongkong

Born and bred in Hong Kong, Steve Leung is a leading international architect, interior and product designer. His works reflect the projects' unique characters with his contemporary touch, taking inspirations from Asian culture and arts. Honoured as the Winner of 19th Andrew Martin International Interior Designer of the Year Award, his projects have been credited with more than 130 international corporate and design awards. He established his own architectural and urban planning consultancy in 1987, later restructured into Steve Leung Architects Ltd. (SLA) and Steve Leung Designers Ltd. (SLD). In 2018, SLD Group was listed on the Main Board of the Hong Kong Stock Exchange. Headquartered in Hong Kong with five branches in Beijing, Shanghai, Guangzhou, Shenzhen and Tianjin and with 600 dedicated designers and professionals, the Group is one of the largest interior design practices in Asia. Steve Leung is enthusiastically engaged in the design industry as the current President of the International Federation of Interior Architects/Designers (IFI) and as one of the founders of "C-Foundation", committed in actively promoting the development of the design profession in Asia and worldwide.

Steve Leung, in Hongkong geboren und aufgewachsen, ist ein führender internationaler Architekt, Innenarchitekt und Produktdesigner. Seine Arbeit spiegelt die einzigartigen Eigenschaften der Projekte wider und gibt ihnen einen zeitgemäßen Schliff, der von fernöstlicher Kultur und Kunst inspiriert ist. Steve Leung ist Gewinner des 19. Andrew Martin International Interior of the Year Award und wurde fernerhin mit mehr als 130 weiteren internationalen Unternehmens- und Designauszeichnungen gekürt. Er gründete 1987 seine eigene Beratungsagentur für Architektur und Städtebau und strukturierte sie später in Steve Leung Architects Ltd. (SLA) und Steve Leung Designers Ltd. (SLD) um. 2018 wurde die SLD Group im Hauptsegment an der Hongkonger Börse notiert. Mit Hauptsitz in Hongkong und fünf Niederlassungen in Beijing, Shanghai, Guangzhou, Shenzhen und Tianjin sowie 600 engagierten Designern und Fachleuten ist die Gruppe eines der größten Innenarchitekturbüros in Asien. Steve Leung engagiert sich mit Begeisterung in der Designindustrie – als der derzeitige Präsident der International Federation of Interior Architects/Designers (IFI) und als einer der Gründer der „C-Foundation", die aktiv zur Förderung des Designberufs in Asien und weltweit beiträgt.

01 Fusital – H377 Series SL Duemilasedici
The door handle collection in collaboration with Fusital is based on a contemporary minimalist design inspired by the bold geometry of Chinese traditional brass hardware and antique door lockset.

Die in Zusammenarbeit mit Fusital produzierte Türgriff-Kollektion basiert auf einem zeitgemäßen, minimalistischen Gestaltungskonzept, das seine Inspiration in der auffallenden Geometrie traditioneller chinesischer Messingwaren und antiker Türschlösser findet.

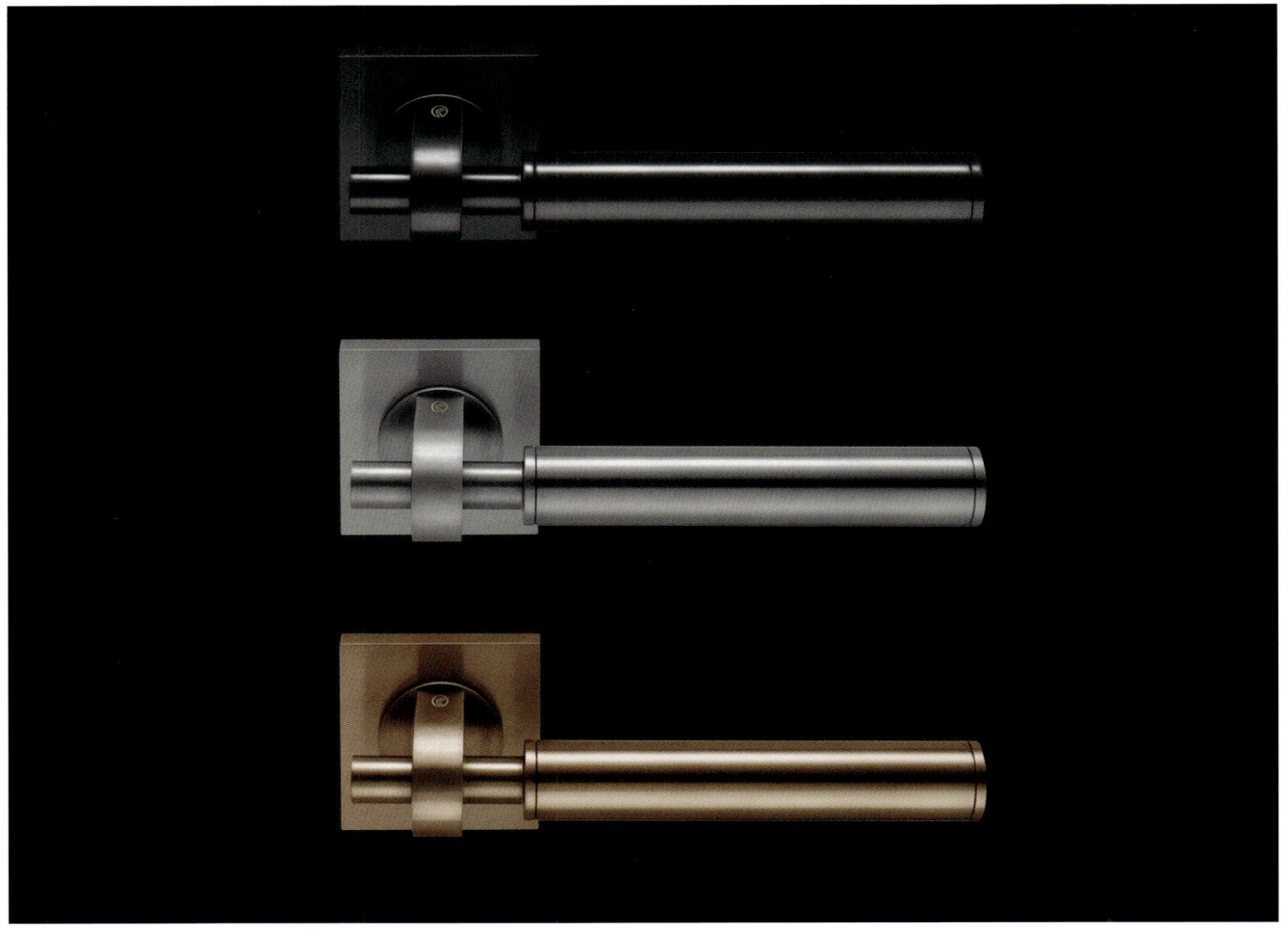

01

"I'm happy that by being a part of this jury, the passion and joy of creation can be passed on to many more designers, globally."

„Ich freue mich, dass ich als Mitglied der Jury die Gelegenheit habe, die Leidenschaft und die Freude am Gestalten an viele weitere Designer zu vermitteln, und das international."

What was the deciding moment of your career?
It was establishing my own studio at 30 and restructuring it to do both architecture and interior design in 1997. I started developing business in Mainland China three years after. It was a life changing moment and I'm thankful that it created interesting and rewarding chapters in the years after.

Are there noticeable differences between customers with different backgrounds?
Clients have different needs and preferences and are influenced by distinctive cultural and lifestyle features. But eventually design is about life, and life is about people, living and experience. In the end, original ideas that respond to people's fundamental needs functionally and more so psychologically will be the most sought-after designs, inspiring a positive change in daily life.

Was war der entscheidende Moment Ihrer Karriere?
Es war die Gründung meines eigenen Studios im Alter von 30 Jahren und dann in 1997 die Umstellung auf sowohl Architektur als auch Innenarchitektur. Drei Jahre später habe ich damit begonnen, das Geschäft in Festlandchina aufzubauen. Es war der Punkt, an dem sich mein Leben verändert hat, und ich bin dankbar dafür, dass es mir in den Jahren danach noch interessante und bereichernde Kapitel beschert hat.

Erkennen Sie Unterschiede zwischen Kunden verschiedener Herkunft?
Kunden haben unterschiedliche Bedürfnisse und Vorlieben und werden von ihren verschiedenen kulturellen Eigenheiten und Lebensformen beeinflusst. Letztlich befasst sich Design aber mit dem Leben und im Leben geht es um Menschen – darum, wie sie leben, und um die Erlebnisse, die sie haben. Am Ende werden originelle Ideen, die funktional und besonders psychologisch auf die grundlegenden Bedürfnisse von Menschen eingehen, die begehrtesten Gestaltungen sein und einen positiven Wandel im Alltag bewirken.

Dr. Thomas Lockwood
USA

Dr. Thomas Lockwood is co-author of the books "Innovation by Design" (2017) and "The Handbook of Design Management" (2011) as well as author of "Design Thinking" (2009), "Corporate Creativity" (2009), and "Building Design Strategy" (2008). He received a PhD, an MPhil and an MBA in Design Management after a BA in Business and Design. Thomas Lockwood is recognised as a thought leader at integrating design and innovation practice into business, and building great design and UX organisations. In 2011, he formed Lockwood Resource, an international consulting and recruiting firm specialising in design and innovation leadership. Previously, he was president of the Design Management Institute (DMI) from 2005 to 2011, a visiting professor at Pratt University, and from 1996 to 2005 a corporate design director at Sun Microsystems and StorageTek, among others. He created high-tech skiwear for the US Olympic Nordic Ski Team, corporate design programmes for Fortune 500 organisations and internationally led conferences and workshops.

Dr. Thomas Lockwood ist Co-Autor der Bücher „Innovation by Design" (2017) und „The Handbook of Design Management" (2011) sowie Autor von „Design Thinking" (2009), „Corporate Creativity" (2009) und „Building Design Strategy" (2008). Nach einem Bachelorabschluss in Unternehmensdesign und Gestaltung machte er seinen MPhil und MBA und promovierte in Designmanagement. Thomas Lockwood gilt als ein Vordenker für die Integration von Design und Innovation in der Wirtschaft und für den Aufbau starker Design- und UX-Unternehmen. 2011 gründete er Lockwood Resource, eine internationale Beratungs- und Personalvermittlungsfirma, die sich auf Design und Innovationsführerschaft spezialisiert hat. Zuvor war er u. a. Präsident des Design Management Institute (DMI) von 2005 bis 2011, Gastprofessor an der Pratt University sowie von 1996 bis 2005 Corporate Design Director bei Sun Microsystems und StorageTek. Er entwickelte Hightech-Skibekleidung für das Olympic Nordic Ski Team der USA sowie Corporate-Design-Programme für Fortune-500-Unternehmen und leitete internationale Kongresse und Workshops.

01 Innovation by Design
"Innovation by Design" explores the integration of innovation, design and corporate culture, and presents the ten ways leaders can develop cultures of innovation.

„Innovation by Design" erforscht die Integration von Innovation, Design und Unternehmenskultur und präsentiert die zehn Wege, mit denen Führungskräfte eine Kultur der Innovation aufbauen können.

02 Design Thinking
"DesignThinking" explores points of view, techniques, methods, and hands-on case studies from international thought leaders.

„DesignThinking" untersucht die Blickweise, Kniffe, Methoden und praktischen Fallstudien internationaler Vordenker.

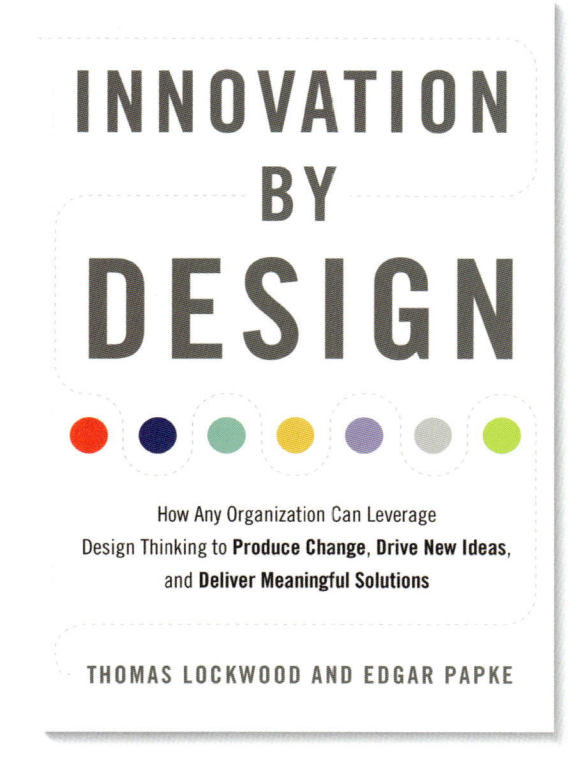

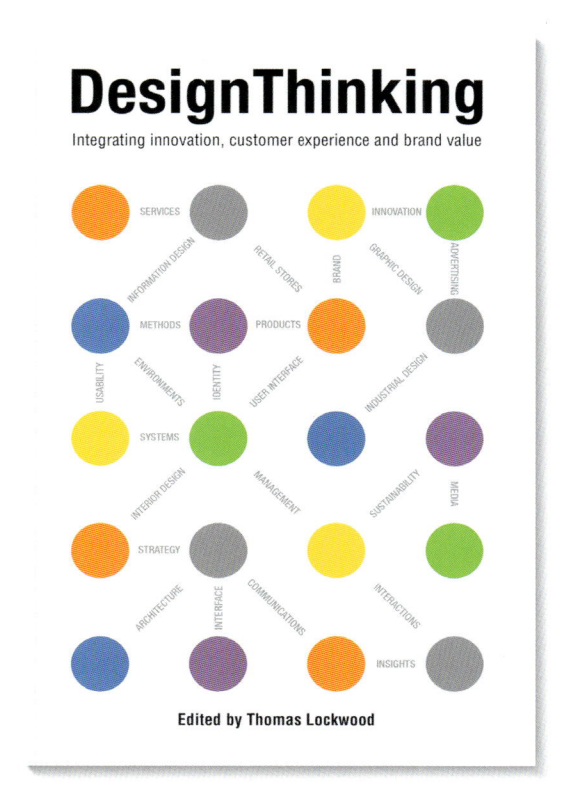

01

02

"Good design solves problems perfectly."

„Gutes Design löst Probleme perfekt."

In your opinion, what would the world look like without innovation?
It would probably look more like the animal kingdom. It is impossible to know what animals think, but as an outsider, I would imagine them to be more content, more peaceful and more observant. Innovation is what advances our societies.

How can a company become an innovation leader in its sector?
By reaching beyond technology innovation and embracing a strategy of open innovation. This requires a shift in focus from sales and what a company can make to a focus on what people actually need. The path means embracing design thinking and human centred design, in order to solve the right problems.

What development could significantly improve our world?
An app to create world peace! Truly, if we all could all just accept one another as we are, rather than imposing our doctrines and individual agendas upon others.

Wie sähe eine Welt ohne Innovation Ihrer Meinung nach aus?
Sie würde wahrscheinlich mehr dem Tierreich ähneln. Es ist unmöglich zu wissen, was Tiere denken, doch als Außenstehender stelle ich mir vor, dass sie zufriedener, ruhiger und aufmerksamer sind. Innovation ist der Motor, der unsere Gesellschaften vorantreibt.

Wie wird man als Unternehmen zum Innovationsführer seiner Branche?
Indem man mehr als nur technische Innovation erzielt und sich eine Strategie der offenen Innovation zu eigen macht. Das erfordert eine Verlagerung des Schwerpunktes weg vom Vertrieb und dem, was ein Unternehmen herstellen kann, hin zu dem, was Menschen wirklich brauchen. Das erreicht man, wenn man auf Designdenken und eine menschenorientierte Gestaltung umstellt, um so die richtigen Probleme zu lösen.

Welche Entwicklung könnte unsere Welt maßgeblich verbessern?
Eine App, die Weltfrieden schafft! Ehrlich, wenn wir einander nur alle akzeptieren könnten, so wie wir sind, anstatt einander unsere Dogmen und persönlichen Einstellungen aufzudrücken.

Wolfgang K. Meyer-Hayoz
Switzerland
Schweiz

Wolfgang K. Meyer-Hayoz studied mechanical engineering, visual communication and industrial design and graduated from the Stuttgart State Academy of Art and Design. After a number of years as an in-house designer in industry, he founded the Meyer-Hayoz Design Engineering Group in 1985. The multiple award-winning company works in the fields of medical engineering, biotechnology, life sciences as well as on the design of machines, robots and other appliances. The company also advises start-ups as well as multinationals in the areas of design strategy, industrial design, user-interface design, temporary architecture and communication design. From 1987 to 1993, Wolfgang K. Meyer-Hayoz was honorary president of the Swiss Design Association (SDA). He serves as jury member on international design panels and is a member of the Association of German Industrial Designers (VDID) and the Swiss Management Society (SMG). In addition, he is a member of the group of supporters for the Institute of Marketing at the University of St. Gallen and chairs change management and turnaround projects in the field of design strategy.

Wolfgang K. Meyer-Hayoz absolvierte Studien in Maschinenbau, Visueller Kommunikation sowie Industrial Design mit Abschluss an der Staatlichen Akademie der Bildenden Künste in Stuttgart. Nach Jahren als Inhouse-Designer in der Industrie gründete er 1985 die Meyer-Hayoz Design Engineering Group. Das vielfach international ausgezeichnete Unternehmen ist in Medizintechnik, Biotechnologie, Life Sciences sowie Maschinen-, Robotik- und Gerätedesign tätig und berät Start-up-Unternehmen ebenso wie Weltmarktführer in den Kompetenzbereichen Design Strategy, Industrial Design, User Interface Design, Temporary Architecture und Communication Design. Von 1987 bis 1993 führte Wolfgang K. Meyer-Hayoz ehrenamtlich als Präsident die Swiss Design Association (SDA). Er engagiert sich als Juror in internationalen Designgremien, ist Mitglied im Verband Deutscher Industrie Designer (VDID) und der Schweizerischen Management Gesellschaft (SMG) sowie aktives Mitglied im Förderkreis des Instituts für Marketing der Universität St. Gallen und moderiert Change-Management- und Turnaround-Projekte im designstrategischen Bereich.

01 Multitron
Incubation shaker for the reliable and easy cultivation of microorganisms and cell cultures, for Infors AG, Switzerland
Inkubationsschüttler für die zuverlässige und komfortable Kultivierung von Mikroorganismen und Zellkulturen, für Infors AG, Schweiz

02 ICM 710/PCM 710
Range of compact control units for burglar alarms, for Securiton AG, Switzerland
Kompakte Bediengeräteserie für Einbruchmeldeanlagen, für Securiton AG, Schweiz

01

02

"It takes time, conviction and mutual esteem to develop a strategic direction for companies through design – our customers need to understand that design services cannot be produced quickly like in a pressure cooker."

„Die strategische Ausrichtung von Unternehmen durch gestalterische Arbeit benötigt Zeit, Überzeugung und stets die gegenseitige Wertschätzung – unsere Kunden müssen also verstehen, dass Designleistungen nicht wie aus einem Schnellkochtopf zu haben sind."

How do you keep reinventing yourself as a designer?
I have always been an inquisitive person. New materials, technologies, possibilities for the use of things and their application to new business models have always fascinated and motivated me to think a step further in the spirit of anticipation.

Where do you find the energy for your impressive commitment to your profession?
I am convinced that designers have a very fine and pronounced sense of intuition so that they notice changes and upheavals in society early on. The awareness and recognition of these changes gives us designers the unique opportunity to develop new solutions, first conceptually and later physically. For me, this process is a "source of energy".

What makes your work so exciting?
Every job is new and different. Every customer has their own specific requests and every company champions new values and value propositions in its own way. It never gets boring!

Wie erfinden Sie sich als Designer immer wieder neu?
Ich war schon immer ein sehr neugieriger Mensch. Neue Materialien, Technologien, Nutzungsmöglichkeiten und deren Anwendung für neue Geschäftsmodelle haben mich immer fasziniert und angespornt, noch einen Schritt weiter zu denken, im Sinne der Antizipation.

Woher schöpfen Sie die Energie für Ihr großes berufliches Engagement?
Ich bin überzeugt, dass Gestalter ein sehr feines und ausgeprägtes Gespür haben und daher Veränderungen und Umbrüche in unserer Gesellschaft früh wahrnehmen. Das Bewusstsein und Erkennen dieser Veränderungen gibt uns als Gestaltern gleichzeitig die einzigartige Chance, hieraus neue Lösungsansätze erst gedanklich und dann physisch zu entwickeln. Diesen Prozess empfinde ich als permanenten „Energiespender".

Was macht Ihren Beruf so spannend?
Jede Aufgabe ist neu und anders. Jeder Kunde hat seine spezifischen Wünsche und jedes Unternehmen vertritt auf seine Weise immer wieder neue Werte und Wertvorstellungen. Langeweile kommt hierdurch nie auf!

Prof. Jure Miklavc
Slovenia
Slowenien

Professor Jure Miklavc graduated in industrial design from the Academy of Fine Arts in Ljubljana, Slovenia, and has nearly 20 years of experience in the field of design. He started his career working as a freelance designer, before founding his own design consultancy, Studio Miklavc. Studio Miklavc works in the fields of product design, visual communications and brand development and is a consultancy for a variety of clients from the industries of light design, electronic goods, user interfaces, transport design and medical equipment. Sports equipment designed by the studio has gained worldwide recognition. From 2013 onwards, the team has been working for the prestigious Italian motorbike manufacturer Bimota. Designs by Studio Miklavc have received many international awards and have been displayed in numerous exhibitions. Jure Miklavc has been involved in design education since 2005 and is currently a lecturer and head of industrial design at the Academy of Fine Arts and Design in Ljubljana.

Professor Jure Miklavc machte seinen Abschluss in Industrial Design an der Academy of Fine Arts and Design in Ljubljana, Slowenien, und verfügt über nahezu 20 Jahre Erfahrung im Designbereich. Er arbeitete zunächst als freiberuflicher Designer, bevor er sein eigenes Design-Beratungsunternehmen „Studio Miklavc" gründete. Studio Miklavc ist in den Bereichen Produktdesign, Visuelle Kommunikation und Markenentwicklung sowie in der Beratung zahlreicher Kunden der Branchen Lichtdesign, Elektronische Güter, Benutzeroberflächen, Transport-Design und Medizinisches Equipment tätig. Die von dem Studio gestalteten Sportausrüstungen erfahren weltweit Anerkennung. Seit 2013 arbeitet das Team für den angesehenen italienischen Motorradhersteller Bimota. Studio Miklavc erhielt bereits zahlreiche Auszeichnungen sowie Präsentationen in Ausstellungen. Seit 2005 ist Jure Miklavc in der Designlehre tätig und aktuell Dozent und Head of Industrial Design an der Academy of Fine Arts and Design in Ljubljana.

01 Carefoot
Integral project of building a brand, corporate identity, products and communication for children's shoes by Austrian company Alpvent. The solution incorporates a convenient size measuring system with an app.
Umfassendes Projekt für den Aufbau der Marke, Corporate Identity, Produkte und Kommunikation der Kinderschuhe der österreichischen Firma Alpvent. Die Lösung schließt ein praktisches App-basiertes Messsystem für Schuhgrößen ein.

01

"I hope that in ten years, product design will be more involved with the real solutions for environmental problems. Designers will also be more connected to the field of robotics and artificial intelligence."

„Ich hoffe, dass sich das Produktdesign in zehn Jahren mehr mit den wirklichen Lösungen für Umweltprobleme auseinandersetzt. Designer werden sich auch mehr mit dem Bereich der Robotertechnik und künstlichen Intelligenz befassen."

What constitutes good design?
Good design is usually a consequence of emotional intelligence and transforms technical innovation in a way that is understandable, pleasant and enjoyable for the user and is not invasive for the environment. Good design is also more than just a summary of different parameters – in the best scenarios it influences us in such a way that it changes the way in which we live to the positive.

What distinguishes your design "signature"?
My design signature is more about the process and approach rather than some typical formal language. I believe in design viewed in context. In that respect I would say that "empathy" is the focus of my work – towards users, environment, technology and identity.

What message would you like to give young designers for their future careers?
I would want to encourage them to be extra curious and sensitive to real needs and to the environment.

Was macht gutes Design aus?
Gutes Design ist generell das Ergebnis emotionaler Intelligenz und verwandelt technische Innovation derart, dass sie für den Nutzer verständlich, angenehm und erfreulich ist, ohne die Umwelt zu belasten. Gutes Design ist auch mehr als die Summe verschiedener Parameter. In den besten Fällen beeinflusst es uns dahingehend, dass es unser Leben positiv verändert.

Was kennzeichnet Ihre gestalterische Handschrift?
Meine gestalterische Handschrift findet sich eher in dem Prozess und Ansatz als in einer charakteristischen Formensprache wieder. Ich glaube an eine Gestaltung, die im Kontext betrachtet werden sollte. In dieser Hinsicht würde ich sagen, dass „Empathie" im Fokus meiner Arbeit steht – Empathie für Nutzer, die Umwelt, Technik und Identität.

Welche Botschaft möchten Sie jungen Designern mit auf den Weg geben?
Ich würde sie dazu ermutigen, besonders neugierig zu sein – und sensibel für echte Bedürfnisse und die Umwelt.

Adriana Monk
Switzerland
Schweiz

Adriana Monk studied product design at the Art Center College of Design in La Tour-de-Peilz, Switzerland, and graduated from Pasadena, USA, beginning her career at the BMW Group Designworks/USA. She subsequently established herself as the automotive industry's leading interior designer for luxury brands such as Rolls-Royce, Jaguar and Land Rover, before pursuing her passion for yachts. In 2008, she founded Monk Design in Switzerland. The agency's focus is on boat interiors, exclusive detailing and graphic design for performance yachts, for both private clients and boats produced in series. With a balanced sense of proportions and aesthetics, Adriana Monk produces new creative solutions. Her work has won several international awards including the World Superyacht Award, Red Dot, iF and the Eurobike Design Award. She is a guest lecturer at the Royal College of Art in London and at the International University of Monaco and also a jury member at competitions like the Design & Innovation Awards of Boat International.

Adriana Monk studierte Produktdesign am Art Center College of Design in La Tour-de-Peilz, Schweiz, und machte ihren Abschluss in Pasadena, USA, bevor sie ihre Karriere bei BMW Group Designworks/USA startete. Anschließend etablierte sie sich als führende Innenarchitektin der Automobilbranche für Luxusmarken wie Rolls-Royce, Jaguar und Land Rover, bevor sie ihrer Leidenschaft für Yachten nachging. 2008 gründete sie Monk Design in der Schweiz. Der Schwerpunkt liegt auf Boot-Interieurs, exklusiven Detailausführungen und Grafikdesign für Performance-Yachten, sowohl für Privatkunden als auch für Serienboote. Mit einem ausgewogenen Sinn für Proportionen und Ästhetik gelangt Adriana Monk zu neuen, kreativen Lösungen. Ihre Arbeit wurde mehrfach international ausgezeichnet, u. a. mit dem World Superyacht Award, Red Dot, iF und dem Eurobike Design Award. Sie ist als Gastdozentin am Royal College of Art in London und der International University of Monaco sowie als Jurorin z. B. des Design & Innovation Awards von Boat International tätig.

01 monk-e-shine lamp, model L1180
Low-voltage reading lamp specifically designed for yachts, produced by Palagi Marine Lights, Italy. The double rotation axis allows for a very wide range of light direction. Clean design with no visible fixings.

Speziell für den Bootsbau gestaltete Niedervolt-Leseleuchte, hergestellt von Palagi Marine Lights, Italien. Dank der 2-Achsen-Rotation ist die Beleuchtungsmöglichkeit sehr groß. Montage ohne sichtbare Schrauben.

01

"Honesty, purity and simplicity are words that resonate with my design discipline. I believe that a design will stand the test of time if it is not only functional but also aesthetically pleasing."

„Ehrlichkeit, Reinheit und Schlichtheit sind Worte, die mit meiner Auffassung von Gestaltung in Einklang stehen. Ich glaube, dass eine Gestaltung nur dann überdauert, wenn sie sowohl funktional als auch ästhetisch überzeugt."

To what do you attach particular importance when judging products?
Judging other people's work is an honour and a very demanding task. By reading the documentation I assess if the design brief has been respected, and whether the product is unique and innovative. By using and handling the products I look for beauty and function as well as quality and the intuitive operation of the product.

Why did you decide to leave the automotive industry and pursue your passion for yachts?
After ten years designing automotive interiors for various luxury brands, I wanted to challenge my creativity. Yachts have always fascinated me: sculptural forms that glide through water. I was awestruck when I first saw a 100-foot carbon-fibre hull. I then proceeded to study naval architecture and get my sailing licence before pursuing my dream: working for Wally Yachts was the stepping stone to leave the automotive industry and open my own design studio, following my passion for yachts.

Worauf legen Sie bei der Bewertung von Produkten besonderen Wert?
Das Werk anderer beurteilen zu dürfen, ist eine Ehre und eine sehr anspruchsvolle Aufgabe. Beim Lesen der Unterlagen bewerte ich, ob die Designvorgaben respektiert wurden und ob das Produkt einzigartig und innovativ ist. Beim Benutzen und Handhaben der Produkte achte ich auf Schönheit und Funktion sowie auf Qualität und die intuitive Bedienung des Produkts.

Warum haben Sie sich dazu entschieden, die Automobilbranche zu verlassen und Ihrer Leidenschaft für Yachten nachzugehen?
Nach zehn Jahren der Gestaltung von Innenräumen für Fahrzeuge verschiedener Luxusmarken wollte ich etwas für meine Kreativität tun. Yachten haben mich schon immer fasziniert: skulpturale Formen, die durch Wasser gleiten. Als ich das erste Mal einen 100-Fuß-Schiffsrumpf aus Kohlefaser sah, war ich sprachlos. Ich habe dann erst Schiffbau studiert und einen Segelschein gemacht, bevor ich meinen Traum verwirklichen konnte: Für Wally Yachts zu arbeiten, war das Sprungbrett für den Abschied aus der Automobilbranche und erlaubte mir, meiner Leidenschaft für Yachten zu folgen und mein eigenes Designstudio aufzubauen.

Prof. Dr. Ken Nah
Korea

Professor Dr. Ken Nah graduated with a Bachelor of Science in Industrial Engineering from Hanyang University, South Korea, in 1983. He deepened his interest in Human Factors/Ergonomics by earning a master's degree from Korea Advanced Institute for Science and Technology (KAIST) in 1985. He received a Ph.D. in Engineering Design from Tufts University, Boston, in 1996. Ken Nah is also a USA Certified Professional Ergonomist (CPE), for the first time as a Korean. He is currently a professor of Design at the International Design School for Advanced Studies (IDAS), Hongik University in Seoul as well as director of the Human Experience and Emotion Research (HE.ER) Lab. Since 2002 he has been the director of the International Design Trend Center (IDTC). Ken Nah was the director general of "World Design Capital Seoul 2010". Alongside his work as a professor, he is also the senior vice-president of the Korea Federation of Design Associations (KFDA) and the Korea Association of Industrial Designers (KAID). Ken Nah has been an advisor on design policy to several ministries of the Korean government since 2000.

Professor Dr. Ken Nah graduierte 1983 an der Hanyang University in Südkorea als Bachelor of Science in Industrial Engineering. Sein Interesse an Human Factors/Ergonomie vertiefte er 1985 mit einem Masterabschluss am Korea Advanced Institute for Science and Technology (KAIST). 1996 promovierte er im Bereich „Konstruktive Gestaltung" an der Tufts University in Boston. Darüber hinaus ist Ken Nah ein in den USA zertifizierter Ergonom (CPE). Derzeit ist er Professor für Design an der International Design School for Advanced Studies (IDAS) der Hongik University in Seoul sowie Direktor des „Human Experience and Emotion Research (HE.ER)"-Labors. Seit 2002 ist er zudem Leiter des International Design Trend Centers (IDTC). Ken Nah war Generaldirektor der „World Design Capital Seoul 2010". Neben seiner Lehrtätigkeit als Professor ist er Senior-Vizepräsident der Korea Federation of Design Associations (KFDA) und der Korea Association of Industrial Designers (KAID). Seit 2000 ist Ken Nah ferner als Berater in Designpolitik für verschiedene Ministerien der koreanischen Regierung tätig.

01 SHAPL Dr. Nah Series 1
Luggage and backpack set
Koffer- und Rucksackset

01

"One trend I have noticed in current design is a seamless assimilation of 'smartness' in products to achieve maximum ease and convenience for users."

„Ein Trend, der mir im aktuellen Design aufgefallen ist, ist die nahtlose Integration von ‚Intelligenz' in Produkte, um Nutzern maximalen Komfort und Anwenderfreundlichkeit zu bieten."

What constitutes an ergonomic product?
Ergonomics, or more appropriately, Human Factors, is defined as a human-centred design discipline seeking for an optimal solution for human users in their working and living environment. Therefore, a product design based on human factors should be easy, convenient, safe, and pleasant to use physically, physiologically, and psychologically and meet emotional wants as well.

How will the product design discipline develop over the ten years to come?
I guess the next ten years will be the most turbulent years for any discipline including design due to big data, AI and convergence. Design should quickly adapt the technology, especially for generative design and engineering analysis, not to mention marketing and business. In a nutshell, design as a discipline will at the same time become general on one hand and very specific on the other hand, which will make it the most challenging and exciting area.

Was macht ein ergonomisches Produkt aus?
Ergonomie oder besser gesagt die Arbeitswissenschaft wird als eine am Menschen orientierte Gestaltungsdisziplin definiert, die versucht, eine optimale Lösung für menschliche Nutzer in ihrem Arbeits- und Lebensumfeld zu entwickeln. Daher sollte ein Produktdesign, das auf Arbeitswissenschaft beruht, einfach, komfortabel, sicher und physisch, physiologisch und psychologisch angenehm zu benutzen sein. Gleichzeitig sollte es auch emotionale Bedürfnisse erfüllen.

Wie wird sich das Produktdesign in den kommenden zehn Jahren entwickeln?
Ich tippe darauf, dass die nächsten zehn Jahre die turbulentesten Jahre in jedem Sektor sein werden, auch in der Gestaltung; und das aufgrund von Big Data, KI und Konvergenz. Design sollte die neue Technologie schnell anwenden und anpassen, besonders für generatives Design und technische Analysen, mal ganz abgesehen von Marketing und der Geschäftswelt. Kurz und gut: Design als Disziplin wird auf der einen Seite sehr allgemein werden und auf der anderen sehr spezifisch, wodurch es zu dem spannendsten, aber auch anspruchsvollsten Sektor werden wird.

Alexander Neumeister
Germany/Brazil
Deutschland/Brasilien

Alexander Neumeister is a high-tech industrial designer, who lives both in Germany and Brazil. A graduate of the Ulm School of Design and a one-year scholarship student at the Tokyo University of Arts, he specialised in the fields of medicine, professional electronics and transportation. Among some of his best-known works are the "Transrapid" maglev trains, the German ICE trains, the Japanese Shinkansen "Nozomi 500", as well as numerous regional trains and subways for Japan, China and Brazil, and the C1 and C2 trains for the Munich underground. Aside from working on projects for large German companies, he was design consultant for Hitachi/Japan for 21 years. From 1983 to 1987, he was board member and later vice-president of the World Design Organization (formerly Icsid). In 1992, Alexander Neumeister and his team received the honorary title "Red Dot: Design Team of the Year". In 2011, he was awarded the design prize of the city of Munich and in 2015, he won the EU's "European Railway Award" in recognition of his contribution to railway design.

Alexander Neumeister arbeitet als Hightech-Industriedesigner und ist in Deutschland wie in Brasilien zu Hause. Als Absolvent der Hochschule für Gestaltung in Ulm und Stipendiat der Tokyo University of Arts für ein Jahr spezialisierte er sich auf die Bereiche Medizin, Professionelle Elektronik und Verkehr. Die Magnetschwebebahn „Transrapid", die deutschen ICE-Züge, der japanische Shinkansen „Nozomi 500", aber auch zahlreiche Regionalzüge und U-Bahnen in Japan, China und Brasilien sowie die U-Bahnen C1 und C2 für München zählen zu seinen bekanntesten Entwürfen. Neben Projekten für deutsche Großunternehmen war er 21 Jahre lang Designberater für Hitachi/Japan. Von 1983 bis 1987 war er Vorstandsmitglied und später Vizepräsident der World Design Organization (ehemals Icsid). 1992 wurden Alexander Neumeister und sein Team mit dem Ehrentitel „Red Dot: Design Team of the Year" ausgezeichnet. 2011 erhielt er den Designpreis der Landeshauptstadt München und 2015 den „European Railway Award" der EU für seine Leistungen auf dem Gebiet des Railway-Designs.

01 Series 800
Train project for Great Western Railways in the UK, where it went into operation 2017. This train works with bimodal propulsion and is driven by both electric and diesel engine power. Depending on the situation, it can be switched from one method of propulsion to the other.
Zugprojekt für die Great Western Railways im Vereinigten Königreich, wo es 2017 in Betrieb genommen wurde. Der Zug hat einen bimodalen Antrieb mit Elektro- und Dieselmotor. Je nach Situation kann er auf den einen oder anderen Antrieb umgeschaltet werden.

01

"In my opinion, good design is the successful combination of materials and function, but it also includes the ability to adapt to different environments and the exclusion of superfluous decorations."

„Gutes Design ist für mich die gelungene Kombination von Materialaufwand und Funktion. Aber auch der Verzicht auf unnötige Dekoration und die Fähigkeit, sich in Umgebungen einzuordnen."

You were responsible for the design of the ICE. What does it feel like to site in the flagship of the Deutsche Bahn?
I designed both the ICE concept train, as well as the ICE-3. My team and I created open seating areas for the design with compartments at the end of one of the carriages – with minimally greater distances between the seats in first class. The design work on the train began in 1996 and now, more than 20 years later, I still enjoy travelling in "my ICE-3". The interior has lost none of its elegance.

What would you still like to achieve professionally?
At over 75, I asked myself how many more trains I still want to design in order to be satisfied. I decided to hand my shares over to my partner and to leave N+P Industrial Design. In Germany, I still advise a former colleague, who works as a freelancer in Munich, and in Brazil I work for two companies in the electronics sector. I have never regretted the decision to step back a bit.

Sie waren für das Design des ICEs verantwortlich. Wie fühlt es sich an, in dem Flaggschiff der Deutschen Bahn zu sitzen?
Ich habe sowohl den ICE-Versuchszug wie auch den ICE-3 gestaltet. Für das Design haben mein Team und ich offene Sitzlandschaften geschaffen mit Abteilen am Ende eines Waggons – für die erste Klasse mit geringfügig größeren Sitzabständen. Das Design startete 1996 und nun, mehr als 20 Jahre danach, macht es mir immer noch Spaß, in „meinem ICE-3" zu reisen. Der Innenraum hat nichts von seiner Eleganz eingebüßt.

Was möchten Sie beruflich noch erreichen?
Mit über 75 Jahren stellte ich mir die Frage, wie viele Züge ich noch gestalten wollte, um zufrieden zu sein. Ich entschloss mich, meine Anteile an meine Partner abzugeben und aus N+P Industrial Design auszusteigen. In Deutschland berate ich noch einen ehemaligen Mitarbeiter, der sich in München selbständig gemacht hat, und in Brasilien arbeite ich für zwei Unternehmen im Elektronikbereich. Die Entscheidung, das alles zu reduzieren, habe ich nie bereut.

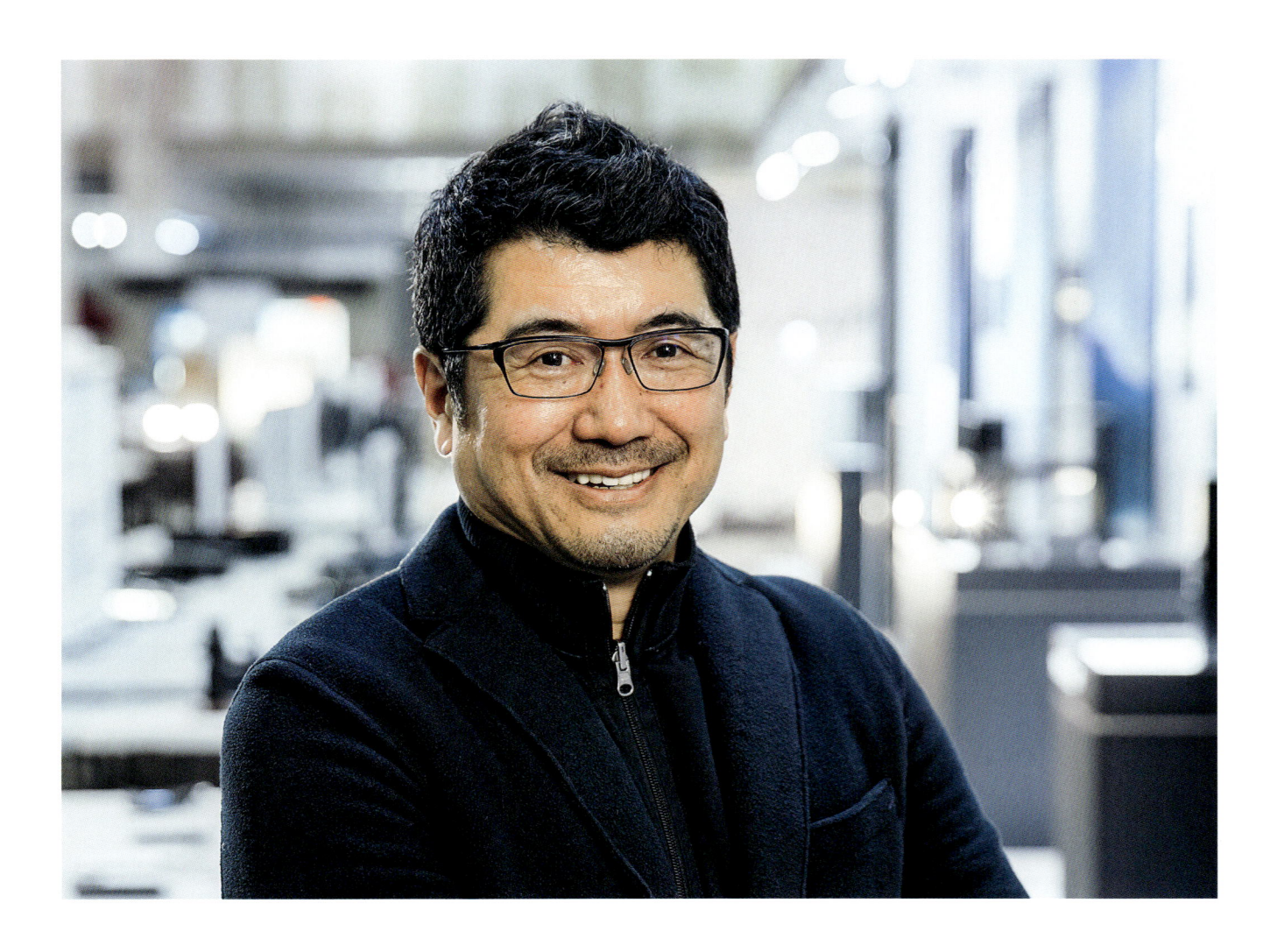

Ken Okuyama
Japan

Ken Kiyoyuki Okuyama, industrial designer and CEO of Ken Okuyama Design, was born in 1959 in Yamagata, Japan, and studied automobile design at the Art Center College of Design in Pasadena, California. He has worked as a chief designer for General Motors, as a senior designer for Porsche AG, and as design director for Pininfarina S.p.A., being responsible for the design of Ferrari Enzo, Maserati Quattroporte and many other automobiles. He is also known for many different product designs such as motorcycles, furniture, robots and architecture. Ken Okuyama Design was founded in 2007 and provides business consultancy services to numerous corporations. Ken Okuyama also produces cars, eyewear and interior products under his original brand. He is currently a visiting professor at several universities and also frequently publishes books.

Ken Kiyoyuki Okuyama, Industriedesigner und CEO von Ken Okuyama Design, wurde 1959 in Yamagata, Japan, geboren und studierte Automobildesign am Art Center College of Design in Pasadena, Kalifornien. Er war als Chief Designer bei General Motors, als Senior Designer bei der Porsche AG und als Design Director bei Pininfarina S.p.A. tätig und zeichnete verantwortlich für den Ferrari Enzo, den Maserati Quattroporte und viele weitere Automobile. Zudem ist er für viele unterschiedliche Produktgestaltungen wie Motorräder, Möbel, Roboter und Architektur bekannt. Ken Okuyama Design wurde 2007 als Beratungsunternehmen gegründet und arbeitet für zahlreiche Unternehmen. Ken Okuyama produziert unter seiner originären Marke auch Autos, Brillen und Inneneinrichtungsgegenstände. Derzeit lehrt er als Gastprofessor an verschiedenen Universitäten und publiziert zudem Bücher.

01 JR EAST
"Train suite Shiki-Shima"

01

"I always seek, sketch and write way before the job comes in. My hands show me the way, like a fortune teller."

„Lange bevor der Auftrag kommt, bin ich ständig auf der Suche, skizziere und schreibe. Meine Hände weisen mir den Weg, genau wie bei einem Wahrsager."

What was the development process for the Ferrari Enzo like?
Single talent doesn't make a good car. It was a miracle to gather spirited geniuses like Luca Cordero di Montezemolo and Sergio Pininfarina and to be part of the team as a designer at the very end of the last century. It will never happen again.

What advice do you most frequently give to customers?
I am a "chef" for a good design. I put up a menu, customers come, we talk, and I give a lot more than they expected with a good surprise.

What do you like about your role as consultant?
Together with the top management, we define a future vision and solutions to get there, sharing confidentiality. For that reason, we only work with one company in each industry. It's like being a family.

Wie sah der Entwicklungsprozess des Ferrari Enzo aus?
Einzelne Talente machen kein gutes Auto. Es war ein Wunder Ende des letzten Jahrhunderts, dass wir sprühende Genies wie Luca Cordero di Montezemolo und Sergio Pininfarina gewinnen konnten – und für mich als Designer, Teil des Teams sein zu können. Das wird nie wieder geschehen.

Welchen Tipp geben Sie Ihren Kunden am häufigsten?
Ich bin der „Koch" für eine gute Gestaltung. Ich stelle ein Menü zusammen, die Kunden kommen, wir reden und ich gebe ihnen sehr viel mehr als sie erwarteten, noch dazu mit einer guten Überraschung.

Was gefällt Ihnen an der Tätigkeit als Berater?
Gemeinsam mit dem Topmanagement definieren wir eine Vision für die Zukunft und die Lösungen, die uns dahinbringen werden – in strengster Vertraulichkeit. Daher arbeiten wir in jeder Branche auch nur mit einem Unternehmen. Man fühlt sich als Teil der Familie.

Simon Ong
Singapore
Singapur

Simon Ong, born in Singapore in 1953, graduated with a master's degree in design from the University of New South Wales and an MBA from the University of South Australia. He is the deputy chairman and co-founder of Kingsmen Creatives Ltd., a leading communication design and production group with 21 offices across the Asia-Pacific region, the Middle East and North America. Kingsmen has won several awards, such as the President's Design Award, Singapore Good Design Mark, SRA Best Retail Concept Award, SFIA Hall of Fame, Promising Brand Award, A.R.E. Retail Design Award and RDI International Store Design Award USA. Simon Ong is actively involved in the creative industry as chairman of the design group of Manpower, the Skills & Training Council of Singapore Workforce Development Agency. Moreover, he is a member of the advisory board of the Design Business Chamber of Singapore and Singapore Furniture Industries Council (Design). Currently, Simon Ong is a board member of the Association of Retail Environments (USA), a board director of Nanyang Academy of Fine Arts and a member of the advisory board to the School of Design & Environment at the National University of Singapore.

Simon Ong, geboren 1953 in Singapur, erhielt einen Master in Design der University of New South Wales und einen Master of Business Administration der University of South Australia. Er ist stellvertretender Vorsitzender und Mitbegründer von Kingsmen Creatives Ltd., eines führenden Unternehmens für Kommunikationsdesign und Produktion mit 21 Geschäftsstellen im asiatisch-pazifischen Raum, dem Mittleren Osten und Nordamerika. Kingsmen wurde vielfach ausgezeichnet, u. a. mit dem President's Design Award, Singapore Good Design Mark, SRA Best Retail Concept Award, SFIA Hall of Fame, Promising Brand Award, A.R.E. Retail Design Award und RDI International Store Design Award USA. Simon Ong ist als Vorsitzender der Designgruppe von Manpower, der „Skills & Training Council of Singapore Workforce Development Agency", aktiv in die Kreativindustrie involviert. Zudem ist er Mitglied des Beirats der Design Business Chamber Singapore und des Singapore Furniture Industries Council (Design). Aktuell ist Simon Ong Vorstandsmitglied der Association of Retail Environments (USA), Vorstandsvorsitzender der Nanyang Academy of Fine Arts und Mitglied des Beirats der School of Design & Environment an der National University of Singapore.

01 Twenty3
at Formula 1 2018 Singapore Airlines Singapore Grand Prix
Scintillating action from the race track can be caught from full-length windows at the restaurants at Twenty3.

Das fulminante Geschehen auf der Rennstrecke kann durch die raumhohen Fenster des Twenty3-Restaurants verfolgt werden.

"A product that surprises me has a standout design that is simple yet well-engineered, while marrying function and aesthetics. Most importantly, it needs to be intuitive for users."

„Um mich zu überraschen, muss ein Produkt ein herausragendes Design vorweisen, das sowohl einfach als auch ausgereift ist. Gleichzeitig sollte es Funktion und Ästhetik in Einklang bringen. Am wichtigsten ist, dass es intuitiv zu benutzen ist."

What are the hallmarks of good design?
Less is more. A well-designed product that resonates with its users will let them realise that their daily lives are made better by using it whether they knew they needed it or not in the first place.

How does a product become a classic?
This status has to be earned and not claimed. The product should be able to stand the test of time amidst the changing consumer mindset and an ever increasing digitally connected world. These are products that end up representing their own category and their design becomes reason enough for users to buy the product.

Do you have a tip for young designers?
Don't lose sight that it is about the user experience (UX). You need to understand who you are designing for and how they interact and experience the product; how they use it, and the relationship the users form with the product.

Was kennzeichnet gutes Design?
Weniger ist mehr. Ein gut gestaltetes Produkt, das mit seinen Nutzern im Einklang ist, wird ihnen zeigen, dass ihr Alltag durch seine Verwendung besser wird, auch wenn sie sich vorher gar nicht bewusst waren, dass sie es brauchten.

Wie wird ein Produkt zum Klassiker?
Dieser Status will verdient sein und kann nicht einfach beansprucht werden. Das Produkt sollte sich langfristig bewähren, trotz der ständig wechselnden Einstellung der Konsumenten und der zunehmend digital vernetzten Welt. Klassiker sind Produkte, die in einer Kategorie für sich stehen und deren Design Grund genug ist, sie zu kaufen.

Haben Sie einen Tipp für junge Designer?
Nie die Benutzererfahrung (UX) aus den Augen verlieren. Sie müssen wissen, für wen sie gestalten und wie ihre Zielgruppe mit dem Produkt umgeht und es erlebt; wie sie es benutzt und welche Beziehung sie zu dem Produkt entwickelt.

Dr. Sascha Peters
Germany
Deutschland

Dr. Sascha Peters is founder and owner of the agency for material and technology HAUTE INNOVATION in Berlin. He studied mechanical engineering at the RWTH Aachen University, Germany, and product design at the ABK Maastricht, Netherlands. He wrote his doctoral thesis at the University of Duisburg-Essen, Germany, on the complex of problems in communication between engineering and design. From 1997 to 2003, he led research projects and product developments at the Fraunhofer Institute for Production Technology IPT in Aachen and subsequently became deputy head of the Design Zentrum Bremen until 2008. Sascha Peters is author of various specialist books on sustainable raw materials, smart materials, innovative production techniques and energetic technologies. He is a leading material expert and trend scout for new technologies. Since 2014, he has been an advisory board member of the funding initiative "Zwanzig20 – Partnerschaft für Innovation" (2020 – Partnership for innovation) commissioned by the German Federal Ministry of Education and Research.

Dr. Sascha Peters ist Gründer und Inhaber der Material- und Technologieagentur HAUTE INNOVATION in Berlin. Er studierte Maschinenbau an der RWTH Aachen und Produktdesign an der ABK Maastricht. Seine Doktorarbeit schrieb er an der Universität Duisburg-Essen über die Kommunikationsproblematik zwischen Engineering und Design. Von 1997 bis 2003 leitete er Forschungsprojekte und Produktentwicklungen am Fraunhofer-Institut für Produktionstechnologie IPT in Aachen und war anschließend bis 2008 stellvertretender Leiter des Design Zentrums Bremen. Sascha Peters ist Autor zahlreicher Fachbücher zu nachhaltigen Werkstoffen, smarten Materialien, innovativen Fertigungsverfahren und energetischen Technologien und zählt zu den führenden Materialexperten und Trendscouts für neue Technologien. Seit 2014 ist er Mitglied im Beirat der Förderinitiative „Zwanzig20 – Partnerschaft für Innovation" im Auftrag des Bundesministeriums für Bildung und Forschung.

01
A special area about future food and 3D printing in the food industry on the occasion of "imm/LivingKitchen" trade fair in January 2019 in Cologne
Sonderfläche zu Future Food und 3D-Druck im Ernährungsbereich anlässlich der „imm/LivingKitchen"-Messe im Januar 2019 in Köln

01

"I believe the most exciting recent development to be 4D printing and the resulting potential for programmable materials. With the help of an exterior impulse, components can change their own shape."

„Der 4D-Druck und die damit zusammenhängenden Potenziale programmierbarer Materialien empfinde ich als die spannendste Entwicklung der letzten Jahre. Mithilfe eines äußeren Impulses können sich Bauteile damit selbsttätig verformen."

What are key activities of your HAUTE INNOVATION agency?
I founded HAUTE INNOVATION with the aim of speeding up the transfer of innovations in materials into marketable products. In the meantime, we have become established as a trend agency for future technologies. Our customers come from the automotive, furniture and construction industries.

What is your objective as a designer?
We don't work as classical designers, but rather carry out trend analyses for our customers and initiate innovation processes. To this end, we organise exhibitions on disruptive technology. For example, we were responsible for a special area at the "imm/LivingKitchen" trade fair in Cologne about future food and 3D printing in the food industry.

Was sind die wichtigsten Aktivitäten Ihrer Agentur HAUTE INNOVATION?
Ich habe HAUTE INNOVATION mit dem Ziel gegründet, Materialinnovationen schneller in marktfähige Produkte zu überführen. In der Zwischenzeit werden wir als Trendagentur für Zukunftstechnologien wahrgenommen und haben Kunden in der Automobil-, Möbel- und Bauindustrie.

Welches Ziel verfolgen Sie als Designer?
Wir arbeiten nicht als klassische Designer, sondern setzen für unsere Kunden Trendanalysen um und initiieren Innovationsprozesse. In diesem Zusammenhang gestalten wir Ausstellungen zu disruptiven Technologien. Hier haben wir zur „imm/LivingKitchen"-Messe in Köln beispielsweise eine Sonderfläche zu Future Food und 3D-Druck im Ernährungsbereich verantwortet.

Dirk Schumann
Germany
Deutschland

Dirk Schumann, born in 1960 in Soest, studied product design at Münster University of Applied Sciences. After graduating in 1987, he joined oco-design as an industrial designer, moved to siegerdesign in 1989, and was a lecturer in product design at Münster University of Applied Sciences until 1991. In 1992, he founded his own design studio "Schumanndesign" in Münster, developing design concepts for companies in Germany, Italy, India, Thailand and China. For several years now, he has focused on conceptual architecture, created visionary living spaces and held lectures at international conferences. Dirk Schumann has taken part in exhibitions both in Germany and abroad with works that have garnered several awards, including the Gold Prize (Minister of Economy, Trade and Industry Prize) in the International Design Competition, Osaka; the Comfort & Design Award, Milan; the iF product design award, Hanover; the Red Dot Design Award, Essen; the Focus in Gold, Stuttgart; as well as the Good Design Award, Chicago and Tokyo. In 2015, he founded Schumann&Wang in Xiamen City, the Chinese subsidiary of Schumanndesign.

Dirk Schumann, 1960 in Soest geboren, studierte Produktdesign an der Fachhochschule Münster. Nach seinem Abschluss 1987 arbeitete er als Industriedesigner für oco-design, wechselte 1989 zu siegerdesign und war bis 1991 an der Fachhochschule Münster als Lehrbeauftragter für Produktdesign tätig. 1992 eröffnete er in Münster sein eigenes Designstudio „Schumanndesign", das Designkonzepte für Unternehmen in Deutschland, Italien, Indien, Thailand und China entwickelt. Seit einigen Jahren beschäftigt er sich mit konzeptioneller Architektur, entwirft visionäre Lebensräume und hält Vorträge auf internationalen Kongressen. Dirk Schumann nimmt an Ausstellungen im In- und Ausland teil und wurde für seine Arbeiten mehrfach ausgezeichnet, u. a. mit dem Gold Prize (Minister of Economy, Trade and Industry Prize) des International Design Competition, Osaka, beim Comfort & Design Award, Mailand, dem iF product design award, Hannover, dem Red Dot Design Award, Essen, dem Focus in Gold, Stuttgart, sowie dem Good Design Award, Chicago und Tokio. 2015 gründete er mit Schumann&Wang in Xiamen City die chinesische Dependance von Schumanndesign.

01
Washbasin and fittings
for JOMOO China
Waschbecken und Armatur
für JOMOO China

01

"Good design is characterised by maximum practical value for the user, sensitive management of resources, durable design, emotion and a clear brand identification."

„Gutes Design zeichnet sich durch größtmöglichen Gebrauchswert für den Benutzer, einen sensiblen Umgang mit Ressourcen, langlebiges Design, Emotionalität und klare Identifizierbarkeit der Marke aus."

What do you design at "Schumanndesign"?
Products with sophisticated functionality for a range of industries. We have often long-standing relationship with international companies in the sanitary, medical and communication technology industries as well as in mechanical and plant engineering. The resulting products are the consequence of close, personal cooperation with customers. I particularly value the international nature of our work and the associated awareness of cultural diversity and values.

How did you come to open a branch office in Xiamen City?
It all started at the "Design Business Week", organised by Red Dot in 2013 in Xiamen, where we first made contact with companies from Xiamen City and other Chinese industrial centres. This led to concrete projects in 2015. As Xiamen is also a centre for the sanitary industry, it seemed natural for us to establish a branch office there. Our operations in southern China have also led to interesting projects and overarching activities in Beijing and Shanghai.

Was gestalten Sie bei „Schumanndesign"?
Produkte mit hohem Anspruch an ihre Funktionalität für unterschiedliche Branchen. Die oft langfristigen Kooperationen mit internationalen Unternehmen liegen in den Bereichen Sanitär, Medizin- und Kommunikationstechnik sowie Maschinen- und Anlagenbau. Die Produkte entstehen in engen, individuellen Kooperationen mit den Kunden, wobei ich die Internationalität und das damit zusammenhängende Verständnis für kulturelle Vielfalt und Werte sehr schätze.

Wie kam es dazu, dass Sie eine Dependance in Xiamen City eröffnet haben?
Der Ursprung geht letztlich auf die von Red Dot 2013 veranstaltete „Design Business Week" in Xiamen zurück, auf der es zu ersten Kontakten zu Unternehmen aus Xiamen City und anderen Industriestandorten in China und 2015 zu konkreten Projekten kam. Da auch Xiamen einen Schwerpunkt im Sanitärbereich hat, war es naheliegend, eine Dependance vor Ort zu etablieren. In der Folge unserer Tätigkeiten in Südchina haben sich auch interessante Projekte und übergreifende Aktivitäten in Beijing und Shanghai ergeben.

Prof. Song Kee Hong
Singapore
Singapur

Professor Song Kee Hong has worked with some of the world's most notable brands, including Dell, Epson, HP, Intel, Lenovo, P&G, Philips, Sanyo, Sennheiser and WelchAllyn, and he has received more than twenty international design awards for his work. His recent portfolio of cross-disciplinary design work spans diverse industries – from consumer electronics to mission-critical domains in healthcare, industrial and security for government systems. Song Kee Hong is currently a deputy head at the Industrial Design Division, National University of Singapore. He is also the design director of Design Exchange. He has over two decades of design experience, including work at global innovation consultancy Ziba and at HP.

Professor Song Kee Hong hat für einige der namhaftesten Marken der Welt gearbeitet, darunter Dell, Epson, HP, Intel, Lenovo, P&G, Philips, Sanyo, Sennheiser und WelchAllyn. Für seine Arbeit wurde er in mehr als zwanzig internationalen Designwettbewerben ausgezeichnet. Zu seinen jüngeren interdisziplinären Projekten zählen Aufträge für verschiedene Branchen von der Unterhaltungselektronik bis hin zu entscheidenden Bereichen wie dem Gesundheitswesen, der Industrie und staatlichen Sicherheitssystemen. Zurzeit ist Song Kee Hong stellvertretender Leiter der Industrial Design Division an der National University of Singapore und gleichzeitig Designdirektor von Design Exchange. Er blickt auf mehr als zwei Jahrzehnte Designerfahrung zurück, die Tätigkeiten bei der globalen Innovations-Unternehmensberatung Ziba und bei HP einschließt.

01 HP Deskjet 9600 Series
Printer
Drucker

01

"Good consumer product design can be very demanding in terms of balancing stunning aesthetics with good user experience."

„Gutes Design für Konsumgüter kann sehr anspruchsvoll darin sein, beeindruckende Ästhetik mit guter Benutzererfahrung in Einklang zu bringen."

To what extent does your work as a designer in the consumer electronics industry differ from your work as a designer in the healthcare sector?
Although much of the technical process such as configuring component layout and ergonomics are similar, that's where the similarity ends. The main differences are in the user scenario and operating environment. When I designed an emergency ambulance, my team had to ride in one to real cases and understand all the critical needs of both the crew and patient; all design decisions are driven by these needs.

What do you like about being a jury member?
Besides the opportunity to view and try thousands of designs from around the world, I like to meet and share experience and insights with my peers from around the world. Always amusing to see that we're so different and yet so similar at the same time!

Inwiefern unterscheidet sich die Arbeit als Designer in der Unterhaltungselektronik von der Tätigkeit als Gestalter im Gesundheitswesen?
Obwohl ein Großteil der technischen Verfahren, z. B. die Anordnung der verschiedenen Komponenten und die ergonomische Gestaltung, sich ähneln, hört die Gemeinsamkeit da auch schon auf. Die Hauptunterschiede betreffen die Nutzungssituation und die Betriebsumgebung. Als ich dabei war, einen Notarztwagen zu gestalten, musste mein Team in einem Krankenwagen zu echten Notfällen mitfahren, um die maßgeblichen Bedürfnisse sowohl des Einsatzteams als auch der Patienten zu verstehen. Alle Designentscheidungen werden von diesen Bedürfnissen gesteuert.

Was gefällt Ihnen an Ihrer Tätigkeit als Juror?
Abgesehen von der Gelegenheit, tausende Gestaltungsprojekte aus der ganzen Welt zu sehen, gefällt mir, dass ich Kolleginnen und Kollegen aus der ganzen Welt treffen und Erfahrungen und Erkenntnisse mit ihnen austauschen kann. Es ist immer amüsant zu sehen, wie sehr wir uns unterscheiden und gleichzeitig doch ähneln!

Dick Spierenburg
Netherlands
Niederlande

Dick Spierenburg, born in 1953, studied architecture at Delft University of Technology and Interior & Product Design at the Royal Academy of Art in The Hague. He worked at the Dutch manufacturer Castelijn for over fifteen years, as managing and creative director. In 1995, he set up and managed three leading permanent interior design exhibitions in Amsterdam, NIC, Pakhuis Amsterdam and Post CS. Parallel to these activities Dick Spierenburg established KBDS with Dutch designer Karel Boonzaaijer in 2001 designing for Arco, Artifort, Castelijn, Gelderland, Hollands Licht, Minotti Italia, Montis and Moroso. In 2009, he founded his own studio. In Germany, he co-ordinated the initiative for a design and interior showroom for international brands "Design Post", and was appointed creative consultant and in 2011 creative director to imm cologne. Since 2014, Dick Spierenburg has been consulting the trade fair Orgatec, and has been focusing on the design of exhibitions such as for the MAKK museum and presentation spaces for Thonet, Linak or Oase.

Dick Spierenburg, 1953 geboren, studierte Architektur an der Technischen Universität Delft sowie Innenarchitektur und Produktdesign an der Königlichen Kunstakademie in Den Haag. Danach arbeitete er mehr als 15 Jahre als Geschäftsführer und Creative Director für den niederländischen Hersteller Castelijn. 1995 baute er drei führende permanente Innenarchitektur-Ausstellungen in Amsterdam, NIC, Pakhuis Amsterdam und Post CS, auf, die er danach auch leitete. Gleichzeitig gründete er gemeinsam mit dem holländischen Designer Karel Boonzaaijer im Jahr 2001 KBDS und gestaltete für Arco, Artifort, Castelijn, Gelderland, Hollands Licht, Minotti Italia, Montis und Moroso. 2009 eröffnete er sein eigenes Designstudio. In Deutschland organisierte er die Initiative „Design Post", ein Design- und Innenarchitektur-Showroom für internationale Marken, und wurde zum Creative Consultant benannt. 2011 wurde er Creative Director der imm cologne. Seit 2014 berät Dick Spierenburg die Fachmesse Orgatec und konzentriert sich auf die Gestaltung von Ausstellungen, u. a. für das MAKK Museum, und von Ausstellungsräumen für Thonet, Linak und Oase.

**01 Pure Editions Club
at imm cologne 2019**
The 2019 design for the Editions Club shows an exciting contrast between volume and lightness: a high cross vault is suggested, but built with paper thin walls. Only a few materials were used to reach the special effect of an intimate room. A stretched hospitality space, serene and light, with an impressive perspective as scenery for seating areas.

Das Design für den Editions Club von 2019 weist einen spannenden Kontrast zwischen Volumen und Leichtigkeit auf: Angedeutet wird ein hohes Kreuzgewölbe, das aus papierdünnen Wänden besteht. Es wurden nur wenige Materialien verwendet, um den besonderen Effekt eines intimen Raumes zu erzeugen. Ein geräumiger Hospitality-Bereich, ruhig und hell, mit einer eindrucksvollen Perspektive als Kulisse für die Sitzecken.

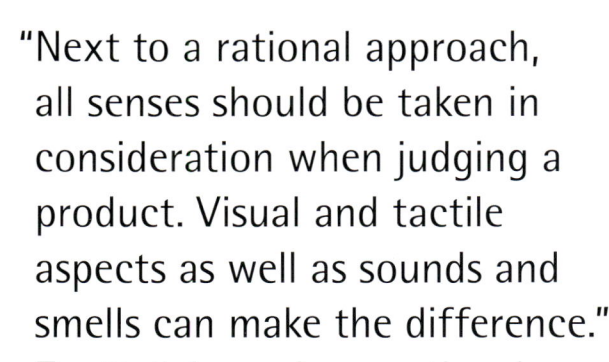

01

"Next to a rational approach, all senses should be taken in consideration when judging a product. Visual and tactile aspects as well as sounds and smells can make the difference."

„Zusätzlich zu einem rationalen Ansatz sollten bei der Bewertung eines Produkts auch alle Sinne ins Spiel kommen. Optische und haptische Aspekte, Klänge und Gerüche können den Unterschied ausmachen."

With what can a piece of furniture persuade you of its merits?
With an innovative character: new possibilities in use and appealing visual aspects. A new product must earn its place with its concept, materialisation, options for use, look & feel and sustainable qualities.

To what extent has the "Bauhaus" movement influenced you?
The principles of Bauhaus have left many traces both in my education and in my work. It is good to question every step you take in the design process but letting intuition speak is equally important. We should not overestimate the influence of Bauhaus in the present time. The world has changed in the last 100 years. Design and architecture should lead and not follow when it comes to societal change and development.

Womit kann ein Möbelstück Sie überzeugen?
Mit einem innovativen Charakter: neuen Möglichkeiten der Anwendung und ansprechenden optischen Eigenschaften. Ein neues Produkt muss seinen Platz verdienen – mit Konzept, Materialisierung, Anwendungsmöglichkeiten, Optik und Haptik und nachhaltigen Eigenschaften.

Stichwort „Bauhaus": Inwieweit beeinflusste die Kunstschule Sie?
Die Bauhaus-Prinzipien haben sowohl in meiner Ausbildung als auch in meiner Arbeit nachhaltige Spuren hinterlassen. Es ist gut, jeden Schritt, den man im Gestaltungsprozess macht, zu hinterfragen. Es ist allerdings genauso wichtig, die Intuition zu Wort kommen zu lassen. Wir sollten den Einfluss des Bauhauses allerdings nicht überschätzen. Die Welt hat sich in den letzten 100 Jahren verändert. Design und Architektur sollten im Wandel der Gesellschaft und bei Entwicklungen führen und nicht folgen.

Leon Sun
China

Leon Sun is Chief Content Officer and Editorial Director of the international home and lifestyle magazine ELLE DECORATION China. He is journalist with over a decade of experience in the interior design industry. By introducing the latest global design and trends into the Chinese market, he actively promotes the development of the domestic interior industry. Amongst others, he realised the special topics "Oriental Gene", "Asia Now" and "Rong He" at ELLE DECORATION China. Furthermore, he is judge of the EDIDA International Design Awards and Vice President of the China Gold Idea Design Award. Graduating in Visual Communication from the Shanghai Donghua University, Leon Sun started his career as Visual Director at ELLE DECORATION China in 2006. From 2011 to 2014, he was Visual Director at AD China.

Leon Sun ist Chief Content Officer und Editorial Director des internationalen Wohn- und Lifestyle-Magazins ELLE DECORATION China. Er ist Journalist mit mehr als einem Jahrzehnt Erfahrung im Sektor Inneneinrichtung. Indem er die international aktuellsten Gestaltungen und Trends auf dem chinesischen Markt vorstellt, unterstützt er die Entwicklung der heimischen Einrichtungsbranche aktiv. Unter anderem realisierte er die Themenspecials „Oriental Gene", „Asia Now" und „Rong He" bei ELLE DECORATION China. Darüber hinaus ist er Juror des EDIDA International Design Awards und Vice President des China Gold Idea Design Awards. Mit einem Abschluss in Visual Communication von der Shanghai Donghua University begann er seine Karriere 2006 als Visual Director bei ELLE DECORATION China. Von 2011 bis 2014 war er Visual Director bei AD China.

01 2019 China Interior Design Annual

ELLE DECORATION China released the 2019 China Interior Design Annual, a special selection of interior design projects. The top designers Tony Chi, Steve Leung, Alan Chan and André Fu reviewed the submitted works and leading designers like Kengo Kuma, Yabu Pushelberg, Kenya Hara and Neri&Hu Stucio shared their insights on excellent China interior designs in all relevant categories.

ELLE DECORATION China ist Herausgeber des 2019 China Interior Design Annual, einer Sonderauswahl von Innenarchitekturprojekten. Die Topdesigner Tony Chi, Steve Leung, Alan Chan und André Fu haben die eingereichten Arbeiten begutachtet, während führende Designer wie Kengo Kuma, Yabu Pushelberg, Kenya Hara und Neri&Hu Studio ihre Einblicke in herausragende chinesische Innenarchitekturprojekte in allen relevanten Kategorien vermitteln.

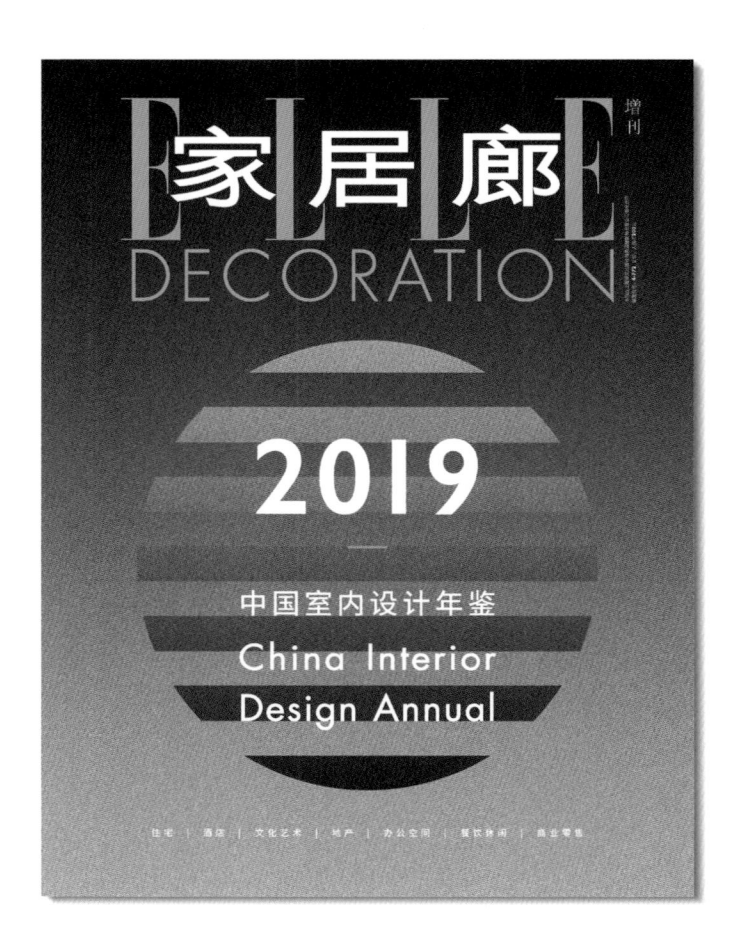

01

"A good designer is always curious. He is an expert in exploring the unknown, creating new things and revealing his unique perspective in the way in which he interprets life and the world through his works."

„Ein guter Designer ist immer neugierig. Er ist Experte im Erforschen von Unbekanntem, im Schaffen von Neuem und im Darstellen seiner einzigartigen Sichtweise, in der er das Leben und die Welt mit seiner Arbeit interpretiert."

What constitutes good design?
Design is about solving problems and offering better services to people. Therefore, a good design is a tool that makes people's life better.

To what do you attach particular importance when judging products?
Firstly, to creativity and innovations in ideas, formats or materials; secondly, to workability and its way of solving problems and considering physical or psychological needs. Thirdly, to the look and whether it immediately catches your eye and, fourthly, to friendliness: a product needs to reflect the relationship between humans and objects and to be environmentally friendly.

Where will the design industry be ten years from now?
Our life will advance along with technological developments which allow us to dream bigger. However, design will evolve in different directions due to its diversity, interacting with technologies, culture and art.

Was macht gutes Design aus?
Bei Design geht es darum, Probleme zu lösen und Menschen einen besseren Service zu bieten. Daher ist gutes Design ein Hilfsmittel, das Menschen das Leben erleichtert.

Worauf legen Sie bei der Bewertung von Produkten ein besonderes Augenmerk?
Erstens auf die Kreativität und die Innovationen, die ein Produkt in Idee, Format und Materialien bietet; zweitens auf Praktikabilität und die Art, in der es Probleme löst und auf physische und psychische Bedürfnisse eingeht. Drittens auf den Look und ob es sofort die Augen auf sich zieht und, viertens, auf die Freundlichkeit – ein Produkt sollte die Beziehung zwischen Mensch und Objekt widerspiegeln und umweltfreundlich sein.

Wo wird die Designbranche in zehn Jahren stehen?
Unser Leben wird mit den technischen Entwicklungen voranschreiten und uns erlauben, größere Träume zu träumen. Design wird sich aufgrund seiner Vielfalt allerdings in verschiedene Richtungen entwickeln und mit Technik, Kultur und Kunst zusammenwirken.

Kazuo Tanaka
Japan

Kazuo Tanaka graduated in 1983 from Tokyo University of the Arts, majored in industrial design. He is president and CEO of the GK Design Group Incorporated, a comprehensive freelance design office in Japan founded in 1952 by Kenji Ekuan. Kazuo Tanaka has been elected president of the Japan Industrial Designers Association (JIDA) and taking on many kinds of activities since 2013. In 2007, he was elected member of the board of directors of the World Design Organization (formerly Icsid) and has been active, also as a regional adviser, in many international programmes. Kazuo Tanaka has also been serving as a board member of Japan Institute of Design Promotion (JDP), and a member of the study group on the relation between industrial competitiveness and design by the Japan Patent Office (JPO) of the Ministry of Economy, Trade and Industry (METI). He also has been involved as a juror in many international design promotion activities and was awarded the Good Design Award Prime Minister Prize, the SDA Grand Prize and many other awards.

Kazuo Tanaka absolvierte sein Studium des Industriedesigns 1983 an der Tokyo University of Arts. Er ist Präsident und CEO der GK Design Group Incorporated, eines übergreifenden unabhängigen Designstudios in Japan, das 1952 von Kenji Ekuan gegründet wurde. Kazuo Tanaka wurde zum Präsidenten der Japan Industrial Designers Association (JIDA) ernannt und geht seit 2013 mehreren Tätigkeiten nach. 2017 wurde er zum Vorstandsmitglied der World Design Organization (ehemals Icsid) gewählt und ist seitdem auch auf regionaler Ebene beratend in vielen internationalen Projekten aktiv. Kazuo Tanaka ist ebenfalls als Vorstandsmitglied des Japan Institute of Design Promotion (JDP) tätig und Mitglied der Studiengruppe zur Beziehung zwischen industrieller Wettbewerbsfähigkeit und Design des Japanischen Patentbüros (JPO) des Ministeriums für Wirtschaft, Handel und Industrie (METI). Als Juror nahm er an einer Vielzahl internationaler Designwettbewerbe teil und erhielt den Good Design Award Prime Minister Prize, den SDA Grand Prize und viele weitere Auszeichnungen.

01 fugan
Fugan Suijo, shipping line of
the Toyama Prefecture, 2015

Fugan Suijo, Schifffahrtsgesell-
schaft der Toyama-Präfektur, 2015

01

"When evaluating products, I first of all prove their functionally, then their aesthetic excellence and social conviction. I then try to see if the product is pioneering by putting these views together."

„Bei der Bewertung von Produkten teste ich zuerst ihre Funktionalität, dann ihre ästhetische Qualität und soziale Überzeugung. Danach versuche ich herauszufinden, ob das Produkt bahnbrechend ist und alle diese Eigenschaften vereint."

Please describe good design:
Good design is the thing that provides excellent social, cultural and economic value. Today's design is evaluated for its comprehensiveness.

What constitutes good teamwork?
While each member has different professions and ideas, each member's deep understanding of his role in the common mission constitutes teamwork.

What does the Red Dot Award represent in your opinion?
The Red Dot Award has always been pointing towards the direction in which design should be heading in changing times. I firmly believe that it has an essential and invariable value.

How do you imagine the future of design?
New technologies and services have been changing the future of design. At the same time, the cultural nature of design, unchanged since the twentieth century, may also become more brilliant.

Beschreiben Sie bitte gutes Design:
Gutes Design ist das, was hervorragenden sozialen, kulturellen und wirtschaftlichen Wert schafft. Design wird heute nach seiner Vollständigkeit beurteilt.

Was macht gute Teamarbeit aus?
Obwohl jedes Teammitglied unterschiedliche Fachkenntnisse und Ideen hat, macht die tiefgründige Kenntnis seiner Rolle in der gemeinsamen Aufgabe die Teamarbeit aus.

Wofür steht der Red Dot Award für Sie?
Der Red Dot Award war schon immer wegweisend für die Richtung, die Design in wechselvollen Zeiten einschlagen soll. Ich bin fest davon überzeugt, dass der Red Dot Award einen maßgeblichen und konstanten Wert hat.

Wie stellen Sie sich die Zukunft des Designs vor?
Neue Technologien und Dienstleistungen beeinflussen die Zukunft des Designs. Gleichzeitig mag der kulturelle Charakter des Designs, der seit dem 20. Jahrhundert unverändert ist, noch fulminanter werden.

Nils Toft
Denmark
Dänemark

Nils Toft is the founder and managing director of Designidea. With offices in Copenhagen and Beijing, the multiple internationally awarded studio works in the key fields of sustainable energy solutions, consumer electronics, medical devices and design psychology, as well as taking on projects in business development, design strategy and exhibition design. Nils Toft graduated as an architect and designer from the Royal Danish Academy of Fine Arts in Copenhagen in 1986 and started his career as an industrial designer, joining the former Christian Bjørn Design in 1987, an internationaly active design studio in Copenhagen. Within a few years, he became a partner of CBD and, as managing director successfully ran the business until 2010. Nils Toft's work has recently been focused on understanding and measuring how people are impacted by design. By measuring physiological parameters such as heart rate, eye movements, neurological activity and electro dermal activity, it is possible to unveil a test person's emotional condition as well as their psychological reactions in relation to products, environments and services.

Nils Toft ist der Gründer und Geschäftsführer von Designidea. Mit Niederlassungen in Kopenhagen und Beijing arbeitet das international mehrfach ausgezeichnete Studio hauptsächlich in den Bereichen Erneuerbare Energien, Unterhaltungselektronik, Medizintechnik und Designpsychologie. Das Studio übernimmt ebenfalls Projekte in den Bereichen Geschäftsentwicklung, Designstrategie und Ausstellungsdesign. Nils Toft machte seinen Abschluss als Architekt und Designer 1986 an der Royal Danish Academy of Fine Arts in Kopenhagen und begann seine Karriere als Industriedesigner 1987 bei dem damaligen Christian Bjørn Design, einem international operierenden Designstudio in Kopenhagen. Innerhalb weniger Jahre wurde er Partner bei CBD und leitete das Unternehmen erfolgreich bis 2010 als Managing Director. In letzter Zeit hat Nils Toft sich in seiner Arbeit auf das Verständnis und Messen der Wirkung von Design auf Menschen konzentriert. Wenn man physiologische Parameter wie z. B. Pulsschlag, Augenbewegung, neurologische sowie elektrodermale Aktivität misst, ist es möglich, emotionale und psychologische Reaktionen der Versuchsperson auf Produkte, die Umgebung und Dienstleistungen zu erkennen.

01 Wittenborg 95
High-quality semi-automatic coffee machines
Hochwertige halbautomatische Kaffeemaschinen

01

"My professional goal is to continually be curious, always seeking new challenges and chasing a continuously moving goal post."

„Mein professionelles Ziel ist es, immer neugierig zu sein, immer neue Herausforderungen zu suchen und ein ständig wechselndes Ziel zu verfolgen."

What does the "Designidea" company stand for?
Designidea is based on the philosophy that in all companies there are great ideas waiting to be discovered and with the help of good designers can be turned into great products.

What, to date, has been the most exciting project of your career?
I have been fortunate enough to work on many different types of exiting projects and that is what has made my career exiting. I am driven by my curiosity and new projects – challenges are what excites me the most.

How do you proceed when evaluating products?
I verify whether the design is of a high quality and clearly expresses the intended idea behind the product.

With what can a designer surprise you?
I am positively surprised and full of admiration when I see a technical product with many constraints that, because of a great design by a talented designer, appears so clear and obvious, that your only response is, "of course".

Wofür steht Ihr Unternehmen „Designidea"?
Designidea basiert auf der Philosophie, dass es in allen Unternehmen großartige Ideen gibt, die nur darauf warten, entdeckt und mithilfe guter Designer in großartige Produkte verwandelt zu werden.

Was war das bisher spannendste Projekt Ihrer Karriere?
Ich habe das Glück, an vielen verschiedenen aufregenden Projekten beteiligt gewesen zu sein. Das ist es, was meine Karriere so spannend macht. Mich treiben Neugier und neue Projekte an. Am aufregendsten finde ich neue Herausforderungen.

Wie gehen Sie bei der Bewertung von Produkten vor?
Ich prüfe, ob die Gestaltung qualitativ hochwertig ist und klar die Intention hinter dem Produkt zum Ausdruck bringt.

Womit kann ein Designer Sie überraschen?
Ich bin positiv überrascht und voller Bewunderung, wenn ich ein technisches Produkt mit vielen Features sehe, das dank eines großartigen Gestaltungskonzepts von einem talentierten Designer so klar und einleuchtend erscheint, dass man nur „na klar" denken kann.

Prof. Danny Venlet
Belgium
Belgien

Professor Danny Venlet was born in 1958 in Victoria, Australia, and studied interior design at Sint-Lukas, the Institute for Architecture and Arts in Brussels. Back in Australia in 1991, Venlet started to attract international attention with large-scale interior projects such as the Burdekin hotel in Sydney and Q-bar, an Australian chain of nightclubs. His design projects range from private mansions, lofts, bars and restaurants all the way to showrooms and offices of large companies. The interior projects and the furniture designs of Danny Venlet are characterised by their contemporary international style. He says that the objects arise from an interaction between art, sculpture and function. These objects give a new description to the space in which they are placed – with respect, but also with relative humour. Today, Danny Venlet teaches his knowledge to students at the Royal College of the Arts in Ghent.

Professor Danny Venlet wurde 1958 in Victoria, Australien, geboren und studierte Interior Design am Sint-Lukas Institut für Architektur und Kunst in Brüssel. Nachdem er 1991 wieder nach Australien zurückgekehrt war, begann er, mit der Innenausstattung großer Projekte wie dem Burdekin Hotel in Sydney und der Q-Bar, einer australischen Nachtclub-Kette, internationale Aufmerksamkeit zu erregen. Seine Designprojekte reichen von privaten Wohnhäusern über Lofts, Bars und Restaurants bis hin zu Ausstellungsräumen und Büros großer Unternehmen. Die Innenausstattungen und Möbeldesigns von Danny Venlet sind durch einen zeitgenössischen, internationalen Stil ausgezeichnet und entspringen, wie er sagt, der Interaktion zwischen Kunst, Skulptur und Funktion. Seine Objekte geben den Räumen, in denen sie sich befinden, eine neue Identität – mit Respekt, aber auch mit einer Portion Humor. Heute vermittelt Danny Venlet sein Wissen als Professor an Studenten des Royal College of the Arts in Gent.

01 L-Hop 2
Toilet roll holder with integrated light for the company Dark
Toilettenrollenhalter mit integriertem Licht für die Firma Dark

01

"Cultural exchange among designers is important to discover what other cultures have to offer and what solutions they have – in order to help us challenge our cultural dogmas."

„Der kulturelle Austausch zwischen Designern ist wichtig, um herauszufinden, was andere Kulturen zu bieten und welche Lösungen sie gefunden haben – das sollte uns helfen, unsere kulturellen Dogmen zu hinterfragen."

Is there a way of instantly recognising your designs? What are their distinguishing features?
My work is sometimes described as organic behaviouristic minimalism. Organic curves are beautiful and sensual but I believe one should use them sparingly. I am also a follower of the ideas of Wabi-Sabi, "the beauty of imperfection". I believe that the distinguishing features of my work are objects that move away from encrusted habits or customs and are therefore often behavioural change makers.

Unpretentious or grandiose – what do you prefer and why?
I would say unpretentious grandiosity would be my preference. Something is grandiose when it does not scream it out loud.

What are the essential features of a well-designed piece of furniture?
Excellence of execution, exceptional concept, emotionally capturing, elegant solution of a problem, environmentally friendly. Well-designed furniture should aim to have most of these E-factors.

Woran sind Ihre Gestaltungen zu erkennen? Was zeichnet sie aus?
Meine Arbeit wird manchmal als organisch behavioristischer Minimalismus bezeichnet. Organische Rundungen sind schön und sinnlich, doch bin ich der Meinung, dass man sie sparsam einsetzen sollte. Ich bin auch ein Anhänger der Ideen von Wabi-Sabi, „der Schönheit des Unvollkommenen". Ich glaube, dass die kennzeichnenden Merkmale meiner Arbeit Objekte sind, die sich von verkrusteten Gewohnheiten oder Gebräuchen entfernt haben und daher häufig zu „Änderungsgestaltern" des Verhaltens werden.

Schlicht oder pompös – was bevorzugen Sie und warum?
Ich würde sagen, dass ich eine Vorliebe für schlichten Prunk habe. Etwas, das pompös ist, ohne es zu laut kundzutun.

Was muss ein gut gestaltetes Möbelstück mitbringen?
Eine ausgezeichnete Umsetzung, ein herausragendes Konzept, es sollte emotional fesseln, eine elegante Lösung für ein Problem bieten und umweltfreundlich sein. Gut gestaltete Möbelstücke sollten einen Großteil dieser Eigenschaften aufweisen.

Dr. Joseph Francis Wong
Hong Kong
Hongkong

Dr. Joseph Francis Wong joined the Hong Kong Design Institute as the Vice Principal in 2017. Prior to this, he was Associate Professor at the City University of Hong Kong, where he taught architectural design and theory for 19 years. Joseph Francis Wong received a Bachelor of Arts in Architecture from Berkeley, a Master of Architecture from MIT and a Doctor of Education from Leicester. He is a Fellow of the Hong Kong Institute of Architects, where he was part of the Board of Internal Affairs and the Board of Educational Affairs and chaired the Environment and Sustainable Design Committee. His research on open building and spatial/visual field analysis has been presented and published in many conferences and journals, including Design Studies, Habitat International, Journal of Architecture as well as Environment and Planning B. In recognition of his contribution to design education, Joseph Francis Wong was awarded the Berkeley Prize International Fellowship in 2014.

2017 trat Dr. Joseph Francis Wong dem Hong Kong Design Institute als Vice Principal bei. Zuvor war er als Associate Professor an der City University of Hong Kong tätig, wo er 19 Jahre lang architektonische Gestaltung und Theorie lehrte. Er machte einen Bachelor of Arts in Architektur in Berkeley, einen Master of Architecture am MIT und einen Doctor of Education in Leicester. Joseph Francis Wong ist Fellow des Hong Kong Institute of Architects, wo er Teil des Board of Internal Affairs und des Board of Educational Affairs war und dem Environment and Sustainable Design Committee vorsaß. Seine Forschung über offene Gebäude und räumliche/visuelle Feldanalyse wurde in vielen Konferenzen und Zeitschriften vorgestellt und veröffentlicht, so in Design Studies, Habitat International, Journal of Architecture sowie Environment and Planning B. In Anerkennung seines Beitrags zur Designlehre erhielt Joseph Francis Wong 2014 den Berkeley Prize International Fellowship.

01 Kai Tak District Cooling Plant, Hong Kong
In collaboration with Andrew Lee King Fun & Associates Architects Ltd., Hong Kong
In Zusammenarbeit mit Andrew Lee King Fun & Associates Architects Ltd., Hongkong

01

"Innovation is a well-considered solution to a problem redefined through rigorous research."

„Innovation ist eine wohlüberlegte Lösung für ein Problem, das durch gründliche Recherche neu definiert wurde."

What does a product have to offer in order to persuade you of its merits?
Simplicity and user considerations. A good product does not need to attempt too much; it's more preferable to do one thing or a few things really well than too many things above average. It must also be clear and sensible about actual usage by users.

How do you proceed when evaluating products?
I would go straight for it, try to understand and use the product before reading the instructions. That's my first criterion. Next, I would correlate design intentions to the actual design itself. The product should definitely stand out in terms of elegant integration of look and feel to functionality.

Was muss ein Produkt mitbringen, um Sie zu überzeugen?
Einfachheit und eine Berücksichtigung der Nutzer. Ein gutes Produkt sollte nicht versuchen, zu viel zu leisten. Es ist besser, eine Sache oder ein paar Dinge richtig gut zu machen, als zu viele Dinge über dem Durchschnitt. Das Produkt sollte auch klar und vernünftig in Bezug auf die Anwendung durch den Nutzer sein.

Wie gehen Sie bei der Bewertung von Produkten vor?
Ich gehe ganz direkt vor und versuche, das Produkt zu verstehen und zu benutzen, bevor ich die Anleitung lese. Das ist mein erstes Kriterium. Als Nächstes versuche ich, den Zusammenhang zwischen Designintention und dem eigentlichen Design zu erkennen. Das Produkt sollte auf jeden Fall aus der Masse hervorstechen – in einer eleganten Integration von Optik, Haptik und Funktionalität.

Alphabetical index manufacturers and distributors
Alphabetisches Hersteller- und Vertriebs-Register

3B S.p.A.
Page/Seite 272

Beijing 17PIN Network Technology Co., Ltd.
Page/Seite 253

A

A-John Enterprise Co., Ltd.
Page/Seite 80

ABB (China) Limited
Page/Seite 136-137

Guangzhou ABO
Sunny Walk Restaurant Co., Ltd.
Page/Seite 75

Above Lights (HK) Limited
Page/Seite 376

Acofusion Lighting
Page/Seite 354

AD Architecture
Page/Seite 78

AEC Lighting Solutions Co., Ltd.
Page/ Seite 367

Aekyung
Page/Seite 77

aeris GmbH
Page/Seite 172-173

Aichi Dobby Ltd.
Page/Seite 238-239

AIGANG GmbH
Page/Seite 108-109

AKD Design GmbH
Modal Concept
Page/Seite 273

Shanghai Allocacoc Industrial Design Co., Ltd.
Page/Seite 373

AM PM Europe GmbH
Page/Seite 307, 328-329

American Standard
Page/Seite 260, 326

Angelo Po
Page/Seite 220-221

Animo
Page/Seite 211

Anyware Solutions ApS
Page/Seite 120

Aquabocci Ltd
Page/Seite 157

Arçelik A.S.
Page/Seite 204

Arkoslight
Page/Seite 336

Arovast Corporation
Page/Seite 234-235

Arpino
Page/Seite 384-385

Studio Arredi S.r.l.
Page/Seite 179

Shenzhen Aukey E-Business Co., Ltd.
Page/Seite 377

Avolt AB
Page/Seite 145

B

Zhejiang Ballee
Sanitary Wares Technology Co., Ltd.
Page/Seite 260

Bear Electric Appliance Co., Ltd.
Page/Seite 233, 237

Georg Bechter Licht
Page/Seite 147

berbel Ablufttechnik GmbH
Page/Seite 222-223

Berker GmbH & Co. KG
Page/Seite 146

Berkshire Innovations, Inc.
Page/Seite 236

Bette GmbH & Co. KG
Page/Seite 294

Bianco Asia Ltd.
Page/Seite 248-249

blomus GmbH
Page/Seite 364

Blue Sanitary Ware
Page/Seite 301

BMW Group
Forschungs- und Technologiehaus
Page/Seite 76

Bodum AG
Page/Seite 200-203

Bodyfriend Co., Ltd.
Page/Seite 255

BORA Vertriebs GmbH & Co KG
Page/Seite 226-227

Robert Bosch Hausgeräte GmbH
Page/Seite 207, 212-213, 252

Bosch Thermotechnology (Beijing) Co., Ltd.
Page/Seite 254, 259

Bradano
Page/Seite 261

Bravat
Page/Seite 261, 329

Breville
Page/Seite 193, 206, 209, 233, 250

Ningbo Bright Electric Co., Ltd.
Page/Seite 366

Richard Brink GmbH & Co. KG
Page/Seite 394

BRITA GmbH
Page/Seite 258

Brizo
Page/Seite 317

Brumberg Leuchten GmbH & Co. KG
Page/Seite 349

BSH Home Appliances (China) Co., Ltd.
Page/Seite 278-279

Bull Group Incorporated Company
Page/Seite 143, 146-147, 160

Bürgenstock Hotels AG
Page/Seite 74

Busch-Jaeger Elektro GmbH
Mitglied der ABB-Gruppe
Page/Seite 122

BUZAO
Page/Seite 342

C

Capdell
Page/Seite 174

Cavius Aps
Page/Seite 148

Centor Holdings Pty Ltd
Page/Seite 84-85

Changhong Meiling Co., Ltd.
Page/Seite 247, 286

Shanghai Chunmi
Electronics Technology Co., Ltd.
Page/Seite 231, 243

Gruppo Cimbali S.p.A.
Page/Seite 211

City of Prague
Page/Seite 388-389

Clean Best (Shenzhen) Technology Co., Ltd.
Page/Seite 258

Xiamen Clease Industries Co., Ltd.
Page/Seite 328

Co-Green Design Consultants
Page/Seite 162

COBRA, spol. s r.o.
Page/Seite 119

Concept 7
Page/Seite 372

Coravin
Page/Seite 253

Corona, Colceramica
Page/Seite 312

Coway
Page/Seite 254

Shenzhen Crastal Technology Co., Ltd.
Page/Seite 194-196

Crestron Electronics, Inc.
Page/Seite 123

D

De'Longhi Appliances
Page/Seite 208

Deceuninck NV
Page/Seite 90-91

Delica AG
Page/Seite 206

Delta Light N.V.
Page/Seite 335

Dessmann (China)
Machinery & Electronic Co., Ltd.
Page/Seite 112, 116

DingTalk (China)
Technology Information Co., Ltd.
Page/Seite 139

DOOYA
Page/Seite 94-101

Dowell Real Estate
Page/Seite 78

Foshan Duo Pu Le Furniture Co., Ltd.
Page/Seite 182-183

Duravit AG
Page/Seite 299

DW Windsor
Page/Seite 365

DXV
Page/Seite 303

E

Easo
Page/Seite 260

Hong Kong Ecoaqua Co., Limited
Page/Seite 258

Qingdao Ecopure Filter Co., Ltd.
Page/Seite 258

AB Electrolux
Page/Seite 215, 229, 251, 268

ERCO S.r.l.
Page/Seite 88

Eumar Santehnika OÜ
Page/Seite 295

Eureka Lighting
Page/Seite 339

Eve Systems
Page/Seite 146

F

Foshan Fanxiaoer
Rice Cooking Robot Technology Co.
Page/Seite 245

Farko Sp. z o.o.
Page/Seite 88

Faro Barcelona
Page/Seite 375

FLUA Lighting Co., Ltd.
Page/Seite 381

Fluxwerx Illumination Inc.
Page/Seite 332-334

FORMANI Holland B.V.
Page/Seite 118

Ningbo Fotile Kitchen Ware Co., Ltd.
Page/Seite 225

Franke Küchentechnik AG
Franke Kitchen Systems
Page/Seite 267

FritsJurgens
Page/Seite 106

G

Geberit International AG
Page/Seite 296, 303

GID International Design
Page/Seite 170

Gira Giersiepen GmbH & Co. KG
Page/Seite 111, 121

Glimakra of Sweden
Page/Seite 153

Godelmann GmbH & Co. KG
Page/Seite 395

Gorenje, d.d.
Page/Seite 229

GPI International Limited
Page/Seite 369

Gree Electric Appliances, Inc. of Zhuhai
Page/Seite 107, 240-241, 256

Grohe AG
Page/Seite 262-263, 314-316, 318-319, 324-325

Groveneer OÜ
Page/Seite 152

Shunde Guoxin Electric Ind Co., Ltd of Foshan
Page/Seite 378

H

Haberdashery
Page/Seite 370-371

Häfele GmbH & Co. KG
Page/Seite 156, 158-159

Haier Group
Page/Seite 280-285, 287-289

Adam Hall GmbH
Page/Seite 366

Hansgrohe SE
Page/Seite 304-305, 320-321, 327, 329

Hase Kaminofenbau GmbH
Page/Seite 171

HDC icontrols
Page/Seite 117

Hero
Page/Seite 204

Hettich Marketing-
und Vertriebs GmbH & Co. KG
Page/Seite 160

Honeywell China
Page/Seite 114

The Hong Kong Research Institute of Textiles
and Apparel
Page/Seite 82-83

Zhejiang Horizon Industrial Design Co., Ltd.
Page/Seite 170

hülsta-werke
Hüls GmbH & Co. KG
Page/Seite 180

I

IKEA of Sweden
Page/Seite 214, 224, 376

Ilcar di Bugatti S.r.l.
Page/Seite 191

International Sustainable
Chemistry Collaborative Centre (ISC3)
Page/Seite 78

interstil
Diedrichsen GmbH & Co. KG
Page/Seite 154-155

Intra Lighting
Page/Seite 339, 342

Nanjing IoT Sensor Technology Co., Ltd.
Page/Seite 116

IP44 Schmalhorst GmbH & Co. KG
Page/Seite 361

J

Beijing Jiangxinxiaozhen e-business Co., Ltd.
Page/Seite 317

Beijing Jinmao
Page/Seite 74

JOMOO Kitchen & Bath Co., Ltd.
Page/Seite 302, 306, 323, 326

Josko Fenster & Türen GmbH
Page/Seite 87

Joyoung
Page/Seite 242, 247, 250

JURA Elektroapparate AG
Page/Seite 210

Alphabetical index manufacturers and distributors
Alphabetisches Hersteller- und Vertriebs-Register

K

Kartell S.p.A.
Page/Seite 174

KEFAN Houseware & Furnishings Intelligent Manufacturing Co., Ltd.
Page/Seite 313

KEMFLO (Nanjing) Enviromental Technology Co., Ltd.
Page/Seite 257

Kenwood Limited
Page/Seite 246

Kesseböhmer GmbH
Page/Seite 158–159

Walter Knoll AG & Co. KG
Page/Seite 168, 179

Kohler Company
Page/Seite 294

Kohler Mira
Page/Seite 322

Koncept
Page/Seite 334

Krinner GmbH
Page/Seite 163

Kriskadecor
Page/Seite 345

Kuhn Rikon AG
Page/Seite 273

L

LAMILUX Heinrich Strunz GmbH
Page/Seite 87

Shenzhen Lankesun Intelligent Technology Co., Ltd.
Page/Seite 219

LaPreva AG
Page/Seite 303

Laufen Bathrooms AG
Page/Seite 307

Lavazza
Page/Seite 207

Hong Kong L.C.Z Group Limited
Page/Seite 361

Guangdong Lehua Intelligent Sanitary Ware Co., Ltd.
Page/Seite 326

Paola Lenti S.r.l.
Page/Seite 178

LG Electronics Inc.
Page/Seite 214, 254, 274–276

LG Uplus
Page/Seite 147

Liantek Electrical Appliances (Shenzhen) Co., Ltd.
Page/Seite 251

Licht+Raum AG
Page/Seite 346

limoss GmbH & Co. KG
Page/Seite 138

Linea Light Group
Page/Seite 343

LIXIL Corporation
Page/Seite 89, 102, 161, 266

Xiamen Lota International Co., Ltd.
Page/Seite 265, 314

Lumi United Technology Co., Ltd.
Page/Seite 121

Lumini
Page/Seite 376, 381

Luxurite (Shenzhen) Smart Home Ltd.
Page/Seite 121, 123

M

Beijing MADV Technology Co., Ltd.
Page/Seite 112

Zhejiang Marssenger Kitchenware Co., Ltd.
Page/Seite 270–271

Mastrad
Page/Seite 218

Mawa Design Licht- und Wohnideen GmbH
Page/Seite 374

Ningbo Mengo Kitchen Equipment Co., Ltd.
Page/Seite 267

GD Midea Consumer Electric MFG, Co., Ltd.
Page/Seite 192

Foshan Shunde Midea Electrical Heating Appliances
Page/Seite 244

Midea Kitchen & Water Heater Appliance Division
Page/Seite 255

Guangdong Midea Kitchen Appliances Manufacturing Co., Ltd.
Page/Seite 232

Hefei Midea Refrigerator Co., Ltd.
Page/Seite 277

Midea Smart Technology Co., Ltd.
Page/Seite 117, 135

Miele & Cie. KG
Page/Seite 211, 216, 268, 279

Guangdong Mingmen Locks Industry Co., Ltd.
Page/Seite 117

Miniso Hong Kong Limited
Page/Seite 372

mmcite 1 a.s.
Page/Seite 386

Modular Lighting Instruments Pits NV
Page/Seite 344

Moorgen
Page/Seite 124–133

Mundus Viridis d.o.o.
Page/Seite 168

N

Naber GmbH
Page/Seite 273

NDS Member of Norma Group
Page/Seite 394

Nektar Natura, d.o.o.
Page/Seite 163

Nescafé Dolce Gusto
Page/Seite 206

Nestlé Nespresso SA
Page/Seite 204, 210

neuform-Türenwerk Hans Glock GmbH & Co. KG
Page/Seite 105

Nien Made Enterprise Norman – Window Fashions
Page/Seite 93, 185

Niko NV
Page/Seite 111, 148–149

Nishikawa Sangyo Co., Ltd.
Page/Seite 184

Nordlux A/S
Page/Seite 341, 381

Nowodworski sp.j.
Page/Seite 341

NUC Electronics Co., Ltd.
Page/Seite 247

Nulite Lighting
Page/Seite 340

NVC Lighting Technology Corporation
Page/Seite 352–353

O

Okamura Corporation
Page/Seite 387

OKE Group GmbH
Page/Seite 184

Oktalite Lichttechnik GmbH
Page/Seite 351

Olansi Healthcare Co., Ltd.
Page/Seite 259

Onankorea
Page/Seite 368

Opple Lighting Co., Ltd.
Page/Seite 354, 356–357, 378

Orea AG
Page/Seite 150–151

Shenzhen ORVIBO Technology Co., Ltd.
Page/Seite 113, 138

Xiamen Oshince Technology Co., Ltd.
Page/Seite 323

P

Panasonic Corporation
Page/Seite 233, 269

PEAKnx DOGAWIST Company
Page/Seite 122

Performance in Lighting S.p.A.
Page/Seite 335

Peters Design GmbH
Page/Seite 343

Philips
Page/Seite 245, 253

Phyn LLC
Page/Seite 259

Pirnar d.o.o.
Page/Seite 103

PVD Concept
Page/Seite 344

Q

Hangzhou Qingguxiaoxiang Technology Co., Ltd.
Page/Seite 328

R

Rabel Systems
Page/Seite 79

raumplus Besitz- und Entwicklungs-GmbH & Co. KG
Page/Seite 169

RAVAK a.s.
Page/Seite 300

Regazzi SA
Page/Seite 92

Ribag Licht AG
Page/Seite 349

Rifeng Enterprise Group Co., Ltd.
Page/Seite 313

Rinnai Korea
Page/Seite 228

Ritzwell & Co.
Page/Seite 166–167, 176

Riviera & Bar
Page/Seite 198

Hangzhou ROBAM Applicances Co., Ltd.
Page/Seite 217, 224

Roca Brasil
Page/Seite 292–293

Romney Opto-electronic Systems Technology (Guangdong) Co., Ltd.
Page/Seite 350

Ningbo Royalux Lighting Co., Ltd.
Page/Seite 358–359, 364

RZB Rudolf Zimmermann, Bamberg GmbH
Page/Seite 347, 396

S

Samsung C&T Corporation Resort Group, Landscape Business (Everscape)
Page/Seite 392–393

Samsung SDS
Page/Seite 115

Sapeli, a.s.
Page/Seite 104

Sapiens Design
Page/Seite 378

Schneider Electric (China) Co., Ltd.
Page/Seite 120, 135

Schneider-Electric
Page/Seite 140–141

Schreiber Innenausbau GmbH
Page/Seite 80

Schüco International KG
Page/Seite 86–88, 110

Schulte Elektrotechnik GmbH & Co. KG
Page/Seite 144

Seazen Holdings Co., Ltd.
Page/Seite 74

Sector Alarm AS
Page/Seite 110

SELF Electronics Co., Ltd.
Page/Seite 351

SharkNinja
Page/Seite 205, 251

Shengtai Brassware Co., Ltd.
Page/Seite 316–317, 327

The Siam Sanitary Fittings Co., Ltd.
Page/Seite 306

Siemens AG
Page/Seite 138

Siemens Ltd., China
Page/Seite 143, 148

Signify
Page/Seite 335, 339–340, 342, 348, 350, 355, 357, 365, 379, 397

Simes S.p.A.
Page/Seite 349, 356

Simon Electric (China) Co., Ltd.
Page/Seite 142

Siterwell Electronics Co., Limited
Page/Seite 149

SK magic
Page/Seite 230

Slamp S.p.A.
Page/Seite 337

SLV GmbH
Page/Seite 365

Smeg S.p.A.
Page/Seite 205, 215, 246

Xiamen Solex High-Tech Industries Co., Ltd.
Page/Seite 264–265

Song's Chinese Cusine
Page/Seite 75

SONNEMAN – A Way of Light
Page/Seite 380

Sonnenglas GmbH
Page/Seite 362–363

KG Spennare AB
Page/Seite 80

Sugatsune Kogyo Co., Ltd.
Page/Seite 106

Zhejiang Supor Electrical Appliances Manufacturing
Page/Seite 243, 250

T

Guangdong Taigroo Electric Technology Co., Ltd.
Page/Seite 244

talsee AG
Page/Seite 297

TCL Corporation
Page/Seite 110, 112

Team 7 Natürlich Wohnen GmbH
Page/Seite 181

Teawith Essentials Association
Page/Seite 188–189

The Retreat at Blue Lagoon Iceland
Page/Seite 72–73

Tojo Möbel GmbH
Page/Seite 169

TON a.s.
Page/Seite 177

Top Electric Appliances Industrial Ltd.
Page/Seite 198

Toto Ltd.
Page/Seite 308–311

Trilux GmbH & Co. KG
Page/Seite 348, 350

Tuya Inc.
Page/Seite 120

Alphabetical index manufacturers and distributors
Alphabetisches Hersteller- und Vertriebs-Register

U
UNAM – National Autonomous
University of Mexico
Page/Seite 81

Unilock
Page/Seite 395

Union Galvanizer Co., Ltd.
Page/Seite 175

Uponor GmbH
Page/Seite 259

Ningbo Utec Electric Co., Ltd.
Page/Seite 360

V
V-ZUG AG
Page/Seite 228

Vatti Corporation Limited
Page/Seite 217, 225, 269

Vauth-Sagel Systemtechnik GmbH & Co. KG
Page/Seite 273

Viega Supply Chain GmbH & Co. KG
Page/Seite 301

VIGOUR GmbH
Page/Seite 298

Villeroy & Boch AG
Page/Seite 295

Vimar S.p.A.
Page/Seite 134

vitamin design
DONA Handelsges. mbH
Page/Seite 181

Vorwerk Temial GmbH
Page/Seite 197

W
Wever & Ducré BVBA
Page/Seite 373

Whirlpool EMEA S.p.A.
Page/Seite 215, 278

WMF Consumer Electric GmbH
Page/Seite 205, 209

X
XAL GmbH
Page/Seite 334, 340, 346

Beijing Xiao Mo Guai Technology Co., Ltd.
Page/Seite 179

Xiaomi Inc.
Page/Seite 114, 231, 373

Guangdong Xinbao
Electrical Appliances Holdings Co., Ltd.
Page/Seite 190, 199

Y
Qingdao Yeelink
Information Technology Co., Ltd.
Page/Seite 142, 372, 377

Hangzhou You Jia Technology Co., Ltd.
Page/Seite 116

Z
Zanotta S.p.A.
Page/Seite 175

Zucchetti Rubinetteria S.p.A.
Page/Seite 307

Zumtobel Lighting GmbH
Page/Seite 338

Zuo Studio
Page/Seite 390–391

Alphabetical index designers
Alphabetisches Designer-Register

2Lion
Page/Seite 218

2nd West
Page/Seite 206

Foshan 3&1 Industrial Design Co., Ltd.
Page/Seite 117

Beijing 17PIN Network Technology Co., Ltd.
Page/Seite 253

A

a·g Licht GbR
Page/Seite 338

A-John Enterprise Co., Ltd.
Page/Seite 80

A1 Productdesign
Reindl + Partner GmbH
Page/Seite 158–159

ABB (China) Limited
Page/Seite 136–137

Above Lights (HK) Limited
Page/Seite 376

Acofusion Lighting
Page/Seite 354

AD Architecture
Page/Seite 78

Klaus Adolph
a·g Licht GbR
Page/Seite 338

AEC Lighting Solutions Co., Ltd.
Page/Seite 367

aeris GmbH
Page/Seite 172–173

AHACKENBERG DESIGN
Page/Seite 205

Qingyun Ai
Rifeng Enterprise Group Co., Ltd.
Page/Seite 313

Aichi Dobby Ltd.
Page/Seite 238–239

AIGANG GmbH
Page/Seite 108–109

Guangzhou Alighting IOT & Technology Co., Ltd.
Page/Seite 350

Shanghai Allocacoc Industrial Design Co., Ltd.
Page/Seite 373

ambigence GmbH & Co. KG
Page/Seite 160

Studio Ambrozus
Page/Seite 222–223

American Standard
Page/Seite 260, 326

Daniel Amosy
Catino
Page/Seite 80

Yoshihiko Ando
LIXIL Corporation
Page/Seite 266

Antec Solutions Ltd.
Page/Seite 236

Aquabocci Ltd
Page/Seite 157

Arçelik A.Ş.
Page/Seite 204

Arkoslight
Page/Seite 336

Arovast Corporation
Page/Seite 234–235

Arpino
Page/Seite 384–385

ARTEFAKT design
Page/Seite 301

AUG Shenzhen Industrial Design Co., Ltd.
Page/Seite 328

Shenzhen Aukey E-Business Co., Ltd.
Page/Seite 377

Avolt AB
Page/Seite 145

AW Design International Ltd.
Page/Seite 236

B

Sooncheol Baek
Samsung C&T Corporation
Resort Group, Landscape Business (Everscape)
Page/Seite 392–393

Bing Bai
Foshan 3&1 Industrial Design Co., Ltd.
Page/Seite 117

Uroš Bajt
Gorenje, d.d.
Page/Seite 229

Zhejiang Ballee
Sanitary Wares Technology Co., Ltd.
Page/Seite 260

Martin Ballendat
Design Ballendat GmbH
Page/Seite 180

Bao Changliang
Haier Innovation Design Center
Page/Seite 281, 283

Kaining Bao
Gree Electric Appliances, Inc. of Zhuhai
Page/Seite 107

Basalt Architects
Page/Seite 72–73

Massimo Battaglia
Studio Volpi
Page/Seite 220–221

Maximilian Bauer
BSH Home Appliances (China) Co., Ltd.
Page/Seite 278

Giuseppe Bavuso
Bavuso Design S.r.l.
Page/Seite 88

Bear Electric Appliance Co., Ltd.
Page/Seite 233, 237

Georg Bechter Licht
Page/Seite 147

Christoph Becke
BSH Home Appliances (China) Co., Ltd.
Page/Seite 278

Christoph Behling Design Ltd.
Page/Seite 296, 303

Berkshire Innovations, Inc.
Page/Seite 236

Arkadi Berman
Eumar Santehnika OÜ
Page/Seite 295

Berrel Berrel Kräutler AG
Page/Seite 348

Ilaria Bertelli
Smeg S.p.A.
Page/Seite 246

Aixia Bian
AEC Lighting Solutions Co., Ltd.
Page/Seite 367

Bianco Asia Ltd.
Page/Seite 248–249

BIG-GAME
Page/Seite 273

Christopher Black
gravity GmbH
Page/Seite 76

Blue Sanitary Ware
Blue Sanitary Design Team Germany
Page/Seite 301

Bodyfriend Co., Ltd.
Page/Seite 255

Bohman Folenius
Page/Seite 375

Bønnelycke Arkitekter ApS
Page/Seite 341, 381

Studio Piet Boon
Page/Seite 118

BORA Vertriebs GmbH & Co KG
Page/Seite 227

Massimo Borrelli
Italdesign
Page/Seite 211

Robert Bosch Hausgeräte GmbH
Page/Seite 207, 212–213, 252

Bosch Thermotechnik GmbH
Page/Seite 254, 259

Bosch Thermotechnology (Shanghai) Co., Ltd.
Page/Seite 254, 259

Nicol Boyd
Office for Product Design
Page/Seite 179

Bradano
Page/Seite 261

Bravat
Page/Seite 261, 329

Breville
Page/Seite 193, 206, 209, 233, 250

Ningbo Bright Electric Co., Ltd.
Page/Seite 366

Richard Brink GmbH & Co. KG
Page/Seite 394

Brizo
Page/Seite 317

Magnus Brock
Richard Brink GmbH & Co. KG
Page/Seite 394

Brumberg Leuchten GmbH & Co. KG
Page/Seite 349

BSH Home Appliances (China) Co., Ltd.
Page/Seite 278–279

Wilfried Buelacher
J&W Design Ltd.
Page/Seite 358–359, 364

Bull Group Incorporated Company
Page/Seite 143, 146–147, 160

Metod Burgar
Wilsonic Design, d.o.o.
Page/Seite 163

Sonja Bürzle
Robert Bosch Hausgeräte GmbH
Page/Seite 252

Busch-Jaeger Elektro GmbH
Mitglied der ABB-Gruppe
Page/Seite 122

Sebastian David Büscher
Page/Seite 361

Büttler Bosshard Industrial Designer
Page/Seite 210

BUZAO
Page/Seite 342

byform productdesign
Page/Seite 156, 273

C

CA PLAN
Page/Seite 77

Cai Zengyi
Shijiazhuang Yiqi Technology Co., Ltd.
Page/Seite 326

Liangliang Cao
Gree Electric Appliances, Inc. of Zhuhai
Page/Seite 240–241

Cao Pu
Zhejiang Supor
Electrical Appliances Manufacturing
Page/Seite 243

Catino
Page/Seite 80

Cavius Aps
Page/Seite 148

Centor Holdings Pty Ltd
Centor Design Team
Page/Seite 84–85

Yu Juung Chang
A-John Enterprise Co., Ltd.
Page/Seite 80

Changhong Meiling Co., Ltd.
Page/Seite 247, 286

Yang Chao
GD Midea Consumer Electric MFG, Co., Ltd.
Page/Seite 192

Cheng Chen
Siterwell Electronics Co., Limited
Page/Seite 149

Gang Chen
JOMOO Kitchen & Bath Co., Ltd.
Page/Seite 326

Guangyu Chen
Gree Electric Appliances, Inc. of Zhuhai
Page/Seite 107

Chen Jian
Zhejiang Supor
Electrical Appliances Manufacturing
Page/Seite 250

Chen Jianquan
Shijiazhuang Yiqi Technology Co., Ltd.
Page/Seite 326

Chen Jun
Haier Innovation Design Center
Page/Seite 289

Prof. Chen Long Hui
Guangdong Xinbao
Electrical Appliances Holdings Co., Ltd.
Page/Seite 190, 199

Nanfei Chen
Gree Electric Appliances, Inc. of Zhuhai
Page/Seite 107, 240–241, 256

Peng Chen
Vatti Corporation Limited
Page/Seite 217, 225, 269

Qianni Chen
Foshan Shunde Midea
Electrical Heating Appliances
Page/Seite 244

Qinhong Chen
Gree Electric Appliances, Inc. of Zhuhai
Page/Seite 241

Xueliang Chen
Vatti Corporation Limited
Page/Seite 217, 225

Xusheng Chen
Gree Electric Appliances, Inc. of Zhuhai
Page/Seite 240–241, 256

Zhida Chen
Xiamen Clease Industries Co., Ltd.
Page/Seite 328

Zhida Chen
Xiamen Solex High-Tech Industries Co., Ltd.
Page/Seite 264–265

Hongyi Cheng
Gree Electric Appliances, Inc. of Zhuhai
Page/Seite 240–241

Cheng Kai
Zhejiang Supor
Electrical Appliances Manufacturing
Page/Seite 243

Cheng Yongli
Haier Innovation Design Center
Page/Seite 288

Kong Chengxiang
Kurz Kurz Design China
Page/Seite 255

China University of Technology
Page/Seite 80

Najung Cho
LG Electronics Inc.
Page/Seite 254

Hyun Choi
LG Electronics Inc.
Page/Seite 274–275

Kyukwan Choi
LG Electronics Inc.
Page/Seite 254, 274–276

Shilton Chong
Top Electric Appliances Industrial Ltd.
Page/Seite 198

Shanghai Chunmi
Electronics Technology Co., Ltd.
Page/Seite 231, 243

Clean Best (Shenzhen) Technology Co., Ltd.
Page/Seite 258

Xiamen Clease Industries Co., Ltd.
Page/Seite 328

Co-Green Design Consultants
Page/Seite 162

483

Alphabetical index designers
Alphabetisches Designer-Register

Florent Coirier
Page/Seite 344

Concept 7
Page/Seite 372

Yiannis Constantinides
Rabel Systems
Page/Seite 79

Coravin
Page/Seite 253

Emidio Corbetta Design
Page/Seite 272

Robert Cornelissen
Serge Cornelissen BVBA
Page/Seite 374

Serge Cornelissen
Serge Cornelissen BVBA
Page/Seite 374

Corona, Colceramica
Corona Design Team
Page/Seite 312

Matej Coufal
Page/Seite 386

Coway
Page/Seite 254

Shenzhen Crastal Technology Co., Ltd.
Page/Seite 194-196

Mirco Crosatto
Linea Light Group
Page/Seite 343

D

Marie Dam Holsting
Light-Point A/S
Page/Seite 361

Simon Davies
GPI International Limited
Page/Seite 369

Mi Dawei
BSH Home Appliances (China) Co., Ltd.
Page/Seite 279

Pieter de Vos
Niko NV
Page/Seite 148-149

De'Longhi Appliances
Page/Seite 208

Deceuninck NV
Page/Seite 90-91

deepdesign
Page/Seite 205, 246

Fien Dekker
Rain(a)Way
Page/Seite 395

Delta Light N.V.
Page/Seite 335

Delugan Meissl Associated Architects
Page/Seite 338

Caike Deng
Bear Electric Appliance Co., Ltd.
Page/Seite 233, 237

Design AG
Frank Greiser & Brigitte Adrian GbR
Page/Seite 154-155

Design Apartment
Page/Seite 74

Design Department
Nan Fung Group
Page/Seite 82-83

Design Group Italia
Page/Seite 72-73

designaffairs GmbH
Page/Seite 138

Arne Desmet
Niko NV
Page/Seite 111, 148-149

Ding Fan
United Design Lab
Page/Seite 188-189

Jie Ding
Foshan Shunde Midea
Electrical Heating Appliances
Page/Seite 244

DingTalk (China)
Technology Information Co., Ltd.
Page/Seite 139

Daniel Dirks
JOMOO Kitchen & Bath Co., Ltd.
Page/Seite 302

Shenzhen Dizan Technology Co., Ltd.
Page/Seite 350, 376

Jianbo Dong
Gree Electric Appliances, Inc. of Zhuhai
Page/Seite 107

Yaxi Dong
Gree Electric Appliances, Inc. of Zhuhai
Page/Seite 107

DOOYA
Ningbo DOOYA
Mechanic & Electronic Technology Co., Ltd.
Page/Seite 94-101

Dots Studio
Page/Seite 175

Dou Zhendong
Haier Innovation Design Center
Page/Seite 282

Johann Dück
JOMOO Kitchen & Bath Co., Ltd.
Page/Seite 302

Foshan Duo Pu Le Furniture Co., Ltd.
Page/Seite 182-183

DW Windsor
Page/Seite 365

DXV
Page/Seite 303

E

Easo
Page/Seite 260

Hong Kong Ecoaqua Co., Limited
Page/Seite 258

Qingdao Ecopure Filter Co., Ltd.
Page/Seite 258

EGGS Design
Page/Seite 110

Karsten Eibach
Krinner GmbH
Page/Seite 163

Max Eicher
BSH Home Appliances (China) Co., Ltd.
Page/Seite 278

AB Electrolux
Page/Seite 215, 229, 251, 268

EliumStudio
Page/Seite 140-141

EOOS Design GmbH
Page/Seite 168

Jan Eugster
2nd West
Page/Seite 206

Eumar Santehnika OÜ
Page/Seite 295

Eureka Lighting
Eureka Lighting Design Team
Page/Seite 339

F

F Mark Ltd.
Page/Seite 338

Faltazi Design Studio
Page/Seite 140-141

Fang Jianping
United Design Lab
Page/Seite 188-189

Yuan Fang
Joyoung
Page/Seite 250

Gao Fanyu
AUG Shenzhen Industrial Design Co., Ltd.
Page/Seite 328

Farko Sp. z o.o.
Page/Seite 88

Fei Zhaojun
Haier Innovation Design Center
Page/Seite 280

Wu Feipeng
Midea Kitchen & Water Heater
Appliance Division
Page/Seite 255

Hongtao Feng
Foshan Shunde Midea
Electrical Heating Appliances
Page/Seite 244

Hua Feng
JOMOO Kitchen & Bath Co., Ltd.
Page/Seite 323

Jiabao Feng
Gree Electric Appliances, Inc. of Zhuhai
Page/Seite 240-241, 256

Jinmei Feng
Gree Electric Appliances, Inc. of Zhuhai
Page/Seite 240-241, 256

Feng Zhiqun
Haier Innovation Design Center
Page/Seite 280

Xu Fenglin
BSH Home Appliances (China) Co., Ltd.
Page/Seite 278-279

Fine Science
Page/Seite 365

Francesco Fiorotto
De'Longhi Appliances
Page/Seite 208

FLUA Lighting Co., Ltd.
Page/Seite 381

Fluxwerx Illumination Inc.
Page/Seite 332-334

Klaus Försterling
BSH Home Appliances (China) Co., Ltd.
Page/Seite 278

Norman Foster
Page/Seite 179

Franke Küchentechnik AG
Franke Kitchen Systems
Page/Seite 267

FritsJurgens
Page/Seite 106

FromD Innovation
Page/Seite 136-137

Prof. Michal Froněk
Olgoj Chorchoj Studio
Page/Seite 388-389

Yihui Fu
JOMOO Kitchen & Bath Co., Ltd.
Page/Seite 306

Takayuki Fujita
Aichi Dobby Ltd.
Page/Seite 238-239

G

G-ART Design International
Page/Seite 74

Gao Rongna
Haier Innovation Design Center
Page/Seite 288

Celine Garland
Brizo
Page/Seite 317

Gloria Gianatti
Sapiens Design
Page/Seite 378

GID International Design
Page/Seite 170

Gira Giersiepen GmbH & Co. KG
Page/Seite 111, 121

Katja Gnielka
Robert Bosch Hausgeräte GmbH
Page/Seite 207

Gorenje, d.d.
Page/Seite 229

GP designpartners gmbh
Page/Seite 307, 328-329

GPI International Limited
Page/Seite 369

Gintaras Grabliauskas
vitamin design
DONA Handelsges. mbH
Page/Seite 181

gravity GmbH
Page/Seite 76

Gree Electric Appliances, Inc. of Zhuhai
Page/Seite 107, 240-241, 256

GRO design
Page/Seite 312

Grohe AG
Page/Seite 262-263, 314-316, 318-319, 324-325

Yingzhi Guan
Schneider Electric
Page/Seite 120, 135

Nicola Guelfo
Italdesign
Page/Seite 211

Shunde Guoxin Electric Ind Co., Ltd of Foshan
Page/Seite 378

H

Cocoon H
Guangdong Taigroo Electric Technology Co., Ltd.
Page/Seite 244

Jeonghoon Ha
Samsung SDS
Page/Seite 115

Sungchoon Ha
Onankorea
Page/Seite 368

Haberdashery
Page/Seite 370-371

Habits S.r.l.
Page/Seite 191

Häfele GmbH & Co. KG
Page/Seite 158-159

Hager Electro SAS
Corporate Design Hager Group
Page/Seite 146

Haier Innovation Design Center
Page/Seite 280-285, 287-289

Adam Hall GmbH
Page/Seite 366

Xiong Hao
Kurz Kurz Design China
Page/Seite 255

Hase Kaminofenbau GmbH
Page/Seite 171

HDC icontrols
Page/Seite 117

Kaipeng He
Top Industrial Design Co., Ltd.
Page/Seite 108-109

Qixing He
Shenzhen Dizan Technology Co., Ltd.
Page/Seite 376

Xuxiang He
Gree Electric Appliances, Inc. of Zhuhai
Page/Seite 241

Yongqiang He
Xiamen Lota International Co., Ltd.
Page/Seite 265, 314

Zexin He
Shanghai Allocacoc Industrial Design Co., Ltd.
Page/Seite 373

Hero
Page/Seite 204

Heikki Herranen
Pistejaviiva
Page/Seite 179

Eduard Herrmann
Page/Seite 386

Joachim Hessemer
LAMILUX Heinrich Strunz GmbH
Page/Seite 87

Colby Higgins
SharkNinja
Page/Seite 205

Tomoharu Hijikata
Aichi Dobby Ltd.
Page/Seite 238-239

Stefan Hillenmayer
designaffairs GmbH
Page/Seite 138

Joel Högberg
Spennare AB
Page/Seite 80

Alphabetical index designers
Alphabetisches Designer-Register

Stefan Hohn
Noto GmbH
Page/Seite 123

Holscher Design
Page/Seite 356

Homwee Technology (Sichuan) Co., Ltd.
Page/Seite 247, 286

Honeywell China
HUE Design Studio
Page/Seite 114

Xiaosong Hong
NVC Lighting Technology Corporation
Page/Seite 352–353

Zhihuai Hong
JOMOO Kitchen & Bath Co., Ltd.
Page/Seite 326

Zhejiang Horizon Industrial Design Co., Ltd.
Page/Seite 170

Prof. Günter Horntrich
Blue Sanitary Ware
Blue Sanitary Design Team Germany
Page/Seite 301

Hangzhou Hotdesign Co., Ltd.
Page/Seite 116

Bangbin Hou
Guangdong Midea Kitchen
Appliances Manufacturing Co., Ltd.
Page/Seite 232

Chao Sheng Hsu
A-John Enterprise Co., Ltd.
Page/Seite 80

Hua Hu
NVC Lighting Technology Corporation
Page/Seite 352–353

Jian Hu
Gree Electric Appliances, Inc. of Zhuhai
Page/Seite 107

Hu Minhui
Haier Innovation Design Center
Page/Seite 285

Quansen Hu
Xiamen Oshince Technology Co., Ltd.
Page/Seite 323

Xiaowu Hu
Guangdong Midea Kitchen
Appliances Manufacturing Co., Ltd.
Page/Seite 232

Caiyun Huang
Bravat
Page/Seite 261

Hongrong Huang
Shunde Guoxin Electric Ind Co., Ltd of Foshan
Page/Seite 378

Jianying Huang
Rifeng Enterprise Group Co., Ltd.
Page/Seite 313

Kunpeng Huang
JOMOO Kitchen & Bath Co., Ltd.
Page/Seite 323

Huang Kunsong
Shijiazhuang Yiqi Technology Co., Ltd.
Page/Seite 326

Huang Yi
Haier Innovation Design Center
Page/Seite 288

Yong Cai Huang
Republican Metropolis Architecture
Page/Seite 75

Yuecheng Huang
Clean Best (Shenzhen) Technology Co., Ltd.
Page/Seite 258

Yujiong Huang
Shunde Guoxin Electric Ind Co., Ltd of Foshan
Page/Seite 378

Huang Zeping
Haier Innovation Design Center
Page/Seite 288

Weihung Hung
Shanghai Chunmi
Electronics Technology Co., Ltd.
Page/Seite 243

Nathanael Hunt
Haberdashery
Page/Seite 370–371

I

IKEA of Sweden
Page/Seite 214, 224, 376

Imago Design GmbH
Page/Seite 227

Guangdong Infinity Mind
Architecture Design Co., Ltd.
Page/Seite 75

Shin Inho
NVC Lighting Technology Corporation
Page/Seite 352–353

INNOCEAN Worldwide
Page/Seite 77

Nanjing IoT Sensor Technology Co., Ltd.
Page/Seite 116

Italdesign
Page/Seite 211

J

J&W Design Ltd.
Page/Seite 358–359, 364

jack be nimble
Page/Seite 350

Raymond Jao
Nien Made Enterprise
Norman – Window Fashions
Page/Seite 93, 185

Lukasz Jaworski
Nowodworski sp.j.
Page/Seite 341

Kevin Jeong
Rinnai Korea
Page/Seite 228

Jianan Ji
Bravat
Page/Seite 329

Chen Jia
Lumi United Technology Co., Ltd.
Lumi United Industrial Design Team
Page/Seite 121

Zhu Jian
Nanjing IoT Sensor Technology Co., Ltd.
Page/Seite 116

Jiang Chunhui
Haier Innovation Design Center
Page/Seite 281–285, 287–289

Li Jiang
JOMOO Kitchen & Bath Co., Ltd.
Page/Seite 306

Jiang Xiaoxia
Haier Innovation Design Center
Page/Seite 287

Beijing Jiangxinxiaozhen e-business Co., Ltd.
Page/Seite 317

Li Jianping
Midea Kitchen & Water Heater
Appliance Division
Page/Seite 255

Junghun Jin
Onankorea
Page/Seite 368

Yang Jin
Beijing MADV Technology Co., Ltd.
Page/Seite 112

Liu Jing
Nanjing IoT Sensor Technology Co., Ltd.
Page/Seite 116

Yuna Jo
LG Electronics Inc.
Page/Seite 214

JOMOO Kitchen & Bath Co., Ltd.
Page/Seite 302, 306, 323, 326

Junghyun Joo
LG Electronics Inc.
Page/Seite 276

Yongjoon Joo
Rinnai Korea
Page/Seite 228

Stefanie Jörgens – Gesunde Lebensräume
Page/Seite 78

Josko Fenster & Türen GmbH
Page/Seite 87

Patrick Jouin
Page/Seite 175

Joyoung
Page/Seite 242, 247, 250

Hanjin Jung
LG Electronics Inc.
Page/Seite 214

Hee Sub Jung
HDC icontrols
Page/Seite 117

K

Aleš Kachlík
Olgoj Chorchoj Studio
Page/Seite 388–389

Wang Kai
BSH Home Appliances (China) Co., Ltd.
Page/Seite 279

Florian Kallus
kaschkasch
Page/Seite 364

Kang Jingru
Haier Innovation Design Center
Page/Seite 282

Sookyeong Kang
LG Electronics Inc.
Page/Seite 254

David Karasek
Page/Seite 386

Kardorff Ingenieure Lichtplanung GmbH
Page/Seite 343

kaschkasch
Page/Seite 364

KEMFLO (Nanjing)
Enviromental Technology Co., Ltd.
Page/Seite 257

Kenwood Limited
Page/Seite 246

Keren Hu
United Design Lab
Page/Seite 188–189

Kesseböhmer GmbH
Page/Seite 158–159

Andreas Kessler
BSH Home Appliances (China) Co., Ltd.
Page/Seite 279

Dan Kestenbaum
SharkNinja
Page/Seite 205

Jeongeun Kim
SK magic
Page/Seite 230

Myong Kyu Kim
Bodyfriend Co., Ltd.
Page/Seite 255

Sanghun Kim
LG Electronics Inc.
Page/Seite 276

Sangwoo Kim
LG Electronics Inc.
Page/Seite 214

Sooyeon Kim
LG Electronics Inc.
Page/Seite 214

Yong Kim
LG Electronics Inc.
Page/Seite 274–275

Sophia Klees
jack be nimble
Page/Seite 350

Philipp Kleinlein
BSH Home Appliances (China) Co., Ltd.
Page/Seite 279

KLID – Kris Lin Interior Design
Page/Seite 78

Miki Kobayashi
Panasonic Corporation
Page/Seite 233

Ernst Köhler
WMF Consumer Electric GmbH
Page/Seite 209

Kohler Company
Kohler Design Studio
Page/Seite 294

Kohler Mira
Kohler Mira Design Team
Page/Seite 322

Lucie Koldová Studio
Page/Seite 177

Ulrich Kollmann
Regazzi SA
Page/Seite 92

Fabian Kollmann
Bosch Thermotechnik GmbH
Page/Seite 254, 259

Koncept
Page/Seite 334

Urša Kovačič
Gorenje, d.d.
Page/Seite 229

Krinner GmbH
Page/Seite 163

Diego Kuo
Shanghai Chunmi
Electronics Technology Co., Ltd.
Page/Seite 231, 243

Kurz Kurz Design China
Page/Seite 255

L

Jean-Jacques L'Henaff
DXV
Page/Seite 303

LAMILUX Heinrich Strunz GmbH
Page/Seite 87

Marco Lärm
BSH Home Appliances (China) Co., Ltd.
Page/Seite 278

W. L. Lau
Antec Solutions Ltd.
Page/Seite 236

Lavazza
Page/Seite 207

Daesung Lee
LG Electronics Inc.
Page/Seite 274–275

Hangbok Lee
LG Electronics Inc.
Page/Seite 214

Jieun Lee
NUC Electronics Co., Ltd.
Page/Seite 247

Johnson Lee
Bianco Asia Ltd.
Page/Seite 248–249

Nari Lee
Coway
Page/Seite 254

Seoyeon Lee
LG Uplus
Page/Seite 147

Seungryun Lee
Samsung SDS
Page/Seite 115

Soyeon Lee
Coway
Page/Seite 254

Pan Lefan
Co-Green Design Consultants
Page/Seite 162

Sascha Leng
Robert Bosch Hausgeräte GmbH
Page/Seite 252

LG Electronics Inc.
Page/Seite 214, 254, 274–276

LG Uplus
Page/Seite 147

Dong Wen Li
Olansi Healthcare Co., Ltd.
Page/Seite 259

Jin Li
Beijing Jiangxinxiaozhen e-business Co., Ltd.
Page/Seite 317

Peilin Li
Honeywell China
HUE Design Studio
Page/Seite 114

Alphabetical index designers
Alphabetisches Designer-Register

Li Pengtao
Haier Innovation Design Center
Page/Seite 284

Qupeng Li
Miniso Hong Kong Limited
Page/Seite 372

Sha Li
Gree Electric Appliances, Inc. of Zhuhai
Page/Seite 107, 240–241, 256

Shenghua Li
Xiamen Solex High-Tech Industries Co., Ltd.
Page/Seite 264

Wanqi Li
Top Industrial Design Co., Ltd.
Page/Seite 108–109

Wenkai Li
Tuya Inc.
Page/Seite 120

Li Xia
Haier Innovation Design Center
Page/Seite 284–285

Li Xiaozhu
Zhejiang Marssenger Kitchenware Co., Ltd.
Page/Seite 270–271

Yao Li
Gree Electric Appliances, Inc. of Zhuhai
Page/Seite 240

Yonghuang Li
Xiamen Lota International Co., Ltd.
Page/Seite 265, 314

Li Yu
United Design Lab
Page/Seite 188–189

Liantek
Electrical Appliances (Shenzhen) Co., Ltd.
Page/Seite 251

Xiaodong Liao
Xiamen Solex High-Tech Industries Co., Ltd.
Page/Seite 265

Licht+Raum AG
Page/Seite 346

Light-Point A/S
Page/Seite 361

Sophia Lim
Joyoung
Page/Seite 242

limoss GmbH & Co. KG
Page/Seite 138

Eugene Lin
KEMFLO (Nanjing) Enviromental Technology Co., Ltd.
Page/Seite 257

Jianfeng Lin
Gree Electric Appliances, Inc. of Zhuhai
Page/Seite 240–241, 256

Lin Jie
Shijiazhuang Yiqi Technology Co., Ltd.
Page/Seite 326

Jiqiao Lin
JOMOO Kitchen & Bath Co., Ltd.
Page/Seite 306

Lin Kai
Shijiazhuang Yiqi Technology Co., Ltd.
Page/Seite 326

Kris Lin
KLID – Kris Lin Interior Design
Page/Seite 78

Ruei-Hsing Lin
China University of Technology
Page/Seite 80

Xian Lin
Xiamen Clease Industries Co., Ltd.
Page/Seite 328

Yun Hui Lin
A-John Enterprise Co., Ltd.
Page/Seite 80

Linea Light Group
Page/Seite 343

Jonathan Lion
2Lion
Page/Seite 218

Mathieu Lion
2Lion
Page/Seite 218

LITE-ON Technology Corp.
Page/Seite 93, 185

Liu Fang
Teawith Essentials Association
Page/Seite 188–189

Liu Haibo
Haier Innovation Design Center
Page/Seite 280

Jiachi Liu
Gree Electric Appliances, Inc. of Zhuhai
Page/Seite 107

Jiahua Liu
Gree Electric Appliances, Inc. of Zhuhai
Page/Seite 107, 240–241, 256

Liu Mingjun
Haier Innovation Design Center
Page/Seite 281

Shengsheng Liu
Gree Electric Appliances, Inc. of Zhuhai
Page/Seite 240–241, 256

Xuefei Liu
Bosch Thermotechnology (Shanghai) Co., Ltd.
Page/Seite 254, 259

Yan Liu
Gree Electric Appliances, Inc. of Zhuhai
Page/Seite 240–241, 256

Liu Yibing
Shijiazhuang Yiqi Technology Co., Ltd.
Page/Seite 326

LIXIL Corporation
Page/Seite 89, 102, 161, 266

LKK Design Shenzhen Co., Ltd.
Page/Seite 112

LKKer Technology Co., Ltd.
Page/Seite 245

Xiaotong Long
Shenzhen Dizan Technology Co., Ltd.
Page/Seite 376

Andres Lopez
Corona, Colceramica
Corona Design Team
Page/Seite 312

Xiamen Lota International Co., Ltd.
Page/Seite 265, 314

Roy Lu
Shenzhen Crastal Technology Co., Ltd.
Page/Seite 194–196

Wang Lu
Joyoung
Page/Seite 247

Wei Lu
Guangdong Midea Kitchen Appliances Manufacturing Co., Ltd.
Page/Seite 232

Wenbo Lu
Gree Electric Appliances, Inc. of Zhuhai
Page/Seite 240

Lu Yue
Haier Innovation Design Center
Page/Seite 283

Gregor Luippold
Robert Bosch Hausgeräte GmbH
Page/Seite 207

James Luk
FLUA Lighting Co., Ltd.
Page/Seite 381

Lumi United Technology Co., Ltd.
Lumi United Industrial Design Team
Page/Seite 121

Lumini
Page/Seite 376, 381

Viktor Lundberg
Avolt AB
Page/Seite 145

Jonatan Lundén
Catino
Page/Seite 80

Jackie Luo
J&W Design Ltd.
Page/Seite 358–359, 364

Yanping Luo
JOMOO Kitchen & Bath Co., Ltd.
Page/Seite 323

Luxurite (Shenzhen) Smart Home Ltd.
Page/Seite 121, 123

Xiaoming Lv
JOMOO Kitchen & Bath Co., Ltd.
Page/Seite 306, 326

M

Ma Lifeng
Haier Innovation Design Center
Page/Seite 281

Niklas Madsen
Superlab
Page/Seite 153

Beijing MADV Technology Co., Ltd.
Page/Seite 112

Ian Mahaffy Industrial Design
Page/Seite 120

Zhejiang Marssenger Kitchenware Co., Ltd.
Page/Seite 270–271

Jean-Marie Massaud
Studio Massaud
Page/Seite 304–305

Mihkel Masso
Mihkel Masso Studio
MMIDS OÜ
Page/Seite 152

Alessandro Mattia
Sapiens Design
Page/Seite 378

Meng Meng
Lumi United Technology Co., Ltd.
Lumi United Industrial Design Team
Page/Seite 121

Meng Xiangbo
Haier Innovation Design Center
Page/Seite 284

Juan Mesa
Corona, Colceramica
Corona Design Team
Page/Seite 312

Kristina Meyer
byform productdesign
Page/Seite 156, 273

GD Midea Consumer Electric MFG, Co., Ltd.
Page/Seite 192

Foshan Shunde Midea
Electrical Heating Appliances
Page/Seite 244

Midea Kitchen & Water Heater
Appliance Division
Page/Seite 255

Guangdong Midea Kitchen
Appliances Manufacturing Co., Ltd.
Page/Seite 232

Hefei Midea Refrigerator Co., Ltd.
Page/Seite 277

Midea Smart Technology Co., Ltd.
Page/Seite 117, 135

Miele & Cie. KG
Page/Seite 211, 216, 268, 279

Nina Mihovec
Wilsonic Design, d.o.o.
Page/Seite 163

Jeff Miller Inc.
Page/Seite 207

Martin Miller
SharkNinja
Page/Seite 251

Anthony Milling
Aquabocci Ltd
Page/Seite 157

Miniso Hong Kong Limited
Page/Seite 372

Jiang Minzhen
Lumi United Technology Co., Ltd.
Lumi United Industrial Design Team
Page/Seite 121

Shinsaku Miyamoto
Ritzwell & Co.
Page/Seite 166–167, 176

mmcite 1 a.s.
Page/Seite 386

Moorgen
Moorgen Deutschland GmbH
Page/Seite 124–133

Ningbo Morgen Industry Design Co., Ltd.
Page/Seite 267

Mathias Mößle
RZB Rudolf Zimmermann, Bamberg GmbH
Page/Seite 396

Stephan Müller
Kardorff Ingenieure Lichtplanung GmbH
Page/Seite 343

Multiple SA
Page/Seite 206

N

Fernando Najera
Hase Kaminofenbau GmbH
Page/Seite 171

Naked Image
Page/Seite 250

Studio Narai
Page/Seite 191

NDS
Member of Norma Group
Page/Seite 394

Prof. Jan Němeček
Olgoj Chorchoj Studio
Page/Seite 388–389

Nestlé Nespresso SA
Page/Seite 204, 210

Thorben Neu
Ritual Creative Inc.
Page/Seite 259

neuform-Türenwerk Hans Glock GmbH & Co. KG
Page/Seite 105

Edmund Ng
Koncept
Page/Seite 334

Kenneth Ng
Koncept
Page/Seite 334

Nien Made Enterprise
Norman – Window Fashions
Page/Seite 93, 185

Michael Nien
Nien Made Enterprise
Norman – Window Fashions
Page/Seite 93, 185

Niko NV
Page/Seite 111, 148–149

Nishikawa Sangyo Co., Ltd.
Page/Seite 184

Patrick Norguet
Studio Norguet Design
Page/Seite 174

Normal Studio
Page/Seite 140–141

Kryštof Nosál
Nosal Design Studio
Page/Seite 300

Noto GmbH
Page/Seite 123

Dan Nourian
NDS
Member of Norma Group
Page/Seite 394

NOVAGUE
Page/Seite 104, 119

Nowodworski sp.j.
Page/Seite 341

NUC Electronics Co., Ltd.
Page/Seite 247

Nulite Lighting
Page/Seite 340

NVC Lighting Technology Corporation
Page/Seite 352–353

Alphabetical index designers
Alphabetisches Designer-Register

O

Nicolas Ochoa
Corona, Colceramica
Corona Design Team
Page/Seite 312

Office for Product Design
Page/Seite 179

Ruy Ohtake
Page/Seite 292–293

Okamura Corporation
Page/Seite 387

OKE Group GmbH
Page/Seite 184

Asli Ökmen
Arçelik A.S.
Page/Seite 204

Oktalite Lichttechnik GmbH
Page/Seite 351

Olansi Healthcare Co., Ltd.
Page/Seite 259

Olgoj Chorchoj Studio
Page/Seite 388–389

Onankorea
Page/Seite 368

Opple Lighting Co., Ltd.
Page/Seite 354, 356–357, 378

Orea AG
Orea Design
Page/Seite 150–151

Mina Orihashi
Aichi Dobby Ltd.
Page/Seite 238–239

Shenzhen ORVIBO Technology Co., Ltd.
Page/Seite 113, 138

Xiamen Oshince Technology Co., Ltd.
Page/Seite 323

Andreas Ostwald
ostwalddesign
Page/Seite 172–173

P

Gerald Palmsteiner
PEAKnx
DOGAWIST Company
Page/Seite 122

Palomba Serafini Associati
Page/Seite 307

Panasonic Corporation
Page/Seite 233, 269

Jinhee Park
LG Electronics Inc.
Page/Seite 276

Sebin Park
Onankorea
Page/Seite 368

Christoph Pauschitz
GP designpartners gmbh
Page/Seite 307, 328–329

PEAKnx
DOGAWIST Company
Page/Seite 122

Pearl Creative
Storti&Rummel GbR
Page/Seite 258

Guogang Peng
Above Lights (HK) Limited
Page/Seite 376

Jiangming Peng
Rifeng Enterprise Group Co., Ltd.
Page/Seite 313

Ran Peng
Midea Smart Technology Co., Ltd.
Page/Seite 117, 135

Wei Peng
Olansi Healthcare Co., Ltd.
Page/Seite 259

Yinshui Peng
Romney Opto-electronic Systems Technology (Guangdong) Co., Ltd.
Page/Seite 350

Carlos Pereira
Arpino
Page/Seite 384–385

Performance in Lighting S.p.A.
Page/Seite 335

Moritz Peters
Peters Design GmbH
Page/Seite 343

Pezy Group
Page/Seite 211

Philips
Philips Design
Page/Seite 245, 253

Phoenix Design GmbH + Co. KG
Page/Seite 226, 320–321, 327, 329

Krit Phutpim
Dots Studio
Page/Seite 175

Pi-Design AG
Page/Seite 200–203

Pirnar d.o.o.
Page/Seite 103

Pistejaviiva
Page/Seite 179

Petter Polson
Catino
Page/Seite 80

Matevž Popič
Gorenje, d.d.
Page/Seite 229

Greta Pötter
PEAKnx
DOGAWIST Company
Page/Seite 122

Fernando Prado
Lumini
Page/Seite 376, 381

Henrik Preutz
IKEA of Sweden
Page/Seite 376

Bastian Prieler
Page/Seite 169

Lidija Pritržnik
Gorenje, d.d.
Page/Seite 229

Prode
Page/Seite 179

Propeller Design AB
Page/Seite 116

PVD Concept
Page/Seite 344

Q

Xu Qinglian
Shenzhen ORVIBO Technology Co., Ltd.
Page/Seite 113, 138

Xiaozhou Qiu
Rifeng Enterprise Group Co., Ltd.
Page/Seite 313

Wang Qiuchen
LKKer Technology Co., Ltd.
Page/Seite 245

Zhengbing Qu
Rifeng Enterprise Group Co., Ltd.
Page/Seite 313

Machiel Quadt
Bradano
Page/Seite 261

R

R&D Design Co., Ltd.
Page/Seite 225

Rabel Systems
Page/Seite 79

Rain(a)Way
Page/Seite 395

raumplus Besitz- und Entwicklungs-GmbH & Co. KG
Page/Seite 169

Regazzi SA
Page/Seite 92

Guillaume Reiner
Schneider-Electric
Page/Seite 140–141

Oliver Renelt
Reneltdesign
Page/Seite 146

Republican Metropolis Architecture
Page/Seite 75

Resideo
Page/Seite 110

Ribag Licht AG
Page/Seite 349

Christine Rieder
BSH Home Appliances (China) Co., Ltd.
Page/Seite 278

Rifeng Enterprise Group Co., Ltd.
Page/Seite 313

Innocenzo Rifino
Habits S.r.l.
Page/Seite 191, 248–249

Rinnai Korea
Page/Seite 228

Ritual Creative Inc.
Page/Seite 259

Sebastian Ritzler
gravity GmbH
Page/Seite 76

Ritzwell & Co.
Page/Seite 166–167, 176

Hangzhou ROBAM Applicances Co., Ltd.
Page/Seite 217, 224

Ray Rodenburgh
Unilock
Page/Seite 395

Hyoungwon Roh
LG Electronics Inc.
Page/Seite 254

Romney Opto-electronic Systems Technology (Guangdong) Co., Ltd.
Page/Seite 350

Zeng Rong
BSH Home Appliances (China) Co., Ltd.
Page/Seite 278

Zheng Rongchun
Shenzhen ORVIBO Technology Co., Ltd.
Page/Seite 113, 138

Tomas Rosén
Office for Product Design
Page/Seite 179

Thorsten Rosenstengel
byform productdesign
Page/Seite 156, 273

Francesco Rota
Page/Seite 178

Sandro Roth
Licht+Raum AG
Page/Seite 346

Prof. Lorenzo Ruggieri
Studio Narai
Page/Seite 191

Li Rui
Co-Green Design Consultants
Page/Seite 162

Johan Runströmer
Avolt AB
Page/Seite 145

David Rusch
NDS
Member of Norma Group
Page/Seite 394

Fabio Rutishauser
2nd West
Page/Seite 206

RZB Rudolf Zimmermann, Bamberg GmbH
Page/Seite 347, 396

S

Rubén Saldaña Acle
Arkoslight
Page/Seite 336

Karl Saluveer
Mihkel Masso Studio
MMIDS OÜ
Page/Seite 152

Samsung C&T Corporation
Resort Group, Landscape Business (Everscape)
Page/Seite 392–393

Samsung SDS
Page/Seite 115

Hiroshi Saotome
Okamura Corporation
Page/Seite 387

Sapiens Design
Page/Seite 378

Johann Scheuringer
Josko Fenster & Türen GmbH
Page/Seite 87

Bureau Kilian Schindler
Page/Seite 273

Felix Schmidt
byform product design
Page/Seite 273

Schmitz Visuelle Kommunikation
Page/Seite 111, 121

Schneider Electric
Page/Seite 120, 135, 140–141

Sebastian Schneider
kaschkasch
Page/Seite 364

Schreiber Innenausbau GmbH
Page/Seite 80

Bernd Schriefer
volume3 design
Page/Seite 295

Schüco International KG
Page/Seite 86–88, 110

Siegfried Schulte
Schulte Elektrotechnik GmbH & Co. KG
Page/Seite 144

Sector Alarm AS
Page/Seite 110

Florian Seidl
Lavazza
Page/Seite 207

SELF Electronics Co., Ltd.
Page/Seite 351

Jaan Selg
Propeller Design AB
Page/Seite 116

Juhun Seo
NUC Electronics Co., Ltd.
Page/Seite 247

Youngwoo Seo
Samsung C&T Corporation
Resort Group, Landscape Business (Everscape)
Page/Seite 392–393

Xin Shao
Vatti Corporation Limited
Page/Seite 269

Wu Shaobin
Shenzhen ORVIBO Technology Co., Ltd.
Page/Seite 113, 138

SharkNinja
Page/Seite 205, 251

Shengtai Brassware Co., Ltd.
Justime Design Team
Page/Seite 316–317, 327

Zhang Shenrong
Kurz Kurz Design China
Page/Seite 255

Shili Shi
Zhejiang Ballee Sanitary Wares Technology Co., Ltd.
Page/Seite 260

Weizhi Shi
LKK Design Shenzhen Co., Ltd.
Page/Seite 112

Tomohiro Shigeura
Panasonic Corporation
Page/Seite 269

Chen Shishi
Midea Kitchen & Water Heater Appliance Division
Page/Seite 255

Chen Shu
Guangdong Taigroo Electric Technology Co., Ltd.
Page/Seite 244

The Siam Sanitary Fittings Co., Ltd.
COTTO Design Team
Page/Seite 306

Alphabetical index designers
Alphabetisches Designer-Register

Siemens AG
Page/Seite 138

Siemens Ltd., China
Page/Seite 143, 148

Signify
Signify Design Team
Page/Seite 335, 339–340, 342, 348, 350, 355, 357, 365, 379, 397

Simes S.p.A.
Page/Seite 349, 356

Simon Electric (China) Co., Ltd.
Simon Electric Group – China Design Team
Page/Seite 142

Siterwell Electronics Co., Limited
Page/Seite 149

SK magic
Page/Seite 230

Slamp S.p.A.
Page/Seite 337

SLV GmbH
Page/Seite 365

Smeg S.p.A.
Page/Seite 205, 215, 246

Luke Smith-Wightman
Page/Seite 338

Xiamen Solex High-Tech Industries Co., Ltd.
Page/Seite 264–265

Büro Sommer
Page/Seite 335

Kibok Song
DXV
Page/Seite 303

Robert Sonneman
SONNEMAN – A Way of Light
Page/Seite 380

Sonnenglas GmbH
Sonnenglas Design Team
Page/Seite 362–363

Johan Spennare
Spennare AB
Page/Seite 80

Philippe Starck
Page/Seite 174

Ralph Staud
BSH Home Appliances (China) Co., Ltd.
Page/Seite 279

Michael Stein Design
Page/Seite 298

Philippe Stephant
SLV GmbH
Page/Seite 365

Sebastian Stoller
limoss GmbH & Co. KG
Page/Seite 138

Pierre Struzka
Multiple SA
Page/Seite 206

studio KMJ GmbH
Page/Seite 299

Gushun Su
Beijing Jiangxinxiaozhen e-business Co., Ltd.
Page/Seite 317

Sugatsune Kogyo Co., Ltd.
Page/Seite 106

Sui Xinyuan
Haier Innovation Design Center
Page/Seite 285

Sun Ke
Haier Innovation Design Center
Page/Seite 287, 289

Superlab
Page/Seite 153

Zhejiang Supor
Electrical Appliances Manufacturing
Page/Seite 243, 250

Scott Swierad
Unilock
Page/Seite 395

T
Guangdong Taigroo Electric Technology Co., Ltd.
Page/Seite 244

Naoki Takizawa Design Inc.
Page/Seite 184

tale Designstudio GmbH
Page/Seite 297

talsee AG
Page/Seite 297

Jianming Tan
Gree Electric Appliances, Inc. of Zhuhai
Page/Seite 107, 240–241, 256

Chung-Han Tang
Design Apartment
Page/Seite 74

Xiao Tao
Midea Smart Technology Co., Ltd.
Page/Seite 117, 135

Michael Taylor
Berkshire Innovations, Inc.
Page/Seite 236

Warren Taylor
Berkshire Innovations, Inc.
Page/Seite 236

TCL Corporation
Shenzhen TCL Digital Technology Co., Ltd.
Page/Seite 110, 112

Teawith Essentials Association
Page/Seite 188–189

Produktdesign Tesseraux+Partner
Page/Seite 181, 294

Dörte Thinius
Busch-Jaeger Elektro GmbH
Mitglied der ABB-Gruppe
Page/Seite 122

Thinkobjects
Page/Seite 168

Matteo Thun
Matteo Thun & Partners
Page/Seite 74

Michael Thurnherr
2nd West
Page/Seite 206

Fuzhong Tian
Gree Electric Appliances, Inc. of Zhuhai
Page/Seite 107

Zhang Tijun
Nanjing IoT Sensor Technology Co., Ltd.
Page/Seite 116

Thomas Tischer
BSH Home Appliances (China) Co., Ltd.
Page/Seite 279

Keishi Tomiya
Toto Ltd.
Page/Seite 308

Top Design Co., Ltd.
Page/Seite 108–109

Top Electric Appliances Industrial Ltd.
Page/Seite 198

Top Industrial Design Co., Ltd.
Page/Seite 108–109

Maria Isabel Toro
Corona, Colceramica
Corona Design Team
Page/Seite 312

Toto Ltd.
Page/Seite 308–311

Lorenzo Truant
Page/Seite 342

Thomas Turner
Haberdashery
Page/Seite 370–371

Tuux
Page/Seite 81

Tuya Inc.
Page/Seite 120

U
Unilock
Page/Seite 395

United Design Lab
Page/Seite 188–189

Greg Upston
Naked Image
Page/Seite 250

Ningbo Utec Electric Co., Ltd.
Page/Seite 360

V
V-ZUG AG
Page/Seite 228

Patrik van Daele
PVD Concept
Page/Seite 344

Arjan van der Wal
FritsJurgens
Page/Seite 106

Erwin van Handenhoven
Hager Electro SAS
Corporate Design Hager Group
Page/Seite 146

Vatti Corporation Limited
Page/Seite 217, 225, 269

Arif Veendijk
Pezy Group
Page/Seite 211

Design Studio Lars Vejen for LIGHT-POINT A/S
Page/Seite 361

Vetica Group
Page/Seite 303

Vimar S.p.A.
Page/Seite 134

vitamin design
DONA Handelsges. mbH
Page/Seite 181

Studio Volpi
Page/Seite 220–221

volume3 design
Page/Seite 295

Prof. Volker von Kardorff
Kardorff Ingenieure Lichtplanung GmbH
Page/Seite 343

Vorwerk Temial GmbH
Vorwerk Design
Page/Seite 197

W
Dietlind Walger-Hutter
aeris GmbH
Page/Seite 172–173

Albert Wan
AW Design International Ltd.
Page/Seite 236

Wan Lulu
Haier Innovation Design Center
Page/Seite 282, 287, 289

Studio Marcel Wanders
Page/Seite 307

Cancan Wang
Bear Electric Appliance Co., Ltd.
Page/Seite 233, 237

Fei Wang
A-John Enterprise Co., Ltd.
Page/Seite 80

Prof. Feng Wang
Foshan Duo Pu Le Furniture Co., Ltd.
Page/Seite 182–183

Hongjun Wang
Beijing 17PIN Network Technology Co., Ltd.
Page/Seite 253

Huijie Wang
Gree Electric Appliances, Inc. of Zhuhai
Page/Seite 240

Lijuan Wang
AIGANG GmbH
Page/Seite 108–109

Mengquan Wang
Gree Electric Appliances, Inc. of Zhuhai
Page/Seite 107

Prof. Ming Chuan Wang
China University of Technology
Page/Seite 80

Pingping Wang
Joyoung
Page/Seite 250

Shuaishuai Wang
Shanghai Allocacoc Industrial Design Co., Ltd.
Page/Seite 373

Wang Shupeng
Haier Innovation Design Center
Page/Seite 289

Xiaowen Wang
Guangdong Infinity Mind
Architecture Design Co., Ltd.
Page/Seite 75

Yan Wang
Shenzhen Dizan Technology Co., Ltd.
Page/Seite 376

Wang Yinpeng
Ningbo Bright Electric Co., Ltd.
Page/Seite 366

Yuanxin Wang
Xiamen Lota International Co., Ltd.
Page/Seite 265

Wang Zhenhao
Haier Innovation Design Center
Page/Seite 285

Zhihua Wang
Shenzhen Aukey E-Business Co., Ltd.
Page/Seite 377

Vincent Weckert
Siemens AG
Page/Seite 138

Wei Xiaobo
Haier Innovation Design Center
Page/Seite 281

Zhang Wei
AUG Shenzhen Industrial Design Co., Ltd.
Page/Seite 328

Wever & Ducré BVBA
Page/Seite 373

Whirlpool EMEA S.p.A.
Global Consumer Design EMEA
Page/Seite 215, 278

Wilsonic Design, d.o.o.
Page/Seite 163, 339

WMF Consumer Electric GmbH
Page/Seite 209

Chung Kin Wong
Shanghai Chunmi
Electronics Technology Co., Ltd.
Page/Seite 231

Euncheuk Woo
Samsung SDS
Page/Seite 115

Faxiang Wu
JOMOO Kitchen & Bath Co., Ltd.
Page/Seite 306

Guojun Wu
Zhejiang Horizon Industrial Design Co., Ltd.
Page/Seite 170

Huanlong Wu
Gree Electric Appliances, Inc. of Zhuhai
Page/Seite 107, 240–241, 256

Jiao Wu
Zhejiang Horizon Industrial Design Co., Ltd.
Page/Seite 170

Lichuan Wu
JOMOO Kitchen & Bath Co., Ltd.
Page/Seite 306, 326

Qingxia Wu
GD Midea Consumer Electric MFG, Co., Ltd.
Page/Seite 192

Tingbin Wu
Miniso Hong Kong Limited
Page/Seite 372

Wanfeng Wu
Bravat
Page/Seite 329

Weijian Wu
NVC Lighting Technology Corporation
Page/Seite 352–353

Wu Xiaoli
Haier Innovation Design Center
Page/Seite 289

Mark Wunderlin
talsee AG
Page/Seite 297

Alphabetical index designers
Alphabetisches Designer-Register

X

XAL GmbH
Page/Seite 334, 340, 346

Qi Xi
Gree Electric Appliances, Inc. of Zhuhai
Page/Seite 256

Rong Xiang
NVC Lighting Technology Corporation
Page/Seite 352–353

Donghong Xiao
Rifeng Enterprise Group Co., Ltd.
Page/Seite 313

Honghe Xiao
Siterwell Electronics Co., Limited
Page/Seite 149

Jianxiang Xiao
JOMOO Kitchen & Bath Co., Ltd.
Page/Seite 323

Xiaomi Inc.
Page/Seite 114, 231, 373, 377

Peihe Xie
AD Architecture
Page/Seite 78

Xing Xie
Bravat
Page/Seite 261

Xie Yugang
Haier Innovation Design Center
Page/Seite 287

Chen Xin
Kurz Kurz Design China
Page/Seite 255

Hao Xin
Shenzhen Crastal Technology Co., Ltd.
Page/Seite 194–196

Guangdong Xinbao
Electrical Appliances Holdings Co., Ltd.
Page/Seite 190, 199

Yao Xingen
BSH Home Appliances (China) Co., Ltd.
Page/Seite 278–279

Changying Xu
Beijing Jiangxinxiaozhen e-business Co., Ltd.
Page/Seite 317

Xu Lujiang
Shijiazhuang Yiqi Technology Co., Ltd.
Page/Seite 326

Xu Xuexiang
Beijing MADV Technology Co., Ltd.
Page/Seite 112

Y

Koji Yamaura
Panasonic Corporation
Page/Seite 233

Yan Hongyan
Haier Innovation Design Center
Page/Seite 289

Zhang Yan
Joyoung
Page/Seite 247

Li Yanchao
Joyoung
Page/Seite 247

Prof. Yang Bin
Guangdong Xinbao
Electrical Appliances Holdings Co., Ltd.
Page/Seite 190, 199

Deqing Yang
Xiamen Oshince Technology Co., Ltd.
Page/Seite 323

Dezhi Yang
Honeywell China
HUE Design Studio
Page/Seite 114

Junji Yang
Clean Best (Shenzhen) Technology Co., Ltd.
Page/Seite 258

Lin Yang
Arovast Corporation
Page/Seite 234–235

Liumei Yang
Easo
Page/Seite 260

Sen Yang
Gree Electric Appliances, Inc. of Zhuhai
Page/Seite 240

Xiaobing Yang
Rifeng Enterprise Group Co., Ltd.
Page/Seite 313

Xiaoqiang Yang
Hangzhou Hotdesign Co., Ltd.
Page/Seite 116

Yang Xue Jin
Zhejiang Supor
Electrical Appliances Manufacturing
Page/Seite 250

Zhihong Yang
Gree Electric Appliances, Inc. of Zhuhai
Page/Seite 107

Yao Yueqiang
Liantek
Electrical Appliances (Shenzhen) Co., Ltd.
Page/Seite 251

Ri Hua Ye
Midea Smart Technology Co., Ltd.
Page/Seite 117, 135

Qingdao Yeelink
Information Technology Co., Ltd.
Page/Seite 142, 372, 377

Inseon Yeo
LG Electronics Inc.
Page/Seite 276

Il Soo Yeom
Bodyfriend Co., Ltd.
Page/Seite 255

Yi Zuowei
Haier Innovation Design Center
Page/Seite 280

Deqing Yin
Beijing 17PIN Network Technology Co., Ltd.
Page/Seite 253

Li Ying
LKKer Technology Co., Ltd.
Page/Seite 245

Jinjiang Yiqi Technology Co., Ltd.
Page/Seite 326

Shijiazhuang Yiqi Technology Co., Ltd.
Page/Seite 326

Yonoh Studio
Page/Seite 345

Seungjin Yoon
LG Electronics Inc.
Page/Seite 276

Zhifu You
Above Lights (HK) Limited
Page/Seite 376

Yu Dong
Haier Innovation Design Center
Page/Seite 287

Jinfeng Yu
Foshan 3&1 Industrial Design Co., Ltd.
Page/Seite 117

Jongyoon Yu
SK magic
Page/Seite 230

Qi Yu
Siemens Ltd., China
Page/Seite 148

Seonil Yu
LG Electronics Inc.
Page/Seite 274–275

Yu Zhaoting
Haier Innovation Design Center
Page/Seite 289

Zhengtie Yu
Bravat
Page/Seite 261

Ji Yun
BSH Home Appliances (China) Co., Ltd.
Page/Seite 279

Yezo Yun
LG Electronics Inc.
Page/Seite 276

Z

Matteo Zaghi
Prode
Page/Seite 179

Shenzhen Zanidea Creative and Cultural Co., Ltd.
Page/Seite 219

Ray Zee
Design Department
Nan Fung Group
Page/Seite 82–83

Jincui Zhan
Rifeng Enterprise Group Co., Ltd.
Page/Seite 313

Aiden Zhang
Qingdao Ecopure Filter Co., Ltd.
Page/Seite 258

Jia Zhang
Guangdong Midea Kitchen
Appliances Manufacturing Co., Ltd.
Page/Seite 232

Jiqing Zhang
Top Design Co., Ltd.
Page/Seite 108–109

Zhang Limei
Haier Innovation Design Center
Page/Seite 281–283

Zhang Mi
Shijiazhuang Yiqi Technology Co., Ltd.
Page/Seite 326

Min Zhang
Gree Electric Appliances, Inc. of Zhuhai
Page/Seite 256

Zhang Xiaoguang
Hero
Page/Seite 204

Zhang Xiaoyue
Haier Innovation Design Center
Page/Seite 285

Youmei Zhang
Gree Electric Appliances, Inc. of Zhuhai
Page/Seite 240–241, 256

Zhang Yu
Shijiazhuang Yiqi Technology Co., Ltd.
Page/Seite 326

Yu Zhang
Gree Electric Appliances, Inc. of Zhuhai
Page/Seite 256

Baowen Zhao
Shanghai Chunmi
Electronics Technology Co., Ltd.
Page/Seite 243

Benqiang Zhao
Hangzhou ROBAM Applicances Co., Ltd.
Page/Seite 217, 224

Binxiang Zhao
Joyoung
Page/Seite 250

Huanyi Zhao
Foshan Shunde Midea
Electrical Heating Appliances
Page/Seite 244

Yang Zhao
Gree Electric Appliances, Inc. of Zhuhai
Page/Seite 240–241, 256

Zhen Xiaojing
Hero
Page/Seite 204

Leihong Zheng
Schneider Electric
Page/Seite 120, 135

Lv Zheng
Joyoung
Page/Seite 242

Wenqiang Zheng
JOMOO Kitchen & Bath Co., Ltd.
Page/Seite 326

Yanhui Zheng
LKK Design Shenzhen Co., Ltd.
Page/Seite 112

Yuxing Zheng
Bravat
Page/Seite 329

Zhaoping Zheng
JOMOO Kitchen & Bath Co., Ltd.
Page/Seite 323

Zhipeng Zheng
JOMOO Kitchen & Bath Co., Ltd.
Page/Seite 326

Puhua Zhong
Rifeng Enterprise Group Co., Ltd.
Page/Seite 313

Suping Zhong
Hangzhou ROBAM Applicances Co., Ltd.
Page/Seite 217, 224

Wenjin Zhong
Shenzhen Crastal Technology Co., Ltd.
Page/Seite 194–196

Yugen Zhong
Tuya Inc.
Page/Seite 120

Lin Zhou
Top Design Co., Ltd.
Page/Seite 108–109

Zhou Shu
Haier Innovation Design Center
Page/Seite 280

Shuaiwen Zhou
Gree Electric Appliances, Inc. of Zhuhai
Page/Seite 240–241, 256

Zhou Zhangling
Zhejiang Marssenger Kitchenware Co., Ltd.
Page/Seite 270–271

Chuanbao Zhu
Xiamen Lota International Co., Ltd.
Page/Seite 265, 314

Yunwei Zhu
JOMOO Kitchen & Bath Co., Ltd.
Page/Seite 302

Zhuang Jingyang
Teawith Essentials Association
Page/Seite 188–189

Luyao Zhuang
LKKer Technology Co., Ltd.
Page/Seite 245

Guo Ziyuan
Kurz Kurz Design China
Page/Seite 255

Zuo Studio
Page/Seite 390–391

Find additional award-winning products and designer portraits in the separate volumes "Doing", "Working", "Enjoying".

Weitere ausgezeichnete Produkte und Designerporträts finden Sie in den Einzelbänden „Doing", „Working", „Enjoying".

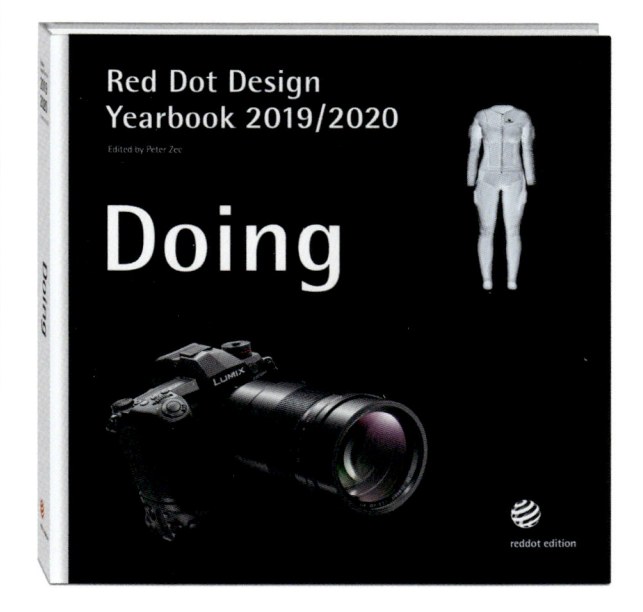

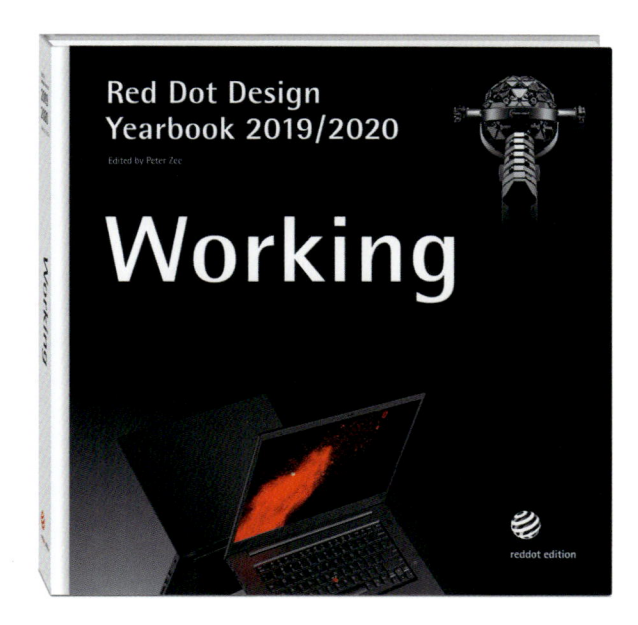

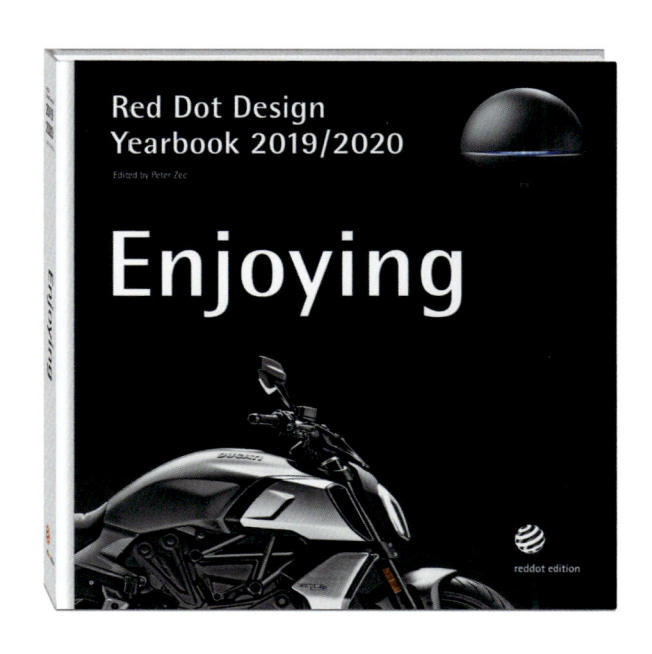

Doing

Babies and children
Baby und Kind

Household
Haushalt

Tableware and cooking utensils
Tableware und Kochutensilien

Garden
Garten

Tools
Werkzeuge

Cameras
Kameras

Communication
Kommunikation

Robots
Roboter

Working

Office
Büro

Computer and information technology
Computer- und Informationstechnik

Industrial equipment, machinery and automation
Industriegeräte, Maschinen und Automation

Materials and surfaces
Materialien und Oberflächen

Heating and air conditioning technology
Heiz- und Klimatechnik

Life science and medicine
Life Science und Medizin

Enjoying

Bicycles
Fahrräder

Vehicles
Fahrzeuge

Sports and outdoor
Sport und Outdoor

Leisure and games
Freizeit und Spiel

Entertainment
Entertainment

Spas and personal care
Wellness und Personal Care

Fashion, lifestyle and accessories
Mode, Lifestyle und Accessoires

Watches and jewellery
Uhren und Schmuck

reddot edition

Editor | Herausgeber
Peter Zec

Project management | Projektleitung
Sophie Angerer

Project assistance | Projektassistenz
Theresa Falkenberg
Ekaterina Haak
Laura-Gabriela Hellbach
Anja Lakomski
Judith Lindner
Samuel Madilonga
Vivien Mroß
Louisa Mücher
Lena Poteralla
Anamaria Sumic
Sabine Wöll
Janik Zeh

Editorial work | Redaktion
Mareike Ahlborn, Essen, Germany
Jörg Arnke, Essen, Germany
Bettina Derksen, Simmern, Germany
Eva Hembach, Vienna, Austria
Karin Kirch, Essen, Germany
Karoline Laarmann, Dortmund, Germany
Bettina Laustroer, Wuppertal, Germany
Kirsten Müller, Essen, Germany
Astrid Ruta, Essen, Germany
Martina Stein, Otterberg, Germany
Corinna Ten-Cate, Wetter, Germany

"Red Dot: Design Team of the Year"
Burkhard Jacob, Krefeld, Germany

Translation | Übersetzung
Heike Bors-Eberlein, Tokyo, Japan
Patrick Conroy, Lanarca, Cyprus
Stanislaw Eberlein, Tokyo, Japan
William Kings, Wuppertal, Germany
Kocarek GmbH (Anna Krepper, Christopher Schuster,
David Lauber), Essen, Germany
Tara Russell, Dublin, Ireland
Philippa Watts, Exeter, United Kingdom
Andreas Zantop, Berlin, Germany
Christiane Zschunke, Frankfurt am Main, Germany

Proofreading | Lektorat
Klaus Dimmler (supervision), Essen, Germany
Mareike Ahlborn, Essen, Germany
Jörg Arnke, Essen, Germany
Wolfgang Astelbauer, Vienna, Austria
Dawn Michelle d'Atri, Kirchhundem, Germany
Annette Gillich-Beltz, Essen, Germany
Sonja Illa-Paschen, London, United Kingdom
Karin Kirch, Essen, Germany
Norbert Knyhala, Castrop-Rauxel, Germany
Regina Schier, Essen, Germany
Anja Schrade, Stuttgart, Germany
SPRACHENWERFT GmbH, Hamburg, Germany

Layout | Gestaltung
Lockstoff Design GmbH, Meerbusch, Germany
Nicole Slink (supervision)
Christina Jörres
Alica Kern
Alexandra Korschefsky
Alina Laase
Stephanie Marniok
Saskia Rühmkorf

Cover | Umschlag
Idea | Idee
Burkhard Jacob, Krefeld, Germany
Implementation | Umsetzung
Lockstoff Design GmbH, Meerbusch, Germany

Photographs | Fotos
Dragan Arrigler (Carefoot, juror Jure Miklavc)

Guglielmo Galliano, Responsible Grafik & Visual
of Ferrari Design (portrait of Flavio Manzoni,
Red Dot: Design Team of the Year 2019)

Altin Manaf (GENESI, juror Masayo Ave)

Peter Molick, (product photo ReThink!, USA,
Volume Working)

Jens Passoth (designer portrait photo of Kees de Boer,
Volume Working)

Singapore GP Pte. Ltd. (Twenty3, juror Simon Ong)

Swiss Krono Group (juror Katrin de Louw)

Masafumi Yamamoto (fugan, juror Kazuo Tanaka)

Jury photographs | Jurorenfotos
eventfotograf.in, Essen, Germany
Schuchrat Kurbanov
Alex Muchnik

In-company photos | Werkfotos der Firmen

Production | Produktion
gelb+, Düsseldorf, Germany
Bernd Reinkens

Lithography | Lithografie
gelb+, Düsseldorf, Germany
Bernd Reinkens (supervision)
Wurzel Medien GmbH, Düsseldorf, Germany
Jonas Mühlenweg

Printing | Druck
Dr. Cantz'sche Druckerei Medien GmbH,
Esslingen, Germany

Bookbindery | Buchbinderei
Conzella Verlagsbuchbinderei, Pfarrkirchen, Germany

Red Dot Design Yearbook 2019/2020
Living: 978-3-89939-213-5
Doing: 978-3-89939-214-2
Working: 978-3-89939-215-9
Enjoying: 978-3-89939-216-6
Set (Living, Doing, Working & Enjoying): 978-3-89939-212-8

© 2019 Red Dot GmbH & Co. KG, Essen, Germany

The Red Dot Award: Product Design
competition is the continuation of the
Design Innovations competition.
Der Wettbewerb „Red Dot Award: Product Design"
gilt als Fortsetzung des Wettbewerbs
„Design Innovationen".

All rights reserved, especially those of translation.
Alle Rechte vorbehalten, besonders die der Übersetzung
in fremde Sprachen.

No liability is accepted for the completeness
of the information in the appendix.
Für die Vollständigkeit der Angaben im Anhang
wird keine Gewähr übernommen.

Publisher & worldwide distribution |
Verlag & Vertrieb weltweit
Red Dot Edition
Design Publisher | Fachverlag für Design
Contact | Kontakt
Sabine Wöll
Gelsenkirchener Str. 181
45309 Essen, Germany
Phone +49 201 81418 22
Fax +49 201 81418 10
E-mail edition@red-dot.de
www.red-dot-edition.com
Book publisher ID no. | Verkehrsnummer
13674 (Börsenverein Frankfurt)

**Bibliographic information published
by the Deutsche Nationalbibliothek**
The Deutsche Nationalbibliothek
lists this publication in the Deutsche
Nationalbibliografie; detailed bibliographic
data are available on the Internet at
http://dnb.ddb.de
Bibliografische Information
der Deutschen Nationalbibliothek
Die Deutsche Nationalbibliothek verzeichnet
diese Publikation in der Deutschen
Nationalbibliografie; detaillierte
bibliografische Daten sind im Internet über
http://dnb.ddb.de abrufbar